Limited Classical Reprint Library

NOTES,

CRITICAL AND PRACTICAL,

ON THE BOOK OF

NUMBERS:

DESIGNED AS A GENERAL HELP TO

BIBLICAL READING AND INSTRUCTION

BY GEORGE BUSH,

LATE PROF. OF HEB. AND ORIENT. LIT. IN N. Y. CITY UNIVERSITY.

Foreword by
Dr. Cyril J. Barber

Klock & Klock Christian Publishers, Inc.
2527 GIRARD AVE. N.
MINNEAPOLIS, MINNESOTA 55411

Originally published by
Ivison & Phinney
Chicago, Ill.
1858

0-86524-099-X

Printed by Klock & Klock in the U.S.A.
1981 Reprint

FOREWORD

The writings of George Bush have seldom failed to bless those who read them. My students have often remarked to me after using one of his commentaries for an assignment how blessed they felt following their research. To this I respond that there is no real reason why research, particularly biblical research, should not be a blessing.

Personally, I too have found Bush's works well worth the time spent consulting them. They are characterized by a happy blend of sound exegesis and a pleasing inclusion of orientalisms seldom found in commentaries; and this combination makes them valuable for personal study as well as exposition.

Charles Haddon Spurgeon must have had a similar experience, for he said that he found Bush's writings to be "of considerable value." In another place in his book, *Commenting and Commentaries*, he remarked: "Bush is a careful illustrator of the Word, and apt at giving the practical lesson. His works are well compiled."

George Bush (1796-1859) was born at Norwich, Vermont. His father had studied law, but had been prevented from practicing his chosen profession on account of ill-health. When George was only nine, tragedy entered the Bush home. George's mother died, and it seems as if young George never fully recovered from his sense of loss. In fact, decades later, one biographer records that "he would often lament his want of a mother's care."

Apprenticed to a printer at age fourteen, Bush was dismissed after three months because he was absent-minded. In a day when the dignity of work was a valued ethic, such dismissal would have been sufficient to bring the opprobrium of the community down upon him. Bush's later prodigious efforts demonstrate that he was not lazy. It seems better, therefore, to conclude that his "absentmindedness" may well have stemmed from a major lack in his life--the absence of someone to love him and make him feel wanted and secure.

After studying in an academy for four years, Bush entered Dartmouth College and graduated from there with highest honors. He then enrolled in Princeton Theological Seminary and, upon graduation, became a tutor in the College of New Jersey (1822-1823).

Following his ordination into the Presbyterian ministry in Salem in 1824, George Bush was called to the pastorate of the Presbyterian Church of Indianapolis, where he served for three years. During this time he married the daughter of the Hon. Lewis Condict of Morristown, New Jersey. Unfortunately, in 1827 tragedy again entered the life of Goerge Bush, for his wife died leaving him their young son to rear.

To a person of such tender emotions, this second bereavement must have come as a heavy blow, and it is not surprising that, in 1831, Bush left Indianapolis for New York City where he became Professor of Hebrew and Oriental Literature in the University. From this time onward a steady stream of books flowed from his pen, among them his *Commentary on the Book of Psalms*, a Hebrew Grammar, and his famous *Notes, Critical and Explanatory on Genesis, Exodus, Leviticus, Numbers, Joshua* and *Judges*.

Dr. Bush's mother had died unsaved, and it is to be regretted that some of her son's efforts were spent in trying to prove that there will not be a resurrection of the dead. His reasoning is preserved in his treatise entitled *Anastasis.* Later, as if dissatisfied with this position, Bush began to embrace the errors of Emanuel Swedenborg, and particularly the doctrine of universalism. Here again the student of his life cannot help but wonder at the powerful effect his mother's untimely passing was still exerting upon him. Fortunately, these aberant views never appeared in any of his commentaries.

Ten years before his own death, Dr. Bush married again. He continued to teach, preach and write until six months before passing into the presence of his Lord. At his death, George Bush left behind him a legacy of devotion and piety. One intimately acquainted with his manner of life wrote:

> In his later years he never opened any book but the Bible, Thomas a Kempis, and the hymnal. It was his habit during life, after family worship, to read the Word in the original. This he continued to do till within six weeks of his departure.

So few able commentaries have been written on the Book of Numbers that we should be thankful such a work as this one has come down to us. In commenting on a related work, Spurgeon said,

> The author read extensively to produce this volume. In his later years he became a Swedenborgian, but there is no trace of that [form of] learning in this or his other comments.

In his evaluation of Bush's exposition of Numbers, the famous "Prince of Preachers" showed the same discernment:

> Although Bush is indebted to many authors, he is by no means a mere collector; his remarks repay you for consultation, . . .

Were it not for George Bush's *Notes on Numbers*, there would be a hiatus in our study and appreciation of this portion of God's inspired revelation of Himself and His dealings with His people. We are thankful, therefore, that we can benefit from all the good that George Bush wrote on this, the fourth book of Moses.

Cyril J. Barber
author, *The Minister's Library*

INTRODUCTION.

§ 1. *Title, Author, Scope, &c.*

The title by which this book is designated by the Jews is וידבר *va yedabbēr, and he spake*, from the first word of the original, or במדבר *bemidbar*, *in the wilderness*, the fifth word of the first verse; the last, probably, from the fact that the contents of the book relate in great measure to the history of the sojourning of the Israelites in the wilderness. The Septuagint terms it ΑΡΙΘΜΟΙ *Arithmoi*, of which the Latin Numeri, and the English Numbers are a translation. The fact is somewhat peculiar, as every one of the other books of Moses is designated by the Greek title in Anglicised form, viz., *Genesis, Exodus, Leviticus, Deuteronomy*. The present book might as well have been called *Arithmoi*, were it not that the Latin rendering *Numeri* (*Numbers*) for some reason had an early preference given it over the Greek, and for this reason it has maintained its ground. The book originally received its denomination mainly from its account of the *numbering*, *mustering*, or *marshalling* of the people on two different occasions, the first in the commencement of the history, the other towards the close. Besides which we meet with various *lists* or *enumerations* of persons and places, that may have entered into the account with those who first adopted the title. We have endeavored, however, in our Notes to show, from the genuine import of the terms employed, that the precise idea conveyed is not so truly that of *numbering*, as of *ordering*, *arranging*, *marshalling*, or, otherwise, *mustering*. As some important results flow from the establishment of this construction, we commend our remarks on this head to particular attention.

The authorship of the book is, like that of some of the preceding, determined by the general current of evidence which assigns the writing of the entire Pentateuch to Moses. It is clearly recognized in the subsequent books as pertaining to that body of documents technically termed "The Law," as for instance we find in Josh. 4 : 12, the following distinct allusion to the arrangement made with the two tribes and a half to settle on the west side of Jordan after first crossing over with their brethren; "And the children of Reuben, and the children of Gad, and half the tribe of Manasseh, passed over armed before the children of Israel, *as Moses spake unto them.*" Compare 2 Chron. 29 : 11. 31 : 3. Ezek. 20 : 13. Matt. 12 : 5.

The time embraced in the book extends from the early part of the second year after the exodus to the beginning of the eleventh month of the fortieth year after that event; it therefore comprehends a period of thirty-eight years and nine or ten months. Most of the transactions, however, recorded in the book seem to have taken place near the beginning and the end of this period. The date of the events mentioned about the middle of the book cannot now be ascertained. Up to ch. 10 : 11, we find the people remaining at Sinai, and it is then stated that on the twentieth day of the second month of the second year they were directed to remove and advance towards the Promised Land. They proceed as far as Kadesh on its borders, where we find them in ch. 13 : 46, and where, on account of gross rebellion, the nation was condemned to wander in the desert for forty years, till the then existing generation should have died away (ch. 14). From this time onward to ch. 20, it is next to impossible to fix with accuracy the order and date of the various transactions, laws, etc. recorded, but at that time we find the Israelites again at Kadesh taking measures to enter Canaan. The book closes with the people resting on the borders of the Promised Land on the east of the Jordan.

As to the time of its being written, the evidence adduced in the Introduction to the "Notes on Leviticus," § 1, relative to the date of the composition of that book, leads obviously to the conclusion, that while the former was written during the encampment at Mount Sinai, the latter, or the present book, was written at the station on the plains of Moab. The authority for this statement is found in Num. 36 : 13, "These are the commandments and the judgments which the Lord commanded by the hand of Moses unto the children of Israel in the plains of Moab by Jordan *near* Jericho." We can glean nothing more definite than this relative to the date of the writing.

§ 2. *General Contents.*

The history presents us with an account of the census-taking of the tribes, the consecration of the Tabernacle, and the offering of the princes at its dedication. It describes the journeys and encampments of Israel under the miraculous guidance of the cloudy pillar, the punishment at Taberah, and the signal vengeance with which, on several occasions, the Most High visited the distrustful murmurs of the people, and that rebellious spirit which so often broke out in sedition against his appointed ministers. The promptitude and severity with which these rebellious outbreaks were rebuked are relieved by the signal mercy and forbearance of Heaven in listening to the prayers of Moses in behalf of the offending people. The narrative is interspersed with various incidents collateral to the main thread of the history, which are full of interest and instruction. Conspicuous among these is the account of the rebellion of Korah and his company, the visitation of the fiery flying serpents, the story of Balaam and his constrained predictions, and the miraculous budding of Aaron's rod. Henry remarks in his usual pithy way that "an abstract of much of this book we have in a few words, Ps. 95 : 10, "Forty years long was I grieved with this generation," and an application of it to ourselves, Heb. 4 : 1, "Let us fear lest we seem to come short." It is worthy also of reflection that while the annals of many distinguished and powerful nations who were cotemporaries of the Israelites at this period, are all utterly lost, here we have preserved to us the records of a handful of people that dwelt in tents, and wandered strangely in a wilderness, but who were thus favored because they were the children of the covenant, and the germ of the Church for countless generations.

§ 3. *Synoptical View.*

Part I.—*Preparation for Departure from Sinai.*

	CHAPTERS
1. Numbering or mustering the people at large, ...	I
2. Order of the tribes in their encampment, ...	II
3. The appointment and ministrations of the Levites, . .	III, IV
4. Various laws respecting the unclean, the woman suspected, and the Nazarite, ...	V, VI
5. The offerings of the princes, and the consecration of the Levites,	VII, VIII
6. Regulations respecting the celebration of the Passover, the signals and order of marching, and the calling of assemblies, .	IX, X

Part II.—*The Departure from Sinai and the Journeying to the Land of Moab, with the Murmurings on the Way.*

1. Murmurings from the wearisomeness of the way and disgust with the manna, ...	XI
2. Sedition of Aaron and Miriam, ...	XII
3. Spies sent to explore the land, ...	XIII
4. The people murmur at their report and are punished, .	XIV
5. Various ceremonial laws, ...	XV
6. Rebellion and punishment of Korah, Dathan, and Abiram, .	XVI
7. Blossoming of Aaron's rod, ...	XVII
9. The duties and the support of the Priests and Levites, .	XVIII
10. Law respecting the water of separation and the sacrifice of the red heifer, ...	XIX
11. Murmuring for want of Water, unbelief of Moses, perfidy of Edom, and death of Aaron, ...	XX
12. Renewed murmurings of the people and their punishment by fiery flying serpents, ...	XXI

Part III.—*Preparation for occupying the Promised Land, and Directions respecting the Occupancy.*

1. The summoning of Balaam by Balak, and his compliance,	XXII
2. Balaam's sacrifice, and his prophetic benedictions, .	XXIII, XXIV
3. The sin of the people with the Midianitish women and their punishment, ...	XXV
4. A new census taken of the people, ...	XXVI
5. Law concerning inheritance, and the inauguration of Joshua, ...	XXVII
6. Various laws respecting offerings, ...	XXVIII, XXIX
7 Law respecting vows, ...	XXX
9. Occupation of part of the promised inheritance by reason of the slaughter of the Midianites, ...	XXXI
10. Allotment of the two tribes and a half in the east of the Jordan, ...	XXXII

§ 4. *Commentators.*

We are obliged to repeat here the remark made in the Introduction to Leviticus, that the commentators on this book are few apart from those who have expounded the several books of the Pentateuch, or the Old Testament at large. Yet we cannot say but our apparatus is sufficiently ample, although every year is adding to its extent. No attempt at unfolding the genuine scope of the Mosaic books can do justice to the theme, which overlooks the resources accumulated by critics and travellers within the last twenty years. In the preparation of the following Notes, the author has pursued the same general plan, and been governed by the same principles which characterize his former volumes on the books of Moses. He is happy to acknowledge his indebtedness to the labors of his predecessors, while at the same time he has thought and spoken for himself, and ventures to claim something more for his work than the mere culling out and remoulding of the best critical or practical remarks of others. Having the inspired original, with its collateral ancient versions, continually before him, he could scarcely fail to reach some results which are peculiar to himself, although in a work intended for plain Bible readers as well as teachers, he has been guarded as to launching forth into veins of mere curious or speculative research. He is admonished by the lessons of advancing years that he has no time for any but useful inquiries, and that even in this department his labors henceforth must be bounded by inevitably narrow limits. He has endeavored, therefore, so to conduct his studies, and so to shape the results, as to subserve the highest interest of the greatest number of his readers.

In the way of critical and ethical helps in his undertaking, the most important have been the following, for the use of several of which he has been indebted to the private and public collections which have been kindly placed at his service.

Walton's Polyglot.
Pool's Synopsis.
Ainsworth on the Pentateuch.
Attersol on Numbers.
Biblia Maxima of de la Haye.
Origen's Homilies on Numbers.
Theodoret's Quæstiones in Numeros.
Le Clerc's Commentary.
Dodd's do.
Patrick's do.
Calmet's do.
Cleaver's do.
Rosenmuller's do.
Gill's do.
Henry's do.
Hewlett's do.

Barrett's Synopsis of Criticism.
Geddes' Translation and Notes.
Michaelis' Laws of Moses.
" Germ. Translation of Scriptures.
Pyles' Paraphrase.
Pool's Annotations.
Babington's Comfortable Notes.
Drusius ad Loca Difficilia.
Saurin's Dissertations.
Parker's Bibliotheca Biblica.
De Wette's German Translation.
Dathius' Latin Translation.
Jurieu's Critical History.
Bishop Hall's Contemplations.
Outram on Sacrifices.
Kitto's Daily Bible Illustrations.

Stackhouse's History of the Bible.
Vatablus' Biblia Sacra.
Pfeiffer's Dubia Vexata.
Junius & Tremellius' Latin Bible.
Haak's Dutch Annotations.
Kidder on the Pentateuch.
Wells' Sacred Geography.
" Help to the Sacred Scriptures.
Robinson's Researches.
Bonar's Sinai and the Desert.
Lewis' Hebrew Antiquities.
Palfrey's Lectures on Hebrew Antiquities.
Kitto's Pictorial Bible.
" Biblical Cyclopædia.
Works of Philo and Josephus.
Bishop Wilson's Bible.

ABBREVIATIONS.

Chald.	The *Chaldee* version, or Targum of Onkelos.
Gr. or Sept.	The *Greek* version of the *Seventy*.
Vulg.	The *Latin* version, commonly called the *Vulgate*.
Arab.	The *Arabic* version of the Polyglot.
Sam.	The *Samaritan* Pentateuch.
Syr.	The *Syriac* version of the Polyglot.
Targ. Jon.	The *Targum* or Paraphrase of *Jonathan*.
Targ. Jerus.	The *Targum of Jerusalem*.

In respect to these various versions and Targums, the reader will find ample information in the Introduction to the Notes on Genesis. They are not all of equal value, but all of them will occasionally throw important light upon passages occurring in the sacred text. The Vulg. and the Gr. are generally quoted in the words of the English translation—the former of the Douay, and the latter of Thomson or Brenton. In quoting from the Targums and the Jewish Expositors, the author has usually availed himself of the version given in Ainsworth's very valuable Notes, to which he has had frequent recourse throughout.

THE BOOK OF NUMBERS.

CHAPTER I.

THE Israelites, at the date of the opening of this book, had remained about a year in the vicinity of Mount Sinai, whither they had arrived within little more than a month after their departure from Egypt. During this time of nearly thirteen months they had erected and furnished the Tabernacle, and had received the various laws and institutions recorded in the preceding books, and had been undergoing a certain preliminary discipline or training in the matters of divine worship, which infinite wisdom saw to be of the utmost importance for them in the circumstances in which they were placed. They had but recently been delivered from a state of degrading bondage, and had come forth from under the hand of their oppressors as a somewhat rude and uncultivated horde, requiring to be put through a kind of educational process before they would be fit to answer, in all respects, the ends of their marvellous selection and segregation as a peculiar people. These ends were in a great measure typical and representative. A "church in the wilderness" was to be formed that should, in its distinguishing economy of rites and ceremonies, laws and judgments, fitly foreshadow that future Christian and spiritual Church, in which it was ordained that all those shadows should be turned into substance. It was indeed a burdensome yoke that was to be imposed upon them, and it is not difficult to perceive that their shoulders must be gradually inured to the load which they were called, for so many ages, to bear. Hence their protracted stay at Sinai, which would naturally tend to *break them in* to the service allotted them in their typical capacity—a capacity in which it appears from the whole drift of the Epistle to the Hebrews they were mainly called to act. For this end it was necessary, moreover, that a certain external order and organization should be adopted, whereby the analogous arrangements of the ulterior spiritual body, of long subsequent development, should be suitably set forth. Hence it was that a special *mustering* and *enumeration* of the people, together with a prescribed *form of encampment*, was ordered at the time of the commencement of the present history, for which we may in addition suggest a number of collateral ends to be answered; as, (1.) That the people might have palpable evidence how fully the Lord had made good his promise to Abraham of multiplying his seed. (2.) That every Israelite might know for himself and be able to declare to his posterity, from what tribe he descended and to what family he belonged, and this more especially with a view that the genealogy of the future Messiah might be clearly ascertained. (3.) That in case of an attack from their enemies, they might know their strength as a military body; in which character however they are to be looked upon as pre-eminently typical of a *church militant,* for nothing can be conceived more abhorrent to the

CHAPTER I.

AND the LORD spake unto Moses in the wilderness of Sinai[a], in the tabernacle of the congregation, on the first *day*

a Ex. 19, 1. Num. 10, 12.

divine love and wisdom than wars and conquests viewed in any other light. They may be permitted, but never approved. (4.) That a more orderly method of march in their journey to Canaan might be secured. "It is a rout and a rabble," says Henry, "not an army, that is not mustered and put in order." With these prefatory remarks we enter upon the critical exposition of the text.

The Mustering of the Tribes.

V. 1. *And the Lord spake unto Moses in the wilderness of Sinai.* The true rendering of this clause depends upon the determination of the question, whether the census here ordered to be taken is the same with that previously mentioned, Ex. 30 : 12. 38 : 26, or an entirely different one—a point about which commentators greatly differ. In the one case, the present would be the correct rendering; in the other it would be, "The Lord *had* said." The identity of the two enumerations is favored by the identity of the sum total of each, viz. 603,550, and by the difficulty of conceiving why a second numbering should be ordered within so short a time—not more than a few months—after the first. But on the other hand, it is disfavored by the express specification of dates. The census mentioned Ex. 30 : 12 and 38 : 26 was evidently ordered in reference to the poll-tax of half a shekel which was to accompany it, and from which a portion of the revenue necessary for the work of the Tabernacle was to be derived. Indeed, it is expressly stated Ex. 38 : 25–27, that the silver sockets of the Tabernacle were made out of the half shekels contributed on this occasion. The census, therefore, which yielded this fund must have been taken previous to the erection of the sacred edifice, and this, we learn, was finished and set up on the first day of the *first* month of the second year of the sojourn in the wilderness. But in the passage before us the command to number the people was given on the first day of the *second* month of the same year, or precisely one month after the erection of the sanctuary. Were it not for this very explicit mention of dates we should be inclined to Mr. Kitto's opinion, who remarks of the present census, that "we may doubt whether the enumeration in Ex. 38 : 26 is the result of a different one. A census must always occupy some time in making, and yet we find an interval of only a few months between the two periods; and if we suppose them different it is impossible to conceive why a second enumeration should so immediately follow the first. Besides, the amount stated in both instances is the same, namely, 603,550—an identity of numbers scarcely possible even in the interval of a few months, had the enumerations been different. We therefore think that the census is the same: it was completed doubtless in time to make the poll-tax available for the works of the Tabernacle, and the result is stated incidentally in Ex. 38 : 26, in connection with the amount; while here we have a more particular account of the same enumeration in order to show the relative strength of the different tribe ." This would be a very probable view of the matter but for the difficulty stated above. If the census was made in time to be available for the work of the Tabernacle, it must have been made prior to the first day of

of the second month, in the second year after they were come out of the land of Egypt, saying,

---

the first month of the second year; but that brings it in conflict with the present, which was not ordered till the first day of the second month. In this emergency Rosenmuller adopts the suggestion of Vater, that the text has been tampered with by some one who, supposing that a new census is here spoken of, took the liberty to affix a false notation of the time. But as we are opposed from principle to all such gratuitous expedients in the way of solving difficulties, it remains, if possible, to find some solution which shall not impeach the integrity of the sacred text, and we have satisfied our own mind that in the command here given as to numbering the congregation, *the previous one was to be assumed as a basis.* As far as the bare numbers were concerned, the tables or register already made out would answer; and this accounts for the fact that the sum total is the same in both cases. Prof. Palfrey here remarks, with great probability, that "the second was not so much a distinct counting, as a more formal verification of the first." "When Eleazar and Ithamar," he adds, "had already so recently made out their enumeration of the people for one purpose, it is altogether unlikely that their lists would be disregarded, and a work so onerous be gone through a second time *de integro.* It is safely to be presumed, that the list first made would be put into the hands of the officers who were to superintend the new enrolment; and that as the number, supposing it to have been accurately stated in the first instance, could not have become materially different in so short a space of time, the main purpose would be to authenticate it, without disturbing it any further than to count, instead of each individual in any company who had died in the interval, the name of some one who had grown up to full age." (*Lect. on Jewish Ant.* vol. I. p. 313.) Thus too Dr. Chalmers (*Script. Readings in loc.*):—"Henry speaks of their being numbered before from Ex. 38:25, 26, and remarks on the perfect coincidence of the two censuses. But may it not have been one census, even the present one? We have only to suppose that the levy, though begun and proceeded with, was not completed till after the enumeration was finished." The object of the measure in the present case was not therefore precisely the same that it was before. *Then* it was to obtain a revenue *per capita* for the service of the sanctuary. *Now* it was with a view to *order* and *arrangement* among the different tribes, as well as to ascertain, perhaps, their relative strength. But this design will disclose itself more fully as we unfold the import of terms in what follows. We simply remark at present that the difference between this and the former numbering we regard as the difference between a *census* and a *muster*. What that is the reader will soon be able to apprehend. ——¶ *In the tabernacle of the congregation.* Heb. באהל מועד *beohel moëd, in the tabernacle of appointment*, or *of stated meeting.* Gr. "Tent or tabernacle of witness," doubtless from its containing the book of the law, which is frequently spoken of as the witness of the covenant established between the Lord and his people. See Note on Ex. 27:21. 'Tabernacle of witness.'—*Coverdale.* 'Tent of the congregation.'—*Ainsworth.* 'Tabernacle of the covenant.'—*Douay.* 'Public tent.'—*Purver.* There were three places in which the Lord gave audience to Moses, and from which he spake to him. One was at

2 Take[b] ye the sum of all the congregation of the children of

b Ex. 30. 12. c. 26. 2. 63. 2 Sam. 24. 2. 1 Chr. 21. 2.

---

the door of the Tabernacle, near which stood the Altar of Burnt-Offerings. Ex. 29 : 42. "This shall be a continual burnt-offering throughout your generations at the door of the tabernacle of the congregation before the LORD: where I will meet you, to speak there unto you." Another was out of the cloudy pillar. Ps. 99, "He spake to them in the cloudy pillar." Comp. Ex. 33 : 9. Num. 12 : 5. This, however, concurred for the most part with the other, inasmuch as the pillar of cloud usually stood at the door of the Tabernacle when the Lord spake thence to Moses, ch. 11 : 17. The third was the Mercy-seat, the principal seat of the oracle, Num. 7 : 89. It was hence that the Most High now addressed the command to Moses.——¶ *In the first day of the second month of the second year.* Heb. "In the one (day) to the second month." Gr. εν μιᾳ, "In the one." The same phraseology occurs several times in the Greek of the New Testament. Thus Matt. 28 : 1, "Toward the *first day* (Gr. one day) of the week." Comp. Mark 16 : 2. John 20 : 1. Acts 20 : 7. Titus 3 : 10, "After the first (Gr. one) and second admonition." Comparing this with Ex. 19 : 1. 40 : 2. Num. 22 : 11, it appears that the Israelites abode in the desert of Sinai very nearly a whole year; for they came into it on the first day of the third month of the first year, and continued there to the twentieth day of the second month of the second year. This second month is called in the Hebrew calendar *Zif*, and answers to a part of our April. It is so called from the *brightness* and *beauty* of the flowers which then make their appearance, as this is the import of *Zif*. Within this period God published the Law from Mount Sinai, commanded the erection of the Tabernacle, which was accomplished in the first day of the second year, and in the subsequent days of the first month the various laws regarding the sacrifices, the distinction of clean and unclean animals, together with all the details of the ritual that form the contents of the after part of the book of Exodus and of the whole of Leviticus, were delivered. But for this comparison of dates we should scarcely be aware of the vast amount of action condensed into so brief a space. It is clear that the sojourn at the foot of the sacred mount was no idle vacation to the chosen people. The intimation is palpable, that in all matters pertaining to divine worship a listless and languid deportment is sadly out of place, and that the utmost activity of mind and heart is called for. "Diligent in business, fervent in spirit, serving the Lord," is the true motto.

2. *Take ye the sum of all the congregation of the children of Israel.* Heb. שאו את ראש *seoo eth rōsh*, lit. *take up, lift up, elevate the head.* The expression would not seem to be in itself the most natural for conveying the idea of census-taking . We should be inclined. from the force of the words, to render the clause, "elevate the headship," that is, taking "head" as an abstract equivalent to *chief, principal*, we would understand it as implying that a special prominence and distinction was to be given to what might be deemed the *headship* of the congregation composed of the males of above twenty years of age, but excluding females, children, and the infirm and aged. These were to be enumerated and registered, which was a kind of *elevation* predicated of this portion of the people, in contradistinction from the others. This construction

Israel, after their families, by the house of their fathers, with the number of *their* names, every male by their polls;

is favored by the Gr. λαβετε αρχην, *take the principality* of all the congregation, by which we suppose to be meant *the principal* or *most distinguishing part*. But however probable this interpretation, it is certain that the majority of the versions agree with the rendering of the English. Thus, Chal. "Take the sum, or computation, of the congregation of the sons of Israel." Syr. "Take the sum of the number of the heads of the whole assembly." Sam. "Take the sum of the congregation," etc. Arab. "Take the sum of the sons of Israel." In this rendering we, on the whole, concur, though with some degree of doubt, and take the leading idea to be that of *capitation.* "Taking the head" is ascertaining the sum total, and it is obvious that the summation of a series of numbers is the bringing them, as it were, into a head. Thus we speak of *heading up* a row or a column of figures. As in the human body all the different parts are developed from the head, and exist in it in potency, so the sum total in any numerical count is in like manner a *head* to all the different parts of which it is composed, and into which it may be resolved. So the word *capital,* from *caput, head,* is familiar with us to denote the amount of wealth belonging to an individual or a company. The parallel usage of the Scriptures in regard to this word is worthy of note, Ps. 139:17, 'How precious are thy thoughts unto me, O God, how great *is the sum of them* (Heb. *roshĕhem, their head*)." Ps. 119:160, "Thy word is true from the beginning;" rather, "*The sum total* (Heb. *rōsh, head*) of thy word is truth." From this general order it is evident from what follows that the Levites were to be exempted, v. 47.——¶ *After their families, by the house of their fathers.* Heb. *lemishpehothâm, according to their families;* Gr. κατα συγγενειας αυτων, *according to their kindreds,* Luke 1:61. The precise distinction here designed to be understood between "their families" and "the houses of their fathers," is not entirely obvious. In the summoning together of the congregation under Joshua, ch. 7:14, for the search which resulted in the detection of Achan, they came by tribes, by families, and by houses, which would seem to imply that families denoted a wider range of kindred than houses. But we find ourselves forced to the conclusion that the phrase "house of their fathers" is merely exegetical of "families;" that is to say, that the way in which the different families in any tribe were distinguished, was by denominating them respectively from that individual who could properly be termed its *father, founder,* or *head.* Otherwise we are at a loss to conceive how the families could be distinguished. Thus in the account of the numbering recorded ch. 26:5–7, we seem to be furnished with a clew to the diction before us; "Take the sum of the people, from twenty years old and upward; as the LORD commanded Moses and the children of Israel, which went forth out of the land of Egypt. Reuben, the eldest son of Israel: the children of Reuben; Hanoch, of whom cometh the family of the Hanochites: of Pallu, the family of the Palluites: of Hezron, the family of the Hezronites: of Carmi, the family of the Carmites. These are the families of the Reubenites: and they that were numbered of them were forty and three thousand

3 From twenty years old and upward, all that are able to go forth to war in Israel: thou and Aaron shall number them by their armies.

---

and seven hundred and thirty." In this paragraph we see how it is that the families in a tribe are distinguished. The eldest son of Reuben is Hanoch, and all his descendants are called from him Hanochites. He was therefore the head or father of that family; and so, of the rest who are mentioned. We know not what to make of any "houses of fathers" apart from these families, upon whom the fathers' names are thus called. These several families might each of them be numerously subdivided into minor branches, but they would still, as we suppose, be called by the name of their common ancestor, which is perhaps intimated in the Gr. version of the present passage, "According to their kindred, according to the houses of their patriarchal fathers."——¶ *With the number of their names.* Heb. *bemispar shēmoth, in, with, by,* or *according to their names.* If our previous suggestions are well founded respecting the relation which this census bears to the preceding, we may reasonably suppose that the actual *number* of the host was ascertained by the number of half shekels received by Moses on that occasion, Ex. 38:25, 26, but the names may not have been recorded, nor even the people duly classified according to the arrangement here prescribed, nor their pedigree accurately ascertained, which was a work that would require a considerable time, at least as compared with the collecting the poll-tax above mentioned.——¶ *By their polls.* Heb. *legulgelothâm, according to their skulls.* This is equivalent to *man* or *person.* Thus Ex. 38:25, "A bekah for every man." Heb. "A bekah for a skull." From the same root comes "Golgotha," *the place of a skull.* Gr. "According to their head." "Head by head."—*Cov.* "Poll by poll."—*Mat.* "Man by man."—*Gen.* The sum total was to be made up of the separate units.

V. 3. *From twenty years and upward.* Heb. "From the son of twenty years." That is, going on in the twentieth year, but not having completed it, which is the force of the original. This became ever after the age at which one was thought fit for war. According to the Jewish writers, sixty was the age when they were considered to be exempt from military service, but this is nowhere stated in the Scriptures.——¶ *All that are able to go forth to war in Israel.* Heb. *kol yotzë tzâbâ, every one going forth host-wise.* "Every one that goeth forth (with) the army."—*Ains.* That is, every one that usually goes forth, every one that is able to go. The present participle in Hebrew denotes an *habitual* course of action, thus involving oftentimes the idea of the future, and occasionally of the past; whence some commentators contend that the phrase here refers properly to those that came forth out of Egypt, as appears from ch. 26:4, where the very same Heb. term is thus rendered. This would of course exclude all that were not of Israel, all that were under twenty, and all that would naturally be incapacitated from disease, old age, and other infirmities. It is to be observed, however, that there is nothing in the original corresponding to "able," which word might therefore more properly have been printed in italics.——¶ *Thou and Aaron shall number them by their armies.* Heb. *tiphkedu othâm letzibothâm,* rendered by Ainsworth, *ye shall muster them by their armies.* The Heb. term (תִּפְקְדוּ *tiphkedu*), rendered in our version "number," does not primarily convey this idea. Recourse to lexicography will show that the leading sense of the word is *to visit*, either with a view to mercy and blessing, or to punishment, and hence *to inspect, to survey, to loak after, to oversee, to preside*, general ideas which include also, from the force of the Hiphil or causative form, the import of *giving in charge, appointing over, ordering, disposing, and commanding.* In the use of the terms *visit* and *visitor* as applied to a class of men constituting a board of revision and superintendence in connection with universities and other incorporated institutions, whose duty it is to mark defects, to rectify wrongs, and to enforce statutes, we find an illustration of the extended meaning which this term bears in the sacred writings. The following examples will throw light upon the usage. Gen. 21:1, "The Lord *visited* Sarah, and did unto Sarah as he had spoken." Gen. 39:4, "And Joseph found grace in his sight, and he served him; and he *made him overseer* over his house, and all that he had he put into his hand." Lev. 26:16, "*I will appoint over* you terror, consumption, and the burning ague." Num. 3:10, "Thou shalt *appoint* Aaron and his sons," i. e. give them their charge; and so very often for *appointing, intrusting*, and *giving charge and power to look after.* Ex. 20:5, "*Visiting* the iniquity of the fathers upon the children." The overseer or visitor is clothed with power to *punish* or *animadvert upon* offenders, in which sense the word often occurs. It is found also in the sense of *mustering* or *numbering*, as in the chapter before us, but this is merely an incidental sense, for it does not strictly signify *to number*, although at the *muster* or *review* the people might be numbered. But the idea of *numbering* has become attached to the term because the *inspection, survey, ordering*, and *disposition* implied in the term was usually an accompaniment of the capitation or census-taking. The proper significance of *pâkad, to visit*, has thus become extended so as to cover a ground for which it was not originally designed. The appropriate term for *numbering* is ספר *sâphar*, with which פקד *pâkad* is not synonymous, the two differing in the manner above stated. The accessory has therefore, in this instance, assumed the place of the principal—a fact which it is desirable for the reader to know. "To *inspect* or *visit* the people," says Mr. Bates (Heb. Lex. *sub voce*), "related as well to their conduct, religious and civil, as to their number, and at such musters, lustrations, purifications, and typical atonements were necessary." See Ex. 30:12. When it is said, therefore, in the passage before us, "Thou and Aaron shall number them by their armies," the import is not so strictly that of *numbering* as of *disposition* and *arrangement;* they were to be *inspected* and *marshalled*, and *set in proper array.* We are happy to be confirmed in the above interpretation by the remarks of a valuable writer of the 17th century (Robert Gell), whose work, entitled "An Essay towards the Amendment of the last English Translation of the Bible," has come into our hand since the above was written. "They render *pâkad, to number*, which though it so signifies, yet in the business of this and the next chapter, it is a word too general, and is more properly to be termed *to visit*, or rather *to muster;* as the Latin phrase imports, "exercitum lustrare," "facere militum recognitionem." So "armilustrum" signifies *mustering*, a viewing of harness, weapons, and soldiers. For they who *mus-*

ter their forces do not only take account *how many* their soldiers are, and so *number* them, but they also take notice and inquire how able, how well appointed, how well furnished they are for war. Besides, the Scripture throughout this and the next chapter useth diverse words, as *mispar* for *number*, and *pâkad* for *visiting* or *mustering*. So that the translation confounds those acts which the Spirit of God distinguisheth." To this he adds that the muster prescribed involved the idea of inspection as to sex, age, pedigree, etc., and as the design of this was to cull out the choice, the flower of the host, the most hale, vigorous, and valiant, or the truly "excellent ones," therefore the term *visiting* or *numbering* is applied to them; for that "such are highly esteemed, loved, cared for, *numbered*, appears from the contrary; as it is said of persons despicable and contemned, *extra numerum esse; nullo numero esse; nullius esse numeri*—military phrases implying such as are of *no reckoning, no account*, who stand for *ciphers*. But the Lord's soldiers are all *numbered, visited, mustered*." That there is an ulterior purport in this, would appear from the usage of the term in the following passage: Luke 12:7, "Even the very hairs of your head are all *numbered*." The idea here is not precisely that of *numbering*, which would of course be useless to Omniscience, but of the minutest inspection, of the most intimate providential cognizance, a knowledge accompanied with the most watchful and tender care. Is. 13:4, "The Lord of hosts *mustereth* (Heb. *mepakkēd*) the host of the battle." The battle here is spiritual, for the Lord wages no other, and mustering the host is arranging, ordering, and arraying the internal states and principles of those who compose it. Again, Is. 40:26, "Lift up your eyes on high, and behold, who hath created these things, that bringeth out their host by *number*." So also Ps. 147:4, "He telleth the *number* of the stars, he calleth them all by their names." That by numbering in these passages is signified to *ordain, order*, or *arrange*, is evident from the fact that it is spoken of the Most High, who does not in reality number or name armies or stars, but inspects, orders, arranges, and disposes the things represented by them, which are of course things pertaining to the kingdom of heaven and the church. As this is the high prerogative of Jehovah himself, who alone is competent to the task, we may gather from this source, perhaps, the true grounds of the reason why David's conduct in numbering the people was viewed by the Lord in so heinous a light. As the people of Israel represented typically the church, and as it is the province of the Lord alone to order the internal conditions and interests of the church, therefore any measure which by its representative significancy would imply that man was invested with that power involved a high degree of presumption, and therefore called for punishment. Such was the character of David's conduct in the transaction referred to. He took it upon him to do that which in its true bearings implied an invasion of the divine prerogative. Hence its enormity. We may farther observe upon this subject of *numbering*, that while it evidently has no special moral character when viewed in itself, yet it is occasionally introduced in such connections as to compel us to seek some sense beyond that of the simple letter. Thus for example, Ps. 90:12, "So teach us to *number* our days, that we may apply our hearts unto wisdom." As man is ignorant of the number of his days on earth, Ps. 71:15, as "the number of his years is hidden," not to the "oppressor" only, but to all other men, it is evident that a man can "number his days" only by ordering and regulating the states of his life from one day to another in such a manner as to meet the demands of true wisdom. Is. 38 : 10, "I said, in the cutting off of my days, I shall go to the gates of the grave; I am deprived of the residue of my years (Heb. *pikkadti, I am numbered* as to the residue of my years)." That is, the term of my existence is ordered and arranged, and in the divine counsels brought to a completion. Dan. 5 : 25, 26, "And this is the writing that was written, Mene, Mene, Tekel, Upharsin. This is the interpretation of the thing: Mene; God hath *numbered* thy kingdom;" i. e. hath brought to an end, hath finished, thy kingdom, after accurately exploring, weighing, and estimating its quality. And so elsewhere.—From the whole, then, we gather that the *numbering* here commanded to Moses and Aaron has respect rather to the visitation, inspection, and orderly arrangement implied in the more genuine import of the term, and that in its typical bearings it refers to that inner process which causes the church to "shine forth fair as the moon, clear as the sun, and terrible *as an army with banners*," in which last expression we are probably to recognize an allusion to the appearance of the hosts of Israel when marshalled in the order described in this and the following chapters. The principle we regard as sound that the nation of Israel sustained a typical relation to the church of after times—the relation, as it were, of a shadow to a substance—and that consequently it is no matter of surprise if we occasionally meet with terms which, though applied in the first instance to the Israelitish economy, yet have not their meaning exhausted in that application, and are therefore to be carried over, as we may say, to the more adequate and substantial subject of the Lord's church under the New Testament. Thus, for instance, the promises in regard to the excessive multiplication of the seed of Abraham cannot be regarded as having been fulfilled in the literal history of that people. Gen. 13 : 16, "And I will make thy seed as the dust of the earth: so that if a man can *number* the dust of the earth, then shall thy seed also be numbered." Gen. 15 : 5, "And he brought him forth abroad, and said, Look now toward heaven, and tell the stars, if thou be able to *number* them: and he said unto him, So shall thy seed be." Num. 23 : 10, "Who can count the dust of Jacob, or *number* the fourth part thereof?" This language can only be considered as holding good of the spiritual and not of the natural Israel. They became indeed a populous nation, but the expressions cited above far transcend the actuality of their literal increase. It is in the Christian church only that they receive a complete fulfilment. The same remark may be made in regard to the perpetuity of David's throne. 2 Sam. 7 : 10, "Thine house and thy kingdom shall be established for ever before thee: thy throne shall be established for ever." Comp. Ps. 89 : 36, 37. Luke 1 : 33. We are compelled to have recourse to an ulterior meaning in order to satisfy the demands of these texts. In giving, therefore, a similar scope to the word *number* in this connection, we consider ourselves warranted by the principle above stated, and which has ever been considered sound by the great mass of Christian expositors. The giving up of this principle is in our view a most injudicious and dangerous concession to the spirit of German rationalism, which would fain eliminate from the Word of God every divine element.

4 And with you there shall be a man of every tribe; every one head[c] of the house of his fathers.

5 And these *are* the names of the men that shall stand with you: Of *the tribe of* Reuben; Elizur[d] the son of Shedeur.

6 Of Simeon; Shelumiel the son of Zurishaddai.

7 Of Judah; Nahshon[e] the son of Amminadab.

8 Of Issachar; Nethaneel the son of Zuar.

9 Of Zebulun; Eliab the son of Helon.

10 Of the children of Joseph: of Ephraim, Elishama the son of Ammihud: of Manasseh, Gamaliel the son of Pedahzur.

11 Of Benjamin; Abidan the son of Gideoni.

12 Of Dan; Ahiezer the son of Ammishaddai.

c Ex. 18. 25. Josh. 22. 14. *d* ch. 2. 10, etc. ch. 7. 30, etc. 10. 18, etc. *e* Ruth 4. 20.

V. 4. *And with you there shall be a man of every tribe.* Heb. "With you there shall be (plur.) a man, a man to a tribe." This is rendered for the most part by the different versions as in ours—"a man of every tribe," as the subsequent verses show to have been the fact; although from the plural usage and the repetition of "man," it might seem that more than one individual was intended for each tribe. But as shown from parallel usage it is doubtless a distributive form of expression involving no special peculiarity of sense. Probably the more exact idea is, "there shall be with you some man or other to each tribe," but whoever he were, he was to be one holding a conspicuous rank in his tribe. This is implied in the appellation "head of the house of his fathers," which however does not signify the first-born in their several tribes, but those who were acknowledged as prominent on some other account, as their wisdom or valor, or some other distinguishing trait.

V. 5. *These are the names of the men that shall stand with you.* To "stand with" is to "assist," which is evident from the fact that the word "assist" itself is etymologically equivalent to "stand with" (*ad* and *sto*).——¶ *Of* (*the tribe of*) *Reuben.* Heb. "To Reuben." Gr. "Of those of Reuben." The supply of "tribe," "sons," "children," or something equivalent is very proper, as appears from comparing v. 10, where instead of simply "of Joseph," as here "of Reuben," we read "of the children of Joseph."—In the ensuing verses to v. 16 we have barely a list of the names of the twelve chiefs, princes, or headmen who were now selected as assistants to Moses and Aaron in the muster enjoined. In regard to these there is nothing of special note demanding attention, excepting, perhaps, that in the order of recital Reuben, Simeon, Judah, Issachar, and Zebulun, the sons of Leah, and Ephraim, Manasseh, and Benjamin, the sons of Rachel, take the precedence of Dan, Asher, Gad, and Naphtali, the sons of the handmaids Billah and Zilpah. In the former enumeration, Ex. 1:2, 3, and in the inscription on the precious stones, Ex. 28:9, 10, the order is very nearly the same, although the name of Asher does not come in here as elsewhere.—Levi and Joseph are omitted; the first because that tribe was to be numbered by itself, and the second, because Joseph's two sons, Ephraim and Manasseh, representing the double portion that pertained to his birthright,

13 Of Asher; Pagiel the son of Ocran.

14 Of Gad; Eliasaph the son of Deuel.

15 Of Naphtali; Ahira the son of Enan.

16 These[f] *were* the renowned of the congregation, princes of the tribes of their fathers, heads[g] of thousands in Israel.

f ch. 7. 2. 1 Chr. 27. 16, etc. g Ex. 18. 21, 25.

---

were substituted in his place, Gen. 48: 5, 6. 1 Chron. 5:1. 2. Gad is also omitted, as his tribe was virtually merged in that of Judah, Num. 2:10–14. "Deuel," v. 14, is called "Reuel," ch. 2:14. The similarity of the letter ד D and ר R would make the exchange of the one for the other easy.

V. 16. *These were the renowned of the congregation.* Heb. *kerüë hâedâh, the called ones of the congregation.* The original word signifies literally *called* or *named*, as if in this instance implying those who were designated by the Lord himself to this function, which would of course have the effect to render them more distinguished and honorable than before. The Latin Vulg. accordingly has "nobilissimi principes multitudinis," *most noble princes of the multitude.* The Gr. επικλητοι, *distinguished, illustrious.* In other connections, as Num. 16:2. 26:9. Ez. 23:23, it is rendered to the same effect, *famous* and *renowned;* but for the most part the English words answering to it are *called, invited, bidden,* and also *guests.* We may here perhaps unite the two senses, and consider the term as denoting persons *renowned* for the wisdom of age, and therefore *called* to consult upon all matters of importance pertaining to the tribes. This is favored by some of the earlier English versions. "Ancient men (or elders)."—*Cov.* "Counsellors."—*Mat.* "The called."—*Ains.* "They who are called."—*Pur.* Rabbi Sol. Jarchi says these were the same personages who in Egypt were beaten by Pharaoh's taskmasters. Ex. 5:14, "And the officers of the children of Israel, which Pharaoh's taskmasters had set over them, were beaten, and demanded, Wherefore have ye not fulfilled your task in making brick, both yesterday and to-day, as heretofore?" ——¶ *Of the congregation.* From the usage of this term in several instances it would appear that it does not always denote the whole congregation, the entire mass of the Israelitish nation, but the deputies or representatives of the several tribes convened and acting in the name of the whole. Michaelis (*Laws of Moses*, P. I. art. 45) draws this inference from the fact that while Moses is said to have spoken "to the whole congregation," yet he could not possibly have been heard by one or two millions of people, and therefore he must have addressed himself to a certain number of persons deputed to represent the rest. These persons he understands to be denoted by "the called of the congregation" here mentioned. Syr. "The celebrated of the assembly." This import of a national council or diet, of a representative character, we regard as probably the correct one. The context will generally determine when it bears this sense.——¶ *Princes of the tribes of their fathers.* Heb. *nesiïë mattoth, princes* or *rulers of the tribes.* "Captains."—*Cov.* "Lords."—*Mat., Cran.* The original is derived from a root signifying *to raise, to elevate,* and denotes accordingly one who is *lifted up* and *officially preferred* above the rest of the people.——¶ *Heads of the thousands in Israel.* Gr. χιλιαρχοι, *chiliarchs.*

17 And Moses and Aaron
took these men which are expressed [h] by *their* names [i]:
18 And they assembled all
the congregation together on
the first *day* of the second
month, and they declared their
pedigrees after their families,
by the house of their fathers,
according [k] to the number of
the names, from twenty years
old and upward, by their polls.
19 As [l] the LORD commanded Moses, so he numbered them
in the wilderness of Sinai.
20 And the children of Reuben, Israel's eldest son, by
their generations, after their
families, by the house of their
fathers, according to the number of the names, by their
polls, every male from twenty
years old and upward, all that
were able to go forth to war;
21 Those that were numbered
of them, *even* of the tribe of

h Rev. 7. 4, etc. i John 10. 3. k ver. 20, etc. l ver. 2.

These "heads" were not only men of note and weight in their tribes, such men as Jethro advised Moses to associate with him in governing the people, Ex. 18:21, but also commanders of the bands or companies of thousands into which the tribes were divided, respecting which see Ex. 18:21, 25. The Heb. term for "thousands" is rendered "families" in Judg. 6:15, though retained in Mic. 5:2, where it is translated by the Gr. "rulers" or "governors," which rendering is sanctioned by the Spirit of inspiration, as it occurs Mat. 2:6.

V. 17. *Which are expressed by their names.* Heb. *nikkebo*, *pricked* or *pierced*, i. e. *designated.* See Note on Lev. 26:11.

V. 18. *And they assembled, etc.* As the command was given by the Lord from the Tabernacle on the first day of the second month, v. 1, so it appears it was immediately executed, or began to be executed, on the same day. True obedience is ever a prompt obedience.——¶ *And they declared their pedigrees.* Heb. *yithyaledu, they genealogized themselves.* That is, recited their pedigree according to their families and houses. The Gr., according to one reading, has επεσκεπησαν, *recounted*, and according to another επηξονουσαν, i. e. referred or conveyed to αξονας, *tables*, denoting a process of registration. As they declared their genealogies, the proper officers took them down. The fair implication is, that in all matters pertaining to the order in which the Lord would have his church arranged, while he in a supreme manner controls and overrules every thing, yet his people are not to forego their own agency, but are to do all in their power to *number* and arrange themselves.——¶ *By their polls.* Heb. "By their skulls." Gr. "From head to head."

V. 20. *And the children of Reuben.* Reuben holds the first place, not because his tribe was the most numerous, for in this respect it fell short of several of the others, but from his being the first-born.——¶ *By their generations, after their families, etc.* See on these subdivisions of the tribes the Note on v. 2. above. "Generations" denotes a larger number than "families," and "families" than "houses," while "houses," or households, comprised all the individuals pertaining to each.

V. 21. *Those that were numbered of them, etc.* Heb. *pekudĕhem le-mattch re-ubĕn, the numbered of them to the tribe of Reuben*, or more correctly *the arranged, the marshalled, the ordered*;

Reuben, *were* forty and six thousand and five hundred.
22 Of the children of Simeon,
by their generations, after their
families, by the house of their
fathers, those that were numbered of them, according to the
number of the names, by their
polls, every male from twenty
years old and upward, all that
were able to go forth to war;
23 Those that were number-
ed of them, *even* of the tribe of
Simeon, *were* fifty and nine
thousand and three hundred.
24 Of the children of Gad,
by their generations, after their
families, by the house of their
fathers, according to the number of the names, from twenty
years old and upward, all that
were able to go forth to war;

---

for we still adhere to the view given above of the purport, in this connection, of the original word. We do not regard it as implying strictly *to number*, but rather to *review*, *marshal*, or *arrange*. The numbering of the previous census we take to be assumed in this transaction, and made its basis. It will be observed that in every instance the phrase "according to the number of the names" occurs, which we take to imply that the number already ascertained was made use of. What can be understood, for example, by the expression predicated of the tribe of Simeon "numbered according to the number of the names," especially when the word for "numbered" (*pekudâv*) is entirely different from that for "number" (*mispar*)? What is it but an unmeaning tautology? But take the term "numbered" here to signify *reviewed*, *marshalled*, *arranged*, and all is clear. In fact, the whole transaction recorded in this chapter, instead of being properly a census appointed for the purpose of ascertaining the numbers of the host, was undoubtedly an *inspection*, *ordering* and *classification* of the whole body, on the basis of a prior census, with reference to the order of the march and the encampment during the sojourn in the wilderness. What else can we infer from the absolute identity of the totals here given with that given in Ex. 38 : 26. In regard to each tribe the object is not to ascertain *de novo* of how many it consisted, but the number already previously ascertained is merely restated. We here, after Ainsworth and Adam Clarke, present a comparative view of the state of the tribes under the present and a still later census recorded ch. 26, which will preclude the necessity of farther comment upon a large portion of the chapter. In the first column the numbers are given in their *decreasing* proportion, in the second the *increase* of some and the *decrease* of others will be seen at a glance.

	1st Census. Ch. I.	*2d Census.* Ch. XXVI.
1. Judah,	74,600	76,500
2. Dan,	62,700	64,400
3. Simeon,	59,300	22,200
4. Zebulun,	57,400	60,500
5. Issachar,	54,400	64,300
6. Naphtali,	53,400	45,400
7. Reuben,	46,500	43,730
8. Gad,	45,650	40,500
9. Asher,	41,500	53,400
10. Ephraim,	40,500	32,500
11. Benjamin,	35,400	45,600
12. Manasseh,	32,200	52,700
Total,	603,550	Tot. 601,730

Judah, as being the most distinguished, is the most numerous tribe, and Manasseh the least so, the difference between them being no less than 42,400. But in the subsequent census, ch. 26;

25 Those that were numbered of them, *even* of the tribe of Gad, *were* forty and five thousand six hundred and fifty.

26 Of the children of Judah, by their generations, after their families, by the house of their fathers, according to the number of the names, from twenty years old and upward, all that were able to go forth to war;

27 Those that were numbered of them, *even* of the tribe of Judah, *were* threescore and fourteen thousand and six hundred[m].

28 Of the children of Issachar, by their generations, after their families, by the house of their fathers, according to the number of the names, from twenty years old and upward, all that were able to go forth to war;

29 Those that were numbered of them, *even* of the tribe of Issachar, *were* fifty and four thousand and four hundred.

30 Of the children of Zebulun, by their generations, after their families, by the house of their fathers, according to the number of the names, from twenty years old and upward, all that were able to go forth to war;

31 Those that were numbered of them, *even* of the tribe of Zebulun, *were* fifty and seven thousand and four hundred.

32 Of the children of Joseph,[n] *namely*, of the children of Ephraim, by their generations, after their families, by the house of their fathers, according to the number of the names, from twenty years old and upward,

m 2 Chr. 17. 14

n Deut. 33. 17.

34, while Judah has the pre-eminence, Simeon the third in number before, has become the least, and Manasseh has risen to the seventh place. During the interval between the two enumerations seven of the tribes had an *increase;* five a *decrease.* Which they were and to what extent the change occurred may be learned from the foregoing table.—It is remarkable that except in the case of Gad in this chapter, and Reuben in ch. 26, all the numbers are whole or round numbers, beginning with *thousands* and ending with *hundreds*—Gad and Reuben alone ending with *tens.* Whether this is to be understood as the *exact* enumeration of the tribes, in which case a special providence is to be recognized in precluding broken numbers, or whether it was designed to give simply round numbers without regard to *units* and *fractions*, it is not easy to determine. We are inclined, on the whole, to adopt Rosenmuller's solution, viz., that as the muster now instituted was in order to select from the whole body of the people those that were "able to go forth to war," and to marshal them into proper array, they were accordingly divided, as is common in all armies, into divisions of thousands and hundreds, leaving the overplus uncounted, even although it may have consisted in some cases of those who were twenty years and upward. This remainder would constitute a corps, from which recruits would be taken to supply the places of those who might die or be otherwise disqualified for military service. This confirms our previous suggestion: that the object of the measure here recorded was not

all that were able to go forth to war;

33 Those that were numbered of them, *even* of the tribe of Ephraim, *were* forty thousand and five hundred.

34 Of the children of Manasseh, by their generations, after their families, by the house of their fathers, according to the number of the names, from twenty years old and upward, all that were able to go forth to war;

35 Those that were numbered of them, *even* of the tribe of Manasseh, *were* thirty and two thousand and two hundred.

36 Of the children of Benjamin, by their generations, after their families, by the house of their fathers, according to the number of the names, from twenty years old and upward, all that were able to go forth to war;

37 Those that were numbered of them, *even* of the tribe of Benjamin, *were* thirty and five thousand and four hundred.

38 Of the children of Dan, by their generations, after their families, by the house of their fathers, according to the number of the names, from twenty years old and upward, all that were able to go forth to war;

39 Those that were numbered of them, *even* of the tribe of Dan, *were* threescore and two thousand and seven hundred.

40 Of the children of Asher, by their generations, after their families, by the house of their fathers, according to the number of the names, from twenty years old and upward, all that were able to go forth to war;

41 Those that were numbered of them, *even* of the tribe of Asher, *were* forty and one thousand and five hundred.

42 Of the children of Naphtali, throughout their generations, after their families, by the house of their fathers, according to the number of the names, from twenty years old and upward, all that were able to go forth to war;

43 Those that were numbered of them, *even* of the tribe of

---

strictly to make out an exact numerical census. This is still farther confirmed by the fact that in every instance of the repetition of the language of v. 21, "those that were numbered of them, even of the tribe of Reuben, were," etc. The Heb. has it, "the numbered of them to the tribe of Reuben was," etc., as if *setting off* or *assigning* to each from the whole or *exact* number of which it consisted, a certain definite *round* number, rejecting the units. This we conceive to be the force of the particle *to.*

V. 22–43. The question may perhaps be asked, why was it necessary to repeat the formula of enumeration in every instance instead of stating in one comprehensive passage that the tribes were all numbered, or that each tribe contributed such a quota, and the sum total was so much? We suggest in reply that, although it might seem at first view that a revelation from heaven, to give all needed knowledge, and yet be comprised within reasonable limits, could not *afford* to devote space to such repetitions as we find here and else-

Naphtali, *were* fifty and three thousand and four hundred.

44 These[o] *are* those that were numbered, which Moses and Aaron numbered, and the princes of Israel, *being* twelve men: each one was for the house of his fathers.

45 So were all those that were numbered of the children of Israel, by the house of their fathers, from twenty years old and upward, all that were able to go forth to war in Israel;

46 Even all they that were[p] numbered were six hundred

o c. 26. 64.

p Ex. 12. 37. 38 26. c. 2. 32. 26. 51. Deut. 10. 22.

---

where, particularly in regard to building the Tabernacle, yet there may be moral considerations amply sufficient to warrant the course pursued. One reason may be, that the Most High is particular to record to the honor of his servants an exact obedience to an exact command. He would, moreover, impressively teach that he is no respecter of persons, that he has the same care of and regard for one as another; that as a common Father he neglects none, but remembers all. He thus removes too all ground of discontent and envy on the score of alleged favoritism. The numbers of the fewest shall be as distinctly and minutely specified as those of the most numerous, and we can easily see that the fulfilment of the divine promise in the multiplication of the peculiar people would engrave itself more deeply on their hearts when each particular tribe was specifically reminded of its own separate increase. A minute recital leads to a more minute contemplation.

V. 44. *These are those that were numbered, etc.* Heb. lit. "These are the marshalled or mustered which Moses mustered and Aaron and the princes of Israel: twelve men; one man each to the house of his fathers were they." Gr. "One man for one tribe according to the tribe of their fathers' houses were they." Here also we express our preference for the rendering *mustered* instead of *numbered.*

Vs. 45, 46. *So were all those that were numbered, etc.* The rendering of these verses is not happy. The strictness of the letter requires the following:—"And they were, all the mustered (ones) of the sons of Israel, to the house of their fathers, from the son of twenty years old and upward, every one that was able to go forth to war in Israel; they were, (I say), all the mustered ones, six hundred thousand, and three thousand, and five hundred and fifty." The increase indicated by the sum total is certainly remarkable, but not such as to require the operation of a miracle. We recognize the effect rather of an extraordinary benediction than of a miraculous generation in the multitudinous progeny of seventy persons during the space of 216 years. The Lord had promised that he would make of the seed of Abraham "a great nation," and the record before us shows that the promise was abundantly fulfilled. This promise was renewed from time to time to the patriarchs for their fuller assurance and consolation, and the result enumerated here is celebrated in worthy strains, by the Psalmist, Ps. 105: 24. 37, "He increased his people greatly and made them stronger than their enemies.—He brought them forth also with silver and gold, and there was not one feeble person among their tribes;" from which we infer, that though the course of nature was not violated, yet its powers were extraordinarily aided

thousand and three thousand
and five hundred and fifty.
47 But [q] the Levites after the
tribe of their fathers were not
numbered among them.
48 For the LORD had spoken
unto Moses, saying,

[q] c. 2. 33. c. 3. 4. 1 Chr. 6. & 21, 6.

49 Only thou shalt not number the tribe of Levi, neither
take the sum of them among the
children of Israel:
50 But [r] thou shalt appoint
the Levites over the tabernacle
of testimony, and over all the

[r] Ex. 38. 21. c. 3. 6, etc.

---

in accomplishing the result. The grand lesson taught by the history is, that the divine promises will all and always be infallibly performed, as will also the divine threatenings. It was said that Caleb and Joshua alone should enter the land of Canaan, Num. 14:30, and such was the precise fact. All the rest, because of their murmuring, idolatry, and disobedience, perished in the wilderness; some having been slain with the sword, some swallowed up of the earth, some consumed with pestilence, some stung by serpents, and some having died a natural death. Consequently neither their eyes saw, nor their feet trod upon, the goodly land of promise, as the Lord had threatened. To friend and to foe the Lord will be sure to be as good as his word. Analogous to the increase of the natural seed of Israel is that also of the spiritual. The church says in heart, Is. 49:21, "Who hath begotten me these?" The Lord's kingdom began to be preached by the twelve apostles and the seventy disciples, and that immortal seed of the word soon begat "many ten thousands of Jews," Acts 21:20, and many more of the Gentiles, even an "innumerable multitude," Rev. 7:9.

V. 47. *But the Levites, etc.* Heb. "But the Levites, according to the tribe of their fathers, were not mustered in the midst of them." This tribe was exempt from military service; accordingly when they were numbered the census included all even from children of one month old. See ch. 3:15. 26:62. The phrase "after, or according to, the tribe of their fathers" is probably a compendious form of expression denoting in brief what is said at length of all the rest, "by their generations, after their families, by the house of their fathers," etc.

V. 49. *Only thou shalt not number the tribe of Levi, neither take the sum of them.* The truth of our previous remarks on the distinction between *numbering* and *mustering* is evident from the language of this verse, in which we cannot suppose that "numbering" and "taking the sum" signify the same thing. The original in the former case is *tiphkod*, which in its different forms we have generally rendered *muster*, *marshal*, etc. for the reasons stated in the note on v. 3. Nothing was to be done towards arranging or marshalling the tribe of Levi together with the others, because they were to be set apart to a peculiar function with which no others were to interfere.

V. 50. *But thou shalt appoint the Levites over, etc.* Heb. *haphkēd*, *shalt give in charge*, or *clothe with a visitorial power*, from the root *pâkad*, *to visit*, and in the causative *to make to visit*, that is, *to set over*. The special functions allotted to each of the several families of the Levites are detailed in the third chapter.——¶ *Tabernacle of testimony.* So called from its being the depository of the Ark of the Covenant, within which were contained the tables of the Law,

vessels thereof, and over all things that *belong* to it: they shall bear the tabernacle, and all the vessels thereof; and they shall minister unto it, and shall encamp[s] round about the tabernacle.

51 And[t] when the tabernacle setteth forward, the Levites shall take it down: and when the tabernacle is to be pitched, the Levites shall set it up: and the[u] stranger that cometh nigh shall be put to death.

52 And the children of Israel shall pitch their tents, every

s ver. 53. t c. 10. 17-21. u c. 18. 22.

---

called "tables of testimony," Ex. 31:18. ——¶ *Over all things that belong to it.* Vulg. "And whatever pertains to the ceremonies." This is perhaps favored by the next clause which is nearly equivalent, and in which "they shall minister unto it" seems to answer to the phrase before us—"they shall bear the tabernacle, and all the vessels thereof, and they shall *minister unto it,*" in effect the same as having charge of the ceremonies connected with it.——¶ *Shall bear, etc.* This service, the burdens of which were appointed by the Lord through Moses, is more particularly specified Num. 4:25. 31. 36. To aid them in it the use of six wagons was allowed to two of the three main Levitical families. Num. 7:7-9.——¶ *Shall encamp round about the tabernacle.* That is, in immediate proximity to it, between it and the stations of the rest of the tribes. The Levites, therefore, may be said to have constituted a kind of sacred legion around the palace of the Great King. Of this arrangement see in what follows, chs. 2 and 3.

V. 51. *And when the tabernacle setteth forward, the Levites shall take it down.* Heb. *ubinsoa hammishkan, and in the journeying of the tabernacle;* i. e. whenever the signal should be given by the motion of the cloudy pillar that the encampment was to be broken up and the tabernacle removed, then it was the business of the Levites to take off and roll up the curtains, to remove the upright boards from their sockets, to gather together all the component parts of the edifice, with its various utensils, and dispose of them in the most convenient way for travelling. So, on the contrary, when a new resting-place was indicated, the Levites, and they alone, were to attend to the re-erection of the tabernacle, and the putting in order of all its appurtenances.——¶ *The stranger.* That is, one who was not of the tribe of Levi. This was their peculiar province, in respect to which every one else was a stranger. So in regard to the priesthood, as distinguished from this inferior ministry or service, both Israelites and Levites were counted "strangers." Thus when Eleazer the priest took the brazen censers which had been profaned by Korah and his company, and made them into plates for covering the altar, it is said that they were "to be for a memorial unto the children of Israel, that *no stranger which is not of the seed of Aaron,* come near to offer incense before the Lord." This exclusiveness of function is recognized also by David, 1 Chron. 15:2, "Then David said, None ought to carry the ark of God but the Levites: for them hath the Lord chosen to carry the ark of God, and to minister unto him for ever."——¶ *Shall be put to death.* Heb. *yumoth, shall be made to die;* without expressly indicating whether directly by the stroke of the divine hand, or by the agency of the magis-

man[v] by his own camp, and
every man by his own standard,
throughout their hosts.
53 But the Levites[w] shall
pitch round about the tabernacle of testimony, that there be
no wrath[x] upon the congregation of the children of Israel:

v c. 2. 2. 24. 2. w ver. 50. x c. 8. 19. 16. 46. 18. 5. 1 Sam. 6. 19.

---

trate. Targ. Jon. "He shall be killed by fire flaming out from before the Lord." The case of Nadab and Abihu, and of Uzzah, 1 Chron. 13:10, would seem to imply that a special interposition of heaven was to be generally understood by the expression.

V. 52. *Every man by his own camp.* That is, at his own camping-place, in his own allotted station. Gr. "In his own order," equivalent to Paul's phrase in speaking of the resurrection, 1 Cor. 15:23, "every man in his own order." The order here referred to is described in the next chapter.——¶ *Every man by his own standard.* Gr. "By his own regiment."

V. 53. *That there be no wrath upon the congregation, etc.;* as there would be danger of if the discrimination between holy and common were not most rigidly observed. The exterior portion of the encampment was not to press too closely upon the consecrated centre. The reason was the same that dictated the prohibition respecting the body of the people approaching too near the sacred mount from which the Law was delivered. Ex. 19:12, 13, "And thou shalt set bounds unto the people round about, saying, Take heed to yourselves that ye go not up into the mount, or touch the border of it: whosoever toucheth the mount shall be surely put to death: there shall not an hand touch it, but he shall surely be stoned, or shot through; whether it be beast or man, it shall not live." The order here prescribed was wholly of a *representative* character, as there is no reason to suppose that the *interior states of mind* of the tribe of Levi were distinguished by any higher degree of spirituality or sanctity than those of the rest of the nation. But a ritual or official sanctity pertained to them, which was a sufficient ground for the command here given, and the *truth* or *mystery* shadowed forth is to be sought in the true spiritual priesthood of the Christian church, which consists of all those who by the graces of their renewed spirits are brought especially near to the Lord, whether belonging to the ranks of the clergy or the laity. The import of the name Levi is *adhesion*, and wherever there is such a cleaving to the Lord from the force of an internal attraction, there are spiritual Levites, and in regard to them the above interdict, we learn, is removed under the New Testament dispensation. Is. 56:3, 6, 7, "Neither let the son of the stranger, that hath joined himself (הנלוה *hannilvâh, conjoined himself, as it were, Levitically*) to the Lord, speak, saying, The Lord hath utterly separated me from his people: neither let the eunuch say, Behold, I am a dry tree. Also the sons of the stranger, that join themselves to the Lord, to serve him, and to love the name of the Lord, to be his servants, every one that keepeth the sabbath from polluting it, and taketh hold of my covenant; even them will I bring to my holy mountain, and make them joyful in my house of prayer: their burnt offerings and their sacrifices shall be accepted upon mine altar; for mine house shall be called an house of prayer for all people." Adhesion, in this relation, is but another term for spiritual

and the Levites[y] shall keep the
charge of the tabernacle of testimony.
54 And the children of Israel
did according to all that the
LORD commanded Moses, so did
they.

y c. 3. 7, 8. 31. 30, 47. 1 Chr. 23. 32. 2 Chr. 13. 10.

CHAPTER II.

AND the LORD spake unto
Moses and unto Aaron, saying,
2 Every[a] man of the children
of Israel shall pitch by his own
standard, with the ensign of

a c. 1. 52.

---

conjunction, which is the effect of love, and all the subjects of genuine love to the Lord and charity to the neighbor are spiritual priests.

V. 54. *And the children of Israel did according to all that the Lord commanded Moses.* His being able thus to refer every thing to a divine command would effectually preclude the charge that Moses designed to elevate and aggrandize his own tribe. The opponents of revelation have always been disposed to accuse Moses of being actuated by mercenary motives, whereas the whole drift of the narrative shows that he was merely an obedient instrument in the Lord's hands for accomplishing his purposes in respect to the chosen people. Heb. 3:5, "Moses verily was faithful in all his house as a servant."

CHAPTER II.

The Ordering of the Encampment.

V. 1. *And the Lord spake unto Moses and unto Aaron.* The former order respecting the mustering was given to Moses alone; the present respecting the arrangement of the camp is given to both Moses and Aaron. The typical bearings of this arrangement had a more important reference to the spiritual order of the church, and therefore Aaron, the high priest, has a prominent part assigned him in the transaction. Moses represents that part of the economy which was more distinctively secular.

V. 2. *Every man of the children of Israel shall pitch by his own standard.* Heb. *al diglo, by his banner.* The origin of the Heb. term is not very obvious, though the Arab. has *dagal, to veil, to cover.* The Gr. renders it by *tagma, an orderly band, a cohort.* Vulg. *turmas, troops.* Chald. *tiksa*, supposed to be derived from the Gr. *taxis, order.* The idea of a *banner, standard, flag*, is generally by commentators attached to the word, and this is confirmed by the parallel usage in the following instances: Ps. 20:5, "We will rejoice in thy salvation, and in the name of our God *will set up our banners* (*nid-gol*)." Cant. 2:4, "He brought me to the banqueting house, and *his banner* (*diglo*) over me was love." Cant. 5:10, "My beloved is white and ruddy, the *chiefest* (*dâgul, a bannered one*) among ten thousands." The twelve tribes were arranged into four divisions, three in each, and each of the four was distinguished by a banner. Comp. vs. 3, 18, 25.——¶ *With the ensign of their fathers' house.* Heb. *be-othoth, in* or *with the signs.* This is usually understood to intimate that not only the several tribes, but also the several families and kindreds had their distinct ensigns or banners. This, however, is doubtful, as the original *othoth* may refer to the signs or devices figured on each of the above mentioned standards. What these were it is now impossible to determine. Ainsworth supposes that they were particular colors corresponding with those of the pre-

their father's house: far [b] off about the tabernacle of the congregation shall they pitch.

b Josh. 3. 4.

cious stones in Aaron's breastplate, on which were engraved the names of the different tribes. This he derives from the Targum of Jonathan, who expatiates thus:—"The standard of the camp of Judah was of linen of three colors, according to the three precious stones in the breastplate (Chalcedony, Sapphire, and Sardonyx), and in it were engraved and expressed the names of the three tribes, Judah, Issachar, and Zebulun; and in the midst thereof was written, 'Rise up, Lord, and let thine enemies be scattered;' in it also was portrayed the figure of a Lion. The standard of the camp of Reuben was of linen of three colors, answerable to the three precious stones in the breastplate (Sardine, Topaz, and Amethyst), and therein were engraved and expressed the names of the three tribes, Reuben, Simeon, and Gad; and in the midst thereof was written, 'Hear, O Israel, the Lord our God is one Lord;' therein also was portrayed the figure of an Hart." And so he proceeds with the rest. Another of the Rabbinical writers, Aben Ezra, says, "there were signs in every standard, and our ancestors have said that in Reuben's standard there was the figure of a Man, etc.; in Judah's standard the figure of a Lion, etc,; in Ephraim's, the figure of a Bullock, etc.; and in the standard of Dan the figure of an Eagle; so they were like the Cherubim which the prophet Ezekiel saw (Ezek. 1:10)." We may perhaps find in this circumstance a clew to the symbolic scenery, Rev. 4:6, 7, where mention is made of four living creatures precisely corresponding with these devices upon the standards of the four tribes here mentioned. Their place in the encampments was between the Tabernacle and the outmost circuit of the tribes. So on the Apocalyptic platform the four beasts are said to have occupied the space in the midst between the throne and the circle or semicircle encompassing it at considerable distance. These "living creatures" were symbols of a vast multitude. As we can only give on the subject of the standards the conjectures of Jewish writers, it is needless to dwell upon it. It is sufficient to know that the several divisions of the host had each of them a banner to serve as a rallying point to their respective tribes, and to remind them of the necessity of an orderly adherence to whatever position the Lord had assigned them. "As a bird wandering from her nest is a man wandering from his place." The following is the rendering of the Gr. of the first two verses of this chapter:—"And the Lord spoke to Moses and to Aaron saying, Let the children of Israel encamp fronting (each other), every man keeping his own rank, according to (their) standards, according to the houses of their families; the children of Israel shall encamp round about the tabernacle of witness."——¶ *Far off about the tabernacle, etc.* Heb. *minneged, from before*, i. e. *aloof, at a distance from.* "Over against round about."—*Ains.* "Away from the presence of."—*Mat.* "On the other side and round about."—*Cran.* "At a distance round about."—*Purv.* The original imports that the tents should be stationed at some distance from the tabernacle, and yet that the doors of the tents should be inwards towards the tabernacle. The following passages show the usage of the word, Ps. 38:11, "My lovers and my friends stand *aloof* (*minneged, from before*) from my sore, and my kinsmen stand afar off;" i. e. they stand at a distance, yet so that their faces look to-

3 And on the east side toward the rising of the sun shall they of the standard of the camp of Judah pitch throughout

wards the smitten one. 2 Kings 2:7, "And fifty men of the sons of the prophets went and stood to view *afar off* (*minneged mĕhâroq, in sight*, or *over against*)." Deut. 32:52, "Yet thou shalt see the land *before* (*thee*) (*minneged*), but thou shalt not go thither," etc. By the distant position a due reverence for the sacred structure was inculcated, and it afforded space also for the intervening camp of the Levites who made a nearer interior enclosure within the general host, and of the same form with the camp itself, which was quadrangular. From the distance which was required to intervene between the body of the Israelites and the Ark of the Covenant in crossing the Jordan (Josh. 3:4), it has been reasonably conjectured that the distance of the camp of Israel from the Tabernacle was two thousand cubits, or an English mile. Rabbi Solomon writes thus on this passage: "Over against; that is, afar off, a mile, as it is said in Joshua, 'yet there shall be a space between you and it, about two thousand cubits by measure.'" The arrangement was such that the Lord dwelt in the midst of his people, who were round about the sanctuary to guard it. Allusion is probably had to this arrangement in Rev. 4:2-4, where the prophet beholds in heaven a central Throne answering to the Tabernacle and Temple, which in Ezek. 43:7 are called God's Throne, and "round about the throne were four and twenty seats (Gr. thrones)," which, as double the number of the twelve tribes, points perhaps to the increase and enlargement of the church under the Gospel, Is. 54:2. Between the Throne and the circuit round about, which Vitringa supposes to have been a semicircular area, were "four living creatures full of eyes," respecting which see a previous note. This feature of the symbolical scenery is evidently most appropriate to the Levites, or the spiritual priesthood represented by them; for as eyes denote inspection and watching, they shadow forth the function of the sacred ministry, which pertained to the tribe of Levi, and not to those of Judah, Reuben, Ephraim, and Dan. But the scenery of the Israelitish camp undergoes various modifications when transferred to the stage of the Apocalyptic visions, and as the whole of the tribes are represented to John by the twenty-four elders, and these elders adumbrate the church as a Kingship, their heads being adorned with "crowns," so the four living creatures may represent the same church viewed more especially as a priesthood, seeing they evidently lead in worship. Yet the two great classes, the Elders and the Living Creatures, are so intimately associated and conjoined in their acts, that we cannot easily regard them as two entirely distinct and separate orders or castes.—Moses and Aaron were on the east, the Gershonites on the west, the Kohathites on the south, and the Morarites on the north side of the Tabernacle.

V. 3. *And on the east side toward the rising of the sun shall they of the standard of the camp of Judah pitch.* Lit. "And they that encamp eastward (or foremost) toward the rising of the sun," etc. Gr. "They that encamp first toward the east shall be the order of the camp of Judah." The original Heb. *kadmah*, denotes either *the east*, or *before, foremost, in front*, i. e. relative to the Tabernacle, which is at the same time equivalent to *east*, as in relation to the west the east is said to be *before* and the west *behind*. The south is

their armies: and Nahshon[c] the son of Amminadab *shall be* captain of the children of Judah.

c c. 1. 7, etc. 10. 14. 1 Chr. 2. 10. Mat. 1. 4. Luke 3. 32, 33.

4 And his host, and those that were numbered of them, *were* threescore and fourteen thousand and six hundred.

---

called the *right side* of the world, Ps. 89: 13, and the north *the left*. Comp. Job 23: 8, 9. The general camp was appointed to be in the form of a square, the four sides of which corresponded with the four cardinal points of the compass. Each side was to consist of the united bodies of three tribes, nearest related by blood to each other. The eastern side, as being the most honorable from its relation to the sun, the grand symbol of the Deity, and from looking toward the Most Holy Place of the Tabernacle, was assigned to the standard of Judah, to which, as to their chief head, were annexed those of Issachar and Zebulun, to pitch on each side of him, the whole amounting to 186,400 men.——¶ *Shall they of the standard of the camp of Judah pitch.* Precedence and pre-eminence are here assigned to Judah as frequently elsewhere in the sacred history. In this we recognize an incipient fulfilment of Jacob's prophecy respecting the rank which he should hold among his brethren, Gen. 49: 8, 9. This prophecy was slow in its accomplishment, though abundantly verified in the end. It is true that in point of numbers this tribe exceeded the rest on their coming out of Egypt, and on the present occasion was appointed to take the lead under the standard of Nahshon. But this was but a dim foreshadowing of the future distinction of Judah, for he was still without kingdom or principality. To the eye of sense, moreover, it would seem as if every thing was so ordered, and that too for a long lapse of time, as to frustrate the accomplishment of the prediction. Moses, of the tribe of Levi, was clothed with the supreme command of the host, and after his death Joshua, of the tribe of Ephraim, was chosen leader, and he was succeeded by a series of Judges who were raised up now from one tribe, and now from another, till we come to Saul, the first king, who was of the tribe of Benjamin. Meantime, the pre-eminence of Judah was kept in abeyance, nor was it till the time of David that the tree of his predicted renown began to bud and blossom. David was of the stock of Judah, and from him descended, according to the flesh, He who was to be the "lion of the tribe of Judah," and in whose spiritual supremacy all these prophecies culminated to a head. In the character of standard-bearer of the armies of Israel Judah also prophetically represents Michael, who leads the heavenly armies in their contests with the Dragon and his army. Rev. 5: 5. 12: 7. 19: 11. So in regard to all the divine promises, though the performance may be long deferred, yet it is certain to be realized at last. "Though it tarry, wait for it." ——¶ *Throughout their armies.* Heb. *letzibothâm.* That is, in the order and disposition of their several bodies or corps, answering to our brigades, battalions, regiments, etc.——¶ *And Nahshon, etc. shall be captain.* By comparing this with the preceding chapter, it will be observed that the commanders-in-chief of the several tribes were the very persons who were selected to preside over the numbering there related; which shows that they were men of distinction among their brethren.

V. 4. *And his host, and those that were numbered, etc.* Rather, "And his host,

5 And those that do pitch
next unto him *shall be* the tribe
of Issachar: and Nethaneel the
son of Zuar *shall be* captain of
the children of Issachar.
6 And his host, and those that
were numbered thereof, *were* fifty and four thousand and four
hundred.
7 *Then* the tribe of Zebulun:
and Eliab the son of Helon *shall*
be captain of the children of Zebulun.
8 And his host, and those that
were numbered thereof, *were* fifty and seven thousand and four
hundred.
9 All that were numbered
in the camp of Judah *were* an
hundred thousand and fourscore
thousand and six thousand and
four hundred, throughout their

---

even they that were mustered." Otherwise, if we suppose the women and children and servants, together with the aged and infirm to be included, it would have made the number much greater. The transition from the words of the Lord himself commanding the order of the encampment, to those of Moses declaring the respective numbers of each division, is not to be overlooked. This remark is to be applied to the whole of the present chapter.

Vs. 5–7. *Children of Issachar—tribe of Zebulun.* Judah, Issachar and Zebulun were all three born of Leah, which rendered it natural that they should be associated under one banner.

V. 9. *An hundred thousand, etc.* This was by far the most numerous of the four grand divisions, as will be evident from a tabular view.

The Camp of	Judah,....	186,400	East.
"	Reuben,..	151,450	South.
"	Ephraim,.	108,100	West.
"	Dan,......	157,600	North.

The excess on the part of Judah is not far from 30,000. This tribe, which led the van, and that of Dan, which brought up the rear, were the most numerous. This would contribute to the safety of the sanctuary, and its attendants marching in the middle between them, according to the well-known rule of military tactics, that the *advanced* and *rear guards* should be stronger than the centre.——¶ *These shall first set forth.* Heb. ראשנה יסעו *rishonâh yissa-u, shall foremost break up;* in reference to striking their tents and thus breaking up the encampment. The original is a term properly used to signify the *plucking up* of the stakes, pins, or fixtures to which the cords of the tents were attached, and by which they were held secure. The corresponding word in Arabic is applied to *plucking teeth out of their sockets.* See Note on Gen. 11:2. See also Barnes on Is. 33:20. As their journeying was mainly towards the East, so the eastern division would naturally be the first to move. As the words stand, they would appear to be uttered by Moses, as the previous part of the verse contains his language in contradistinction from that of the Lord; yet understood as a command they would seem to be more appropriate to Jehovah himself. Rosenmuller, however, takes the clause as spoken by Moses in his own person, and translates it in the past instead of the future, in which latter form it is found in the original. We incline to favor this construction. Considering the words as those of Moses, we would take them in the narrative sense as equivalent to—"those uniformly set forth first;" i. e. it was appointed to them, it was made their duty, and it was their uniform

armies. These shall first[d] set
forth.
10 On the south side *shall be*
the standard of the camp of Reuben according to their armies:
and the captain of the children
of Reuben *shall be* Elizur the
son of Shedeur.
11 And his host, and those
that were numbered thereof,
were forty and six thousand and
five hundred.
12 And those which pitch by
him *shall be* the tribe of Simeon: and the captain of the children of Simeon *shall be* Shelumiel the son of Zurishaddai.
13 And his host, and those
that were numbered of them,
were fifty and nine thousand
and three hundred.
14 Then the tribe of Gad:
and the captain of the sons of
Gad *shall be* Eliasaph the son
of Reuel.
15 And his host, and those
that were numbered of them,
were forty and five thousand and
six hundred and fifty.
16 All that were numbered
in the camp of Reuben *were* an
hundred thousand and fifty and
one thousand and four hundred
and fifty, throughout their armies. And they shall set forth
in the second[e] rank.
17 Then[f] the tabernacle of
the congregation shall set for-

d c. 10. 14. *e* c. 10. 18. *f* c. 10. 17, 21.

practice. See ch. 10:14. This is the frequent usage of the Heb. future when employed to denote an action that is of repeated or customary occurrence. See Nordheimer's Heb. Grammar, Vol. II. p. 167.

Vs. 10–16. *On the south side shall be the standard of the host of Reuben, etc.* The south side of the camp was to consist of the companies of Reuben, with those of Simeon and Gad on either side of him, pitching under his banner, though under their own commanders. These formed the second great camp, called the camp of Reuben, consisting of 151,450 men, who were in all their marches to occupy the second rank. To the tribe of Reuben is assigned the precedency in this division, while those of Simeon and Gad are adjoined to it. Reuben was the firstborn, and by birth was entitled to take the lead of all the tribes, but having lost his birthright by transgression, the first place fell to Judah, and the second rank became his. Simeon was the next brother to him, of the same mother, and Gad was the firstborn of Zilpah, maid to that mother (Leah.) This relationship probably governed the arrangement.—It will be observed that the order of falling in, when the tribes took up their march, was from the East to the South, thence to the West, and so on to the North, "according," says Ainsworth, "to the course of the sun, and the climates of the world."

V. 14. *Eliasaph, the son of Reuel.* See ch. 1:14, where he is called Deuel, the similarity of the Heb. D (ד) and R (ר) doubtless having caused the interchange of the one for the other.

V. 16. *They shall set forth in the second rank.* Heb. *sheniyim yissâ-u, they shall break up second.* See Note on v. 9. This closes the account of the second division.

V. 17. *Then the tabernacle of the congregation shall set forward.* Heb. *nâsa, shall break up;* i. e. by plucking up the

ward with the camp of the Levites in the midst of the camp; as they encamp, so shall they set forward, every man in his place by their standards.

18 On the west side *shall be* the standard of the camp of Ephraim according to their armies: and the captain of the sons of Ephraim *shall*

---

pins as in the case of the other tents, for the Tabernacle was a tent, though of a different construction from all others. The Tabernacle was to follow the two divisions above mentioned, and to be followed by those of Ephraim and Dan; but the particular mode of transporting the Tabernacle and its appendages will be more fully considered in the Notes on ch. 10:14–21. It appears that in one respect they did not march as they pitched; for then there was a camp on each side of the Tabernacle, but when they marched there was none on the sides, but two divisions went before it, and two behind. This, however, does not describe the exact order, as we shall see on ch. 10. When the host was encamped a central position was assigned to the Sanctuary, in reference to which it is said of the Church, Ps. 46:5, "God is *in the midst of her*, she shall not be moved." The original word here employed (*bekirbâh*) is used to denote the interior parts of the body, the seat of the various viscera, as the heart, the stomach, the womb, etc., implying that the divine presence is central to his church, constituting its inmost heart and life. The place, then, of the Tabernacle, the grand symbol of the Lord's habitation among his people, was not in a corner of the host, nor upon one side, nor outside, but in their very midst. So it is said, Lev. 26:11, 12, "And I will set my tabernacle among you: and my soul shall not abhor you. And I will walk among you, and I will be your God, and ye shall be my people." Thus placed, with the Shekinah enshrouded in it, it served as a more striking pre-intimation of Him who was to be called "Emmanuel, God with us."——¶ *In the midst of the camp.* It appears from ch. 10, that this is to be understood with some qualification, as in the march the Tabernacle was in fact carried in two separate portions, one by the sons of Gershon and Merari, and the other by the Kohathites. Still the expression "in the midst" is entirely proper in reference to the fact.——¶ *As they encamp, so shall they set forward.* This doubtless is to be understood of the Levites instead of the tribes at large.——¶ *Every man in his place.* Heb. *al yâdo, upon his hand*, i. e. towards the *side* or *quarter* to which he belongs.

Vs. 18–24. There is but little to be noted in respect to this third division, except that Ephraim has the precedence assigned him instead of Manasseh, which, however, was according to Jacob's blessing (Gen. 48:19, 20). With him were associated Manasseh and Benjamin, all three being descended from Rachel.

V. 18. *On the west side.* Heb. *yâmmâh, seaward*, i. e. towards the Mediterranean, which lay to the west of Canaan. See Note on Gen. 12:8. The west side of the camp was to contain the tribes of Ephraim, Manasseh, and Benjamin—all three descended from Rachel—under their several heads or captains, now united, for the sake of order, under the standard of Ephraim, and making the third great division, consisting of 108,100 men. This, therefore, was the smallest body of all the four, being about 80,000 less than that of Judah.

be Elishama the son of Ammihud.

19 And his host, and those that were numbered of them, *were* forty thousand and five hundred.

20 And by him *shall be* the tribe of Manasseh: and the captain of the children of Manasseh *shall be* Gamaliel the son of Pedahzur.

21 And his host, and those that were numbered of them, *were* thirty and two thousand and two hundred.

22 Then the tribe of Benjamin: and the captain of the sons of Benjamin *shall be* Abidan the son of Gideoni.

23 And his host, and those that were numbered of them, *were* thirty and five thousand and four hundred.

24 All that were numbered of the camp of Ephraim *were* an hundred thousand, and eight thousand and an hundred, throughout their armies. And they shall go forward in the third[g] rank.

[g] c. 10. 22.

25 The standard of the camp of Dan *shall be* on the north side by their armies: and the captain of the children of Dan *shall be* Ahiezer, the son of Ammishaddai.

26 And his host, and those that were numbered of them, *were* threescore and two thousand and seven hundred.

27 And those that encamp by him *shall be* the tribe of Asher: and the captain of the children of Asher *shall be* Pagiel the son of Ocran.

28 And his host, and those that were numbered of them, *were* forty and one thousand and five hundred.

29 Then the tribe of Naphtali: and the captain of the children of Naphtali *shall be* Ahirah, the son of Enan.

30 And his host, and those that were numbered of them, *were* fifty and three thousand and four hundred.

31 All they that were numbered in the camp of Dan *were* an hundred thousand and

V. 24. *And they shall go forward in the third rank.* Heb. *shelishim yissa-u, shall break up third.* There is no adequate reason for rendering the original in this place by "go forward" when precisely the same word in vs. 9 and 16 is rendered by "set forth." It is far better, as a general rule, not to break the uniformity of rendering where it can well be avoided.

Vs. 25–31. The last of the four divisions is made up of the tribes of Dan, Asher, and Naphtali—three sons of Jacob by the handmaids Bilhah and Zilpah—and furnishing the largest number of men except the division of Judah, viz. 150,600 men. They were appointed, therefore, in all their marches, to bring up the rear, as Judah led the van, for the greater security of the Sanctuary, which was to be guarded by them.

"The collective encampment enclosed a large open square, in the centre of which stood the Tabernacle. The position which the Tabernacle thus occupied still remains the place of honor in grand oriental camps, and is usually oc-

fifty and seven thousand and six hundred. They shall go [h] hindmost with their standards.

h c. 10. 25.

---

cupied by the king or general. The distance between it and the common camp was indicative of respect and reverence. The interior was not, however, wholly vacant, being occupied by the small camps of the Levites, who had the charge and custody of the Tabernacle, and pitched their tents around it; the tents of Moses, Aaron, and the priests occupying the most honorable place, fronting the entrance to the Tabernacle, or rather to the court which contained it. The Jewish writers say that the circumference of the entire encampment was about twelve miles; a statement which seems sufficiently moderate, when we recollect the hollow square in the centre, and consider the vast extent of ground required for the tents of two millions of people."—*Pict. Bible.*

The accompanying sketch will afford the reader an idea approximating the truth of the plan and order of the encampment, whenever they pitched during their march through the desert.

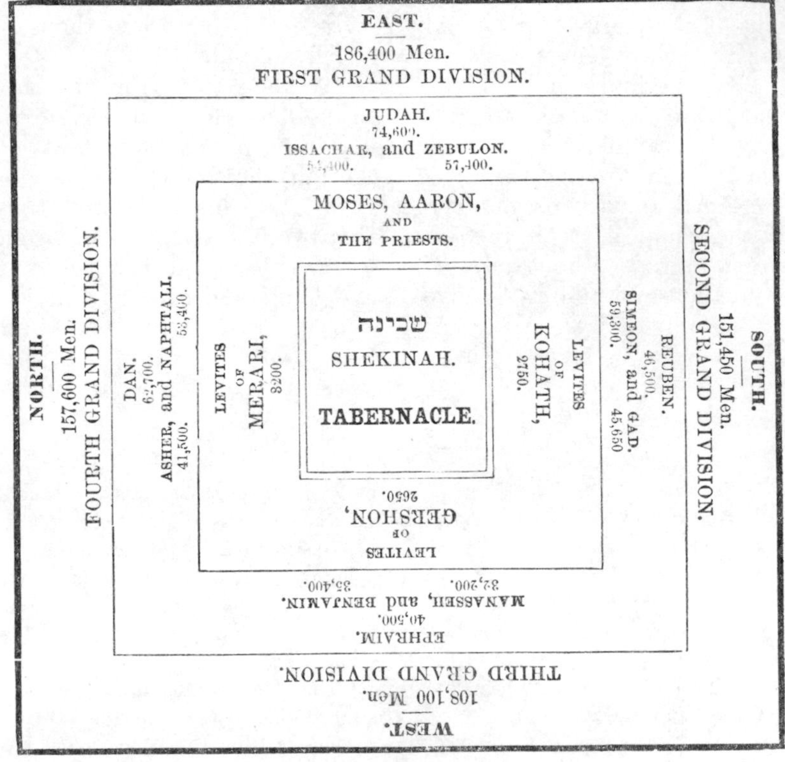

V. 31. *They shall go hindmost with their standards.* Heb. *lâaharonâh yisu ledigleham, they shall break up (march) to the rear of their standards,* i. e. of the standards of the preceding tribes, called "theirs" from their all forming one

32 These *are* those which
were numbered of the children
of Israel by the house of their
fathers; all [i] those that were
numbered of the camps, throughout their hosts, *were* six hundred thousand and three thousand and five hundred and fifty.
33 But the Levites were not
numbered among the children
of Israel; as the LORD commanded Moses.
34 And the children of Israel
did according to all [k] that the
LORD commanded Moses: so [l]
they pitched by their standards,
and so they set forward, every
one after their families, according to the house of their
fathers.

CHAPTER III.

THESE also *are* the generations of Aaron and Moses in the day *that* the LORD spake with Moses in Mount Sinai.

i Ex. 38. 26. c. 1. 46, 4 . 11. 21.
k Ps. 119. 6. *l* c. 24. 2, 5, 6.

---

united body. On any other construction it is not easy to see how "standards" in the plural should be ascribed to one division, when it is clear that each had but a single standard.

V. 32. *These are those that were numbered, etc.* Heb. "These are the mustered ones." Gr. αυτη η επισκεψις, *this is the survey* or *visitation.* See Note on ch. 1 : 2.——¶ *By the house of their fathers.* Collective singular for the plural. Gr. κατ' οικους, *according to the houses.*

V. 33. *But the Levites were not numbered among the children of Israel.* Heb. *bethok benë Yisrâel, in the midst of the sons of Israel,* implying that the Levitical tribe was *centrally interfused* in the midst of the general mass of the tribes. Typically understood it denotes that the true priesthood of the church exists in the midst of the body, instead of constituting a class distinct from the body. The priesthood consists in the priestly function which is to be exercised by those who are possessed of certain gifts and endowments that enable them to edify their brethren.

V. 34. *And the children of Israel did according to all that the Lord commanded Moses.* As the obedience of Israel in making and setting up the Tabernacle is borne witness to on a former occasion (Ex. 39 : 42, 43), so here also their exact compliance with the divine directions as to an orderly encamping round about it, and marching before and after it. The practical lesson inculcated throughout is the beauty and the benefit of order in all things pertaining to the Church. The camp of Israel, viewed in its external aspect, was arranged with so much regularity and beauty, that Balaam upon beholding it was led to exclaim, Num 24 : 5, "How goodly are thy tents, O Jacob, and thy tabernacles, O Israel!" A similar exclamation would be drawn from us if we could see, in clear vision, the exquisite and heavenly disposition of the true church in its internal economy.

CHAPTER III.

The family Stock of Aaron.

V. 1. *These also are the generations of Moses and Aaron.* That is, these are the offspring of Aaron, and the genealogy of the Levites, as also the narrative, the rehearsal, of the events, acts, or transactions, that occurred in respect to them. In this sense we find "generations" employed Gen. 5 : 1.

2 And these *are* the names of the sons of Aaron; Nadab[a] the first-born, and Abihu, Eleazar, and Ithamar.

3 These *are* the names of the sons of Aaron, the[b] priests which were anointed, whom he consecrated to minister in the priest's office.

4 And Nadab and Abihu died[c] before the LORD, when they offered strange fire before

a Ex. 6. 23. *b* Ex. 28. 41. Lev. 8. 2, etc. *c* Lev. 10. 1, 2. c. 26. 61. 1 Chr. 24. 2.

6:9. 25:18, where see Notes.—The inspired historian being now about to enter upon a recital of the appointed order and functions of the tribe of Levi, who were exempted from the former numbering or muster, first pauses to advert to the family of Aaron as the head of the priestly caste. He then goes on to relate their numbering and the order of their ministration in the department to which they were devoted.——¶ *In the day that the Lord spake with Moses in Mount Sinai.* That is, when he spake on a former occasion; a clause introduced probably with a view to intimate that Nadab and Abihu, mentioned in the next verse, were then living, whereas they were now dead. It is as if he had said, "These are the generations of Aaron and Moses that were then alive in the day that the Lord spake with Moses in Mount Sinai." It is evident that at the time when this part of the history commences Moses was not in the mount, but in the midst of the camp.

V. 2. *And these are the names of the sons of Aaron.* As the first verse naturally leads us to expect an account of Moses' posterity as well as Aaron's, it becomes a question why that of Aaron only is given. To which it is answered, that Moses' lineage is probably included under the general name of the *Amramite*, v. 27, embracing all the children and grandchildren of *Amram*, with the exceptions only of Moses and Aaron. The "generations" or descendants of Moses are perhaps thus obscurely mentioned from the fact of their being but common Levites, the priesthood being given exclusively to Aaron's posterity, for which reason we may suppose that he is here named before Moses, though generally mentioned after him.

V. 3. *Whom he consecrated.* Heb. "Whose hand he filled." Upon this phraseology, see the Note on Ex. 29:9. Gr. "Whom they perfected, or accomplished, as to their hands."——¶ *To minister in the priest's office.* This is expressed in the Heb. by a single word, *lekahën*, the root from whence comes *kohën, a priest.* It is a term of peculiar significancy, and sometimes implies *prince* as well as *priest.*

V. 4. *And Nadab and Abihu died before the Lord, etc.* Of which, see Lev. 10:1, 2. Numb. 26:61. 1 Chron. 24:1, 2. As they offered strange fire, they perished by strange fire, showing that men's punishments often bear a striking analogy to their sins.——¶ *And they had no children.* This is mentioned that it might be known in all subsequent time, that none were to be admitted to the office of the priesthood, but such as could trace their genealogy to Eleazar or Ithamar. Had Nadab and Abihu left any sons, they would have inherited their fathers' office before Eleazar. The Rabbins say, "Whoever is foremost in inheritance, is foremost for honor or dignity."——¶ *In the sight of Aaron their father.* Heb. "Before the face of." That is, while Aaron lived. So it is said of Haran (Gen. 11:28) that he died "before the

the Lord in the wilderness of Sinai, and they had no children: and Eleazar and Ithamar ministered in the priest's office in the sight of Aaron their father.

5 And the Lord spake unto Moses, saying,

6 Bring[d] the tribe of Levi near, and present them before Aaron the priest, that they may minister unto him.

d c. 8. 6. 18. 2, etc. Deut. 33. 10. Mal. 2. 4.

---

face of Terah," i. e. while Terah was alive. So "before the moon and the sun" (Ps. 72:5, 17,) i. e. while those bodies continue to give their light. Gr. "With Aaron." In 1 Chron. 24:19, they are said to have ministered "under Aaron." Heb. "By the hand of Aaron." From these two descended so large a company of priests, that in the days of David they were distributed into twenty-four courses, sixteen of Eleazar and eight of Ithamar. The Hebrew Doctors say, "Over every course there was one President. And they went up to Jerusalem to serve by course every week. And every sabbath day they changed; one course went out, and the next after them came in." Comp 1 Chron. 9:22, 25. 2 Kings 11:5, 7. The words carry with them the implication, that they exercised their ministry so entirely in conjunction with their father, that they were little liable to such dangerous lapses as had been fatal to Nadab and Abihu. They kept under their father's eye, and took instructions from him in all they did. Their brethren, perhaps, were out of their father's sight when they offered strange fire.

The Gift of the Levites to Aaron for the Service of the Tabernacle.

Vs. 5, 6. *Bring the tribe of Levi near, etc.* Heb. *hakrëb, cause to approach.* The word has the double import of *local approximation* and of *setting apart* and *offering* to the Lord in a special dedication to his service. See Note on Ex. 29:8. Indeed, so emphatically is the tribe of Levi spoken of in this character, as solemnly dedicated to the service of the Sanctuary, that the very terms are applied to them which are elsewhere employed to denote the sacrificial offerings. Thus ch. 8:11, "And Aaron shall *offer* (Heb. *wave*) the Levites before the Lord for an *offering* (Heb. *wave-offering*) of the children of Israel, that they may execute the service of the Lord." Having spoken of Aaron and his immediate descendants, he now comes to give order respecting the rest of the tribe of Levi, who had been omitted in the late muster.——¶ *Present them.* Heb. *haamadtâ otho, cause him* (or *it*) *to stand* before Aaron, etc. The whole tribe is spoken of in the singular. Gr. *steseis autous, thou shalt place, set,* or *station them.* The original, in the Hiphil or *causative* conjugation, is frequently rendered *to present,* as also *to set, to establish, to appoint.* This tribe had on a former occasion (Ex. 32:29) "consecrated" themselves to God by a signal act of obedience, in consequence of which they had now secured to themselves the "blessing" which they were then promised.——¶ *That they may minister unto him.* Heb. *ve-shërethu otho, and they shall minister* (*to* or *wait upon*) *him.* There is nothing of special importance in the meaning of this term, except that it is a different term in the original from "minister," "ministered" in vs. 3, 4, which implies the ministry or service of the priests instead of that of the Levites, which was of a low-

7 And they[e] shall keep his
charge, and the charge of the
whole congregation before the
tabernacle of the congregation,
to do[f] the service of the tabernacle.

8 And they shall keep all the
instruments of the tabernacle of
the congregation, and the charge
of the children of Israel, to do
the service of the tabernacle.
9 And thou shalt give[g] the

e 1 Chr. 26. 20, 22. f c. 1. 50.

g c. 8. 19. 18. 6, 7.

---

er order. It were desirable that words differing in the original, even though by a slight shade, should be represented by different words in a version. In this case it is to be observed, however, that the Heb. שרת *shârath*, is frequently applied to the ministry of the priests, though the other word כהן *kâhan*, is never applied to that of the Levites.

V. 7. *And they shall keep his charge.* Heb. *shâmeru eth mishmarto, they shall keep his keeping.* In Lev. 18:30 it is rendered, "Ye shall keep my *ordinance.*" Elsewhere the original is rendered *ward, watch, safeguard, office.* The leading idea is that of something imposed as a matter of strict observance, custody, and care. A part of this charge was evidently keeping watch day and night at the door of the tabernacle. Lev. 8:35. By keeping the charge of Aaron and of the whole congregation is meant the performance of those duties and services about the sanctuary which would otherwise have devolved upon the principals in whose behalf they acted. This clause, therefore, would more properly be rendered, "*even* the charge of the whole congregation," as it is in one of the old English versions. As it now reads, the "charge of the whole congregation" seems to imply the charge which would have devolved upon the whole congregation, provided the Levitical tribe had not been substituted for this purpose in their stead. This, however, does not exclude the additional idea in regard to Aaron, that he may have delivered to them a solemn charge or commandment respecting their services which they are here required to obey.——¶ *Before the tabernacle of the congregation.* This expresses very precisely the nature of their office, which was to minister *before* the sanctuary and not *in* it, like the priests.——¶ *To do the service.* Heb. *laabōd eth abodath, to serve the service.* We give the literal rendering simply to let the English reader know what it is; and so in multitudes of other cases.

V. 8. *All the instruments of the tabernacle.* That is to say, the tabernacle itself and all its contents, which are particularly described vs. 25, 26, 31, 36, 37. The Levites, as the servants of the priests, were to perform the most common and laborious offices. It was a special part of their charge to take down, put up, and carry the tabernacle with its various utensils.——¶ *And the charge of the children of Israel.* That is, the general charge of the children of Israel, the charge which would otherwise have been theirs, but which was transferred to the Levites.

V. 9. *And thou shalt give the Levites unto Aaron, and to his sons.* Being first virtually presented to the Lord as his peculium, they are now, by his command, bestowed as a gift upon the priests, ch. 8:19. So ministers under the N. T. are called "gifts," Eph. 4:8, 11.——¶ *They are wholly given.* Heb. *nethunim, nethunim, given, given.* A Hebraism well represented in our version by "wholly given," implying a

Levites unto Aaron, and to his
sons: they *are* wholly given
unto him out of the children of
Israel.
10 And thou shalt appoint
Aaron and his sons, and they
shall wait on their priest's office; and the stranger [h] that

h ver. 38. Eph. 2. 19. Heb. 10. 19–22.

cometh nigh shall be put to
death.
11 And the LORD spake unto
Moses, saying,
12 And I, behold, I have
taken the Levites [i] from among
the children of Israel instead of
all the first-born that openeth

i ver. 41. c. 8. 16.

---

complete dedication. In like manner the Gibeonites devoted by Joshua to menial services about the sanctuary were also called *Nethinim, given.*——¶ *To him.* Heb. לוֹ *lo*, for which the Gr. evidently read לִי *li, to me*, as it has μοι, *to me.*

V. 10. *And thou shalt appoint Aaron and his sons.* Heb. *tiphkod, shalt cause to preside* or *superintend;* the term which we have so fully explained in the Note on ch. 1:3. Gr. *katastēseis, thou shalt constitute* or *set.* It is to be remarked, however, that others render it by *thou shalt number*, or *muster*, as the term is precisely the same with that which occurs ch. 1:49, "Only thou shalt not *number* (Heb. *tiphkod*) the tribe of Levi." In that case the Levites were not to be included in the general census; in the present case they also were to be numbered apart by themselves. But we doubt if the precise idea of *numbering* is intended to be conveyed by the term in this connection. The dominant import of the original, as we have seen, is *to order, arrange, adjust in a visitorial way*, and this we incline to adopt as the true sense in the present passage. Moses, as clothed with a visitorial or superintending power, was to *order* the priestly functions of Aaron and his sons according to the divine will.——¶ *And they shall wait upon their priest's office.* Heb. *shameru eth kehonnethâm, they shall keep their priesthood*, i. e. "for every thing of the altar and within the veil," ch. 18:7.——¶ *The stranger that cometh nigh.* That is, to take upon him the duties of the priests. Gr. "That toucheth." By the *stranger* is to be understood any and every one who was not "of the seed of Aaron," as explained ch. 16:40; for "no man taketh this honor unto himself, but he that is called of God, as was Aaron." Even the common Levite was excluded as well as the rest of Israel from the sacred function of the priests. Comp. ch. 18:3, "And they (the Levites) shall keep thy charge, and the charge of all the tabernacle: only they shall not come nigh the vessels of the sanctuary and the altar, that neither they, nor ye also, die."——¶ *Shall be put to death.* That is, by the magistrate, or, by the immediate hand of God, as in the case of Korah and his company.

The Substitution of the Levites for the First-born.

V. 12. *I have taken the Levites from among the children of Israel.* Heb. *mittōk, from the midst;* a more emphatic form of expression than "from among." The Levites are frequently spoken of subsequently as an element *centrally interfused* throughout the whole mass of the people. As to their substitution for the first-born and the grounds of it, see the note on Ex. 13:2. It is very generally conceded that prior to the establishment of the priesthood of Aaron and

the matrix among the children of Israel: therefore the Levites shall be mine;

13 Because all the first-born[k] *are* mine: *for* on the day that I smote all the first-born in the land of Egypt I hallowed unto me all the first-born in Israel, both man and beast; mine shall they be: I *am* the LORD.

14 And the LORD spake unto Moses in the wilderness of Sinai, saying,

15 Number the children of Levi after the house of their fathers, by their families: every

k Ex. 13. 2, 12. Lev. 27. 26. Luke 2. 23.

---

his sons, the first-born in the patriarchal families officiated in that capacity. The Talmud says, "Before the Tabernacle was erected, the use of private Altars and High Places was permitted, and the eldest of each family performed the sacrifices." (*Tract. Milikim in Mishna*, 14.) See Note upon Ex. 24: 5, respecting the "young men" sent by Moses to perform the office of sacrificers. The conclusion seems fair that priesthood was one of the privileges of primogeniture. We are aware that this opinion is questioned by Outram, Patrick, and others, but their objections do not strike us as satisfactory.——¶ *That openeth the matrix.* Heb. *peter rehem, the opening*, or *opener, of the womb;* in apposition with the first-born," by which is to be understood the first-born of the father, and not merely the first-born of the mother.

V. 13. *On the day that I smote all the first-born in the land of Egypt.* This clause assigns the reason why the first-born were especially set apart and dedicated to the Lord. As Moses says to Pharaoh that the Most High had raised him up (or, Heb. "caused him to stand, to survive") when he was as good as dead by reason of the destructive plagues, so here the first-born of Israel, that were graciously exempted when the first-born of Egypt were destroyed, in the midst of whom they were, are claimed as the special property of Jehovah, inasmuch as they might be considered by their parents as having been virtually taken from them by the avenging stroke. It was not because they were intrinsically better than the first-born of the Egyptians that they were spared, but merely out of the sovereign good pleasure of the Lord himself, who "giveth not account of any of his matters." He therefore says of them, "Mine they shall be." A separate and independent reason is given for the substitution of the Levites in their stead, to wit, the devoted zeal they had manifested on the occasion of the iniquity connected with the worship of the golden calf, Ex. 32: 26. Deut. 33: 9, on which see Notes.——¶ *I hallowed unto me all the first-born.* That is, sanctified and set apart from all profane and secular use, and appropriated as something holy.

The Numbering or Muster of the Levites.

V. 15. *Number the children of Levi.* Heb. *pekōd, visit, muster.* The command is here directed solely to Moses, but it is evident from v. 39 and ch. 4: 34, that the duty was performed by Moses and Aaron, and by the princes of the congregation.——¶ *After the house of their fathers.* Gr. *kat' oikous, according to the houses.* They were counted after the houses of their fathers and not of their mothers, inasmuch as if a woman of the tribe of Levi were

male [l] from a month old and upward shalt thou number them.

16 And Moses numbered them, according to the word of the LORD, as he was commanded.

17 And these [m] were the sons of Levi by their names; Gershon and Kohath and Merari.

18 And these *are* the names of the sons of Gershon, by their families; Libni [n], and Shimei.

19 And the sons of Kohath by their families; Amram, and Izehar, Hebron, and Uzziel.

20 And the sons of Merari by their families; Mahli, and Mushi. These *are* the families of the Levites according to the house of their fathers.

l ver. 39. c. 26. 62. *m* Gen. 46. 11. Ex. 6. 16. *n* Ex. 6. 17–19.

married to a man of the tribe of Judah, or any other tribe, her son was not reckoned a Levite. Maimonides, the great expounder of the Hebrew Canons, says, "Priests and Levites and Israelites may lawfully go in one to another (i. e. to marry) and that which is born goeth after the male, etc., as it is written, According to the house of their fathers; the house of his father, that is, his family, and not the house of his mother."——¶ *Every male from a month old.* Heb. *mibbën 'hodesh, from the son of a month.* Male children were not reputed wholly purified from their uncleanness till they were a month old, Lev. 12 : 4, when the first-born were brought and presented before the Lord, Luke 2 : 22, and when also they were redeemed. The main reason, therefore, of the Levites being numbered or mustered from this age doubtless was, that as they were substituted for the first-born of the other tribes, and *their* redemption was appointed from a month old, the same period is fixed upon in this case. To this we may add, that as the males of all the other tribes were numbered "from twenty years and upward," had the Levites been numbered in the same way, they would have fallen far short of the count of the first-born of the twelve tribes.

V. 16. *According to the word of the Lord.* Heb. *al pi Yehovah, according to the mouth of the Lord.* Gr. "By the voice of the Lord."

The Descendants of Levi.

V. 17. *And these were the sons.* Heb. *va-yihyu ëlleh, and these became* or *were made to be.* A nice shade of meaning is conveyed by this phraseology. As a general fact, in enumerations of this kind, the substantive verb is omitted in the original and "are" in the present tense supplied, as in the next verse, where it is said, "And these *are* the names," etc. So if nothing more was intended in the present passage than the simple specification of the three sons of Levi, it would doubtless have read, "And these *were* the sons," etc. The true meaning, therefore, we think is given in the Vulg. version, which renders it "inventi sunt," *were found to be*, i. e. *were made out to be*, by consulting the genealogical tables to ascertain their names, for they themselves were not now living. Allusion is probably had to Gen. 46 : 11. Ex. 6 : 16.——¶ *Gershon, and Kohath, and Merari;* whose descendants are ordinarily termed the *Gershonites*, the *Kohathites*, and *Merarites.*

V. 20. *According to the house of their fathers.* Gr. "According to the houses of their fathers;" as above, v. 15.

21 Of Gershon *was* the family of the Libnites, and the family of the Shimites: these *are* the families of the Gershonites.

22 Those that were numbered of them, according to the number of all the males, from a month old and upward, *even* those that were numbered of them, *were* seven thousand and five hundred.

23 The families of the Gershonites[o] shall pitch behind the tabernacle westward.

24 And the chief of the house of the father of the Gershonites *shall be* Eliasaph the son of Lael.

25 And the charge of the sons of Gershon[p] in the tabernacle of the congregation *shall be* the tabernacle[q], and the tent[r], the covering thereof, and the hanging for the door of the tabernacle of the congregation.

o c. 1. 53. *p* c. 4. 24–26. *q* Ex. 25. 9. *r* Ex. 26. 1, etc.

The Families of the House of Gershon, their Number, Position, and Charge.

V. 22. *Those that were numbered of them according to the number, etc.* Heb. *pekudĕhem bemispar, the mustered ones of them in* (i. e. *according to*) *the number.* This makes it still plainer that there was a real distinction between the acts denoted by these two words, and which we have endeavored all along to set forth by rendering the one by *muster* and the other by *number.* Of the nature of this distinction, see Note on ch. 1:3. Inspection, adjustment, arrangement, are mainly implied by the first, and enumeration by the second. Granting, however, that the distinction is somewhat subtle and obscure, still it is desirable that a translation should in some way indicate the fact that different words are employed in the Hebrew.

V. 24. *And the chief of the house, etc.* An officer in chief was to be set over each of the families, and over all these chiefs a supreme or presiding inspector, v. 32. The exact order and regularity established throughout the camp, in the disposition of the tribes, the services of the Levites, etc. is every where to be observed. The phrase "house of the father" is probably equivalent to "father-house," and as to its import, see Note on ch. 1:2.

V. 25. *In the tabernacle of the congregation, (shall be) the tabernacle, and the tent, and the covering thereof.* The terms here employed may lead to some confusion in the mind of the reader. The original has three distinct words applied to denote the different parts of the tabernacle.—(1.) *Ohel moëd, tent of the congregation,* here rendered "tabernacle of the congregation." This is applied to the edifice as a whole. (2.) *Mishkan, habitation,* sometimes also denoting the whole tabernacle, but here the inner set of ten curtains made of fine twined linen, and described Ex. 26:1, 7, 14. 36:8, 14, 19. (3.) *Ohel, tent,* used to designate the next outer set made of goat's hair. To these may be added *mikseh, covering,* the term applied to the outer envelope of ram's skins spread over the whole. See Note on Ex. 26:1, where a fuller account is given. The care of the curtains and hangings in general fell to the lot of the Gershonites.——¶ *The hanging for the door.* Of this see the Note on Ex. 26:36, and of the hangings of the court and the curtain for the entrance, see Note on Ex. 27:9.

26 And the hangings[s] of the court, and the curtain for the door of the court, which *is* by the tabernacle, and by the altar round about, and the cords[t] of it, for all the service thereof.

27 And of Kohath[u] *was* the family of the Amramites, and the family of the Izeharites, and the family of the Hebronites, and the family of the Uzzielites: these *are* the families of the Kohathites.

28 In the number of all the males, from a month old and upward, *were* eight thousand and six hundred, keeping the charge of the sanctuary.

29 The families of the sons of [v] Kohath shall pitch on the side of the tabernacle southward.

30 And the chief of the house of the father of the families of the Kohathites *shall be* Elizaphan the son of Uzziel.

31 And their[w] charge *shall be* the ark[x], and the table[y], and the candlestick, and the altars[z], and the vessels of the sanctuary wherewith they minister, and the hanging[a], and all the service thereof.

32 And Eleazar the son of Aaron the priest *shall be* chief

s Ex. 27. 9, etc. *t* Ex. 35. 18. *u* 1 Chr. 26. 23.

v c. 1. 53. *w* c. 4. 15. *x* Ex. 25. 10. *y* Ex. 25. 23, 31. *z* Ex. 27. 1. 30. 1. *a* Ex. 26. 32.

V. 26. *And the cords of it.* That is, of the tabernacle, and not of the altar. The affixed pronoun in Hebrew often refers not to the nearest noun, but to one more remote. See *Glassius Phil. Sac.* p. 155. ed. Dath.

The Families of the House of Kohath, their Number, Position, and Charge.

V. 27. *And of Kohath was the family of the Amramites.* A precedency is given to this family because Moses and Aaron pertained to it, they being the sons of Amram. The branch of the family here alluded to must have been the descendants of Moses, for they were mere ordinary Levites, whereas those descended from Aaron, and called his "sons," were priests.

V. 28. *Keeping the charge of the sanctuary.* Heb. *kodesh, the holy,* or, *the holiness.* Gr. "the holies." The abstract is here used for the concrete. Thus, Is. 60:17, "peace" and "righteousness" are used as abstracts for "men of peace and righteousness."

V. 29. *Southward.* Heb. *tĕmânâh, to the right.* The points of the compass, according to Scriptural usage, are supposed to be determined by the position of one who looks to the east. In this case the south will be to the right. So Ps. 89:12, "The north and the *south* (Heb. *yâmin, the right*), thou hast created them."

V. 30. *Elizaphan the son of Uzziel.* This man was of the fourth and youngest family of the Kohathites, and yet was preferred to the chief rank among them. This, according to some of the Hebrew writers, gave offence to Korah, who was of the second family, or that of Izhar, and prompted the rebellion of which he was the leader, recorded in ch. 16:1–11.

V. 32. *Chief over the chief of the Levites.* Heb. "Chief of the chiefs," which is an expression implying somewhat less of official pre-eminence. Eleazar, who was appointed to this dignity, was

over the chief of the Levites,
and have the oversight of them
that keep the charge of the sanctuary.
33 Of Merari [b] *was* the family of the Mahlites, and the family of the Mushites: these *are*
the families of Merari.
34 And those that were numbered of them, according to the
number of all the males, from a
month old and upward, *were* six
thousand and two hundred.
35 And the chief of the house
of the father of the families of
Merari *was* Zuriel the son of
Abihail: *these* [c] shall pitch on
the side of the tabernacle northward.
36 And *under* the custody
and [d] charge of the sons of Merari *shall be* the boards of the
tabernacle, and the bars thereof,
and the pillars thereof, and the
sockets thereof, and all the vessels thereof, and all that serveth
thereto,
37 And the pillars of the
court round about, and their
sockets, and their pins, and their
cords.
38. But those that encamp
before the tabernacle toward the
east, *even* before the tabernacle

b 1 Chr. 6. 19. *c* c. 1. 53. *d* c. 4. 31, 32.

more than a Levite, being a priest, and hence arose the distinction between *high-priest* and *second priest*, as intimated 2 Kings 25:18.——¶ *Of the Levites*, Heb. *hallĕvi, the Levi.* The name of the individual becomes collective by prefixing the article ה *h.* So in all such words as *Gershonites, Libnites, Kohathites, Hebronites, Merarites, etc.* They are the names of the heads of the families with the article prefixed. In 1 Chr. 12:27, "the Aaronites" is "Aaron" in the original without the article.——¶ *Have the oversight.* Heb. *pekuddah, visitation* or *visitorial oversight*, from the root *pâkad*, on the import of which we have had such frequent occasion to remark. See Note on ch. 1:3. The original is often rendered in the Gr. by *episkopē, bishopric*, implying *the office of overseer.*

The Families descended from Merari, their Number, Position, and Charge.

V. 33. *These are the families of Merari.* There is nothing peculiarly worthy of note to be remarked respecting this branch of the Levites, except that it was fewest in number of all the rest, being 1300 less than the children of Gershon. They had charge of the framework of the tabernacle. As their burden on this account was heavier than that of their brethren the Gershonites, therefore they were allowed four wagons and eight oxen for their service, whereas the Gershonites had only two wagons and four oxen. See ch. 7:7, 8.

The Encampment of Moses and Aaron.

V. 38. *Toward the east.* Heb. *kēdemâh*, which may also be rendered *in front, foremost*, a rendering probably to be preferred on account of the occurrence of the word "eastward" in the next clause. The east, in the Scriptures, is always supposed to take the precedence of the other quarters, as it is there that the sun rises, and the sun from the earliest ages has ever been accounted the most striking symbol of the Deity. The position now assigned to Moses and Aaron was of course the

of the congregation eastward, *shall be* Moses, and Aaron and his sons, keeping [e] the charge of the sanctuary for the charge of the children of Israel; and the stranger [f] that cometh nigh shall be put to death.

e ver. 7, 8. f ver. 10.

39 All [g] that were numbered of the Levites, which Moses and Aaron numbered at the commandment of the LORD, throughout their families, all the males from a month old and upward, *were* twenty and two thousand.

g c. 26. 62.

---

most honorable, being between the standard of Judah and the door of the tabernacle, which it was their province to guard.——¶ *Keeping the charge of the sanctuary for the charge of the children of Israel.* The original is variously rendered by the versionists;—"Keeping the charge of the sanctuary, for the charge of the sons of Israel."—*Ains.* "That they may wait upon the sanctuary and the children of Israel."—*Cov.* "Wait on the sanctuary instead of the children of Israel."—*Mat.* "Wait to keep the sanctuary and to keep the children of Israel."—*Cran. Bish.* The Latin Vulg. has;—"Having the custody of the sanctuary in the midst of the sons of Israel." The idea is undoubtedly that of a charge allotted to Moses and Aaron and his sons, which would otherwise have devolved upon the Israelites as a body.

V. 39. *Moses and Aaron.* The reader of the original Hebrew will observe that there are in this place a number of extra diacritical points over the word Aaron, which doubtless have some peculiar significancy, but what they indicate it is not possible to ascertain with certainty. Some of the Rabbinical writers say it is to denote that Aaron himself was not embraced in the numbering of the tribe; but as we find no reason given for this opinion, it can pass for nothing more than a conjecture, although it may be in itself true. J. H. Michaelis, in the notes to his invaluable edition to the Heb. Bible, approves the suggestion of Hiller, who regards these points as a Masoretic symbol to indicate the absence of the entire word in other manuscripts; and accordingly it is actually found wanting in the Samaritan, Codex, and in vs. 14, 16 of this chapter, Aaron is not named with Moses. Kennicott also observes that the word is omitted in the most ancient Hebrew manuscript in the Bodleian library. There are fifteen of these words in the whole Hebrew text, printed with dots over every letter, thus ואהרן *ve-aharon*, whereas normally there should be but one dot over the whole word.——¶ *Twenty and two thousand.* A difficulty here arises from the fact that the sum total resulting from the enumeration of the several families as given above is 22,300. Thus,

Gershon,..............	7,500
Kohath,................	8,600
Merari,................	6,200
	22,300

The prevailing mode among commentators of reconciling the discrepancy is to suppose that the *first-born of the Levites themselves* were deducted from the gross census of the tribe, and their number, if in proportion to the other tribes, would not have been far from three hundred. It would have come sufficiently near to it to warrant the present expression. By the fact of their being the first-born, they belonged to God of course (Ex. 13 : 2. 34 : 20), and could not be exchanged for the first-born of other tribes, and substituted in their stead, as other Levites were. We know of no more probable solution than this, and yet it is not quite satisfactory, for why should the first-born be enumerated in the census of the several families and yet not counted in the aggregate sum? And why did God order all the males to be numbered, without at the same time making express exception of the first-born? Again, it is thought scarcely credible that out of 22,000 Levites there should have been no more than 300 first-born. But to this it is suggested that those only were reputed the first-born in this and the other tribes who were born *subsequent* to the slaughter of the Egyptian first-born, as it was from this date that the Lord claimed them as his own; and on this supposition 300 may have been but a fair proportion. But after every explanation the point must be left in some degree of uncertainty. Happily, it is not one of any great importance.—It is worthy of notice, that the Levites were the fewest in number of any of the tribes, being but 22,000, whereas the least of the others had 32,600, and the greatest 74,400; and to make the disparity still more striking, out of these 22,000 there were but 8,580 that were fit for service in the sanctuary (ch. 4: 47, 48.) We may safely admit a providential ordering in this, for if this tribe had increased proportionally to the rest, there would have been more Levites by far than the first-born of all the tribes. Michaelis and Palfrey, in their peculiar mode of commenting on the Laws of Moses would make more of the following suggestion than we are inclined to attribute to it. "The sacred authority was a balance in the commonwealth, which must not be suffered to become a preponderating weight. It furnished great advantages for political usurpation, if other circumstances should favor. Accordingly, it was most safely committed to that division of the people, which was much the least formidable through its numerical force." (*Palf.* Lect., Vol. I. p. 323.) We recognize the leading drift of all these institutes as spiritual, and not political. We may here recapitulate, in brief compass, the principal items pertaining to the Levites.

1. Numbers.
   - Gershonites, 7500.
   - Kohathites, 8600.
   - Merarites, 6200.

2. Position when encamped.
   - Gershonites, behind westward, v. 23.
   - Kohathites, southward, v. 29.
   - Merarites, northward, v. 35.
   - Moses and Aaron, in front eastward, v. 38.

3. Charges.
   - Gershonites; the tent, coverings, veil, hanging of the court, etc.
   - Kohathites; the ark, table, altar. and instruments of the sanctuary,
   - Merarites; the boards, bars, pillars, sockets, etc.

4. Special Prerogatives of Kohath.
   1. Excelled in the multitude of families, or chief fathers, having four, whereas each of his brethren had but two.
   2. Excelled in multitude of children, having 8600, that is, 1100 more than his elder brother Gershon, and 2400 more than Merari.
   3. Of him came Moses, "king in Jeshurun," Aaron the priest, and Miriam the prophetess. Thus all the priests were of this family. Ex. 6:18, 20. Num. 26:58, 59.
   4. His families had the chief place about the sanctuary, to wit, the south quarter, next to

40 And the LORD said unto Moses, Number[h] all the first-born of the males of the children of Israel, from a month old and upward, and take the number of their names.

41 And[i] thou shalt take the Levites for me (I *am* the LORD) instead of all the first-born among the children of Israel; and the cattle of the Levites instead of all the firstlings among the cattle of the children of Israel.

42 And Moses numbered, as the LORD commanded him, all the first-born among the children of Israel.

43 And all the first-born

h ver. 15. *i* ver. 12, 45.

Moses, Aaron, and the priests. ch. 3:29.

5. They had charge of the most holy things within the Tabernacle, as the ark, table, candlesticks, altar of incense, etc.

6. Whereas the whole tribe of Levi had 48 cities allotted them in Canaan, Kohath's posterity had 23 of these; the priests, 13; the other Kohathites, 10: so that he had, as it were, a double portion, as much as both his brethren, Josh. 21:

The Numbering of the First-born of Israel and the Substitution of the Levites.

V. 40. *Number all the first-born, etc.* Heb. *pekōd, muster.* If the idea is precisely that of numbering, it is not easy to see why it should be said in the next clause, "Take the *number* (*mispar*) of their names." This goes strongly to confirm our previous suggestion on the subject. The object of this enumeration was that their number and that of the Levites might be compared, so that the proper adjustment might be made between them.——¶ *From a month old and upward.* This period is designated, because the first-born males were to be a month old before their parents were bound to redeem them: if they died before, they were not to pay any thing for them.

V. 41. *And thou shalt take the Levites for me.* Heb. לִי *li, to* or *unto me.* Chald. "Thou shalt bring near the Levites before me." The expression in a previous passage, v. 12, "I have taken the Levites," denotes rather the divine purpose of taking, which was then communicated to Moses, whereas the language in this connection conveys a command to Moses to declare this purpose to the people, and to have it executed by actually making the exchange. ——¶ *And the cattle of the Levites, etc.* This does not imply that the cattle were actually to be sacrificed, or taken away from the Levites, but simply that they should be accounted as the Lord's cattle. They were to be considered as alienated, though still left on the hands of their former owners. This is a very proper light in fact in which to view all our worldly possessions; as really belonging to the Lord, but left in trust with us.

V. 42. *And Moses numbered—all the first-born, etc.* Heb. *yiphkōd, mustered;* on which see above. It will be observed that it is not said that he numbered either the cattle, or the firstlings of the cattle, of the Levites, inasmuch as the exchange was not made by precisely substituting one for one, but was made in the gross, by taking *all* the cattle of the Levites for *all* the firstlings of the Israelites' cattle.

V. 43. *And all the first-born males by the number of names, etc.* The phrase-

males, by the number of names, from a month old and upward, of those that were numbered of them, were twenty and two thousand two hundred and threescore and thirteen.

44 And the LORD spake unto Moses, saying,

45 Take [k] the Levites instead of all the first-born among the children of Israel, and the cattle of the Levites instead of their cattle; and the Levites shall be mine: I *am* the LORD.

46 And for those that are to be redeemed [l] of the two hundred and threescore and thirteen of the first-born of the children of Israel, which are more [m] than the Levites;

47 Thou shalt even take five [n]

k ver. 41.

l Ex. 13. 13. c. 18. 15. m ver. 39–43. n Lev. 27. 6. c. 18. 16.

---

ology of the original is here again peculiar from the use of the substantive verb *to be* (ויהי *va-yehi, was* (*were*) which, as in v. 17 implies more than simply the fact of *existence*, namely, the *making out to be, the ascertaining*, or *determining*, for it is very seldom indeed that this verb is employed in the specification of numbers. The phrase "by the number of names" we suppose to refer to a list or census previously made, and as the subsequent term "numbered" is in the original a different word (לפקדיהם *liphkedĕhem, according to their mustered ones*), the distinction between *numbering* and *mustering*, so completely lost sight of in our English version, is still, we think, designed to be kept up.——¶ *Twenty and two thousand two hundred and threescore and thirteen.* It is no doubt a circumstance well calculated to excite surprise, that out of a body of upwards of 600,000 men, reckoning from twenty years old and upward, there should not have been more than this number of first-born sons. Accordingly, various solutions have been proposed to account for the fact. Ainsworth and others recognize in it a special providence, designed to bring the first-born of Israel at large and the first-born of the Levites more upon a par in point of numbers. This is a pious suggestion which may be well founded, although even in that case other considerations are not precluded; as (1.) there may have been an unusually large proportion of female first-born, which of course are not reckoned. (2.) It is probable that those only come into the count who were born *subsequent* to the slaughter of the Egyptian first-born, which occurred a few months previously, and not those who were born before; for thus reads the law, Ex. 13:2, "Whatsoever openeth the womb (i. e. hereafter) both of man and beast shall be mine."

The Redemption of the Supernumeraries.

V. 45. *Take the Levites, etc.* That is, he was to take the two and twenty thousand Levites above mentioned instead of so many first-born. As for the cattle, they were not numbered as before remarked, but exchanged in the lump. ——¶ *And the Levites shall be mine.* Chald. "And the Levites shall minister before me."

V. 46. *And for those that are to be redeemed.* Heb. lit. "And the redeemed." But the participle in the Heb. has often the force of the future. Gr. "And the redemptions (or ransoms.") And so afterwards, vs. 48, 49, 51.

V. 47. *Thou shalt even take five shekels apiece.* Heb. "Thou shalt take five,

shekels apiece by the poll; after
the shekel of the sanctuary shalt
thou take *them*: (the shekel [o] *is*
twenty gerahs:)
48 And thou shalt give the
money, wherewith the odd number
of them is to be redeemed,
unto Aaron and to his sons.
49 And Moses took the redemption
money of them that
were over and above them that
were redeemed by the Levites:
50 Of the first-born of the
children of Israel took he the
money; a thousand three hundred
and threescore and five

o Ex. 30. 13. Lev. 27. 25. Ezek. 45. 12.

---

five shekels."——¶ *By the poll.* Heb. *legulgoleth, by the head* (lit. *the skull.*) Gr. *kata kephalēn, by the head.* This sum of five shekels became ever after the fixed price of redemption, as appears from ch. 18:16. This amount had recently (Lev. 27:6) been appointed as the valuation of a man-child from a month to five years old. As this was the least of the valuations, it showed that the Most High would burden his people as little as possible with the impositions he saw fit to lay upon them. The arrangement now ordained furnished the precedent of a permanent tax, intended to be laid on the first-born in after times, as one of the perquisites of the priesthood. "In the first instance it could not have been onerous, the number of supernumeraries, on whom it was assessed, being so small, and the whole amount being probably levied on all the first-born, since one had no better right than another to consider himself redeemed by the substitution of a Levite in his place. Once established, the tax would be one likely to be cheerfully paid, both on account of the interesting associations belonging to its original institution, and the happy circumstances under which a parent would be called on to pay it for his heir. On the one hand, it would furnish a perpetual revenue to the priesthood, considerable in amount; while on the other it would come from those whose domestic expenses were not yet such as to render it burdensome."—*Palfrey.*——¶ *The shekel is twenty gerahs.* Or, *twenty pence.* The *gerah* was a piece of silver supposed to have weighed about 16 barley-grains, while the *shekel* weighed 320 grains. Concerning the shekel, see Note on Gen. 20:16.

V. 48. *And thou shalt give the money.* Heb. *keseph, the silver.* This was but reasonable, inasmuch as the Levites being given to Aaron and his sons by the Lord (vs. 6, 7), the money that was paid to make up what was lacking in their proportion to the first-born of right belonged to them.——¶ *Wherewith the odd number of them is to be redeemed.* Heb. "(The money) of the redeemed of the supernumeraries among them. Gr. "The redemptions (or ransoms) of those that are over."

V. 49. *Of them that were over and above, etc.* Heb. *hă-odephim, that exceeded.* The original word is the same that occurs in the preceding verses where the overplus of first-born is mentioned. In these different verses it is variously rendered by "more than," "odd number," and "them that were over and above." The root *ădaph*, signifies *to be superabundant* or *superfluous, to exceed.* In the process of redemption the first-born were redeemed as far as their number would reach; the rest, forming the excess over the Levites, were redeemed by money.

V. 50. *Of the first-born.* Heb. *bekor*, in the singular, whereas the Gr. ren-

shekels, after [p] the shekel of the
sanctuary:
51 And Moses gave [q] the money of them that were redeemed, unto Aaron and to his sons, according to the word of the LORD, as [r] the LORD commanded Moses.

p ver. 46, 47. *q* ver 48. *r* Mal. 4. 4.

CHAPTER IV.

AND the LORD spake unto Moses and unto Aaron, saying,
2 Take the sum of the sons of Kohath from among the sons of Levi, after their families, by the house of their fathers,
3 From [a] thirty years old and

a c. 8. 24. 1 Chr. 23. 3. 24. 7.

---

ders plurally παρα των πρωτοτοκων, *from the first-born (sons)*, as implying all. As to the precise manner in which this affair of the redemption of the first-born was conducted, it is not possible to speak with certainty. Some of the Jewish writers say it was done by lot, so many scrolls having inscribed on them "A son of Levi," and so many, "Five shekels;" but the assertion rests probably upon conjecture or tradition, and cannot have authority with us at the present day. Still such *may* have been the method.——¶ *A thousand three hundred and threescore and five shekels.* Two hundred and seventy-three, which was the surplus number to be redeemed, multiplied by five gives just this total.

V. 51. *The money of them that were redeemed.* Gr. "The silver, the redemptions (or ransoms) of them that were superfluous (or over and above.") This was given to Aaron, because the Levites were given to him, v. 9, and when the requisite number of persons fell short, the deficiency was supplied by this redemption money. The redeeming men in this manner by silver foreshadowed a better redemption by Christ, the Lord, and is probably referred to by the apostle Peter when he says (1 Pet. 1:18, 19), "Ye know that ye were not redeemed with corruptible things, as silver and gold, etc., but with the precious blood of Christ."——¶ *According to the word of the Lord.* Heb. "According to the mouth of the Lord." Gr. "By the voice of the Lord."

CHAPTER IV.

The Duties of the respective Levitical Families in Connection with the Tabernacle.

V. 2. *Take the sum, etc.* Heb. *nâso eth rosh, take the head.* See Note on ch. 1:2. Chald. "Receive the count (or reckoning) of the sons of Kohath;" whose families stand foremost here, because they carried the holiest things. Of Kohath's pre-eminence, see Note on ch. 3:28. Though Gershon was the eldest, yet Kohath has the precedence by reason of the sanctity of his function.——¶ *After their families, by the house of their fathers.* See Note on ch. 1:2.

V. 3. *From thirty years old and upward, even until fifty years old.* Heb. "From the son of thirty years to the son of fifty years;" of which phrase see Note on Gen. 5:32. All the commentators here advert to an apparent discrepancy between this passage and ch. 8:24, where five-and-twenty is the age specified, and 1 Chron. 23:24. 2 Chron. 31:17. Ezra 3:8, where twenty is designated as the age at which these services were to commence. The Greek, with a view apparently to conciliate this passage with ch. 8:24, reads *twenty-five* instead of *thirty*, while Le Clerc supposes that *twenty-five* in the latter place to be a wrong reading for *thirty*. But the intimation of error in the manuscript is merely conjectural. The Jewish writers, for the most part, in order

upward even until fifty years old, all that enter into the host,

to reconcile these various statements, maintain that Moses here speaks of entering upon their full ministration, which being laborious, involving the carrying the burden of the sanctuary, required the utmost vigor of body and discretion of mind; it therefore began at thirty. But in ch. 8:24 the age of twenty-five, they say, denotes the time when they entered upon the preliminary work of learning the duties which they were afterwards to perform. Thus Maimonides says, "A son of Levi cometh not into the court unto his service, until they have first taught him five years, as it is said Num. 8:24, 'from five and twenty years old;' but whereas it is said Num. 4:3, 'from thirty years old,' lo, five are for him to learn; and he entereth not upon his service till he hath grown great (attained his full stature) and become a man; as it is said, Num. 4:19, 'Every *man* according to his service.'" Chaskuni, another rabbi, says moreover, "At twenty-five years old they entered all of them to do the lighter works, as to watch that no stranger came into the sanctuary, etc. etc., and at thirty years of age they were in their strength, and did bear the sanctuary," etc. This solution is on the whole satisfactory, and the arrangement indicated continued till the time of David, who, near the close of his life, recognized the present ordinance, 1 Chron. 23:3, but as the service had then, when there was no tabernacle to carry, become lighter and the demand for them at the same time increased, the period was fixed at twenty years instead of thirty. The following are the words of the sacred historian relative to that subject, 1 Chron. 23: 24, 27. "These *were* the sons of Levi after the house of their fathers; *even* the chief of the fathers, as they were counted by number of names by their polls, that did the work for the service of the house of the Lord, from the age of twenty years and upward. For David said, The Lord God of Israel hath given rest unto his people, that they may dwell in Jerusalem for ever: And also unto the Levites; they shall no more carry the tabernacle, nor any vessels of it for the service thereof. For by the last words of David the Levites were numbered from twenty years old and above." This would appear to have been done by divine direction, 1 Chron. 28:13, 19, in order that by beginning early to be instructed they might be the more fit at thirty to serve the Lord and his people. The age of thirty, therefore, became probably from this circumstance somewhat *canonical* for full induction into the priestly office, as we learn was the case with John the Baptist and with our Lord himself.—— ¶ *Until fifty years old.* At this period of life the strength and vigor of manhood begins somewhat to decay, and it was therefore ordered that they should be henceforth exempted from the harder kinds of service, but they still retained a lighter species of ministry about the tabernacle, of which see ch. 8:24, 27. ——¶ *All that enter into the host.* Heb. *kol bo letzâbâ*, *every one that cometh to the army.* "All that are meet for the war."—*Cov.* "All that were able to war."—*Mat.* "All that are able to go forth to the war."—*Cran.* The term is military, but as it is spoken of the Levites, the import is spiritual, denoting that kind of ministry or service which the priesthood was expected to perform, for which reason the Greek renders it *pas eisporeuomenos leitourgein, every one that entereth in to liturgize,* i. e. to officiate sacerdotally. In v. 23, the original phrase embracing this word is ren-

to do the work in the tabernacle of the congregation.

4 This [b] *shall be* the service of the sons of Kohath in the tabernacle of the congregation, *about* the [c] most holy things.

5 And when the camp setteth forward, Aaron shall come, and his sons, and they shall take down the covering vail [d], and cover the ark [e] of testimony with it;

6 And shall put thereon the covering of badgers' skins, and

b ver. 15. c ver. 19.

d Ex. 26. 31. Is. 25. 7. Heb. 9. 3. 10. 20 e Ex. 25. 10–16.

dered "to war the warfare," and this probably gave rise to the N. T. diction, in which the work of the ministry is called, 1 Tim. 1:18, "warring a good warfare," and where we find mention also of "fighting a good fight of faith," of "the weapons of our warfare," of "good soldiers of Jesus Christ," etc.; all which speak of the Christian life as a spiritual warfare.——¶ *To do the work.* Gr. *panta ta erga, all the works.* Chald. "To serve the service." Vulg. "To stand and to minister." This is exegetical of the warfare above mentioned as holy and spiritual. Accordingly, the bishop's office is called by Paul "a good work," 1 Tim. 3:1, as it is to "labor in the word and doctrine," 1 Tim. 5:17.——¶ *In the tabernacle of the congregation.* Not precisely *in* the tabernacle, but *about* it, for none but the priests were allowed to enter within.——¶ *(About) the most holy things.* Heb. *kodesh hakkodoshim, holiness of holinesses.* This stands in the original in apposition with tabernacle, which is called "most holy" from the holiness of the various utensils, etc. which it contained. See the usage ch. 3:28. 10:21, where "sanctuary" is the collective name for all the sacred contents of which it was the receptacle, such as the ark of the covenant, the altar, the table of shew-bread, the candlestick, etc. "In the tabernacle of witness, which is most holy."—*Cov. Mat.* Bp. Patrick, however, suggests, with considerable show of probability, that the omission of the word "about" would give a preferable sense;—"This shall be the service of the sons of Kohath, etc. (even) the most holy things," the ark and its appurtenances. Comp. vs. 19, 20, in the latter of which it is called "the holy," and in the former "the holy of holies," as here.

V. 5. *And when the camp setteth forward.* Heb. *bansaa, in the breaking* or *pulling up.* See the term explained in the Note on ch. 2:17. "When the host breaketh up."—*Cov.* "When the host removeth."—*Mat.* The signal for setting forward was the removal of the pillar of cloud.——¶ *Aaron shall come, and his sons.* The express law prohibiting any one except the high-priest once a year, entering into the most holy place, which held good while the cloud rested on the tabernacle, must have admitted an exception when it was about to be taken up. Then the inferior priests might enter to prepare the sacred vessels for removal.——¶ *Shall take down.* Heb. *horidu, shall cause to descend.*——¶ *The covering veil.* Heb. *paroketh hamâsok,* that is, the veil that hung between the holy and most holy place, as described Ex. 26:31, where see Note. Gr. "shadowing veil." Heb. 9:3, "The second veil." It was made of blue, purple, scarlet, and fine linen.

V. 6. *And shall put thereon the covering of badgers' skins.* As to the material indicated by the term "badgers' skins," see Note on Ex. 25:5. Here the term does not mean the covering of

shall spread over *it* a cloth wholly of blue, and shall put in the
staves [f] thereof.
7 And upon the table [g] of [h]
shew-bread they shall spread a
cloth of blue, and put thereon
the dishes, and the spoons, and
the bowls, and covers to cover
withal: and the continual bread
shall be thereon:
8 And they shall spread upon
them a cloth of scarlet, and cover the same with a covering of
badgers' skins, and shall put in
the staves thereof.
9 And they shall take a cloth
of blue, and cover the candlestick [i] of the light, and his lamps,
and his tongs, and his snuff-dishes, and all the oil vessels thereof, wherewith they minister unto
it:

f 1 K. 8. 7, 8. *g* Ex. 25. 23–30. *h* Lev. 24. 5–8. *i* Ex. 25. 31–38.

badgers' skins made for the tabernacle, which was carried by the Gershonites (vs. 24, 25), but one made for the purpose of concealing and sheltering the ark when it was carried. The proper rendering would therefore be, "And shall put thereon *a* covering of badgers' skins," as in v. 8.——¶ *Shall spread over it a cloth wholly of blue.* This was one among the "clothes of service" mentioned Ex. 31:10, on which see Note. This covering of blue, it seems, in the case of the ark, was put on over the coarser skin-covering, in order doubtless to invest that symbol with higher honor as a type of Christ, in whose heart was the divine law (Ps. 40:8), as the two tables were enshrined in the sacred chest. Rabbi Bechai intimates that this *blue*-colored cloth spread over the ark was an emblem of the skies which are spread as a curtain between us and the Majesty on high. ——¶ *And shall put in the staves thereof.* Heb. *vesâmu baddauv, and adjust the staves thereof;* i. e. dispose them rightly under the covering, that they might be laid on their shoulders; for the staves were never taken out of the rings, to which they were no doubt in some way fitted to prevent slipping.

V. 7. *And upon the table of shew-bread.* Heb. *shulhan pânim, the table of faces,* or *of presence,* instead of *the table of the bread of faces,* or *presence,* of the, etc., of the import of which see Note on Ex. 25:30, where a full explanation is given. Instead of *blue* the Sept. here renders by *purple.* As it is not said, like the other, to have been *wholly of blue,* it was doubtless something of a different color.——¶ *And covers to cover withal;* or, Heb. "to pour out withal." Probably some kind of cups or goblets are intended, into which wine was poured. See on this point the Note on Ex. 25:29. "Goblets and pots to pour with."—*Bish.* "Goblets and cups to pour the libaments." —*Dou.* "Libation-vessels."—*Gr.*—— ¶ *The continual bread.* That is, the bread which was to stand continually in the divine presence, the old being changed for new every sabbath. The Israelites were doubtless able to procure corn enough from the adjacent countries, even when in the wilderness, to make the shew-bread and to present the daily meal-offerings. The land of Midian, where Moses' father-in-law dwelt, was not far distant.

V. 8. *Shall spread upon them a cloth of scarlet.* Of the import of the original for "scarlet," see Note on Ex. 25:4. The ark only and the table of shew-bread had three coverings; the rest of the sacred utensils had but two. None but the table had a covering of scarlet.

10 And they shall put it and
all the vessels thereof within a
covering of badgers' skins, and
shall put *it* upon a bar.
11 And upon the golden al-
tar [k] they shall spread a cloth of
blue, and cover it with a covering of badgers' skins, and shall
put to the staves thereof:
12 And they shall take all
the instruments [l] of ministry,
wherewith they minister in the
sanctuary, and put *them* in a
cloth of blue, and cover them
with a covering of badgers' skins,
and shall put *them* on a bar:
13 And they shall take away
the ashes from the altar, and
spread a purple cloth thereon:

k Ex. 30. 1-5.

l Ex. 25. 9. 1 Chr. 9. 29.

Of the various minor articles specified in these verses, see a minute explanation in the Notes on Ex. 25, throughout.

V. 10. *And shall put it upon a bar.* Heb. *al hammot, upon a bar, lever,* or *bier.* The original is a different word from that employed to denote the *staves* inserted in rings, and implies some kind of hand-vehicle carried between two. It is the word used ch. 13:23, to denote the instrument of carriage on which the grapes were borne by the spies, though there translated *staff.*

V. 12. *All the instruments of ministry.* By these are probably to be understood the various utensils or vessels not elsewhere particularly specified, such as are spoken of 2 Kings 25:14, 15, among the different articles enumerated as being carried away from the temple at Jerusalem to Babylon.

V. 13. *Shall take away the ashes from the altar.* That is, from the brazen altar, or altar of sacrifice, which stood in the court, and of which the ashes were to be often cleansed; but especially upon removals.——¶ *Spread a purple cloth thereon.* The brazen altar only was covered with purple, as the table only was with scarlet, v. 8. It was probably owing to the large infusion of red that these colors were occasionally used interchangeably for each other. Thus Mat. 27:28, "They put on him a *scarlet* robe;" for which in John 19:2, we read, "They put on him a *purple* robe." So also Mark 15:17, "They clothed him with *purple.*" Some have supposed that purple was employed in this instance as a color that would naturally be formed by *a fire smothered in blue,* and infer that the sacred fire, which was to be kept always burning, and of which nothing is expressly said in this connection, was in fact carried on the depressed or concave grate of the altar, where it might be covered over with some kind of lid, and still leave the upper surface of the altar even. But we consider it after all as doubtful whether the injunction respecting the continual burning of the altar-fire (Lev. 6:13) is to be so strictly construed as to forbid the supposition that it might go out during the actual journeyings of the people, and be rekindled again from heaven, as at first, when they became stationary, and so resumed their daily worship. The law of the daily sacrifices (Ex. 29:38) was equally express as to its being perpetually observed, and yet the observance was no doubt occasionally interrupted during their marches. Should we be satisfied that the holy fire had at any time disappeared or gone wholly out, still we do not perceive that this would any more have affected its legal perpetuity, than would circumcision cease to be a sacramental or covenant sign because it was dropped for a

14 And they shall put upon it all the vessels [m] thereof, wherewith they minister about it, *even* the censers, the flesh-hooks, and the shovels, and the basons, all the vessels of the altar; and they shall spread upon it a covering of badgers' skins, and put to the staves of it.

15 And when Aaron and his sons have made an end of covering the sanctuary, and all the vessels of the sanctuary, as the camp is to set forward; after that, the sons of Kohath [n] shall

m Ex. 38. 3. 2 Chr. 4. 19.

n c. 7. 9. 10. 21. Deut. 31. 9. Josh. 4. 10. 2 Sam. 6. 13. 1 Chr. 15. 2, 15.

---

course of years in the wilderness. They were both of divine appointment, and both ordained to be of lasting perpetuity, but both, we suppose, might temporarily *lapse* without doing away the grounds of the language implying such perpetuity. An occasional exception does not destroy a general rule.

V. 14. *Censers.* This word is rendered by "fire-pans," Ex. 27:3, on which see Note.—It is remarkable that Moses says nothing in this connection respecting the Laver, which was one of the principal of the sacred vessels. The omission is supplied in the Greek version, as at the end of this verse it reads, "And they shall take a purple cloth, and cover the Laver and his base (foot), and they shall put it into a blue cover of skin, and put it on bars." Upon what authority this addition rests is not known. Capellus, Grotius, and Houbigant, however, agree in supposing that this clause has in some way slipped out of the Masoretic copies of the Hebrew text, and with them Rosenmuller is disposed to coincide. The fact is certainly somewhat singular, when elsewhere the Laver is especially enumerated among the other articles here spoken of. In the absence of any satisfactory light on the point, we may perhaps safely give some weight to the pious suggestion of Ainsworth that the Laver is not mentioned because it was not to be covered, as were all the other sacred things here specified. "It may be conjectured that the Laver is left uncovered and always open to the eyes of the people, that it might be a lively representation of God's grace in Christ, continued and opened as an ever-springing fountain; that by the washing of the new birth, by repentance and faith in this blood, we may in all our travels, at all times, cleanse our hands and feet (our works and ways), as the sacrificers did from the Laver, Ex. 30:19, 20; that albeit the face of the church is sometimes hid (as the tabernacle wrapped up), and the light of the Word shineth not, nor public worship performed, yet always God's elect having faith in him may wash and purge themselves in Christ's blood unto forgiveness of sins, sanctification of the spirit, and salvation."

V. 15. *Have made an end of covering the sanctuary.* Heb. *hakkodesh, the sanctity* or *holiness.* Gr. *ta hagia, the holy things.* See v. 4, also ch. 3:28. We may safely recognize a spiritual import in this veiling from the public eye of Israel the holy things of their economy. As Moses' covering his face with a veil denoted that "the children of Israel could not steadfastly look to the end (i. e. the scope or drift) of that which is abolished," or, in other words, were incompetent to grasp its typical significancy, so the Tabernacle in like manner and for a like reason was folded up and shrouded with veils and coverings from

come to bear *it*: but they shall not touch[o] *any* holy thing, lest they die[p]. These[q] *things are* the burden of the sons of Kohath in the tabernacle of the congregation.

o 2 Sam. 6. 6, 7. 1 Chr. 13. 9, 10. p Heb. 12. 29. q c. 3. 31.

---

the gaze of the people. They were not in a state to penetrate its mysteries to their spiritual good, and therefore the sight was precluded. But the end and accomplishment of these types we are now enabled, by the light of the Gospel, to discern, even "the revelation of the mystery, which was kept secret since the world began, but now is made manifest, and by the scriptures of the prophets, according to the commandment of the everlasting God, made known to all nations for the obedience of faith." Accordingly in the Apocalyptic vision we have God's Throne and the true Tabernacle set forth in all their unveiled glory, Rev. 4:2, etc. So also Rev. 11:19, "And the temple of God was opened in heaven, and there was seen in his temple the ark of his testament."——¶ *But they shall not touch any holy things.* Heb. *hakkodesh, the sanctity.* Gr. *ta hagia, the holy things,* implying the totality of the sacred things. It does not mean the tabernacle particularly, having, if any thing, a more especial reference to the ark of the covenant, which was the heart and core of the whole typical establishment, to which it belonged. A comparison of the following passages will show conclusively the soundness of this construction, 1 Kings 8:8, "And they drew out the staves, that the ends of the staves were seen out in *the holy* (*place.*") According to the Heb. it is *min hakkodesh, from the holy,* i. e. projecting out from the holy. The parallel text, 2 Chron. 5:9, has it thus:—" And they drew out the staves (of the ark), that the ends of the staves were seen *from the ark* (Heb. *min hââron, from the ark.*") The prohibition now uttered was of equivalent bearing with that respecting Mount Sinai, which, by reason of the divine presence associated with it at the time, might not be touched upon pain of death, Ex. 19:12. Heb. 12:18. The meaning is, that they were not to touch the things themselves that were covered, although in order to carry them they must of course touch the staves. These, we may suppose, were sometimes, during the transportation, held in their hands, and sometimes borne on their shoulders, as they became fatigued with one or the other mode.——¶ *Lest they die.* Heb. *vâmëthu, and they die.* Chald. and Gr. "That they may not die." The "not" in this kind of phraseology is sometimes inserted, and sometimes omitted. The judgment here threatened was executed upon Uzzah, a Levite, who for putting forth his hand to steady the ark was immediately smitten of God and died. 1 Chron. 13:10.——¶ *These* (*things*) *are the burden of the sons of Kohath.* Gr. *tauta arousin, they shall bear these things,* implying upon their own shoulders, and not by means of wagons or any other mode of conveyance. This was clearly the general province of the sons of Kohath, as a part of the Levitical order contradistinguished from the priests. But judging from several portions of the subsequent history, it does not appear that this arrangement was of such inviolable sanctity as never to be infringed upon, for the following passages have only to be consulted to make it evident that the priests did, on particular occasions, assume the office of the Levites in bear-

16 And to the office of Eleazar, the son of Aaron the priest, *pertaineth* the oil [r] for the light, and the sweet [s] incense, and the daily meat-offering [t], and the anointing oil [u], *and* the oversight of all the tabernacle, and of all that therein *is*, in the sanctuary, and in the vessels thereof.

17 And the LORD spake unto Moses and unto Aaron, saying,

r Ex. 25. 6. Lev. 24. 2. *s* Ex. 30. 34. *t* Ex. 29. 40. *u* Ex. 30. 23.

---

ing the ark. Deut. 31 : 9. Josh. 3 : 3. 1 Chron. 15 : 12, 15. It was undoubtedly fitting in itself that the most worthy things should be handled by the most worthy persons, provided their numbers were such as would enable them to do it. But as this was not the case at the outset of the Jewish polity, the burden was devolved upon an inferior class, to which it was mainly, though not exclusively, confined in all after times. David's setting the ark on a cart (2 Sam. 6 : 13. 1 Chron. 13 : 7) was his infirmity, for he afterwards confesses (1 Chron. 15 : 13) that "the Lord our God made a breach upon us, for that we sought him not after the due order." But his error being corrected in this matter, he subsequently returned to the primitive order, causing the priests and the Levites to "sanctify themselves to bring up the ark of the Lord God of Israel" (1 Chron. 15 : 13), which it would seem they did conjointly.

The Office of Eleazar.

V. 16. *And to the office of Eleazar——(pertaineth) the oil, etc.* Lit. "And the office (Heb. *pekuddath, charge, oversight, visitation,*) was the oil, etc." Gr. "And Eleazar, the son of Aaron, was overseer (*episcopos, bishop*) — his oversight (*episcopē, bishopric*) was the oil," etc. The use of these ecclesiastical terms helps us to apprehend the spiritual import which runs through the whole.——¶ *The oil for the light:* that is, for the golden candlestick with its bowls, or lamp-sconces. The Jewish writers say that the four following things were to be carried by Eleazar himself, to wit, "The oil of the light and the oil of anointing, the one in his right hand and the other in his left; and the incense in his bosom, and the meat-offering on his shoulder."——¶ *And the daily meat-offering.* Heb. *minchath hattâmid, the meat (meal) offering of the continual.*——¶ *The oversight of all the tabernacle.* Heb. *pekuddath,* the same word which in the beginning of the verse is translated "office."——¶ *In the sanctuary.* Heb. *bekodesh, in the sanctity,* or *holiness;* that is, *in regard* to the holiness, by which is meant especially the ark of the covenant, the holiest of the holy things. "Sanctuary" here is evidently something distinct from "tabernacle," as otherwise we have a mere repetition. ——¶ *In the vessels thereof.* That is, *in regard* to the vessels thereof; by which is meant the vessels pertaining to the tabernacle and not to the sanctuary. The remarks of Ainsworth on the typical purport of all this are very appropriate:—"In this office Bishop Eleazar was a figure of Christ, 'the Bishop of our souls' (1 Pet. 2 : 25), unto whom it pertaineth to give grace (the oil of the Spirit) for understanding the Scriptures (Luke 4 : 18. 24 : 45. John 1 : 16); to put odors of sweet incense, to the prayers of all saints by his mediation (Rev. 8 : 3. 1 Tim. 2 : 5); to present his Church as a pure meat (meal) offering and sacrifice unto his Father (Eph. 5:

18 Cut ye not off the tribe of the families of the Kohathites from among the Levites:
19 But thus do unto them, that they may live, and not die, when they approach unto the most[v] holy things: Aaron and his sons shall go in, and appoint them every one to his service and to his burden:
20 But they shall not go in to[w] see when the holy things are covered, lest they die.

v ver. 4.

w Ex. 19. 21. Lev. 10. 2. 1 Sam. 6. 19.

26, 27. 1 Cor. 5:7); to give the anointing oil of the Holy Ghost for our sanctification and the rejoicing of our hearts (John 7:39. 1 John 2:27); to oversee all churches and ministers, and all actions in churches where he is present and walks among them till the world's end. Matt. 28:10. Rev. 1:13. 2:1, 2, etc."

A Special Charge to Moses and Aaron.

V. 18. *Cut ye not off, etc.* Heb. *al takrithu, cause ye not to be cut off.* Gr. *mē olothreusate, destroy not.* That is, be careful lest by your negligence the people give way to vain curiosity, and thus expose themselves to be cut off by a divine interposition, as happened in the case of Nadab and Abihu. The practical lesson taught in these words is a very solemn one, to wit, that we ourselves become chargeable with those judgments which befall our fellow-men through our procurement, which are occasioned by our heedlessness or neglect. "Those who do not what they can to keep others from sin, do what they can to cut them off."—*Henry.*——¶ *The tribe of the families of the Kohathites.* Gr. "Ye shall not destroy of the tribe the family of Kaath." The form of the expression in the original is peculiar, and would indicate that the word "tribe" is here to be taken in a more restricted sense than usual, as equivalent to *stock.* The whole of the Levites properly constituted a *tribe,* and yet in this instance we read of a tribe being cut off "from among the Levites," showing clearly that it must bear a narrower sense than it ordinarily does.

V. 19. *That they may live and not die.* On the import of this phrase see Note on Deut. 33:6. The Targum of Jonathan thus expounds it:—"That they may live in the life of the righteous, and not die with flaming fire," in reference to Lev. 10:2.——¶ *Appoint them every one to his service, etc.* Heb. "Place or put them man, man, upon his service and upon his burden;" so that all disorder and confusion of service might be avoided. Maimonides says, "The Levites are to be warned that they do not each other's work, as that the singer help not to do the porter's work, nor the porter the singer's; as it is written, *Every man unto his service and his burden.* The Levites that do the priest's service, or a Levite that employeth himself in that work which is not his own, are in danger of death by the hand of God."

V. 20. *They shall not go in to see.* So also in Ex. 19:21, the people were charged not to "break through unto the Lord to gaze," and the men of Bethshemesh, because they "looked into the ark of the Lord," were smitten to the number of upwards of 50,000 men, 1 Sam. 6:19. The real internal ground of this prohibition is the contrariety of state between a holy God and sinful men. As their minds were incapable of perceiving the sacred mysteries couch-

21 And the LORD spake unto Moses, saying,
22 Take also the sum of the sons of Gershon, throughout the houses of their fathers, by their families;
23 From thirty[a] years old

[a] ver. 3.

ed under the symbols, so it was fitting that the symbols themselves should be withholden from their eyes.——¶ *When the holy things are covered.* Heb. כבלע *keballa, as the swallowing up;* a peculiar phraseology, of which the true import is not very easy to be determined. The general usage of the term may be judged of from the following instances: Ch. 16:30, "But if the Lord make a new thing, and the earth open her mouth, and *swallow them up," etc.* Job 20:15, "He hath *swallowed down* riches." Ex. 7:12, "But Aaron's rod *swallowed up* their rods." Ps. 106:17, "And the earth opened and *swallowed up* Dathan." Job 7:19, "How long wilt thou not depart from me, nor let me alone till I *swallow down* my spittle?" In other cases it is rendered by *devour, destroy,* and *spend.* Its general purport is that of *absorbing,* and thence *abolishing, making way with,* and *causing suddenly to disappear.* It is nowhere else rendered by *cover* except in the present passage, though that sense is somewhat countenanced by the version of Onkelos, "While they cover the sacred vessels," and by the Syriac and the Arabic, "When the holy is covered." Yet for reasons soon to be given we doubt if this is the true sense, and Michaelis in his "Supplement to the Hebrew Lexicons" (sub voce בלע) says this sense is unknown to all oriental tongues. Gesenius intimates that the expression may perhaps be elucidated from the phraseology in Job, "till I have swallowed my spittle," i. e. for a moment's time, a proverbial mode of speech in vogue among the Arabs. According to this the sense would be, "They shall not see, *for one moment,* the holy things." But the true rendering we take to be this:—"They shall not go in to see, as it were, to swallow, the holy things;" i. e. they shall not presume to gratify themselves with a hasty view, with a quick and furtive glance, as if they would swallow the objects with their eyes. The two ideas of *swallowing* and of *suddenness* are obviously included in the expression, and this is corroborated by the Greek, "They shall by no means go in to look suddenly upon the holy things, and die." The concealment thus enjoined plainly pointed to the darkness of that dispensation. "That which is now brought to light by the gospel, and revealed to babes, was then hid from the wise and prudent. They saw only the coverings, not the holy things themselves; but now Christ has 'destroyed the face of the covering.'"—*Henry.*

The Mustering and the Charge of the Gershonites.

V. 22. *Take also the sum of the sons of Gershon.* The literal rendering of the Heb. is here preferable:—"Take the sum of the sons of Gershon, of them also;" implying that although the Kohathites (the sons of the second brother) were first numbered, because they were to carry the holiest things, yet the Lord would not overlook the other families nor permit their ministry to be discharged any more irregularly. They also were to be carefully enumerated and assigned their particular charges.

V. 23. *Shalt thou number them.* Heb. *tiphkod, shalt thou muster.* Gr. *episkepsai, survey.*——¶ *All that enter in to*

and upward until fifty years old,
shalt thou number them; all
that enter in to perform the service, to do the work in the tabernacle of the congregation.
24 This *is* the service of the
families of the Gershonites, to
serve, and for burdens.
25 And [y] they shall bear the
curtains of the tabernacle, and
the tabernacle of the congregation, his covering, and the covering of the badgers' skins [z] that
is above upon it, and the hanging for the door of the tabernacle of the congregation.
26 And the hangings [a] of the
court, and the hanging for the
door of the gate of the court,
which *is* by the tabernacle, and
by the altar round about, and
their cords [b], and all the instruments of their service, and all
that is made for them: so shall
they serve.
27 At the appointment of

y c. 3. 25, 26. z Ex. 26. 14.

a Ex. 27. 9. b Ex. 35. 18.

perform the service. Heb. *litzbo tzaba, to war the warfare.* Gr. *leitourgein, to liturgize,* i. e. to minister sacerdotally. Vulg. Qui ingrediuntur et ministrant in tabernaculo fœderis, *all who go in and minister in the tabernacle of covenant.* "All that are meet for the war to have an office in the tabernacle of witness."—*Cov.* "All that are able to go forth in war, for to do service in the tabernacle." —*Mat.* See Note on v. 3.——¶ *To do the work.* "To serve the service."—*Ains.* This is doubtless exegetical or explanatory of the "warfare" just before mentioned. A succeeding phrase in this manner is often inserted with the express design of elucidating a preceding one.

V. 24. *This is the service, etc.* Gr. *leitourgia, liturgy,* i. e. sacred ministry. ——¶ *To serve, and for burdens.* A definite distinction is undoubtedly to be understood here between *service* and *burden,* the former referring to their ministry in the Tabernacle while it stood, in which they assisted the priests, and also took down and set up the sacred structure (ch. 10:21); and the latter denoting their carrying the edifice and its furniture, when it was to be removed.

V. 25. *Shall bear the curtains of the tabernacle.* That is, the ten fine curtains that formed the inward hangings of the Tabernacle (Ex. 26:1, 2, etc.). As nothing is said of Aaron or his sons being employed to take them down and make them ready for carriage, it may be presumed that all this was done by the Gershonites. The foregoing prohibition did not include the curtains of the Tabernacle.——¶ *And the tabernacle.* Not the boards, the framework, of the Tabernacle, which fell to the charge of the Merarites (v. 31), but the eleven curtains of goats' hair which covered the boards, and which are here called collectively the Tabernacle (Ex. 26:7, 8, etc.). See Notes on ch. 3:25, 26.

V. 26. *And all the instruments of their service, and all that is made for them.* Or perhaps more correctly, "All that is to be done by them." Gr. "All the vessels of service that they minister with they shall attend to." "All the instruments that serve for them, and all that belongeth to their occupying."—*Cov.* "All the instruments that serve unto them, and all that is made for them."—*Mat.* It is not easy to fix the precise shade of meaning intended.

V. 27. *At the appointment of Aaron, etc.* Heb. *al pi, at the mouth.* Chald. "At the word."——¶ *In all their bur-*

Aaron and his sons shall be all the service of the sons of the Gershonites, in all their burdens, and in all their service: and ye shall appoint unto them in charge all their burdens.

28 This *is* the service of the families of the sons of Gershon in the tabernacle of the congregation; and their charge *shall be* under the hand of Ithamar [c], the son of Aaron the priest.

29 As for the sons of Merari, thou shalt number them after their families, by the house of their fathers;

30 From thirty [d] years old and upward even unto fifty years old shalt thou number them, every one that entereth into the service, to do the work of the tabernacle of the congregation.

31 And this [e] *is* the charge of their burden, according to all their service in the tabernacle of the congregation: the [f] boards of the tabernacle, and the bars thereof, and the pillars thereof, and sockets thereof,

32 And the pillars of the court round about, and their sockets, and their pins, and their cords, with all their instruments [g], and with all their ser-

c ver. 33. d ver. 3.

e c. 3. 36, 37. f Ex. 26. 15. g Ex. 25. 9.

---

dens, and in all their service. Rather, "*as to* all their burdens, and *as to* all their service." Gr. According to all their ministrations, and according to all their works."——¶ *And ye shall appoint unto them in charge all their burdens.* Heb. *pekadtem*, the same word which is elsewhere rendered *number*, and which we have for the most part rendered *muster*, denoting not so strictly *enumeration* as *arrangement*, *marshalling*, *etc.* See Note on ch. 1 : 3. Gr. "Thou shalt take account of them (Gr. *episkepsē*) by name in all their works," as in v. 32. The original rendered "in charge" (*bemishmereth*) denotes literally *in* or *with observation*, and may be understood of the *care*, *diligence*, and *exactitude* with which the appointments of Aaron and his sons were to be carried out relative to the Gershonites and their functions.

V. 28. *This is the service.* Gr. *leitourgia, liturgy.*——¶ *And their charge.* Or, their observation, their custody.——¶ *Under the hand.* That is, under the government and direction. So in v. 33.

The Mustering and the Charge of the Merarites.

V. 29. *Thou shalt number.* Heb. *tiphkod, thou shalt muster.* "Thou shalt appoint."—*Cov. Mat.* See Note on v. 37.

V. 30. *From thirty years old and upward.* Gr. "Twenty-five years;" on which see Note on v. 3.——¶ *Every one that entereth into the service.* Heb. "Every one that entereth into the warfare." See Notes on vs. 3, 23. The original here is precisely the same with that in v. 3, and which is there rendered "all that enter into the host," in which appears a striking instance of that want of uniformity which is so conspicuous throughout our common version.

V. 31. *The boards of the tabernacle, etc.* Of the various articles mentioned here and in v. 32, see a particular account in Ex. 26, throughout. The charge of this family was evidently the most cumbersome of any, and therefore they were accommodated with wagons for the purpose, ch. 7 : 8.

V. 32. *And by name ye shall reckon*

vice: and by name ye shall reckon the instruments of the charge of their burden.

33 This *is* the service of the families of the sons of Merari, according to all their service in the tabernacle of the congregation, under the hand [h] of Ithamar, the son of Aaron the priest.

34 And Moses and Aaron, and the chief of the congregation, numbered the sons of the Kohathites, after their families,

h ver. 28. Josh. 3. 6.

and after the house of their fathers,

35 From thirty [i] years old and upward even unto fifty years old, every one that entereth into the service, for the work in the tabernacle of the congregation:

36 And those that were numbered of them, by their families, were two thousand seven hundred and fifty.

37 These *were* they that were

i ver. 47.

---

the instruments. Heb. *beshĕmoth, by names.* Chald. "By their names." "By name ye shall reckon the things that they must wait upon to bear.—*Mat.* "All the vessels and implements they shall receive by account, and so shall carry them."—*Vulg.* As the sockets, pillars, pins, cords, etc. pertaining to the Tabernacle were very numerous, and many of them small, they were liable to get misplaced, neglected, or lost, and therefore it was commanded that an *inventory* should be made out of all these particulars, as a security against the risks to which they would naturally be subject.——¶ *Shall reckon.* Heb. *tiphkedu, shall muster.* It is important to keep before the eye of the reader the peculiar use of this word.

The Number of the Kohathites.

V. 33. *This is the service of the families of the sons of Merari.* That is, in taking down and carrying the tabernacle, which was done under the superintendence of Ithamar, who had the oversight both of the Gershonites and Merarites, as Eleazar had of the Kohathites, vs. 16, 28.

V. 34. *And Moses and Aaron —— numbered.* Heb. *yiphkod, mustered;* to which the act of numbering was subordinate. See previous Notes.

V. 35. *Every one that entereth into the service.* Heb. כל הבא לצבא *kol habbâ letzâbâ, every one that entereth this warfare.* Gr. *leitourgein, to liturgize.* See Note on vs. 3, 30.

V. 36. *And those that were numbered of them —— were, etc.* Heb. *va-yihyu pekudĕhem, and these were of the mustered ones of them,* that is, these were made to be, or found to be, according to the explanation given in the Note on ch. 3:43. The process denoted by the term *pâkad,* which we have rendered by *muster,* seems first to have been accomplished, and then their number subsequently ascertained. It does not appear that the above word in itself denotes both processes.——¶ *Two thousand seven hundred and fifty.* By comparing this with ch. 3:28, it appears that out of 8600, the total number of the Kohathites, there were only about a fourth part fit and able for service.

V. 37. *These (were) they that were numbered, etc.* It will be observed that while the verb "were" is inserted in the preceding verse it is omitted here, which goes to confirm our suggestion, that its import in certain connections is not simply *to be,* but *to be made,* or *to*

numbered of the families of the Kohathites, all that might do service in the tabernacle of the congregation, which Moses and Aaron did number, according to the commandment of the LORD by the hand of Moses.

38 And those that were numbered of the sons of Gershon, throughout their families, and by the house of their fathers,

39 From thirty years old and upward even unto fifty years old, every one that entereth into the service, for the work in the tabernacle of the congregation,

40 Even those that were numbered of them, throughout their families, by the house of their fathers, were two thousand and six hundred and thirty.

41 These [k] *are* they that were numbered of the families of the sons of Gershon, of all that might do service in the tabernacle of the congregation, whom Moses and Aaron did number, according to the commandmeut of the LORD.

42 And those that were numbered of the families of the sons of Merari, throughout their families, by the house of their fathers,

43 From thirty years old and upward even unto fifty years old, every one that entereth into the service, for the work in the tabernacle of the congregation,

44 Even those that were numbered of them, after their families, were three thousand and two hundred.

45 These *be* those that were numbered of the families of the sons of Merari, whom Moses and Aaron numbered, according to the word of the LORD [l] by the hand of Moses.

46 All those that were numbered of the Levites, from Moses and Aaron and the chief of Israel numbered, after their fam-

k ver. 22.

l ver. 29.

---

be made out to be, as the result of some previous process. The act indicated by the term *pâkad* seems to be, *to ascertain by inspection* or *visitation what individuals were fit and competent to perform certain offices.* This is the idea we attach to the word *muster.* The actual enumeration of these individuals, though accompanying the muster, was not identical with it. A similar phraseology occurs in vs. 38–40.

The Number of the Gershonites.

V. 40. *Two thousand six hundred and thirty.* From ch. 3 : 22, it appears that the total of the Gershonites was 7500. Of these a little more than one third were fit to serve in the Tabernacle.

The Number of the Merarites.

V. 44. *Three thousand and two hundred.* Here also out of 6200 Merarites (ch. 3 : 34) only somewhat more than half were found fit for service in their appropriate sphere. In a tabellated form the numbers stand thus:—

KOHATHITES, ...	Able men,	2,750	
	Unable,	5,850	
	Total, ...		8,600
GERSHONITES, ...	Able men,	2,630	
	Unable,	4,870	
	Total, ...		7,500
MERARITES, ...	Able men,	3,200	
	Unable,	3,000	
	Total, ...		6,200
	Grand total, ...		22,300

ilies, and after the house of their
fathers,
47 From [m] thirty years old
and upward even unto fifty years
old, every [n] one that came to do
the service of the ministry, and
the service of the burden in the
tabernacle of the congregation,
48 Even those that were numbered of them, were eight thousand and five hundred and fourscore.
49 According to the com-
mandment of the LORD they were
numbered by the hand of Moses,
every one according to his service [o], and according to his burden: thus were they numbered
of him, as the LORD commanded
Moses.

m ver. 3. 23, 30. 1 Chr. 23. 3, 27. *n* Rom. 12. 6-8. 1 Cor. 12. 4-31.

o ver. 15, 24. 31. ver. 1. 21.

Thus, out of the whole number of the Levites, amounting to 22,300, only 8,580 were fit for service, leaving 13,720 unfit, either from being too old or too young, or otherwise disqualified. "Of the many that add to the numbers of the church, there are comparatively but few that contribute to the service of it. So it has been, and so it is; many have a place in the tabernacle that do but little of the work of the tabernacle."—*Henry.* The family of Merari, though numerically smaller than either of the other families of Levi, had yet a greater number of able men than either of them; for out of 6200 males of a month old and upwards, we find 3200 who were neither too young nor too old for the service of the sanctuary; which was more than one half the whole number. In this the divine wisdom conspicuously appears; for the Merarites were charged with the heaviest part of the burdens, such as the boards, bars, sockets, etc.; and though wagons were afterwards provided for them, yet their duties in loading and unloading would be peculiarly onerous. It was requisite, therefore, that those charged with this responsibility should be adapted to it both in numbers and strength. In most cases, in any given number of families, the young and the aged exceed those in middle life; but here it is otherwise, as more than half the Merarites were strong men, between the ages of thirty and fifty. This we may regard as the result of a special ordering of the divine Providence.

V. 47. *Every one that came to do the service of the ministry, and the service of the burden.* Heb. *laabod abodath abodah, to serve the service of the service,* i. e. the most laborious service, even that of the burden. The *service* is here probably to be distinguished from the *burdens* according to the explanation given in the Note on v. 19. Gr. "Every one that goes in to the service (*ergon, work*) of the works, and the *charge of* the things that are carried in the tabernacle of witness."

V. 49. *According to the commandment.* Heb. *al pi, at* or *upon the mouth.* Gr. "By the voice."——¶ *They were numbered by the hand of Moses, etc.* Heb. "He mustered them by the hand of Moses, every one according to his service and according to his burden." "He mustered" (i. e. one mustered) is an impersonal form of expression equivalent to "they were mustered," as rendered in our version; but it is always desirable to exhibit the exact literal sense of a passage. From the tenor of the verse it is still farther apparent that the import of "muster" in this connection, is not precisely to "number," but to *arrange, order,* and *marshal,* in reference to the discharge of certain functions.

CHAPTER V.

AND the LORD spake unto Moses, saying,

2 Command the children of Israel, that they put out of the camp every leper[a], and every one that hath an issue[b], and whosoever is defiled by the dead.[c]

a Lev. 13. 3, 46. c. 12. 14. Deut. 24. 8, 9. *b* Lev. 15. 2. *c* Lev. 21. 1. c. 9. 6, 10. 19. 11-13 31. 19.

CHAPTER V.

The Removal of the Unclean from the Camp.

V. 2. *Command the children of Israel, etc.* The camp of Israel having been now arranged according to the divine program, with the sanctuary in the centre, as the palace of "the Great King," orders are given with a view to preserve its sanctity inviolate. According to laws enacted on these subjects at different times, lepers and persons otherwise unclean were to be excluded from the camp. For this exclusion the following reasons may be cited. (1.) *Physical;* the diseases were *contagious*, and therefore there was a necessity for putting those afflicted with them apart, that the infection might not be communicated. (2.) *Spiritual;* the camp was the habitation of God, a being of infinite purity, and therefore in honor of him who had thus condescended to dwell with them, nothing impure should be permitted to remain. (3.) *Typical;* the camp was the emblem of the church, where nothing that is defiled should enter, and in which nothing that is unholy should be tolerated. Comp. ch. 12:14. Lev. 13:46. Deut. 24:8, 9. 2 Kings 7:3. That Moses was to *command* the children of Israel to do this shows the weightiness of the matter in the divine estimation; and it is very natural to infer that so stringent a law in regard to external or natural purity would tend to produce a more careful study of internal or moral purity, the one being emblematical of the other, and therefore by association of ideas intimately connected with it.——¶ *Every leper.* For a full account of the leprosy and the laws pertaining to it, see Note on Lev. 13, throughout.——¶ *Every one that hath an issue.* See Note on Lev. 15:2.——¶ *Whosoever is defiled by the dead.* Heb. *tâmë lânephesh, defiled by a soul.* The usage is very peculiar, but a reference to the following passages will show beyond dispute that the usual Heb. word for soul does in several instances denote a *dead body*, Lev. 21:11. 22:4. Num. 6:6. Hag. 2:13. An attempted solution of the grounds of this usage will be found in my work entitled, "The Soul; or, an Inquiry into Scriptural Psychology," p. 62. It is obvious that these legal pollutions represented our pollution by sin of whatever kind, and the exclusion of persons affected by these different species of defilements from the camp pointed to a similar allotment in regard to those who are spiritually defiled, and thus liable to be cast out of the Church, into which it is said that "any thing that defileth may in no wise enter," Rev. 22:27. "Henceforth there shall no more come into thee the uncircumcised and the unclean," Is. 52:1. As in the preceding chapters the chosen people are exhibited as a great, numerous, and highly favored people, so we are taught in this and several following chapters that they were to be a holy people; that is, that they were to be externally and ceremonially holy; they were to be strict in the observance of all the divine rites and institutions, as the condition of enjoying the tokens of the Lord's presence among them, and the outward

3 Both male and female shall
ye put out, without [d] the camp
shall ye put them, that they defile not their camps, in the midst
whereof I [e] dwell.
4 And the children of Israel
did so, and put them out without the camp: as the LORD
spake unto Moses, so did the
children of Israel.
5 And the LORD spake unto
Moses, saying,
6 Speak unto the children of
Israel; When [f] a man or woman
shall commit any sin that men

d 2 K. 7. 3. 2 Chr. 26. 21. e Lev. 26. 11, 12. 2 Cor. 6. 16.

f Lev. 6. 2.

---

blessings of his Providence which were promised to their obedience. As a matter of historical fact it does not appear that the nation of Israel, as a nation, were at all distinguished by a corresponding internal sanctity and purity. Their religious character has probably always been substantially what it now is. But their *representative* function could still be discharged independent of their personal qualities. Hence it is that we meet with such an ordinance as the present. The purity of the Jewish camp pointed typically to the purity of the Christian church.

V. 3. *Both male and female shall ye put out.* Heb. *mizzâkâr ad nekëbâh teshallehu, from male to female shall ye send out.* The command here given took effect upon Miriam as related ch. 12:15.——¶ *Without the camp shall ye put them.* Heb. *el mihootz, to without,* that is, to a place without the precincts of the camp.——¶ *That they defile not their camps.* Heb. "And let them not defile (or, make unclean) their camps." That is, as we suppose, at whatever place they might encamp during their journeyings, they were always to be careful and observe the same exemplary purity by excluding the causes and occasions of pollution. Yet the fact is not to be overlooked that many distinguished expositors, both Jewish and Christian, give another reason for the use of the plural in this connection. They say that there were three camps: (1.) The camp of the Shekinah, or of the Lord's divine presence, viz., the Sanctuary with its courts. (2.) The camp of Levi, who, with his sons, camped round about the sanctuary. (3.) The camp of Israel, which encompassed them all. A threefold division somewhat analogous was recognized in reference to the Temple and its precincts in aftertimes. Lepers were accounted so unclean, that they were not admitted into any of these three camps, but shut out of them all, Lev. 13:46. But he that had an *issue*, or seminal flux, Lev. 15:2, was only shut out of the first two, the camp of the Lord and the camp of the Levites; while he might remain in the camp of Israel. He that was "defiled by the dead," Lev. 21:1, was only excluded from the first, but not from the other two.——¶ *In the midst whereof I dwell.* That is, by the visible symbol of the divine presence. Chald. "My Shekinah dwelleth among you." As the divine presence consecrates whatever comes in contact with it, it behoves all uncleanness and iniquity to hide its head before him.

Restitution to be made in the case of Trespasses.

V. 6. *When a man or woman shall commit any sin that men commit.* Heb. "A man or a woman, when they shall do (any) of all the sins of man." That is, any of the sins which men, as frail and fallen beings, are prone to commit.

commit, to do a trespass against the LORD, and that person be guilty;

7 Then they shall confess [g] their sin which they have done: and he shall recompense [h] his trespass with the principal thereof, and add unto it the fifth *part*

g Lev. 5. 5. 26. 40. Josh. 7. 19. Job 33. 27. Ps. 32. 5. Prov. 28. 13. 1 John 1. 9.

h Lev. 6. 5–7. 7. 7.

Gr. "Of all human sins;" sins incident to humanity. Pool and others give the expression a little different shade of import, and understand by "sins of man" sins against men, sins whereby other men are wronged and injured. It is therefore an example of what is termed a genitive of the object, being classed with the following, "Blasphemy of the Spirit," i. e. blasphemy *against* the Holy Ghost. Comp. Mat. 12:31, and Mark 3:29. Luke 10:12. "Power of all flesh," John 17:2, i. e. power *over* all flesh. "Power of spirits," Mat. 10:1, i. e. power *over* or *against* spirits, Luke 9:1. "Prayer of God," Luke 6:12, i. e. prayer *directed to* God. "Spoil of the poor," Is. 3:14, i. e. spoil *taken from* the poor. "Violence of the children of Judah," Joel 3:19, i. e. violence *against* them, as it is also translated. This construction is favored by vs. 7, 8; but it is not very material which is adopted.——¶ *To do a trespass against the Lord.* Heb. "To transgress a transgression;" that is, to commit (or, by committing) a transgression, as in Lev. 6:2, where see Note. Chald. "To falsify a falsehood," that is, to speak or deal falsely. On the force of the Heb. term see Note on Lev. 5:15. Gr. "Despising shall despise," as also in Lev. 6:2.——¶ *Against the Lord.* See this phrase explained in the Note on Lev. 6:2. It implies that wrongs done to the neighbor are in fact sins against God. The Chaldee understands this of frauds and deceptions practised upon others by means of a false oath, which would seem to be countenanced by Lev. 6:2, where the same command is given. The prevarication and falsehood supposed in such a case, the denial of having received a deposit in trust, would be an aggravated offence against the Lord, who requires universal equity and honesty.——¶ *And that person be guilty.* Heb. *nephesh hahiv, and that soul.* That is, according to Pool, shall be sensible of his guilt, or be convicted of his conscience. Otherwise it would amount simply to a tautology, for the being really guilty is implied in the previous expression, "when one shall commit any sin." Rosenmuller, however, interprets it, "And shall in this manner have contracted guilt." Compared with the following verse this appears to be the most probable construction.

V. 7. *Then they shall confess their sin, etc.* Heb. *hithvaddu, shall make themselves to confess,* implying somewhat of self-compulsion. Although here made a condition in a particular case, yet confession is the invariable requisite to remission in all cases. "Whoso that confesseth and forsaketh (sins) shall have mercy," Prov. 28:13. It is evident that the design of the divine Lawgiver was to encourage confession in regard to such offences as could not be discovered by the testimony of witnesses. This was merciful and wise. It tended to relieve the mind of a sense of guilt, and to promote an ingenuous disposition. In order still farther to effect this object, it will be observed that the fine in case of theft is much less than it would have been had not the crime been acknowledged, but had been proved in a court of justice.——¶ *Shall recompense his trespass* Heb. *hashib eth*

thereof, and give *it* unto *him* against whom he hath trespassed.

8 But if the man have no kinsman to recompense the trespass unto, let the trespass be recompensed unto the LORD, *even* to the priest; beside the ram of the atonement, whereby an atonement shall be made for him.

9 And every offering of all

---

ashomo, shall restore his trespass (or, *his guiltiness*), meaning the thing for which he is guilty. On the whole subject of *ashams*, trespasses, and trespass-offerings, see the introductory observations to Lev. 5, where the nature of these offences and the prescribed offerings is fully discussed. See also Note on Lev. 6:4. Maimonides says, "The *asham* (*guiltiness*) here spoken of is the thing taken by rapine or the price thereof."——¶ *With the principal thereof.* Heb. *berosho, in his head*, i. e. with the sum total in all its items, every whit. See Note on ch. 1:2, on the peculiar use of "head" in the sense of *sum.*——¶ *And add unto it the fifth part thereof.* See the Notes on Lev. 6: 4, 5. This penalty was enjoined both as a compensation to the injured party for being deprived of the use of his property for a longer or shorter time, and as a proper though mild punishment to the offender, with a view to prevent the recurrence of similar wrongs. It is enacted in Ex. 22:1, that "If a man shall steal an ox, or a sheep, and kill it, or sell it; he shall restore five oxen for an ox, and four sheep for a sheep." But in this instance the law evidently contemplates the case of a high-handed and wilful act of theft, where the perpetrator is convicted by legal process, and not by his own confession, of the crime; whereas, in the passage before us, the fraudulent act is regarded as of milder form, and is extenuated by the voluntary confession of the guilty party.

V. 8. *But if the man have no kinsman.* Heb. *goël, redeemer.* On the import of this term, see Note on Gen. 9:5. It denotes the person who, according to oriental custom, assumes the office of redeemer, avenger, and general agent in behalf of one who is deceased. On this ground the Hebrews apply this law mainly to the *stranger*, supposing there would not be apt to be any one in Israel without kinsmen of some kind, either parent, brother, child, or other relative; "but this," says Jarchi and Maimonides, "is meant of the stranger that dieth and leaveth no heirs."——¶ *Let the trespass be recompensed unto the Lord, even unto the priest.* The Lord and the priest are here, as it were, identified, from the fact that the priest was the Lord's representative or deputy, acting on his behalf and in his name. The case contemplated is where the man to whom an injury had been done was dead, and he who had committed it was required to make satisfaction to his heir, if he had one, by restoring the principal and adding a fifth part to it. In case he had no heir and no kinsman to act the part of a Goël, the restoration was to be made to the Lord, in the person of his representative the priest, though Jewish writers say, with much plausibility, that it was afterwards equally distributed among all the priests who were then serving in their course. ——¶ *Beside the ram of atonement.* Comp. Lev. 6:6, 7. The guilty party had offended both God and man by his trespass. By restitution he was to satisfy the latter, and by atonement the former.

V. 9. *Every offering.* Heb. *terumah,*

the holy things of the children
of Israel, which they bring unto
the priest, shall [i] be his.
10 And every man's hallowed
things shall be his: whatsoever
any man giveth the priest, it
shall be his.
11 And the LORD spake unto
Moses, saying,
12 Speak unto the children
of Israel, and say unto them, If
any man's wife go aside, and
commit a trespass against him,

i Ex. 29. 28. Lev. 6. 17, 18. 7. 6–14. c. 18. 8, 9, 19. Deut. 18. 3, 4. Ezek. 44. 29, 30. Mal. 3. 8–10. 1 Cor. 9. 13.

---

heave-offering, taken here in a large sense so as to include the *wave-offering*, both which, according to Ex. 29:26–28, fell to the portion of Aaron. Chald. "Separation, or separated thing." Gr. "And every first-fruit according to all the hallowed things."——¶ *Which they bring unto the priest.* Heb. *yakribu*, *bring near*, *cause to approach*, i. e. by way of religious offering. As before remarked, it was offered to the Lord in the person of the priest. Comp. ch. 18. Gr. "Whatsoever they shall offer to the Lord, to the priest to him shall it be."——¶ *Shall be his.* That is, his who officiates as offerer at the time. Compare with this what is said about the provision for the priests, Ezek. 44: 28–30, "I am their inheritance: and ye shall give them no possession in Israel: I am their possession. They shall eat the meat-offering, and the sin-offering, and the trespass-offering; and every dedicated thing in Israel shall be theirs. And the first of all the first-fruits of all things, and every oblation of all, of every sort of your oblations, shall be the priest's: ye shall also give unto the priest the first of your dough, that he may cause the blessing to rest in thine house." These verses appear to have no specially intimate connection with the foregoing, but having spoken of a recompense to be made under certain circumstances to the priest, he takes occasion to deliver some other laws in which the priests were concerned.

V. 10. *Every man's hallowed things shall be his.* That is, every man's hallowed things are to be considered, in the first instance, as being his own, and subject to his own voluntary disposal; but when he has determined to make a present of any of them to the Lord, then they fall to the share of that priest into whose hand it is delivered, who is to consider it his. The former verse speaks of the holy things of the children of Israel in general, this of what any particular person bestowed upon a priest.

The Trial of Jealousy.

V. 12. *If any man's wife go aside.* Heb. *ish, ish, a man, a man*, that is, as rightly rendered, the wife of *any* man—a not unusual Hebrew idiom. Adultery was a crime expressly forbidden by the seventh commandment, and the punishment assigned by the law to both the adulterer and the adulteress was death by stoning, when the commission of the crime was discovered. But sometimes the crime might be suspected, and a spirit of jealousy, with or without just cause, might come over the mind of the husband. In such a case express provision was made, by this law, for determining the guilt or innocence of the wife; and although God might have declared her innocence or guilt at once, yet he chose that it should assume the form of a public trial, that the attention of the people might be the more called, both to the crime of adultery, as also to his own presence and active agency in the administration of the law he had given them. The connection of this enactment with the preceding is not very obvious, but it may be that inasmuch as the preceding verses allude to various kinds of frauds, this may be introduced here as the most aggravated form of that iniquity which a man could have practised upon him. The law in itself is one of the most remarkable of all the Mosaic institutes. It goes on the assumption that as the Lord is the author of marriage, so he will show himself the revenger of the breach of it; and it would naturally carry with it, so far as the predicted results ensued, indubitable evidence of miraculous agency, and consequently afford full proof of the divinity of its origin; and if this particular law were divine, it could not well fail to make out the same character for the whole system. Here is a crime threatened with a punishment which could only fall upon it through a special divine interposition, and such a fact would establish a permanent supernatural administration of the affairs of the Jewish nation. It is one of the earliest specimens on record of what is termed *the trial by ordeal*. Ordeal (Lat. *ordalium*) is plausibly supposed to be derived from the Saxon *ordal* or *ordel*, compounded of *or*, *great*, and *dæl*, *judgment*, implying the *greatest*, *most solemn*, and *decisive* mode of *judgment*. It always implied an appeal to the *immediate interposition* of God, and was therefore resorted to only in momentous cases, where there was no sufficient *evidence* whereby accused parties could be convicted of guilt. Such were the cases of jealousy described in this chapter. "Cases would frequently occur," says Mr. Kitto, "where the husband might suspect adultery without being able to prove it, and in that case, the man and wife could not fail to live miserably together, or else the man would feel inclined to act on his own impressions, and take the law into his own hands. To meet such a case, a trial was instituted, by which the innocence or guilt of a suspected wife might be established beyond question. The trial of a case of only suspected guilt, and incapable of proof, could not be other than an *ordeal;* and no one who pays attention to this awful process can doubt that it must have had a powerful effect for the intended purpose, or believe that any really guilty woman could go through it and brave its results. It must have been an awful thing even to the innocent, who knew that the result would clear their character from suspicion; and this was perhaps intended in order that their conduct might not only be free from actual guilt, but that they might avoid all conduct calculated to give cause for suspicion. We read no instance in which the trial took place; and if the administration of the ordeal were really infrequent, we may regard that as an evidence of its practical utility. For it would seem that the trial and its result were so dreadful, that the guilty rather confessed their crime, as they were earnestly exhorted to do, than go through it. The innocent only would then drink the bitter water; and as it produced no marked effect upon *them*, this may have led to the gradual disuse of the trial, under the impression that it had ceased to be operative. The Jews, however, say that this form of trial continued in use till towards the latter end of the second temple; for they were of opinion that the bitter water would have no effect if the husband himself were guilty of a similar crime; and they add that the adulteries of men became so common, that the ordeal ceased to distinguish the guilty woman from the innocent."—*Pict. Bible.* Although there is good reason to believe, with Spencer, that the ordeal, as a purgation of crime, ex-

13 And a man[k] lie with her carnally, and it be hid from the eyes of her husband, and be kept close, and she be defiled, and *there be* no witness against her, neither she be taken *with the manner;*

k Lev. 18. 20.

isted in the customs of heathen nations prior to its enactment among the Jews, yet it is probable that this appointment embodied in a divine code has served as an authority, or rather as a precedent, for various similar usages which have prevailed in later times for the detection of crimes, such as witchcraft, for instance, of which it was impossible to produce satisfactory proof. We have grounds for abundant gratitude, that under the milder dispensation in which our lot is cast, no such direct appeals to a divine decision find a warrant.

V. 13. *And a man lie with her carnally.* Heb. "A man lie with her (with) the lying of seed."——¶ *And be kept close.* Heb. נסתרה *nisterah, she hath been hidden*, or, *acted mysteriously, has mystified.* Concealment, mystery, is the leading idea, and in fact the very word *mystery* is supposed to be derived from the root of the original Hebrew *sâthar, to hide, to conceal.* It has evidently a close relation with *mistor, a hiding-place,* formed directly from the above root by prefixing מ = *m.*——¶ *And there be no witness against her.* For if there were, she must have been punished by being put to death. See the law Lev. 18 : 20 and 20 : 10. The remark may here be made, that the case described in this verse is not to be considered as *actual*, but *hypothetical*, that is, the husband has some reason to *suspect* that his wife has gone aside; she has gone aside in his opinion; for it is clear from the context that he had no proof of it, nor indeed does the law seem intended for unequivocal cases, as in all such cases the punishment was death, as just observed; and it is a saying of the Hebrew doctors that "the bitter waters are never used except in doubtful cases." The ensuing verse makes it evident that the man is harboring a suspicion which may or not be well founded. In this state of suspense he is directed what to do.——¶ *Neither she be taken (with the manner.)* The concluding phrase "with the manner" conveys no intelligible sense as the words are now understood. They might be omitted without any apparent detriment to the sense. It is in fact a peculiar idiomatic phrase occurring in the older English writers, and now almost wholly obsolete, except in law documents, to which it originally and properly belongs. It is equivalent to being taken in the act. Johnson, in his Dictionary, under the word "manner," gives a definition almost identical with that of Blackstone, who says of certain methods of prosecution, that "one was when a thief was taken *with the mainour*, that is, with the thing stolen upon him *in manu, in his hand.*" "Mainour," it seems, was the ancient spelling, which Blackstone says comes from the French *mainœuvre, a manu,* and this gradually became changed into *manier*, and then into *manner.* Whishaw's "Law Dictionary" has the following:—"Manner (from the Fr. *manier* or *mainer*, i. e. *manu tractare.*) To be taken *with the manier*, is where a thief, having stolen any thing, is taken with the same about him, as it were in his hands; which is called *flagrante delicto.*" So in "Nares' Glossary," which contains the fullest exhibition of the usage of the phrase, it is said, "To be taken *with* or *in the manner*, is to be caught in a criminal fact; originally in a theft with the thing stolen in hand." To the above, we may add the follow-

14 And the spirit of jealousy[l] come upon him, and he be jealous of his wife, and she be defiled: or if the spirit of jealousy come upon him, and he be jealous of his wife, and she be not defiled;

l Prov. 6. 34, 35. Cant. 8. 6. Zeph. 3. 8.

---

ing from "Junius' Letters" (Let. 68), which goes to confirm all that is said above. "It is worth the reader's attention to observe how nearly, in the ideas of our ancestors, the circumstance of 'being taken with the maner" approached to the conviction of the felon. It fixed the authoritative stamp of verisimilitude upon the accusation; and by the common law, when a thief was taken *with the maner* (that is, with the things stolen upon him *in manu*) he might, so detected *flagrante delicto*, be brought into court, arraigned and tried without indictment; as by the Danish law, he might be taken and hanged upon the spot, without accusation or trial."

V. 14. *And the spirit of jealousy come upon him.* Heb. ועבר עליו רוח-קנאה *ve-âbar âlauv ruach kinâh, and the spirit of jealousy pass upon him.* Gr. "And the spirit of jealousy (rather, zealousy—ζηλωσις) come upon him." By the "spirit of jealousy" is implied a jealous or zealous affection of mind, one by which the subject of it is powerfully impelled. In like manner the Scriptures elsewhere speak of "the spirit of wisdom, the spirit of counsel, the spirit of knowledge," Is. 11:2. Eph. 1:17; "the spirit of fornications," Hos. 4:12; "the spirit of fear," 2 Tim. 1:7; "the spirit of meekness," Gal. 6:1; "the spirit of slumber," Rom. 11:8; and in 1 Cor. 14:12, "spirits" are put for the gifts and movings of the Holy Spirit. Jealousy is a zealous affection taken sometimes in a good and sometimes in an evil sense, as zeal is sometimes spoken of as good and sometimes as evil, John 2:17. 2 Cor. 7:11. Gal. 5:20, and is called *bitter zeal*, James 3:14. The Hebrew has one term (*kinah*) by which to express *zeal, jealousy, envy,* and *emulation.* Thus Phineas was "*zealous* for his God," ch. 25:11; Elias was "very *zealous*" for him, 1 Kings 19:10; Joshua was *envious* for Moses' sake, Num. 11:29; and jealousy is an affection termed "hard (or cruel) as the grave, the coals whereof are coals of fire," Song 8:6. Jealousy is said also to be "the rage of a man; therefore he will not spare in the day of vengeance," Prov. 6:34. The same affection is ascribed, by the figure termed anthropopathy, to the Lord himself, who is termed "a jealous God," Ex. 20:5. In all these cases the original word is the same with that in the present passage. The phrase "spirit of jealousy" belongs to a mode of speech which is usual when any strong, vehement, or violent affection, passion, or prompting takes possession of a man, as though his whole soul was carried away by it, and he had scarcely the power of resistance. At the same time, we are doubtless at liberty to recognize an allusion to the power and influence of evil spirits who are present and active in instigating all such promptings of our fallen nature, exciting them when there is no ground, and aggravating them when there is. If we are authorised to recognize the influence of the Holy Spirit in all such affections as are termed the spirit of wisdom and meekness, the spirit of knowledge and understanding, the spirit of grace and supplication, the spirit of prophecy, of faith, and of a sound mind, so on the other we may properly refer the opposite affections to an opposite source, and see an evil demon in an evil disposition,——¶ *And he be jealous of his*

15 Then shall the man bring his wife unto the priest, and he shall bring her offering[m] for her, the tenth *part* of an ephah of barley meal: he shall pour no oil upon it, nor put frankincense thereon; for it *is* an offering of jealousy, an offering of memorial, bringing[n] iniquity to remembrance.

m Lev. 5. 11.

n 1 K. 17. 18. Ezek. 29. 16. Heb. 10. 3.

wife, and she be defiled. Two distinct cases are evidently supposed, one in which the woman *has* committed adultery, giving thereby occasion for a just and well-founded jealousy; the other in which she *has not* been guilty of the crime, and consequently given no legitimate cause for distrust. Both these suppositions are involved in the language of the present verse. But whatever were the *facts* in the case, the prescribed course was the same.——¶ *And she be defiled.* That is, whether she be defiled.——¶ *And she be not defiled.* Or whether it be only his suspicion. The language is all along to be understood of the impressions of the husband, and not of the actual fact.

V. 15. *Then shall the man bring his wife unto the priest.* Together with the witnesses, if any, who were prepared to testify to the act. According to the Jewish writers, the priest first endeavored to persuade her to confess the truth, suggesting hypothetically various apologies and extenuations for her, and if she confessed, saying, "I am defiled," she was not put to death, but simply divorced, with the loss of her dowry; if she said, "I am pure," they then proceeded.——¶ *The tenth part of an ephah of barley meal.* A coarse offering of barley-meal, without oil or frankincense, is here prescribed in accordance with the nature of the transaction and the state of the parties. As all the circumstances were *disagreeable,* so the offering was not of the usual palatable material. It was unaccompanied by the other usual requisites, because it was no grateful offering of thanksgiving, but an expression of humiliation, grief, and shame. The Hebrew writers say, "meal, not flour; barley, not wheat: she hath done the act of a beast, and her oblation is the meal of a beast." It may here be asked, Why the jealous wife was not equally privileged to arraign her husband and put him to an oath of purgation similar to that here prescribed for the woman. To this it may be replied (1), that women generally speaking are more prone to suspicion and jealousy than men, and therefore more liable to make an improper use of such a liberty. (2.) Because, among the Jews the marital pre-eminence and authority was so marked, that the greatest violence would have been done to the husband's prerogative by such a concession to the wife. (3.) Because, an injury to the conjugal relation on the part of the wife was a more heinous offence than one on the part of the husband, inasmuch as he was thereby made liable to father another man's issue, and to leave his inheritance and estate to children that were not his. (4.) Because, wives under the instigation of jealousy, had not so much power to oppress and wrong their husbands, as the husbands had to wrong their wives. The law was prompted by a prevailing kindly regard to the welfare of woman.——¶ *An offering of memorial bringing iniquity to remembrance.* The character and design of the offering determined its quality. It was an offering composed of the lowest and meanest kind of grain, such as was used by the

16 And the priest shall bring her near, and set her before the LORD:

17 And the priest shall take holy water in an earthen vessel; and of the dust that is in the

poorest of the people, and therefore adapted to remind the woman of the humiliating circumstances into which, for the time being, she was brought. It was to have no oil, because oil was a symbol of love or charity, and its accompanying joy and gladness, in which her reputed conduct showed her lacking; while frankincense denoted that sweet spiritual savor which renders all offerings acceptable to the Lord, and this also was supposed to be wanting so long as her innocence was in question. It was an offering that brought iniquity to remembrance, not only in the conscience of the guilty party, but also in the minds of others, who would be impressed by its heinousness. Again, it was a memorial offering in that it was a solemn appeal to the Most High, reminding him that he had engaged to judge, and expecting from him a discovery of the woman's sin, if sin had been committed, or of her justification if she were innocent. See Notes on Lev. 5:11 and 2:2.

V. 16. *And the priest shall bring her near, and set her before the Lord.* Heb. "Cause her to stand." Most commentators understand the original pronoun *othâ*, *his* or *it*, of the offering and not of the woman; consequently they render "bring it" and "set it before the Lord," instead of "her," as she is commanded to be set before the Lord in v. 18. The Hebrew will admit of either interpretation, and it is not possible to pronounce absolutely which is the true one. He was to place her by the sanctuary, the Lord's dwelling-place, that she might consider herself as in his immediate presence, and that she and all the spectators might solemnly await his decision. "Before the Lord," signifies at the altar of burnt-offerings standing before the door of the Tabernacle. She was thus to consider herself as standing and about to hold up her hand at the bar of God's judgment-seat, where no prevarication was to be allowed.

V. 17. *And the priest shall take holy water.* Heb. *mayim kedoshim, holy waters,* plur. Chald. "Waters of the laver." Gr. "Clean living water," which would seem to imply that the translators understood it of the "water of separation" mentioned ch. 19:9, which was sprinkled with the ashes of the red heifer and applied to those who were *separated* from the congregation for uncleanness, that after being washed and cleansed with it they might be again received. But it is with more probability called "holy" as being taken from the laver, and thence separated from common to sacred uses. It was from thus being appropriated that it acquired the epithet "holy." Intrinsically it had no more holiness than any other water. This water was to be put in an earthen vessel, inasmuch as what was coarse and plain was most suitable to the occasion. The baseness of the vessel tended to set forth the degradation of the party on supposition of her guilt, and being of a fragile material it could be easily broken after being thus employed, so that no monument of the crime should remain. Comp. Lev. 6:28. 11:33. 15:12.——¶ *Of the dust that is in the floor of the tabernacle.* The design of putting dust into the water was to signify the reproach and shame she lay under. Ainsworth remarks, that as dust was the serpent's food, so it was implied that if she had hearkened to the serpent's temptation, she might expect to partake of the ser-

floor of the tabernacle the priest shall take, and put *it* into the water:

18 And the priest shall set the woman before the LORD[o], and uncover the woman's head, and put the offering of memorial in her hands, which *is* the jealousy-offering: and the priest shall have in his hand the bitter water that causeth the curse.

o Heb. 13. 4. Rev. 2. 19-23.

---

pent's curse. Yet it was to be dust taken from "the floor of the tabernacle," whence it acquired a certain degree of sanctity, and thus an honor was put upon every thing pertaining to the place which God had chosen to put his name there, and an awe inspired of the divine judgments. "Nothing could be more unexceptionable than taking dust from the floor, and this in presence of the woman and her friends. This was very unlike the case of the ordeals among the heathen, when the persons accused were required to drink things naturally pernicious; to handle hot iron; or to dip their hands into boiling water, hot oil, etc., when nothing but a miracle, or some artifice, would save the innocent; whereas here, nothing but a miracle could hurt the guilty. It was therefore an excellent method to set the mind of the husband at ease, in a case which is frequently the occasion of much distress."—*Priestly.*——¶ *Put it into the water.* Heb. *el hammâyim, to the water;* as the Rabbinists say, "He put it upon the top of the water, that it might be seen upon the upper part of the water." And again, "If he put in the dust before the water, it was unlawful."

V. 18. *And the priest shall set the woman before the Lord.* Heb. "Shall cause to stand." She was to be placed before the door of the tabernacle with her face towards the ark, where was the symbol of the divine presence. This was a place of constant resort, and the publicity of the exposure would not only tend to affect duly her own feelings, but operate also as a warning to others not "to do after her lewdness."——¶ *And uncover the woman's head.* A covering upon the head of a woman was regarded as a sign of subjection to her husband and of corresponding protection upon his part towards her. It intimated a tender relation which was supposed to be broken for the time being, and a certain degree of *exposure to judgment* coupled with deep degradation, indicated by the act of denuding the head. The act would also naturally carry with it the implication, that if guilty it would be in vain any longer to attempt to hide her sin, as the divine Detector would now disclose the facts, and discover to the eyes of all Israel whether she were unjustly accused or not. In addition to this, the Jewish writers say that her hair was loosed, her garments torn open to the breast, and whatever ornaments of gold or jewels she wore were taken from her, all with a view to render her external condition accordant with her supposed moral state.——¶ *And put the offering of memorial in her hand.* This offering having been brought by her husband for her, v. 15, she was now to take and offer, emblematical of her offering herself to the Lord's trial, as the oblation was to be presented to him.——¶ *And the priest shall have in his hand.* "All the while that her head is bare, and the meal-offering in her hands, the water is to be in a vessel in the priest's hand, that she may see the water."—*Maimonides.*——¶ *The bitter water that causeth the curse.* Heb. *më hammârim, waters*

19 And the priest shall charge her by an oath[p], and say unto the woman, If no man have lain with thee, and if thou hast not gone aside to uncleanness *with another* instead of thy husband, be thou free from this bitter water that causeth the curse:

20 But if thou hast gone aside *to another* instead of thy husband, and if thou be defiled,

p Mat. 26. 63.

of bitternesses. Gr. *to udor tou elegmou, water of conviction,* so called from its *convincing* of guilt. Some of the Hebrew writers intimate that the water was made bitter by the infusion of wormwood or something else of similar quality, but the far preferable opinion is, that it was so called from its effects, for if she were guilty, the drinking of the water would prove fatal, and death is said to be *bitter,* 1 Sam. 15 : 32, "And Agag said, Surely the *bitterness of death* is past." Eccl. 7 : 26, "And I find *more bitter than death* the woman," etc. The same is said of afflictions, Is. 38 : 15, 17, "I shall go softly all my years in the *bitterness of my soul.*" "Behold, for peace I had *great bitterness.*" Solomon, speaking of an harlot, says, Prov. 5 : 4, "Her end is *bitter as wormwood,*" that is, both to herself and to her victims. We may reasonably conclude, therefore, that "waters of bitternesses," an intensitive form of expression, denote waters which produced the most bitter and baneful effects, as a just penalty for the offence. Comp. vs. 24, 27. ——¶ *That causeth the curse.* Heb. *hamorerim,* rendered by Ainsworth, *bitter curse-bringing.* Syr. "Exploring." Sam. "Declaring;" both pointing to the effect of the water as determining or revealing the guilt of the delinquent. This, however, is to be attributed to no inherent virtue of that kind in the water itself; it was due only to the divine power operating in and with it that it produced such baleful results.

V. 19. *And the priest shall charge her by an oath.* Heb. *hishbia, shall adjure, shall cause to swear.* Gr. "Shall adjure her in or by the curses of this oath." The priest was thus, in the most solemn manner, to adjure the woman to tell the truth, and to denounce the curse of God against her if she were guilty, at the same time declaring to her what would be the effect of her drinking the water. Maimonides says that in after times, when the Jews had, in their dispersion, lost their own language, this adjuration was to be uttered in a language that she understood, in order that she might intelligently say *Amen.*——¶ *If no man.* That is, no other man than thy husband. Thus Gen. 36 : 6, "went into the country from the face," etc. Chald. "into another country."——¶ *With another instead of thy husband.* Heb. *tahath ishĕkâ, under thy husband;* that is, by the substitution of another for thy husband. The usage is illustrated by the following passages; Gen. 4 : 25, "God hath appointed me another seed *instead of* Abel;" Heb. "*under* Abel." Ez. 23 : 5, "And Aholah played the harlot *when she was mine;*" Heb. "*under me.*" Hos. 4 : 12, "They have gone a whoring *from under their God;*" that is, by adopting some other one in his place.——¶ *Be thou free from this bitter water.* Heb. "Be thou innocent," that is, free, guiltless, clear; this water shall be innocuous to thee; thou shalt receive no harm from it. The imperative for the future.

V. 20. *Instead of thy husband.* Heb. "under thy husband," as in the preceding verse.——¶ *Some man have lain*

and some man have lain with
thee beside thine husband:
21 Then the priest shall
charge [q] the woman with an
oath of cursing, and the priest
shall say unto the woman, The
LORD make thee a curse [r] and
an oath among thy people, when
the LORD doth make thy thigh
to rot, and thy belly to swell:
22 And this water that causeth the curse shall go into thy

q Josh. 6. 26. 1 Sam. 14. 24. Neh. 10. 29.

r Jer. 29. 22.

with thee. Heb. "Some man have given with thee his lying." See Note on v. 13; also on Lev. 15:18.

V. 21. *Then the priest shall charge the woman, etc.* This is not to be understood as an additional adjuration, but merely the continuation of that begun v. 19. Purver renders the verse more accurately thus: "Thus shall the priest go on, causing her to swear with an oath of cursing; the Lord make thee a curse and an oath among thy people, by his making thy thigh fall and thy belly swell."——¶ *The Lord make thee a curse and an oath.* The context here contains a species or formula of adjuration which the priest administered to the accused party. It was equivalent to saying, "The Lord make thee such an object of cursing, that men may make thee a model of imprecation, saying, if I swear falsely, let God punish me, as he did such a woman." So Is. 65:15, "Ye shall leave your name for a curse (or an oath) to my chosen;" i. e. for an oath of execration.——¶ *Make thy thigh to rot and thy belly to swell.* The precise nature of the punishment here threatened is not perhaps fully conveyed by the words employed in our common version. The "rotting" of the thigh is in the Hebrew the "falling" of the thigh, and if we understand "thigh" in the euphemistic sense in which it is used Gen. 46:26, "the souls which came out of Jacob's *thigh*," we may infer that *prolapsus uteri*, or *falling of the womb*, was the real effect implied in the language of this clause and *ovarian dropsy* signified by the other. So it is understood by Horsley and others. We find the sense of "rot" given to this word no where else but in the present connection, though it is often used as equivalent to "die." If it be understood of the thigh, properly speaking, it denotes doubtless the *withering* or *shrinking away* of the muscles and fat, but in that case it is difficult to conceive why the effect should be confined to one thigh, instead of embracing both, although the original word is singular. The evidence, therefore, on the whole, preponderates in favor of the first construction. The term "rot" implies an ulcerating process, for which we find no authority in the general usage of the original. It seems, also, somewhat accordant with the laws of the divine Providence, that the penalty of transgression should be visited upon the offending part, if it be localized at all. In the Greek, the epithet applied to the belly is "burst" instead of "swollen," and this is supposed by the Rabbinical writers to have been the actual effect, of which, however, there is no special proof. It is also a tradition of the same writers, that the water which Moses made the Israelites to drink with the powder of the golden calf, Ex. 32:20, produced a similar effect.

V. 22. *Shall go into thy bowels.* To this there appears to be an obvious allusion in Ps. 109:18, "As he clothed himself with cursing like as with a garment, so *let it come into his bowels like water.*"——¶ *And the woman shall say,*

bowels[s], to make *thy* belly to swell, and *thy* thigh to rot. And the[t] woman shall say, Amen, amen.

s Ps. 109. 18. t Deut. 27. 15.

23 And the priest shall write these curses in a book, and he shall blot *them* out with the bitter water:

Amen, amen. Gr. γενοιτο, γενοιτο, *so be it, so be it.* The response is probably doubled to express her full consent and concurrence with the import of the malediction. Some have supposed an allusion to both parts of the adjuration, viz. that which freed her if innocent, and that which condemned her if guilty, but this is unnecessary; such reduplications are common. "This is an instance of what we have already mentioned, that an oath was not pronounced at length by the persons who took it, but it was read or pronounced to them by a proper officer. When he had finished, the party swearing appropriated its terms as his own by saying, AMEN, AMEN!—"So let it be"—or some equivalent expression. Although, however, this was the formulary of assent to an oath, it did not, in all cases, bear that force, being sometimes merely a protestation. The word *Amen*, like the words *Hallelujah* and *Hosanna*, has been retained in the religious services of the Western Christian church, and is understood as an expression of assent on the part of the people to that which the minister has said in their name; thus formally adopting his expressions. It was probably thought that the word, as well as the others we have mentioned, possessed in the original a peculiar emphasis and force, for which it would be difficult to find a precise equivalent in any European tongue."—*Pict. Bible.* It is difficult to conceive how a woman could respond *Amen* in such circumstances, if she were really guilty, unless she had become so hardened in sin as to be utterly reckless what she uttered. But if she confessed that she had been defiled, or, which was equivalent, if she declined drinking, then, according to the Hebrew tradition, she was permanently separated from her husband, but without dowry.

V. 23. *And the priest shall write these curses in a book.* Heb. *bassepher, in a scroll* or *tablet.* The Hebrew denominates all writings by the term we translate "book," whether long or brief, whether bills, bonds, letters, etc. Comp. Deut. 24:1. 2 Sam. 11:14. Is. 39:1, in all which the original is *sepher, book.* "The whole context," says Mr. Kitto, "is quite averse to rendering the Hebrew word by "book" in this place. The word is generally applicable to every roll, scroll, or tablet in which any thing was written; and the context must in all cases determine the probability as to what is intended. The Rabbinical writers think that the curse in this awful ceremony was written on a scroll of vellum or parchment. This we may very well doubt; but without at present inquiring whether the art of preparing vellum was known at this time, it seems more probable that, for such a temporary purpose as the present, the writing was made on a tablet of wood, properly prepared. Such tablets were very anciently used, and still are so, in some countries, not only for writing intended to be soon obliterated, but for that which is designed to be permanent. Whatever was used in the present instance, it was certainly nothing at all resembling in its form the idea which the word "book" suggests to our minds."——¶ *Shall blot (them) out with the bitter water.* Heb. *mâhâh el më hammârim, shall wipe them out to*

24 And he shall cause the woman to drink the bitter water that causeth the curse: and the water that causeth the curse

(or *into*) *the bitter water*. The process of obliteration was such that the characters written were to be wiped or scraped off into the bitter water, and this water was then to be drank by the woman. She would in consequence drink the very *words* of the execration. "It would seem from this that the ink made no permanent marks on the skin, linen, wood, or whatever other substance the words were written on. It is precisely the same with the ink now in use in the East. In its composition no calx of iron, or other material that could make a permanent dye, is employed, and although the writing made with it has an intense and brilliant black color, which will remain unchanged for ages, the characters may at any time be sponged or washed out with water. We have, while writing this note, tried this; and find it quite easy to obliterate, by the slightest action of the moistened finger, words which were written several years since, at different times, with inks procured in different countries of Western Asia. It is unnecessary, therefore, to suppose, with some who judge only from our own ink, that the ink employed on the present occasion was prepared in a peculiar manner, and used only on this occasion."—*Pict. Bible*. The import of this part of the ceremony is well interpreted by Henry, to wit, that it was the curse which impregnated the water and gave it its strength to effect what was intended; signifying at the same time, that if she was innocent the curse should be blotted out, and never appear against her, as it is written, "I am he that blotteth out thy transgressions for mine own sake, and will not remember thy sins;" while on the other hand, if she were guilty, the curse as it was written being infused into the water, it would enter with it into her bowels, even "like oil into her bones," Ps. 109:18, as we read of a curse entering into a house, Zech. 5:4. These remarks will afford a sufficient answer to the question, why the curse should be written and afterwards blotted out. If it were to be blotted out, why should it be written? If it were to be written, why should it be blotted out? It appears that the act had a double significancy, the writing implying one thing, and the obliteration another.

V. 24. *Shall cause the woman to drink the bitter water*. Previous to which, however, it appears that the jealousy-offering mentioned v. 26 was to be presented. The following note by Mr. Kitto will be read with interest in this connection: "There is still a strong impression entertained among the inhabitants of Africa, and some Asiatic countries, that the full force of a charm, or of a prayer or a curse, is obtained by having it written, and by washing the writing off in water, and drinking the draught. The idea on which this is founded is sufficiently intelligible when the virtue of a written charm is believed—and such belief is by no means rare in countries nearer home than those of Africa or Asia. It is then an obvious act of the mind, or rather of superstition, to conclude that the virtue inhering in the written charm may be best imbibed by its words being swallowed, which they cannot well be by any process more convenient than washing them off in water. Travellers, particularly African travellers, abound in instances of their being applied to for written charms, by drinking the words of which the applicants believed they would obta n some desired good, some security from evil, or a remedy against

shall enter into her, *and become* bitter.

25 Then the priest shall take the jealousy-offering out of the woman's hand, and shall wave[u] the offering before the LORD, and offer it upon the altar:

26 And the priest shall take an handful of the offering, *even* the[v] memorial thereof, and burn *it* upon the altar, and afterward shall cause the woman to drink the water.

27 And when he hath made her to drink the water, then it shall come to pass, *that*, if she be defiled, and have done trespass against her husband, that

u Lev. 8. 27.

v Lev. 2. 2, 9.

---

disease. One instance from Mungo Park will illustrate this subject: 'At Koolkorro my landlord brought me his writing-board that I might write him *a saphie* to protect him from wicked men. I wrote the board full, from top to bottom, on both sides; and my landlord, to be certain of having the full force of the charm, washed the writing from the board into a calabash, with a little water, and having said a few prayers over it, drank this powerful draught; after which, lest a single word should escape, he licked the board until it was quite dry.'" (Travels, p. 236.)—*Pict. Bible.*——¶ *Shall enter into her,* (*and become*) *bitter.* Heb. "Shall enter into her to bitterness." Chald. "Shall enter into her to cursing;" that is, they shall work in her the evil and bitter effects of a curse.

V. 25. *Shall wave the offering before the Lord.* Shall move it to and fro in token of presentation or dedication to the Lord. "The priest took the ministering vessel wherein the meat-offering was, and put it upon her hands, and the priest put his hands under hers, and waved it."—*Maimonides.*

V. 26. *Shall take an handful.* This handful was to be the memorial immediately after spoken of. See Note, Lev. 2:2, where the nature of the "memorial" is explained. The portion of the offering that remained after the memorial-handful was taken out was eaten by the priest, unless the husband was a priest, when it was scattered among the ashes. This offering, in the midst of the transaction, was a solemn acknowledgment that the whole affair was to be conducted under the Lord's auspices, and that he was appealed to as a God "from whom no secret is hid."

V. 27. *Then it shall come to pass, etc.* All things being thus performed according to the tenor of the divine directions, the issue was to be awaited. If the woman charged with the crime was really guilty, the water she drank would prove in effect a deadly poison to her, operating in the manner above described, in addition to which the Jewish writers say that her face would turn pale and yellowish, her eyes were ready to start from her head, and the cry was raised, "Carry her forth, carry her forth, lest she defile the court of the temple," i. e. by dying within its precincts. Such signal effects could not of course be attributed to the water viewed in itself, but only to the efficacy of the divine operation working in and with the external agent. The mingled water and dust had in themselves no more power to produce the effects described than had the clay and spittle, employed by our Saviour, to open the eyes of the blind. The effect in either case was equally supernatural. It is a tradition of the Jews that the adulterer also died the same day and hour that

the water that causeth the curse
shall enter into her, *and become*
bitter, and her belly shall swell,
and her thigh shall rot: and the
woman shall be a curse [w] among
her people.
28 And if the woman be not
defiled, but be clean; then she
shall be free, and shall conceive [x] seed.
29 This *is* the law of jealousies, when a wife goeth aside [y]
to another instead of her husband, and is defiled;
30 Or when the spirit of jealousy cometh upon him, and he
be jealous over his wife, and
shall set the woman before the
LORD, and the priest shall execute upon her all this law.
31 Then shall the man be
guiltless from iniquity, and this
woman shall bear [z] her iniquity.

w Deut. 28. 37. Is. 65. 15. Jer. 24. 9. 29. 18, 22. 42. 18. Zech. 8. 13. Is. 57. 8. *x* Ps. 113. 9. *y* ver. 19.

z Lev. 20. 17–20.

---

the adulteress did, and in a similar manner; which may or may not have been the fact. The Jewish doctors add also, that the waters had this effect upon the adulteress only in case the husband had not offended in the same way.

V. 28. *Then she shall be free.* That is, shall receive no harm from the draught; as in v. 19. *Dou.*, "Shall not be hurt."——¶ *Shall conceive seed.* Heb. *nizreâh zera, shall be sown with seed.* Chald. "Shall prove with child." The Jewish writers speak in high terms of the effects of this water upon the innocent woman, as may be seen from the words of Maimonides:—"If she be undefiled, when she hath drunk she will wax strong, and her face wax clear; and if she have any sickness, it will leave her; and she shall conceive and bear a man-child; and if she were wont to have hard travail, she shall have speedy travail; and if she were wont to bring forth females, she shall bring forth males."

V. 29. *When a woman goeth aside to another instead of her husband.* Heb. "Goeth aside under her husband." Our version gives the correct idea, but somewhat paraphrastically. See Note on v. 19.

V. 30. *Shall set the woman before the Lord.* Heb. "Shall cause to stand;" i. e. in the manner and for the end before described.——¶ *Shall execute upon her all this law.* Heb. "Shall do unto her all this law."

V. 31. *Then shall the man be guiltless.* That is, he shall be blameless in this matter, inasmuch as he has done what in him lay towards detecting and removing the evil which he suspected in his wife.

The law which we have now considered is fertile of suggestion. (1.) It involved a striking proof of that special providence which governed the affairs of the Jews. The inquest was not referred to the scrutiny or ingenuity of human judges, but was carried to the tribunal of God himself for his express decision. There was clearly nothing in the water itself when thus mixed that could have the effect described, or indeed, any injurious effect at all. The effect was wholly supernatural. The offender might brave the trial, though conscious of her sin, in unbelief of the declared providential results, but she would nevertheless assuredly find there was a God in Israel who would verify and vindicate his own ordinance. It is supposed that the crime committed had been so secret that no human being, except the guilty persons, were cognizant of it. It is supposed, also, that no clew to the discovery of it could possibly be found. But the issue of the ordeal brings the truth into the light of noonday. Could any doubt remain whether the Lord's hand was in the detection of the crime? Every such instance would tend to work the powerful conviction in the minds of all the Israelites that the Most High ruled indeed among them, and that his providence would fulfil all his threatenings, as well as all his promises. (2.) Such a direct appeal to the Lord himself would serve to mark, in the strongest manner, the guilt of adultery. Not only was that sin punished with death when discovered, but here was a particular mode appointed for its detection when suspected, in which God thought it not below him to act immediately as judge, and to inflict a fearful punishment upon the transgressor. What could serve more effectually to stamp the impress of a peculiar enormity upon this above most other forms of evil in the sight of heaven? (3.) It would operate as a powerful preservative of public morals. It is the hope of concealment that gives an edge to temptation. A thief will not steal, if he knows that he must infallibly be detected; nor will the adulterer or seducer lay their plans for compassing the ruin of their victims, if they know that they cannot possibly conceal their guilt. In view of such a law as this, all parties would be put upon their guard. Every man of common feeling would shrink from being the occasion of exposing a woman to so unerring a test and so certain and dreadful a punishment. He could not but feel for the danger into which he would bring his partner in guilt, and fear the sting of a perpetually accusing conscience in case he should be the cause of her condemnation and death. And then its influence upon females would be exceedingly great. It would tend to preserve them not only from the actual commission of the sin, but from the slightest approximation towards it. How careful and circumspect must every wife have been rendered by knowing that she might at any time be subjected to such an ordeal even upon suspicion, and what shame and punishment, and what a miserable death was before her, if she became guilty. Add to this, that whenever an instance of the execution of this law occurred, all who saw it, both male and female, would be deeply affected by it; the innocent would feel themselves yet more afraid of the sin and be more fully resolved to abstain from it. All Israel would hear and fear, and do no more so wickedly. (4.) It would be a guardian of domestic peace, and a great comfort to the oppressed. The "spirit of jealousy" is a formidable enemy to family quiet. It corrodes and eats out all domestic happiness, and among a people so hard-hearted as the Jews, and so ready to put away their wives on the slightest occasions, would naturally lead to the most cruel treatment. But when a woman of blameless character was made the victim of her husband's jealousy, with what holy confidence would she drink the appointed cup, and make her appeal to Him who searches the heart! With what triumph would she depart from the tabernacle when God himself had borne a public testimony to her innocence!——The Jewish "law of jealousy" has now ceased, but let us not suppose that the Lord is any less observant of sin, any less opposed to it, or any less intent upon its punishment. His providential interpositions may not be so immediate or so visible in this world as they were among the Jews; but in the world to come, if not before, every transgressor will learn, that "his sins shall find him out." Not more plainly did the Most High make manifest the guilt of the adulteress under this law than he will bring out the wickedness, however secret, of adulterers and adulteresses, and all other transgressors of every kind, in the fearful revelations of the future. So likewise they who labor under *false* accusations; they may securely commit their cause to God. Any person may be unjustly accused, and not always having at hand the means of clearing himself, he may lie long under the weight of injurious suspicions, but the truth will eventually come to light, and every wrong be abundantly redressed.

CHAPTER VI.

The Law of the Nazarite.

Among the religious practices of the Jews, that of *making vows*, from a voluntary prompting, was one of the most remarkable. It does not appear, indeed, that vows originated with that nation; they seem rather to have been one form in which the religious sentiment of all nations and ages was prone to express itself. But, though not a product of the Mosaic system, yet it was adopted into it and laws made for its conduct. These vows consisted of some solemn engagement voluntarily assumed by those who made them, or of the consecration of some person or thing to some particular use or service, such as might redound to the honor of God. The vow of the Nazarite, described in the present chapter, is one of the most remarkable of these, especially when viewed in its typical relations. The vow of the Nazarite involved the dedication of a person to God, either temporarily or permanently, and implied in its own nature a peculiar aspiration towards a closer conjunction with heaven in the acts of piety and devotion than was ordinarily enjoyed by those who were occupied simply with the common routine of life and its duties. It was for the time being a separation from and a renunciation of the pleasures of the world, and of all fleshly gratifications and indulgences. The Nazarite was one who had purposed, for the good of his soul, to lead an ascetic life and to "mortify his members which were on the earth," living in all purity and holiness, and manifesting to the utmost that character and conduct which under the Gospel consists in "denying ungodliness and worldly lusts, and living soberly, righteously, and godly in this present world." The various abstinences involved in the Nazarite vow will be considered in detail as we proceed, but we here remark on the institution in general, that it was designed to prefigure the Lord the Saviour, who, though not observant of the laws relating to that order of men, was nevertheless consecrated by divine designation and by voluntary engagement to the service of God in the work of human redemption, to which he was devoted without intermission, and from which he desisted not till he could say, "It is finished." In pointing typically to him, it points also to his people. The formal vow and its ceremonies have now indeed ceased; but the general duty of devoting ourselves to the Lord, in all the branches of a holy life, still subsists in all its binding force, being founded on the most powerful obligations and motives. "Ye are bought with a price," says the Gospel, "therefore glorify God in your body and your spirit which are his." It inculcates an entire separation from the world in its corrupt principles, its erroneous lessons, its vain pleasures, its ambitious projects, its sinful works. Its language is, "Come out from among them, and be ye separate, saith the Lord, and

CHAPTER VI.

AND the LORD spake unto Moses, saying,

2 Speak unto the children of Israel, and say unto them, When either man or woman

---

touch not the unclean thing, and I will receive you, and will be a father unto you, and ye shall be my sons and daughters, saith the Lord almighty." The spirit of this injunction is plainly Nazaritic, containing an express allusion to the separation and the danger of uncleanness which were incident to that class of men. Although we cannot fairly draw from this chapter an absolute prohibition of the use of wine, or of other worldly enjoyments of a harmless kind, yet we are taught from it to study a holy superiority to all *the pleasures of sense* as tending to subject the soul to the body, and thus retard our ascent to heaven. Though not required to abandon the world and its secular cares, yet we are required to "use the world as not abusing it," and to repose our burdens on the Lord. Though not called to that singularity of dress which marked the Nazarite to public view, yet neither are we called to be conformed to every idle fashion, or to run into all the absurdities which characterize the world. Though we are not to shrink from various contacts forbidden to the Jewish votary, yet we are to keep at the remotest distance from all moral pollution, in the profound dread of walking unworthy of our holy profession, and bringing dishonor upon the Lord's venerable name. Thus let us walk, and as the Nazarite, after his term of separation was fulfilled, "might drink wine," so after the short period of mortification and self-denial here we shall "enter into the joy of our Lord," even into "his presence, where there is fulness of joy and pleasures for evermore."

V. 2. *When either man or woman shall separate.* Heb. *yaphli, shall signally separate.* See Notes on Ex. 8 : 22. Lev. 27 : 2, where the import of the original term is largely unfolded. The root from which *yaphli* comes (*pâlâ*), signifies the doing of something extraordinary and marvellous, and is the word that occurs Lev. 27 : 2, concerning the making of a *singular vow*, and conveys doubtless the idea of one's acting from an extraordinary zeal for God and religion. To *separate*, in this connection, is to exempt in a special and marvellous manner. Gr. "Whosoever shall greatly vow a vow." A vow is a religious promise made to God, and it is here supposed that it might be made by either a man or a woman; but it is presumed in this case that the parties are free, each in their own power or at their own disposal; as otherwise a superior might annul the vow of an inferior by the law recorded Num. 30 : 4, etc. So in respect to this particular kind of vow the Hebrew canons say, "The father (of a child) or the husband (of a wife) may disannul the Nazariteship of his child or his wife, if he will, as in other ways." Philo, in his treatise "On Animals fit for Sacrifice," after describing the voluntary or votive oblations which were occasionally made by the people, goes on to say, "And when they have no longer any materials left in which they can display their piety, they then consecrate and offer up themselves, displaying an unspeakable holiness, and a most superabundant excess of a God-loving disposition, on which account such a dedication is fitly called *the great vow;* for every man is his own greatest and most valuable possession, and this even he now gives up and abandons." The more particular na-

shall separate *themselves* to vow a vow of a Nazarite[a], to separate *themselves* unto the LORD;

a Judg. 13. 5. Acts 21. 23, 24.

ture of the Nazarite vow will be considered in what follows.——¶ *Of a Nazarite.* Heb. *nazir*, from the root *nâzar*, *to separate*, denoting one who was especially *separated* and *set apart*, either by the act of his parents or his own, to the worship and service of God, and that either for life or for a temporary season. Such vows are recognized in the Mosaic laws, although there is good reason to believe that they were of far more ancient origin. That the present, at any rate, was not the first occasion of the institution is evident from the fact, that the ordinance here mentioned was given in the *second* year after the departure from Egypt; but in an earlier law concerning the Sabbatical year, which was made in the *first* year, a figurative expression drawn from Nazaritism occurs, in calling the vines which in that year were not to be pruned, vines or grapes of *separation* or *Nazariteship*. (See Note on Lev. 25:5.) This implies that the thing itself must have been already in vogue, and that too, probably, for a long time. Spencer also shows, in his great work on the "Hebrew Laws," that the custom of special consecration prevailed from the earliest ages among the Gentile nations, so that under the Mosaic dispensation the object was to regulate a pre-existing custom, that it should not minister to superstition or idolatry, and to establish a usage which carried with it a rich typical significancy. On this head Mr. Kitto remarks, that the practice was probably allowed to the chosen people, "with a reference to the true God, in order to take away occasion for its being preserved in honor of idols. A rooted custom, in itself harmless, but applied to purposes of evil, may with less difficulty have its object altered than be wholly eradicated. In viewing the laws of Moses, it is always useful, so far as may be possible, to distinguish those which originate usages, from those which only correct, modify and alter usages already existing."—*Pict. Bible.* It does not appear that the assumption of the Nazarite vow is anywhere positively enjoined or recommended, yet neither is it discouraged where one's spirit moved him, from devout impulses, to undertake it. From the following allusions we may infer that the institution was in itself capable of being made subservient to a good and acceptable use. Lam. 4:7, "Her *Nazarites* were purer than snow, they were whiter than milk, they were more ruddy in body than rubies, their polishing *was* of sapphire." Am. 2:11, "And I raised up of your sons for prophets, and of your young men for *Nazarites*." Of the Nazarites who were such by reason of a vow made by their parents, Samson, Jeremiah, John the Baptist, and probably Samuel, are conspicuous instances: of examples of voluntary Nazaritism we meet with scarcely any in the sacred history, though the case of Paul, Acts 18:18, approaches it, as it is said of him that he had shorn his head in Cenchrea in consequence of having made a vow. But it is certain that there is nothing of this nature that is now obligatory on Christians, although *monastic* institutions would seem to have had their origin in promptings very similar to those which operated with the Jewish Nazarite. To the due accomplishment of this kind of vow, we learn that the following requisites were indispensable.

1. Total abstinence from wine and every thing that could intoxicate. This

interdiction was so severe, that they were not only obliged to avoid the use of any strong liquor, and were to taste no vinegar made of wine, nor wine made by macerating grapes in water, after the juice had been pressed out, but they were not even permitted to eat moist or dried grapes, nor paste or sauce that had any of the juice of grapes in it, nor pulp or stone, or even so much as the bark of the vine.

2. Letting the hair grow without cutting. No razor, or scissors, or any other instrument was to come upon the head till the expiration of the vow, which was seldom less than thirty days.

3. Avoiding the touch of a dead body, whereby pollution might be contracted. He was not at liberty to enter a house where a corpse lay, nor to follow it to the grave, nor, if we may believe the Hebrew writers, was he so much as to wear mourning even at the decease of his nearest relatives or friends.

The reasons of these prohibitions, as well as the ceremonies observed during the continuance and at the close of the vow, will be considered in the sequel.

Writers of the school of Michaelis and Palfrey, who have a very dim perception of the spiritual drift of the Mosaic institutes, are prone to recognize in this a civil and prudential use in addition to the religious; and we may safely admit that the sobriety and temperance which the Nazarites were obliged to observe were very conducive to health. But whether they were intended to be celebrated by the prophet for their fair and ruddy complexion, when it is said (Lam. 4:7) that they were "whiter than milk and more ruddy than rubies," inasmuch as these are sure signs of a sound and healthy constitution, may well be questioned. We are prompted ourselves to recognize a far deeper import in these expressions, while at the same time, we would not undervalue any of the secondary or incidental results that may have accrued from the usage.

But in our view the principal importance of this institution arose from its typical or representative significancy. The Jews as a nation were but little addicted to ascetic devotion, and it was probably only now and then that an individual was found disposed thus to sequester himself from the routine of ordinary life and give himself up for a longer or shorter time to the rigid exercise of a purely religious course. Nevertheless, as the Nazarite institute had obtained in the world, the divine wisdom saw that important ends could be answered by incorporating it into the Levitical system as a foreshadowing mainly of that pre-eminent consecration which was to distinguish Him who was "holy, harmless, undefiled, and separate from sinners." One of the appellations by which he was to be known was that of "Nazarene," and although we are well aware that other grounds may be assigned for this title, yet we see no sufficient reason for excluding this from among those grounds. The original term *nâzar*, as we have observed, signifies *to separate, to set apart* or *dedicate to a holy use*. It is clear from the prophetical writings that the Messiah was to be a person of eminent sanctity. He is called by the Psalmist "the Holy One," and the actual record of his life shows that *holiness* was his grand distinguishing trait. How reasonable, then, to suppose, that an epithet derived from the word *nâzar* may be applied to him by the pen of inspiration in calling him a "Nazarene." It is admitted that our Lord's external life was not conformed to the rules of the order, for he ate and drank like other men, and mingled indiscriminately with all classes, though still in such a manner that it could ever be said of him

3 He shall separate *himself* from [b] wine, and strong drink, and shall drink no vinegar of wine, or vinegar of strong drink, neither shall he drink any liquor

b Jer. 35. 6-8. Amos 2. 12. Luke 1. 15.

---

that he was "undefiled and separate from sinners." Still we may recognize the *substance* of the Nazaritical character in his ineffably pure and spotless life, wherein we recognize the *essential verity* of all that was typically reflected in the qualities and actions of such men as Joseph, Sampson, Samuel, Jeremiah, and John the Baptist, who are regarded as personal prefigurations of the Lord himself. It is perhaps for the reason that the Nazariteship of Christ is to be seen in his *general* character and deportment instead of a specific conformity to the laws of the institution, that commentators have been unable to point to any *express prediction* in the prophets which could be said to have been fulfilled by his being called a Nazarene. It may have been solely upon the ground of the general tenor of the ancient oracles respecting him. Add to this, that when it is said, "he shall be *called* a Nazarene," it is equivalent to its being declared that he shall *actually be* such, as verbs of *naming* are in multitudes of cases used for verbs of *being*. Comp. Is. 56 : 7 with Luke 19 : 40. From all this the reader will perceive the light in which we regard the Nazarite law as mainly important.

V. 2. *Unto the Lord.* Chald. "Before the Lord." Targ. Jon. "To the name of the Lord." This indicates the motive and end proposed in a Nazaritic vow, which was a nearer approach to the Lord with a view to his honor and glory, to the expression of gratitude for mercies received, and for the strengthening of faith and love, and all the graces and virtues of the servant of God. On this subject the Hebrew writers teach, "He that saith, Lo, I will be a Nazarite if I do so, or if I do it not, and the like, he is a wicked man, and such Nazariteship is like wicked men's. But he that voweth to the Lord by way of holiness is honest and commendable; and of him it is said, the crown of his God is upon his head (Num. 6 : 7), and the Scripture compareth him with a prophet, Am. 2 : 11." It appears from 1 Macc. 3 : 49, that in public calamities this vow was more severely kept.

V. 3. *He shall separate* (*himself*) *from wine and strong drink.* Heb. "Shall be a Nazarite from wine," etc. Gr. "Shall be sanctified from wine." Vulg. "Shall abstain from wine and from every thing that will make a man drunk." On the original term *shekar*, here rendered *strong drink*, see the Note on Lev. 10 : 9. In strict propriety the term *shekar* denotes strong drink made from any kind of fruits, such as dates, etc., but the Hebrews restrict it in this connection to such only as is made of the fruit of the vine. "Three species of things are forbidden to the Nazarite, viz., pollution, shaving, and the fruit of the vine; but strong drink made of dates, or such like, is lawful for the Nazarite; and the strong drink forbidden him by the law is strong drink made with mixture of wine."—*Maimonides.* The same writer observes, that by the sobriety and sanctity thus enjoined, and especially by their avoidance of dead bodies, the Nazarites were raised, as it were, to the dignity of the high priest, who was laid under similar restrictions. The special design of the prohibition is supposed to have been that they might reduce to subjection the sensual man, retain their faculties

of grapes, nor eat moist grapes, or dried.

4 All the days of his separation shall he eat nothing that is

clear and unclouded, and thus be better qualified for that devout study of the law to which they would naturally addict themselves during the period of their separation. "By this prohibition," says Ainsworth, "God taught the Nazarites sanctification in mortifying the lusts of the flesh; for the drinking these beverages endangereth men to "forget the law" of God, Prov. 31: 45, to mock and to rage (as "wine is a mocker and strong drink raging"), Prov. 20:1, they "take away the heart," Hos. 4:13; and the priest and the prophet through them "err in vision and stumble in judgment," Is. 28:7. Therefore Daniel in his mourning drank no wine, Dan. 10:3; John Baptist, the Nazarite, drank no wine, and was therefore counted a mourner, Luke 7:32, 33, and the Nazarites, by this abstinence, were taught, instead of wine, "to be filled with the Spirit," Eph. 5:18, and with the love of the Lord, which is "better than wine," Cant. 1:2.—— ¶ *Vinegar of wine.* Heb. חמץ, *hometz*, which implies *acid fermentation.*—— ¶ *Vinegar of strong drink.* Both these drinks were forbidden because they had virtually the same intoxicating effect with the principal liquors themselves. ¶ *Liquor of grapes.* Or, Heb. "preparation of grapes." Gr. "Whatsoever is made of grapes." Vulg. "Any thing that is pressed out of the grape." The import of the original is that of something macerated or steeped in water almost to solution. Grape-skins steeped in water after the juice is pressed out, form the drink here alluded to.—— ¶ *Nor eat moist grapes nor dried.* This was doubtless forbidden on the ground that the grapes either in a moist or dried state (as raisins) might tend to stir up the appetite for the juice, or wine, and it conveys the important lesson, that we are not only to avoid sin with the utmost care and caution, but every thing that borders upon it and leads to it, every thing that would serve as an occasion, or operate as a temptation, to it. "Abstain from every appearance of evil." The Hebrew doctors teach that "it is unlawful for a Nazarite to stand in the company of them that drink wine, but he is to keep away, for there is a stumbling-block before him. Our wise men have said (moreover) that he should not come near a vineyard."—*Maimonides.*

V. 4. *All the days of his separation.* Heb. נזרו *nizro*, *of his Nazariteship.* Gr. "Of his vow."——¶ *Eat nothing that is made of the vine tree.* That is, nothing which is *yielded* or *produced* by the vine, for a tree is said to *make fruit* when it yields or brings it forth. See Note on Gen. 1:11. Instead of *vine tree* the literal rendering is *vine of the wine*, to which, however, *vine tree* is equivalent. The only other passage in which this phrase occurs is, Judg. 13: 14, "She may not eat of any thing that *cometh of the vine* (Heb. "that cometh of the vine of the wine"), implying in both cases not so much *artificial preparations* of the fruit of the vine as its native growth or product. From the above passage in Judges it appears that the mothers also of such as were sanctified to be Nazarites from the womb were required, during their pregnancy, to abstain from the things which were forbidden to the Nazarites themselves, inasmuch as the unborn child was sustained by the mother's food and drink. It is easy to infer that its symbolical import was that of a full and complete renunciation of worldly pleasures from the commencement of the new birth

made of the vine tree, from the kernels even to the husk.
5 All the days of the vow of his separation there shall no razor [c] come upon his head: until the days be fulfilled, in the which he separateth *himself* unto the LORD, he shall be holy, *and* shall let the locks of the hair of his head grow.

c Judg. 16. 17, 19. 1 Sam. 1. 11.

---

through the whole period of sanctification.——¶ *From the kernels even to the husk.* Or, from the stones to the outer skin. "From the grape-stones to the rind."—*Gid. Booth.* This is but a repetition of the charge given in the preceding verse relative to abstaining from whatever might serve as an occasion or provocation to sin. So we are commanded not only to avoid pollution, but to "hate even the garment polluted by the flesh," 1 Thes. 5:22. Thus too are idols not only to be renounced, but "ye shall defile also the covering of thy graven images of silver, and the ornaments of thy molten images of gold." As occasionally gleams of light are reflected upon these laws from the comments of the Rabbins, we furnish the reader with suitable specimens. "All things forbidden of the vine are equal one with another; so that if he put green grapes with dry, or with unripe grapes, and with kernels and husks, and eat of this mixture but so much as an olive, he is to be beaten. Also if he drink a quarter of a log of the mixture of wine with vinegar, he is beaten. If he eat the like quantity but of the husks, which are the outward skins, or of the kernels, which are the seeds within, he is beaten."—*Maimonides.* It appears also from Judg. 13:4, 14, that as the Nazarite was not to taste of wine, so neither was he to eat any unclean thing, which was an additional sign of the sanctification implied in the observance.

V. 5. *All the days of the vow of his separation.* Heb. *neder nizro, vow of his Nazariteship.* Gr. "Of his sanctity, or purity."——¶ *Shall no razor come upon his head.* Heb. "Pass upon his head." On this the Rabbins say: "The Nazarite that shaveth his head is to be beaten, whether it be with razor or with scissors; likewise if he pluck off his hair with his hand, he is to be beaten." ——¶ *Until the days be fulfilled.* There is nothing explicit in Scripture as to the length of time which the Nazarite's vow might embrace. The shortest term fixed by the Jewish writers is thirty days, but from the example of Paul it would appear that it might be for a week only, Acts 22:26, 27. The period, however, was in fact left optional with the votary, though we are naturally led to suppose it was of sufficient duration, in ordinary cases, to allow of the growth of the hair to a considerable length, so that there should be enough to be burnt at the conclusion of the term, v. 18.——¶ *Shall let the locks of the hair of his head grow.* Heb. "Letting his locks grow, the hair of his head." The reasons assignable for this appointment are various. (1.) It served as a sign of mortification to worldly delights, as the cutting off or pulling out of the hair was a usual accompaniment of deep sorrow and affliction, of humiliation and self-abasement. It is, moreover, a fact unquestionable, that all forms of ascetic and monastic life tend to the cultivation of the hair and the beard, although the tonsure is characteristic of certain orders of religious devotees. Particular causes may operate in these cases, but there can be no doubt that the *tendency* is what we have stated. (2.) It was a testimony to the

6 All the days that he separateth *himself* unto the LORD he shall come at no dead body [d].

7 He shall not make himself unclean for his father, or for his mother, for his brother, or for his sister, when they die; because the consecration of his God *is* upon his head.

d Lev. 21. 1, 2, 11. c. 9. 6. 19. 11, 16.

---

purity which the Nazarite professed, for when the Nazarite (v. 9), or the leper (Lev. 14:8, 9) was cleansed from impurity, the hair was shaven off; wherefore the keeping it from being shaven implied that the parties had kept themselves from uncleanness. Accordingly, when the Lord would denote the rejection of Israel, as being unclean before him, he did it by this sign of cutting off the hair with a razor, Is. 7:20. Ez. 5:1–10. (3.) It was to be kept unshorn as a symbol or badge of the peculiar strength and virtue which should mark a prevailing holiness of spirit and life. The case of Samson illustrates this idea of the import of the long hair of the Nazarite, although it is carefully to be borne in mind that the strength was not intrinsically in the hair, any more than the healing virtue by which Naaman was cured of his leprosy was in the Jordan, but in the divine potency which cooperated with the outward sign. (4.) As the long hair of woman is regarded in the Scriptures as a sign of her husband's power over her, and her subjection to him (1 Cor. 11:5–10), so the Nazarite's hair might properly be regarded in the same light, as a token of his special subjection to the Lord, to whose power and auspices he had committed himself by his vow.

V. 6. *Shall come at no dead body.* Heb. *al nephesh mēth, at the soul of a dead person.* Another instance of the peculiar usage by which the original word for "soul" is applied to a *dead body.* On this usage see Note on Lev. 21:1. Num. 5:2. Targ. Jon. "Shall not come at the son of man that is dead." All death refers the mind naturally to sin, and that which is pure and holy cannot come in contact with that which is sinful without pollution. Others might touch dead bodies without contracting any thing more than a temporary ceremonial pollution; indeed, some must do this, or the dead would remain unburied; but it was forbidden to the Nazarite on the pain of forfeiting all the honor and advantage of his vow. The tendency was to remind them of the necessity of keeping their consciences pure from dead works, and of not touching the unclean thing.

V. 7. *Shall not make himself unclean, etc.* That is, by touching, mourning for, or burying them. This rule would teach them to moderate their affections and griefs, on account of earthly relatives, and to consider themselves more entirely consecrated to their Father in heaven. In this respect they stood upon a par with the high priest himself, Lev. 21:11. ——¶ *Because the consecration of his God is upon his head.* Heb. *nezer, the Nazariteship,* or *separation.* Gr. "The vow." Chald. "The crown of his God;" as the original, *nezer*, is also rendered, Lev. 21:12. The allusion is to the unshorn locks of hair upon his head, constituting the principal external badge of the Nazarite. The high priest was in like manner distinguished by what is "the *crown* (*nezer*) of the anointing oil of his God," and both the one and the other in their consecration were types of Christ, on whose head it is said, Ps. 132:18, "the *crown* (*nezer*) shall flourish." So also Christians, "made kings and priests unto God," have "on their heads *crowns* of gold," Rev. 1:6. 4:4.

8 All the days of his separation [e] he *is* holy unto the LORD.
9 And if any man die very
suddenly by him, and he hath
defiled the head of his consecration; then he shall shave [f] his

e 2 Cor. 6. 17, 18.

f Acts 18. 18.

V. 8. *Holy unto the Lord.* The leading idea conveyed by the term "holy" in this connection is undoubtedly that of external ceremonial holiness, evinced in scrupulously abstaining from what was forbidden, while at the same time, if an inward and spiritual sanctity could be superadded to this it would redound so much the more to the advantage of the votary. But the Jews, as a general fact, were a people very little receptive of the deeper internal workings of spiritual life. Their function was rather representative or typical, and this function could be discharged independent of the interior state of the subjects.

V. 9. *If any man die very suddenly by him.* Heb. "If the dead dieth by him suddenly unawares." That is, by apoplexy, violence, or in any other way. A provision is here made for the cleansing of a Nazarite in case he happened unavoidably to contract a ceremonial pollution by the touch of a dead body. Should such a thing occur at any time after the commencement of his separation, the uncleanness would nullify the proceedings up to that point, and he would have to begin anew. The ceremonies for such an occasion are here prescribed.——¶ *Hath defiled the head of his consecration.* Heb. *rosh nizro, the head of his Nazariteship.* Gr. "Immediately shall the head of his vow be defiled." It was requisite that he should be strictly exempt from pollution by the dead during all the days of his Nazariteship. In the case supposed there was evidently no blame to be attached to the person who happened to be providentially present at the death of a fellow-being; still defilement was imputed and purification enjoined. It is a legitimate, practical inference from this, that even sins of infirmity, or faults in which we are overtaken by surprise, and to which we are moved by no ill-intention, are a proper ground of repentance and humiliation.——¶ *Shall shave his head in the day of his cleansing, etc.* The sense of the original is not perfectly clear, but the probable import is, that the shaving of the head was not to take place immediately upon the occurrence of the defilement, but on the seventh day afterwards, at the close of the season for which he was to consider himself unclean. According to this the final clause of the verse, "on the seventh day shall he shave it," is merely exegetical of the preceding. Theodoret, however, and some others suppose a twofold shaving to be indicated, the one on the first day of his uncleanness and the other on the last. But in this case, it is difficult to understand why the first day that he was to be considered unclean should be called "the day of his cleansing." The shaving now enjoined was to cleanse from the incidental pollution contracted, and was entirely different from the shaving prescribed upon the fulfilment of the vow, v. 18, which was to be done at the door of the Tabernacle, where also the hair was to be burnt. "When the Nazarite shall shave himself for his uncleanness, he need not shave him at the door of the Sanctuary, nor cast his hair into the fire. But whether he be shaved within or without the Sanctuary, his hair is unlawful to be put to any use, but must be buried."—*Maimonides.* The import of all this was equivalent to that of the shaving of the

head in the day of his cleansing, on the seventh day shall he shave it.

10 And on the eighth day he shall bring two [g] turtles, or two young pigeons, to the priest, to the door of the tabernacle of the congregation:

g Lev. 5. 7. 14. 22. 15. 14, 29.

11 And the priest shall offer the one for a sin-offering, and the other for a burnt-offering, and make an atonement for him, for that he sinned by the dead, and shall hallow his head that same day.

12 And he shall consecrate unto the LORD the days of his

---

leper when cleansed, Lev. 14, signifying the renunciation of one's own righteousness by any works he can perform, and the acknowledgment of pollution even in his best doings. Comp. Phil. 3:8, 9.——¶ *The seventh day.* The day when all who were defiled by the dead were made clean by the sprinkling of holy water, ch. 19:11, 12, 19.

V. 10. *Shall bring two turtles.* That is, two turtle-doves. The appointment accords with that which the law made for atonement in behalf of those who had unclean issues, and went through a process of cleansing on account of them. See Notes on Lev. 15:14, etc. "When a Nazarite is defiled with any uncleanness for which he is to shave himself, one is to sprinkle upon him on the third day, and on the seventh day (Num. 19:12), and he is to shave off the hair of his head, in the seventh day, and to wash in the seventh day, after he is sprinkled, as do all that are defiled by the dead, and when his sun is set, he shall bring his offerings on the eighth day, and they are two turtles, or two young doves."—*Maimonides.*

V. 11. *And the priest shall offer.* Heb. *âsâh, shall do.* This is a peculiar phraseology, made use of where mention is made of sacrificial rites. It is equivalent to *sacrificabit, parabit, mactabit* in Latin, i. e. *to make ready and offer up in sacrifice.* The parallelism in the following passages will unfold the usage. 1 Chron. 21:23, "Let my lord *do* that which is good in his eyes." 2 Sam. 24:22, "Let my lord the king *take and offer up* what seemeth good unto him." So also Ps. 66:15, "I will *offer* (Heb. *will do*) bullocks with goats." The same word occurs Ex. 29:36. Gen. 18:7. 27:17.——¶ *For that he sinned by the dead.* Heb. על נפש *al nephesh, upon* or *over a soul.* Chald. "By the dead." The act is termed *sinning,* though not with strict propriety, as it was merely a casual and undesigned contraction of legal uncleanness. The original term is חטא *hâtâ, to miss, to fail of one's aim,* and such was the effect in the present instance. Though done without his agency and against his will, yet in the eye of the law it was a defilement, and as such was to be atoned for. It was designed to make men very cautious how they came in contact with any thing that should cause pollution.——¶ *Shall hallow his head.* Heb. *kiddēsh, shall sanctify.* By "his head" is meant "the head of his Nazariteship," as v. 9. The observance of his vow was to commence anew by the consecration of the hair of his head, which was to be suffered to grow without cutting henceforth to the expiration of the period embraced in his vow. Rabbi Sol. Jarchi says, "Sanctify his head, i. e. to begin again the count of his Nazariteship." This is confirmed by the ensuing verse.

V. 12. *And he shall consecrate.* Heb. *hizzir, shall separate as a Nazarite,* the original root from which comes *nâzir,*

separation, and shall bring a lamb of the first year for a trespass-offering [h]: but the days that were before shall be lost, because his separation was defiled.

13 And this *is* the law of the Nazarite, when the days of his separation are fulfilled [i]: he shall be brought unto the door of the tabernacle of the congregation;

14 And he shall offer his offering unto the LORD, one he-lamb of the first year without blemish for a burnt-offering, and one ewe-lamb of the first year

h Lev. 5. 6.

i Acts 21. 26.

---

the Nazarite. The import is, that he shall begin, with the eighth day, a new term of self-consecration or separation, to continue for the same length of time that he had first vowed.——¶ *For a trespass-offering.* Which was the proper offering for involuntary sins. Lev. 8:15. 22:14.——¶ *The days that were before shall be lost.* Heb. *yippelu, shall fall,* or *fall out.* Chald. "Shall be frustrated." Gr. "Shall not be reckoned." Vulg. "Shall be made void." This single act of defilement, however insignificant it might appear in itself, would still be sufficient to annul all that he had done before, so that it should be accounted for nothing. "It teaches us," says Henry, "that 'if a righteous man turn away from his righteousness,' and defile himself with dead works, all his righteousness that he hath done shall be 'lost to him,'" Ezek. 33:13.

V. 13. *This is the law of the Nazarite, etc.* That is, that which follows is the law in regard to the closing ceremonies of the Nazariteship, the specified period having expired. It points out the manner in which the votary was to express his gratitude to God, on the fulfilment of his vow, and receive an orderly discharge.——¶ *He shall be brought.* Heb. *yâbi otho, he shall bring him.* As the original leaves it doubtful who are meant by "he" and "him," three different modes of interpretation have been suggested. (1.) That the man brought himself, which is apparently, though not certainly favored by the Gr. (2.) That the priest brought him. (3.) That the word "him" should rather be rendered "it," referring to the lamb which the man was to bring as an oblation. We prefer the construction which makes the subject of the verb indefinite, "one shall bring him," i. e. he shall be brought, as our version has it.

V. 14. *He shall offer.* Heb. *hikrib, shall bring near,* the appropriate term for sacrificial and other offerings. See Note on ch. 8:9, 10.——¶ *Of the first year.* Heb. "Of his first year," and so in the subsequent clause respecting the she-lamb, "of her first year."——¶ *For a burnt-offering.* One of each of the three great classes of offerings mentioned Lev. 1:3:4: is here prescribed, corresponding to the threefold prohibitions of wine, tonsure, and corpse-defilement specified above. The design of them is well expressed by Patrick:—"A *burnt-offering,* as an acknowledgment of God's sovereign dominion. A *sin-offering,* imploring pardon for any omissions of which he might have been guilty during his vow; and a *peace-offering,* in thankfulness to God, who had given him grace both to make, and to keep, and to fulfil this vow." The duty of bringing these offerings, though the vow had been fulfilled without any pollution, would teach the Nazarite that so far from meriting any thing by his pious consecration of himself, a secret

without blemish [k] for a sin-offering, and one ram without blemish for [l] peace-offerings,

15 And a basket of unleavened bread, cakes [m] of fine flour mingled with oil, and wafers of unleavened bread [n] anointed with oil, and their meat-offering, and their [o] drink-offerings.

16 And the priest shall bring *them* before the LORD, and shall offer his sin-offering, and his burnt-offering.

17 And he shall offer the ram *for* a sacrifice of peace-offerings unto the LORD, with the basket of unleavened bread: the priest shall offer also his meat-offering, and his drink-offering.

18 And the Nazarite shall shave [p] the head of his separation *at* the door of the taberna-

k Lev. 4. 3, 28, 32. Mal. 1. 13, 14. 1 Pet. 1. 19. l Lev. 3. 6. m Lev. 2. 4. n Ex. 29. 2. o c. 15. 5, 7, 10.

p Acts 21. 24.

and unseen guiltiness still clave to him even in his best and most perfect works, and though "he knew nothing by himself (i. e. against himself), yet was he not thereby justified, but he that judged him was the Lord." 1 Cor. 4 : 4.

V. 15. *And their meat-offering and their drink-offerings.* The possessive "their" in this connection seems to refer to the *burnt-offering* and *peace-offering* mentioned in the preceding verse, and which were always to have the meat-offering (meal-offering) and drink-offering as an accompaniment, besides the basket of unleavened bread, with the cakes and wafers. See Lev. 7 : 12. Num. 15 : 2, 3, etc.

V. 16. *Shall bring (them.)* Heb. *hikrib*, lit. *shall cause to come near;* a term which is interchanged with "offer," 1 Chron. 16 : 1, "they *offered* (*yakribu*) burnt-sacrifices," etc. compared with 2 Sam. 6 : 17, "And David *offered* (*yaal*) burnt-offerings," etc.——¶ *Shall offer his sin-offering.* Heb. "Shall *do* his sin-offering." See Note on v. 11. For an account of the nature and use of the sin-offering, see Note on Lev. 4 : 1. This, though mentioned second, was offered first, according to the Hebrew writers:—"He killed the sin-offering first, and after the burnt-offering, and after that the peace-offerings, and after that he was shaved."—*Maimonides.* Having made his peace with God by the sin-offering, the other two which followed were made acceptable.

V. 17. *Shall offer the ram.* Heb. "Shall *do* the ram," as in the preceding verse. On the nature and design of the peace-offering, see Note on Lev. 3 : 1. It was here a token of thankfulness that he had been enabled to fulfil his vow, and a kind of rejoicing festival before the Lord, as the flesh of the peace-offerings was eaten by him who brought the sacrifice after the Lord and the priest had had their portions.——¶ *With the basket of unleavened bread.* From Lev. 8 : 26, it would appear that not the whole contents of the basket were thus offered to the Lord, but one of each kind of the cakes was dedicated to him as a wave-offering, and the rest was eaten by the offerer and his friends invited on the occasion.——¶ *The priest shall offer.* Heb. "Shall *do.*" From this it is obvious that the meat-offering (meal-offering) and the drink-offering were distinct from the basket of unleavened bread, although Boothroyed and Geddes are disposed to identify them.

V. 18. *The Nazarite shall shave the head of his separation.* Heb. "Of his Nazariteship." That is, the hair of his head, which was the grand visible dis-

cle of the congregation; and
shall take the hair of the head
of his separation, and put *it* in
the fire which *is* under the sacrifice of the peace-offerings.

19 And the priest shall take
the sodden [q] shoulder of the
ram, and one [r] unleavened cake
out of the basket, and one unleavened wafer, and shall put
them upon the hands of the Nazarite, after *the hair of* his separation is shaven:

20 And the priest shall wave
them *for* a wave-offering before
the LORD: this *is* holy for the
priest, with the wave-breast and
heave-shoulder: and after that
the Nazarite may drink wine.

21 This *is* the law of the
Nazarite who hath vowed, *and*

q 1 Sam. 2. 15. r Ex. 29. 23–28.

---

tinguishing badge of his separation or consecration to the Lord as a Nazarite. The Hebrews call this "the shaving of purity," for having now fulfilled his vow, this hair was holy, not having been defiled like that which he was ordered to shave off before, v. 9. The ceremony, therefore, was like cancelling a bond when the condition is performed.——¶ *At the door of the tabernacle.* That the act might receive an appropriate notoriety; that it might be publicly known that he had completed his vow. After the Tabernacle was succeeded by the Temple, this was done in the precincts of the latter. Acts 21:26.——¶ *Put it in the fire which is under the sacrifice of the peace-offerings.* Being considered consecrated and holy it was consigned to the fire, where it was consumed in honor of the Lord whom the fire represented. The fire, however, in this case, was not the fire of the altar, which was too pure for such an oblation, but the common fire under the pot or caldron in which the peace-offerings were boiled. This might be called, in one sense, holy, because it was employed to boil holy meat, and for that reason was more sacred than common fire.

V. 19. *Shall take the sodden shoulder.* That is, the *boiled* shoulder, which was the left, the right, called the *heave-shoulder*, v. 20, being by a previous law (Lev. 7:32, 33) appropriated raw to the priest. In this case, accordingly, the left shoulder was added to the right as a special token of the Nazarite's thankfulness to heaven for the many mercies vouchsafed.——¶ *After (the hair of) his separation is shaven.* Heb. "After his Nazariteship is shaven." The thing signified being put for the sign.

V. 20. *And the priest shall wave them.* On the import of the words "wave," "waving," "wave-offering," see Notes on Ex. 29:24–28. Whatever were the distinction between *wave-offering* and *heave-offering*, the act was performed by the priest's putting his hands under those of the offerer, thus intimating that the acceptance of all our services is through the mediation of our great High Priest, Jesus Christ, by whom we are to offer "the sacrifice of praise to God continually."——¶ *This is holy for the priest.* Heb. *kodesh, holiness;* that is, a holy portion for the priest to eat.——¶ *With the wave-breast and heave-shoulder.* Heb. "Upon, or in addition to, the breast of waving and shoulder of heaving," which were the perquisites of the priests, of all the peace-offerings.——¶ *May drink wine.* Heb. "Shall drink," i. e. if he pleases, being now discharged of his vow and restored to his former freedom, to live as other men.

V. 21. *This is the law of the Naza-*

of his offering unto the LORD for his separation, beside *that* that his hand shall get: according to the vow which he vowed, so he must do after the law of his separation.

22 And the LORD spake unto Moses, saying,

23 Speak unto Aaron and unto his sons, saying, On this wise ye shall bless [s] the chil-

[s] Lev. 9. 22. Deut. 10. 8. 21. 5. Josh. 8. 33. 1 Chr. 23. 13.

---

rite, etc. The common rendering and interpretation of this verse does not strike us as satisfactory. It is for the most part understood to mean that all the observances above mentioned he was bound to comply with, however poor he might be, besides which he might add whatever his circumstances and inclinations might prompt him to over and above what was thus prescribed. ('Beside that that his hand shall get.') But to this it is a serious objection, that the preceding law makes no allusion to any such additional voluntary offerings, and yet the writer is professing to recite the terms of the law. We propose, therefore, the following, as the literal and more correct rendering of the passage:—"This (i. e. what is said above) is the law of the Nazarite who shall vow, (and the law of) his gift (*korbano, his korban*) unto the Lord according to his Nazariteship, beside that which his hand shall have attained; according to the vow which he shall have vowed, so shall he do according to the law of his Nazariteship." The phrase, "beside that that his hand shall get," denotes, we think, that which fell within the measure of his ordinary ability. Over and above what he ordinarily did in the way of gifts or oblations, he was especially bound as a votary to discharge punctiliously all the requirements above specified which were involved in his vow. The phraseology in the clause "for his separation" (*al nizro*), which we have rendered "according to his Nazariteship," is in the original closely akin to that which occurs in the final clause of the verse, "after the law of his separation (*al torath nizro*"). If the preposition על *al* may be properly rendered in one case *after*, i. e. *according to*, we see not why it may not be also in the other.——¶ *According to the vow which he vowed.* Heb. *kepi nidro, according to the mouth of his vow.* That is, according to the tenor, purport, and intention of his vow. It is reiterating the general declaration, that he must conform, with the utmost strictness, to the terms of the vow which he has voluntarily made. On the general purport of the latter part of this chapter, in which various offerings are commanded, the following remarks of Calvin will be seen to be very appropriate: "Here we clearly perceive, that however cheerfully and earnestly men endeavor to offer themselves altogether to God, yet they never attain to the goal of perfection, nor arrive at what they desire, but are always exposed to God's judgments, unless He should pardon their sins. Even when the work of the Nazarites is complete, God commands them to confess their guilt, and suffers not this service to intrude into the place of merit, but requires of them a sacrifice, that they may borrow from elsewhere what belongs not to themselves, though they appear to be the most perfect of all men."—*Harm. of Pent.*

The Formula of Blessing pronounced upon the People.

V. 23. *On this wise shall ye bless, etc.* The Lord here prescribes the form of

dren of Israel, saying unto them,

24 The LORD bless[t] thee, and[u] keep thee;

t Ps. 134. 3. u Ps. 121. 7. John 17. 11.

---

blessing which Aaron and his sons were to pronounce upon the people, especially at the close of the daily services. The office of benediction was in a peculiar manner committed to them, as appears from Deut. 22 : 5, "And the priests the sons of Levi shall come near; for them the Lord thy God hath chosen to minister unto him, and *to bless in the name of the Lord*." And 1 Chron. 23 : 13, "Aaron was separated, that he should sanctify the most holy things, he and his sons for ever, to burn incense before the Lord, to minister unto him, *and to bless in his name* for ever." In this act they represented one grand prerogative of Christ, the great High Priest of the Church, who is pre-eminently the fountain of blessing, and "in whom all the nations of the earth are (to be) blessed." The uniform practice of the Apostles in blessing the people, leads us to infer that it was to be continued under the Christian dispensation; and accordingly, in conformity to their example, the Christian Church has universally retained the custom of closing the service with a pastoral benediction. Not that ministers can, by any power or authority of their own, convey a blessing; but as stewards of the mysteries of God, and mediums between himself and his people, they may still act as the appointed vehicles of blessings which he sees fit to impart. The priestly benediction was in itself very simple, yet as the divine appointment it undoubtedly brought down many blessings upon those upon whom it was pronounced. And shall we suppose that the Most High will put any less honor upon his ordinances under the Gospel? Let not then the benediction be slighted, as though it were a mere signal for the breaking up of the congregation, but be looked upon as the expression of the Lord's good will to each of his worshippers involving the exhortation to *do* as well as to *learn* his commandments. The threefold repetition of the name "Jehovah" undoubtedly carries with it an allusion to the divine mystery set forth in the august titles Father, Son, and Holy Spirit, as evangelically explained by the apostle, 2 Cor. 13 : 14, "The grace of our Lord Jesus Christ, and the love of the Father, and the communion of the Holy Ghost be with you all." Indeed, the Hebrew writers confess that as the name "Jehovah," in this connection, is differently pointed each time, some mystery unknown to them is couched under it. Under the Christian dispensation this mystery is unfolded. The term "bless," though here predicated of the priests, is properly to be understood of the Lord himself, and the part of the priests was simply that of *invocation*, for they could not bless of themselves. At the same time, as they acted as official intercessors, and spake in the name of Him who *commanded* the blessing," the prayer on that account involved a virtual promise, and was uttered with a certain authority which gave assurance of its accomplishment. This blessing was pronounced in a standing posture, with uplifted hands, and probably with a loud voice, and the face turned towards the people. Deut. 10 : 8. Lev. 9 : 22. With the Levitical priests this was typical. In our Lord himself it was veritably fulfilled. Luke 24 : 50, "And he led them out as far as to Bethany; and he lifted up his hands, and blessed them."

V. 24. *The Lord bless thee, and keep*

25 The LORD make his face[v] shine upon thee, and be gracious[w] unto thee;

v Ps. 31. 16. 67. 1. 80. 3, 7, 19. 119. 135. Dan. 9. 17 w Gen. 43. 29. Ex. 33. 19. Mal. 1. 9.

26 The LORD lift up[x] his countenance upon thee, and give thee peace[y].

x Ps. 4. 6. 89. 15. y Ps. 29. 11. Is. 26. 3, 12. John 14. 27. Phil. 4. 7. 2 Thes. 3. 16.

---

thee. The blessing is here pronounced in the singular ("thee"), although its import is of course plural. In this respect it is like the precepts of the Decalogue, which address themselves to every man in his individual capacity, the implication being in either case that no one is to lose himself in a multitude, but to make a personal application of whatever is included in the blessing or the command. The leading import of *blessing*, when spoken of the Lord, is *abundant increase* and *multiplication* of good things both temporal and spiritual. "The Lord bless thee and keep thee," therefore, is equivalent to, the Lord bestow upon thee plentifully the favors of his providence and his grace, and kindly guard and preserve thee in the happy enjoyment of them. The original term for "keep" is often employed to signify the tutelary care, the faithful guardianship, which the Most High exercises towards those who put their trust in Him. Thus, Ps. 121 : 7, "The Lord shall *preserve* thee from all evil, he shall *preserve* thy soul."

V. 25. *The Lord make his face to shine upon thee, etc.* Heb. *yâër pânauv ëlëkâ, make his face* (lit. *faces*) *to be light* (*lightsome* or *luminous*) *to thee.* The Targ. Jon. adds, "when thou art studying the law, and reveal to thee its hidden things." The ancient versions, though somewhat various in the form of expression, evince a substantial agreement. Chald. "The Lord display his Shekinah (or Divine Majesty) upon thee, and have compassion upon thee." Syr. "The Lord illuminate thee with his countenance, and vivify thee." Arab. "The Lord kindle the splendor of his countenance upon thee, and be propitious to thee." Gr. "The Lord make his face to shine upon thee, and be merciful to thee." The *face* of God sometimes denotes his anger, Lev. 20 : 6. Ps. 21 : 10. 34 : 17, and sometimes his favor, Ps. 21 : 7. But the *light* or *the shining* of his face usually carries with it the idea of loving-kindness and salvation in Christ, as Ps. 80 : 7, "Cause thy face to shine, and we shall be saved." Comp. Ps. 44 : 3. It is equivalent to, "smile upon thee," and this implies the opposite to the hiding of the face, and covering it with a cloud. The term *gracious*, it will be observed, has, in most of the ancient versions, the sense of *pity, compassion, mercy,* while with us it has somehow received a sense in conformity with the idea of *atonement* or *propitiation* upon which it is supposed to be built, and therefore is usually explained, in this connection, as implying the *forgiveness of sin.* Probably, however, the leading idea is that of *benignity*, and the clause may be paraphrased, "The Lord bless thee with the sensible effects of his favor, and visit thy soul with an influence like that of the sun upon the face of nature, cheering and enlivening it."

V. 26. *The Lord lift up his countenance upon thee, and give thee peace.* Heb. "The Lord lift up his countenance to thee, and put, or dispose, unto thee, peace." Chald. "The Lord take away his anger from thee, and impart to thee peace." Vulg. "The Lord turn his countenance to thee, and give thee peace." The phrase "lift up the countenance," when spoken of men, implies a free, open, and cheerful air and de-

27 And they shall put my name [z] upon the children of Israel, and I will [a] bless them.

z Deut. 28. 10. 2 Chr. 7. 14. Is. 43. 7. Dan. 9. 18, 19.

a Gen. 12. 2. 3. c. 23. 20. Ps. 5. 12. 67. 7. 115. 12, 13. Acts 3. 26. Eph. 1. 3.

portment, the opposite of downcast and melancholy, as Job 29 : 24. 2 Sam. 2 : 22; so when spoken of God it imports that favor and complacency which produce such an elevation of face in the subject of it, being attended with an inward calm of conscience, a peace and assurance which could flow from no other source. This *peace* is but another name for all manner of prosperity and welfare, being opposed to war, to discord and enmity, to tumult and confusion, and also to adversity. This threefold invocation, therefore, is very comprehensive in its range of import, being laden with the richest blessings which heaven can impart to men. "There be many that say, Who will show us any good? Lord, lift thou up the light of thy countenance upon us." We may here remark, that some interpreters are of opinion, that the last clause of each benediction explains the foregoing, as if it were said, "The Lord bless thee, by keeping thee; the Lord make his face to shine upon thee, by being gracious unto thee; the Lord lift up his countenance upon thee, by giving thee peace." This may be admitted, without at the same time superseding any of the other senses which we have attributed to the language. "As I came along the road, I met Rāman, and he lifted up his face upon me; but I knew not the end;" which means, he looked pleasantly. Does a man complain of another who has ceased to look kindly upon him, he says, "Ah! my friend, you no longer lift up your countenance upon me."—*Roberts.*

V. 27. *They shall put my name upon the children of Israel.* Heb. *sâmu, shall put,* or *impose;* a phraseology of a peculiar kind, implying mainly the *invocation* of the divine name upon the chosen people, whereby is understood the ministerial or mediatory communication, in a measure, of the very qualities and attributes for which the *name* of Jehovah stands. Chald. "They shall put, or impose, the blessing of my name." We may doubtless suppose that the threefold blessing above mentioned involved the essential import of the name Jehovah, so that in pronouncing that blessing they did in effect impart the virtue of that divinely significant name; and it may be questioned whether this verse is not, in fact, the Lord's own interpretation of the purport of the blessing which he ordered to be pronounced, and which is given in the preceding verses. It is not, at any rate, clear what *more* is intended to be conveyed by the language of this verse than is embraced in the true sense of the three preceding. Ainsworth remarks, that it is apparently meant of the priests' gesture in lifting up their hands "towards the people," as did Aaron, Lev. 9 : 22, as a sign that the name and blessing of God was imposed upon them. But this was probably done in the benediction itself, and therefore cannot well indicate a distinct act here. Why may we not regard the benediction pronounced by Aaron and his sons upon the children of Israel as a dim, but real foreshadowing and revelation of that great truth which lies at the very foundation of the Christian system—the love of the Everlasting Father, the grace of the Incarnate Son, the comfort, the teaching, and the communion of the Holy and Blessed Spirit—not as three Gods, but as one God viewed under a threefold

CHAPTER VII.

AND it came to pass on the day that Moses had fully set up [a] the tabernacle, and had anointed it [b], and sanctified it,

a Ex. 40. 18. b Lev. 8. 10, 11.

aspect. According to this suggestion, God the Father is referred to in the 24th verse—"The Lord bless thee and keep thee;" the Son, the Redeemer, is referred to in the 25th verse—"Make his face to shine upon thee, and be gracious unto thee;" and the Holy Spirit is alluded to in the 26th verse—"Lift up the light of his countenance upon thee, and give thee peace." This view appears to us a reasonable one, and therefore, on the whole, we would read the passage as if written, "And (thus) shall ye put my name," etc. That is, by pronouncing the above blessing ye shall in effect put my triune name upon the children of Israel, and thereby challenge them as mine; as especially bound and consecrated to me in the acknowledgment of my divine nature and perfections.——¶ *And I will bless them.* Targ. Jon. "I will bless them in or by my Word." Gr. "I the Lord will bless them." That is, both the people and the priests. For the strengthening of their faith the Lord promises to bless the blessing of his appointed servants.

CHAPTER VII.

The Offering of the Princes at the Dedication of the Tabernacle.

V. 1. *On the day.* That is, about the time. The Tabernacle was fully set up on the first day of the first month of the second year after the departure from Egypt, Ex. 40 : 17, 18. The history here seems to revert to that period, and yet we are not to interpret it in such a strictness of sense as to confine what is here said to the space of a single day; for the anointing or consecrating process occupied seven days (Lev. 8 : 35), and the dedication here spoken of took place after that. It must be understood, therefore, that after the Tabernacle had been erected, and consecrated with all its appurtenances, the priests anointed, their services defined, the tribes registered and arranged under their several standards, the Levites distinguished into their appropriate classes; that "in that day," or about that time, the chief heads of the different tribes entered upon the work of dedication as described in what follows.—The general scope of the Israelitish history as typical of the Christian church undoubtedly warrants the idea of such a bearing in the present narrative. The Tabernacle, it will be observed, is first set up, and then, with all its implements and utensils, anointed and sanctified, and thus made fit to be consecrated to the holy uses for which it was designed. The actual dedication followed, and this was signalized by the voluntary gifts of the heads of the tribes, as recorded in the present chapter. The ceremony of unction in the O. T. is a standing symbol of the effusion of the Holy Spirit in his purifying and gladdening influences. As applied to the Tabernacle and its contents it points typically to the inauguration of Christ as head of his church, and in and through him to the universal church itself, which is the fulness of his spiritual body. The representative import of the Altar is not materially different, though it has a more especial reference to the Lord and the church in respect to the *worship* rendered by the one and received by the other. We may say, then, that the dedication of the altar is the consecration of the church. The day of the anointing of the altar denotes

and all the instruments thereof, both the altar and all the vessels thereof, and had anointed them, and sanctified them,

---

the time of the Lord's inauguration, when, after the resurrection and ascension, the Holy Spirit was poured out in rich abundance, and his precious gifts imparted to believers. "As a recompense in the same" their hearts were also opened "as the hearts of a willing people," and they were ready to bestow at once their goods and themselves upon the Lord as a holy dedication. "Thy people," says the Psalmist, Ps. 110:3, "shall be willing in the day of thy power;" Heb. "shall be a people of voluntarinesses, or liberalities;" and it is perhaps with a tacit reference to this noble, liberal, generous spirit and prompting that the chiefs of the tribes are here termed "princes." The character thus typically given to the Christian church in its primitive period, when its disciples were in this respect of one heart and one mind, ready to possess all things in common, is to be considered as virtually the character of the Lord's disciples in all ages; for of them it may be properly said, "the liberal soul deviseth liberal things." In the present case, it might be said of the Israelites, as of the early Christians, that "their deep poverty abounded to the riches of their liberality," for though they had little to spare, yet they gave it with a princely generosity. The inventory is here made out, and the names of the donors stand recorded to their honor, as we often see in modern times the names of contributors to missionary and other benevolent enterprises published to the world, not to trumpet or eulogize their benefactions, but to attest their zeal, and serve as an encouraging example to others. On this subject we quote the apposite remarks of Mr. Cummings, in his "Scripture Readings on Numbers," (in loc.):—"Some people seem to think, that to publish one's name in a list, or in an advertisement, as the donor of so much to a charitable object, is wrong. It may be right or wrong; in the thing itself there is nothing necessarily wrong, nor is there any thing necessarily right. If it be done from vain glory, it is wrong; but if it be done simply as expressing one's gratitude to God, and one's sympathy with His cause, then it has precedents in the Old Testament, it has a precedent in the New. That woman's name, who anointed the Saviour's feet with the precious perfume, is recorded, and recorded as a precedent for us. And it may be done to induce others, who have more in their coffers, but at present less liberality in their hearts, to go and do likewise. We are not called upon ostentatiously to display what we do; that is sin: it is not only sin, it is absurd; but we are at the same time called upon to let our light, whether it be bright or dim, so shine before men, that others seeing our good works—our names recorded in the annual list—may glorify not us, but our Father who is in heaven. And if these men, the princes of the ancient tribes of Israel, gave so much, and so liberally—for it was a vast amount of gold and of silver—to that tabernacle that was to be taken down, how should we rejoice in every opportunity, as it presents itself, in the Providence of God, of contributing to build up a living temple of living stones on Christ the foundation rock, until that completed and perfected temple shall sound with the praises of Him that redeemed it—'Grace, grace unto it.'"——¶ *Had anointed it.* That is, with oil, according to the command, Ex. 30:23–28, the execution of which is related Lev. 8:10, 11. As the Tabernacle and the Al-

2 That the princes [c] of Israel, heads of the house of their fathers, who *were* the princes of the tribes, and were over them that were numbered, offered:
3 And they brought their offering before the LORD, six covered wagons, and twelve oxen; a wagon for two of the princes, and for each one an ox; and they brought them before the tabernacle.

c c. 1. 4, etc.

---

tar were the principal things, and what sanctified the oblations (Mat. 23 : 17, 19), therefore the princes' offerings were deferred till these were duly set up and inaugurated.

V. 2. *That the princes, etc. —— offered.* See ch. 1 : 16, where the same term occurs, which Geddes renders "patriarchal chiefs." The word "offered," which in our version is the last word in the verse, is in the Hebrew the first. Accordingly, Ainsworth renders, "Then offered the princes," etc.——¶ *Heads of the house of their fathers.* For "heads of the *houses.*" See Note on ch. 1 : 20.——¶ *And were over them that were numbered.* Heb. "That stood by, upon, or over them that were mustered." As this is the same term that occurs ch. 1 : 5, in speaking of the numbering of the people by Moses and Aaron and their assistants, "these are the names of the men that shall *stand* with you," the inference would seem fair, that the writer intended to say these were the same persons who officiated with Moses and Aaron on that occasion. Gr. "That presided over the *visitation,*" i. e. the muster. Vat. "That stood by while the people were numbered." Calvin, however, does not recognise any allusion to these twelve assistants. His explanation is, that after the people were numbered, and separated into their several divisions, these were chosen as the chiefs of the tribes. This may have been so, and yet the men chosen may have been the twelve above mentioned.

V. 3. *And they brought their offering.* Heb. *korbânâm, their korban.* The design of this offering was to perform a public service, by affording convenient vehicles to transport the heavier materials of the Tabernacle when it was removed from place to place.——¶ *Before the Lord.* That is, before the door of the Tabernacle, as appears from the final clause of the verse.——¶ *Six covered wagons.* Heb. *shesh egloth tzâb.* The original *tzâb* is from a root signifying *to swell, to grow turgid.* It is employed in reference to the swelling of the adulterous woman under the operation of the waters of jealousy, and is the term rendered *tortoise,* Lev. 11 : 29, from the *turgid* form of his shell. The similar form of a *covered wagon* will show the ground of its usage in this sense in the present instance. The same word in Is. 66 : 20, is translated "litter." The Gr. has αμαξας λαμπηνικας, *coach wagons,* the epithet implying, according to lexicographers, a kind of vehicles such as were used by illustrious men and women. Though comparatively of a rude structure, they were doubtless the best and most costly that could be furnished under the circumstances.——¶ *And twelve oxen.* "It appears that each cart was drawn by two oxen, and a greater number does not seem to have been employed on any of the different occasions mentioned in Scripture. Oxen seem to have been generally used for draught in ancient times among other nations as well as the Hebrews; and they still continue to be employed in

4 And the LORD spake unto Moses, saying,

5 Take *it* of them, that they may be to do the service of the tabernacle of the congregation; and thou shalt give them unto the Levites, to every man according to his service.

6 And Moses took the wagons and the oxen, and gave them unto the Levites.

7 Two wagons and four oxen he gave unto the sons of Gershon, according to their service [d]:

8 And four wagons and eight oxen he gave unto the sons of Merari [e], according unto their service, under the hand of Ithamar the son of Aaron the priest.

9 But unto the sons of Kohath he gave none; because [f] the service of the sanctuary belonging to them *was*, *that* they should bear upon their shoulders.

d c. 4. 24–28. e c. 4. 29–33. f c. 4. 4–15.

dragging the few carts which are in use in some parts of Western Asia."—*Pict. Bible.*——¶ *A wagon for two of the princes.* Heb. "A wagon upon two of the princes;" i. e. according to, or for two. Such is the peculiar force of the Heb. particle *al.* From which it appears that there was a certain kind of concert in this presentation of the wagons, as if each two of the princes combined to furnish a wagon, while each one contributed an ox.

V. 5. *Take it of them.* It is perhaps in reference to this expression that Jonathan in his Targum says that Moses at first refused the presents, to which Rab. Sol. Jarchi adds, that "he received them not from their hand till he was commanded by the mouth of God." The words imply, perhaps, some demurring on the part of Moses until he had taken time, according to his usual custom on all doubtful points, to consult the Lord, and definitely ascertain his will.——¶ *That they may be to do the service.* Heb. "And let them be to serve the service." Gr. "And they shall be for the ministerial work of the Tabernacle of testimony." Vulg. "To serve in the ministry of the Tabernacle."——¶ *To every man according to his service.* Heb. "According to the month of his service." That is, according to the measure and proportion of his service; or, in other words, according as every one had a greater or less burden to carry. Accordingly, to the Gershonites, who had the lightest burden, the curtains and hangings, ch. 4: 24–28, he gave but two wagons and four oxen.

V. 8. *Four wagons and eight oxen he gave unto the sons of Merari.* The largest allowance of wagons was made to this family both because it was the most numerous, and was charged with the heaviest burdens, ch. 4:31, 32, 48. The boards, bars, pillars, sockets, etc., fell to their lot.——¶ *According unto their service.* Heb. "According to the month of their service."——¶ *Under the hand of Ithamar.* Heb. "In the hand of Ithamar," that is, under his guidance and direction. He had the general superintendence of both the Gershonites and the Merarites, ch. 4: 28, 33.

V. 9. *Because the service of the sanctuary, etc.* Heb. *abodath hakkodesh, the service of the holy,* that is, of the holy things, such as the Ark, Table, Candlestick, Altar of Incense, etc. Gr. "Because they have the ministrations of the holy (του αγιου).——¶ (*That*) *they should bear upon their shoulders.* This was with a view to the greater honor

10 And the princes offered for dedicating[g] of the altar in the day that it was anointed, even the princes offered their offering before the altar.

g Deut. 20. 5. 1 K. 8. 63. 2 Chr. 7. 5, 9. Ezra 6. 16. Neh. 12. 27. Ps. 30. title.

and dignity of the Ark and of the Law contained in it. The violent motion of a wagon might injure the exquisite workmanship of the sacred chest, and shake and ruffle the ephod and breastplate, which by carrying on the shoulder would be effectually avoided. From the fearful judgment that befell Uzzah, 2 Sam. 6 : 3, 7, it would appear that the order as to this mode of transportation was exceedingly strict. The bearing of the Ark and the other holy things was not, however, so exclusively the province of the Kohathites that it might not be assumed by the priests, the sons of Aaron, on certain special occasions, as appears from Josh. 3 : 3.

V. 10. *The princes offered for dedicating of the altar, etc.* Heb. *eth hanukkath, the initiation,* or *consecration.* Although our version renders the clause "*for* dedicating," etc., yet there is nothing in the original to answer to "for," and the true sense undoubtedly requires the rendering :—" Offered the dedication of the altar," etc., i. e. the sacrifices which constituted the dedication-offering, or, as Geddes proposes, the initial-offering, by a figure of speech similar to that by which the Heb. "sin" is sometimes used to signify a "sin-offering." The usage in regard to the original term (from the root *hânak*) is peculiar and somewhat important. When spoken of men it denotes *catechising, initiation, instruction, training up* to any new thing to which they were previously unaccustomed. Thus Prov. 22 : 6, *Train up* (*hanōk*) a child in the way he should go," etc., where the margin has *catechise.* When applied to other things, as temples, altars, houses, etc., it indicates the first using or enjoying of them, which was usually done with some special solemnities. Thus, Solomon "*dedicated* the house of God," 2 Chron. 7 : 5, and kept "the *dedication* of the altar seven days," 2 Chron. 7 : 9; and at the return from Babylon "they kept the *dedication* of the house of God with joy, and offered at the *dedication* thereof an hundred bullocks," etc., Ezra 6 : 16, 17. In like manner the people kept "the *dedication* of the wall of Jerusalem with gladness, thanksgiving, singing, cymbals, psalteries, and harps," Neh. 12 : 27–43. David also composed the thirtieth Psalm on the occasion of the *dedication* of his house; and it appears from Deut. 20 : 5, that all the Israelites were in the habit of *dedicating* their dwelling-houses. In the time of the Maccabees "they kept the *dedication* of the altar eight days," with sacrifices and gladness, and ordained it to be so kept yearly, 1 Mac. 4 : 54, 56–59, which ordinance was observed in our Lord's time, John 10 : 22, in what is termed "the feast of the *dedication.*" A like ceremony obtained among the Gentiles, as is evident from what is said Dan. 3 : 2, 3, of Nebuchadnezzar's "*dedicating* the image" which he had set up. We may trace the continuance of these usages in the custom of dedicating or consecrating churches and chapels, and other public buildings, and in the ceremonies connected with the 'opening' of roads, markets, bridges, and occasionally with the launching of ships. In all these cases the original word is the same with that employed in this passage. The custom is expressed in Greek by εγκαινισμος, and the feast by εγκαινεια, Lat. encænia, from καινος, *new*, implying *renova-*

11 And the LORD said unto Moses, They shall offer their offering, each prince on his day, for the dedicating of the altar.

12 And he that offered his offering the first day was Nahshon [h] the son of Amminadab, of the tribe of Judah;

h c. 1. 7. 2. 3.

---

tion, restoration, or the *re-appropriation* of any thing to its intended use. So the solemnity of covenant-making at Mount Sinai, related Ex. 24:3–8, is called by the Apostle, Heb. 9:18, a *dedication;* as he says "it was not *dedicated* without blood," and Christ is said to have "*dedicated* a new and living way" into the holy heavens, Heb. 10:20. So in the present case, in order that the altar might be consecrated for the oblations of Israel at all times, the princes of the twelve tribes are moved to *dedicate* it with gifts and sacrifices of various kinds, continued with great solemnity for twelve days, thus representatively testifying their faith and joy in Christ, who was symbolized by the altar, and by whom they should offer the sacrifice of praise to God continually, Heb. 13:10–15. It is to be observed, however, that this is a distinct offering from that of the wagons above-mentioned. Rabbi Sol. Jarchi observes: "After they had voluntarily given the wagons and oxen to carry the Tabernacle, their heart stirred them up to offer voluntary offerings to the altar to dedicate it." Though not expressly intimated, it is yet to be presumed that the offerings made by the princes on this occasion were not exclusively an expression of their own personal promptings, but made on the behalf and at the expense of the tribes to which they severally belonged. Calvin appropriately remarks, that "although mention is only made of the 'princes,' it is probable that each of them presented what the whole tribe had subscribed, since there was no person at that time wealthy enough to give so much gold and silver of his own."—*Harm. of Pent.*——¶ *In the day that it was anointed.* Heb. "In the day of its being anointed." That is, about or near the time; not precisely on the very day. See Note on v. 1.

V. 11. *And the Lord said unto Moses, They shall offer their offering, each prince on his day.* Heb. "One prince for a day, one prince for a day, shall they offer their offering." Repeated for the sake of emphasis and the greater solemnity of the proceeding, as well as to indicate the equal right which all the princes and tribes had in the altar to be dedicated. It would probably be better to render the first clause of the verse, "For the Lord *had* said," intimating that God had previously required this tribute of the people. As it now stands, it would seem as if Moses had not been ordered to receive it before it was actually presented by the princes and the people. A preferable sense results from considering the whole verse as parenthetical, with the pluperfect rendering.——¶ *For the dedicating of the altar.* The dedication here mentioned is not to be understood as if the altar was now for the first time to be inaugurated into its stated use. This had in fact been done before, and seven days spent in the ceremony; but the idea conveyed is that of its *beginning to be used* after having been previously set apart and sanctified.

V. 12. ¶ *Nahshon, the son of Amminadab.* It will be noticed that in every other instance throughout the chapter, the title "prince" is attached to the

13 And his offering *was* one silver charger, the weight thereof *was* an hundred and thirty *shekels*, one silver bowl of seventy shekels, after the shekel[i] of the sanctuary: both of them *were* full of fine flour mingled with oil, for a[k] meat-offering:

i Ex. 30. 13. *k* Lev. 2. 1.

name of the person designated. Here it is omitted, for which the reason may be, that the distinction of offering first involved in itself a kind of principality, inasmuch as the tribe of Judah, in the person of Nahshon, represented the Lord the Saviour, descended from him, and who was, "in all things to have the pre-eminence." Chazkuni, a Rabbinical writer, remarks thus upon the fact:—"He is not called prince, that he might not be puffed up because he offered first; and all the others are called princes, for that they submitted themselves and offered after him." It is not, however, very easy to perceive how the recording or not recording of his title should have had any effect in the way of inflating his spirit, when for aught that appears the history of the transaction might have been written years after its occurrence.——¶ *Of the tribe of Judah.* Heb. *lematteh, for the tribe.* Several versions render it "*of* the tribe," but the above is the most literally exact, and doubtless the true sense. As such it confirms the remark made above, that the offerings were not made so much by the princes in their own names, as in the names of the tribes to which they pertained, and over which they presided. It will be observed that the offering of the chiefs of tribes, each in his day, is not in the order of their births, or as they stand in ch. 1, but according to the order in which they were ranged around the Tabernacle, ch. 2, beginning at the east, proceeding thence to the south, next to the west, and ending at the north. This order we may present in tabellated form, thus:—

1. Judah: *Nahshon*, v. 12........	East.
2. Issachar: *Nethaneel*, v. 18.....	
3. Zebulun: *Eliab*, v. 24........	
4. Reuben: *Elizur*, v. 30........	South.
5. Simeon: *Shelumiel*, v. 36.....	
6. Gad: *Eliasaph*, v. 42........	
7. Ephraim: *Elishama*, v. 48....	West.
8. Manasseh: *Gamaliel*, v. 54...	
9. Benjamin: *Abidan*, v. 60.....	
10. Dan: *Ahiezer*, v. 66..........	North.
11. Asher: *Pagiel*, v. 72..........	
12. Naphtali: *Ahira*, v. 78........	

This ceremony of offering was continued for twelve successive days, on each of which the prince or chief at the head of his tribe, forming a grand procession, marched forward and laid his rich offering upon the common altar, in regard to which all the tribes stood on a footing of dignified equality. And in order still further to cement the union of the whole body of the people, each day of the celebration was made a day of festivity for the whole, by the Feast Offering which made part of the tribute.

V. 13. *One silver charger.* Heb. *kaarath, dish, platter,* or *deep bowl.* Gr. "Trublion," which in Mat. 26:23, is rendered *dish.* Its precise use has not been clearly determined, but it would seem to have been designed for receiving the fine flour of which the meat (meal) offering was made, or for the mixing of the flour into a paste. See Ex. 25:29.——¶ *An hundred and thirty shekels.* About sixty-five ounces.——¶ *One silver bowl.* Heb. *mizrok, bowl, basin.* Gr. "Phiale," translated *vials,* Rev. 16, which however does not convey a correct idea to the English reader, as the vessels intended were of very

14 One spoon of ten *shekels* of gold, full of incense [l]:

l Ex. 30. 34.

15 One young bullock, one ram, one lamb of the first year, for [m] a burnt-offering:

m Lev. 1. 2, 3.

different construction from our vials. "Goblets" would be a rendering nearer the truth. The use of these vessels in the holy things was to hold the blood which was carried to the altar and there poured out or sprinkled, Ex. 27 : 3. It is obvious, too, from the concluding clause, that it was used for containing the fine flour mingled with oil, the memorial of which was to be burnt in the fire of the altar, Lev. 2 : 2.——¶ *Shekel of the sanctuary.* Heb. *shekel hakkodesh, shekel of the holiness* or *sanctity;* that is, the shekel employed as a standard in regard to the weight of all holy things.——¶ *For a meat offering;* that is, for a meal-offering, or mincha, which was to be an accompaniment of the burnt-offering and peace-offering mentioned vs. 15, 17.

V. 14. *One spoon.* Heb. *kaph, cup;* a vessel for holding incense, called a spoon from its concavity. See Note on Ex. 25 : 29. Geddes and Boothroyd render by "incense-pot." As this was of gold, it doubtless pertained to the altar of incense, and not to the brazen altar standing in the outer court; and this would indicate that both altars were now dedicated, that is, began to be first used for the purposes of the whole congregation. As to the use of incense in connection with the meat-offering, see Note on Lev. 2 : 1, et seq. If these dedication-offerings have, on the whole, as we have endeavored to show, a Christian aspect, then it may be presumed that these various vessels of gold and silver come into the general category of typical, and we see nothing more probable than the suggestions of the old commentator Rabanus Maurus, who says :—" These different kinds of vessels, made for offering libations, were intended to denote the varying capacities of men in respect to the reception of divine things. One and the same kind of teaching is not equally adapted to all classes of men. The wise, the simple, the rich, the poor, the sound, and the infirm, require different modes of instruction. The rude race of the Jews, abiding under the shadow of the Law, were to be trained in one way; in quite another way is a Christian people, beholding the mysteries of the Law unfolded in the verity of the Gospel, to be nurtured into a perfect man." He then goes on to explain the symbolical purport of the different kinds of vessels, the bowls, goblets, cups, etc., intimating that they here represent the various capacities of truth distinguishing different persons in the church, all of whom, however, are prompt to present their several faculties to the Lord to be filled from the fulness of his Spirit, and then solemnly dedicated to his service.

V. 15. *One young bullock, etc.* The offerings here mentioned, the plate and the sacrifices, of which latter there were no less than twenty-one, were very costly, and must have constituted a magnificent donative for a people now sojourning in a wilderness beyond the bounds of civilization. "The occasion must have been one of great and striking solemnity, and, from the account here given, reminding us strongly of the annual festival of Nurooz in Persia, when the king sits in great state and glory, with the nobles of his court attending in their most gorgeous attire, and thus receives in succession a long

16 One kid of the goats for
a [n] sin-offering:
17 And for a sacrifice of
[o] peace-offerings, two oxen, five rams, five he-goats, five lambs of the first year. This *was* the offering of Nahshon the son of Amminadab.
18 On the second day Nethaneel [p] the son of Zuar, prince of Issachar, did offer.
19 He offered [q] *for* his offering one silver charger, the weight whereof *was* an hundred and thirty *shekels*, one silver bowl of seventy shekels, after the shekel of the sanctuary; both of them full of fine flour mingled with oil, for a meat-offering:
20 One spoon of gold of ten *shekels*, full of incense:
21 One young bullock, one ram, one lamb of the first year, for a burnt-offering:
22 One kid of the goats for a sin-offering:
23 And for a sacrifice of peace-offerings, two oxen, five rams, five he-goats, five lambs of the first year. This *was* the offering of Nethaneel the son of Zuar.
24 On the third day Eliab [r] the son of Helon, prince of the children of Zebulun, *did offer:*
25 His offering *was* one silver charger, the weight whereof *was* an hundred and thirty *shekels*, one silver bowl of seventy shekels, after the shekel of the sanctuary; both of them full of fine flour mingled with oil, for a meat-offering:
26 One golden spoon of ten *shekels*, full of incense:
27 One young bullock, one ram, one lamb of the first year, for a burnt-offering:
28 One kid of the goats for a sin-offering:
29 And for a sacrifice of peace-offerings, two oxen, five rams, five he-goats, five lambs of the first year. This *was* the offering of Eliab the son of Helon.
30 On the fourth day Elizur [s] the son of Shedeur, prince of the children of Reuben, *did offer:*
31 His offering [t] *was* one silver charger, of the weight of an hundred and thirty *shekels*, one silver bowl of seventy shekels, after the shekel of the sanctuary; both of them full of fine

n Lev. 4. 25. *o* Lev. 3. 1. *p* c. 1. 8. 2. 5. *q* ver. 13, etc. *r* c. 1. 9. 2. 7. *s* c. 1. 5. 2. 10. *t* ver. 13, etc.

---

series of costly offerings, which the princes who govern the provinces of his empire send, at that season, to the capital for his acceptance, and which are of such value as to form one of the principal portions of his yearly revenue."—*Pict. Bible.*

V. 17. *And for a sacrifice of peace-offerings.* The victims here are much more numerous than in the case of the burnt-offerings or the sin-offerings for the reason that the priests, the princes, and as many of the people as were invited had their share of them, and feasted together before the Lord with great rejoicing.

V. 18. *On the second day Nethaneel —— did offer.* It may here be remark-

flour mingled with oil, for a meat-offering:

32 One golden spoon of ten *shekels*, full of incense:

33 One young bullock, one ram, one lamb of the first year, for a burnt-offering:

34 One kid of the goats for a sin-offering:

35 And for a sacrifice of peace-offerings, two oxen, five rams, five he-goats, five lambs of the first year. This *was* the offering of Elizur the son of Shedeur.

36 On the fifth day Shelumiel[u] the son of Zurishaddai, prince of the children of Simeon, *did offer:*

37 His offering[v] *was* one silver charger, the weight whereof *was* an hundred and thirty *shekels*, one silver bowl of seventy shekels, after the shekel of the sanctuary; both of them full of fine flour mingled with oil, for a meat-offering:

38 One golden spoon of ten *shekels*, full of incense:

39 One young bullock, one ram, one lamb of the first year, for a burnt-offering:

40 One kid of the goats for a sin-offering:

41 And for a sacrifice of peace-offerings, two oxen, five rams, five he-goats, five lambs of the first year. This *was* the offering of Shelumiel, the son of Zurishaddai.

42 On the sixth day Eliasaph[w] the son of Deuel, prince of the children of Gad, *offered:*

43 His offering[x] *was* one silver charger, of the weight of an hundred and thirty *shekels*, a silver bowl of seventy shekels, after the shekel of the sanctuary; both of them full of fine flour mingled with oil, for a meat-offering:

44 One golden spoon of ten *shekels*, full of incense:

45 One young bullock, one ram, one lamb of the first year, for a burnt-offering:

46 One kid of the goats for a sin-offering:

47 And for a sacrifice of peace-offerings, two oxen, five rams, five he-goats, five lambs of the first year. This *was* the offering of Eliasaph the son of Deuel.

u c. 1. 6. 2. 12. v ver. 13, etc. w c. 1. 14. 2. 14. x ver. 13, etc.

---

ed that every tribe, through its prince or chief, offers precisely the same kind of offering, and in the same quantity, and that the offering of each is distinctly described, although it necessitates a repetition in the same words, whereas we should doubtless have supposed that, after specifying the first, the sacred writer would have said:—"And so in like manner with all that followed; each one made the same offering." But infinite wisdom has seen fit to adopt another course, and it may have been upon the same principle with that to which we have adverted, ch. 1:20–43, with which compare Note on Ex. 36:8–38. The witnessing of the actual processions and offerings continued from day to day would have produced a deep and solemnizing impression upon the mind, and it may be that the leisurely perusal of the distinct account of each,

48 On the seventh day Elishama [y], the son of Ammihud, prince of the children of Ephraim, *offered:*

49 His offering [z] *was* one silver charger, the weight whereof *was* an hundred and thirty *shekels*, one silver bowl of seventy shekels, after the shekel of the sanctuary; both of them full of fine flour mingled with oil, for a meat-offering:

50 One golden spoon of ten *shekels*, full of incense:

51 One young bullock, one ram, one lamb of the first year, for a burnt-offering;

52 One kid of the goats for a sin-offering:

53 And for a sacrifice of peace-offerings, two oxen, five rams, five he-goats, five lambs of the first year. This *was* the offering of Elishama, the son of Ammihud.

54 On the eighth day *offered* [a] Gamaliel, the son of Pedahzur, prince of the children of Manasseh:

55 His offering [b] *was* one silver charger, of the weight of an hundred and thirty *shekels*, one silver bowl of seventy shekels, after the shekel of the sanctuary; both of them full of fine flour mingled with oil, for a meat-offering:

56 One golden spoon of ten *shekels*, full of incense:

57 One young bullock, one ram, one lamb of the first year, for a burnt-offering:

58 One kid of the goats for a sin-offering:

59 And for a sacrifice of peace-offerings, two oxen, five rams, five he-goats, five lambs of the first year. This *was* the offering of Gamaliel, the son of Pedahzur.

60 On the ninth day Abidan [c], the son of Gideoni, prince of the children of Benjamin, *offered:*

61 His offering [d] *was* one silver charger, the weight whereof *was* an hundred and thirty *shekels*, one silver bowl of seventy shekels, after the shekel of the sanctuary; both of them full of fine flour mingled with oil, for a meat-offering:

62 One golden spoon of ten *shekels*, full of incense:

63 One young bullock, one ram, one lamb of the first year, for a burnt-offering:

64 One kid of the goats for a sin-offering:

65 And for a sacrifice of peace-offerings, two oxen, five rams, five he-goats, five lambs of the first year. This *was* the offering of Abidan, the son of Gideoni.

66 On the tenth day Ahie-

y c. 1. 10. 2. 18. *z* ver. 13, etc. *a* c. 1 10. 2. 20. *b* ver. 13, etc.

c c. 1. 11. 2. 22. *d* ver. 13, etc.

---

when set before us in written recital, was presumed to be productive of a somewhat similar effect.

V. 48. *On the seventh day.* As twelve days were occupied in the celebration, one, or perhaps two sabbaths must have intervened in the time, and yet it appears that the ceremonies suffered no interruption on that account. But the Lord is "Lord also of the sabbath," and

zer [e], the son of Ammishaddai, prince of the children of Dan, *offered:*

67 His offering [f] *was* one silver charger, the weight whereof *was* an hundred and thirty *shekels*, one silver bowl of seventy shekels, after the shekel of the sanctuary; both of them full of fine flour mingled with oil, for a meat-offering:

68 One golden spoon of ten *shekels*, full of incense:

69 One young bullock, one ram, one lamb of the first year, for a burnt-offering:

70 One kid of the goats for a sin-offering:

71 And for a sacrifice of peace-offerings, two oxen, five rams, five he-goats, five lambs of the first year. This *was* the offering of Ahiezer, the son of Ammishaddai.

72 On the eleventh day Pagiel [g], the son of Ocran, prince of the children of Asher, *offered:*

73 His offering [h] *was* one silver charger, the weight whereof *was* an hundred and thirty *shekels*, one silver bowl of seventy shekels, after the shekel of the sanctuary; both of them full of fine flour mingled with oil, for a meat-offering:

74 One golden spoon of ten *shekels*, full of incense.

e c. 1. 12. 2. 25. *f* ver. 13, etc. *g* c. 1. 13. 2. 27. *h* v. 13, etc.

75 One young bullock, one ram, one lamb of the first year, for a burnt-offering:

76 One kid of the goats for a sin-offering:

77 And for a sacrifice of peace-offerings, two oxen, five rams, five he-goats, five lambs of the first year. This *was* the offering of Pagiel the son of Ocran.

78 On the twelfth day Ahira [i] the son of Enan, prince of the children of Naphtali, *offered:*

79 His offering [k] *was* one silver charger, the weight whereof *was* an hundred and thirty *shekels*, one silver bowl of seventy shekels, after the shekel of the sanctuary; both of them full of fine flour mingled with oil, for a meat-offering:

80 One golden spoon of ten *shekels*, full of incense:

81 One young bullock, one ram, one lamb of the first year, for a burnt-offering:

82 One kid of the goats for a sin-offering:

83 And for a sacrifice of peace-offerings, two oxen, five rams, five he-goats, five lambs of the first year. This *was* the offering of Ahira, the son of Enan.

84 This *was* the dedication of the altar, in the day when it

i c. 1. 15. 2. 29. *k* ver. 13, etc.

---

the work which he himself appoints for that day is holy work, suitable for that sacred season.

V. 84. *This was the dedication of the altar.* Targ. Jon. "This was the dedication of the anointing of the altar." It was dedicated by the oblations and sacrifices above recited, which, though simple and plain, were of great value, leaving us to infer that we are to serve

was anointed, by the princes of Israel: twelve chargers of silver, twelve silver bowls, twelve spoons of gold;

85 Each charger of silver *weighing* an hundred and thirty *shekels*, each bowl seventy: all the silver vessels *weighed* two thousand and four hundred *shekels*, after the shekel of the sanctuary:

86 The golden spoons *were* twelve, full of incense, *weighing* ten *shekels* apiece, after the shekel of the sanctuary: all the gold of the spoons *was* an hundred and twenty *shekels*.

87 All the oxen for the burnt-offering *were* twelve bullocks, the rams twelve, the lambs of the first year twelve, with their meat-offering: and the kids of the goats for sin-offering, twelve.

88 And all the oxen for the sacrifice of the peace-offerings *were* twenty and four bullocks, the rams sixty, the he-goats sixty, the lambs of the first year sixty. This *was* the dedication

---

God with the chiefest and choicest of our possessions, and that too in a large and liberal spirit. Comp. Ex. 25:22. ——¶ *In the day when it was anointed.* That is, at or about the time when it was anointed, for as the pageant occupied twelve days, the term "day" must of course be taken in an extended sense. "*When* it was anointed," is plainly equivalent to "*after* it was anointed."

V. 85. *All the silver vessels weighed, etc.* The sum total of all these various offerings in silver, gold, and cattle, may be thus exhibited:—

12 Silver Chargers, each	130	shekels.
12 Silver Bowls,	" 70	"
12 Gold Spoons,	" 10	"
Total Shekels of Silver,		2400
" " of Gold,		120

Of beasts for sacrifice:

Bullocks,	12
Rams,	12
Lambs,	12
Goats,	24
Rams,	60
He-Goats,	60
Lambs,	60
Total,	240

"By this," says Adam Clarke, "it is easy to see, that though the place in which they now sojourned was a wilderness, as to cities, villages, and regular inhabitants, yet there was plenty of pasturage, else the Israelites could not have furnished these cattle, with all the sacrifices necessary for different occasions, and especially for the passover, which was celebrated during their sojourning in the desert, and which itself must have required an immense number of lambs, when each family of 600,000 males was obliged to provide one," (ch. 9.) It is not, however, to be disguised, that there are serious difficulties to be encountered in the attempt to show how such a vast multitude of cattle as would be requisite for the purposes of the people of Israel could be subsisted in this desert, rocky region. Mr. Stanley, in his recent work on Sinai and Palestine, alludes to this subject, and though he does not consider any solution of the problem yet given as wholly satisfactory, yet he offers several suggestions calculated greatly to weaken the force of the objections brought against the Mosaic history on this score. He remarks, that there is abundant evidence that the resources

of the altar, after that it was anointed [l].

89 And when Moses was gone into the tabernacle of the congregation to [m] speak with him, then he heard the voice of one speaking unto him from off the mercy-seat [n] that *was* upon the ark of testimony, from between the two cherubims: and he spake unto him.

l ver. 1. *m* c. 12. 8. Ex. 33. 9, 11. *n* Ex. 25. 22.

CHAPTER VIII.

AND the LORD spake unto Moses, saying,
2 Speak unto Aaron, and say unto him, When thou lightest the lamps[a], the seven lamps shall give light over against the candlestick.
3 And Aaron did so: he lighted the lamps thereof over against the candlestick, as the LORD commanded Moses.

a Ex. 25. 37. 40. 25.

---

of the peninsula were anciently far greater than they are now.

V. 89. *And when Moses was gone into, etc.* Heb. *bebo Mosheh, in Moses' going in.* The meaning undoubtedly is, that from this time henceforth, whenever Moses went into the Tabernacle to consult the divine oracle, he was privileged to hear the voice speaking to him, as here described.——¶ *To speak with him.* That is, with God.——¶ *Heard the voice of one speaking with him.* Gr. "Heard the voice of the Lord speaking." Targ. Jon. "Heard the voice of the Spirit speaking." This was in accordance with the prerogative vouchsafed to Moses of being admitted to more intimate converse with the Lord than any of the rest of the prophets. See ch. 12:8.——¶ *From off the mercy-seat.* Heb. "From above the mercy-seat." In this was fulfilled the promise made Ex. 25:21, 22, "And thou shalt put the mercy-seat above upon the ark —— and there I will meet with thee, and I will commune with thee from above the mercy-seat, from between the two cherubims." For this reason, the most holy place of the Sanctuary, where the ark and the mercy-seat were stationed, was called *debir, speaking-place* or *oracle,* from the root *dābar, to speak.* Into this sacred recess Moses alone was then thus privileged to enter. But now every Christian has in effect all the rights that Moses had. The humblest believer is a priest in the truest and only existing sense of the word; and has access as a priest into the immediate presence of God. The monopoly of the few is now the privilege of all mankind that believe. The narrow gate that once gave access to a single nation, is now opened so wide that all nations may pass freely through it.

CHAPTER VIII.

The Lighting of the Lamps and the Workmanship of the Candlestick.

V. 2. *When thou lightest the lamps.* Heb. "In thy causing the lamps to ascend." See the import of this phrase fully explained in the Notes on Ex. 25:37. Gr. "When thou shalt set up, or put up, the lamps." Chald. "When thou shalt kindle the lamps." The lamps or sconces containing the oil, were so constructed as to be capable of being detached, and taken down from the branches, to be filled and then *raised up* (*made to ascend*) to their proper places on the candlestick.——¶ *Shall give their light over against the candlestick.* Heb. "Over against the face (lit. faces) of the candlestick." The meaning is not entirely obvious from the literal rendering, but the explanations drawn from the Rabbinical comments throw a satisfactory light upon it. "Over against the candlestick" we take to be equivalent to "towards the central shaft," for the term "candlestick" is occasionally applied by way of eminence to the shaft from which the branches issued. See Notes on Ex. 25 : 31–37. At other times it stands for the whole structure. The meaning undoubtedly is, that the wicks should be so disposed in the lamp-cups or sconces that they should incline to the edge nearest the centre, and thus should shine towards the candlestick emphatically so called. The central lamp, it is supposed, was lighted from the fire of the altar, and all the others from that. We give in this connection the form of the candlestick as we have been enabled to deduce it from the words of the sacred historian, as contained Ex. 25 : 31–40.

CANDLESTICK.

The Hebrew doctors say, "The six lamps that were fastened unto the six branches that went out of the candlestick, all of them had their faces towards the middlemost lamp which was on the branch (the shaft) of the candlestick; and this middlemost lamp, the face of it was towards the Most Holy Place, and it is called the western lamp."—*Maimonides.* In like manner Sol. Jarchi says, "Over against the face of the candlestick, that is, the middle lamp, which is none of the branches, but of the body of the candlestick. The seven lamps shall give light; the six which are upon the six branches, the three that are eastward having the wicks in them turned towards the middlemost; and so the three that are westward having the tops of the wicks towards the middlemost." The same thing is briefly expressed in the latter clause of Ex. 25 : 37. It is indeed said that "the *seven* lamps shall give their light" in the manner above described, but we are still at liberty to understand this with the due discrimination as implying that the words strictly considered hold good

4 And this work of the [b] candlestick *was of* beaten gold, unto the shaft thereof, unto the flowers thereof, *was* [c] beaten work: according unto the pattern [d] which the LORD had showed Moses, so he made the candlestick.

b Ex. 25. 31. *c* Ex. 25. 18. *d* Ex. 25. 40.

of the *six* branches only in their relation to the central shaft. Similar modes of diction could easily be cited. Thus, what our Lord says of the twelve apostles sitting upon twelve thrones and judging the twelve tribes of Israel, must be understood as exclusive of Judas. The opposite interpretation to this is, that by giving light over against the candlestick is meant, causing the light to fall upon the north side of the Tabernacle, especially illuminating the table of show-bread, whereas the candlestick itself stood upon the south side. This is the sense affixed to the passage by the Vulg., which, however, is rather a paraphrase than a translation:—"When thou shalt place seven lamps, let the candlestick be set up on the south side. Give orders, therefore, that the lamps look over against the north, towards the table of the loaves of proposition; over against that part shall they give light, towards which the candlestick looketh." For ourselves, we give a decided preference to the other construction. The typical bearing of the candlestick with its lamps is largely unfolded in our Notes on Ex. 25:31–37, and in consistency with that the suggestion flows easily from what is here said, that as the central shaft more especially represents the Lord the Saviour, who is to the church what the vine is to the branches, and as whatever of spiritual light and heat is possessed by his ministering servants flows from him, so it is eminently proper that they should by a reciprocal turning or inclination, reflect their light towards its divine source, as in grateful acknowledgment of its derivation therefrom.

V. 4. *And this work of the candlestick (was of) beaten gold.* Or, as the Heb. will admit, "This was the work of the candlestick, (viz. it was) beaten gold," etc. For a detailed account of the fabrication of the candlestick, see Ex. 25:18, 31–39. 37:17–24, where, in our Notes, we have endeavored to show that the epithet "beaten" implies simply *hard, solid,* as the Gr. has it, and that it implies the *nature of the material* and not the *mode of construction.* The candlestick with the branches, bowls, knops, and flowers, was constructed of one piece, although not by beating or hammering, but the lamps were formed apart, like the tongs and snuff-dishes. So one of the Rabbinists says, "The lamps were vessels by themselves, and might be removed from the branches."—*Chazkuni.*——¶ *Unto the shaft thereof, etc.* That is, both the shaft and the flowers. The word "unto" is equivalent to "including," and the clause is thus expounded by Sol. Jarchi:—"As if he should say, the body of the candlestick, all of it, and all that pertained to it."——¶ *According unto the pattern.* Heb. *kammareh, according to the sight, show, vision, appearance;* the word being derived directly from the root *rââh, to see.* The reference, however, is undoubtedly to the visionary pattern or model exhibited to Moses in the mount, Ex. 25:40, although in this latter passage the original word for *pattern* is *tabnith,* and not that which is here so rendered.——¶ *Which the Lord had showed Moses.* Heb. "Which the Lord had caused Moses to see." The phraseology of the Hebrew implies a peculiar effect wrought upon

5 And the LORD spake unto Moses, saying,
6 Take the Levites from among the children of Israel, and cleanse them.
7 And thus shalt thou do unto them, to cleanse them: Sprinkle water [e] of purifying upon them, and [f] let them shave

[e] c. 19. 9, 17, etc. [f] Lev. 14. 8, 9.

---

his interior vision, by which he was enabled to behold what otherwise would have been beyond his power. He was favored with a spiritual perception. The objects seen were seen by the inward and not by the outward eye, and to this he was incompetent unless the Lord had *made* him to see.

The Consecration of the Levites.

V. 6. *Take the Levites, etc.* That is, not the whole body of the Levites, but all besides the priests, who had been consecrated on a former occasion, Lev. 8. To them the other Levites were to be adjoined as ministers and assistants, ch. 3 : 6, etc., and *their* consecration forms the subject of the present chapter.——¶ *From among the children of Israel.* We see in this the basis of the familiar distinction of the chosen people into the different classes mentioned 1 Chron. 9 : 2, "The Israelites, the priests, Levites, and the Nethinims." ——¶ *And cleanse them.* Or, "purify them," i. e. in the manner about to be described. Although it was required, as a general rule, that all the people, when they approached the sanctuary, should be free from any ceremonial uncleanness, 2 Chron. 23 : 19, yet there was a manifest propriety in the ministers of the Lord's house complying with the words of the prophet, Is. 52 : 11, "Be ye clean that bear the vessels of the Lord;" and such a purification was represented by this external washing of the body in water. So the apostle makes "pureness" one of the requisite characteristics by which the ministry is to be distinguished, 2 Cor. 6 : 4, 6. "The mere circumstance of birth did not entitle the Levites to enter abruptly upon the duties which devolved on them. They were to receive a sort of consecration, which is described in this chapter, and which, although solemn, is different from, and more simple than, that which the priests received. They were properly purified by sprinkling and shaving, and after suitable offerings and sacrifices, were presented before the Lord. They were not washed, or anointed, or invested with official robes, like the priests."—*Pict. Bible.*

V. 7. *Sprinkle water of purifying upon them.* Heb. "Sprinkle upon them the sin-water;" that is, the water of purification from sin; which we learn from ch. 19 : 9, 10, was prepared from the ashes of a red heifer, cedar-wood, hyssop, and scarlet. It is called "sin-water" (Heb. *më 'hattaath, waters of sin*) as the sacrifice of atonement for sin is called "sin-offering." Indeed, we may say with Adam Clarke, that as the heifer herself was sacrificed, and her blood sprinkled seven times before the Tabernacle, ch. 19 : 3–6, she may be considered as a proper *sacrifice for sin*, and consequently the water thus prepared be termed the *water of the sin-offering.* "As the *ashes* were kept ready at hand for purifying from all legal pollutions, the preparation might be considered as a *concentration* of the essential properties of the sin-offering, and might be resorted to at all times with comparatively little expense or trouble, and no loss of time. As there were so many things by which legal pollution might be contracted, it was

all their flesh, and let them wash their clothes, and *so* make themselves clean.

8 Then let them take a young bullock with his meat-offering [g], *even* fine flour mingled with oil, and another young bullock shalt thou take for a sin-offering.

g Lev. 2. 1.

---

necessary to have always at hand, in all their dwellings, a mode of purifying at once convenient and unexpensive. As the *water* by which the Levites were here purified must have been the water prepared from the ashes of the red heifer, this ordinance was undoubtedly instituted *before* this time, though not described till chap. 19 : 1–10 of this book; but that chapter might be in connection with any of the preceding ordinances, as well as where it is now found."—*A. Clarke.*——¶ *Let them shave all their flesh.* Gr. "Let them shave all their body." "Let a razor go over their whole body."—*Cov.* "Make a razor to run along upon all the flesh of them."—*Mat., Cran.* "Let them cause a razor to pass over all their flesh."—*Ains.* This was another symbol of purification similar to that of the leper, who shaved off all his hair as well as washed his flesh, as a part of the process of his cleansing, Lev. 14 : 8, 9. The same ceremony was ordained also in the case of the polluted Nazarite, ch. 6 : 9. One of the Hebrew doctors remarks, that there was a moral significancy in the act, to wit, that the Levites were thereby admonished "to cast away all worldly cares, as much as might be, and give themselves wholly to their sacred ministry." The example may also be properly understood as teaching that all Christians, and especially all Christian ministers, should "purify themselves from all filthiness of flesh and spirit, perfecting holiness in the fear of God," 2 Cor. 7 : 1. It is worthy of remark, that Herodotus says expressly of the Egyptian priests, that they shave their whole body every third day, lest any vermin or other foulness should cleave to the worshippers of the gods. As to the Levites, it does not appear that the direction here given was to be observed except on special occasions.——¶ *Let them wash their clothes.* Another rite prescribed in purifying the unclean. Comp. Ex. 19 : 10, in allusion to which it is said of the redeemed, Rev. 7 : 9, 14, 15, their garments are "washed and made white in the blood of the Lamb," that they may "serve him day and night in his temple."

V. 8. *Let them take a young bullock.* Heb. "A youngling the son of the herd." That is, of the second year. See Note on Ex. 29 : 1, where the same offering was brought for the priests. This was to constitute a burnt-offering or holocaust "to make an atonement for the Levites, and as the Jewish Rabbins say, "For the consecration of their service."——¶ *With his meal-offering.* That is, meal-offering, composed of fine flour mingled with oil, and which was understood to be an accompaniment of course of the burnt-offering. The ordinary meal-offering for a bullock was "three-tenth deals of fine flour mingled with oil," and for a drink offering "half a hin of wine," ch. 28 : 12, 14. See Notes on Lev. 2.——¶ *Another young bullock.* Heb. "A second bullock the son of the herd." This, though mentioned second, was offered first, v. 12. Lev. 8 : 14, 18. 14 : 19. The only case in which a bullock was offered for a sin-offering was that in which the priest, and through him the whole congregation had sinned, Lev. 4 : 3, 13, 14, 22, 23, and the reason

9 And [h] thou shalt bring the Levites before the tabernacle of the congregation: and [i] thou shalt gather the whole assembly of the children of Israel together:
10 And thou shalt bring the Levites before the LORD: and the children of Israel shall put [k] their hands upon the Levites:
11 And Aaron shall offer [l] the Levites before the LORD *for* an offering of the children of Is-

h Ex. 29. 4, etc. 40. 12. *i* Lev. 8. 3 *k* Lev. 1. 4. *l* ver. 15.

that this kind of offering was made on this occasion was, that it was offered for the Levites in a body who represented, as it were, the whole congregation.

V. 9. *And thou shalt bring the Levites.* Heb. *hikrabtâ, thou shalt bring near*, or *cause to approach;* a sacrificial term almost constantly in use in speaking of the offerings made upon the altar. It denotes that the Levites were viewed in the light of a species of sacrifice dedicated and devoted to the Lord. For this purpose they were to be brought like other sacrifices to the door of the tabernacle, which is usually to be understood by the phrase "before the Lord."——¶ *Thou shalt gather the whole assembly.* The occasion was one in which the whole body of the people were equally interested, for the Levites being now to be taken for the first-born, it was proper that the whole congregation should signify their concurrence in the transaction. This was according to the established rule in law, *Quod omnium interest, ab omnibus fieri debet, what concerns all ought to be done by all.* In like manner the congregation was assembled at the consecration of the priests, Lev. 8:3, 4.

V. 10. *The children of Israel shall put their hands upon the Levites.* Heb. *sâmeku, shall lean* their hands, etc. That is, not the whole body of the people, but some of the chief of them, the elders, in the name of the rest. Ainsworth suggests from Chuzkuni that the first-born performed that office, as the Levites were substituted in their place and made atonement for them, vs. 18, 19. The act of imposition of hands in this instance denoted a certain kind of transfer from one party to another of a right, function, or prerogative which originally pertained to the transferring party. The act, therefore, as Mr. Kitto suggests, had virtually the same significancy as that of the Levites in laying *their* hands on the bullocks which were to be sacrificed for them (v. 12), or to suffer and die for them; and the application from the first-born to the Levites would express, not only the consecration of the latter, but their substitution to attend to the service of the sanctuary in the room of the first-born. The Levites represented typically the ministers in the Christian church; and the transaction before us carries with it the implication, that the functions which they discharge are inherently appropriate to the whole body to which they pertain, and that it was never intended that they should be absolutely and entirely alienated to a particular class perpetuating itself by an ordination rite in which the people at large have no share. Even when the imposition of hands devolves upon those who have been themselves set apart in this manner, it should still be distinctly understood that the act is performed *in the name and behalf* of the mass of the people. Under the present dispensation all true Christians are "kings and priests unto God," and they should not lightly part with their birthright.

V. 11. *And Aaron shall offer the Le-*

rael, that they may execute the service of the LORD.

12 And the Levites shall lay their hands upon the heads of the bullocks: and thou shalt offer the one *for* a sin-offering,

---

vites, etc. Heb. *hĕniph, shall wave.* A sacrificial term applied to the wave-offering, respecting which see Notes on Ex. 29:23–28. The original is rendered in the Gr. by *aphoriei, shall separate,* which is transferred into the N. T. in reference to the *setting apart* of Barnabas and Saul (Paul) for the work to which the Lord had called them, Acts 13:2. In like manner Paul speaks of himself, Rom. 1:1, as "*separated* unto the Gospel of God." As the leading idea of the Heb. term is that of *agitation,* so the Gr. applied to ministers and apostles denotes more than simple separation, viz., the trials, tossings, and afflictions which, for the most part, should accompany their dedication to the special service of the Lord and the church. The rendering of the Arab. is here remarkable:—"And Aaron shall lead them about by a circuitous leading," implying that they were conducted about through the camp, somewhat as in the East a bride is conducted in a procession from her father's house to the house of the bridegroom, to whom she is ever after to be solemnly dedicated and devoted. The agitation or waving to and fro indicated by the original Heb. term implied the solemn consecration of the things waved to God, as a sacrifice; and therefore the Levites were presented to him under the same consideration as were the first-born. As, however, it was impossible for Aaron to wave them as he did the ordinary sacrifices, and yet the term would seem to express something which he did to them, it is not unlikely that they were made to perform some kind of locomotion, although it might not have been precisely that indicated by the Arabic version. Patrick suggests, that Aaron "lifting up his hands, and turning about to all sides, as he did when he offered a wave-offering, they, at his command, imitated the same motion, and so were offered up to God, and became wholly his." Le Clerc, however, conjectures that they were led round about the altar, thus favoring the construction of the Arabic, which we on the whole are inclined to adopt.——¶ *For an offering.* Heb. *tenuphâh, a wave-offering.* See Note on ch. 3:6. Gr. *apodoma, a gift,* as the ministers of the church are also called Eph. 4:8, 11.——¶ *That they may execute the service.* Heb. "That they may serve the service." Gr. "That they may be to work, or do, the works of the Lord;" as also in v. 15. The same phraseology occurs in the original of 1 Cor. 16:10, "For he worketh the work of the Lord, as I also do." The language of 1 Cor. 9:13, is equivalent:—"Do ye not know that they which minister about holy things, live," etc.

V. 12. *Shall lay their hands upon the heads.* Heb. "Upon the head," sing. doubtless because the ceremony was performed upon the head of each one separately.——¶ *Thou shalt offer.* Heb. "Thou shalt do." See Note on ch. 6: 11, 16, 17. As the words are addressed to Moses, the meaning is, that he should cause the sacrifice to be offered by the hands of Aaron the priest. There is something which strikes us as very plausible in the suggestion of Vitringa and Patrick, that the Levites were themselves considered in this transaction as an *expiatory sacrifice;* for being given to God instead of the first-born, in the sanctification of whom the whole family was sanctified, and their sin in a certain sense expiated, the offering of the Le-

and the other *for* a burnt-offering, unto the LORD, to make an atonement for the Levites.

13 And thou shalt set the Levites before Aaron, and before his sons, and offer them *for* an offering unto the LORD.

14 Thus shalt thou separate [m] the Levites from among the children of Israel: and the Levites shall be mine [n].

15 And after that shall the Levites go in to do the service of the tabernacle of the congregation: and thou shalt cleanse them, and offer [o] them *for* an offering.

16 For they *are* wholly given

m c. 16. 9.

n c. 3. 45. o ver. 11, 13.

vites in this manner was to be considered as having the same effect as had the offering of the first-born, viz. the sanctification and atonement of the people at large. This idea seems to be countenanced by the phraseology of v. 19, "to make atonement for the children of Israel," which may properly be understood as equivalent to making atonement *in behalf* of the children of Israel, i. e. viewing the Levites themselves as the atoning sacrifice, and not the ministers by whom it is made. In the present verse the Levites are evidently regarded as a sacrificial offering, and yet, as they were not devoted to death, any more than the first-born, but still lived, therefore the sin-offering and the burnt-offering were substituted in their stead. Upon these they accordingly laid their hands, that the sin which the children of Israel laid upon them (v. 10) might in the same way be transferred to the victims, which thus became the real sacrifices. The soundness of the proposed interpretation will depend upon the true import of the phrase *lekappër al, to make atonement upon, for*, or *in behalf of*, whether it refers to the sacrifice or to the sacrificer. We incline, though not without some wavering, to the former. As to the actual usage, there is no doubt that the making atonement is predicated both of sacrifice and of the officiating priest.

V. 13. *And thou shalt set.* Heb. "Thou shalt cause to stand," i. e. thou shalt present, as a token of their being given to him and to his sons, as in v. 19. See also ch. 5:16, 18, 30.——¶ *And offer them (for) an offering unto the Lord.* Heb. "And thou shalt wave them (as) a wave-offering." This sense of the original makes it probable that the true rendering is, "*After* thou hast waved them for a wave-offering," implying that they were presented to Aaron and his sons after having been thus offered to the Lord. It is doubtless in allusion to this that Paul, in writing to the Romans, says, "I beseech you, brethren, by the mercies of God, that ye present your bodies *a living sacrifice*, holy, acceptable unto God, which is your reasonable service."

V. 14. *The Levites shall be mine.* Chald. "Shall be ministers before me." See Note on ch. 16:9.

V. 15. *And thou shalt cleanse them and offer them.* Heb. "Wave them." Gr. "Give them before the Lord." As this is evidently no new order for their cleansing, the sense is unquestionably, "Thou having cleansed them, and offered them." See vs. 7, 11.

V. 16. *For they (are) wholly given unto me.* Heb. "For they are Nethinim, Nethinim to me;" repeated for the sake of emphasis. On the import of "Nethinim" see Note on ch. 3:9. Gr. "For these are given to me for a present."

unto me from among the children of Israel; instead [p] of such
as open every womb, *even instead of* the first-born of all the
children of Israel, have I taken
them unto me.
17 For all the first-born [q] of
the children of Israel *are* mine,
both man and beast: on the day
that I smote every first-born in
the land of Egypt I sanctified
them for myself.
18 And I have taken the Levites for all the first-born of the
children of Israel.
19 And I have given [r] the
Levites *as* a gift to Aaron and
to his sons from among the children of Israel, to do the service
of the children of Israel in the
tabernacle of the congregation,
and to make an atonement for
the children of Israel: that [s]
there be no plague among the
children of Israel, when the
children of Israel come nigh
unto the sanctuary.
20 And Moses, and Aaron,
and all the congregation of the
children of Israel, did to the
Levites according unto all that
the LORD commanded Moses

p c. 3. 12, 45. Luke 2. 23. q Ex. 13. 2, 12–15. c. 3. 13. r c. 3. 9.

s c. 1. 53. c. 16. 46. 18. 5. 2 Chr. 26. 16.

——¶ *Instead of such as open every womb.* Heb. "Instead of the opening of every womb;" on which phraseology see Note on ch. 3 : 12. The ensuing phrase, "first-born," is in apposition with this and explanatory of it.

V. 19. *And I have given the Levites (as) a gift.* Heb. "And I have given the Levites as Nethinim." Gr. "And I have given the Levites presented as a gift." Being first solemnly set apart and dedicated to the Lord, they are now given back by him to the donors, teaching us, that whatever we give up to the Lord in the spirit of a grateful surrender, will be sure to be returned to us with interest.——¶ *To do the service of the children of Israel.* Heb. "To serve the service." Gr. "To do the works." Vulg. "To serve me for Israel," i. e. to serve me in the holy rites instead of Israel themselves. The service of the children of Israel is the service which they would have been required to perform had not the Levites been chosen in their stead.——¶ *To make an atonement.* Heb. *lekappër, to make atonement.* The insertion of the particle "an" is superfluous, as the word expresses a continuous function. It confirms the interpretation suggested above, v. 12, that the making atonement by the act of sacrificing was not the province of the Levites, but of the priests. They were to serve as a kind of perpetual medium of atonement.——¶ *That there be no plague, etc.* Chald. "No death." That is, that the people may be secured from the stroke of divine judgments by every thing being done in exact accordance with the prescribed order, all others except the proper commissioned persons being precluded from officiating in and about the Tabernacle. This plainly teaches that the surest preservation against disastrous visitations is a strict compliance with the divine injunctions. Germane to this is the case of Phineas, ch. 25 : 7, 8, 13, who, in slaying the offenders "stayed the plague," and is thereupon said to have "made an atonement for the children of Israel."——¶ *When the children of Israel come nigh unto the sanctuary.* Heb. *el hakkodesh, unto the holiness;* that is, to the place and to the

concerning the Levites, so did
the children of Israel unto them.
21 And the Levites were
[t] purified, and they washed their
clothes; and Aaron offered [u]
them *as* an offering before the
LORD; and Aaron made an
atonement for them to cleanse
them.
22 And after [v] that went the
Levites in to do their service in
the tabernacle of the congregation before Aaron, and before his
sons: as [w] the LORD had commanded Moses concerning the
Levites, so did they unto them.
23 And the LORD spake unto
Moses, saying,
24 This *is it* that *belongeth*
unto the Levites: from [x] twenty
and five years old and upward
they shall go in to wait upon
the service of the tabernacle of
the congregation.

t ver. 7. *u* ver. 11, 12. *v* ver. 15. *w* ver. 5, etc. *x* c. 4. 3. 1 Chr. 23. 3, 27.

---

things of holiness, which the Gr. renders *pros hagia, to the holinesses.* The danger incurred by the infraction of this command is impressively taught, Lev. 10:1. 1 Chron. 13:20.

V. 21. *And the Levites were purified.* Heb. *yithhatte-u, purified themselves,* or, "had themselves purified." That is, from sin, as the original root signifies, of which the outward rite was the sprinkling of sin-water upon them, v. 7.——¶ *And Aaron offered them as an offering.* Heb. "Waved them (as) a wave-offering." See on v. 12. Gr. "Gave them as a gift."——¶ *And Aaron made an atonement for them to cleanse them.* Heb. *letaharâm*, a different word from that above rendered "purified." The term "cleanse" expresses the effect produced upon the subjects of the "atonement," which in the first instance involves the idea of "reconciliation." But in our relations with the Most High, we are not to be content with the mere fact of expiation; we are to aim at moral purification as the ultimate end contemplated by atonement.

V. 22. *After that went the Levites in, etc.* In conformity with the directions given above, v. 15.——¶ *To do their service.* Heb. "To serve their service." Gr. *leitourgein tēn leitourgian autōn, to liturgize their liturgy*, i. e. to minister their ministry. See Note on ch. 4:3.——¶ *Before Aaron and before his sons.* In their presence, and by their direction, just as they themselves ministered "before the Lord."

The Age at which the Levites' Service was to commence, and the Period of its Continuance.

V. 24. *This (is it) that (belongeth) unto the Levites.* That is to say, add this to what has been already prescribed concerning them.——¶ *From twenty and five years old.* Heb. "From a son of twenty-five years." So also in v. 25. The meaning is, that from this period they might enter upon their service, and perform its lighter labors, such as taking care of the Tabernacle, excluding strangers and the unclean, etc., but were not to assume the heavier duties, such as loading or unloading the wagons, transporting the materials, and the like, for this required that they should have attained the age of thirty, as appears from ch. 4:3.——¶ *They shall go in to wait upon the service.* Heb. "He (i. e. every one) shall go in to war the warfare in the service." Upon this phraseology see Note on ch. 4:3, 23. Gr. *energein, to energize, to work vigorously.*

25 And from the age of fifty years they shall cease waiting upon the service *thereof*, and shall serve no more:
26 But shall minister with their brethren in the tabernacle of the congregation, to keep [y] the charge, and shall do no service[z]. Thus shalt thou do unto the Levites touching their charge.

CHAPTER IX.

AND the LORD spake unto Moses in the wilderness of

y c. 1. 53. 18. 4. 1 Chr. 23. 32. Ezek. 44. 8, 11.

z 1 Tim. 4. 15.

V. 25. *From the age of fifty years.* Heb. "From a son of fifty years." Precisely the same form of phraseology which occurs in the preceding verse, and which is there rendered, "from twenty and five years old."——¶ *They shall cease waiting upon the service.* Heb. "He (i. e. every one) shall return from the warfare of the service;" that is, shall return home, withdrawing from the service of the Tabernacle. Gr. *apostēsetai, shall stand away, withhold himself from, his liturgy (ministry).* The verb occurs in the original of Luke 2:37, where it is said of Anna the prophetess, that she "*departed* not from the temple." The import doubtless is, that from this time they were to cease from the hardier and heavier labors of the sanctuary, such as the transportation, etc., though they might still perform the lighter ministrations. "That which is spoken in the law of the Levites from fifty years old, that 'he shall return,' etc., is not meant but for the time that they carried the Sanctuary from place to place, and it is not a commandment of force in the generations following. But in the subsequent ages a Levite was not disallowable by years, neither by blemishes, but by voice; when his voice failed by reason of extreme old age, he was disabled from serving in the sanctuary. And it seemeth to me that he is not disallowable save for singing the song, but he might be of the porters."—*Maimonides.*

V. 26. *But shall minister with their brethren.* Heb. "But he shall minister with his brethren," sing. for plur. as above. This ministry is explained by what follows; it consisted in "keeping the charge," i. e. taking care of the Tabernacle, to which they were to serve as a kind of guard.——¶ *And shall do no service.* Heb. "And shall not serve the service;" by which is meant, they shall not be required to perform any more hard service, their age beginning to require ease and rest. This is confirmed by the Rabbinical glosses, the purport of which is, that the service here mentioned is the service of bearing the holy things on the shoulders, but they were to keep the charge (custody), to encamp round about the tent, to sing, and to beware that no stranger came into the Tabernacle.

CHAPTER IX.

The Passover again commanded, with a special Qualification.

V. 1. *And the Lord spake unto Moses.* Or, Heb. "The Lord had said," for it is quite obvious that the transactions referred to in the first fourteen verses of this chapter took place prior to the numbering of the people recorded in the first two chapters of the book. The command for numbering and ordering of the tribes there related was given on "the first day of the *second month,*" ch. 1:1, 2. This it appears was issued

Sinai, in the first month of the
second year after they were come
out of the land of Egypt, saying,
2 Let the children of Israel
also keep the passover at his appointed season [a],
3 In the fourteenth [b] day of
this month, at even, ye shall

a Ex. 12. 3. Deut. 16. 1. b 2 Chr. 30. 2, 15.

"in the *first month.*" But it is no unusual thing to find such transpositions in the sacred writers. One of the Hebrew doctors observes, "There is no order of former and latter in the Law." And Houbigant says, "It is enough to know that these books contain an account of things transacted in the days of Moses, though not in their regular or chronological order." The order concerning the passover is recorded here simply as an introduction to the rule prescribed for such as had been prevented, by a particular cause, from keeping the passover at the proper time. The law respecting pollution by a dead body was given subsequent to the law respecting the passover, and hence a new question arose which had to be settled. It is in connection with the decision of this question that the reference to the original institution occurs. In this record we read, "And it shall come to pass, when ye be come to the land which the Lord will give you, according as he hath promised, that ye shall keep this service." The rite was indeed once observed in Egypt on the night of their departure, but as there was no express intimation that it was to be kept in the desert, a special divine warrant would be requisite for the purpose. Such a warrant was given on this occasion, and from Josh. 5 : 10–12, it would appear that no other passover was celebrated during the whole period of the wandering till they had entered the promised land.

V. 2. *Let the children of Israel keep the passover.* Heb. "Let the children of Israel make or do the passover." On the origin and import of the term "passover," see Note on Ex. 12 : 11——¶ *At his appointed season.* That is, on the fourteenth day of the first month, in memory of their signal deliverance from Egypt, as also of their exemption from the desolating judgment which befell the first-born of that country. Gr. "According to its hour." The Hebrew writers say that the occurrence of the Sabbath on the same day with the season of the passover was not to interfere with its observance.

V. 3. *In the fourteenth day of this month.* The narrative here is retrospective, and the "this month" designated is the first month, on which the Lord issued the command, and to which the reader is supposed to be carried back.——¶ *At even.* Heb. "Between the two evenings." That is, in the afternoon, between the time of the sun's beginning to decline, which was called the first evening, and that of his setting, which was called the second. See Note on Ex. 12 : 6. As the passover referred to the Lord as its substantial reality, so the hour of its being offered pointed forward to his coming "in these last days," Heb. 2 : 1, 2, that is, towards the evening of the world, and to the fact of his crucifixion at the ninth hour, or about three o'clock, P. M.——¶ *According to all the rites of it, etc.* Heb. "According to all the statutes of it." Gr. "According to the law thereof." That is, according to all the prescribed rites and ordinances, such, for instance, as those mentioned Ex. 12 : 43–50, where the very term here rendered "rites (*hukkāh*) occurs, and where the refer-

keep it in his appointed season: according to all the rites of it, and according to all the ceremonies thereof, shall ye keep it.
4 And Moses spake unto the children of Israel, that they should keep the passover.
5 And [c] they kept the passover on the fourteenth day of the first month, at even, in the wilderness of Sinai; according to all that the LORD commanded Moses, so did the children of Israel.
6 And there were certain men who were defiled [d] by the dead body of a man, that they could not keep the passover on that day: and [e] they came before Moses and before Aaron on that day:
7 And those men said unto him, We *are* defiled by the dead body of a man: wherefore are

c Josh. 5. 10.

d c. 5. 2. 19. 11, 16. John 18. 28. e Ex. 18. 15, 19. c. 27. 2, 5.

---

ence is principally had to the *persons* who were to partake of the passover. ——¶ *According to all the ceremonies thereof.* Heb. "According to all the judgments thereof." The import of the term "judgments" in this connection is not perfectly obvious. It is not improbably to be understood of the unleavened bread, bitter herbs, and other accompaniments by which it was to be distinguished. In the permanent obobservance of the passover certain specialities peculiar to the first institution, such as the sprinkling of the door-posts with blood, taking it in a standing posture, etc. were to be excepted.

V. 4. *That they should keep the passover.* Heb. "That they should make, or do, the passover," as frequently before. This, Ainsworth remarks, was for the sanctification of the whole body of the people in their own persons, as the priests and Levites had been sanctified to their several ministries.

V. 6. *And there were certain men who were defiled by the dead body of a man.* Heb. "Who were unclean by the soul of man;" a peculiar usage of the original, in regard to which see the Note on ch. 5:2. Vulg. "Behold some who were unclean by occasion of the soul of a man." The corresponding Gr. is ψυχη, *psychē*, *soul*, which is also rendered *dead body.* Persons thus defiled were unclean seven days, Lev. 19:11, were precluded access to the sanctuary, ch. 5:2, and were not allowed to eat of the holy things, Lev. 7:20. In the emergency that had thus arisen they had recourse to Moses and Aaron for directions what to do, as it devolved upon them to take cognizance of such cases, as appears from the tenor of Lev. 11:1, 2, etc. Yet it would seem that Moses was mainly appealed to, for he only answered.

V. 7. *Wherefore are we kept back?* Heb. *lâmâh niggâra, wherefore are we abated, abridged,* or *made to fall short?* The leading idea of the original is that of *diminution, curtailment,* and consequent *deprivation.* Vulg. "Wherefore are we defrauded?" Gr. "Shall we therefore fall short, or fail?" i. e. in regard to the privilege of offering, in which the original indicates a *want of fulness.* The demand was a reasonable one under the circumstances. Their defilement might have been involuntarily contracted by burying a dead body, which was still their duty, and why should this preclude them from participating in religious rites, to which they were disposed to pay a due regard? It is to be remembered that the law excluding the polluted from the camp, ch.

we kept back, that we may not offer an offering of the LORD in his appointed season among the children of Israel?

8 And Moses said unto them, Stand still, and I will hear what the LORD will command concerning you.

9 And the LORD spake unto Moses, saying,

10 Speak unto the children of Israel, saying, If any man of you or of your posterity shall be unclean by reason of a dead body, or *be* in a journey afar off, yet he shall keep the passover unto the LORD.

11 The fourteenth [f] day of the second month, at even, they

f ver. 3.

5:2, had not yet been enacted, although it would seem that some portion of the people, from an innate or anticipative impression of its indecorum, were disposed to debar them from the privilege. But as the command of observance was strict they found themselves in a dilemma. If they neglected to eat, they were liable to judgment; if they ate in their present circumstances, they were equally exposed. What should they do?——¶ *That we may not offer an offering of the Lord.* Heb. *korban Yehovah, the gift of Jehovah.* So called as being commanded by the Lord, and observed to his honor and glory, and termed therefore, Ex. 12:27, "the *sacrifice* of the Lord's passover." Gr. "The gift of the Lord."

V. 8. *Stand still.* Heb. *amdu, stand, stay;* i. e. wait in patient expectation. Chald. "Tarry till I hear." Vulg. "Stay till I consult the Lord." An intimation of profound deference to the divine will, in virtue of which he would venture upon no decision in a doubtful case without first consulting the Lord in his appointed way. The Targ. Jon. on this place remarks, that the judges of the Sanhedrim "should not be ashamed to ask concerning the judgment which is too hard for them; for Moses, who was the master of Israel, had need to say, 'I have not heard.'"

V. 10. *If any man of you be unclean.* Heb. "A man, a man, when he shall be unclean." The phrase "or of your posterity" occurs in the original in the latter part of the verse.——¶ *By reason of a dead body.* Heb. "Upon or for a soul." See Note on ch. 5:2. Gr. and Chald. "By the soul of a man," i. e. of a dead man, as v. 6. Targ. Jon. "By the pollution of a man that is dead." This specific case only is mentioned, but all similar ones seem to be included. ——¶ *Or be in a journey afar off.* Heb. "Away afar off." That is, at such a distance that he could not reach the tabernacle on the day appointed, or beyond the limits of his own country, for it appears from Deut. 12:5, 6. 16:2, that the passover could not be kept any where out of Judea. The Hebrew doctors make the least distance that could be called "a journey afar off" to be fifteen miles.

V. 11. *The fourteenth day of the second month.* It was therefore established by the Lord as a standing ordinance, that all such Israelites as, at the time of the passover-feast, were either under any legal defilement, or abroad at a considerable distance from the Tabernacle, or in circumstances which hindered their attendance upon it at the stated time, should have a *second* day appointed for its observance, viz. the fourteenth day of the second month, when it was to be celebrated by the parties concerned with the same ceremonies as it had been by the rest of the nation.——¶ *At*

shall keep it, and *eat* it with unleavened bread [g] and bitter *herbs*.

12 They shall leave none [h] of it unto the morning, nor break [i] any bone of it: according to all the ordinances of the passover they shall keep it.

13 But the man that *is* clean, and is not in a journey, and forbeareth to keep the passover, even the same soul [k] shall be cut off from among his people: because he brought not the offering of the LORD in his appointed [l] season, that man shall bear [m] his sin.

14 And if a stranger shall sojourn among you, and will keep the passover unto the LORD; according to the ordinance of the passover, and according to the manner thereof, so shall he do: ye shall have one [n] ordinance, both for the stranger, and for him that was born in the land.

15 And on the day that the tabernacle was reared up, the

g Ex. 12. 8. h Ex. 12. 10. i Ex. 12. 46. John 19. 36. k Ex. 12. 15. l ver. 7. m c. 5. 31. n Ex. 12. 49.

---

even. Heb. "Between the two evenings." See on v. 3. Gr. "Towards evening."——¶ *With unleavened bread and bitter herbs.* See Note on Ex. 12:8.

V. 12. *Shall leave none of it unto the morning.* If any were left till then it was to be burnt. See Note on Ex. 12: 10.——¶ *According to all the ordinances of the passover.* Heb. "According to the statute of the passover." Gr. "According to the law of the passover (pascha)." This is to be understood of all the rites proper to the offering and eating of the paschal lamb, but not to the keeping of the seven days of unleavened bread.

V. 13. *The man that is clean and is not in a journey, etc.* Gr. "In a far journey." This case doubtless implies others of like negligence or presumption.——¶ *Forbeareth.* Heb. *hâdal, ceaseth, faileth.* Gr. "Cometh short." Comp. v. 7, where in the Sept. the same word occurs.——¶ *Shall be cut off.* Either by the sentence of the judges, or by the judgment of heaven. See Note on Gen. 17:14.——¶ *From among his people.* Heb. "From his peoples." Meaning the *tribes* of Israel, called the "peoples of Israel," Acts 4:27, where the original is plural, though the rendering is singular.——¶ *Shall bear his sin.* That is, the punishment due to his sin. See Lev. 22:9.

V. 14. *If a stranger shall sojourn among you.* Gr. "If a proselyte come unto you in your land." Syr. "If one shall dwell among you who has been converted unto me." The allusion is to such strangers or foreigners as had become proselytes to the faith of Israel, and had submitted to circumcision according to the law laid down Ex. 12: 48, 49. We are to recognize in this a pre-intimation of the future calling in of the Gentiles to the Lord's true church.

The Manner in which the Cloudy Pillar conducted the Movements of the Host.

V. 15. *On the day that the tabernacle was reared up.* Heb. "On, or in, the day of his (Moses') rearing up the tabernacle." This was the first day of the first month of the second year after their departure from Egypt. This is mentioned here as Moses is about to speak of the removal from Sinai, of which the removal of the cloud, that

cloud covered [o] the tabernacle,
namely, the tent of the testimony: and at even [p] there was upon the tabernacle as it were the appearance of fire, until the morning.
16 So it was alway: the cloud [q] covered it *by day*, and the appearance of fire by night.

o Ex. 40. 34. *p* Ex. 13. 21. 40. 38. Neh. 9. 12, 19. Ps. 78. 14.

q Deut. 1. 33.

had rested upon the Tabernacle from the day of its first erection, was to be the signal. Of this cloud, with its symbolical uses, see the extended essay on the "Shekinah," at the end of the first vol. of the "Notes on Exodus."——¶ *The tent of the testimony.* Heb. "The cloud covered the tabernacle (*mishkan*, see Note on Ex. 26:1) to, or for, the tent of the testimony;" by which we may reasonably understand a distinction equivalent to saying, that over that part of the Tabernacle where the ark was, i. e. the Most Holy Place, the cloud rested. Having before hung on high over the camp, it now descended and settled upon the Tabernacle, covering it as with a garment. This is confirmed by the Gr. which renders, "And (or even) the house of the testimony," i. e. the department of the sacred edifice where the ark, with the tables of testimony, was deposited. Within this holy recess the divine presence was symbolized by another cloud of more glorious aspect resting over the mercy-seat. See Note on Lev. 16:2. Gr. "The cloud covered the tabernacle, the house of the testimony."——¶ *As it were the appearance of fire.* Heb. *kemareh, as the appearance*, from the root *râäh, to see.* The term here employed is the same with that which is rendered *pattern*, ch. 8:4, when speaking of the visionary model shown to Moses in the mount, after which he was to construct the Tabernacle and its various appendages. In that case, it is obvious that it was no material object which was presented to the outward eye, but something spiritual exhibited to the interior vision; so in the present instance we infer that the pillar of cloud was not a material substance, but something having the *appearance*, the *semblance* of one, such as the divine power was competent to produce. Of the precise *nature* of that which appeared we are altogether ignorant, as we are also of that of the symbol of the divine presence, which rested over the ark of the covenant, and which was in some way visible. It is probable that a very close and accurate investigation of the sense of the several original words rendered *to see*, would lead to the conclusion that *mental vision* is more frequently indicated in the language of holy writ than we have ordinarily supposed. Consult 2 Kings 6:17, for the case of Elisha's servant, who saw by spiritual vision the mountain covered by chariots and horses of fire. The cloud here spoken of was a dark columnar mass by day, and a pillar of fire by night to the senses of the Israelites. It signified both the presence and protection of the Most High in behalf of Israel.

V. 16. *So it was alway: the cloud covered it (by day.)* The words "by day" are wanting in the original, probably for the reason that the preceding term "alway" (Heb. *tâmid*) implies and is generally rendered "day by day." It is also readily supplied from Ex. 40:38. The continuance of this signal of the divine favor, notwithstanding the unworthiness of the people, is thus gratefully recorded by Nehemiah, ch. 9:19, "Yet thou in thy manifold mercies forsookest them not in the wilderness: the pillar of the cloud departed

17 And when [r] the cloud was
taken up from the tabernacle,
then after that the children of
Israel journeyed: and in the
place where the cloud abode,
there the children of Israel
pitched their tents.
18 At the commandment of
the LORD the children of Israel
journeyed, and at the commandment of the LORD they pitched:
as long as the cloud abode upon
the [s] tabernacle they rested in
their tents.
19 And when the cloud tarried long upon the tabernacle
many days, then the children of
Israel kept the charge [t] of the
LORD, and journeyed not.
20 And *so* it was, when the
cloud was a few days upon the
tabernacle; according to the

r Ex. 40. 36-38. c. 10. 11, 33.
s 1 Cor. 10. 1. t c. 1. 53. 3. 8. Zech. 3. 7.

---

not from them by day, to lead them in the way; neither the pillar of fire by night, to show them light, and the way wherein they should go."

V. 17. *And when the cloud was taken up from the tabernacle.* Heb. "And according to the being taken up of the cloud from upon (or over) the tabernacle." Gr. "Went up from the tent." ——¶ *Journeyed.* Heb. *yis-u, plucked up,* frequently rendered *departed, removed, set forward.* On its true import see Note on ch. 2 : 9.——¶ *In the place where the cloud abode.* Heb. *yishkon, shechinized,* from the root *shâkan,* usually rendered *to dwell, to abide,* i. e. *to tabernacle,* from which comes *Shechinah,* a term of profound significance, of which see Note on Ex. 25 : 8. The cloud, as the usual accompaniment and symbol of the divine glory, doubtless gave rise to the prophetic imagery in which the coming of the Lord is announced as taking place "in the clouds of heaven," Dan. 7 : 13. Rev. 1 : 7. So he is also said to be "clothed with a cloud, and his feet as pillars of fire," Rev. 10 : 1.——¶ *The children of Israel pitched their tents.* Set up the Tabernacle and encamped round about it.

V. 18. *At the commandment of the Lord.* Heb. *lepi, at the mouth.* Chald. "At the word of the Lord." Gr. "By the commandment of the Lord." The signs by which the Lord makes known his will and his words, according to the language of the Psalmist, Ps. 105 : 27, "They showed his signs among them (Heb. the words of his signs), and wonders in the land of Ham." The moving of the cloud was the signal of the divine pleasure that the camp also should move and take up their march to another station; which they did and went on as long as the cloud moved, stopping when it stopped.

V. 19. *And when the cloud tarried long.* Heb. "And in the cloud's prolonging (its stay)."——¶ *The children of Israel kept the charge of the Lord.* Heb. "Observed the observation." Chald. "Kept the charge (or observation) of the word of the Lord." The idea doubtless is, that they persisted, with the most exemplary patience, in the observance of all the prescribed rites and ceremonies, without presuming to anticipate the divine order for breaking up. They kept the charge of the Lord by obeying his will as to their movements.

V. 20. *And so it was, when the cloud was a few days upon the tabernacle.* Heb. "Days of number," i. e. days easily numbered, a Heb. idiom for few days. See Note on Gen. 34 : 30. This verse is to be viewed in close connection with the preceding. The purport

commandment of the LORD they abode in their tents, and according to the commandment of the LORD they journeyed.

21 And *so* it was, when the cloud abode from even unto the morning, and *that* the cloud was taken up in the morning, then they journeyed; whether *it was* by day or by night that the cloud was taken up, they journeyed.

22 Or *whether it were* two days, or a month, or a year, that the cloud tarried upon the tabernacle, remaining thereon, the children of Israel abode [u] in their tents, and journeyed not: but when it was taken up, they journeyed.

23 At the commandment of the LORD they rested in the tents, and at the commandment of the LORD they journeyed: they kept [v] the charge of the LORD, at the [w] commandment of the LORD by the hand of Moses.

u Ex. 40. 36, 37. *v* ver. 19. *w* Ps. 77. 20.

is, that the obedience of the people was equally marked whether the cloud tarried many or few days at any one station. In either case they awaited patiently the appointed indication.

Vs. 21–23. *Whether (it was) by day or by night.* Night travelling is not uncommon in the East, where the heat of the day is very severe.——¶ *Two days, or a month, or a year.* It is obvious from this that their times of tarrying at the different stations were very unequal. At one time they rested eighteen years together; at another but one day; at another one night. In this there is evidently nothing capricious or unstable to be charged upon the people, as their movements were constantly regulated by the divine direction, and this again was undoubtedly governed by reasons of infinite wisdom, though not expressly made known. The fact of the encampings and the removals of the host being thus controlled by the divine dictation and guidance, is reiterated again and again in these concluding verses. Maimonides says the reason of this particularity is, that it was designed to confute the opinions of the Arabians and others that the Israelites were so long detained in the wilderness—which the Arabic writers have termed the "Wilderness of Wandering"—because they had lost their way, and therefore spent years in vaguely rambling over the peninsula. This, he observes, is a very idle conceit, as the way from Mount Horeb to Kadesh Barnea was a well known and frequented route, and not above eleven days' journey; so that it is not to be supposed that they could have missed it, and far less should have wandered in a bewildered condition for forty years. As the whole history, however, of the wanderings of the children of Israel in the wilderness was obviously intended to be typical of the varied experience of the Lord's people in their life-journeying through the world, so we may regard these apparently zigzag marches and longer or shorter tarryings at different stations, as pointing to that vast diversity of *states* through which the Lord's pilgrims pass on their way to the heavenly Canaan. At one time they make a brief pause or halt in a particular state; at another they take up a long abode in such a state, and the plucking up the stakes and loosening the cords of the tents denote the breaking away and disentanglements which occur when they make a transition from one stage to another of their spiritual progress.

CHAPTER X.

AND the LORD spake unto Moses, saying,

2 Make thee two trumpets of silver: of a whole piece shalt thou make them, that thou mayest use them for the calling [a] of

a Is. 1. 13.

The conduct of the Israelites in thus yielding an implicit obedience to the divine will in this respect is worthy of all commendation, and stands in striking contrast with their too frequent perverseness and rebellion in other periods of their history. However tedious and irksome their travel or abiding, and however impatient of arriving at the promised land, yet they submitted themselves to the constant direction of their heavenly Guide, and never presumed to move but under his conduct. The history affords a lesson of universal application. Let us ever defer to divine guidance, and we shall not fail to be led in the right way; we shall be protected as under the shadow of omnipotence; we shall be relieved of a thousand anxious cares which will be sure to spring up in the attempt to order our own footsteps; and we shall enjoy the sweet inward assurance that all things are working together for our good, as those that love God and put their trust in him.

CHAPTER X.

The making of Silver Trumpets commanded.

V. 2. *Make thee two trumpets of silver.* Heb. *hatzotzeroth.* The trumpet of the Hebrews was made of metal, the cornet (Shophar) of horn. See Lev. 23:24. Josephus speaks of this instrument thus:—"Moses was the inventor of the form of their trumpet, which was made of silver. Its description is this: In length it was a little less than a cubit. It was composed of a narrow tube, somewhat thicker than a flute, but with so much breadth as was sufficient for the breath of a man's mouth: it ended in the form of a bell like common trumpets. Its sound was called in the Hebrew tongue, *Asosra.*"—*J. A.*, B. III. c. 12. There were but two of these now first made, as Aaron had but two sons who were priests, and by whom they were to be blown, v. 8, viz. Eleazer and Ithamar, but at a subsequent period, when the Levitical establishment had become much enlarged, we read of "a hundred and twenty priests sounding with trumpets," 2 Chron. 5:12. Their general uses were for summoning assemblies and giving notice for decampments and marches; and considering the vast extent of the encampment, some signal of this kind must have been indispensable. From Is. 58:1. 27:13, it is to be inferred that the trumpet points typically to the preaching of the gospel as the instrumentality by which sinful men are to be called into the Lord's kingdom.——¶ *Of a whole piece shalt thou make them.* Heb. *mikshâh, of hard or solid work.* On the true import of this term, see note on Ex. 25:31. Though there rendered "beaten work," yet it undoubtedly implies a fabric that was cast instead of being hammered into form. The trumpets were cast in one piece like the golden candlestick, which would probably render the sound more distinct and loud. ——¶ *For the calling of the assembly.* This was the first of the special uses to which the trumpets were devoted. But inasmuch as the camp was of several miles extent, and as the sound of two trumpets could not be heard over the whole distance, it is probable that

the assembly, and for the journeying of the camps.
3 And when they shall blow [b]
with them, all the assembly shall
assemble themselves to thee at
the door of the tabernacle of the
congregation.
4 And if they blow *but* with
one *trumpet*, then the princes,
which are heads [c] of the thousands of Israel, shall gather
themselves unto thee.
5 When ye blow an alarm [d],
then the camps that lie on the
east [e] parts shall go forward.
6 When ye blow an alarm
the second time, then the camps
that lie on the south [f] side shall

b Jer. 4. 5. Joel 2. 15.

c Ex. 18. 21. c. 1. 16. *d* Joel 2. 1. *e* c. 2. 3. *f* c. 2. 10.

---

notice was extended by progressive acclamations from one party to another till the utmost borders were reached. Compare with this the language of the prophet:—"Blow the trumpet in Zion, sanctify a fast, call a solemn assembly; gather the people, sanctify the congregation, Joel 2 : 15, 16.——¶ *For the journeying of the camps.* Heb. *lemassa*, *for the breaking up*, from the root before indicated, ch. 2 : 17. This was the second use of these instruments. If it be asked, what necessity there was for the sounding of trumpets when the encampment was to be broken up, inasmuch as the removal of the cloud indicated the removal of the host, we reply that the sound of the trumpet was not to notify the time of marching, but to indicate the order in which the several divisions were to move. Thus, upon the sounding of the first signal, the camp of Judah was to move; upon the second, that of Reuben; and so of the rest. There were, therefore, three things to be observed in connection with their removals:—1. The Lord's lifting the cloud, ch. 9 : 18, 22.—2. The sound of the trumpets, ch. 10 : 2, 5, 6.—3. The prayer of Moses, ch. 10 : 35.

V. 3. *And when they shall blow.* That is, the priests, as expressly ordered, v. 8. The Gr., however, has, "When thou shalt blow," referring to Moses, who might be said to blow through the priests whom he had appointed. The original term for "blow" (*tâka*) signifies primarily to *drive forcibly, to thrust in*, as the pins or stakes of a tent, a dagger, a nail, etc.; hence also applied to the violent driving or impinging of the wind, by which locusts are driven into the sea, or the breath into a trumpet.——¶ *With them.* That is, with both of them; for when but one was blown, the princes only assembled, v. 4.

V. 4. *If they blow* (*but*) *with one* (trumpet.) The Vulg. has it, "If thou sound but once;" but the Gr. better, "If thou shalt sound with one," as this accords with the Hebrew.

V. 5. *When ye blow an alarm.* Heb. *teruäh*, implying not, as in the other case, a long, even, and continuous blast, but a broken, quavering, and interrupted one, a sound of a more exciting and animating character, which our translators have not improperly expressed by "sounding an alarm."——¶ *The camps that lie upon the east part shall go forward.* These were the tribes of Judah, Issachar, and Zebulun, ch. 2 : 3–7. The term "camps" is apparently employed to signify the several distinct divisions that occupied the different quarters round about the Tabernacle.

V. 6. *On the south side.* This was occupied by Reuben, Simeon, and Gad, ch. 2 : 10. It would be reasonable to suppose, that after the mention of the camps on the east and south, mention

take their journey: they shall
blow an alarm for their journeys.
7 But when the congregation
is to be gathered together, ye
shall blow, but ye shall not
sound an alarm.
8 And the sons of Aaron,
the [g] priests, shall blow with
the trumpets; and they shall
be to you for an ordinance for
ever throughout your generations.
9 And if ye go to war [h] in
your land against the enemy
that oppresseth [i] you, then ye
shall blow an alarm with the
trumpets; and ye shall be re-

g c. 31. 6. Josh. 6. 4. 1 Chr. 15. 24. 2 Chr. 13. 12.

h 2 Chr. 13. 14. i Judg. 2. 18. 10. 8, 12. Ps. 106. 42.

---

would be made in like manner of those on the north and west; but these are for some reason omitted in the Hebrew, though supplied as follows in the Gr., "And ye shall sound a third alarm, and the camps pitched westward shall move forward; and ye shall sound a fourth alarm, and they that encamp toward the north shall move forward." This addition, however, has not been acknowledged by the Samaritan, nor by any other of the versions but the Coptic. Nor are there any various readings in the collections of Kennicott and De Rossi which countenance the Gr. in supplying the desideratum. Bp. Patrick supposes that the omission in the original is virtually supplied in the ensuing clause:—"They shall blow an alarm for their journeys," which he understands as equivalent to saying that they shall blow a *third* and *fourth* alarm for the moving of the other two standards. It is, however, an equally plausible interpretation, that these words amount to no more than a brief recapitulation of the order just given. Yet the Vulg. countenances the idea of Patrick:—"And after this manner shall the rest do, when the trumpets shall sound for a march."

V. 7. *But when the congregation, etc.* A manifest distinction between simply *blowing* and *blowing an alarm* appears in the language of this verse. The nature of this distinction is explained above, vs. 3, 5. The sound in the one case was long and equable, in the other short, broken, and sharp. Adam Clarke remarks that "from the similarity in the words, some suppose that the Heb. *teruah* was similar to the Roman *taratantara*, or sound of their *clarion*." It is possible that this distinction may be alluded to by Paul, 1 Cor. 14:8, where he says, "If the trumpet shall give an uncertain sound, who shall prepare himself to battle?" that is, if the milder and gentler sound is given when the rough and broken one is required.

V. 8. *And the sons of Aaron, the priests, shall blow.* The office of blowing the trumpets was restricted exclusively to the priestly order, probably with a view to intimate that the act had a typical reference to the preachers of the Word in subsequent ages.——¶ *An ordinance for ever.* Heb. "A statute of eternity." The outward symbolical use was to continue to the coming of Christ and the spiritual, or that which was the substance of the shadow, to abide ever after. This would make it an everlasting ordinance.

V. 9. *And if ye go to war, etc.* Heb. "If ye come to war." Gr. "If ye go forth to war." But "coming" is often expressed by the term that is rendered elsewhere by "going," as Jon. 1:3, "And found a ship *going* (Heb. *bâäh*, *coming*) to Tarshish."——¶ *Against the enemy that oppresseth you.* Heb. "The

membered [k] before the LORD your God, and ye shall be saved [l] from your enemies.

10 Also [m] in the day of your gladness, and in your solemn days, and in the beginnings of your months, ye shall blow with the trumpets over your burnt-offerings, and over the sacrifices of your peace-offerings; that they may be to you for a [n] me-

k Gen. 8. 1. Ps. 106. 4. 136. 23. *l* Luke 1. 70, 71. *m* Lev. 23. 24. c. 29. 1. 1 Chr. 15. 24. 2 Chr. 5. 12. 7. 6. 29. 26. Ezra 3. 10. Neh. 12. 35. Ps. 81. 3. 89. 15.

n Ex. 28. 29. Acts 10. 4.

distresser that distresseth you." Gr. "The adversaries that resist you." This is to be regarded as the third use of these instruments, viz. to serve as a signal of war, of which we read striking instances in the war of Israel against the Midianites, Num. 31 : 6; and of Judah against Jeroboam, 2 Chron. 13 : 12, when they said, "Behold, God himself is with us for our captain, and his priests with sounding trumpets to cry alarm against you." According to the Hebrew writers this calamity of war is to be considered as including within it all other forms of national judgments:— "As if he should say, every thing that shall distress you, as famine, and pestilence, and locusts, and the like; ye shall cry out for them, and sound an alarm."—*Maimonides.*——¶ *And ye shall be remembered before the Lord your God.* Chald. "The remembrance of you shall come up for good before the Lord." The Lord will be merciful to you and grant your request. Such is the import of the divine remembrance. See Note on Gen. 8 : 1. It is doubtless to be inferred that fasting, prayer, and repentance, were to be practised on all such occasions. That seasons of general humiliation were appointed of the Lord is evident from the language of the prophet Joel, in whose day palmer-worms, locusts, canker-worms, and caterpillars wasted the fruits of the earth, and drought, like fire and flame, burnt up the pastures and trees of the field, for which the people were exhorted to fast and pray, accompanied with *blowing of trumpets, sounding alarms, etc.*, Joel 1 : 4–20. 2 : 1–16.

V. 10. *Also in the day of your gladness.* Gr. "In the days of your gladness." Vulg. "If at any time ye shall have a banquet." This was the fourth use of these sacred implements. Allusion is had, in the first clause, to occasions of public rejoicing, such as the dedication of the first temple, 2 Chron. 5 : 12, 13; to the return from the captivity and the foundation of the second temple, Ezra 3 : 10, 11; and to the "dedication of the wall of Jerusalem," Neh. 12 : 27, 35.——¶ *And in your solemn days.* That is, days of solemnities, or ordinary feasts and fasts, such as are enumerated in the 23d ch. of Leviticus, or as were subsequently to be appointed, ch. 28 : 11, 14. Deut. 16 : 11.——¶ *In the beginnings of your months.* That is, on the feast of new moons, which were observed with special sacrifices appointed by divine authority. Of these see ch. 28 : 11–14. Comp. Ps. 81 : 3, "Blow up the trumpets in the new moon, in the time appointed, on our solemn feast day." These seasons were at first ushered in with the sound of trumpets alone, but subsequently the Lord through David and the prophets ordered other instruments to be employed, as psalteries, harps, cymbals, flutes, and timbrels, 2 Chron. 7 : 6. 16 : 5, 6. Ps. 149 : 3.——¶ *Over your burnt-offerings, etc.* Examples of this are recorded 2 Chron. 19 : 25–28. 5 : 12, 13. As the peace-offerings were sacrifices of thanksgivings, it was very suitable

morial before your God: I *am*
the LORD your God.

11 And it came to pass on
the twentieth *day* of the second
month, in the second year, that
the cloud [o] was taken up from off
the tabernacle of the testimony.

12 And the children of Israel took their journeys out of

o Ex. 40. 36, 37. c. 9. 17–20.

---

that they should be accompanied with the sound of the trumpets as a symbol of holy hilarity.——¶ *That they may be to you for a memorial.* That is, that the Lord, by whose sovereign authority these commands are given, may graciously accept your offerings and vouchsafe the tokens of his kind remembrance, when he sees that his service is your delight and joy.

The Removal of the Camp from Sinai to Paran.

V. 11. *And it came to pass on the twentieth day, etc.* Twelve months lacking ten days was the period that the Israelites had now lain encamped at the base of Mount Sinai, when the divine command is given to them to break up the encampment and set forward on their journey to the promised land. The Samaritan version here introduces the following words from Deut. 1 : 6–8, "The Lord our God spake unto us in Horeb, saying, Ye have dwelt long enough in this mount; turn and take your journey," etc. We know of no authority for this insertion.——¶ *The cloud was taken up from off the tabernacle.* Heb. "Was made to ascend." This was of course the Lord's own act, signifying that it was his good pleasure that the people should commence their march, ch. 9 : 17. But they were not left solely to the indications of the cloud. It was at this time that the words above cited from Deut. 1 : 6–8, were addressed to them. Accordingly the people were called both by word and sign from Sinai, the place of bondage, so rendered by reason of the Law's being there delivered, Gal. 4 : 24, 25, to the land of promise prefiguring the state of grace and freedom in Christ Jesus.

V. 12. *Took their journeys.* Heb. *Took their journeys according to their journeyings.* The original word is the common one for *breaking up.* Bp. Horsley renders it, "Decamped according to their decampments," which he understands to be equivalent to, "in due order." Le Clerc supposes it to imply, slowly, and according to the rate at which so vast a multitude could proceed. By another construction the sense is that they marched according to the journeys or stations which are more precisely recounted ch. 11 : 34, 35. 12 : 16. 3 : 15, seqq. The reader must be left to choose between these several suggestions. We incline to the latter.——¶ *The cloud rested.* Heb. ישכן *yishkon, shekinized,* as above, ch. 9 : 15–23, where see Note.——¶ *In the wilderness of Paran.* Gr. Φαραν, *Pharan,* to which corresponds the modern Feiran, the name of one of the principal Wadys, or valleys, in the rocky region of the Peninsula, although there is no adequate evidence to prove that the wilderness of Paran or Pharan was the same as the *wady* of Feiran. Previous to reaching this point they had encamped at two different stations, viz. the first at Kibroth-hattaavah, ch. 33 : 16, the second at Hazeroth, ch. 11 : 35. From v. 33 it appears that the station here called Paran was three days' journey from Sinai. As to the exact localities of the places mentioned here and elsewhere in the narrative of the wanderings, it is scarcely possible to identify them with any de-

the wilderness of Sinai [p], and the cloud rested in the wilderness of Paran [q].

13 And they first took their journey according to the commandment of the LORD [r] by the hand of Moses.

14 In the first *place* went the [s] standard of the camp of the children of Judah, according to their armies: and over his host *was* Nahshon the son of Amminadab.

15 And over the host of the

p Ex. 19. 1. q c. 12. 16. r c. 2. 9-34. s c. 2. 3, 9.

gree of certainty. We can only avail ourselves of the results of the researches of modern travellers by whom the country has been explored; and even these we shall for the most part rather refer to than transcribe into our own pages. Prof. Robinson's map of the Sinaitic region will be indispensable to the reader who would gain an accurate idea of the country made so memorable by the events recorded by Moses. It appears, on the whole, that the Paran here mentioned was the name of an extensive wilderness tract, in which the Israelites had several encampments, rather than of one single station, like Taberah or Hazeroth.

V. 13. *And they first took their journey, etc.* By comparing this with ch. 2:9 (on which see Note) it would appear that Horsley's interpretation is correct, to wit, that vs. 13 and 14 are tantamount to each other, and that the literal rendering would be, "And foremost decamped, according to the commandment of Jehovah by Moses; Foremost, I say, decamped the standard," etc. The original word for "first" in the two verses is precisely the same, and if it does not mean the same in both, it is difficult to determine its true sense in v. 13. Boothroyd renders it, "Thus, for the first time, they marched according to the command of Jehovah by Moses." But this is scarcely consistent with Ex. 17:1. The Gr., the Vulg., and the Syriac agree with Horsley.——¶ *By the hand of Moses.* That is, by the ministry of Moses; Moses being employed as an intermediate. It was through him that the Lord communicated to the people the order of their march and the use of the appointed signal. Moses, also, when the host began to move, uttered the invocation recorded in v. 35. "The reason," says a distinguished commentator, "why to speak by the hand of any one denotes by his means, or mediately, is, because by hand is signified power, thus by the hand of any one, vicarious power, which is the same thing with mediately, for what is done mediately is done by the power of another in himself; hence it is that in the Word this form of speech is adopted, as in the books of the kings, where mention is occasionally made of the Word which Jehovah spake by the hand of any one, as which he "*spake by the hand* of Ahijah the prophet," 1 Kings 14:18. "*By the hand* of Ahijah the Shilonite," 1 Kings 15:29. "*By the hand* of Jehu the prophet," 1 Kings 16:7, 12. "*By the hand* of Joshua," v. 34 of the same chapter. "*By the hand* of Elias," 1 Kings 17:16. "*By the hand* of Jonah the prophet," 2 Kings 14:25

V. 14. *In the first (place) went the standard of the children of Judah.* That in all things Judah, as the progenitor of our Lord, might have the pre-eminence.——¶ *According to their armies.* Or, by a more literal rendering, "The standard of the camp of the children of Judah decamped at the head of their armies," that is, of all the tribes, but

tribe of the children of Issachar *was* Nethaneel the son of Zuar.

16 And over the host of the tribe of the children of Zebulun *was* Eliab the son of Helon.

17 And the tabernacle was taken [t] down, and the sons of Gershon and the sons of Merari set forward, bearing [u] the tabernacle.

18 And the standard [v] of the camp of Reuben set forward according to their armies: and over his host *was* Elizur the son of Shedeur.

19 And over the host of the tribe of the children of Simeon *was* Shelumiel the son of Zurishaddai.

20 And over the host of the tribe of the children of Gad *was* Eliasaph, the son of Deuel.

21 And the Kohathites set forward, bearing the sanctuary [w]: and *the other* did set up the tabernacle against they came.

22 And the standard [x] of the camp of the children of Ephraim set forward according to their armies: and over his host *was* Elishama the son of Ammihud.

23 And over the host of the tribe of the children of Manasseh *was* Gamaliel the son of Pedahzur.

24 And over the host of the tribe of the children of Benjamin *was* Abidan the son of Gideoni.

25 And the standard [y] of the camp of the children of Dan set forward, *which was* the rereward [z] of all the camps through-

t c. 1. 51. *u* c. 4. 24. 7. 6–8. *v* c. 2. 10–16. *w* c. 4. 4–15. *x* c. 2. 18–24. *y* c. 2. 25–31. *z* Josh. 6. 9. Is. 58 8.

---

more immediately of Judah, Issachar, and Zebulun, who constituted the first grand division. As the order in which the several divisions marched is minutely detailed in ch. 2 : 1–31, it will be unnecessary to dwell on the order here recited. We shall therefore comment but briefly upon these verses.

V. 17. *And the tabernacle was taken down.* Heb. *hurad, was made to come down* or *descend.* That is, the curtains were taken off and the boards removed from the sockets, and thus the whole fabric taken down.——¶ *And the sons of Gershon, etc.* They followed immediately after Judah's division, that when they had arrived at the camping-place they might proceed at once to set up the Tabernacle and have it ready against the Kohathites came up with the sacred utensils with which it was to be furnished.

V. 21. *Bearing the sanctuary.* Heb. *hammikdosh, the sanctity,* by which is undoubtedly meant the sacred vessels, the ark, the candlestick, the table, the altar of incense, etc. Gr. τα ἅγια, *the holy things.* As the term "sanctuary" would naturally be regarded as synonymous with "tabernacle," it is not so suitable a rendering of the original as "holy things."——¶ *And (the other) did set up the tabernacle, etc.* That is, the Gershonites and Merarites before mentioned, v. 17.

V. 25. *The rear-ward of all the camps.* Heb. *measseph, the gatherer,* or *gathering host,* equivalent to *rear-guard.* Gr. "The last of all the camps." See the peculiar significancy of this word fully explained in the Note on Josh. 6 : 9. It was the duty of the division of Dan, which closed up the rear, to see to all the feeble, the stragglers, etc., which

out their hosts: and over his host *was* Ahiezer the son of Ammishaddai.

26 And over the host of the tribe of the children of Asher *was* Pagiel the son of Ocran.

27 And over the host of the tribe of the children of Naphtali *was* Ahira the son of Enan.

28 Thus *were* the journeyings of the children of Israel according to their armies, when they set forward.

29 And Moses said unto Hobab, the son of Raguel [a] the Midianite, Moses' father-in-law, We are journeying unto the place of which the LORD said, I [b] will give it you: come thou with us, and we will do thee

a Ex. 2. 18. b Gen. 12. 7.

---

the Lord would not suffer to be overlooked in the general movement of the host.

V. 28. *Thus (were) the journeyings.* Heb. "These were the journeyings." That is, this was the order in which their journeyings were conducted.——¶ *When they journeyed.* Heb. "And they journeyed." Implying that whenever they journeyed the same order was observed.

Moses' Invitation to Hobab.

V. 29. *And Moses said unto Hobab, the son of Raguel.* As to the real person intended to be designated by this name, and his true relationship to Moses, we have nothing positive to add to the considerations adduced upon the subject in the Note on Ex. 2 : 18, to which the reader is referred. It involves a question which can probably never be determined with absolute certainty. Those who hold that Hobab was the son of Jethro, instead of Jethro himself, which, on the whole, we regard as the most probable opinion, maintain that the original word (*'hothēn*) for "father-in-law" may with equal propriety be rendered "brother-in-law," or "near relative," as such seems to be its import in Judg. 1:16. 4:11, to which add Gen. 19:14. But the term "father-in-law," in this connection, for aught we see, may as well be referred to Raguel (Reuel) as to Hobab, and this would assign to it its usual meaning. It would seem, therefore, on the whole, as most probable, that as forty years had elapsed since Moses' connection with this family was formed, his father-in-law (Ex. 2:18) Reuel or Raguel (the same word in the original is used in both places) was dead, or disabled by infirmities, and that the person here called Hobab was in fact the brother of Zipporah, consequently the brother-in-law of Moses.——¶ *Come thou with us, and we will do thee good.* This invitation is rich in practical suggestions. As Israel in the wilderness is a type of the Christian Church in its pilgrim state, and Canaan of the heavenly country, we recognize in these words the benevolent concern which every good man feels in behalf of his fellow-men, that they also may be sharers in the blessings which he is taught to anticipate. Christianity is the religion of love; and it is impossible that one who has himself become, in his own humble estimation, a partaker of the heavenly inheritance, should not earnestly long and strive to enlist others in the pursuit of those incorruptible treasures which have become so precious to himself. If the Pharisees could compass sea and land to make one proselyte, and after all render him more a child of hell than before, shall Christian benevolence

good: for the LORD hath spoken good [c] concerning Israel.

30 And he said unto him, I will not go; but I will depart to mine own land, and to my kindred.

31 And he said, Leave us not, I pray thee: forasmuch as thou knowest how we are to encamp in the wilderness, and thou mayest be to us instead of eyes [d].

c Ex. 6. 7, 8.

d Job 29. 15.

be a principle less powerful to win heedless souls from the way of perdition, and persuade them into the way of peace and life? Such will be the spontaneous prompting of every child of the kingdom. Tasting himself the blessedness of living to the Lord, he will ardently long to bring all he can to the experience of the same blessedness. Especially will he be anxious for relatives and friends, that they may join him in the journey to heaven, and he will plead with them by holding forth the eternal good which he trusts to reap at the end of his pilgrimage.——¶ *For the Lord hath spoken good concerning Israel.* Heb. "Upon Israel." This is rendered by Geddes and Boothroyd, "Jehovah hath promised good things to Israel." This may be a correct paraphrase, but the Heb. has no word signifying *to promise,* and therefore employs the term *dâbar, to speak, to say.*

V. 30. *And he said unto him, I will not go.* This appears not to have been a final refusal. From the subsequent history there is good reason to conclude, that although he at present declined the urgent invitation, and departed, according to his purpose, to his own land and kindred, yet that he afterwards returned and rejoined the chosen people, and either in his own person, or that of his descendants, entered with them into the promised possession. From Judg. 1:16. 4:11. 1 Sam. 15:6, it is evident that his posterity, under the name of "Kenites," had an abiding place among the tribes of Israel, even as late as the time of Saul. It is always pleasant to read the indications of a return to the way of life on the part of those who have at one time seemed resolved to forsake it. We hail with delight every instance, where the man who at first refuses to enter the vineyard afterwards repents and goes.

V. 31. *Thou mayest be to us instead of eyes.* "An aged father says to his son, who wishes to go to some other village, 'My son, leave me not in my old age; you are now my eyes.' 'You are on the look-out for me, your eyes are sharp.' It is said of a good servant, 'he is eyes to his master.'"—*Roberts.* The plea of Moses with Hobab is twofold, first, the good he would gain for himself, and, second, the good he would do to Israel. Every possible motive, involving truth, should be employed to win upon the ungodly, and induce them to unite their lot with the people of God. Still, it becomes in this case a fair question, how the services of Hobab could be required as a guide, when the marchings and the encampings of the host were governed entirely by the cloudy pillar, as we learn from the preceding chapter was the fact. To this it may be replied, in the language of Adam Clarke, that "the cloud directed their *general* journeys, but not their *particular* excursions. Parties took several journeys while the grand army lay still." (See chs. 13, 20, 31, 32, etc.) Add to this, that as the spots in the desert most suitable for the encampment of so large a body of people might

32 And it shall be, if thou go with us, yea, it shall be, that what goodness the LORD shall do unto us, the same[e] will we do unto thee.

e Judg. 1. 16. 4. 11.

not always be in the immediate vicinity of water, they would naturally need such a person as Hobab, a principal person in his tribe, who was perfectly at home over the whole region they were now traversing, and who would of course be able to direct them to the watering-places, as also to the places where fuel might be found, large quantities of both which would be indispensably requisite to meet the demands of so immense a collection of men, women, and children. This would be the more necessary, as from the scarcity of water in those regions, the Arabs were in the habit of digging pits or cisterns, which, when they left, they would close up with stones or sands, so that it would be difficult to discover them again. These hidden places Hobab, as having been born and brought up in the desert, would be apt to be better acquainted with, or more easily able to find, than the stranger people who now required his services. It is beyond question, moreover, as we have before intimated, that a large portion of the supplies of cattle for sacrifice were obtained from the nomade tribes sojourning along the route of the Israelites, and a resident of the region would be of great service in treating with these people in this behalf. In this circumstance we find, if we mistake not, a clew to the rendering of the Gr. in the present passage, *esē en hemin presbutēs*, commonly translated, *thou shalt be an elder among us*, but which we would render, *thou shalt be a legate* or *messenger among us*, i. e. *an agent, a negotiator*, in managing this kind of traffic. At the same time, this version need not exclude the idea of his acting as an elder or counsellor in any emergencies that might arise, where his experience and judgment might be of use. The following extract from the travels of Bruce in Abyssinia will throw light upon the general purposes answered by the employment of guides in desert countries:—"A *hybeer* is a guide, from the Arabic word *hubbar*, *to inform*, *instruct*, or *direct*, because they are used to do this office to the caravan travelling through the desert, in all its directions, whether to Egypt and back again, the coast of the Red Sea, or the countries of Sudan, and the western extremities of Africa. They are *men of great consideration*, knowing perfectly the situation and properties of all kinds of water, to be met on the route, the distances of wells, whether occupied by enemies or not, and if so, the way to avoid them with the least inconvenience. It is also necessary to them to know the places occupied by the simoom, and the seasons of their blowing in those parts of the desert; likewise those occupied by moving sands. He generally belongs to some powerful tribe of Arabs inhabiting these deserts, whose protection he makes use of, to assist his caravans, or protect them in time of danger; and handsome rewards are always in his power to distribte on such occasions." Even the miraculous conduct of the Divine Providence does not supersede human instrumentality when it can be properly employed, as we see in the case of the appointment of Judges at the suggestion of Hobab's father on a former occasion.

V. 32. *The same will we do unto thee.* To which the Targ. of Jonathan adds, "in the division of the land." Vulg. "We will give thee what is best of the riches which the Lord shall deliver to us." If we transfer this from the lite-

33 And they departed from the [f] mount of the LORD three days' journey; and the ark of the covenant of the LORD went before [g] them in the three days' journey, to search out a resting-place for them.

34 And the cloud [h] of the

f Ex. 3. 1.

g Deut. 1. 33. Josh. 3. 3–6. h Ex. 13. 21. Neh. 9. 12, 19.

ral to the spiritual it will imply, that in the allotment of the heavenly inheritance an equal share shall fall to those who from being "aliens from the commonwealth of Israel and strangers from the covenants of promise" became "fellow-citizens with the saints and of the household of God." Nor is it possible for the people of God to hold out any stronger inducements to their fellow-men than the prospect of sharing with them in the blessedness promised.

The Blessing of Moses at the Removing and Resting of the Ark.

V. 33. *And they departed from the mount of the Lord.* Chald. "From the mountain whereon the glory of the Lord had been revealed." That is, Mount Horeb, from whose summit the Law had been given forth.——¶ *Three days' journey.* Heb. "Three days' way." This is a repetition of what had been mentioned before, vs. 11–13.——¶ *And the ark of the covenant of the Lord went before them.* It is not clear that this language is to be understood after the exactest import of the letter. The usual place of the ark was not in the van, but in the centre of the host, which arrangement, however, some of the Jewish writers suppose to have been departed from on this occasion, as it was also on another, viz. when the people crossed the Jordan on their entrance into Canaan, Josh. 3 : 6. But the supposition is not necessary, as the phrase "went before them" may properly signify no more than that it was carried *conspicuously in sight* of the people. "The plain meaning seems to be," says Bp. Patrick, "that the Lord, as their king and governor, led them by the cloud, which was always over the ark; just as a general leads his army, though he be not in the front of it, but in the midst, from whence he issues out his orders."——¶ *To search out a resting place for them.* Chald. "To prepare a place." Gr. "To consider a place." The literal meaning of the original is *rest*, instead of a *place of rest*, but these meanings are occasionally interchanged. Thus Ps. 132 : 8, "Arise, O Lord, into thy *rest*," i. e. thy place of rest. Comp. Gen. 8 : 9. 1 Chron. 28 : 2. Mic. 2 : 10. Zech. 9 : 1. Should it be suggested that this was rather the office of the cloud than of the ark, it is replied, that the ark and the cloudy pillar are to be conceived as acting together in this matter, as the ark always moved under the column. The phraseology is anthropomorphic, or spoken of the Lord after the manner of men. The term signifies properly, to search by *turning* in one direction and another, as a person in looking for a lost article turns round and round, going several times over the same ground. Omniscience, of course, has no occasion to search, and as to the ark and the cloud it could only be said of them metaphorically. In like manner, the Most High speaks in Ezek. 20 : 6, of having brought forth his people out of the land of Egypt into a land he had *espied* for them. Comp. Deut. 1 : 33, where the same phraseology occurs.

V. 34. *And the cloud of the Lord* (*was*) *upon them by day, etc.* Chald. "The

LORD *was* upon them by day, when they went out of the camp.

35 And it came to pass, when the ark set forward, that Moses said, Rise [i] up, LORD, and let thine enemies be scattered, and

i Ps. 68. 1, 2. 132. 8.

cloud of the glory of the Lord." The general fact here mentioned is still more particularly stated Ex. 13:21, 22, "And the Lord went before them by day in a pillar of a cloud, to lead them the way; and by night in a pillar of fire, to give them light; to go by day and night: He took not away the pillar of the cloud by day, nor the pillar of fire by night, from before the people." This cloud is said to have been "upon" or "over" them, and doubtless in such a way as to shelter them from the burning rays of the sun. This may be farther inferred from the words of the Psalmist, Ps. 105:3, "He spread a cloud for a covering; and fire to give light in the night." At the same time it displayed itself in a special manner over the ark in the form of a column. The analogy between the office of the cloudy pillar in guiding the march of the Israelites through the wilderness, and that of our Lord himself in conducting his people in their spiritual pilgrimage is perceptible from his own words, John 10:2–11, where he compares himself to a shepherd calling his sheep by name, and leading them forth, causing them to go in and out, and to find pasture. See also Is. 4:5, 6. Ps. 78:52.——¶ *When they went out of the camp.* Heb. "In their departure from the encampment;" or the places where they had temporarily pitched their tents.

V. 35. *And it came to pass when the ark set forward, that Moses said, etc.* That is, this was his uniform practice on such occasions. This is rendered by the Jerusalem Targum, "And it came to pass, when the ark was taken up, that Moses lifted up his hands in prayer, and said, Rise now, O Word of the Lord, in the strength of thy power, and scatter the enemies of thy people."——¶ *Rise up, Lord.* Or, stand up, opposed to sitting still, and equivalent to manifesting himself for the help and comfort of his people, and for the overthrow and destruction of his enemies. The Lord's apparently *taking vengeance* upon his adversaries is elsewhere expressed by his *rising up;* as Job 31:14, "What shall I do when God *riseth up?*" Ps. 7:6, "*Arise,* O Lord, in thine anger, lift up thyself because of the rage of mine enemies." Comp. Ps. 10:12. 17:13. 44:27. A striking parallel to this occurs Ps. 68:1, where the resurrection and ascension of the Lord are mystically set forth, showing that the words before us receive an ultimate fulfilment in him. The Targ. of Onkelos, or Chald. renders it, "Be thou revealed, O Lord." Targ. Jon. "Be thou revealed now, O Word of the Lord, in the strength of thine anger."——¶ *And let thine enemies be scattered.* The Chald., as we have seen, has here, "the enemies of thy people," and afterwards, "those that hate them," implying that the enemies and persecutors of the Lord's people are in effect his enemies. See Zech. 2:8. Mat. 25:45. Acts 9:4. Rosenmuller remarks in regard to the original word here rendered "scattered" (*phutz*), that it properly denotes the action of waters in overflowing their banks, and is thence figuratively applied to bodies of men rushing in impetuous crowds and pressing out of the pathway on either side like a raging stream that bursts over its banks. When spoken of the dispersion of enemies it implies a routing and discomfiture that

let them that hate thee flee before thee.

36 And when it rested, he said, Return, O LORD, unto the many thousands of Israel.

shall drive them one way and another like the inundations of a flood. So, when typically viewed, the language suggests that the death and resurrection of the Saviour is the breaking and dissipation of the combined forces of his enemies, according to Ps. 68:2, 3, 13, 15, while on the other hand it is a "gathering together in one of the children of God that were scattered abroad," John 11:51, 52. Is. 11:10, 11.

V. 36. *Return, O Lord, unto the many thousands of Israel.* Heb. "Ten thousand thousands." Chald. "Return, O Lord, dwell with thy glory among the ten thousand thousands in Israel." The Heb. original omits the preposition "unto" before "the many thousands," but it is probably to be understood, the Syriac and some other versions supplying it. A similar omission occurs Ex. 4:19, where "into" before "Egypt" is wanting in the original. It is not, in fact, very unusual before verbs of motion. Comp. Hos. 7:11, 16, in the original. The Gr. however, gives a different turn to the words, "And in the resting he said, Turn again (i. e. cause to return), O Lord, the thousands (and) tens of thousands in Israel." This is a possible construction, as the verb rendered "return" (*shûb*) is used actively, though for the most part in such cases followed by the word "captivity," as Deut. 30:3. Ps. 14:7. 126:1. We deem the former preferable. The import of the prayer is, that the Divine Presence, whose movement in the cloud was a signal of warfare against all adversaries, would upon their halting return to its chosen rest and place, and abide as the safety, comfort, and glory of the chosen people. Spiritual *warfare* and spiritual *rest* are the fundamental ideas. Though predicated primarily of the Lord, yet they hold good also of his people, with whom in all things he is most intimately conjoined. "The welfare and happiness of the Israel of God consist in the continual presence of God among them. Their safety consists not in their numbers, though they are *thousands, many thousands,* but in the favor of God and his gracious return to them, and residence with them. These thousands are ciphers, he is the figure, and upon this account, 'Happy art thou, O Israel, who is like unto thee, O people.'"—*Henry.*

CHAPTER XI.

AND [a] *when* the people complained, it displeased the LORD: and the LORD heard *it;*

a Deut. 9. 22.

CHAPTER XI.

The Murmuring of the People and its Consequences.

V. 1. *And (when) the people complained, it displeased the Lord.* Or, according to Ainsworth, "And the people as complaining (i. e. murmuring, fretting themselves) was evil in the ears of Jehovah." It may otherwise be rendered, "And the people were (became) as murmuring evil in the ears of Jehovah." Thus the Gr. "The people murmured evil things before the Lord." This is favored by Horsley, who says, "The passage would be better rendered, 'And the people murmured wickedly in the ears of Jehovah.'" So also Geddes, "Meanwhile the people began to mutter evil in the hearing of the Lord." Or, finally, "And the people were as murmurers, (which was) evil in the

and his anger [b] was kindled; and the fire [c] of the LORD burnt

b Ps. 78. 21. c Lev. 10. 2. 2 K. 1. 12.

ears of the Lord." The original, *kemithonenim*, here rendered *complained* (lit. "were as complainers"), is in a reflexive conjugation implying, as Luther has it, that they "made themselves impatient." They allowed their feelings to act inwardly upon themselves, working their own minds into a restless, discontented, murmuring state, which, however, was not vented so much in open complaints, as in a certain half-suppressed, obscure, and secret repining and fretting, which is conveyed by the force of the original particle, כ, *k*, *as it were*. It seems to be implied that this fretfulness did not so much express itself in the ears of men as in those of the Lord himself, and though it was, as it were, but whispered or buzzed in his ear, yet "he heard it," heard it as though most audibly and distinctly uttered. All this is in effect comprised in the idea intended to be conveyed by the original, but it is obvious how inadequate must be any translation that does not run into a paraphrase. No special reason is given by the sacred writer for the murmuring on this occasion, but one is assigned by the Vulg., "There arose a murmuring of the people against the Lord, as it were repining at their fatigue." It may have been that their hearts were discouraged at being obliged to take somewhat long and tiresome stages at the outset; but whatever were the causes of their discontent, we know that they had a thousandfold more occasion for thanksgiving and praise than for disaffection and complaint. But such is human nature, of which we all partake more or less, and to which we are prone to give way. Let us remember, however, that the Lord sees and takes account of these secret murmurs which are not openly uttered, and may visit them openly as truly as he hears in secret and rewards openly the prayers of the humble and penitent.

——¶ *The fire of the Lord burnt among them.* Chald. "A fire from before the Lord." Heb. *tibar, burned*, from whence was derived the name of the place, "Taberah," *burning*, where this visitation occurred, v. 3. The current of commentators here favor the idea of some literal and visible bursting forth of fire, either from the cloudy pillar or in a flash of lightning, which instantly consumed the offenders, as Nadab and Abihu were consumed by a similar stroke of the divine indignation. Any fire sent by the Lord, is a fire of the Lord, and though some think it was a fire wholly supernatural; others that it was lightning; others that it was the simoom, or hot wind of the desert, yet we incline to a different opinion, and take the judgment here mentioned to be not external, but internal; supposing the *fire* spoken of to be what Job terms "a fire not blown," or but another term for *any kind of wasting effect of the Lord's displeasure*. In what particular form this was manifested it is now impossible to say, but it was such as to carry with it a conviction of its origin, and to lead to implore earnestly its abatement. The Psalmist, in allusion to this judgment, says, Ps. 78 : 21, "So *a fire was kindled* against Jacob, and anger also came up against Israel," where we do not recognize the import of literal fire, any more than when we read in the language of the apostle that "Our God is a consuming fire." By this we are simply to understand that he is terrible in his judgments towards his adversaries. This view is confirmed, if we mistake not, by general usage. Thus, Ps. 78 : 62, 63, "He gave his peo-

among them, and consumed *them that were* in the uttermost parts of the camp.

2 And the people cried unto Moses, and when Moses prayed unto the LORD, the fire was quenched.

3 And he called the name of the place Taberah: because the fire of the LORD burnt among them.

4 And the mixed [d] multitude that *was* among them fell a lust-

[d] Ex. 12. 38.

---

ple over also unto the sword; and was wroth with his inheritance. *The fire consumed their young men;* and their maidens were not given in marriage." Ps. 66:12, "Thou hast caused men to ride over our heads; *we went through fire,* and through water." Ps. 97:3, "*A fire goeth before him,* and burneth up his enemies round about." In all these cases *fire* is but another term for *divine judgments.*——¶ *Consumed (them that were) in the uttermost parts of the camp.* Heb. *tokēl, ate, devoured.* So also the Gr. "Devoured a part of the camp." The extremity of the camp may be mentioned as the part of it occupied more especially by the "mixt multitude," v. 4, with whom it is probable the murmuring more particularly prevailed. Bochart, however, has adduced considerable evidence that the original word here rendered "the uttermost parts" does not always signify an *extremity,* but *any part, every part, in all, throughout.* Probably the true idea is, therefore, that the fire *consumed some in every part of the camp.*

V. 2. *The fire was quenched.* Heb. *yishka, sunk, subsided, went out,* from a root usually signifying *to drown,* or *be drowned,* which implies, of course, a sinking into the water. Whatever the precise form of the judgment were, it now received a manifest and complete check or abatement in consequence of the intercession of Moses.

V. 3. *And he called the name of the place Taberah.* Or, "and one called." Gr. "And the name of that place was called." The station in this case had probably no particular name before the occurrence of the incident here recorded. And so in numerous other instances.

V. 4. *And the mixed multitude that (was) among them fell a lusting.* Heb. "Lusted a lusting," i. e. lusted greatly and inordinately. Respecting this "mixed multitude," see Note on Ex. 12:38, where a full account is given of them. The original term is but inadequately rendered by this appellation. In the former passage it is *ereb rab, a great mixture* or *rabble.* Here it is *asaphsooph, the collected* or *gathered people,* the force of which can only be conveyed by such strictly analogous terms as *riff-raff,* or *ruff-scuff.* The doubling of word-forms in the Heb., as in other Eastern languages, intensifies the meaning, and makes them equivalent to superlatives. Thus *adam* signifies *red,* but in Lev. 13:19 *adamdameth* signifies *exceeding red.* So here *asaphsooph* implies a very large collection of what Bochart calls "populi colluvies undecunque collecta," *the dregs* or *scum of the people from every quarter.* One of the older English versions (Rogers') renders the clause, "And the rascal people that was among them fell a lusting." The word denotes a *mongrel horde* of retainers or hangers-on, who from various motives had followed the sojourning host from Egypt, and who, having little knowledge of God or interest in his promises, were the first to feel the difficulties and privations of

ing: and the children of Israel also wept again, and said,

the way, and thence to fret and murmur.——¶ *And the children of Israel also wept again, and said, etc.* Heb. "Returned and wept." The import of "returned" in this connection is undoubtedly that of *changed their mind, relapsed.* That is, they were wrought upon by the contagious example of the mixed multitude to such a degree as to *fall away from a previous state of mind,* and involve themselves in the rebellious conduct here spoken of. If we take the expression as it stands in our version, "wept again," the inquiry is very natural, When did they weep before? Nothing is previously said of their weeping. But the interpretation we suggest is abundantly confirmed by the usage of the original term, of which scores of instances could be easily adduced. Let the following serve as a specimen. It will be seen that the true idea is that of *a change of mind,* which in the present instance is that from a better to a worse. Ps. 78:34, "When he slew them, then they sought him, and they *returned* and inquired early after God." Eccl. 4:1, "So I *returned* and considered all the oppressions that are done under the sun," etc. as v. 7, "Then I *returned,* and I saw vanity under the sun." Eccl. 9:11, "I *returned,* and saw under the sun that the race is not to the swift, nor the battle to the strong," etc. Is. 19:22, "And the Lord shall smite Egypt: he shall smite and heal it: and they shall *return* even to the Lord, and he shall be entreated of them, and shall heal them." Is. 55:7, "Let the wicked forsake his way, and the unrighteous man his thoughts; and let him *return* unto the Lord, and he will have mercy upon him; and to our God, for he will abundantly pardon." Mal. 3:18, "Then shall ye *return* and discern between the righteous and the wicked, between him that serveth God and him that serveth him not." Judg. 11:35, "And it came to pass when he (Jepthah) saw her, that he rent his clothes, and said, Alas, my daughter! thou hast brought me very low, and thou art one of them that trouble me; for I have opened my mouth unto the Lord, and I cannot *go back* (Heb. *return*)." Ezek. 14:6, "Therefore say unto the house of Israel, thus saith the Lord God: *Repent* (Heb. *return*) and *turn* yourselves from your idols; and *turn away* your faces from all your abominations." Ezek. 18:30, "Therefore, I will judge you, O house of Israel, every one according to his ways, saith the Lord God. *Repent* (Heb. *return*) and *turn* yourselves from all your transgressions; so iniquity shall not be your ruin." In all these cases it is obvious that the word *return* is significant of a mental act. It implies a change of sentiments and views, or in other words a change of state. Although in the letter it is the appropriate term for local removal, yet in a more interior import it unequivocally designates a purely mental process. Viewing the words in this light, we can see the ground on which some commentators have proposed to render them by *aversi sunt, defecerunt, turned away in aversion, revolted,* i. e. were subjects of a mental alienation from the Lord. Instead of weeping compassionately *over* the disaffected multitude, they wept perversely *with* them, and thus contributed to provoke the divine displeasure. "A few factious, discontented, ill-natured people, may do a great deal of mischief in the best societies, if great care be not taken to discountenance it. This Egyptian rabble were the disordered sheep that infected the flock, the leaven that leavened the whole lump."—*Henry.* There

Who [e] shall give us flesh to eat?

5 We remember the fish, which we did eat in Egypt

e 1 Cor. 10. 6.

was in reality no lack of food or water for them; but they had become dainty; they had taken a surfeit of the manna; their soul loathed "this light food," as they slightingly call it on another occasion, and they longed for the fish, the flesh, and the vegetables of Egypt.——¶ *Who shall give us flesh to eat?* That is, O that we had flesh to eat!—the expression of a vehement, impatient desire, mixed with a degree of despair. Compare with this the allusions Ps. 106:14. 78:18-20. A general clamor was started of how hard it was that they should be kept to one kind of diet till they absolutely loathed it, and reproaches were cast upon their leader to the effect that he had decoyed them from a plentiful country, where the sea and the river fed them with a variety of fish, and the soil abounded with the best of herbs, salads, and fruits, all which they had exchanged for a miserable, meagre kind of fare, on which they were in danger of famishing. So grossly does a discontented spirit not only undervalue present comforts, but falsify the truth in regard to one's condition.

V. 5. *We remember the fish, etc.* They stirred up and inflamed their lust by studiously calling to mind the dainties they formerly enjoyed in Egypt. But even in this they imposed upon themselves, for, as Henry remarks, "they did not remember the brick-kilns, and the task-masters, the voice of the oppressor, and the smart of the whip. These are forgotten by the ungrateful people."——¶ *For nothing.* Heb. *hinnom, gratis*, i. e. which cost them nothing but the trouble of taking. As to the great use of fish as an article of food by the Egyptians, the fact is repeatedly affirmed by Herodotus. They ate them either salted or dried in the sun without any other preparation. Indeed, the Egyptians are the first people whom history mentions as curing any kind of meat with salt for preservation. The salt they used was fossil salt, obtained from the African deserts. Sea salt was abhorred by them, probably from some religious consideration, just as the priests abstained entirely from fish, the reason of which is doubtless to be sought from some ancient idea that the spiritual correspondence of fish rendered them unsuitable as an article of diet to the priesthood.——¶ *The cucumbers.* Arabia and Egypt produce abundance of cucumbers, which, owing to the mellowing effects of the sun's rays, are softer than those with us, and of more easy digestion. It is said by travellers that they are eaten in the East in almost incredible quantities.——¶ *Melons.* The water-melon is no doubt intended. This fruit grows abundantly in the Levant and Egypt. It is about the size, and somewhat of the appearance of a pumpkin. The interior is a pulp of blooming red, and rich in juice. "A traveller in the East who recollects the intense gratitude which the gift of a slice of melon inspired while journeying over the hot and dry plains—or one who remembers the consciousness of wealth and security which he derived from the possession of a melon while prepared for a day's journey over the same plains—*he* will readily comprehend the regret with which the Hebrews in the Arabian desert looked back upon the melons of Egypt." The following account of the uses of melons in Egypt is from Hasselquist. "By melons we are probably to understand the

freely; the cucumbers, and the melons, and the leeks, and the onions, and the garlic:

---

water-melon, which the Arabians call *batech*. It is cultivated on the banks of the Nile, in the rich clayey earth which subsides during the inundation. This serves the Egyptians for meat, drink, and physic. It is eaten in abundance during the season, even by the richer sort of people; but the common people, on whom Providence has bestowed nothing but poverty and patience, scarely eat any thing but these, and account this the best time of the year, as they are obliged to put up with worse fare at other seasons. This fruit likewise serves them for drink, the juice refreshing these poor creatures, and they have less occasion for water than if they were to live on more substantial food in this burning climate."——¶ *Leeks*. The original word occurs sixteen times, but is nowhere rendered "leek" but here. In one instance it is translated "herb," in another "hay," and in another "a court;" but in all the other instances it is translated "grass." As grass, however, could not have been what the Israelites desired, it is supposed by some commentators that "greens," implying lettuce, succory, endive, or salads in general, is what is meant. In the uncertainty that obtains on this point we give the following extract from Roberts. "To an Englishman the loss of these articles would not give much concern, and he is almost surprised at the Israelites repining at their loss, as at the loss of great delicacies. The people of the East do not in general eat flesh, nor even fish, so that when they can procure it they consider it a delicacy. Cucumbers are eaten in abundance in hot weather, and melons are most delicious and plentiful. I have never seen leeks in the East, and I am doubtful whether they are to be found; but whether or not, there is much difference of opinion as to the translation of the word. D'Oyly and Mant have a quotation to this effect:—'Whether the following word, rendered *leeks*, have that signification, may be doubted. Some think it was the *lotus*, which is a water plant, a kind of water-lily, which the Egyptians used to eat during the heats of summer.' In the Universal History, (vol. i. p. 486,) it is said, that those 'Egyptians who dwelt in the marshes, fed on several plants which annually grow, particularly the *lotus*, of which they made a sort of bread.' Of the Arabs also, (in the same work,) it is recorded—'They make a drink of the Egyptian *lotus*, which is very good for inward heat.' It has a bulbous root, and is highly esteemed as an article of food. As it grows in *tanks*, it can *only* be had in the hottest weather, when the water is dried up; and in this we see a most gracious provision, in allowing it to be taken when most required. Its cooling qualities are celebrated all over India, and the Materia Medica says of it, 'This is an excellent root, and is also prescribed medicinally, as cooling and demulcent.' The natives eat it boiled, or in curry, or make it into flour for gruels. I am, therefore, of opinion, that it was the *lotus* of Egypt respecting which the Israelites were murmuring." In this opinion Mr. Kitto is inclined to concur, conceding at the same time, that the authority of the Septuagint, which renders it by *prasa*, *leeks*, is not easily disposed of. He refers to Scheuchzer and others, "who think that the word here denotes a plant of the *lotus* kind, which grows very abundantly in the low lands of Egypt, and which was of very delicate taste, and held in

6 But now[f] our soul *is* dried away: *there is* nothing at all, beside this manna, *before* our eyes.

f c. 21. 5.

great estimation. They ate its root, and also made a kind of bread with it. Homer describes the lotus as the first of the plants that grew for the pleasure of the gods. The Arabs, when they can get it, make with it a drink which they highly relish. In India, also, the natives eat it boiled, or in curry, or make it into flour for gruels."—*Pict. Bible.* ——¶ *Onions.* "Whoever has tasted onions in Egypt must allow that none can be had better in any part of the universe. Here they are sweet, in other countries they are nauseous and strong; here they are soft, whereas in the north, and other parts, they are hard of digestion. Hence they cannot in any place be eaten with less prejudice and more satisfaction than in Egypt. They eat them roasted, cut into four pieces, with some bits of roasted meat, which the Turks in Egypt call *kobab,* and with this dish they are so delighted, that I have heard them wish they might enjoy it in paradise. They likewise make soup of them in Egypt, cutting the onions in small pieces; this I think one of the best dishes I ever ate."—*Hasselquist.* This is confirmed by Mr. Kitto. "In warm countries the onion often constitutes a staple article of diet. The sun has the same mellowing effect upon it as upon the cucumber, so that its savor is more bland than when grown in this country, and its use far less likely to affect the stomach with any disagreeable consequences. Most of the people of Western Asia are remarkably fond of onions. We have known poor Arabs wait for more than an hour, till the refuse of onions employed in cooking should be thrown away."——¶ *Garlic.* "The original word occurs but this once in the Scriptures, where it is undoubtedly correctly rendered. Its botanical character is too well known to require description. It is now usually distinguished in the kitchen-garden by the name of 'eschalot' or 'shallot.' A variety of this plant cultivated in France is called 'the onion of Egypt.' They are eaten like onions, and are peculiarly agreeable to the palate. Garlic was so much in request among the ancients, that Homer makes it a part of the entertainment which Nestor served up to his guest Machaon. It formed a favorite viand to the common people among the Greeks and Romans."—*Pict. Bible.*

V. 6. *But now our soul is dried away.* The *soul* is often used for the body, or the whole man, and as denoting that principle which is the seat of the appetite or desire of meat, drink, and other things. See "Bush on the Soul" *passim.* Comp. Ps. 102:4, where the same original word is rendered "withered." Also for the *soul's* requiring food, etc. Ps. 78:18. "In great hunger or thirst the people say, 'Our soul is withered.' 'More than this, sir, I cannot do; my spirit is withered within me.' 'What! when a man's soul is withered, is he not to complain?'"—*Roberts.*——¶ *There is nothing at all, besides this manna, before our eyes.* Heb. "There is nothing at all; only our eyes are unto the manna." We see nothing else, we expect nothing else, but this same monotonous manna, of which we have become sick of the sight. For the eyes to "be unto any one" is to cherish hope and expectation, as Ps. 25:15. 141:8. The form of the expression is very peculiar, and evidently carries with it the import of contempt towards the Lord's kind provision for

7 And the manna *was* as coriander-seed, and the colour thereof as the colour of bdellium [g].

8 *And* the people went about, and gathered *it*, and ground *it* in mills, or beat *it* in a mortar,

[g] Gen. 2. 12.

their wants. The manna thus furnished was a corporeal nourishment representing that which was spiritual, and thus serving as a type of our Lord himself according to his own declaration, John 6 : 32, 33, confirmed by Paul, 1 Cor. 10 : 3, who calls the manna "spiritual bread" because it represented such bread. The loathing the manna, therefore, and longing for the luxuries of Egypt, denoted the rejection of Christ and the benefits of his salvation, the true substance of these Old Testament symbols.

V. 7. *And the manna was as coriander-seed.* Not in color, but in size and shape. See Notes on Ex. 16 : 14, 31. The coriander is cultivated mostly in the south of Europe, and in some parts of England, on account of its seeds, which are required in large quantities by confectioners, druggists, and distillers. It is reared also in gardens on account of its leaves, which are used in soups and salads. The seeds are globular, grayish-colored, and about the size of pepper-corn. The taste and smell are both agreeable, depending on the presence of a volatile oil, which is separated by distillation.—This and the two following verses are evidently parenthetical, being designed to give such an account of the various properties and modes of preparation of the manna, as to evince its great value as an article of diet, and thus to rebuke the people for their light esteem of it.——¶ *And the color thereof.* Heb. "And the eye thereof," i. e. the aspect or appearance, as it is rendered by the Chald. and the Gr. For a similar usage in regard to "eye," see Ex. 10 : 5, with the explanatory Note. It is there rendered "face,"—"the *face* of the earth," meaning the *visible surface* of the earth. Lev. 13 : 55. Ezek. 1 : 16. 8 : 2. 10 : 9.——¶ *Bdellium.* Heb. "Bedolach," on which see Note on Gen. 2 : 12, where we have endeavored to show that the substance meant is the *pearl.* The Gr. however, here renders it *crystal.*

V. 8. *And the people went about, etc.* Heb. "Went to and fro," i. e. in the way of search and espial. The term is applied in some cases to the act of the eyes in looking and exploring on one side and the other, and in Dan. 12 : 4, to the perusal of a book, though rendered "run to and fro." But the true idea is probably that of turning over pages back and forth, and thus passing to and fro through a volume. See 2 Chr. 10 : 9. Zech. 4 : 10.——¶ *Ground it in mills, etc.* "The eastern mill consists of two circular stones, about eighteen inches in diameter, and three inches thick. The top stone has a handle in it, and works round a pivot, which has a hole connected with it to admit the corn. The *mortar* also is much used to make rice flour. It is a block of wood, about twenty inches high and ten inches in diameter, having a hole scooped out in the centre. The pestle is a stick of about four feet long, made of iron-wood, having an iron hoop fixed to the end."—*Roberts.* If the manna, as we are expressly informed, pointed typically to our Lord, we see nothing absurd or unreasonable in the idea that the grinding and beating it, and subjecting it to the various processes here mentioned, shadowed forth the afflictions through which he was called to pass in being prepared to become to us the bread of life, John 6 : 48–51. Heb.

and baked *it* in pans, and made cakes of it: and [h] the taste of it was as the taste of fresh oil.

9 And when the dew [i] fell upon the camp in the night, the manna fell upon it.

10 Then Moses heard the people weep throughout their families, every man in the door

h Ex. 16. 31. i Ex. 16. 14.

2:9, 10. 1 Pet. 3:18. Nor is it to be overlooked that the word here rendered "beat" —— "beat it in a mortar"—is the same with that which is applied, Is. 53:5, to the sufferings of our Lord when he is said to have been "*bruised* for our iniquities." It is remarkable, in regard to the manna, that while it was so hard that it could be ground in a mill, yet it was at the same time of such a consistence that it would melt in the morning rays of the sun if not seasonably gathered.——¶ *Baked it in pans.* Or, *boiled* or *cooked it.* The original is used to signify *baking* in 2 Sam. 13:8, but for the most part it denotes *boiling.*——¶ *Made cakes of it.* Or, as Geddes and Boothroyd, "made hearth-cakes." (Rosen. *placentas sub cineritias, cakes baked in the ashes.*)——¶ *The taste of it was as the taste of fresh oil.* Heb. "As the taste of the best moisture of oil." That is, fresh oil which has no rank savor. The Heb. term *leshad* denotes the choicest oily humor in man's body, Ps. 32:4, and so here it implies the best and sweetest moisture of oil. It had also, we learn, the taste of "wafers with honey," Ex. 16:31. The Gr. here translates it "wafers of oil," and the Chald. "paste or oil-cakes." It was therefore pleasant and wholesome food, and the taste of *oil* and *honey* points to that sweet spiritual relish which the soul perceives in feeding upon Christ as the true manna from heaven.

V. 9. *And when the dew fell upon the camp, etc.* Heb. "Descended." Pool and Ainsworth, by comparing Ex. 16:13, 14, suppose there was a double fall of dew, and that the manna was imbedded, as it were, between the two layers, whence it is called, Rev. 2:17, "hidden manna." But this suggestion takes for granted that the final clause, "the manna fell upon it," implies the falling of the manna upon the dew, whereas, it may as properly mean that it fell upon the camp, which, it must be remembered, covered a vast extent of ground—ten or twelve miles square at least. It is probable that the true idea is conveyed by the Vulg. which renders the verse, "And when the dew fell in the night upon the camp, the manna also fell with it." In the morning, when the sun's rays began to act, the dew would naturally be exhaled, and the manna, as a residuum, would remain spread over the surface of the earth. It is indeed said in the parallel account in Exodus (16:13) that "in the morning the dew lay round about the host," but in the nature of the case this must be understood with some kind of qualification, as otherwise, those whose tents were pitched near the centre of the camp would have had several miles to travel every morning to obtain it. We may reasonably suppose that in a region so broken and rocky, the host would encamp more or less in groups, and the manna might fall "round about" the camping ground of these several groups, and yet at the same time fall over the whole extent of the camp, just as it is evident the quails did when they were sent in such numbers by the Lord previous to the first fall of the manna, Ex. 16:13.

V. 10. *Moses heard the people weep*

of his tent: and the anger of the LORD was kindled [k] greatly; Moses also was displeased [l].

11 And Moses said unto the LORD, Wherefore hast thou afflicted thy servant? and wherefore have I not found favour in thy sight, that thou layest the burden of all this people upon me?

12 Have I conceived all this people? have I begotten them, that thou shouldest say unto me, Carry [m] them in thy bosom,

k ver. 1. Is. 5. 25. l Ps. 139. 21. m Is. 40. 11.

throughout their families. Heb. "By, or according to, their families;" from which it would appear that the spirit of disaffection had spread very extensively among the people.——¶ *Every man in the door of his tent.* Therefore openly, and not covertly, as would have been the case had they indulged their murmurs within doors.——¶ *Moses also was displeased.* Heb. "And in the eyes of Moses (it was) evil." He had done for the people the best in his power, and as he could do nothing without the divine appointment, he could not but feel extremely vexed in view of the ungrateful conduct of the people. Acting all along *for* the Lord, he would naturally feel *with* him in the present provocation.

V. 11. *Wherefore hast thou afflicted thy servant?* That is, wherefore hast thou suffered thy servant to be afflicted?—recognizing a providential permission, which is the only way that the Lord ever afflicts any. He is often said in Scripture to do what he does not prevent being done, what he wisely allows. Still, though we can sympathize in the grievances of Moses, we cannot justify the tone of his remonstrances in what follows. It is to be observed that the literal rendering of this clause is, "Why hast thou done evil to thy servant?" The evil, however, which is to be attributed to the Lord, is not the evil of sin, but merely the evil of trouble and affliction with which he sees fit to exercise the graces of his people. Comp. Jer. 18:8. Is. 45:7. Amos 3:6.——¶ *Wherefore have I not found favor in thy sight, etc.* Why heardest thou not my prayer of deprecation when I so earnestly besought thee to excuse me from being placed at the head of this people? Ex. 3:11. 4:10.

V. 12. *Have I conceived all this people?* Chald. "Am I the father of all this people? Are they my sons?" Are they my children, that I should be charged with the responsibility of supplying all their wants?——¶ *Have I begotten them?* Or, Heb. "Have I brought them forth?" Both terms are perhaps more intrinsically appropriate to the mother, although in spiritual generation the distinctive functions of father and mother seem not to be always very clearly marked. Thus Paul says, 1 Cor. 4:15, "Ye have not many fathers; for in Christ Jesus have I begotten you through the Gospel." But in Gal. 4:19, he says, "My little children, of whom I travail in birth again, until Christ be formed in you." The wording, however, of the entire verse seems intended to describe the office of a *nursing-father.*——¶ *Carry them in thy bosom.* That is, carefully, tenderly, lovingly. This Moses might be said to do in an inferior sense, but how infinitely far does he come short therein of Him of whom it is said, Is. 40:11, "He shall feed his flock like a shepherd: he shall gather the lambs with his arm, and carry them in his bosom, and shall gently lead those that are with young."——

as a nursing father [n] beareth the
sucking child, unto the land
which thou [o] swarest unto their
fathers?
13 Whence [p] should I have
flesh to give unto all this people? for they weep unto me,
saying, Give us flesh, that we
may eat.
14 I [q] am not able to bear all
this people alone, because *it is*
too heavy for me.
15 And if thou deal thus

n Is. 49. 23. 1 Th. 2. 7. o Gen. 13. 15. 26. 3. p Mat. 15. 33.

q Ex. 18. 18. Dan. 1. 9-12.

¶ *As a nursing father beareth the sucking child.* Strikingly indicative of the mildness, gentleness, and love which should characterize rulers, and especially rulers in the church. Is. 49:23, "And kings shall be thy *nursing fathers*, and queens thy nursing mothers." So also the apostle, 1 Thes. 2:7, 11, "We were gentle among you, even as a nurse cherisheth her children: we exhorted, and comforted, and charged every one of you, as a father doth his children." Accordingly, Ainsworth cites from Maimonides the following rule relative to the deportment of the governors of the church:—"It is not lawful for a man to govern with stateliness over the congregation, and with haughtiness of spirit, but with meekness and fear. And every pastor that bringeth more terror upon the congregation than is for the name of God, he shall be punished, and shall not see himself to have a wise son. It is not lawful for him to govern with contemptuous carriage, although they be the common people of the land; neither may he tread upon the heads of the holy people; (for) although they be unlearned and base, they are the sons of Abraham, Isaac, and Jacob, and (are) the armies of the Lord, who brought them out of the land of Egypt by great might and by strong hand; but he must bear the toil of the congregation and their burden, as Moses, our master, of whom it is said, 'As a nursing father beareth the sucking child.'" The Targum of Jon. for "nursing father" has "pedagogue," the term used by Paul in speaking of the Law; Gal. 3:24, "The law was our *school-master* to bring us to Christ."

V. 13. *Whence should I have flesh to give unto all this people?* Even if the flocks and herds should afford a supply to a part of the host, they would by no means be sufficient for *all.* This is indeed a becoming acknowledgment on the part of Moses, of his inability to supply the wants of the people, but it has the air of implying that the Lord expected him to do it, for which he had no sufficient grounds. So far, then, it savored of infirmity, and was open to rebuke. The Lord, however, dealt very graciously with him, as appears from the sequel.——¶ *For they weep unto me.* Heb. "They weep upon me." The phraseology is the same with that Judg. 14:16, "And Samson's wife *wept before him.*" Heb. "Wept upon him." It implies an importunate pressing or bearing down upon one with urgent solicitations.

V. 14. *I am not able to bear all this people alone.* "Had the work been much less, he could not have gone through it in his own strength; but had it been much greater, through God strengthening him he might have done it."—*Henry.*

V. 15. *And if thou deal thus with me.* If thou still leavest me to bear the whole of this burden. It is remarkable that the word "thou" here addressed to the Most High is in the original in the feminine instead of the masculine

with me, [r] kill me, I pray thee, out of hand, if I have found favor in thy sight; and let me not see my wretchedness.

16 And the LORD said unto Moses, Gather unto me seventy[s] men of the elders of Israel, whom thou knowest to be the elders

r 1 K. 19. 4. Jonah 4. 3.

s Ex. 24. 1, 9.

gender—*at* instead of *attâh.* A similar usage occurs Deut. 5 : 27, where the people, terrified with the divine majesty in the delivery of the Law, said unto Moses, "Speak *thou* (Heb. *at*) unto us." The reason of the peculiarity is mere matter of conjecture. The Rabbins say it was owing to a special trepidation and confusion which interfered with distinct utterance. Kennicott and others suppose an error in the manuscripts. We must leave it undetermined.——¶ *Kill me, I pray thee, out of hand.* That is, forthwith, immediately. "Out of hand" is an old English phrase, equivalent to "outright." The original for "kill" is reduplicated, "killing kill me," in order to express more forcibly the vehemence of the desire. It is as if he should say, I shall take it as the greatest kindness if thou wilt at once remove me from the world—an expression of impatience which cannot be justified even in view of the sorest trials to which he was subjected.——¶ *Let me not see my wretchedness.* Heb. "Let me not see my evil." That is, let me not live to become a miserable creature. To "see good" is to enjoy it; to "see evil" is to suffer it. So also to "see death" is to die, Ps. 50 : 23. 89 : 49. 91 : 16. Luke 2 : 26. Comp. the speech of Elijah, 1 Kings 14 : 4. We feel for the vexations of Moses, but we recognize at the same time his infirmity in asking for release from his troubles in such a disorderly way. His language is probably equivalent to that used in Ex. 32 : 32, "Blot me out of the book which thou hast written," but is susceptible of a more favorable construction than is often put upon it; q. d. "Lord, if thy decree against this people may not be reversed; if justice demand their utter extermination; let my eyes be first closed in peace. Subject me not to the severe mortification of surviving all my nation, and of enduring the insults and scorn of our enemies. In mercy take me first out of the world, where I should only lead a life of sorrow and regret, heavier than death itself." The opposite meaning which some would elicit from the words may be thus expressed:—"Lord, grant the pardon of this people to the prayers of thy servant, who would rather submit to everlasting misery than fail to obtain his request." The sentiment implied in this language finds no warrant either in the letter or the spirit of the teachings of the Scriptures.

The Appointment of seventy Elders as Assistants to Moses.

V. 16. *Gather unto me seventy men of the elders of Israel.* Chald. "Gather before me." Targ. Jon. "Gather in my name seventy worthy men." We read no rebuke of Moses on this occasion, for although his conduct was faulty, yet the Lord's forbearance was such that he was willing to pass by his offence as far as any outward manifestation was concerned. The inward reproach of his own conscience he might still be left to feel. It is a matter of considerable debate among commentators, whether this body of seventy elders was one of mere occasional creation and temporary duration, or whether it was henceforward perpetual, and the same in fact with the Sanhedrim or great national council of the Jews, of which we read

of the people, and officers over them; and bring them unto the

in the New Testament. The Jewish writers generally, and many Christian writers of eminence are of the latter opinion. The former appears, however, the more probable hypothesis, as no mention is made of the existence of such a council in all the Old Testament, and this silence cannot well be accounted for consistently with the actual existence of such a body. Add to this, that the Sanhedrim was a judicial institution having control of matters of justice and cases of appeal. The present appears to have been simply a kind of senate formed to aid Moses in bearing the burdens and responsibilities of the station to which he was elevated, and which we can easily apprehend must have been extremely arduous and onerous.——¶ *Whom thou knowest to be the elders of the people.* That is, men of mature age, of grave and exemplary deportment, of ripened wisdom, who would know how best to use the authority committed to them; men who should be elders in fact as well as in name. It is evident from Ex. 24:1, that there was already existing a class of persons called "elders," and that out of these a selection was to be made on the present occasion.——¶ *And officers over them.* Heb. *soterauv, his officers,* the same as the *soterim* mentioned Ex. 5:6, on which see Note. Targ. Jon. "That had been set over them in Egypt;" as if their sufferings there in behalf of their brethren had entitled them to this distinction. "Among the persons that appear in the Israelitish Diet, besides those already mentioned, we find the *soterim,* or *scribes.* They were different from the judges; for Moses had expressly ordained (Deut. 16:18) that in every city there should be appointed, not only judges, but *soterim* likewise. It is very certain that Moses had not originally instituted these officers, but already found them among the people while in Egypt. For when the Israelites did not deliver the required tale of bricks, the *soterim* were called to account, and punished, Ex. 5:6–14. Now, as *satar* in Arabic, signifies *to write;* and its derivative, *mastir, a person whose duty it is to keep accounts, and collect debts,* I am almost persuaded that these *soterim* must have been the officers who kept the genealogical tables of the Israelites, with a faithful record of births, marriages, and deaths; and, as they kept the rolls of families, had, moreover, the duty of apportioning the public burdens and services on the people individually. An office exactly similar, we have not in our governments, because they are not so genealogically regulated; at least we do not institute enumerations of the people by families. But among a people whose notions were completely clannish, and among whom all hereditary succession, and even all posthumous fame, depended on genealogical registers, this must have been an office fully as important as that of a judge. In Egypt, the Levites had not yet been consecrated and set apart from the rest of the tribes; there, of course, the *soterim* must have been chosen either out of every family, or, perhaps, merely according to the opinion entertained of their fitness for the office. In the time of the kings, however, we find them generally taken from the tribe of Levi, 1 Chron. 23:4. 2 Chron. 19:8–11. 34:13. This was a very rational procedure, as the Levites devoted themselves particularly to study; and among husbandmen and unlearned people, few were likely to be so expert at writing, as to be intrusted with the keeping of registers so important. Add to this, that in later times, the genealogical ta-

tabernacle of the congregation, that they may stand there with thee.
17 And [t] I will come down and talk with thee there: and I will take of the spirit [u] which *is* upon thee, and will put *it* upon them; and they shall bear the

t ver. 25. Gen. 11. 5. 18. 21. Ex. 19. 20.
u 2 K. 2. 9, 15. Is. 44. 3. Joel 2. 28.

bles were kept in the temple. We find these *soterim* mentioned in many other passages besides those quoted above. In Num. 11:16, they are the persons of respectability from among whom the supreme senate of Seventy is chosen. In Deut. 1:15, mention is made of *soterim* appointed by Moses in the wilderness, although the people had previously had such magistrates in Egypt; most probably he only filled the places of those who were dead. In Deut. 20:5, we see them charged with orders to those of the people that were selected *to go to war;* which is perfectly suited to my explanation of the nature of their office. In Deut. 29:10, 31:28, Josh. 8:33, 23:2, we find them as representatives of the people in the Diets, or when a covenant with God is entered into. In Josh. 1:10, they appear as the officers who communicated to the people the general's orders respecting military affairs; and this, again, corresponds to the province of muster-masters. In 2 Chron. 26:11, we have the chief *soter*, under whose command the whole army stands after the general, if indeed he himself be not so. In 1 Chron. 27:1, the name of the office alone is mentioned."—*Michaelis.*——¶ *Bring them unto the tabernacle of the congregation.* Heb. "Take them unto the tabernacle." That they might there be, as it were, consecrated to the Lord in the most public manner, so that there should be no doubt among the people as to their authority.——¶ *That they may stand there with thee.* Heb. *ve-hithyatzebu*, *and they shall make themselves to stand, they shall present themselves.* The Hebrew writers give a peculiar emphasis to the phrase "with thee" in this connection, as if it imported that they were to be men of like wisdom, weight, and estimation with Moses, though in an inferior degree.

V. 17. *I will come down.* Chald. "I will reveal myself." Targ. Jon. "I will reveal myself in the glory of my majesty." From v. 25 it appears that this revelation or descent was in connection with the cloudy pillar, which might have been at the same time lowered somewhat nearer to the surface of the earth.——¶ *And talk with thee there.* It is clear from what follows that the Lord, in the symbol of his presence, came down and communed with Moses, according to his promise, but what he said is not made known.——¶ *And I will take of the spirit which is upon thee, and will put it upon them.* Heb. *âtzalti*, *I will separate, set apart, keep, reserve,* of the spirit which is upon thee, etc. That is, he would endow them with the same spirit of government, or with those gifts of wisdom, judgment, counsel, courage, etc., which were bestowed upon Moses, though not to the same degree. They were to be partners, but not equals, in the divine donation. "Spirit" is often used for gifts of the Holy Spirit, or spiritual gifts (*charismata*), for "there are diversities of gifts, but the same Spirit." So "spirits" is used to denote spiritual gifts, 1 Cor. 12:4, "The *spirits* of the prophets are subject to the prophets." The communication of the spirit of Moses to the seventy elders does not imply any diminution as it respected him. The Jewish writers illustrate the matter by saying that "Moses in that hour was like

burden of the people with thee, that thou bear *it* not thyself alone.

18 And say thou unto the people, Sanctify [v] yourselves against to-morrow, and ye shall eat flesh: for ye have wept in the ears [w] of the LORD, saying, Who shall [x] give us flesh to eat? for *it was* well with us in Egypt: there-

v Ex. 19. 10. w Ex. 16. 7. x ver. 4, 5.

unto the lamp that was left burning on the candlestick (in the sanctuary); from which all the other lamps were lighted, yet the light thereof was not lessened a whit." In point of strict truth, however, there was not *any thing* actually taken from Moses. It is merely the language of appearance, founded upon the similarity of the phenomena. In like manner it is said that the Lord God formed Adam of the dust of the ground, not that he was really so formed, for in the original it is, he "formed him dust of the ground," that is, to be of the same material with the dust, so that when he died, he might be said to be resolved into it. So the spiritual gifts evinced by these elders were of the same kind with those of Moses, and therefore they are *said* to be taken from him. The inference is very plain, that divine gifts and qualifications are indispensable for those who are called to act as leaders and superintendents in the Lord's church, and that those who are not possessed of these qualifications are not called.——¶ *And they shall bear the burden of the people with thee.* Heb. "They shall bear with thee in the burden." The preposition "in," however, does not affect the sense, as appears from the usage in Ezek. 18:19, 20, "The son shall not bear the iniquity of the father," where the literal rendering is, "shall not bear *in* the iniquity of the father." The allusion is to the complaint of Moses in vs. 11, 14, and an assurance given that the men now selected shall take part in the burdensome cares and fatigues growing out of the government of an unruly people.

V. 18. *Sanctify yourselves against to-morrow.* Chald. "Prepare yourselves." On the import of this phrase see Note on Ex. 19:10. It denotes preparation in the sense of superinducing upon their minds a state of devout reflection, and external abstinence from whatever would interfere with the sanctity which they were then required to study. So, to "sanctify a war," as in Jer. 6:4. 51:28. Joel 3:9, is to engage in a war with holy motives, to enter into it in such a state of mind, have such an eye to the divine glory, that it should be a *consecrated war.* Alas! how totally unlike the great mass of wars that have been waged among men! The reason why this sanctification was now commanded probably was, that if they duly repented of the sin of their rebellion, and thus approached the Lord in a humble and contrite frame, the promised flesh might not prove a judgment and a curse to them, but a lawful comfort and luxury. Otherwise the command, "Sanctify yourselves" would be equivalent to, "Prepare to meet thy God, O Israel;" i. e. in a way of judgment, and not of mercy.——¶ *Ye have wept in the ears of the Lord.* The parallel clause in v. 20 is, "ye have wept before" the Lord, as the Chald. also renders it here. All unreasonable complaints and murmurings, though vented ostensibly against the Lord's ministers, or addressed to no one in particular, are in reality uttered towards the Lord himself, and come up into his ears.——¶ *The Lord will give*

fore the LORD will give you flesh,
and ye shall eat.
19 Ye shall not eat one day,
nor two days, nor five days, neither ten days, nor twenty days;
20 *But* even a whole month,[y]
until it come out at your nostrils, and it be loathsome unto
you: because that ye have despised the LORD which *is* among
you, and have wept before him,
saying, Why came we forth out
of Egypt?
21 And Moses said, The people, among whom I *am*, *are* six

y Ps. 78. 29. 106. 15.

---

you flesh, and ye shall eat. This was indeed a compliance with the desires of the people, but of the same nature with that which is spoken of at a subsequent period, when he is said to have "given them a king in his anger." A significant allusion to this kind of indulgence occurs also, Ps. 106 : 16, "He gave them them their request, but sent leanness into their souls." The prayers of the wicked may be answered, but in such a way that nothing shall be more to be dreaded. The divine promises to the evil are virtual threatenings.

V. 19. *Ye shall not eat one day, nor two days, etc.* As they did about a year before, Ex. 16 : 12, 13, when the people had been thus feasted for one day.

V. 20. *Until it come out at your nostrils.* Denoting a nausea and surfeit. "What does this mean? Is it not a figurative expression, to show that they were to eat till fully satisfied? Bishop Patrick says, 'Till you be glutted and cloyed with it.' Is it not a striking illustration that this figure of speech is used at this day to convey the same meaning? A host says to his guests, 'Now friends, eat *mookamattam*, to the nose,' literally, to eat till they are full up to the nose. 'O, sir, how can I eat any more? I am full to the nose, I have no more room.' Of a glutton, it is said, 'That fellow always *fills up to the nose!*'"—*Roberts.* Bp. Patrick's note is this:—"Till you be glutted with it, and vomit it up so violently, that it shall come not only out at your mouth, but at your nostrils." This is perhaps somewhat favored by the original *zârâ*, in the ensuing clause, which several of the versions render, "in dispersionem," *for a scattering*, deriving it from *zârâh*, *to be diffused*, or *spread abroad.*——¶ *And it be loathsome unto you.* Heb. "And it shall be unto you for a loathing." Gr. "It shall be unto you for a cholera (εις χολεραν), which Hesychius defines as a violent *disorder of the bowels.* The effect, we may presume, to have been what we should now express by *cholera morbus.* Chald. "It shall be unto you for an offence." "What a righteous thing it is with God to make that loathsome to men which they have inordinately lusted after. God could make them despise flesh as much as they had despised manna."—*Henry.* ——¶ *Because that ye have despised the Lord.* Heb. *meastem*, *contemptuously refused*, or *set at nought.* Chald, "Ye have rejected the Word of the Lord." Gr. "Ye have disobeyed the Lord." The word in the Heb. is the same with that which occurs 1 Sam. 8 : 7, "For they have not *rejected* thee, but they have *rejected* me." It is a serious reflection that our complaining of the divine dispensations amounts, in the Lord's sight, to a positive contempt of him.——¶ *Which is among you.* That is, by the visible symbol of his presence. Chald. "Whose divine majesty dwells among you." Their sin, therefore, was a kind of spiritual *lese-majesty.*

V. 21. *The people among whom I (am)*

hundred[z] thousand footmen; and thou hast said, I will give them flesh, that they may eat a whole month.

z Ex. 12. 37. c. 1. 46.

22 Shall[a] the flocks and the herds be slain for them, to suffice them? or shall all the fish of the sea be gathered to-

a 2 K. 7. 2. Mark 8. 4. John 6. 7, 9.

are six hundred thousand, etc. That is, so many who were able to carry arms; which, by a fair proportion, would require of the aged, of women and children, and the mixed multitude, enough to make a grand total of near three millions of people. In view of the demands of such an immense host, the faith of Moses seems to have wavered. Either from the discomposure of his spirit by reason of the affronts of the people, or from a fear that they might be commanded to feed upon the cattle required for sacrifice, or from sheer incredulity, he is prompted to inquire how it can be possible that so many mouths should be fed with flesh for a whole month together. All the cattle we have, says his unbelief, will come short of the requirement, and all the fish of the Red Sea would be insufficient for it.

V. 22. *Shall all the fish of the sea be gathered together for them?* That is, gathered together in shoals. Harmer's note on this passage is worthy of being transcribed. "When Moses mentioned Israel's being fed with fish, collected from the Red Sea, he seems to have supposed something of an extraordinary kind; but analogous to what had happened to several people, in small companies, not any thing miraculous. In answer to the divine declaration, Moses proposed a difficulty in accomplishing this promise, in the natural course of things, not as imagining it could not be done by a miracle; he could not but know, that he that rained down manna, could, by a miracle, gorge them with flesh; but in the common course of things, or in the natural, though more unusual operation of Providence, could it be brought about? That was what puzzled Moses. Some flocks, and a few oxen, they had with them for the solemnities of sacrifice; but could a part of them, with any addition that might be procured from the people on the skirts of the desert, be sufficient to support them a whole month? Fish might be obtained from the Red Sea, from which, it seems, they were not very distant, but could it be expected they would come in such numbers to the shore, within their reach, as fully to satisfy the cravings of their appetites, day after day, for a whole month?——'We remember the fish we did eat in Egypt freely,' was a part of their moan, Num. 11:5. If Moses knew what the common people of Egypt now know, and which their sages in ancient days must, at least, have remarked, he could be no stranger to that change of place that may be observed as to fish, and their crowding together at certain times; and to some such a natural, but surprising and unknown occurrence, as to the inhabitants of this sea, the words of Moses seem to point: 'Shall the flocks and herds be slain for them? . . . or shall all the fish of the sea be gathered together,' by some natural impulse, to this place, for a month or more, which none of us have had any notion of, nor received any information about, to *suffice them?* Such is, I apprehend, the spirit of these words."——¶ *To suffice them.* Heb. *u-mâtzâ lâhem, and shall one find for them?* For parallel instances of this usage, see Josh. 17:16. Judg. 21:14, with my Note upon each passage. The remark of Philip, John 6:7, 9, im-

gether for them, to suffice
them?
23 And the LORD said unto
Moses, Is[b] the LORD's hand waxed short? thou shalt see now
whether[c] my word shall come to
pass unto thee or not.
24 And Moses went out, and
told the people the words of the
LORD, and gathered the seventy
men of the elders of the people,
and set them round about the
tabernacle.
25 And the LORD came down
[d] in a cloud, and spake unto him,
and took of the spirit that *was*

b Is. 50. 2. 59. 1. *c* Ezek. 12. 25. 24. 14.

d ver. 17.

---

plies a similar staggering of faith:—"Two hundred pennyworth of bread is not sufficient for them (the great multitude) that every one of them may take a little." In both cases, however, the doubts were soon silenced.

V. 23. *Is the Lord's hand waxed short?* Gr. "Shall not the Lord's hand be sufficient?" Chald. "Shall the Word of the Lord be hindered?" *Hand*, by a well known figure of speech, is often used as significant of power, as being the instrument by which power is put forth (Deut. 32:36. Josh. 4:24. 8:20), while the original term for *shortened* implies that which is *lessened* or *scanted*, and is thus rather applicable to what the hand signifies than to the hand itself. In Mic. 2:7, it is spoken of the Lord's Spirit—"Is the Spirit of the Lord *straitened* (Heb. *shortened*)?" but for the most part, as here, the word is predicated of the Lord's hand. Thus, Is. 59:1, "Behold, the Lord's hand is not *shortened*, that it cannot save." Is. 50:2, "Is my hand *shortened* at all, that it cannot redeem? or have I no power to deliver?" where the latter clause explains the former. "Even true and great believers sometimes find it hard to trust God under the discouragements of second causes, and 'against hope to believe in hope.' Moses himself can scarcely forbear saying, 'Can God furnish a table in the wilderness?' when this was become the common cry. No doubt this was his infirmity."—*Henry*.

V. 24. *And Moses went out.* But whether from his own tent or the sanctuary is uncertain. The Targ. Jon. renders it, "He went out from the tent of the Shekinah," into which it may be supposed he had gone to pour out his prayers into the Lord's bosom. He no doubt "went out" also in the person of the emissaries who were dispatched to various parts of the camp to gather in the seventy elders, and as they were convened at the Tabernacle of the congregation, the presumption is that it was thence that Moses is said to have gone out. The place of their congress was the place of his egress.——¶ *Set them round about the tabernacle.* Heb. "Made them to stand." All important assemblies were wont to meet at the Tabernacle. Comp. ch. 27:2.

V. 25. *And the Lord came down in a cloud.* Or, perhaps better, "in *the* cloud." The manifestation in this case was no doubt similar to that mentioned Ex. 33:9, "And it came to pass, as Moses entered into the tabernacle, the cloudy pillar descended, and stood *at* the door of the tabernacle, and (the Lord) talked with Moses," where see my Note. Comp. also Ps. 99:7, "He spake to them in the cloudy pillar."——¶ *When the spirit rested upon them, they prophesied.* Heb. *yithnabbe-u, were made* or *impelled to prophesy*, the Hithpael, or reflexive conjugation having here the same signification as the Niphal or passive, except that in the Hithpael

upon him, and gave *it* unto the seventy elders: and it came to pass, *that*, when [e] the spirit rested upon them, they prophesied, and did not cease.

26 But there remained two *of the* men in the camp, the

e 1 Sam. 10. 5, 6, etc.

the idea is more distinctly of an impulsive power *within* the subject, and the Niphal of one *without*. It is therefore peculiarly applicable to that state of *possession*, or *spiritual excitation*, which prompts extraordinary utterances. Prophesying, in this sense, was one of the special gifts or operations of the Lord's Spirit in its illapse upon the minds of men. The usual word for *prophet* in the original Hebrew is *nâbi*, which is really of a *passive import*, implying one who speaks from a divine impulse, and utters things entirely beyond the scope of his own unassisted ability. He is not so much a *speaker* as one *spoken through*. Thus it is said, Joel 2 : 29, "Upon the handmaids in those days I will pour out my Spirit," that is, Acts 2 : 18, "I will pour out my Spirit, *and they shall prophesy*." So Acts 19 : 6, "And when Paul had laid his hands upon them, the Holy Ghost came on them; and they spake with tongues, *and prophesied*." In like manner, when Saul was anointed king, it was said to him, 1 Sam. 10 : 6, "The Spirit of the Lord will come upon thee, *and thou shalt prophesy*, and shalt be turned into another man." Accordingly it is added, v. 10, "And the Spirit of God came upon him, *and he prophesied*." The term evidently is not restricted to the sense of *foretelling future events*, but implies also any kind of utterance prompted by a divine influence, and especially the unfolding the meaning of the sacred Word. Thus Paul, 1 Cor. 14 : 3, "He that *prophesieth* speaketh unto men to edification, and exhortation, and comfort." Analogous to the elders here appointed were the "helps and governments," spoken of by Paul (1 Cor. 12 : 28) as established in the early Christian church.——¶ *And did not cease.* Heb. *lo yâsâphu, did not add*, that is, did not continue to prophesy in that manner after that day. In like manner it is said, Deut. 5 : 22, that God pronounced the ten commandments, and "added no more" (Heb. *lo yâsŏph*), by which is to be understood, that he spake no more to the people in that peculiar manner. So also it is said of Saul, 1 Sam. 10 : 13, "And when he had *made an end of prophesying*, he came," etc. The gift indicated was probably designed to be of merely temporary duration. Gr. "And they added no more." And Sol. Jarchi, a noted Jewish commentator says, "They did not add;" i. e. they "prophesied not save that day only." This would be sufficient to afford an attestation that they were moved by a divine impulse, and this testimony it was important the people should have. With this coincides the comment of Theodoret, "The seventy did not prophesy beyond this day, because God promoted them not to prophesy, but to govern, which St. Paul also reckons among other gifts bestowed upon Christians," 1 Cor. 12 : 26. It is, however, to be remarked, that this rendering is not uniform. The Chald. exhibits a sense directly opposite,—"And they ceased not," and this is the sense adopted by our translators, unless indeed we suppose with Patrick that the true idea which they attached to the phrase is, "They did not cease all that day while they stood round about the tabernacle." After all, a shade of doubt as to the genuine import of the phrase will still hang over it.

V. 26. *But there remained two (of the) men in the camp.* That is, two out of the

name of the one *was* Eldad, and the name of the other Medad: and the spirit rested upon them; and they *were* of them that were written, but went not out unto the tabernacle: and [f] they prophesied in the camp.

27 And there ran a young man, and told Moses, and said, Eldad and Medad do prophesy in the camp.

28 And Joshua the son of Nun, the servant of Moses, *one* of his young men, answered and said, My lord Moses, forbid [g] them.

29 And Moses said unto him, Enviest thou for my sake?

f Jer. 36. 5, 6.

g Luke 9. 49. John 3. 26.

---

seventy elders before designated. This, however, does not appear in the wording of the original Hebrew, which has simply, "And there remained two men." To intimate the true sense our translators have inserted the words "of the" before "men." The reason of their withholding themselves from the meeting at the Tabernacle is not stated, but whatever it were, the circumstance gave occasion for a manifestation of the Lord's good pleasure, with which we should not otherwise have been favored. It is not improbable that as Saul, when the appointment was about to be made, withdrew and "hid himself among the stuff," so the persons here mentioned were kept back by a similar reserve or repugnancy. But the Lord by his Spirit found them out, and the divine influence soon showed its effects upon them. Though among "them that were written," that is, designated, nominated, for the purpose, yet refusing to come they were seized with the spirit of prophecy and gave vent to it in the midst of the camp.

V. 28. *And Joshua the son of Nun, the servant of Moses, (one) of his young men, answered, etc.* Heb. *mibbehoorauv, of his chosen ones.* It is probable he was one of the "able men" whom Moses chose at the suggestion of Jethro to preside over certain classified portions of the people, Ex. 18:25. The term there employed is *yibhar, chose,* and *mibbehoor, chosen,* is from the same root.——¶ *My lord Moses, forbid them.* Targ. Jon. "My lord Moses, request mercy from before the Lord, and forbid them the spirit of prophecy." Joshua, it would seem, spoke from a commendable zeal for the honor of Moses, but rashly and precipitately. He no doubt thought that these men's prophesying or teaching in the camp tended to make those gifts common, and thus disparage Moses in the eyes of the people; or, he may have thought the proceeding was schismatic, as being calculated to divert the people from the Tabernacle, the appointed place of meeting, where the rest of the seventy elders were assembled. The prompting under which he acted seems to have been very similar to that which moved the disciples in forbidding one to cast out devils in Christ's name because he followed not with them, Luke 9:49, 50. Mark 9:50. And it would appear from the answer both of Moses and of our Lord, that some degree of jealousy rested in the heart of Joshua, as well as of the disciples.

V. 29. *Enviest thou for my sake?* Rather, "Art thou jealous, or zealous, for my sake?" This is the force of the original term which is employed to signify a fervent or highly excited state of jealous, envious, or indignant feeling. Moses knew the men better, and was aware of the true source of their

Would [h] God that all the LORD's people were prophets, *and* that the LORD would put his spirit upon them!

30 And Moses gat him into the camp, he and the elders of Israel.

31 And there went forth a wind from the LORD, and brought [i] quails from the sea, and let *them*

h 1 Cor. 14. 5.

i Ex. 16. 13. Ps. 78. 26-29. 105. 40.

---

inspiration; consequently he designed to administer a gentle rebuke to Joshua for giving way to too earnest a spirit of zealous or jealous regard for his honor. He intimates, therefore, that the number, be it ever so great, of those who were possessed of such extraordinary endowments was so far from being a source of uneasiness to him that he rejoiced in it, and heartily wished there were more of them. We derive from the words of Moses the practical intimation that we are not secretly to grieve at the gifts, graces, or usefulness of others; that we are not to be unduly excited at the weaknesses or infirmities of others; and that we are not to be forward to condemn and silence those that differ from us, as if they did not follow the Lord because they do not follow him with us. "Shall we reject those whom Christ hath owned, or restrain any from doing good because they are not in every thing of our mind?"—*Henry.*——¶ *That the Lord would put his spirit upon them.* That is, the gifts of his spirit. Chald. "His spirit of prophecy." Paul, in like manner, wished that all the church could "prophesy," saying, "Follow after charity, and desire spiritual gifts, but rather that ye may prophesy," 1 Cor. 14:1.

V. 30. *And Moses gat himself into the camp.* Heb. "Was gathered;" implying that he and the elders, now brought under a special influence from above, were moved as in a kind of passive way, to convey themselves from the Tabernacle into the midst of the camp, there to enter immediately upon the administration to which they had been called. The original word is the same with that which is applied, ch. 12:14, 15, to Miriam, and rendered in the one case "received in," and in the other "brought in."

The Quails brought.

V. 31. *And there went forth a wind from the Lord.* Heb. *ve-ruah nâsa, and a wind broke up;* that is, was let forth with violence, as seems to be implied by the use of a term which is ordinarily applied to the *striking of tents* preparatory to departure, which was usually executed no doubt with very considerable dispatch. The word for "wind" is the same with that employed above to signify "spirit," and there may have been an allusion intended to the contrast between the *spiritual influence* imparted to the elders on this occasion, and that *violent inflation* from the Lord which brought on the quails, and thus spent itself eventually upon the people. The same word occurs in relation to the same event, Ps. 78:26–28, "He caused an east wind *to blow* (Heb. *yissa*) in the heaven: and by his power he brought in the south wind. He rained flesh also upon them as dust, and feathered fowls like as the sand of the sea: and he let it fall in the midst of their camp, round about their habitations." The Lord, even in working miracles, does not always dispense with the use of means. He could easily have commanded the appearance of the quails without the agency of the wind, but it seemed

fall by the camp, as it were a day's journey on this side, and

good to his wisdom to make one physical power subordinate to another.——¶ *And brought quails from the sea.* That is, from across the sea, or from the direction of the sea, not out of the waters. They came from the African side of the Red Sea. Heb. *selâv*, a term which Bochart traces to *shâlâh*, which signifies *to live peacefully*, or *to abound*, because in warm countries no bird is more abundant. It is more probable, however, that the Hebrew name refers to the *foolish and ruinous security* in which the quail is known to indulge. When she lights upon a field abounding in grain, she resigns herself to the power of appetite without fear or suspicion. Absorbed entirely in the enjoyment of the moment, she betrays herself with her incessant singing, and is easily enticed into the snare of the fowler. The Israelites, in feeding upon them, showed a similar recklessness, and as Ephraim is compared by the prophet, Hos. 7 : 11, to "a silly dove without heart," i. e. without understanding, so may they be compared to "a silly *quail* without heart." "These birds," says Kitto, "as well as the way of taking and preparing them, must have been well known to the Israelites while in Egypt. At the proper season these migratory birds resorted to Egypt in such vast flocks, that even the dense population of Egypt was unable to consume them while fresh, but they salted and dried great quantities for future use. It is still the same in those countries; and modern travellers, on witnessing the incredible numbers of these birds, have expressed their conviction that, as the text describes, such a suitable wind as the Almighty sent, could only have been necessary to furnish even the great Hebrew host with a sufficient supply of quails to last for a month."—*Pict. Bible.* Ludolph, in his History of Ethiopia, who is followed by Saurin, Bp. Patrick, and others, endeavors to make out that the original term denotes *locusts* instead of *quails*, but the current of authority goes decidedly in favor of the latter rendering. The following considerations serve to confirm it. (1.) The term *selâv* nowhere else in the sacred volume signifies the locust, nor does the root from which it comes favor this interpretation, for no creature is more *restless* than the locust. Besides, the creature which in one passage is called *selâv* is called *oph, bird*, in another; but the latter term properly denotes the *fowls of heaven* and not *winged insects.* Ps. 78 : 27, "He rained flesh also upon them as dust, and *feathered fowls* (Heb. *oph canaph, fowl of wing*) like as the sand of the sea." (2.) It does not appear that insects are ever called in Scripture *oph canaph. Canaph* properly signifies *a wing*, which may be contracted or expanded, for the purpose of covering and protecting the body; which does not seem to accord with the wings of insect tribes. (3.) On the hypothesis of Ludolph, it may be considered as an inexplicable circumstance that Moses, in a country swarming with locusts, did not seem to think of them, when he asked with surprise: "The people among whom I am, are six hundred thousand footmen; and thou hast said, I will give them flesh, that they may eat a whole month. Shall the flocks and the herds be slain for them to suffice them? or shall all the fish of the sea be gathered together for them to suffice them?" Moses knew that the innumerable swarms of locusts which devour the land of Egypt and the surrounding countries, were the sport of every wind, and that a steady gale could waft as many into the desert,

as it were a day's journey on the other side, round about the camp, and as it were two cubits *high* upon the face of the earth.

as would suffice all the thousands of Israel. Why then did he not mention the locusts, and present his supplication for a favorable breeze? This circumstance cannot be accounted for, but on the supposition that locusts were not the object of their desire, nor in the contemplation of Jehovah. We rest, therefore, in the conclusion, that *quails* and not *locusts* are intended by the sacred writer.——¶ *Let* (*them*) *fall by the camp.* Heb. *yittash, be spread abroad, diffused.* The word occurs 1 Sam. 30 : 16, "And when he had brought him down, behold they (the company) *were spread abroad* (Heb. *netushim*) upon all the earth, eating, and drinking, and dancing," etc.——¶ *A day's journey.* Heb. "The way of day." And so in the next clause. The phrase is somewhat ambiguous, as we are not informed whether the day's journey means the space over which an individual could travel in one day, in which case it would be much greater—or the whole army could traverse, which would be much less. If the journey of an individual is intended, it might be about thirty miles; but if the sacred historian refers to the whole army, a third part of this space is as much as they could march in one day in the sandy desert, under a vertical sun. In the opinion of Bochart, this immense cloud of quails covered a space of at least forty miles' diameter; for a day's journey is at least twenty miles. Ludolph thinks, it ought to be reduced to sixteen miles; and others, to half that number, because, Moses refers to the march of Israel through the desert, encumbered with their women and children, their flocks and herds, and the baggage of the whole nation; which must have greatly retarded their movements, and rendered the short distance of eight miles more than sufficient for a journey of one day. It is equally doubtful, whether the distance mentioned by Moses, must be measured from the centre or from the extremities of the encampment; it is certain, however, that he intends to state the countless numbers of these birds which fell around the tents of Israel.——¶ *And as it were two cubits* (*high*) *upon the face of the earth.* The first impression produced by these words would undoubtedly be, that the quails fell in such abundance that they were actually *heaped up* on the surface of the earth to the height of two cubits. But the Hebrew admits of another rendering, which we, with Mr. Kitto, are inclined to adopt, especially as it has the sanction of Jarchi, a Jewish commentator:—"They flew so high as against a man's heart, that he was not fatigued in getting them, either by reaching high or stooping low." So also the Vulg. "And they flew in the air two cubits high above the ground." But more to the purpose is the following note from the "Pictorial Bible." "As we understand, it would seem that the birds were so exhausted, or rather they were so strictly kept by the Divine power within the limit of a day's journey from the camp, that even when roused or attempting flight, they could not rise more than three feet from the ground, and were thus easily caught by nets or by the hand. . . . In support of the view we have been led to take, we may add, that if the birds had lain two cubits deep upon the ground, the far greater part of them must have been dead before they could have been collected, and would therefore have been unfit for food, since the Israelites could eat nothing that had died of suffoca-

32 And the people stood up all that day, and all *that* night, and all the next day, and they gathered the quails: he that gathered least gathered ten [k] homers: and

k Ex. 16. 36.

tion, or the blood of which had not been poured out."

V. 32. *And the people stood up all that day, etc.* Rather, "rose up" (Heb. *yâkom*); that is, they *engaged earnestly* in the work, and were intent upon gathering the fowls for thirty-six hours. This is not unfrequently the import of the original term.——¶ *He that gathered least gathered ten homers.* Or, "ten heaps," as the original word *homer* is properly distinguished from *omer*, a much smaller measure, and from *hamor, an ass*, or the load that was commonly laid upon that animal. But some writers make it equal to the *cor*, which is more than double the weight, and is the common load of a camel. But it was not necessary that every one should gather ten camel loads of quails; for God had promised his people flesh for a month, and would have fulfilled his promise had he bestowed on every individual the third part of a *cor*, or camel's burden. The truth of this assertion will appear, when it is considered, that every Israelite received for his daily subsistence, an omer of manna, which is the tenth part of an ephah. But an ephah is the tenth part of a *cor;* and by consequence, a *cor* contains an hundred *omers*. If then, an *omer* is sufficient for one day, a *cor* must be sufficient for an hundred days, that is, for more than three months. Hence, if every Israelite gathered *ten cors* of quails, they collected thirty times more than God had promised. Bochart endeavors to remove this difficulty, by observing, that Moses, in this verse, speaks only of the heads of families, leaving out of his enumeration, the women, children, and slaves. But it is evident, that Moses did not use the word people, in this restricted sense; for he states, that the wrath of the Lord was kindled against the people that gathered the quails. Dissatisfied, therefore, with this solution, Bochart proposes another with which he is better pleased: The ten *homers* are not ten *cors*, but ten *heaps;* for in this sense, the word is sometimes used. Thus, in the prophecy of Habakkuk, ch. 3:15, homer signifies a *heap* of many waters; and in the book of Exodus, ch. 8:14, a *heap* of frogs. Onkelos and other interpreters accordingly render it in this passage, *ten heaps*. If this be admitted, Moses has not determined the quantity of these birds which every one gathered; but only says, that every one at least gathered ten heaps, that is, by a familiar phrase among the Hebrews, a very great number; for ten is often used in Scripture for many. This version ought, perhaps, to be preferred, both on account of what has been already stated, and because the *cor* is a measure of corn, not of flesh. The view now given is of some value; for if every Israelite gathered ten *cors* of quails, the number of these birds must have been so great as to exceed all belief. But it has been shown, that instead of *ten cors*, an Israelite did not collect and use the third part of one. It is not meant to limit the power of God; but surely no violence should be offered to human belief, by requiring more from it, than God has revealed in his word. The quantities collected must have been at any rate immense, and give new force to the language of the Psalmist, Ps. 78:27, "He rained flesh upon them as dust, and feathered fowls like as the sand of the sea." In indulging themselves in feasting upon

they spread *them* all abroad for
themselves round about the camp.
33 And while [l] the flesh *was*
yet between their teeth, ere it
was chewed, the wrath of the
LORD was kindled against the
people, and the LORD smote the
people with a very great plague.

34 And he called the name of
that place Kibroth-hattaavah;
because there they buried the
people that lusted.
35 *And* the people journeyed
[m] from Kibroth-hattaavah unto
Hazeroth; and abode at Hazeroth.

l Ps. 78. 30, 31.

m c. 33. 17.

---

this new luxury it is evident that their appetites scarce knew bounds. The consequence was what might be anticipated; they ate to surfeiting, and the surfeiting was fatal.——¶ *And they spread (them) all abroad round about the camp.* Heb. "Spread for themselves a spreading." Evidently implying that they were thus spread in order to be dried in the sun for preservation. "This is the first indication in Scripture of animal food being prepared so as to be preserved for future occasions. Our earliest information concerning the Egyptians describes them as salting and drying, for future use, great quantities of fish and fowl. A nomade people, as the Hebrews were when they went down to Egypt, never think of any such process, even at the present day. It is therefore natural to conclude that they learnt this simple and useful art from the Egyptians. We are disposed to conclude with Calmet (in his note on the place), that the Hebrews salted their quails before they dried them. We have here, then, the earliest indication of processes, the benefits resulting from which have become so diffused and familiar, that it costs an effort of recollection to recognize them as benefits."—*Pict. Bible.*

V. 33. *Ere it was chewed.* Heb. *terem yikkârēth, ere it was cut off;* which Pool and others understand of the supply of quails—before it ceased at the end of the month. Thus Joel 1:5, "Howl, all ye drinkers of wine, because of the new wine; for *it is cut off* (Heb. *nikrath*) from your mouth," that is, taken away, made to cease. So also the Vulg. "As yet the flesh was between their teeth, neither *had that kind of meat failed.*" Yet the present rendering is admissible, though not we think quite so probable, as the term nowhere else occurs in the sense of *chewing*. The Psalmist thus alludes to this portion of the sacred history:—"So they did eat, and were well filled: for he gave them their own desire; they were not estranged from their lusts. But while the meat was yet in their mouths, the wrath of God came upon them, and slew the fattest of them, and smote down the chosen men of Israel;" where it is observable, that the original word for "chosen" (*bahurim*) is the same with that rendered "young men," v. 19.——¶ *The Lord smote the people with a very great plague.* Heb. "Smote with a very great smiting." "With a very great slaughter."—*Cov., Mat.* The term "plague" in our translation is of very indefinite import, equivalent to *stroke* or *judgment*. It was doubtless some kind of bodily disease or pestilence, the legitimate effect of their surfeit. As Attersoll remarks, "their sweet meat had sour sauce."

V. 34. *And he called the name of that place Kibroth-hattaavah.* That is, "graves of lust." Vulg. "Sepulchres of concupiscence." There is a distinct

CHAPTER XII.

AND Miriam and Aaron spake against Moses because of the Ethiopian woman whom he had married: for he [a] had married an Ethiopian woman.

a Ex. 2. 21.

allusion to the term in Ps. 78:29, 30, "So they did eat, and were well filled; for he gave them *their own desire* (Heb. *taavâthâm*); they were not estranged *from their lust* (Heb. *mittaavâthâm*)." The words "he called" may be rendered impersonally "one called," i. e. the name of the place was called. That is to say, The name of the place was made a memorial of the sin and the punishment by which it was distinguished.

CHAPTER XII.

The Sedition of Miriam and Aaron against Moses, and its Consequences.

V. 1. *And Miriam and Aaron spake against Moses.* Heb. "And Miriam spake and Aaron." The form of the expression implies that Miriam took the lead in the disaffection, which is confirmed by the fact, that she and not Aaron was smitten with the plague of leprosy, v. 10. Here also, as in the case of our first parents, the woman was the first in the transgression. The sin recorded in the previous chapter was a sin of the bodily appetites breaking out among the lower orders of the people; the sin here mentioned was a sin of ambition and vainglory originating with the chief personages of the host, for these three held the pre-eminence among the people. Mic. 6:4, "For I brought thee up out of the land of Egypt, and redeemed thee out of the house of servants; and I sent before thee Moses, Aaron, and Miriam." It is of course impossible to determine precisely the grounds of this disaffection, for although his marriage with an Ethiopian woman was the ostensible occasion, yet from the next verse, it would seem that they mainly found fault with Moses' undue assumptions as the Lord's messenger. The suggestion is not very improbable that some resentment was felt on account of Aaron's not having been consulted in the choice of the seventy elders, and also from the fact that Moses was wont to advise with his wife's relations, Jethro and Hobab, on important emergencies; for which reason Miriam had now stirred up a quarrel, wherein not daring to assail him in person, they make his marriage with one of a foreign race the pretence for their rebellious conduct. "The unkindness of our friends is sometimes a greater trial of our meekness than the malice of our enemies."—*Henry.*——¶ *Because of the Ethiopian woman whom he had married.* Heb. "Because of the woman the Cushite." And thus it is rendered by most of the oriental versions, while the Sept., Vulg. and Gr. Vers. adopt the term *Ethiopian.* "Cushite" comes from Cush, the son of Ham. The name is applied in Scripture not only to a portion of Africa, but to a part of Arabia also, which is explained by the descendants of Cush having left their name in certain regions where they sojourned some time prior to their final passage into Africa. It is a difficult point to determine whether by this Cushite woman is to be understood Zipporah, or another whom he had married subsequent to Zipporah's death. If it were Zipporah, how can we suppose that after Moses had been married to her for forty years, the union should have been brought up as the ostensible ground of the present quarrel? We are

2 And they said, Hath the LORD indeed spoken only by Moses? hath he not spoken [b] also by us? And the LORD heard [c] *it*.

b Ex. 15. 20. Mic. 6. 4. Is. 37. 4. Ezek. 35. 12, 13. c c. 11. 1. Ps. 94. 7-9.

on the whole inclined to the opinion that it was another woman of Cushite origin who is here alluded to, and that the whole transaction was ordered or overruled with reference to a typical bearing, which is distinctly recognized in the commentaries of several of the early Christian fathers, viz. that Moses should stand as a type of Christ, Aaron of the Jewish priesthood, Miriam of the Jewish synagogue or body of the people, and the Ethiopian or Cushite woman of the Gentile church espoused by faith to the Lord. This view is entirely consistent with the general typical tenor of the Old Testament, wherein so many gospel mysteries are shadowed forth. The Jews, as is well known, resented the adoption of the church of the Gentiles, the mystical Ethiopian or black bride of the Lord, of whom, however, it is said in the Song of Solomon, ch. 1 : 5, "I am black, but comely, O ye daughters of Jerusalem," so that we are not required to understand by *black* an unsightly or repulsive hue, as if Moses had married a negress, but simply one of that complexion which was common among the natives of the Arabian peninsula, and which is probably to be witnessed in the swarthy countenances of the tribes that rove over that region at the present day. It is remarkable that the Chald. translates the passage, "Because of the beautiful woman whom he had married; for he had married a beautiful woman." The commentators are all at a loss to account for this version, and we share ourselves in their perplexity, unless it may be in some way based upon mystical grounds. We may remark, in this connection, that Josephus, Philo, and others, take the woman here spoken of to be, not Zipporah, but another whom he subsequently married. Indeed, it is not easy to satisfy one's self on what ground Zipporah should have been termed an Ethiopian or Cushite unless it were certain that the specific territory of Midian, where she was born, was also called after Cush, of which we doubt if there is sufficient evidence to establish the fact.——¶ *For he had married an Ethiopian woman.* Heb. "Had taken," i. e. to wife, or had married. This is often the distinctive sense of the original, as 1 Chron. 2 : 19, 21. 2 Chron. 11 : 20. Neh. 6 : 18. 10 : 30. Perhaps the case of Moses in this instance may be, in some respects, paralleled by that of Hosea, ch. 1 : 2, 3.

V. 2. *Hath the Lord indeed spoken only by Moses?* The original is still more emphatic. "Hath the Lord indeed spoken only by Moses alone?" It is observable, also, that the Heb. phrase for "by Moses" (*be-Mosheh*) may be rendered "in Moses," implying an inward revelation by the Spirit. It is, however, variously rendered by the versions, "through Moses," "to Moses," and "with Moses." Rosenmuller supposes the sense to be, that inasmuch as they also enjoyed the privilege of divine revelations they could perceive that he had entered into this marriage against the will of the Lord, and solely by the impulse of his own mind, and consequently that they did right to condemn it.——¶ *Hath he not spoken also by us?* Or, Heb. "in us," as David says, "The Spirit of the Lord spake *by me* (בִּי, *bi, in me*), and his word was in my tongue." The drift is, are we not prophets as well as he? For this character is predicated both of Aaron and Miriam, Ex. 4 : 15, 16. 15 : 20. Mic. 6 : 4. They would intimate

3 (Now the man Moses *was* very meek above all the men which *were* upon the face of the earth.)

---

that Moses had mixed and debased the holy seed, which they had not done. As if they should say, Why should he take all power to himself and appoint elders as he pleases, without consulting us? Is he alone acquainted with the mind of God? Are we not also equal sharers in that honor? But surely if they were endowed as they claim with a prophetical spirit equal to that of Moses, how could they fail to be aware that the whole matter had been ordered by the immediate direction of the Lord himself, and that Moses was merely a servant for carrying out his mandates. Their murmuring, therefore, was evidently not so much against Moses as against the Lord.——¶ *And the Lord heard it.* That is, took notice of their words and of their deportment towards Moses. It is not absolutely necessary to suppose that this language was uttered orally, although the presumption is that it was; but from ch. 11:1, we learn that the Lord is said to *hear* what merely passes in the thoughts without being expressed in words. It is a rich source of comfort to a good man that the reproaches of his enemies come to the ears of the Most High before they do to his own, even before they are uttered.

V. 3. *Now the man Moses was very meek, etc.* Heb. *ânâv*, Gr. πραυς, Lat. mitissimus, all implying the quality of *meekness, gentleness, patient endurance, etc.* It comes from a root signifying *to afflict, to humble, to depress, to oppress,* and Adam Clarke and some others are inclined to take the word in this connection as equivalent to *depressed* or *afflicted*, that is, by reason of the oppressive burden laid upon him in the care and government of the people, and because of their ingratitude and rebellion towards him. In this case the drift of Moses is not to laud himself, but simply to advert to the grievous trials of his situation. It is known to the Hebrew scholar that that language exhibits the two forms ענו *ânav*, and עני *âni*, of which the former is usually rendered *meek, humble, poor*, while the latter is rendered *poor, afflicted, humble, lowly, needy.* It is evident, therefore, that there is an intimate relation between the two words and that one is easily interchangeable with the other. Accordingly we may admit on safe grounds that the idea of *affliction* is involved in that of *meekness*, which the usage of the original sufficiently confirms. Thus the Heb. *âni*, Zech. 9:9, "Behold, thy King cometh unto thee: he is just, and having salvation; *lowly*, and riding upon an ass," is rendered by πραυς, *meek*, Mat. 21:5, showing that *âni* and *ânâv* are interchanged by the sacred writers. Luther renders by "geplagter," *plagued, vexed, harassed, annoyed.* It is supposed that by this interpretation the credit of Moses is saved on the score of modesty; for how, it is asked, could a good and wise man, like Moses, pass such an encomium upon himself? "Let another praise thee, and not thine own mouth; a stranger, and not thine own lips." So abhorrent, indeed, is this language conceived to be to all just ideas of the character of Moses, that many judicious expositors have supposed that the passage was not written by Moses, but inserted by some other hand in after times; a suggestion apparently favored by the fact that the clause is parenthetical, and the sense of the context complete without it, as also that the peculiar expression "the man Moses" nowhere else occurs. It may be remarked, however, that the

4 And [d] the LORD spake suddenly unto Moses, and unto Aaron, and unto Miriam, Come out ye three unto the tabernacle of the congregation. And they three came out.

d Ps. 76. 9.

encomium, as it stands, seems to be extorted from Moses as a necessary vindication of himself from unjust reproach rather than volunteered from a principle of vainglory or overweening self-conceit. In a somewhat similar vein Paul occasionally speaks of himself in view of injurious aspersions cast upon him (2 Cor. 11 : 10, 23. 12 : 11, 12). It is urged by objectors, that even admitting the words to have proceeded from the pen of Moses, they are hardly sustained by what we elsewhere learn of his character, which in several instances discovered traits quite the reverse of meekness, evincing in fact a peculiar irascibility. But we think it will be found in these cases that whatever excitement he manifested was merely the working of a commendable zeal for the Lord of hosts, which is perfectly consistent with the most genuine meekness. Every man ought to be stirred up to a holy indignation when God is offended and dishonored. We may say, too, that the penmen of holy writ are not to be held amenable to precisely the same rules as are prescribed to other writers, for they were guided by a divine influence in which their personality was in a great measure sunk; and as they were oftentimes moved to proclaim their own faults and infirmities, we see nothing indecorous in their sometimes using the language of self-commendation, when it is clear, from the whole tenor of their writings, that they were not prompted by self-complacency, that they were superior to the praises or reproaches of men, and were in fact mere organs through whom another power than their own acted. The passage before us, therefore, may be regarded rather as the testimony of the Holy Spirit respecting Moses, than as Moses' testimony respecting himself. And may not the omniscient Spirit testify in this case? Who will presume to deny the truth of the statement? To all which we may add, that, taken in the connection in which they stand, the words may be considered as offering a reason why Moses took no notice of the charges brought against him, committing himself to the protection of the Lord, who heard the aspersions cast upon his servant, and who took his vindication into his own hands. Accordant with this is the rendering of the Vulg., "And when the Lord heard this (for Moses was a man exceeding meek above all men that dwelt upon the earth), immediately he spoke to him, and to Aaron and Mary," etc. This implies that Moses was a man of so much meekness and resignation, that he forbore to act in the matter, and calmly relinquished every thing to the divine direction.

V. 4. *And the Lord spake suddenly, etc.* Thus showing the severity of his displeasure, which brooked no delay, and precluding every intimation that Moses had first complained to God and sought revenge. Thus the Lord shows himself to be a "swift witness" against evil-doers. Comp. Ps. 50 : 19–21. "The more silent we are in our own cause, the more is God engaged to plead it."—*Henry.*——¶ *Come out ye three, etc.* The order was doubtless given by some direct communication to the parties. They were all three summoned as in a judicial manner to appear before the Lord, and from the style of the summons it might have seemed that they

5 And the LORD came down
[e] in the pillar of the cloud, and
stood *in* the door of the tabernacle, and called Aaron and
Miriam: and they both came
forth.
6 And he said, Hear now my
words: If there be a prophet
among you, *I* the LORD will
make myself known unto him in
a vision [f], *and* will speak unto
him in a [g] dream.
7 My servant Moses *is* not

e c. 11. 25.

f Gen. 15. 1. 46. 2. Job 33. 15. Ezek. 1. 1. Luke 1. 11, 22. Acts 10. 11, 17. g Gen. 31. 11. 1 K. 3. 5. Job 33. 15.

were all equally guilty, but the sequel soon made it apparent that the innocent will be separated from offenders whenever the Lord rises to judgment.

V. 5. *And the Lord came down in the pillar of the cloud.* Chald. "And the Lord revealed himself." The pillar of cloud which usually rested over the Tabernacle, and more especially over the Most Holy Place, here removed itself, and together with the indwelling Shekinah descended and took its station at the door of the Tabernacle.——*And they both came forth.* But from whence? From their own tents, or from the Tabernacle? Not the latter, for they were ordered, v. 4, to come "unto" the Tabernacle, but not "into" it. But if it be understood of Moses' or any other tent, it is stated already, v. 4, that "they three came out." Our inference therefore is that the coming forth of Aaron and Miriam, in the present case, was merely an advancing or coming forward from whatever place they may have been occupying at the moment, perhaps from the midst of a surrounding crowd.

V. 6. *If there be a prophet among you.* Heb. *im yihyeh nebiakem, if there shall be a prophet-of-you,* having the pronoun suffixed instead of separate. Chald. "If there shall be prophets to you." Gr. "If there shall be a prophet of you to the Lord." That is, if a prophet, or a class of prophets, shall be a distinguishing appendage of you, the people, as a body, then I will make known myself, etc. The language does not truly intimate any doubt of the fact of there being prophets among them, but the Lord would have it understood that he did not communicate his mind to all alike, but with such a diversity as to constitute a remarkable distinction between Moses and others. On the import of the term "prophet," see Note on Gen. 20:7.——¶ *(I) the Lord will make myself known unto him in a vision, (and) will speak unto him in a dream.* The phraseology in the original is peculiar from the absence of the personal pronoun "I," although it is clear from the grammatical forms that our present reading is correct. "In a vision." Chald. "In visions." The original *marâh* is a derivative from the root *râăh, to see,* and is for the most part rendered *sight* or *appearance.* It does not, like "dream," necessarily imply a state of sleep, but rather a state of trance or ecstasy which might come upon a man while fully awake, and in which, by means of a peculiar opening of the spiritual senses, he was made to see various objects or scenes that stood forth objectively to his view, and which were replete with an inner significancy. Images and forms were exhibited to the percipient power of the mind, but unaccompanied by any voice. Dreams, on the other hand, occurred in sleep, and by divine operation were made a medium of communications from heaven.——¶ *Will speak unto him in a dream.* Or, Heb. *edabbēr bo, will speak in him.*

V. 7. *My servant Moses is not so.*

so, who *is* faithful [h] in all mine
house [i].
8 With him will I speak
mouth [k] to mouth, even apparently, and not in dark speeches; and the similitude of the

h Heb. 3. 2, 5. *i* 1 Tim. 3. 15. 1 Pet. 2. 4, 5.

k Ex. 33. 11. Deut. 34. 10.

That is, the same conditions do not hold in regard to Moses. My mind and will are not made known to him by either of the two methods above mentioned. He is, therefore, if any thing, more than a prophet, having the prerogative of a much higher kind of intercourse with heaven than is accorded to any other person.——¶ *Who is faithful in all mine house.* That is, in all my church, for that such is the import of the expression is clear from 1 Tim. 3:15, "That thou mayest know how thou oughtest to behave thyself *in the house of God, which is the church of the living God.*" Chald. "In (or among) all my people." Targ. Jon. "In all the house of Israel my people." The original for "faithful" is *nĕĕmân*, from *âman*, denoting *firmness, stability, reliability.* It occurs 1 Sam. 3:20, "And all Israel, from Dan even to Beer-sheba, knew that Samuel was *established* (Heb. *nĕĕmân*) to be a prophet of the Lord." Hence in the present form *fidelity* or *trustworthiness.* Moses was more especially reputed faithful from the fact of his doing nothing of himself, or of his own motion, but only as required of the Lord. To this passage the language of the apostle, Heb. 3:1–6, has a direct reference:—"Wherefore, holy brethren, partakers of the heavenly calling, consider the Apostle and High Priest of our profession, Christ Jesus; who was faithful to him that appointed him, as also Moses was faithful in all his house. For this man was counted worthy of more glory than Moses, inasmuch as he who hath builded the house hath more honor than the house. For every house is builded by some man; but he that built all things is God. And Moses verily was faithful in all his house, as a servant, for a testimony of those things which were to be spoken after; but Christ as a son over his own house; whose house are we, if we hold fast the confidence and the rejoicing of the hope firm unto the end."

V. 8. *With him will I speak mouth to mouth.* That is, openly, plainly, familiarly, and without the intervention of any medium. He shall have free and frequent access to me; I will speak to him as one friend speaketh to another; and he shall be permitted to consult me on all needful occasions without reserve or perturbation. All which will be evident tokens of a privilege in which my faithful servant is to have no competitor. See this language explained in the Note on Ex. 33:11.——¶ *Even apparently.* Heb. *u-marĕh, and (according to) appearance*, the same word as occurs v. 6, and implying that visionary representations, such as the pattern of the Tabernacle, would be one of the features of revelation granted him.——¶ *And not in dark speeches.* Heb. *ve-lo behidoth, and not by enigmas.* Ainsworth remarks that the term in the original implies *sharpness*, and intimates the necessity of sharpness of wit both in propounding and expounding such enigmatical or parabolical sayings as are intended by it, i. e. something conveyed in figurative language designed to exercise the ingenuity of the hearer or reader. Its usage may be seen in the following examples; Judg. 14:12, 13, etc. "And Samson said unto them, I will now put forth *a riddle* unto you, etc. And they said unto him, Put forth thy *riddle*, that we may hear it." Ezek. 17:2, 3, "Son of man, put forth a *rid-*

LORD shall he behold: wherefore then were ye not [l] afraid to speak against my servant Moses?

l 2 Pet. 2. 10.

dle, and speak a parable unto the house of Israel; and say, Thus saith the Lord God, A great eagle with great wings, long-winged, full of feathers, which had divers colors, came unto Lebanon," etc. Aben Ezra, in explaining the difference between *marĕh, appearance*, and *hidâh, riddle* or *parable*, says that the model of the Tabernacle shown to Moses on the mount was a specimen of the former, and the parable of the great eagle with great wings of the latter. All dark and hidden doctrine is called also by the same original term, as Ps. 49:4, "I will incline mine ear to a parable; I will open my *dark saying* upon the harp." This passage when quoted Mat. 13:35, for *dark sayings* has *kekrummena, hidden things;* and Paul thus incidentally throws light upon it, 1 Cor. 13:12, "And now we see through a glass *darkly* (Gr. *en ainigmati, in a riddle*), but then face to face." This is virtually the same distinction as that announced here between the vision of Moses and that of other prophets.——¶ *And the similitude of the Lord shall he behold.* Heb. *temunath, likeness, image.* Gr. "And he hath seen the glory of the Lord." The precise idea intended to be conveyed in these words is not obvious. Comparing the passage with Deut. 4:12, 15, it is evident that Moses was to be empowered to see something of the Divine manifestation which the people were not, for it is said, "The Lord spake unto you out of the midst of the fire; ye heard the voice of the words, *but saw no similitude;* only ye heard a voice." A similitude, however, of some kind Moses was privileged to behold, although the privilege is to be understood in a sense which shall not conflict with declarations like the following: Ex. 33:20, "For there shall no man see me, and live." John 1:18, "No man hath seen God at any time; the only begotten who is in the bosom of the Father, he hath declared him." John 5:37, "Ye have neither heard his voice at any time, nor seen his shape." Col. 1:15, "Who is the image of the invisible God." 1 Tim. 6:16, "Whom no man hath seen, or can see." In all these passages we suppose the seeing denied is seeing the Lord as he is in his essence, to which no created being is competent. "Similitude," therefore, as the opposite of this must imply something which could be seen, though not perhaps with the natural eye. Sol. Jarchi remarks of the term in its present connection, that it denotes "the sight of God's back parts," mentioned Ex. 33:20-23, to our Note on which we would especially refer the reader, as the subject is treated at length. Probably we approach the nearest to the true idea of the language when we suppose that the "similitude of the Lord" here spoken of does in fact point to Christ, as the "*image* of the *invisible* God," as the "express *image* of his person," and who was pleased thus by anticipation to reveal himself in some shaded but intelligible manner to the spiritual perception of Moses. If it be said that similar precursive manifestations were made to other prophets besides Moses, our reply is, that our Lord in those cases manifested himself in the person of an angel, and they knew not that it was any *more* than an angel, whereas Moses was enabled to recognize the Lord himself in the angel.——¶ *Wherefore then were ye not afraid to speak against my servant Moses?* Heb. "To speak against my servant, against

9 And the anger of the LORD was kindled against them; and he departed.

10 And the cloud departed from off the tabernacle; and, behold, Miriam *became* leprous [m], *white* as snow: and

m Deut. 24. 9. 2 K. 5. 27. 2 Chr. 26. 19-21

Moses;" a more emphatical form of expression. A similar phraseology occurs elsewhere. Gen. 21:10, "The son of this bond-woman shall not be heir with my son, (even) with Isaac." 2 Sam. 7:23, "What nation in the earth is like thy people, (even) like Israel?" Sol. Jarchi thus comments on the words:—"He saith not, 'Against my servant Moses;' but 'against my servant, against Moses;' against my servant, though he were not Moses; against Moses, for though he were not my servant, (yet) it were meet ye should fear before him; how much more seeing he is my servant."

V. 9. *And he departed.* That is, withdrew the standing token of his gracious and glorious presence by removing the cloudy pillar from its station at the door of the tabernacle. This was done in a hasty manner, without waiting to hear any answer that they might be disposed to make. It is well known what a significant mark of our displeasure it is when, having rebuked a party for some aggravated offence, we turn abruptly away, giving no opportunity for a reply. "The removal of God's presence from us is the sorest and saddest token of his displeasure against us. Woe unto us if he depart; and he never departs, till we by our sin and folly drive him from us."—*Henry.*

V. 10. *And the cloud departed from off the tabernacle.* Targ. Jon. "The cloud of the glory of the divine presence of the Lord." That is, it not merely receded from its temporary station at the door of the Tabernacle, but it reared itself aloft to even a greater height than usual above the sacred edifice.——¶ *And behold Miriam (became) leprous, (white) as snow.*" The rendering would perhaps be more emphatic by omitting the italics,—"The cloud departed, and, behold, Miriam leprous as snow!" This was the worst and most incurable kind of leprosy, as we learn from Ex. 4:6. 2 Kings 5:27, and those who were afflicted with it were excluded the camp as unclean, Lev. 13:2, on which see Note. Chazkuni, a Jewish writer, says that the leprous condition of Miriam was the immediate occasion of the withdrawal of the cloud:—"It is not the way of the earth that holiness should stay in an unclean place." The judgment in this case fell upon Miriam as she was doubtless first in the transgression; and it is clear from Deut. 24:9, where the law of Lev. 13, concerning leprosy is rehearsed, that it was calculated and designed to make a deep impression on the minds of the parties and the people:—"Remember what the Lord thy God did unto Miriam by the way, after that ye were come forth out of Egypt." Aaron's exemption, notwithstanding his sin, was probably owing to his repentance, as intimated in the ensuing verse. "Miriam was stricken, Aaron escaped, both sinned; his priesthood could not rescue him, the greatness of his dignity did but add to the heinousness of his sin; his repentance freed him. I wonder not to see Aaron free, while I see him penitent; this very confession saved him before from bleeding for idolatry, which now preserves him from leprosy for his envious repining. The universal antidote for all the judgments of God is our humble repentance."—*Bp. Hall.*——¶ *And*

Aaron looked upon Miriam, and, behold, *she was* leprous.

11 And Aaron said unto Moses, Alas, my lord, I beseech thee, lay not the sin upon us, wherein we have done foolishly[n], and wherein we have sinned.

12 Let her not be as one dead, of whom the flesh is half consumed when he cometh out of his mother's womb.

n 2 Sam. 24. 10. Prov. 30. 32.

Aaron looked upon Miriam, etc. Heb. *va-yiphen, and turned towards.* Bp. Patrick takes the phrase as implying that Aaron "looked upon" Miriam with a view to *judge* of the nature of the disease according to the law contained Lev. 13 : 2, etc. which makes it the duty of the priest to inspect carefully the indications betokening leprosy. But we find on recurrence to that chapter that the term for "look" is invariably *râäh, to see,* and in no case *pânâh,* which occurs here. We conclude, therefore, that nothing more is intended in the present passage than to intimate, that Aaron simply looked upon or turned his attention to his sister, and saw with amazement that she was covered with the marks of the most inveterate leprosy.

V. 11. *Alas, my lord, I beseech thee, etc.* As much as to say, Have pity upon us, miserable wretches. He supplicates Moses as his superior, and humbly begs his pardon, at the same time deprecating the imputation of the sin which he sincerely acknowledges and bewails. Thus it is that those who exalt themselves shall be abased, that those who vilify the servants of God shall often be constrained to seek their help. Many who in their health and pride have despised and reproached a faithful minister of God, have often, in sickness or affliction, been glad to send for him and avail themselves of his prayers and intercessions. "His sad deprecation prevailed, both to clear himself and recover Miriam. The brother sues for himself and his sister to that brother whom they both emulated, for pardon from himself and from that God who was offended in him. Where now is that equality which was pretended? Behold, he that so lately made his brother his fellow, now makes him his god. 'Lay not this sin upon us; let her not be as one dead;' as if Moses had imposed this plague, and could remove it. Never any opposed the servants of God, but one time or other they have been constrained to confess a superiority."—*Bp. Hall.*——¶ *Wherein we have done foolishly.* Gr. "Because we have acted ignorantly." Aaron probably intended to be ingenuous in his confession, but the language employed savors of some degree of extenuation by imputing it rather to folly and weakness than to positive presumption. No one can do evil without at the same time doing foolishly, but it is well in our confessions to concentrate our thoughts rather upon the evil than upon the folly of our doings.

V. 12. *Let her not be as one dead.* Heb. *kemëth.* Such she may be said to have become legally, being excluded from communion with her people, defiling all that came in contact with her, as a dead body, and liable to become literally a corpse by the deadly effects of the disease.——¶ *Of whom the flesh is half consumed when he cometh out of his mother's womb.* This clause gives some countenance to the rendering of the Gr. "Let it not be as it were like death, as an abortion coming out of his mother's womb, when (the disease) devours the half of the flesh." That is,

13 And Moses cried unto the
LORD, saying, Heal [o] her now,
O God, I beseech thee.
14 And the LORD said unto
Moses, If her father had but
spit in her face, should she not
be ashamed seven days? let her
be shut out [p] from the camp sev-

o James 5. 15.

p Lev. 13. 46.

let her not be as an abortion or still-born child which has lain long dead and half wasted away in its mother's womb.

V. 13. *And Moses cried unto the Lord.* Besought the Lord with earnestness and importunity, as being grieved for her affliction, and regarding the Lord as standing aloof, so as to prompt additional importunity.——¶ *Heal her now, O God, I beseech thee.* The original word for both "now" and "I beseech," is the same—*nâ*, which is properly a particle of entreaty rather than of time, though generally rendered *now*. Targ. Jon. "And Moses prayed and besought mercy before the Lord, saying, I beseech for mercy of the merciful God; I beseech God that hath power of the spirits of all flesh, heal her, I beseech thee." Moses kindly prayed that Miriam might be healed. Though the punishment was inflicted to sustain his honor and authority, he had none of the littleness and malevolence of mind that could rejoice in her affliction. He might indeed have reproached her, insisting that she had only received her desert; but on the contrary he pities and prays for her, thus exemplifying the Christian precept, "Love your enemies; bless them that curse you, and pray for them that despitefully use you and persecute you."

V. 14. *If her father had but spit in her face, etc.* That is, if she had, by some undutiful conduct, provoked her father to be angry with her and to spit in her face as a token of his anger, she would certainly be ashamed for some time to look him in the face; how much more then ought she to be ashamed when she lies under this severe token of my displeasure? If she would in that case continue for seven days overwhelmed in shame, how reasonable that she should be excluded from the camp for the same period, the period appointed for the legal cleansing from such impurities. Comp. Lev. 13:4, 5, 21, 26. 14:8. Num. 6:9. 19:11. "Miriam had greatly offended God, and, therefore, she was to be as a daughter, whose father had spit in her face. In Deut. 25:9, the widow was to spit in the face of her late husband's brother, if he refused to marry her. And Job (30:10) in his great misery says of his enemies, 'they spare not to spit in my face;' and in reference to our Saviour, they did 'spit in his face.' The most contemptuous, the most exasperating and degrading action, which one man can do to another, is to *spit in his face.* A person receiving this insult is at once worked up to the highest pitch of anger, and nothing but the rank or power of the individual will prevent him from seeking instant revenge. Indeed, such is the enormity attached to this offence, that it is seldom had recourse to, except in extreme cases. A master, whose slave has deeply offended him, will not beat him, (for that would defile him,) but he spits in his face. When his anger is at the greatest height, he will not even condescend to do that, but orders a fellow-servant, or some one near, to spit in his face. Is a person too respectable for this indignity; then the offended individual will spit upon the ground. Schoolmasters, also, when very angry with a scholar, do not, as in England,

en days, and after that let her
be received in *again*.
15 And Miriam was shut out
from the camp seven days: and
the people journeyed not till
Miriam was brought in *again*.
16 And afterward the people
removed from Hazeroth, and
pitched in the wilderness of
Paran.

CHAPTER XIII.

AND the LORD spake unto
Moses, saying,

---

begin to beat him, but spit in his face, or order some one else to do it. To a person making use of offensive language, bystanders say, 'Spit in his face.'"—*Roberts.*——*After that let her be received in* (*again*). Heb. *tēāsēph, let her be gathered.* Gr. "She shall come, or enter in." On the import of this word, see Note on Josh. 6:9. Targ. Jon. "And I will cause to stay, for thy sake, the cloud of my glory, and the tabernacle, and the ark, and all Israel, until the time that she is healed, and afterward she shall be gathered in."

V. 15. *And Miriam was shut out of the camp seven days.* Gr. "Separated, set apart." An example of stern justice, without respect to persons, for even kings, when they had become lepers, even without fault of their own, were required to withdraw and dwell apart from the body of the people. 2 Chron. 26:20, 21. The incercession of Moses was graciously accepted, yet so as that the Lord would show his displeasure at the offence, and maintain the honor and authority of his government. She was to be excluded from the camp for seven days, and during that time to dwell alone, as having been visited with that loathsome and defiling disease. Thus her offence was proclaimed by the publicity of her punishment; and she who some time before had borne so honorable a part in the congregation, is now disgraced before them all. Even those that are nearest and dearest to the Lord will not escape with impunity if they transgress, as others might be thereby dangerously emboldened. "If the judgment had been at once inflicted and removed, there would have been no example of terror for others. There is no policy in a sudden removal of just punishment: unless the rain so fall that it lie and soak into the earth, it profits nothing."—*Bp. Hall.*——¶ *The people journeyed not.* Heb. "Brake not up." Sol. Jarchi here remarks that "the Lord imparted this honor to her because she once stayed for Moses when he was cast into the river, as it is written, And his sister stood afar off," etc.

V. 16. *And afterward the people removed from Hazeroth, and pitched in the wilderness of Paran.* In order that all the people might be duly admonished by means of the sin and the punishment of Miriam, they were not permitted to remove from Hazeroth till the days of her separation or cleansing were fulfilled, when they removed and pitched in the wilderness of Paran. Respecting these localities, see Notes on ch. 10:12. 11:35.

CHAPTER XIII.

The Spies sent out to search the Land.

V. 1. *And the Lord spake unto Moses, saying, etc.* Having surmounted all the difficulties of the dreary and barren wilderness that interposed, we find the Israelites now encamped at Kadesh, or

2 Send [a] thou men, that they may search the land of Canaan, which I give unto the chil-

a c. 32. 8.

Kadesh Barnea, on the southern borders of Canaan, and having but a few leagues to travel before entering it. At this point, as we are here informed, the Most High gave commandment to Moses to dispatch twelve men as spies to make a preliminary survey of the land and bring back a report of its character, condition, and inhabitants, of the best modes of access to it, and of the most hopeful methods of effecting its conquest. But by comparing the subsequent narrative, Deut. 1 : 19–24, it appears that this motion did not originate with the Lord, nor yet with Moses, but with the people in a body. We there read as follows :—"And when we departed from Horeb, we went through all that great and terrible wilderness, which ye saw by the way of the mountain of the Amorites, as the Lord our God commanded us ; and we came to Kadesh-Barnea. And I said unto you, Ye are come unto the mountain of the Amorites, which the Lord our God doth give unto us. Behold, the Lord thy God hath set the land before thee: go up and possess it, as the Lord God of thy fathers hath said unto thee ; fear not, neither be discouraged. And ye came near unto me every one of you, and said, We will send men before us, and they shall search us out the land, and bring us word again by what way we must go up, and into what cities we shall come. And the saying pleased me well : and I took twelve men of you, one of a tribe : and they turned and went up into the mountain, and came unto the valley of Eshcol, and searched it out." From this it appears that Moses, in the first instance, acted and spake in the spirit of heroic trust in the divine declaration. exhorting the people to go forward at once and take possession of the promised inheritance. But this spirit found no suitable response in the minds of his followers, as is evident from the measure now proposed, a measure plainly indicative of a cowardly fear that would still disguise itself under the semblance of a prudential policy. "What needed they doubt of the goodness of that land, which God told them did flow with milk and honey? What needed they doubt of obtaining that which God promised to give? When we will send forth our senses to be our scouts in matters of faith, and rather dare trust men than God, we are worthy to be deceived."—*Bp. Hall.* The same writer well observes that "that which the Lord moves unto, prospers ; but that which we move him to first, seldom succeedeth," as was most sadly evinced in the present instance. Their unbelief cost them a forty years' prolonged wandering in the wilderness.

V. 2. *Send thou men.* Heb. "Send thou for thee or for thyself;" which Sol. Jarchi thus expounds, "I command thee not ; if thou pleasest, send ; forasmuch as Israel came and said, We will send men," etc. It was in fact a case in which the Lord "chose their delusions" by permitting them to have their own way. The Lord consented, that is, did not prevent, because he saw the people were intent upon the project, and he yielded to the importunity of their hearts, just as he did to that of Balaam when he was inwardly so desirous of going with the messengers of Balak. It was as if he had said, "Since you harbor such distrust of me, and are so ready to think that I would impose upon you by vain assurances, send forth

dren of Israel: of every tribe of their fathers shall ye send a man, every one a ruler among them.

---

the men, as you propose, and satisfy yourselves in your own way." We have little idea how fearful it is to have the Lord side with our evil promptings by the permissions of his Providence. It were better really that his Providence should fight with our propensities than that it should apparently fall in with them.——¶ *That they may search the land of Canaan.* Heb. *yâthuru*, which has the import of *circling around*, and in this connection of *circumspection*, that is, of *exploring by looking and travelling about.* It is applied to mental investigation, Eccl. 1:13, "I gave my heart to seek and *search out* by wisdom concerning all things that are done under heaven." Comp. Eccles. 7:25. A still more striking parallel occurs Ezek. 20:6, "In the day that I lifted up mine hand unto them to bring them forth of the land of Egypt into a land that *I had espied* for them," where the Gr. has, "Which I prepared for them." Vulg. "Which I had provided for them." Syr. and Chald. "Which I gave unto them." This declaration through the prophet goes to aggravate their offence, for the Lord's having already *espied* the land for his people made it superfluous for them to send spies for the purpose. The land in question is called the "land of Canaan" for the reason, that the Canaanites were the mightiest of the seven nations which now occupied it.——¶ *Of every tribe of their fathers shall ye send a man, etc.* Heb. "One man, one man, to a tribe;" a Hebrew phrase rightly rendered in our version. A man for each tribe would preclude all complaint of partiality, which, however, must be understood to the exclusion of Levi, as this tribe was to have no inheritance in the land, Deut. 18:1.——¶ *Every one a ruler among them.* It was fit that men of authority and prudence should be intrusted with an enterprise of so much moment. Obscure names might bring discredit upon the testimony rendered. They were not, however, persons of the very first rank in their several tribes, for these were called *princes*, but yet they belonged to the ruling class, perhaps to those who in Ex. 18:25, are called "heads of the people." "The basest sort of men are commonly held fit enough for intelligencers; but Moses, to make sure work, chooseth forth the best of Israel, such as were like to be most judicious in their inquiry, and most credible in their report. Those that ruled Israel at home, could best descry for them abroad. What should direct the body but the head?"—*Bp. Hall.* The persons selected for the enterprise were not, therefore, striplings, who might be easily alarmed, nor were they men who had no character or position to maintain; but the chief rulers among the tribes of Israel. He placed in the van of the experiment those in whom, on account of age, experience, wisdom, talent, he could most implicitly trust. And in order that the matter might be quite plain and beyond cavil, he gives a catalogue of all the names of the chiefs, the rulers, and fathers of the tribes that were to be sent on the expedition, and to bring back a faithful report. But the result showed that however this measure was designed for the best, yet the persons selected proved unworthy of the trust reposed in them, and their rank and standing in the congregation gave more weight to their evil report, and thus led to the most disastrous consequences. Alas, how few are the faithful in the Lord's house!

3 And Moses by the commandment of the Lord sent them [b] from the wilderness of

b Deut. 1. 23.

V. 3. *And Moses by the commandment of the Lord, etc.* Heb. "At the mouth of Jehovah." This must of course be understood with the qualifications above intimated. The command did not properly originate with the Lord, but he saw fit to *wink at* the perverse promptings of the people, though the language employed would seem to convey the idea that the measure was enjoined by the divine *will* and not merely tolerated by the divine *permission.* Chald. "According to the word of the Lord." Gr. "By the voice of the Lord." Vulg. "Moses did what the Lord had commanded, sending from the desert of Pharan principal men," etc. It would perhaps be preferable to preserve the order of the original: "And Moses sent them from the wilderness of Paran by the commandment (at the mouth) of the Lord." Drusius here remarks that the Lord commanded this expedition of the spies only as he commanded a bill of divorce to be given when a man of the Jews repudiated his wife. It was not so much the *divorce* which he commanded as the *bill.* So here; it was not so much the sending of the spies which God commanded, as it was the selection of a certain class of men to be employed on the occasion, seeing they *would* have somebody. Not unlike this is the solution of Sol. Jarchi, who explains this phrase, "by the permission of the Lord." So in the Jewish Commentary called Phesikta, it is said, "The election of the spies was according to the mouth of the Lord; not that God commanded them to send them. If thou sayest, why did he not forbid them to send? (It is answered), To accomplish (or fulfil) their desire, and to render them their recompense, and to give unto Joshua and Caleb a good reward." The people had hitherto reposed full trust in the guidance of their Angel-Conductor, and left it to him by what way they should go up, and into what cities they should come. They seem not to have doubted that he who had brought them thus far on their way, would not fail to land them safe within the precincts of the promised land. But at this point the workings of unbelief began to manifest themselves. They now began to feel that they could not trust further than they could see. Yet the Lord yielded to their perverseness, and allowed his promise to be put to the proof, and not only so, but he added his own special directions in the matter; thus showing by his example that rulers and teachers may sometimes give way to the unreasonable demands of the people, with a view to their learning by experience what they refuse to learn from competent testimony. As the incident has a typical bearing, we may suggest, moreover, that the believing Christian may commit an error by indulging an undue anxiety to become acquainted with the particulars of his heavenly home. Though it be well to cast forward our thoughts from time to our heavenly inheritance, to search out with an eye of faith the goodly land, and to attain to some foretaste of its celestial fruits, yet it is not to be forgotten that our main concern is with the present field of duty, trial, and combat, and if satisfied with the promises we shall press on under the divine guidance, and leave the result to a covenant God, who will not fail our expectations. What other inference can we draw from the fact, that the measure here recorded did not originate with the divine wisdom, though it was pleased, in a sense, to adopt it?——¶ *From the*

Paran: all those men *were* heads of the children of Israel.

4 And these *were* their names: of the tribe of Reuben, Shammua the son of Zaccur.

5 Of the tribe of Simeon, Shaphat the son of Hori.

6 Of the tribe of Judah, Caleb the son of Jephunneh.

7 Of the tribe of Issachar, Igal the son of Joseph.

8 Of the tribe of Ephraim, Oshea [c] the son of Nun.

9 Of the tribe of Benjamin, Palti the son of Raphu.

10 Of the tribe of Zebulun, Gaddiel the son of Sodi.

11 Of the tribe of Joseph, *namely*, of the tribe of Manasseh, Gaddi the son of Susi.

12 Of the tribe of Dan, Ammiel the son of Gemalli.

13 Of the tribe of Asher, Sethur the son of Michael.

14 Of the tribe of Naphtali, Nahbi the son of Vophsi.

15 Of the tribe of Gad, Geuel the son of Machi.

16 These *are* the names of the men which Moses sent to spy out the land. And Moses called Oshea the son of Nun, Jehoshua.[d]

c ver. 16.

d ver. 8. Ex. 17. 9.

---

wilderness of Paran. Upon the locality of the wilderness so denominated, see Note on ch. 10:12. It is evident from ch. 32:8. Deut. 9:23, that the spies were sent from Kadesh-Barnea, which lay not far from the southern border of Canaan.——¶ *All those men were heads of the children of Israel.* Gr. αρχηγοι, *chief rulers.* Not the *princes* mentioned ch. 1, for their names were different; but those now sent were men of rank and consideration in their respective tribes, though falling short of the highest.

V. 4. *And these were their names.* Of the ensuing list of names there is nothing important to be said. Levi is omitted as usual, and as to the rest, probably no special reason can be given for the order in which they stand.

V. 11. *Of the tribe of Joseph, (namely), of the tribe of Manasseh, etc.* The phraseology doubtless appears somewhat strange, as the appellation "tribe of Joseph" belongs no more to Manasseh's branch of it than to Ephraim's, which is mentioned v. 8. The name of Joseph was common to each (Ezek. 37: 16, 19. Rev. 7:8), but Ainsworth supposes that Manasseh here has a certain precedence because he was the first-born. Pool, on the other hand, suggests that it might have been with a view to aggravate the sin of Manasseh in joining in such report as was brought back, so unworthy of a descendant of Joseph.

V. 16. *And Moses called Oshea the son of Nun, Jehoshua.* Heb. *hoshëa, salvation*, or, as others render it, *save thou*, and *yehoshua, the salvation of the Lord*, or, *the Lord will save;* the one being in effect a prayer, the other a promise. The change is made by the insertion of one of the letters composing the incommunicable name "Jehovah." In Neh. 8:17 he is called *Jeshua*, and in the Gr. version Ιησους, *Jesus*, which is followed also in the New Testament, as Acts 7: 45. Heb. 4:8. See Note on Josh. 1:1, where the name is more fully explained. The words in this connection ought probably to be regarded as parenthetical and translated "And Moses *had* called," etc. for the name *Joshua* occurs Ex. 17:9, on the occasion of the battle

17 And Moses sent them to spy out the land of Canaan, and said unto them, Get you up this *way* southward[e], and go up into the mountain[f]:

18 And see the land, what it *is*; and the people that dwelleth therein, whether they *be* strong or weak, few or many;

19 And what the land *is* that they dwell in, whether it *be* good or bad; and what cities *they be* that they dwell in, whether in tents, or in strong holds;

e ver. 22. f Gen. 14. 10. Deut. 1. 24. Judg. 1. 9, 19.

---

with the Amalekites. The change of names was a well-known mark of honor, and Moses was doubtless moved by the spirit of prophecy to dignify Joshua in the way he did, as in the divine purpose he was destined to serve, in his capacity as champion of Israel and their leader into the land of promise, as an eminent type of Jesus, the Saviour, whose name he shares, in conducting all those who sincerely follow him to an heavenly inheritance.

V. 17. *Get you up this* (*way*) *southward.* Heb. בנגב *bannegeb, in the south.* That is, by the way of the south, meaning the southern part of the land of Canaan, which was very dry and barren, as is implied in the import of the original term which signifies *dry, parched.* In their present position this was the nearest portion of the promised land, and from this they were to journey north.——¶ *Go up into the mountain.* That is, into the mountainous region—a collective singular. The mountainous tract was possessed by the Amorites, Canaanites, and Amalekites, Num. 14:40, 45. Deut. 1:44.

V. 18. *And see the land.* That is, survey, inspect it, with minute attention. Ascertain all you can of its situation, inhabitants, soil, and the best points of access. The word "land," as the object of their search, it will be observed, occurs here, in v. 19, and in v. 20, with an import somewhat varied. In the first instance it denotes the land in respect to its inhabitants, whether healthy, robust, and hardy, or puny and weak, whether numerous or few; in the second, it refers more especially to the general air and aspect of the country, and how it was settled, whether the people lived in cities, in tents, or in fastnesses and fortified places; in the third, to the soil, whether rich or poor, a fact to be ascertained by the woods and fruits it produced, and of which they were required to bring back specimens.——¶ *And the people that dwelleth therein.* Or, Heb. "Even the people that dwelleth thereupon."——¶ *Whether they be strong or weak.* Heb. "Whether it be strong or weak." That is, the people spoken of collectively as one body.

V. 19. *Whether it be good or bad.* That is, whether it be desirable or undesirable, especially on the score of salubrity from air, water, etc.—— ¶ *What cities* (*they be*) *that they dwell in, whether in tents or in strong holds.* But if they dwelt in cities, how could it be a matter of inquiry whether they dwelt at the same time in tents? This difficulty has been perceived by both versionists and commentators, and accordingly the Chald. renders it, "And what kind of cities they dwell in, whether walled or unwalled." So also the Gr. and the Vulg. And this we are forced to regard as the true construction. As in the former clause the question is concerning the land, whether it be good or bad; so here the question would seem to be respecting the cities, whether they

20 And what the land *is*, whether it *be* fat [g] or lean, whether there be wood therein or not: and be ye of good courage [h], and bring of the fruit of the land. Now the time *was* the time of the first ripe grapes.

21 So they went up, and searched the land, from the wil-

g Neh. 9. 25, 35. Ezek. 34. 14. *h* Deut. 31. 6, 7, 23.

be open and unwalled like a nomade encampment, or whether they are walled and fortified with a view to repel invaders. The weight of authority is decidedly in favor of this sense.

V. 20. *Whether it be fat or lean.* This respects the quality of the soil, which if "fat" is fertile, and if "lean," barren. Chald. "Whether it be rich or poor." So Neh. 9 : 25, "And they took strong cities and a fat land."——¶ *Whether there be wood therein or not.* Heb. "Whether there be tree (collect. sing. for *trees*) therein or not." Chald. and Gr. "Trees." Targ. Jon. "Trees of food," i. e. fruit trees. But the sense of *fruit trees* is conjectural; it is sufficient to understand the words of woody or champaign.——¶ *Be ye of good courage.* Heb. *hithhazzaktem, strengthen, encourage yourselves.*——¶ *Bring of the fruit of the land.* Heb. "Take of the fruit of the land." The bringing of it is rather inferred than expressed.——¶ *The time was the time of the first ripe grapes.* Heb. "The days were the days," etc., when, as one of the Jewish commentators remarks, "they had need to have courage, because the keepers of the vineyards then kept watch."

V. 21. *From the wilderness of Zin.* Heb. *tzin.* This is a different wilderness from that called "the wilderness of Sin (Heb. *sin*)," Ex. 16 : 1, which extended in a long, narrow plain, between the eastern shore of the Red Sea and the neighboring mountains almost to the southern termination of the peninsula. As to the wilderness of Zin, we quote the words of Mr. Kitto. "We have already indicated, generally, what we must now more precisely state, that the Desert of Zin must be identified with the low sandy plain or valley which extends from the Dead Sea to the Gulf of Akaba, and through which the river Jordan appears at one time to have flowed to the Red Sea. This plain is through its whole extent bounded on the east by the mountains of Seir, which so shut it in as to render a passage eastward from the valley impracticable to any large and encumbered body except through the valley (El Ghoeyr), in which the ancient city of Petra formerly stood; and failing, afterwards, to obtain leave to pass through which, the host of Israel was obliged to retrace its steps and go round the southern extremity of the chain near the head of the gulf of Akaba. The plain on its other or western side is bounded by a lower chain of hills which separate it from the Desert of Paran. The average breadth of this plain is about five miles. It is wholly destitute of water, and in every respect answers to the Scriptural account of the Desert of Zin, which, as distinguishing it from that of Paran, could never be definitely understood until Burckhardt's researches furnished the information which has contributed so materially to the elucidation of a very important but previously obscure portion of Sacred writ."—*Pict. Bible.*——¶ *Unto Rehob.* "Elsewhere called Beth-rehob. This place is also mentioned in Judg. 18 : 28. Josh. 19 : 28. 2 Sam. 10 : 8, in such a manner that its general situation cannot be questioned, although we are not acquainted with its precise site. It must have stood in the north of the Holy Land, within Mount Hermon, near the

derness of Zin [i] unto Rehob [k], as men come to Hamath.

22 And they ascended by the south, and came unto Hebron,

i Josh. 15. 1 k Josh. 19. 28.

pass leading through that mountain to Hamath beyond, and not far from Dan. It was the capital of a Syrian kingdom, and continued to be such long after the city, in the division of the land, had fallen to the lot of Asher, that tribe being unable to drive out the old inhabitants. It seems to be mentioned as a distinct kingdom in 1 Sam. 10:8; and one of those which leagued with the Ammonites against David; but it is probable that, in common with the other small Syrian states there enumerated, it was tributary to the kingdom of Zobah with which they acted on that occasion, and afterwards to that of Damascus, by which Zobah was superseded."—*Pict. Bible.*——¶ *As men come to Hamath.* "This is another capital of a small Syrian kingdom, beyond Mount Hermon, and having Rehob on the south and Zobah on the north. The approach to it from the south is through a pass in Mount Hermon, called the entrance of 'Hamath,' and 'the entering in of Hamath,' which, being the passage from the northern extremity of Canaan into Syria, is employed, like Dan, to express the northern boundary of Israel. The kingdom of Hamath appears to have nearly corresponded, at least in its central and southern parts, with what was afterwards called Cœle-Syria, or the great plain or valley between Libanus and anti-Libanus; but stretched northward so far as the city of Hamath on the Orontes, which seems to have been the capital of the country. This city was called Epiphania by the Greeks, and is mentioned under that name by Josephus and the Christian fathers. It has now, like many other sites in Asiatic Turkey, recovered its ancient name, which tradition had preserved. No part of this kingdom was allotted to the Israelites, with whom the Hamathites seem to have lived on very good terms. Toi, who was their king in the time of David, sent his son with presents to congratulate that monarch on his victory over the Syrians of Zobah, who, it would seem, had been dangerous neighbors to Hamath. (See 2 Sam. 8:9.) The present government of Hamath comprises one hundred and twenty inhabited villages, and seventy or eighty that have been abandoned. The western part of the territory is the granary of Northern Syria, although the harvest never yields more than ten for one, in consequence of the immense numbers of mice, which sometimes wholly destroy the crops. Hamath, the capital, is situated on both sides of the Orontes, and is built partly on the declivity of a hill, and partly on the plain. The town is large, and (for the country) well built, though the walls are chiefly of mud. There are four bridges over the Orontes, and a stone aqueduct, supported on lofty arches, for supplying the upper town with water. There are few ancient remains, the materials having been taken away to be employed in modern buildings. Burckhardt thinks that the inhabitants of the town could not amount to less than 30,000."—*Pict. Bible.*

V. 22. *And they ascended by the south, and came unto Hebron.* Heb. *va-yabo, and he came*, or, *one came;* a phraseology supposed to indicate that the spies did not all move in a body, but that they at least occasionally separated, one going in one direction, and another in another, and then again rendezvousing together. In this case it would appear from Josh. 14:9, 12, 14,

where Ahiman, Sheshai, and Talmai, the children of [l] Anak, *were*. (Now Hebron [m] was built seven years before Zoan [n] in Egypt.)

23 And they came unto the

l Josh. 11. 21. *m* Josh. 21. 11. *n* Ps. 78. 12. Is. 19. 11.

Caleb was more especially intended, as Hebron afterwards fell to his inheritance on the ground of his having now visited it. Others, however, suppose that the verb was originally written in the plural, and that the final letter has in course of time dropped away. As to the location of Hebron, see Note on Gen. 23 : 2.——¶ *Where Ahiman, Sheshai, and Talmai, the children of Anak, (were).* The "children of Anak" here mean the *descendants* of Anak. Gr. "The generation of Anak." Chald. "The sons of the giant, or mighty man." They were the posterity of Arba, from whom Hebron had the name of Kirjath-Arba, i. e. the city of Arba, and whose son was Anak, the head of one of the chief families of Canaan, being distinguished for their great stature, prowess, and valor. So formidable were they on these accounts that it became a proverbial saying in that region, "Who can stand before the children of Anak?" Deut. 9 : 2.——¶ *Now Hebron was built seven years before Zoan in Egypt.* This clause was probably inserted in order to countervail the boast of Egypt of being the most ancient nation in the world. Whatever might be pretended, for instance, respecting the antiquity of this Zoan, which was afterwards called Tanis, still here was a city in Canaan of seven years prior origin.

V. 23. *And they came unto the brook of Eshcol.* Heb. *nahal*, signifying both a stream or torrent of water, and the valley through which it runs, whether permanently or only occasionally in the time of floods and freshets. "Eshcol" signifies *a cluster, a bunch*, and this name was given to the place as a memorial of the incident recorded v. 24. Gr. "The valley of the cluster." Robinson, in speaking of his departure from Hebron for Jerusalem, says, (Trav. v. I. 316):—"As we issued from the town, the path for a short distance was full of mud and puddles from a spring near by; and to us, coming out of the desert, this was quite a refreshing sight. The road leads up the valley for a short time; and then up a branch coming from the N. E. The path is here paved; or rather laid unevenly with large stones, in the manner of a Swiss mountain road. It passes between the walls of vineyards and olive-yards; the former chiefly in the valley, and the latter on the slopes of the hills, which are in many parts built up in terraces. These vineyards are very fine, and produce the largest and best grapes in all the country. This valley is generally assumed to be the Eshcol of the Old Testament, whence the spies brought back the cluster of grapes to Kadesh; and apparently not without reason. The character of its fruit still corresponds to its ancient celebrity; and pomegranates and figs, as well as apricots, quinces, and the like, still grow there in abundance." It would seem that their arrival at this valley, which lay in the southern quarter of Canaan, must have been on their return from the exploration of the northern sections, as they would not of course carry the grapes all the way with them.——¶ *And cut down from thence a branch with one cluster of grapes.* The probability is, that what was cut down was a branch of the vine with a number of clusters hanging upon it, but which were so thick that they had the appearance of one. The original word cannot

brook of Eshcol, and cut down from thence a branch with one cluster of grapes, and they bare it between two upon a staff; and

be shown to signify precisely what we understand by "cluster;" it may as properly be translated "bunch," implying a number of clusters, not to advert to the fact that a strictly correct rendering of the Hebrew would perhaps be, that "they cut down a branch *even* a bunch of grapes, one;" for although the copulative "and" occurs between "branch" and "cluster," yet we are certainly not to understand they cut down a branch *and* a cluster, as separate acts. The term "one" plainly implies that the cutting off the branch was the cutting off the clusters that adhered to it, of which there doubtless were several. Still, it is beyond question that the grapes, and consequently the clusters did then, and do still, in that country, attain to an extraordinary size, as will be apparent from the note on this passage from the "Pictorial Bible." "The cluster was doubtless very large; but the fact of its being borne between two upon a staff is less exclusively an evidence of size than is usually considered. It was an obvious resource to prevent the grapes from being bruised in being transported to a considerable distance. Nevertheless, even under the present comparative neglect of the vine in Palestine, it is allowed that grapes and clusters of most extraordinary size are common—as indeed they often are in other parts of Western Asia, as compared with any that we are accustomed to see. The district in which the brook Eshcol is found, and particularly the valley through which that brook flows, is still noted for the superiority of its grapes. Doubdan, in traversing the country about Bethlehem, found a most delightful valley full of aromatic herbs and rose-bushes, and planted with vines, which appeared to him of the choicest kind. He was not there in proper time to make any observations on the size of the clusters; but he was assured by the monks that they still found some, even in the present neglected state of the country, weighing ten or twelve pounds. This valley corresponds to what is commonly thought that of the brook Eshcol. Reland also says, that a merchant who had resided several years at Ramah, in this neighborhood, assured him that he had there seen bunches of grapes weighing ten pounds each. Forster mentions that he knew a monk who had spent eight years in Palestine, and had been at Hebron in the same district, where he saw clusters as large as two men could conveniently carry. We are at liberty to doubt this, if we please, as the majority of travellers concur in stating the weight of the largest clusters produced in Palestine at about ten or twelve pounds, or, at most, as a sufficient burden for *one* man; and because the statement looks as if *made for the text* by one who did not consider, that although two men did carry the cluster of grapes from Eshcol, it does not necessarily follow that the cluster was a full burden for them. Whatever opinion be entertained about the size of the cluster in question, it is agreed that the vines of Canaan are remarkably distinguished for the size of their grapes and clusters. This has been noticed even by travellers from the richest vine-growing countries of Europe; and we may therefore readily conceive how the Israelites must have been impressed by the sight of them, when it is recollected that Egypt, from which they came, was never remarkable for its vines, and that the grapes, though far from bad, are

they brought of the pomegranates, and of the figs.

24 The place was called the brook Eshcol, because of the cluster of grapes which the children of Israel cut down from thence.

25 And they returned from searching of the land after forty days.

26 And they went and came to Moses, and to Aaron, and to all the congregation of the children of Israel, unto the wilderness of Paran, to Kadesh [o]; and brought back word unto them, and unto all the congregation, and showed them the fruit of the land.

o c. 20. 1, 16.

---

very small. The vines of Canaan are of different kinds and colors, white, red, and deep purple; the last are much more common than the others. The most esteemed of all is called *Sorek* in the Scriptures, and probably derived that name from being produced in the valley watered by the river of that name; and those of Eshcol were probably of the same valuable species, the brook so called being merely one of two which, by their junction, form the river Sorek. This is the common opinion; but it must be confessed that we know nothing precisely about this brook, except that it was somewhere in the vine district of the country which afterwards belonged to Judah. Some commentators hesitate to say whether there was any brook at all, as the Hebrew word נחל, *nahal*, means as well a valley as a brook; but we conceive that the word means here, and in some other places, a valley *with* a brook, that is, a brook which, like most others in Palestine, is dried up in the warm season."——¶ *And (they brought) of the pomegranates and the figs.* On the pomegranate, see note on Ex. 28 : 33.

V. 24. *The place was called, etc.* That is, was subsequently called, after the Israelites got possession of the land.

V. 25. *And they returned from searching of the land after forty days.* From what is said, v. 20, that "the time was the time of the first ripe grapes," it is probable the spies were sent forth about the beginning of August and returned about the middle of September, as that is about the time that grapes, pomegranates, and figs ripen in those countries.

The Report of the Spies.

V. 26. *And they went and came, etc.* That is, they travelled and came; the first verb being rather of an expletive nature.——¶ *To Kadesh.* "This is the nearest approach which the Israelites made to the Promised Land at this time. The intermediate stations were—1, the Desert of Paran (ch. 10 : 12); 2, Taberah (ch. 10 : 33); 3, Kibroth-Hattaavah (ch. 11 : 34); 4, Hazeroth (ch. 11 : 35). Nothing is positively known concerning these stations, but very much has been guessed. One thing, however, seems clear, that the Hebrews took the direct route northward from Sinai to Kadesh-barnea, which we may assume to have been somewhere on the southern border of Canaan, although it is much disputed whether there is not another Kadesh, and, if there be but one, where that one should be placed."—*Pict. Bible.*——*And brought back word unto them.* Heb. "And returned them word," where the original presents the peculiar usage of two objectives or accusatives under the regimen of one verb—*othâm, them,* instead of *lâhem, to them.*——¶ *And*

27 And they told him, and said, We came unto the land whither thou sentest us, and surely it floweth [p] with milk and honey; and this [q] *is* the fruit of it.
28 Nevertheless the people [r] *be* strong that dwell in the land, and the cities *are* walled, *and* very great: and moreover we saw the children of Anak [s] there.
29 The Amalekites [t] dwell in the land of the south; and the Hittites, and the Jebusites, and the Amorites, dwell in the moun-

p Ex. 33. 3. q Deut. 1. 25, etc. r Deut. 9. 1, 2. s ver. 33. t Ex. 17. 8. c. 14. 43.

showed them the fruit. Heb. "Caused them to see."

V. 27. *And they told him, and said.* Heb. *va-yesapperu lo va-yomeru, and they recited,* or *related, to him,* i. e. to Moses, as the representative of the whole congregation.——¶ *We came unto the land whither thou sentest us.* It is not a little remarkable that men who proved themselves so cowardly, should have had the courage to risk their persons in exploring the country. But it is probable they were sustained by the undaunted spirit and determination of Caleb and Joshua, though they basely arrayed themselves against them on their return.——¶ *Surely it floweth with milk and honey.* The display of the rich fruit formed of itself an emphatically good report of the land, as to natural advantages and productiveness; and this was confirmed by the verbal statements of the spies. But their tone soon alters when they come to speak of the inhabitants. The rising delight of the congregation, occasioned by such a report, attested by such visible evidence of its truth, is suddenly cast down by the sad tenor of what follows.

V. 28. *Nevertheless the people be strong, etc.* This was of course the language of the faint-hearted spies, and not of Caleb or Joshua. The words were probably true in themselves, but they were evidently spoken with a view to dishearten the people, especially the mention of the giant sons of Anak. "Forty days they spent in this search, and this cowardly unbelief in the search shall cost them forty years' delay of the fruition. Who can abide to see the rulers of Israel so basely timorous? They commend the land, the fruit commends itself, and yet they plead difficulty. 'We are not able to go up.' Their shoulders are laden with the grapes, and yet their hearts are overlaid with unbelief. It is an unworthy thing to plead hardness of achieving, when the benefit will more than requite the endeavor. Our land of promise is above; we know the fruit thereof is sweet and glorious, the passage difficult. The giantly sons of Anak (the powers of darkness) stand in our way. If we sit down to complain, we shall one day know that 'without shall be the fearful.' "—*Bp. Hall.*

V. 29. *The Amalekites dwell, etc.* Heb. "Amalek dwells;" collect. sing.; and so in all the national designations that follow. Respecting the Amalekites, see Note on Ex. 17 : 8. They are not here spoken of as being actually inhabitants of the land of Canaan, but as dwelling upon its *south* border, where if Israel attempted an approach, they would be very liable to encounter the opposition of these ancient enemies of their race, from whose assaults they had already suffered since leaving Egypt, Ex. 17 : 8–16. "Because they had been smitten by Amalek (Deut. 25 : 17, 18), the spies do now make mention of him to make them afraid."—*Sol. Jarchi.*——¶ *In the mountains.* Heb. "In the moun-

tains; and the Canaanites dwell
by the sea, and by the coast of
Jordan.
30 And Caleb [u] stilled the
people before Moses, and said,
Let us go up at once and possess it; for we are well [v] able to
overcome it.
31 But the men that went
up with him said, We be not
able to go up against the people;
for they *are* stronger than we.

u Josh. 14. 7, 8.

v Rom. 8. 37.

tain," i. e. the mountainous region, collect. sing. as in v. 17. The mountains alluded to are, for the most part, the range lying on the south and south-east part of Canaan, which at this time were inhabited by the several nations specified. The Jebusites, however, had pitched farther in the interior, and held the region about Jerusalem. These were the most formidable of all the native population. Of the Amorites, we find the Lord saying through the prophet Amos, ch. 2:9, "Yet destroyed I the Amorite before them, whose height was like the height of the cedars, and he was strong as the oaks."——¶ *The Canaanites dwell by the sea.* That is, the nation specifically called by this name, Gen. 15:20. They were situated partly on the coast of the Mediterranean, and partly in the vicinity of the Jordan.——¶ *By the coast of Jordan.* Heb. "By the hand of Jordan;" i. e. by the *side* of Jordan, or by or upon the side along which the Jordan ran. The word "coast" in this sense is now quite obsolete.

V. 30. *And Caleb stilled the people before Moses.* Heb. "Made the people to be silent to Moses;" implying that the report just made had produced a disaffection among the people which was now upon the point of venting itself before Moses, and perhaps against him, when Caleb boldly stepped forward and assuaged "the tumult of the people." "Joshua was silent, and wisely spared his tongue for a further advantage; only Caleb spoke. I do not hear him say, Who am I to strive with a multitude? What can Joshua and I do against ten rulers? It is better to sit still, than to rise and fall; but he resolves to swim against this stream, and will either draw friends to the truth, or enemies upon himself. True Christian fortitude teaches us not to regard the number or quality of the opponents, but the equity of the cause; and cares not to stand alone, and challenge all comers; and if it could be opposed by as many worlds as men, it may be overborne, but it cannot be daunted: whereas, popularity carries weak minds, and teaches them the safety of erring with a multitude."—*Bp. Hall.*——¶ *Let us go up at once and possess it.* Heb. "Going up let us go up;" to express which emphatical phrase our translators have introduced the words "at once."——¶ *For we are well able to overcome it.* Heb. "Prevailing we shall prevail over it," i. e. the land; which, however, the Gr. renders by "them." In connection with this we may properly exhibit the testimony which Caleb records of himself, Josh. 14:7, 8, "Forty years old was I when Moses the servant of the Lord sent me from Kadesh-barnea to espy out the land; and I brought him word again as it was in mine heart. Nevertheless my brethren that went up with me made the heart of the people melt: but I wholly followed the Lord my God."

V. 31. *We be not able to go up against the people; for they (are) stronger than*

32 And [w] they brought up an evil report of the land which they had searched unto the children of Israel, saying, The land, through which we have gone to search it, *is* a land that eateth up the inhabitants thereof; and

w Deut. 1. 28.

---

we. "See the idle pleas of distrust. Could not God enable them? Was he not stronger than their giants? Had he not promised to displace the Canaanites, to settle them in their stead? How much more easy is it for us to spy their weakness, than for them to espy the strength of their adversaries? When we measure our spiritual success by our own power, we are vanquished before we fight. He that would overcome must neither look upon his own arm, nor the arm of his enemy, but to the mouth and hand of him that hath promised and can perform."—*Bp. Hall.*

V. 32. *And they brought up an evil report of the land.* Heb. *va-yotzi-u dibbath, and they caused to go forth an evil report.* The original for "bringing up an evil report" is in Prov. 10:18, rendered "uttering a slander." The same term is used of the report which Joseph brought of his brethren, Gen. 37:2, although there, and also Num. 14:37, the epithet for "evil" is affixed, which is omitted here. Chald. "And they put an evil name." Gr. "And they brought a horror of that land which they had searched." The evil report consisted of the particulars recited in the remaining clauses of the verse.——¶ *A land that eateth up the inhabitants thereof.* An expression which cannot well mean, as some have supposed, that the country was lacking in fertility, and apt to eat up and consume its inhabitants by famine; for they had before acknowledged it to be "a land flowing with milk and honey." Nor does the suggestion of others appear very probable, that it denotes a peculiar insalubrity of the climate, to which it appears from Mr. Roberts the eastern Asiatics apply a similar phraseology. "Of a very unhealthy place it is said, 'That evil country eats up all the people.' 'We cannot remain in these parts, the land is eating us up.' '*I* go to that place! never! it will eat me up.' Of England it is said, in reference to her *victories*, 'She has eaten up all countries.'" There is no good evidence that the phrase bore the same signification among the Hebrews, nor, if in a hurried journey through the country, they had witnessed the ravages of a plague, would that have been a peculiarly disheartening circumstance, as it would merely have shown the Divine Providence thinning out the ranks of their enemies, and leaving fewer to oppose their entrance. We are therefore inclined to adopt the interpretation of Le Clerc, who supposes it to be understood of the destructive wars which frequently raged among these and the adjacent nations, sweeping off the inhabitants as if by a desolating plague. Thus the Amorites had conquered the Moabites, Num. 21:26, and the Caphtorims the Avims, Deut. 2:23, and one tribe was almost constantly rooting out another, Deut. 2:18–23. This sense receives confirmation from the usage in Ezek. 36:13–15, where the land of Israel is thus apostrophized: "Thus saith the Lord God; Because they say unto you, *Thou land devourest up men*, and hast bereaved thy nations; therefore thou shalt devour men no more, neither bereave thy nations any more, saith the Lord God. Neither will I cause men to hear in thee the shame of the heathen any more,

all the people that we saw in it *are* men of a great stature[x].
33 And there we saw the giants, the sons of Anak[y], *which* *come* of the giants; and we were in our own sight as grasshoppers[z], and so we were in their sight.

x Deut. 9. 2. y ver. 22. z Is. 40. 22.

neither shalt thou bear the reproach of the people any more, neither shalt thou cause thy nations to fall any more, saith the Lord God." It is obvious that in these words the Most High makes a remote allusion to the very reproach that is here cast upon the land of Canaan, as if the surrounding heathen had occasion to load his own people with the same aspersions as did the spies the original inhabitants. This reproach should now be taken away. The prevalence of wasting judgments such as war, pestilence, and famine, should no longer give occasion to say that the land devoured its inhabitants; in all which the idea of the destructive effects of war is prominent. Language very similar, and of similar import, occurs in the conditional threatening against the chosen people, Lev. 26 : 37, 38, "And they shall fall one upon another, as it were before a sword, when none pursueth: and ye shall have no power to stand before your enemies. And ye shall perish among the heathen, and *the land of your enemies shall eat you up.*" To which we may add, that the Chald. here renders, "It is a land that killeth its inhabitants;" which doubtless implies a land wherein the inhabitants kill each other.——¶ *And all the people that we saw in it (are) men of great stature.* Heb. *anshë middoth, men of measures;* i. e. men above the ordinary standard as to height and dimensions. Comp. Is. 45 : 14, "Thus saith the Lord, The labor of Egypt, and merchandise of Ethiopia, and of the Sabeans, *men of stature* (*anshë middah*) shall come over unto thee." Jer. 22 : 14, "That saith, I will build me *a wide house* (*baith middoth, a house of measures*)." Gr. "Exceeding tall." The statement was evidently exaggerated, as it was only the Anakim or Nephilim that answered to this description, but when men's fears are excited, and they wish to produce an impression upon others, they are prone both to magnify and to multiply the objects of their dread. The transition from *some* to *all* is then very easy.

V. 33. *And there we saw the giants.* Heb. "Nephilim;" the term applied to the giants that lived before the flood, men of violence, oppression, and cruelty. See Note on Gen. 6 : 4.——¶ *The sons of Anak, (which come) of the giants.* That is, we saw there the formidable sons or descendants of Anak, a race of men of such enormous stature and strength, that they are evidently to be accounted of the same stock with the Nephilim, or the giants of the olden time, of whom we have so often heard. ——¶ *We were in our own sight as grasshoppers, etc.* Or, Heb. "locusts," as the original is rendered 2 Chr. 7 : 13. The expression is plainly hyperbolical, to which there can be no difficulty in affixing the right sense. It would seem a little problematical how they should have known that they appeared so diminutive in the eyes of these gigantic people. But it will perhaps be sufficient to suggest that it was asserted as a mere *inference*, and not an unnatural one under the circumstances. The estimate of greatness on the one side would give rise to that of littleness on the other.

CHAPTER XIV.

AND all the congregation lifted up their voice, and cried; and the people wept [a] that night.

2 And all the children of Israel murmured [b] against Moses and against Aaron: and the whole congregation said unto

a c. 11. 4.

b Ps. 106. 24, 25.

CHAPTER XIV.

The Murmuring and Mutiny of the People at the Report of the Spies.

V. 1. *And all the congregation lifted up (their voice).* Heb. *tissâ, lifted up.* There is nothing in the original to answer to "voice," although it is undoubtedly understood. The verb is used in other instances in a similar manner. Thus, Is. 42 : 2, "He shall not cry, nor *lift up* (*yissâ*), nor cause his voice to be heard," etc. So Is. 42 : 11, "Let the wilderness and the cities thereof *lift up* (their voices), where our translators have inserted "their voices" in italics, as might have been properly done in the present passage. We find the full phrase, however, in other connections, as Gen. 21 : 10, "She *lifted up her voice*, and wept." It is worthy of notice, that as the people on this occasion *lifted up their voice* in rebellious complaint against the Lord, so he, Ps. 106 : 26, *lifted up his hand* in token of their exclusion by a righteous decree from the land promised to them in the persons of their fathers. The terms in the original are the same.——¶ *And cried.* Heb. "And gave their voice." This form of expression occurs in reference to any loud voice, noise, or cry, whether as predicated of any creature, or represented as proceeding from the Lord himself. Thus, Ps. 18 : 14, "The Most High *gave his voice.*" Jer. 2 : 15, "The young lions roared upon him, (and) *yelled.*" Heb. "gave forth their voice." Ps. 104 : 12, "The birds —— *sing* (Heb. 'give forth their voice') among the branches." Ps. 77 : 17, "The clouds poured out water; the skies *sent out a sound* (Heb. "gave forth a voice)." Hab. 3 : 10, "The overflowing of the water passed by; the deep *uttered his voice*" (Heb. "gave forth his voice)." So, likewise, men are said to "give a voice," upon causing a proclamation to be issued, 2 Chron. 24 : 9. From the force of the expression, therefore, it is evident that the people on this occasion broke forth into open outcries of a rebellious nature, proclaiming thereby their own fickleness, cowardice, imbecility, and shame. Instead of lifting up their ensigns with a heroic resolve to march forward to the land of promise, defying all enemies in the name of the Lord, they sat down in impotent despair, and like so many frightened and fretting children, gave way to sobs and tears! "The rods of their Egyptian task-masters had never been so fit for them as now for crying. They had cause, indeed, to weep for their infidelity; but now they weep for fear of those enemies they saw not. I fear, if there had been ten Calebs to persuade, and but two faint spies to discourage them, those two cowards would have prevailed against those two solicitors: how much more, now ten oppose and but two encourage!"—*Bp. Hall.*——¶ *The people wept that night.* Heb. "In or through that night." Gr. "That whole night."

V. 2. *And all the children of Israel murmured against Moses and against Aaron.* In murmuring against their leaders, they murmured against God by whom those leaders were appointed. This is clear from the language of Moses,

them, Would God that we had died in the land of Egypt! or, would God we had died in this wilderness!

3 And wherefore hath the LORD brought us unto this land, to fall by the sword, that our wives and our children should be a prey? were it not better for us to return into Egypt?

Ex. 16:8, "For the Lord heareth your murmurings which ye murmur against him; and what are we? your murmurings are not against us, but against the Lord." The false and cowardly representations of the spies operated to infect the entire mass of the congregation, so that nothing was heard but mourning and lamentation over the sad lot to which they were doomed in being thus led forth to perish, men, women, and children, at the hands of a cruel enemy. ——¶ *Would God that we had died in the land of Egypt.* The more carefully the language of these malcontents is weighed, the more aggravated does it appear. They were wrought up by their disaffection to a point of absolute madness. They speak as if it had been actually better that they had been slain with the first-born in Egypt, or in the wilderness with those who had lately died of the plague for lusting, than run the hazard of holding on their way to Canaan. They forgot that Omnipotence could bring them in thither as triumphantly as it had brought them out of Egypt. The past, with all its miracles of mercy, is hidden from their eyes, and the dreadful future, painted by unbelief, is all that stands before them. Never had people been so honored, favored, and blest, as had the nation of Israel since their departure out of Egypt, and yet, so light is all this in their eyes, that they now mourn that they had not died before they had experienced it! "They wish rather to die criminals under God's justice than live conquerors in his favor. How base were the spirits of those degenerate Israelites, who, rather than die (if it come to the worst) like soldiers in the field of honor, with their swords in their hands, desire to die like rotten sheep in the wilderness!"—*Henry.* Who can wonder that, as appears from the sequel, vs. 28, 29, they soon had their wish?

V. 3. *And wherefore hath the Lord brought us unto this land?* "The foolishness of man perverteth his way; and his heart fretteth against the Lord." How strikingly is this illustrated in the narrative before us! They blasphemously reflect upon their Divine Benefactor, as if he had brought them hither *on purpose* that they might fall by the sword, and that their wives and children should fall a prey to the ferocious adversaries whom they were called to encounter. "Thus do they in effect charge that God who is Love itself, with the worst of malice, and Eternal Truth with the basest hypocrisy; suggesting that all the kind things he had said to them, and done for them, hitherto, were intended only to decoy them, and to cover a secret design carried on all along to ruin them."—*Henry.* The parallel history, Deut. 1:27, gives us still more distinctly the language they uttered on this occasion, "And ye murmured in your tents, and said, Because the Lord hated us, he hath brought us forth out of the land of Egypt, to deliver us into the hand of the Amorites, to destroy us."——¶ *To fall by the sword.* That is, *that we should fall*, or, in other words, *die*, by the sword. The more ordinary form of expression would be, *to cause us to fall*, but these forms are occasionally interchanged with each other.——¶ *Were it not better for us to return in-*

4 And they said one to another, Let us make a captain, and let us return [c] into Egypt.

c Deut. 17. 16. Neh. 9. 17. Acts 7. 39.

5 Then Moses and Aaron fell on their faces [d] before all the assembly of the congregation of the children of Israel.

d c. 16. 4, 22

to Egypt? Heb. "Were it not good?" It is observable how many obvious considerations they lose sight of in this proposition. As for instance, could they expect the presence of the pillar of cloud to conduct them on their way? Could they look to be supplied with manna from heaven? Would the Lord again divide the waters of the Red Sea for them? Could they anticipate a peaceful passage along the territories of the warlike nations that bordered their path? And should they even succeed in setting their feet again on Egyptian ground, would they find their ancient oppressors any more favorably disposed towards them? Would they have forgotten the death of their first-born? Would they have buried the remembrance of the fathers, children, brothers, husbands, who had perished in pursuing them? But thus infatuated are men when their hearts are set in them to do evil. Like brute-beasts, they mind only that which is present, and the office of memory and reason appears to be suspended.

V. 4. *And they said one to another.* Heb. "And they said (every) man to his brother." On this phraseology, see Note on Lev. 18:18.——¶ *Let us make a captain.* Heb. "Let us give a head." Chald. "Let us appoint or constitute a head (principem)." Gr. "Let us give (or appoint) a leader." Targ. Jon. "Let us appoint a king over us for head." On the incidents here related the sacred writer, in a subsequent age, thus comments, Neh. 9:16, 17, "But they and our fathers dealt proudly, and hardened their necks, and hearkened not to thy commandments, and refused to obey, neither were mindful of thy wonders that thou didst among them; but hardened their necks, and in their rebellion appointed a captain to return to their bondage." It does not appear that in point of fact their rebellion proceeded farther, in this respect, than taking counsel concerning the choice of a leader and head, but in the divine estimation, it is regarded as a deed actually done. Their conduct was no less than a formal renunciation of the divine authority, and as they thus "despised the pleasant land, and believed not his word; but murmured in their tents, and hearkened not unto the voice of the Lord, therefore he lifted up his hand against them, to overthrow them in the wilderness," and we cannot but bow in humble acquiescence with the decree which excluded that generation from entrance upon the promised inheritance.

The Deportment of Moses and Aaron, Joshua and Caleb, on this Occasion.

V. 5. *Then Moses and Aaron fell on their faces.* Heb. "And Moses fell and Aaron upon their faces." The motive for this prostration was not so much to sue with great earnestness to the people to forbear their rebellion, as to pray devoutly to the Lord in their behalf, deprecating the sore displeasure which their base and ungrateful conduct had provoked. It had been, no doubt, more befitting that the Israelites themselves should have fallen down on their faces and humbly supplicated the pardon, both of the Lord and his servants, but in this, as in thousands of other cases,

6 And Joshua [e] the son of
Nun, and Caleb the son of Jephunneh, *which were* of them that searched the land, rent their clothes:
7 And they spake unto all
the company of the children of Israel, saying, The land, which we passed through to search it, *is* an exceeding good land.
8 If the LORD delight [f] in us,
then he will bring us into this land, and give it us; a land which floweth with [g] milk and honey.
9 Only rebel [h] not ye against
the LORD, neither fear [i] ye the

e ver. 30. 38.

f Deut. 10. 15. 2 Sam. 15. 25, 26. 22. 20. 1 K. 10. 9. Ps. 147. 11. g c. 13. 27. h Deut. 9. 23. i Deut. 20. 3.

the transgressors were less impressed with the enormity of their guilt than those transgressed against. Moses and Aaron, therefore, fell down upon their faces in the presence of the whole assembly, that the offenders might be awakened to a sense of their danger, and be excited to cry mightily to heaven for mercy. It is ever characteristic of a gracious heart to mourn for the sins of others as well as for its own. If we know the iniquities of others, and do not mourn for them, we in a sense make them our own, and thus become partakers of other men's sins. If we mourn for them, we discharge ourselves from responsibility on account of them; they are theirs, and not ours. Moses and Aaron, therefore, bowed themselves on this occasion in prostration both of body and spirit. The more ordinary posture of prayer among the nation of Israel seems to have been *standing*, but in cases of special emergency, when they were deeply distressed and exceedingly anxious for a favorable response, they resorted to *kneeling;* and in the utmost ardor and importunity of prayer, they *fell upon their faces,* as we learn by the example of our Lord himself, Mat. 26 : 39. Luke 22 : 41. The reason of this is, that true humiliation of heart prompts corresponding outward gestures, and when the soul is conscious to itself of its desert of hell, the man sinks himself as deep down in that direction as possible.

V. 6. *Rent their clothes.* A well known token of excessive grief, sorrow, or indignation, prompted especially by the hearing of blasphemy against God. In Jer. 36 : 24, it is mentioned as a sign of culpable apathy on the part of Jehoiakim, and his servants, that on hearing the words of the Lord's prophets against Judah, "they were not afraid, *nor rent their garments.*"

V. 7. *And they spake unto all the company.* Nothing could well be a stronger proof of their undaunted courage and incorruptible fidelity than daring thus, in the face of so vast a multitude, to bear a testimony directly opposite to that which had been given by the faithless spies.——¶ *Is an exceeding good land.* Heb. "Is a good land, very, very." Gr. "Exceeding, exceeding good;" that is, every way desirable. This is the mode of expressing the superlative degree in Hebrew.

V. 8. *If the Lord delight in us.* Chald. "If the good pleasure of the Lord (lit. before the Lord) be with us." Gr. "If the Lord choose us." Vulg. "If the Lord be propitious to us." The meaning is, if we are careful not to forfeit the divine favor by our remissness or disobedience.

V. 9. *Only rebel ye not.* Chald. "But rebel ye not against the Word of the

people of the land; for they *are* bread [k] for us: their defence is departed from them, and the LORD *is* with us [l]: fear [m] them not.

k c. 24. 8.

l Gen. 48. 21. Deut. 20. 1-4. 31. 6, 8. Judg. 1. 22. 2 Chr. 15. 2. 32. 8. Ps. 46. 7, 11. Is. 8. 9, 10. 41. 10. Am. 5. 14. Zech. 8. 23. Rom. 8. 31. *m* Is 41. 14.

Lord." Gr. "Be ye not revolters, or apostates, from the Lord." Give way to no murmuring or discontented thoughts; nor think or speak of returning to Egypt.——¶ *They are bread for us.* Heb. "They are our bread." That is, we shall devour and consume them as a hungry man does bread. As if they should say, We seemed, indeed, but as grasshoppers to them, but we say unto you that they shall be bread for us; we shall utterly destroy them. The expression is doubtless designed to stand in direct opposition to what was said by the faithless spies, ch. 13:32, "The land through which we have gone to search it, is a land that eateth up the inhabitants thereof." Gr. "They shall be food for us." Vulg. "For we are able to eat them up as bread." Chald. "They are delivered into our hand." A similar phraseology is not unusual. Num. 24:8, "He (Israel) shall *eat up* the nations his enemies." Ps. 79:7, "For they have *devoured Jacob*, and laid waste his dwelling place." Ps. 14:4, "Who *eat up my people* as they eat bread." Deut. 7:16, "And thou shalt *consume all the people* which the Lord thy God shall deliver thee."——¶ *Their defence is departed from them.* The original Hebrew (צִלָּם *tzillâm*) is far more expressive:—"Their shadow, or shade, has departed from them." That is, their defence, covert, protection, rendered by the Chald. "Their strength has departed from them." Vulg. "All aid or protection has gone from them." The Gr. has a rendering peculiar to itself:—"For their time (i. e. season of prosperity) has withdrawn from them;" implying that their iniquities had come to the full, and they had nothing more to hope from the Divine favor. Among the old English versions, Matthews', Bishop's, and Geneva have, "Their shield is departed from them." Comp. Ps. 91:1, "He that dwelleth in the secret place of the Most High shall abide *under the shadow* of the Almighty." Ps. 121:5, 6, "The Lord is thy keeper; the Lord is *thy shade* upon thy right hand. The sun shall not smite thee by day, nor the moon by night." The metaphor seems to have been derived originally from the effects of the cloudy pillar in affording a cool and refreshing shade from the ardors of the sun as they journeyed through the desert. But the idea of *protection* was equally associated with this marvellous cloud, in which the divine presence was supposed to be especially resident. "The margin reads 'shadow;' but as this word has a common application, which the original has not in view, perhaps 'shade' would be better; but as even this is not unambiguous, perhaps the paraphrase 'protecting shade' would be best of all. The force of this and other similar allusions in the Bible is in a great degree lost upon those who, under the scorching sun of the east, have not had occasion to experience that the shelter of some shady place is an enjoyment of such essential importance, as to be only inferior in value and gratification to that of drink to one who is dried up with thirst under the same circumstances. Hence, in the language of Asia, we generally find that the word 'shade,' or 'shadow,' is used as a metaphor to express defence and shelter; but it must be admitted that it is not always easy to understand where a person's *own* shadow, or a protecting

10 But all the congregation bade stone them [n] with stones. And [o] the glory of the LORD appeared in the tabernacle of

n Ex. 17. 4.

o c. 16. 19. 42. 20. 6.

shade *for* him is expressed. Both senses seem to be in use, the former implying the protection and favor he has the power to bestow, and the latter the protection and favor which he enjoys. Hence, in Arabia and Persia particularly, complimentary expressions continually refer to the shadow, in such phrases as—'May your shadow be continually extended;' 'May your shadow never be diminished;' 'May your shadow be extended over the heads of your well-wishers;' 'May your shadow be a continual shelter to me,' etc. Sometimes the phrase runs: 'May the shadow of your prosperity'—'of your protection,' etc. Mr. Roberts notices a similar use of the word in India, where a poor man, speaking of a rich friend, says, 'He is my shadow,' that is, he is my defence; 'My shadow is gone,' meaning, he has lost his defence; 'Alas! those poor people have lost their shadow,' etc. The Sultan of Turkey and the Shah of Persia are both styled 'The Refuge of the World,' unquestionably with a primary reference to a shadow: indeed both these monarchs lay claim to the title of 'The Shadow of God" (*Zd-ullah*); and the idea which such a title is intended to convey will, after this explanation, be comprehended without difficulty."—*Pict. Bible.*——¶ *And the Lord is with us.* Chald. "And the Word of the Lord is for our help."

V. 10. *All the congregation bade stone them with stones.* Heb. "All the congregation said to stone them with stones." That is, proposed. They would thus reward the exemplary fidelity and firmness of these true-hearted servants of the Most High, who were mainly intent upon turning from the heads of their brethren the storm of divine displeasure which they saw impending. "Though Moses and Aaron entreat upon their faces, and Joshua and Caleb persuade, yet they move nothing. The obstinate multitude, grown more violent with opposing, is ready to return them stones for their prayers. Such have been ever the thanks of fidelity and truth. Crossed wickedness proves desperate; and, instead of yielding, seeks for revenge. Nothing is so hateful to a resolute sinner, as good counsel."—*Bp. Hall.*——¶ *And the glory of the Lord appeared in the tabernacle of the congregation.* It would seem that their murderous purpose would have been accomplished had they not been deterred by a sudden manifestation of the divine glory, which spoke to their perception the language of fearful threatening. The Shekinah, which usually abode within the Tabernacle, now displayed itself in connection with the cloudy pillar, that seems on this occasion to have lowered itself from its usual elevation, and taken its station immediately *over* or *upon* the Tabernacle, and not *in* it, as we read in our version; as otherwise it could not have been seen by the congregation, as we are nevertheless assured it was. Gr. "And the glory of the Lord appeared in the cloud on the tabernacle of witness." Chald. "And the glory of the Lord was revealed." Arab. "Then appeared the splendor of God." For an account of this as a visible phenomenon, see Note on Ex. 16:10. The great and glorious Being, who was invisibly present while the sin conceived in their hearts was working out its fruits, now shows himself to have been all along cognizant of its operation, and he becomes fearfully manifest. Thus the

the congregation before all the children of Israel.

11 And the LORD said unto Moses, How long will this people provoke [p] me? and how long will it be ere they believe me [q], for all the signs which I have showed among them?

12 I will smite them with the pestilence, and disinherit them, and will make of [r] thee a greater nation and mightier than they.

p Zech. 8. 14. Heb. 3. 16. *q* Ps. 106. 24. John 12. 37. *r* Ex. 32. 10.

guilty conscience realizes the divine Being present to itself when a sinful act has been committed as it does not before. The pain of remorse is aggravated by the reflection, that the Lord *might* have been previously seen with the eye of faith to the prevention of that sin which now fills the soul with anguish. Another inference drawn from the narrative is, that the Lord is prone to appear in behalf of his servants when reduced to their utmost straits. For wise ends he withholds the sensible tokens of his presence till danger is fully ripe, till their condition seems absolutely hopeless, and then he triumphantly comes forth from his secret place and rescues and vindicates them.

V. 11. *How long will this people provoke me?* Heb. "Despise, blaspheme, or contemptuously treat me." Gr. "Irritate me." Vulg. "Detract me." The general import is that of contemning, with special marks of indignity. It occurs Is. 5 : 24. 52 : 5. Prov. 1 : 30. 15 : 5.——¶ *How long will it be ere they believe me?* Heb. "How long will they not believe me?" Chald. "How long will they not believe in my Word?" Gr. "How long will they not believe me?" The unbelief now evinced is frequently alluded to elsewhere as the grand procuring cause of their exclusion from the land of promise. Thus, Deut. 1 : 32, "Yet in this thing ye did not *believe* the Lord your God." Heb. 3 : 18, 19, "And to whom sware he that they should not enter into his rest, but to them that *believed not?* So we see that they could not enter in *because of unbelief*." Jude v. 5, "I will therefore put you in remembrance, though ye once knew this, how that the Lord, having saved the people out of the land of Egypt, afterwards destroyed them that *believed not*."——¶ *For all the signs, etc.* Heb. "In all the signs." So at a subsequent period it is said of the posterity of this people, John 12 : 37, "Though he had done so many miracles before them, yet they believed not on him."——¶ *Among them.* Heb. *bekirbo, in the midst of him,* i. e. of the people spoken of collectively.

V. 12. *I will smite them with the pestilence.* Heb. "I will smite him, etc." Collect. sing. comp. v. 15. For "pestilence" here the Gr. and Chald. both exhibit "death." See the usage illustrated in the Note on Ex. 5 : 3. The event showed that this is not to be understood as an absolute and irrevocable determination, but simply as a commination, like that of the destruction of Nineveh within forty days, with the implied condition of exemption in case of speedy repentance or powerful intercession.——¶ *Disinherit them.* Heb. *oriskennu.* Chald., Gr., and Vulg., "Will destroy or consume them." The true import is, that he would deprive them of the land promised to their fathers. On the peculiar usage of the original term see Note on v. 24.——¶ *Will make of thee a greater nation, etc.* Heb. "Will make thee to a nation," etc. Gr. "I will make thee and thy father's house," etc. So also the

13 And Moses [s] said unto the
LORD, Then [t] the Egyptians shall
hear *it*, (for thou broughtest up
this people in thy might from
among them;)
14 And they will tell *it* to
the inhabitants of this land; *for*
they have [u] heard that thou,
LORD, *art* among this people;
that thou, LORD, art seen [v] face
to face; and *that* thy cloud [w]
standeth over them; and *that*
thou [x] goest before them, by
daytime in a pillar of a cloud,
and in a pillar of fire by
night.
15 Now, *if* thou shalt kill
all this people as one man, then

s Deut. 9. 26, 28. t Deut. 32. 27. Ezek. 20. 9, 14. u Josh. 2. 9, 10.

v Ex. 33. 11. w c. 10. 34. x Ex. 13. 21, 22. Ps. 78. 14.

Sam. A similar declaration is made to Moses Ex. 32 : 10, on the occasion of the people's sin in the matter of the golden calf. It is equivalent to saying, that rather than the promise given to Abraham should fail of accomplishment, he would raise up from Moses a new offspring of the same stock, who should inherit the blessings which Israel had forfeited. The noble disinterestedness of Moses appears conspicuous in his reply. He is much more concerned for the divine honor than his own.

V. 13. *The Egyptians shall hear* (*it*). The language here is somewhat abrupt, as we should have anticipated that Moses would have prefaced his pleading with something like this: "If thou shalt smite them, O Lord, with the pestilence as thou dost threaten, then the Egyptians shall hear," etc. But in his impassioned state of mind he seizes at once upon the purpose of God as expressed in the preceding verse, and draws from it the consequences now stated in order to avert it.

V. 14. *And they will tell* (*it*), *etc.* Or, Heb. "They will say;" i. e. they will say what follows in v. 16, for verses 14, 15 are properly parenthetical.——¶ *To the inhabitants of this land.* That is, probably, of the land of Arabia, on the extreme boundaries of which they now were. Others, however, suppose the land of Canaan to be meant, with which the Egyptians had more or less of intercourse. The point will remain doubtful after all our efforts to settle it clearly.——¶ *That thou, Lord, art among this people.* Chald. "That thou, Lord, abidest with thy majesty among this people."——¶ *Art seen face to face.* Heb. "Eye to eye." That is, in the most open, plain, and visible manner, without any interposing medium. Chald. "That with their eyes they have seen the majesty of thy glory." By the Targ. Jon. this is referred to the giving of the Law upon Sinai. It was then especially that this manifestation was made.——¶ *Thy cloud standeth over them.* Affording them shelter and protection; rendered by the Targ. Jon., "that they should not be hurt either by heat or by rain." Comp. Ex. 13 : 21, 22. Num. 9 : 17, etc.

V. 15. *Now* (*if*) *thou kill* (*all*) *this people as one man.* The conditional "if" does not occur in the original, which requires the literal rendering "thou hast killed this people as one man," that is, by the terror of the threatening just uttered. If thou adherest to thy purpose, such will be the destructive effect. He then goes on to state what the consequences will be as respects the nations which shall hear of it. From this it appears that the present rendering is substantially cor-

the nations which have heard
the fame of thee will speak,
saying,
16 Because [y] the LORD was
not able to bring this people into the land which he sware unto
them, therefore he hath slain
them in the wilderness.
17 And now, I beseech thee,
let the power [z] of my LORD be
great, according as thou hast
spoken [a], saying,

y Deut. 9. 28. Josh. 7. 9.

z Mic. 3. 8. Mat. 9. 6, 8. a Ex. 34. 6, 7.

---

rect, and would not be improved by the omission of "if."——¶ *Which had heard the fame of thee.* Heb. "The hearsay or report of thee." Chald. "Which have heard the fame of thy might." Gr. "Which have heard thy name."

V. 16. *Because the Lord was not able, etc.* Heb. "From the not being able of the Lord to bring this people," etc. By a close inspection of the context, v. 13–19, it will appear that Moses founds his plea upon three especial considerations: 1. The disparagement to which the Divine name and glory would be subjected in the estimation both of the Egyptians and the Canaanites, as if he *could not* accomplish his promises. This would give them occasion to blaspheme. 2. The dictates of the gracious long-suffering and forgiving nature of God. 3. The precedent (vs. 17, 18) of the past train of the divine providences, wherein pardon had been repeatedly granted them from the day of their leaving Egypt to the present. On this threefold ground he builds his plea for mercy to be shown to the sinning people.

V. 17. *Let the power of my Lord be great.* Or, "let the might," etc., as the original is the same word with that which occurs in v. 13, and is there rendered *might.* The Heb. for "Lord" in this passage is "Adonai," on which see Note on Gen. 15 : 2. "Let thy power be great" is equivalent to, let thy power be *manifested* to be great. Gr. "Let thy strength be exalted." It becomes, however, a question what the greatness of the divine power has to do with the forgiveness of the people's sin. It is doubtless a great error to refer such an act to omnipotence, as moral attributes are mainly involved in it. The true solution, we are satisfied, is, to understand the ability and the power spoken of in this connection as virtually synonymous with *willingness.* When Moses says, v. 16, "because the Lord was not *able* to bring this people into the land which he sware unto them," we are not, we think, to understand it of what may be termed the Lord's *natural*, but of his *moral* ability; not, so to speak, of a physical incapacity, but of an interior mental unwillingness to bestow upon them a favor of which they had shown themselves so signally undeserving. As far as mere omnipotence was concerned, it required no greater exercise of that to conduct them into Canaan than to slay them by desolating judgments in the wilderness. It is not then this kind of inability which the heathen would impute to the Lord, but simply the inability of a repugnant will. And it will probably be found that in nearly, if not quite, every instance in which the original word is applied to the Most High, it denotes the ability or inability which is involved in the *disposition* as being favorable or averse. So when he prays that the Lord would "magnify his power" in the forgiveness of the present transgression, he means nothing more than that he would put forth his

18 The LORD *is* long-suffering, and of great mercy, forgiving [b] iniquity and transgression,
and by no means clearing *the*
guilty ; visiting [c] the iniquity
of the fathers upon the children
unto the third and fourth *gene-*
ration.
19 Pardon [d], I beseech thee,
the iniquity of this people, according unto the greatness of
thy mercy, and as thou hast forgiven this people from Egypt
even until now.
20 And the LORD said, I
have pardoned, according [e] to
thy word :
21 But *as* truly *as* I live
all [f] the earth shall be filled with
the glory of the LORD.

b Mic. 7. 18. *c* Ex. 20. 5. Jer. 23. 2. *d* Ps. 78. 38. *e* Ps. 106. 23. Jas. 5. 16. *f* Ps. 72. 19 Is. 66. 18, 19.

moral proclivity or *propension* impelling him to pardon. Any other idea of *power* in such a connection is gross and materialistic.

V. 18. *The Lord (is) long-suffering, etc.* Heb. "Long of anger." See the terms employed in this verse fully explained in the Note on Ex. 34 : 6, 7.

V. 19. *From Egypt even until now.* That is, from the time of leaving Egypt. This is frequently the force of the Heb. preposition "from."

V. 20. *I have pardoned according to thy word.* That is, I will not destroy them all as one man ; I will not cut off the whole nation as I at first threatened, but will punish only those who have now so grossly rebelled, leaving it to their posterity to inherit the land. In this connection the words of the Psalmist may properly be cited, Ps. 106 : 23, "Therefore he said that he would destroy them, had not Moses his chosen stood before him in the breach to turn away his wrath, lest he should destroy them."

V. 21. *As truly as I live, etc.* Heb. "And assuredly I live, and all the earth shall be filled," etc. A form of oath frequently appropriated to the Most High, as Ezek. 13 : 3. 20 : 33. 5 : 11. Accordingly it is said, Jer. 4 : 2, "And thou shalt swear, The Lord liveth," etc. So when it is said, Is. 45 : 23, "I have sworn by myself," the apostle, quoting the words, Rom. 14 : 11, says, "For it is written, As I live, saith the Lord." The version of the Arab. is peculiar: "Nevertheless by my eternal duration (or existence) and by my splendor which fills the whole earth have I sworn." As the lifting up of the hand was a usual accompaniment of taking an oath, so we find both conjoined Deut. 32 : 40, "For I lift up my hand to heaven, and say, I live for ever." Hence it is said of the oath which the Lord sware, Ps. 106 : 26, "Therefore he lifted up his hand against them, to overthrow them in the wilderness." Ezek. 20 : 15, "Yet also I lifted up my hand unto them in the wilderness, that I would not bring them into the land which I had given them."——¶ *All the earth shall be filled with the glory of the Lord.* The import of this declaration in this connection is not at once perfectly obvious. From the rendering of the subsequent verse, which ostensibly gives a *reason* for the present declaration, it would seem that the earth was to be filled with the divine glory as a consequence of the condign punishment of the men who had not hearkened to his voice. By others it is understood of the glory which he would procure to himself by means of the miraculous and illustrious things that he would do for his people in conducting them into the land of

22 Because all those men which have seen my glory, and my miracles which I did in Egypt and in the wilderness, have tempted me now these ten times, and have not hearkened to my voice;
23 Surely [g] they shall not see the land which I sware unto their fathers, neither shall any of them that provoked me see it.
24 But my servant Caleb [h], because he had another spirit with him, and hath followed me fully, him will I bring into the

g Deut. 1. 35, etc. Ps. 95. 11. Ezek. 20. 15. Heb. 3. 17, 18.

h c. 32. 11, 12.

---

promise. (See Note on Ex. 16 : 7.) We may perhaps consider both ideas as included. The earth should be filled with the report of the glorious and righteous acts of the Lord in punishing the offenders and crowning the residue of his people with the most signal mercies. The Lord receives glory just in proportion as the majesty and justice of his administration are acknowledged among men.

V. 22. *Which have seen my glory and my miracles.* That is, probably, "have seen my glory, *even* my miracles." The Lord's glory shone forth in the miraculous works which he performed.——¶ *These ten times.* These many times; a definite number for an indefinite, as in Gen. 31 : 7, "And changed my wages *ten times*," i. e. frequently. Job 19 : 3, "These *ten times* have ye reproached me." Lev. 26 : 26. Although it is remarkable that an exact enumeration brings out the number ten as the number of instances in which they had sinned and been forgiven.

V. 23. *Surely they shall not see.* Heb. "If they shall see." A formula of swearing equivalent to a divine oath that they shall not see, i. e. shall not enjoy, the land, as explained by David, Ps. 95 : 11, "Unto whom I sware in my wrath, if they shall enter into my rest," which the apostle cites, Heb. 3 : 18, "To whom sware he that they should not enter into his rest?" "If" in such connections has the force of a negative. As the land of Canaan was a representative of heaven, the exclusion of the rebellious Israelites from that land was a shadow of the exclusion of all the unbelieving and disobedient from the kingdom of heaven.

V. 24. *But my servant Caleb, because he had another spirit with him.* Heb. "Because there was another spirit with him." That is, he was actuated by a very different spirit from the rest of the spies. His was a bold, resolute, courageous spirit, while theirs was a base, cowardly, and pusillanimous spirit. The Arab. renders the clause, "But my servant Caleb, inasmuch as he had another sentiment (or opinion), by reason of which he followed my obedience," etc. The same testimony is doubtless to be understood as applicable to Joshua, though not here named, for the reason probably that he was not classed with the mass of the people, but was a constant attendant upon Moses. He is expressly included in the promise, ch. 32 : 12.——¶ *And hath followed me fully.* Heb. "Hath fulfilled after me." That is, hath exhibited a full, constant, and complete obedience in this matter; hath neither turned aside, halted, or come short in following or complying with my commands. The same original phrase occurs Deut. 1 : 3. Josh. 14 : 8, 9, 14, on which latter passage see Note. The contrary is asserted of Solomon, 1 Kings 11 : 6, "And Solomon did evil in the

land whereinto he went; and his seed shall possess it.

25 (Now the Amalekites and the Canaanites dwelt in the

---

sight of the Lord, and *went not fully after* the Lord, as did David his father." Heb. "Fulfilled not after the Lord." The like unfavorable testimony is borne of the people at large, ch. 32 : 11, "Surely none of the men that came up out of Egypt, from twenty years old and upward, shall see the land which I sware unto Abraham, unto Isaac, and unto Jacob; because *they have not wholly followed me.*" Heb. "They have not fulfilled after me." We may here remark that the Gr. exhibits "He followed me obsequiously." Chald. "He hath perfectly fulfilled, or accomplished, after my fear." Chazkuni, a Jewish writer, renders, "He hath accomplished the word after me," and compares it with 1 Kings 1 : 14, "Behold, while thou yet talkest there with the king, I also will come in after thee and *confirm thy words.*" Heb. "Fill up thy words."——¶ *And his seed shall possess it.* Heb. *yorishenâh, shall inherit it,* as rendered both by the Gr. and Chald.; or, *shall cause to inherit it,* i. e. shall leave it to their posterity for an inheritance. The usage of this word is peculiar, as by a figure called *antiphrasis* it denotes according to its relations either the act of *inheriting* or *disinheriting.* In the latter sense the word occurs above, v. 12, and in the present passage it would bear the sense of disinheriting and driving out the inhabitants, and seizing upon it, as in Josh. 8 : 7, "Then ye shall rise up from the ambush and *seize* upon the city." Heb. *horashtem,* including the twofold idea of *expelling* the inhabitants and *taking possession* for themselves, with which coincides the language of Caleb, Josh. 14 : 12, "If so be the Lord will be with me, then I shall be able to *drive them out,* as the Lord said." Heb. *horashtim, shall disinherit them.* For further illustrations of the usage in question comp. Gen. 15 : 3. Deut. 2 : 24, 31. 1 Kings 21 : 15. Is. 14 : 21. Deut. 2 : 21, 22. Judg. 14 : 15. Sol. Jarchi in the present passage interprets the word in the sense of disinheriting or driving out: "They shall drive out the Anakims and the people that are therein." The promise which the Lord now confirmed with an oath to Caleb was conveyed to him in the Lord's name by Moses, and therefore in Josh. 14 : 9, the swearing itself is attributed to Moses: "And Moses sware on that day, saying, Surely the land whereon thy feet have trodden shall be thine inheritance, and thy children's for ever, because thou hast wholly followed the Lord my God." See Note *in loc.*

V. 25. *Now the Amalekites and the Canaanites dwelt in the valley.* Heb. *yoshïb* (*were* or *are*) *sitting.* The construction is somewhat doubtful, as it is not clear who is the speaker. If the clause is but a continuation of the Lord's words, as many commentators suppose, it should be read without a parenthesis, and in the present tense, —"dwell in the valley." If, on the other hand, it is interjected by Moses, the present rendering is most correct. For ourselves we give the preference to the former, regarding it as equivalent to saying: "Inasmuch as the Amalekites and Canaanites are at present occupying a position in the valley on the opposite side of the mountain, and will be apt to fall upon you with an overpowering force if you attempt to climb and cross the mountain, therefore for your own safety turn to-morrow and advance into the wilderness by the way of the Red Sea." It is true, that the Canaanites are said, v. 45, to

valley.) To-morrow turn you, and get you into the wilderness by the way of the Red Sea.

---

dwell in the mountain, but in either case we consider the term "dwell" as equivalent to "sit" in the sense of temporarily occupying a position, like those who lie in wait. Thus Josh. 8 : 9, "And they went to lie in ambush, and *abode* (*yĕshebu*) between Bethel and Ai." On the apparent discrepancy between vs. 25 and 45 Chazkuni remarks as follows: "The most of them abode (sat) in the valley, and some of them in the mountain, and those few warred against them (the Israelites); and therefore it is written, 'which sat in that mountain,' to imply that there were some of them which sat in another place; or, it may be, they dwelt in the valley, and when they heard that the sons of Israel came against them, they went up into the mountain, and lay in wait for them there; and we find that 'sitting' sometimes means 'lying in wait,' as it is written Ps. 10 : 8, 'He *sitteth* in the lurking-places of the villages.'" The two peoples here mentioned, upon the tidings of the approach of the Israelites, had got together and posted themselves in the valley lying on the other side of the mountain range at the foot of which the tribes were now encamped, and were resolved to fall upon them at their first advance onwards, for which purpose a portion of them had no doubt stationed themselves on the mountain to watch the movements of the host. ——¶ *To-morrow turn you, etc.* We see in this a memorable token of the Lord's goodness, inasmuch as at the same time that he was so highly displeased with them, he was still very unwilling that they should fall into the hands of their enemies. They were now encamped in Kadesh, from whence they had sent the spies, and though it is said they should commence a retrograde march "to-morrow," yet it is probable the term is to be understood in a somewhat indefinite sense as equivalent to *hereafter, henceforward,* or *at an early day,* as in Ex. 13 : 14, "And it shall be when thy son asketh thee *in time to come* (*mâhor, to-morrow*), saying, etc." It is at any rate clear that they did not move at once according to the letter of the command, but that they abode many days at Kadesh after their defeat, and before they began to compass Mount Seir.——¶ *By the way of the Red Sea.* That is, by the way *towards* the Red Sea. And so generally throughout the Scriptures, "the way *of*" is equivalent to "the way *towards.*" The original for "get you" is "journey for yourselves." As to the precise direction in which they were now commanded to travel, and the various subsequent routes taken in the wilderness during the lapse of the ensuing thirty-eight years, we must content ourselves with referring to the geographical investigations of Wells, Robinson, Kitto, Stanley, and others, who have devoted their special attention to this department of biblical inquiry. It has not comported with the general scope of our studies to endeavor to unravel the complexities of the wanderings of Israel over the Arabian peninsula for forty years, till they entered the precincts of Canaan. It is not improbable that the labyrinthian character of the mazes and meanders through which they were led partook of the typical character of their residence in Egypt and their deliverance therefrom, and was intended to represent the confused and irregular course, now forward and now backward, of the soul in the earlier stages of the regenerate life. The

26 And the LORD spake unto
Moses and unto Aaron, saying,
27 How long [i] *shall I bear
with* this evil congregation,
which murmur against me?
I have heard [k] the murmurings of the children of Israel,
which they murmur against
me.
28 Say unto them, *As truly
as* I live, saith the LORD, as ye
have spoken in mine ears, so
will I do to you:

i Mat. 17. 17. k Ex. 16. 12.

---

exodus of the nation from Egypt, the passage through the Red Sea, the destruction of Pharaoh and his host, and the immediately subsequent events are all but universally acknowledged to shadow forth analogous phases in the experience of the Christian, and we see not why the representative principle should not hold in regard to the whole of their desert history, as well as in regard to its preliminaries and commencement. We accordingly incline to regard very favorably the following remarks of Ainsworth (in loc.) on the present peculiar crisis in their sojournings: "In this Red Sea the people had been baptized, 1 Cor. 10 : 1, 2. Ex. 14. Baptism was 'unto repentance,' and with confession of sins, and into the death of Christ, Mat. 3 : 6, 11. Rom. 6 : 3. So this sending them back into the wilderness towards the Red Sea, was to humble them by repentance, that through faith in Christ they might have entrance into the kingdom of heaven; otherwise they should perish for ever, as their carcases perished in the wilderness."

The Lord renews his Threatening.

Vs. 26, 27. *And the Lord spake unto Moses and unto Aaron, saying, etc.* Hitherto from v. 11, the Lord appears to have spoken continuously in a somewhat private way to Moses alone, receiving and replying to his earnest plea contained vs. 13–19. Here, we conceive, commences a new address to Moses and Aaron conjointly, and intended to be imparted by them to the people, v. 39.——¶ *How long (shall I bear with) this evil congregation, etc.* Heb. "How long to this evil congregation?" That is, how long shall I pardon, vs. 19, 20; or, how long shall I bear with? An imperfect form of speech such as men are wont to employ under the influence of a strongly impassioned state of mind. Comp. Ex. 32 : 32. Ps. 6 : 4. 90 : 13.——¶ *Which murmur against me.* Heb. *mallinim âlâi, which cause (the people) to murmur against me.* So also in the ensuing clause the idea is that of a murmuring which is first entertained by one party and thence communicated and propagated to others. It implies the spreading of a disaffection like the widening of the waves on the surface of a lake.

V. 28. *(As truly as) I live, saith the Lord.* The usual formula of a divine oath, as in v. 21. It is here that the Lord swears in his anger that they shall not enter into his rest. Comp. Ps. 95 : 11. Heb. 3 : 18. Num. 32 : 10, 11.——¶ *As ye have spoken in mine ears, so will I do to you.* Heb. "If I do not so unto you as ye have spoken in mine ears." The Lord is here pleased to take them at their word; their wish was that "they might die in the wilderness," v. 2. Here their own imprecation comes upon them, as it did upon their descendants afterwards when they wished that Christ's blood might be upon their own and their children's heads, Mat. 27 : 25. "No less may befall those desperate profane varlets, whose rhetorical flour-

29 Your carcases shall fall in this wilderness; and all that were [l] numbered of you, according to your whole number, from twenty years old and upward, which have murmured against me,

30 Doubtless ye shall not come into the land *concerning* which I sware to make you dwell therein, save Caleb the

l c. 1. 45.

---

ish in their common discourse is frequently interlarded with a wish that "God would damn them;" which is all the mercy they desire from God. Such self-cursing seldom escapeth God's vengeance."—*Ness.*

V. 29. *Your carcases shall fall in this wilderness.* This is rendered in the Gr. version by κωλα, *kola*, which properly signifies *limbs* or *members*, as of the human body, but in several instances it is used synecdochically for *carcase, corpse, dead body*, as Lev. 26 : 30. 1 Sam. 17 : 46. Is. 66 : 24. Heb. 3 : 17. Their language was, v. 3, "Would to God we had died in this wilderness," and now their expressed desire is to be granted them.——¶ *And all that were numbered of you, etc.* Heb. *vekol pekudekem lekol misparkem, and* (*or even*) *all your mustered ones according to all your number.* The distinction between "mustering" and "numbering" is here lost sight of in our common version, though intrinsically marked and important. In mustering, marshalling, or arranging a host, it would be very natural to take a census also, but the two things are essentially distinct, though both are involved in the present clause.——¶ *From twenty years old and upward.* Amounting, as we learn ch. 1 : 46, to 603,550, exclusive of the Levites who were not numbered at this time, and when they were numbered, they were numbered not from twenty years old, but from a month old and upward. Consequently neither the Levites nor the children under twenty, nor the wives of the offenders were included in the severe sentence here denounced, but only the adult men above twenty. This accounts for the fact that we find Eleazar, who is mentioned at the numberings of the Levites, ch. 3 : 32, alive at the dividing of the land of Canaan. It is evident, therefore, that the language of the following passage, ch. 26 : 63–65, is to be limited by the explanation now given: "These are they that were numbered by Moses and Eleazar the priest, who numbered the children of Israel in the plains of Moab by Jordan near Jericho. But among these there was not a man of them whom Moses and Aaron the priest numbered, when they numbered the children of Israel in the wilderness of Sinai. For the Lord had said of them, They shall surely die in the wilderness. And there was not left a man of them, save Caleb the son of Jephunneh, and Joshua the son of Nun."

V. 30. *Doubtless ye shall not come into the land, etc.* Heb. "If ye shall come in," having, as we have before remarked, the force of a negative.——¶ (*Concerning*) *which I sware.* Heb. "Lifted my hand." Chald. "Sware by my Word." See Note on Gen. 14 : 22. So Deut. 32 : 40, "I lift my hand to heaven, and say, I live for ever."——¶ *To make you dwell therein.* Heb. *leshakkan*, the root word from whence is derived "shekinah," respecting which see appendix to the Notes on Ex. 20. The swearing here alluded to was a swearing not to these particular men, but to the patriarchs in behalf of their posterity. The oath was fulfilled to that posterity,

son of Jephunneh, and Joshua the son of Nun.

31 But your little ones, which ye said should be a prey, them will I bring in, and they shall know the land which ye have despised [m].

32 But *as for* you, your carcases, [n] they shall fall in this wilderness.

33 And your children shall wander in [o] the wilderness forty years, and bear your [p] whore-

m Ps. 106. 24.

n 1 Cor. 10. 5. *o* c. 32. 13. Ps. 107. 40. *p* Jer. 3. 1, 2. Ezek. 23. 35. Hos. 9. 1.

---

though not to every individual of it. As Grotius remarks, the land was promised by oath, "non personis, sed populo," *not to persons, but to the people.* Such a promise is not violated even in case a large proportion of the people are excluded.

V. 31. *But your little ones.* Your children under twenty years of age, v. 3. The very children about whose safety they had shown so much distrust and manifested such irreligious solicitude, should be the persons that should certainly inherit the promised land, though a long and trying period should first intervene.——¶ *They shall know the land which ye have despised.* That is, shall know and enjoy the good of the land. Gr. "Shall inherit." Compare with this the statement of Moses, Deut. 1:39, "Moreover, your little ones, which ye said should be a prey, and your children, which in that day had no knowledge between good and evil, they shall go in thither, and unto them will I give it, and they shall possess it."

V. 32. *But (as for) you, your carcases, they shall fall, etc.* Heb. "And your carcases, you, shall fall;" where the latter "you" is exegetical of "carcases," implying the exemption of the children—*you* or *yourselves* only.

V. 33. *Your children shall wander in the wilderness forty years.* Heb. "Shall be feeding." Gr. "Shall be fed." Chald. "Shall tarry or abide." The original term is not the appropriate term for *wandering*, but is still related to it, as sheep obtain their *food* by *wandering* from place to place over their pasture grounds. This was especially the case with the flocks of the Arabian shepherds, who inhabited a region so wild, rocky, and barren, that they could not long remain in one place, but were obliged to strike their tents and seek new grazing places, as one after another would be speedily exhausted. Chazkuni explains it:—"As sheep feed sometimes here and sometimes there, so your sons shall remove hither and thither, till their carcases be consumed." An allusion somewhat analogous is perhaps to be recognized Hos. 4:16, "The Lord will feed them as a lamb in a large place." That is, dispersed, in their captivity, among the conquering countries, among the Assyrians and Medes, who occupied a very large country. They would not be satisfied with the sheepfold of Canaan, and, therefore, says the Lord, they shall have more room; they shall go into a large place, but it shall be a place of captivity. They shall be as a lamb alone in the wilderness, succorless, helpless, surrounded by dangers, and with no eye near to pity, no hand to help it. They shall be carried into captivity, and shall there be lamenting and mourning, and in danger from prowling wolves, but there shall be none to regard, none to deliver.——¶ *Forty years.* That is, reckoning from the time of their coming out of Egypt; of which period one year and a half had

doms, until your carcases be wasted in the wilderness.

34 After the number of the days in which ye searched the land, *even* forty [q] days, each day for a year, shall ye bear your iniquities, *even* forty years; and ye shall know my breach [r] of promise:

q c. 13. 25.

r Jer. 18. 9, 10. Lam. 3. 31–33.

already elapsed. Deut. 2 : 14, "And the space in which we came from Kadesh-barnea, until we were come over the brook Zered, was thirty and eight years." Comp. Num. 10 : 11.——¶ *And bear your whoredoms.* That is, the punishment of your whoredoms. Chald. "Shall take upon them your iniquities." A well kown figurative expression for idolatry and other gross forms of transgression and apostasy. Comp. Jer. 3 : 9. Ezek. 16 : 15–17. Ex. 34 : 15, 16. Lev. 17 : 7.——¶ *Until your carcases be wasted.* Heb. *ad tōm.* The root of this verb is the word which generally denotes what is *perfect, complete, finished, consummated.* It is well rendered by *wasted,* i. e. *consumed,* in the present passage.

V. 34. *After the number of the days.* Heb. lit. "In, or by, the number." Gr. "According to the number."——¶ *Forty days, each day for a year.* So Ezek. 4 : 6, "I have appointed thee each day for a year," where the prophet was symbolically to bear the iniquity of Israel as many days as they had sinned years. In this usage we find authority for interpreting "days" in prophecy as denoting "years." See Dan. 9 : 24, etc. Rev. 11 : 3.——¶ *Ye shall know my breach of promise.* Heb. *tenu-âthi, my breach.* As the original term occurs only here and in Job 33 : 10, where it is rendered, "Behold, he findeth *occasions* against me," it is difficult to fix with precision the genuine meaning of the clause. We are left, therefore, to a choice among a great diversity of renderings. For instance, Gr. "Ye shall know the indignation of mine anger." Chald. "Ye shall know that ye have murmured against me." Vulg. "Ye shall know my revenge." In the various English versions we have the following:—*Cov.*, "That ye may know what it is, when I withdraw my hand." *Mat.*, "Ye shall feel my vengeance." *Cran.*, "Ye shall know my displeasure." *Purv.*, "Ye shall know a rupture with me." Ainsworth renders it as in our version, but italicizes and parenthesizes the words "of promise:"—"Ye shall know my breach (of promise)." As there is nothing to answer to these words in the original, it is not easy to perceive the grounds on which our translators have inserted them without the usual indications conveyed by italic letters. They doubtless supposed that the "breach" implied a "breach of promise," but this cannot be shown to be the legitimate purport of the term, although if it were, the expression is still susceptible of a sense consistent with the general tenor of Scripture, and one that leaves the Divine perfections unimpeached. The divine promise or covenant relative to the possession of the land of Canaan was conditioned upon the obedience of the people to the laws, statutes, and ordinances which the Lord appointed them. If they failed in their engagements, the Lord was released from his, and nothing more than this is meant by his "breach of promise." The Most High is never the first to fail in the performance of what he has engaged to do for his creature, but he may justly forsake those that forsake him. This is the only possible "breach

35 I [s] the LORD have said, I
will surely do it unto all this evil
[t] congregation, that are gathered together against me; in this
wilderness they shall be consumed, and there they shall
die.
36 And the men [u] which Moses sent to search the land, who
returned and made all the congregation to murmur against
him, by bringing up a slander
upon the land,
37 Even those men, that did
bring up the evil report upon
the land, died [v] by the plague
before the LORD.
38 But Joshua the son of

s c. 23. 19. *t* ver. 27. *u* c. 13. 31, 32.

v 1 Cor. 10. 10. Heb. 3. 17. Jude 5.

of promise" that can be laid to the Lord's charge, and even this is the language rather of apparent than of real truth. The root verb to which the original noun is referred occurs in the following connections:—Num. 32 : 7, "Wherefore *discourage ye* (marg. *break*) the heart of the children of Israel from going over into the land," etc. Ch. 30 : 5, "But if her father *disallow* her in the day that he heareth," etc.; i. e. if he disannul her promise.

V. 35. *I the Lord have said.* Chald. "I the Lord have decreed by my Word."——¶ *I will surely do it.* Heb. "If I do not this;" which has the force of an affirmative, as the Gr. renders it, "I will surely do." That is, I will surely do or execute what I have threatened. ——¶ *That are gathered together against me.* That is, gathered in a mutinous and seditious manner. The gathering was ostensibly against Moses and Aaron, but in reality against Jehovah himself who had commissioned his servants to lead and govern the people in his name.——¶ *In this wilderness shall they be consumed.* This sentence or decree is so frequently repeated that they might know that it was peremptory and irreversible. "So we see that they could not enter in because of unbelief." "Let us labor, therefore, to enter that rest, lest any man fall after the same example of unbelief." Heb. 3 : 19. 4 : 11.

V. 37. *Died by the plague before the Lord.* Heb. *bammaggēphâh, by the stroke;* that is, by some signal and fearful stroke of divine judgment, but not probably by any disease technically termed "the plague." This is more particularly intended by the word *devar, pestilence,* which occurs, v. 12, above. The present term is not one that denotes a disease of any kind, but an extraordinary judgment. The original word is translated *slaughter* 1 Sam. 4 : 17, and *stroke* Ezek. 24 : 16. Its usage 2 Chron. 21 : 14, shows that the idea couched under it is general and not specific: "Behold, with a great *plague* will the Lord smite thy people;" that is, with some fearful judgment. So in the present case, it is stated that the ten unfaithful emissaries perished by some special visitation or stroke of the divine displeasure. Having fomented and ripened the mutiny, they became the first sacrifice to the avenging justice of heaven.——¶ *Before the Lord.* That is, before the Tabernacle, where the glory of the Lord appeared. So it is said of Uzzah, 1 Chron. 13 : 14, that "he died there *before the Lord,*" whereas in the parallel narrative 2 Sam. 6 : 7, it is said that "he died there *before the ark of God.*"

V. 38. *But Joshua the son of Nun, etc.* The literal rendering of this verse is decidedly preferable: "But Joshua the son of Nun, and Caleb the son of Je-

Nun, and Caleb the son of Jephunneh, *which were* of the men
that went to search the land,
lived [w] *still.*
39 And Moses told these sayings unto all the children of Israel: and the people mourned [x]
greatly.
40 And they rose up early
in the morning, and gat them up
into the top of the mountain,
saying, Lo, we *be here*, and will

w c. 26. 65. Josh. 14. 6, 10.

x Ex. 33. 4. Is. 26. 16.

---

phunneh, lived of those men that went to search the land." These faithful messengers, notwithstanding their former association with those who now perished, lived, i. e. remained alive safe and in health. And they survived not only the other spies, but all the rebellious Israelites, and went in and took possession of the promised inheritance, Josh. 14 : 10. 19 : 49.

V. 39. *And Moses told these sayings unto all the children of Israel.* That is, made known to the multitude the calamity that had happened and the reasons of it; communicating to all quarters of the camp the sentence which had now gone forth from the Lord's lips, and which had probably as yet been but partially circulated among the immense host consisting of two or three millions of people.——¶ *And the people mourned greatly.* Syr. "And the people sat down in excessive grief." Being overwhelmed with anguish in view of the doom which they had so foolishly brought upon themselves, and which they were assured was irreversible. Knowing this to be the fact, they did not sue to Moses to pray for them, as they had done on other occasions, ch. 11 : 2. They had now abundant and just cause for weeping, whereas before, v. 1, their weeping was causeless.

V. 40. *And they rose up early in the morning, and gat them up, etc.* Heb. "Went up;" i. e. set about it, made all their preparations for it, and actually proceeded a considerable distance towards the summit. Men are often said in Scripture to do what they intend and endeavor to do. See this illustrated in the Note on Gen. 37 : 21. Struck with a temporary panic, a transient fit of slavish fear, as the sequel clearly proves, the people now were as forward to advance as they had been backward before, and though dissuaded by Moses from their rash attempt, they obstinately ventured forth; with what results we are soon informed.——¶ *Lo, we (be here).* Heb. *hinnenu, behold! we*, or, *behold us!*——¶ *And will go up unto the place which the Lord hath promised: for we have sinned.* That is, we are now prepared to do what the Lord commanded, and trust that he will make his promise good. We acknowledge that we have sinned in not at once complying with the divine mandates, and in murmuring and rebelling as we have done, but as we confess our guilt and folly now, and are disposed to make up for our past delinquencies by an exemplary obedience henceforth, we look for the divine favor. But alas, they were obedient and valiant too late! Having sinned against the clearest light and the most emphatic warnings, their transgressions could not be retrieved by the forced repentance and reformation which they now evinced. "The decree was gone forth, the consumption determined; they did not seek the Lord while he might be found, and now he would not be found. Oh, if men would but be as earnest for heaven while their day of grace lasts, as they will be when it is over; would be as

go up unto the place which the LORD hath promised: for we have sinned.

41 And Moses said, Wherefore now do ye transgress the commandment [y] of the LORD? but it shall not prosper.

42 Go not up, for the LORD *is* not among you; that ye be not smitten before your enemies.

43 For the Amalekites and the Canaanites *are* there before you, and ye shall fall by the sword; because [z] ye are turned

y ver. 25.

z 2 Chr. 15. 2.

solicitous to provide themselves oil while the bridegroom tarries as they will be when the bridegroom comes, how well would it be for them!"—*Henry*.

V. 41. *And Moses said.* By comparing this with the parallel narrative, Deut. 1:41–43, it will be seen that Moses acted under special instructions in saying what he did on this occasion: "But as for you, turn you, and take your journey into the wilderness, by the way of the Red Sea. Then ye answered and said unto me, We have sinned against the Lord, we will go up and fight, according to all that the Lord our God commanded us. And when ye had girded on every man his weapons of war, ye were ready to go up into the hill. And the Lord said unto me, Say unto them, Go not up, neither fight; for I am not among you; lest ye be smitten before your enemies. So I spake unto you; and ye would not hear, but rebelled against the commandment of the Lord, and went presumptuously up into the hill."——¶ *Wherefore do ye now transgress the commandment of the Lord?* Heb. "Wherefore (is) this (that) ye are now transgressing the mouth of the Lord?" Gr. "Why do ye transgress the word of the Lord?" Chald. "Why do ye transgress the decree of the word of the Lord?" The commandment which they were here transgressing was that, v. 25, requiring them to turn back to the Red Sea and not think of entering Canaan at present. The use of "mouth" for "commandment" is very frequent.——¶ *But it shall not prosper.* That is, the step on which you are now intent; the project of ascending the mountain and assaulting your enemies. Gr. "It shall not be auspicious to you." Syr. "Ye shall not carry out the thing proposed to its termination." We can never presume upon the Lord's blessing in accomplishing that which is engaged in contrary to his will.

V. 42. *For the Lord is not among you.* Heb. "The Lord is not in your midst." Chald. "The Shekinah of the Lord is not among you." The cloudy pillar removed not, but remained stationary, which should have served to them as an indication that the divine presence was not with them, and that the attempt was presumptuous.——¶ *That ye be not smitten before your enemies.* Chald. "Lest ye be broken (routed) before your enemies." Gr. "And ye shall fall before the face of your enemies." As if he should say, "The Canaanites are before you to attack you, and the Lord is not among you to protect you and fight for you, and therefore look to yourselves that 'ye be not smitten before your enemies.' Those that are out of the way of their duty are from under God's protection, and go at their peril. It is dangerous going where we cannot expect God should go along with us."—*Henry*.

V. 43. *The Amalekites and the Canaanites (are) there before you.* That is,

away from the LORD, therefore
the LORD will not be with
you.
44 But they presumed to
go up unto the hill-top: nevertheless the ark [a] of the covenant of the LORD, and Mo-
ses, departed not out of the
camp.
45 Then the Amalekites came
down, and the Canaanites which
dwelt in that hill, and smote
them, and discomfited them,
even unto Hormah [b].

a c. 10. 33.

b c. 21. 3. Judg. 1. 17.

---

have got the start of you, have preoccupied the post which you would seize; implying that their folly in expecting to dispossess a strong and warlike people who had got into their hands all the strongholds, was equal to their presumption in going counter to the express command of heaven.——¶ *Because ye are turned away from the Lord.* Heb. "Because ye are turned from after the Lord." Chald. "Because ye are turned from after the service of the Lord." Gr. "Because ye have turned away unbelievingly or disobediently from the Lord."——¶ *Therefore the Lord will not be with you.* Chald. "The Word of the Lord will not be for your help."

V. 44. *But they presumed to go up.* Heb. *va-yaphilu*, from the root *âphal*, which occurs only here and Hab. 2:4, where it is rendered "lifted up"—"Behold, his soul which is *lifted up* is not upright in him." The derivative "Ophel" as a proper name (2 Chron. 33:14) denotes a *mount, eminence,* or *rising ground*, applied to a locality near Jerusalem, and as a common noun used to signify the kind of *swellings* termed *emerods* (*hæmorrhoids*) or *piles.* Hence as a verb it implies *to be elevated* or *elated mentally; to be proud, arrogant, presumptuous, etc.*, and hence rendered by Ainsworth "loftily presumed." Chald. "They dealt wickedly or turbulently." The leading idea is that of an *audacious adventuring* upon what is forbidden. The Jewish writers, however, represent the verb as involving the idea of *darkness* or *obscurity*, one of them rendering it, "They went dark, or obscure, inasmuch as they went without leave from God," and another, "They set forward in the dark before day-dawning." Hence probably the origin of the Vulg. rendering, "Illi contenebrati ascenderunt," *they being blinded went up.* The former is doubtless the correct interpretation, as the other appears to have arisen from confounding the present root עפל *âphal*, with אפל *âphal, to be dark* or *obscure.* ——¶ *Nevertheless the ark of the covenant of the Lord, and Moses, departed not out of the camp.* The ark moved only with the removal of the cloud, and Moses moved only with the ark; so that those who did advance did it on their own responsibility, and in direct opposition to the tokens of the divine will.

V. 45. *Then the Amalekites came down, and the Canaanites.* Under the denomination of Canaanites are included also the Amorites, as we learn from Deut. 1:44, "And the Amorites, which dwelt in that mountain, came out against you and chased you, as bees do, and destroyed you in Seir, even unto Hormah."——¶ *Which dwelt in that hill.* Heb. "Which sat in, or on, that mountain." Implying not so much a permanent abode as a temporary occupation for an ambuscade, as we have already remarked, v. 25.——¶ *And smote them, and discomfited them.* The latter term is peculiarly expressive, as

CHAPTER XV.

AND the LORD spake unto Moses, saying,

2 Speak unto the children of Israel, and say unto them, When ye be come into the land of your habitations, which I give unto you,

---

it occurs in the following passage, Is. 30:14, "And he shall break it as the breaking of the potter's vessel, which is broken in pieces." Deut. 9:21, "And I took your sin, the calf which ye had made, and burnt it with fire, and stamped it, and ground it very small, even until it was as small as dust." It implies, therefore, a complete routing and breaking to pieces.——¶ *(Even) unto Hormah.* That is, unto the place which was afterwards called "Hormah," or *destruction,* in memory of the signal slaughter which befell them there.

CHAPTER XV.

Particular Laws relative to Offerings and Sacrifices.

In the preceding chapter we learn that in consequence of the grievous provocation given to the Most High, he had determined to destroy them, and in token thereof had sentenced the offenders to perish in the wilderness, making, at the same time, a merciful reservation in behalf of their children. Accordingly, with a more special reference to that part of the congregation who were to inherit the land, he here repeats and explains some of the laws concerning offerings, which were to be observed after they had actually become settled in Canaan. This implied that notwithstanding past misdemeanors and proneness to rebel, the Lord was still disposed to be reconciled to them, and therefore gives them a virtual assurance that those who did not fall in the wilderness should be eventually planted in Canaan, and that he would there smell the sweet savor of their sacrifices, and make good to them all his promises.

V. 1. *And the Lord spake unto Moses, etc.* The time and the place to which these directions to Moses are to be referred are not clearly intimated in the narrative, but most commentators suppose that they were given during the stay of Israel at Kadesh, where we learn that they abode "for many days" after the events recorded in the preceding chapter.

V. 2. *When ye be come into the land of your habitations.* The tenor of this command would make it certain that they for whom it was intended should be brought into the land promised them, and that a system of worship should be there established. The language employed has led several of the early expositors, together with Calmet, to doubt whether the rites and ceremonies prescribed here and in the preceding books were actually observed prior to their settlement in the land of promise. It is conceived by them that as the circumstances of the people during their wanderings would make it extremely difficult to comply with these regulations, therefore the laws themselves were designed to be prospective in their operation, and only fully obeyed in a more fixed and permanent state of things. "It would appear," says Michaelis, "that the directions here given were not yet obligatory in the wilderness, inasmuch as the Israelites must have been deficient in flour and wine. They had herds and thus could offer cattle; but they had neither agriculture, nor olive-yards, nor vineyards;

3 And [a] will make an offering by fire unto the LORD, a burnt-offering, or a sacrifice in performing a vow [b], or in a free-

a Lev. 1. 2, 3.

b Lev. 7. 16. 22. 18, 21.

consequently it would have been hard for an Israelite who offered a lamb or a goat to have afforded the requisite addition of flour, oil, and wine." On this head it is scarcely possible to give a definite decision, though we think it implied in many places of the Pentateuch that the *principal* sacrifices and offerings were daily observed. But whether this holds in regard to all the details of the system, there is no doubt room for question. The parallel between this portion of the history and the following passage from the prophet Ezekiel, ch. 20 : 33–44, is worthy of notice: "As I live, saith the Lord God, surely with a mighty hand, and with a stretched-out arm, and with fury poured out, will I rule over you: and I will bring you out from the people, and will gather you out of the countries wherein ye are scattered, with a mighty hand, and with a stretched-out arm, and with fury poured out. And I will bring you into the wilderness of the people, and there will I plead with you face to face. Like as I pleaded with your fathers in the wilderness of the land of Egypt, so will I plead with you, saith the Lord God. And I will cause you to pass under the rod, and I will bring you into the bond of the covenant. And I will purge out from among you the rebels, and them that transgress against me: I will bring them forth out of the country where they sojourn, and they shall not enter into the land of Israel: and ye shall know that I am the Lord. As for you, O house of Israel, thus saith the Lord God; Go ye, serve ye every one his idols, and hereafter also, if ye will not hearken unto me: but pollute ye my holy name no more with your gifts, and with your idols. For in mine holy mountain, in the mountain of the height of Israel, saith the Lord God, there shall all the house of Israel, all of them in the land, serve me: there will I accept them, and there will I require your offerings, and the first fruits of your oblations, with all your holy things. I will accept you with your sweet savor, when I bring you out from the people, and gather you out of the countries wherein ye have been scattered; and I will be sanctified in you before the heathen. And ye shall know that I am the Lord, when I shall bring you into the land of Israel, into the country for the which I lifted up mine hand to give it to your fathers. And there shall ye remember your ways, and all your doings, wherein ye have been defiled; and ye shall loathe yourselves in your own sight for all your evils that ye have committed. And ye shall know that I am the Lord, when I have wrought with you for my name's sake, not according to your wicked ways, nor according to your corrupt doings, O ye house of Israel, saith the Lord God."

V. 3. *Will make an offering by fire unto the Lord.* Heb. "Will make a fire unto the Lord." The word "offering" is not expressed in the original, but is evidently understood. Chald. "An oblation before the Lord." This comprehends all the sacrifices which were burnt upon the altar, either in whole or in part.——¶ *A burnt-offering.* Of the import of the term, and of the general law of the burnt-offering, see the Note on Lev. 1 : 1. It was the principal and most ancient of all the offerings, consisting of an animal which was wholly burnt upon the altar every

will-offering, or in your solemn feasts[c], to make a sweet savour[d] unto the LORD, of the herd, or of the flock;

4 Then shall he that offereth his offering unto the LORD bring a meat-offering[e] of a tenth-deal

c Lev. 23. 8, 12. d Ex. 29. 18.

e Ex. 29. 40. Lev. 23. 13.

morning and evening.——¶ *Or a sacrifice.* Understand a *sacrifice of peace-offering*, as the Chald. explains it. See the law concerning these, Lev. 3. The original *zebach, sacrifice,* when occurring in absolute form is often put for *peace-offerings*, as Ex. 18 : 12, on which see Note. Consult also Lev. 17 : 5, 8. 23 : 37. Deut. 12 : 27. Such is the import here, for the meat and drink-offerings about to be specified were not added to the sin or trespass-offerings, except in the case of the cleansing of the leper.——¶ *In performing a vow.* Heb. "In separating a vow." See this phraseology more fully explained in Note on Lev. 27 : 2. The true idea is that of *paying, performing, fulfilling* a vow, but as the particular animal of the herd or flock which was vowed for a sacrifice was to be singled out and set apart from common use, therefore the term *to separate,* which originally applied to the object became gradually applied to the vow itself. Gr. "A sacrifice to magnify a vow."——¶ *Or in a free-will offering.* That is, an offering not required by any law, but which a person might be prompted spontaneously to present as the expression of a grateful heart.——¶ *Or in your solemn feasts.* Of these see a full account Lev. 23, with the accompanying Notes. So the peace-offerings of the passover mentioned Deut. 16 : 1, 2, etc. And the burnt-offerings were to have meat and drink-offerings with them.——¶ *To make a sweet savor unto the Lord.* Heb. "To make a savor of rest to the Lord." Gr. "To make a smell of fragrance to the Lord." Chald. "That it may be accepted with favor before the Lord." See Note on Gen. 8 : 21.

V. 4. *Then shall he that offereth his offering, etc.* That is, of any of the above-mentioned species. The meat-offerings (i. e. meal-offerings) were of two kinds, some being offered alone, respecting which the law is given Lev. 2 : 1, 2, etc., and others being added as a constant accompaniment to the burnt-offerings and peace-offerings, in respect to which the present directions are given. The intent of this law is, to prescribe what proportion the meat-offering and the drink-offering should bear to the several sacrifices to which they were annexed. The general rule that regulated the whole subject was this: That all sacrifices of beasts burnt upon the altar, whether by way of vow, or voluntary gift, being of the nature of a spiritual feast, were each of them to have a meat-offering as an appendage, consisting of flour, oil, and wine, in the following proportions, viz. to every lamb or kid a tenth-deal or omer of flour (about five pints), a quart of oil, and a quart of wine; to every ram, double the quantity of flour, the third of a gallon of wine, and as much of oil; to a bullock the largest sacrifice, three omers of flour, half a gallon of oil, and as much of wine; and so on, the same quantities being prescribed for each, whatever the number of the beasts offered at the altar. But the particulars will be more minutely considered as we proceed.——¶ *Of a tenth-deal of flour.* That is, the tenth part of an ephah, as expressly stated ch. 28 : 5, which was an omer; Ex. 16 : 36. The

of flour mingled with the fourth *part* of an hin of oil[f].

5 And the fourth *part* of an hin of wine for a drink-offering shalt thou prepare, with the burnt-offering or sacrifice, for one lamb.

6 Or for a ram, thou shalt prepare *for* a meat-offering two tenth deals of flour mingled with the third *part* of an hin of oil.

7 And for a drink-offering thou shalt offer the third *part* of an hin of wine, *for* a sweet savour unto the LORD.

8 And when thou preparest a bullock *for* a burnt-offering, or *for* a sacrifice in performing a vow, or [g] peace-offerings unto the LORD;

9 Then shall he bring [h] with a bullock a meat-offering of three tenth deals of flour mingled with half an hin of oil.

10 And thou shalt bring for a drink-offering half an hin of wine, *for* an offering made by fire, of a sweet savour unto the LORD.

11 Thus [i] shall it be done for one bullock, or for one ram, or for a lamb, or a kid.

12 According to the number that ye shall prepare, so shall ye do to every one according to their number.

13 All that are born of the country shall do these things after this manner, in offering an offering made by fire, of a sweet savour unto the LORD.

14 And if a stranger sojourn with you, or whosoever *be* among you in your generations, and will offer an offering made by fire, of a sweet savour unto the LORD; as ye do, so he shall do.

15 One [k] ordinance *shall be*

f Lev. 14. 10. c. 28. 5, etc. g Lev. 7. 11. h c. 28. 12, etc. i c. 28. k ver. 29. Ex. 12. 49. c. 9. 14.

Hebrew writers here remark, that "whosoever would voluntarily offer a meat-offering, might not bring less than a tenth-deal."——¶ *Fourth (part) of an hin of oil.* A hin was a liquid measure of the sanctuary containing one gallon and two pints; a fourth part of this of course was one quart and half a pint.

V. 5. *Wine for a drink-offering.* Heb. *lennesek, for an effusion, for a poured-out offering or libation,* because it was poured out on the altar, but not on the fire. The priest had none of it.

V. 12. *According to the number.* That is, that proportionable to the number of bullocks, rams, sheep, or goats, should be the quantity of the *meat-offering* and *drink-offering;* for bread and wine ought to bear a due proportion to the meat set on the table.

V. 13. *All that are born of the country.* Heb. "Every native-born (Israelite)." This is clearly prospective, as the native-born of the country refers to those who should be born in Canaan and not in the wilderness.

V. 14. *If a stranger sojourn with you.* Gr. "If there be a proselyte among you in your land;" that is, the Gentile converted in whole or in part to the religion of Israel.——¶ *Or whosoever be among you.* That is, a foreigner that shall be permanently settled among you in contradistinction to the temporary sojourner, who may still be a proselyte.——¶ *In your generations.* That is, throughout your generations; in all succeeding ages. So also in v. 15.

V. 15. *One ordinance (shall be both) for you of the congregation.* The word-

both for you of the congregation, and also for the stranger that sojourneth *with you*, an ordinance for ever in your generations: as ye *are*, so shall the stranger be before the LORD.

16 One law and one manner shall be for you, and for the stranger that sojourneth with you.

17 And the LORD spake unto Moses, saying,

18 Speak unto the children of Israel, and say unto them, When [l] ye come into the land whither I bring you,

19 Then it shall be, that, when ye eat of the bread of the

l Deut. 26. 1, etc.

---

ing of the original is peculiar, and may be rendered, "O congregation, one ordinance, or statute, shall be for you, etc." Or, as the main word stands as a nominative absolute, it may be rendered, "As to the congregation, one ordinance shall be for you," etc. For a fuller account of the laws pertaining to proselytes among the chosen people, see the various treatises of Jewish antiquities. The drift of this law would naturally tend to the encouragement of proselytes of other nations to come in and embrace the religion of the true God. It was hereby ordained that all such persons should have the same religious privileges, so far as the ceremonies, sacrifices, and services were concerned, as were accorded to the native-born Israelites; and this privilege they were to enjoy from age to age as long as that dispensation lasted.

The Law of the Offering of the first of the Dough for a Heave-offering.

V. 18. *When ye come into the land, etc.* Heb. "In your coming, or entering in." A new ordinance is here imposed by divine authority, viz. that the people, when they had entered the land, should offer to the Lord a cake made of the first of their dough—a law of which no mention is made by Moses in any other place than this. It is in fact a direction respecting a new perquisite to the priests. It had before been commanded (Lev. 23:17) that at every Pentecost two loaves should be brought to them by each householder, from the first-fruits of the wheat harvest. That provision is now so extended as to give them a similar claim to a loaf made from the first gatherings of all kinds of grain, its size, as far as we know, being left to the giver's discretion. This law, like the last, and like the similar one of older date, was first to go into effect after the establishment in Canaan. It is evidently a law of the same nature with that respecting the first harvest-fruits, namely, that as every corn-grower in the land of Canaan was required to present some part of his first ripe corn every year to God for the use of the priests, so it is now ordained, as a kind of supplement to the same law, that out of the first bread that any man made of his new corn, a part of the dough should be taken and presented to the priest in waiting, ready baked, and before he had baked any for his own use. This the priest was to present as an offering to the Lord by *waving* it up towards heaven, after the manner of a *heave* or *wave-offering*, and then was to have it as a portion for himself.

V. 19. *When ye eat of the bread of the land.* That is, of the bread-corn, the produce of the land, as in Is. 28:28, "Bread is bruised," i. e. bread-corn, as rendered in the common version. So also Ps. 104:14, "That he may

land [m], ye shall offer up an heave-offering unto the LORD.
20 Ye shall offer up a cake of the [n] first of your dough *for* an heave-offering: as *ye do* the heave-offering [o] of the threshing-floor, so shall ye heave it.
21 Of the first of your dough

m Josh. 5. 11, 12. *n* Prov. 3. 9, 10. *o* Lev. 23. 10.

bring forth *food* out of the earth." Heb. "Bread."——¶ *Ye shall offer up an heave-offering unto the Lord.* Heb. "Ye shall heave an heave (offering) unto the Lord." Gr. and Chald. "Shall separate;" it being separated by the owner, and offered to the Lord, and thus made to form one of the "heave-offerings" which the Lord gave to his priests. It was therefore holy. The Jewish writers allude thus to this enactment: "Whosoever separated a cake he first blessed God who sanctified them by his commandments, and commanded them to separate a cake."—*Maimonides.* "An heathen that separated a cake, though in the land of Israel, it was no cake."—*Idem.*——¶ *Unto the Lord.* Chald. "Before the Lord." That is, in his presence, under his auspices, they were first heaved or lifted up to the Lord, the creator of heaven and earth, in token of his supremacy, and in acknowledgment of his goodness, and then made over to the priests without being laid upon the altar, like the other sacrifices. Indeed, it was not necessary that this offering should be made, in after times, at the Temple at Jerusalem, but wherever the offerer resided; and as the priestly class was dispersed all over the land, there was no difficulty in finding those to whom it was to be dispensed. Comp. Ezek. 44:30, "Ye shall also give unto the priest the first of your dough." Comp. also Neh. 10:37. This explains v. 21, below.

V. 20. *Ye shall offer up a cake of the first of your dough.* This is on the general principle involved in the precept, Prov. 3:9, "Honor the Lord with thy substance, and with the first-fruits of all thine increase;" the effect of which would be to sanctify all the rest; "For if the first-fruit be holy, the lump (dough) is also holy," Rom. 11:6. See this subject still further considered in the Notes on Lev. 23:16, 17. As a reward for thus consecrating the first of every thing to the Lord it is said, Prov. 3:10, "So shall thy barns be filled with plenty, and thy presses shall burst out with new wine." The custom of the Israelites was to bestow of their corn, first-fruits, tithes, and other gifts to the priests, Levites, and poor, upon their first reaping and threshing the harvest. See Ex. 13:19. Lev. 13:22. Num. 18:12, 26. Afterwards when they made their bread they separated this cake; and as the Levites separated a heave-offering out of their tithe, Num. 18:26, so the poor that gleaned the fields separated of their dough for a like purpose.——¶ *As ye do the heave-offering of the threshing-floor.* That is, of the corn in the threshing-floor. So Deut. 16:13, "Thou shalt observe the feast of tabernacles seven days, after that thou hast gathered in thy corn and thy wine." Heb. "After thou hast gathered in thy *floor* and thy *vineyard.*" As it was their duty religiously to separate the first-fruits of their corn on the threshing-floor, so also of the dough in their houses.

V. 21. *Of the first of your dough ye shall give, etc.* As this was a new law not given before, so it is repeated several times to give it more emphasis and importance in the eyes of the people; and that its sanctity was highly appreciated is evident from the fact that it

ye shall give unto the LORD an heave-offering in your generations.

22 And if ye have erred[p], and not observed all these com-

p Lev. 4. 2, etc,

was observed by the Israelites after their return from Babylon, Neh. 10:37, "And that we should bring the *first-fruits of our dough* and our offerings," etc. "This seems to have been done in every private family; and the Jews consider a woman as infamous who neglects to do it. At this day the Jews are so observant of this rite, that when they have dough enough to make a cake, they do it as soon as they have water enough to do it. According to the construction and practice of the modern Jews, this cake was given to the priests, though some throw it into the fire. It is understood by them to mean that the first portion of every lump of dough exceeding the bulk of forty eggs was to be given to the priests or Levites in order to sanctify the rest." —*Priestley*. That somewhat of a mystical import was couched in the ordinance is obvious from Paul's allusion, Rom. 11:16, where he applies the first-fruits and the lump of dough to Israel, and it is confirmed by the language of the prophet, Jer. 2:2, 3, "Thus saith the Lord; I remember thee, the kindness of thy youth, the love of thine espousals, when thou wentest after me in the wilderness, in a land that was not sown. Israel was holiness unto the Lord, *and the first-fruits of his increase:* all that devour him shall offend." The phrase, "All that devour (Heb. eat) him," seems to refer to the rule that no one was to eat of the first-fruit of the harvest but the priest. This mystical sense is also recognized by the Jewish commentators: "The commandment of the cake signified in mystery the congregation of Israel, called the first-fruits of the world; which when it is put into the oven that burneth with the fire of the holy blessed God, it is necessary to separate therefrom a cake, that it be not partaker of severe judgment; and therefore is a blessing reserved in the world."—*Rab. Menahem.* But we are taught to go beyond the Jewish nation to find the reality of the emblematic cake: "Of his own will begat he us with the word of truth, that *we should be a kind of first-fruits of his creatures,*" Jas. 1:18.

Sacrifices for Sins of Ignorance.

V. 22. *And if ye have erred.* That is, done unadvisedly through ignorance, error, or oversight, to which is opposed the "doing presumptuously," or "sinning with a high hand," mentioned v. 30. A law had been previously given respecting sins of ignorance, Lev. 4, and it is an obvious question, in what respects that law differed from the present. We may observe in reply, (1.) that the law in Leviticus seems rather to contemplate sins of commission, and this sins of omission. (2.) The present law appears to have reference to such sins of ignorance as might be committed by the whole congregation, while the other is applicable to the sins of individuals. This view seems to be confirmed by the fact, that in the verse before us the collective "ye" is employed, while in the subsequent verse, 27, where the case of an individual is recognized, the term used is "any soul," as it is also in Lev. 4:2. The ceremonial observances enjoined upon the nation were so numerous, complicated, and various, that it might easily be supposed some of them would by degrees be forgotten and disused; consequently if, in process of time, upon consulting the law, there should appear

mandments, which the LORD hath spoken unto Moses,

23 *Even* all that the LORD hath commanded you by the hand of Moses, from the day that the LORD commanded *Moses*, and henceforward among your generations;

24 Then it shall be, if *aught* be committed by ignorance without the knowledge of the congregation, that all the congre-

---

to have been a general neglect of any of the divine appointments, a sacrifice must be offered for the whole congregation. We may suggest, moreover, that the law contemplated perhaps the extension of the meaning of "sins of ignorance" on the part of the congregation, making them cover the case of the commission of any offence within its borders, when the criminal had escaped detection. When such an offence occurred, one which might be considered to involve the responsibility of the nation at large, its sense of the fault was to be manifested in a manner somewhat different from what had been before prescribed, and one more costly and imposing. Instead of a bullock only for a sin-offering, which had been previously ordained, a sin-offering of a kid is now to be substituted, accompanied with the holocaust of a bullock, with the addition of its appropriate meal and drink offerings, as these had been lately prescribed. This was a striking feature of the present enactment, that it tended to make the whole community feel itself charged with the responsibility of the conduct of each of its members. It became liable to a certain form of penalty for the transgression, by certain individuals, of the divinely appointed statutes and ordinances with which they were bound sedulously to comply.——¶ *And not observed all these commandments.* Heb. "Have not done all these commandments." As intimated above, the words of this law differ from those in Lev. 4: 2, 23, they having reference to things which *should not be done*, and these to things which *should be done;* or in other words, the one pointing to sins of *commission*, and the other to sins of *omission.* The implication is very clear, that when commanded duties are neglected through ignorance or inadvertence, the delinquent is not entirely guiltless on that account. His culpability is not so great as that of the knowing or wilful transgressor, but he still needs the application of the virtue of the great sacrifice represented by the bullock and the kid.

V. 24. (*If aught*) *be committed by ignorance without the knowledge of the congregation.* Heb. "By error from the eyes of the congregation." In like manner Lev. 4: 13, "If the whole congregation of Israel sin through ignorance, and *the thing be hid from the eyes of the assembly,*" where the subjoined Note fully explains the phraseology. The reference is probably to some neglect on the part of one or more individuals, of the public services or ceremonies of religion, or some deviation from the prescribed statutes, occasioned either by the remissness of rulers, the misinterpretation of the laws, or the abounding iniquity of the times.——¶ *Shall offer one young bullock.* It is worthy of remark that the Jewish writers generally understand this ordinance of strange worship which required to be expiated by the sacrifice of a bullock for a burnt-offering and a goat for a sin-offering. Outram (*On Sacrifices*, B. I. c. 14, §§ 1, 2) coincides in this opinion, and his remarks are

gation shall offer one young bullock for a burnt-offering, for a sweet savour unto the LORD, with [q] his meat-offering, and his drink-offering, according to the manner, and one kid [r] of the goats for a sin-offering.

25 And the priest shall make an atonement for all the congregation of the children of Israel, and it shall be forgiven them; for it *is* ignorance [s]: and they shall bring their offering, a sacrifice made by fire unto the LORD, and their sin-offering before the LORD, for their ignorance:

26 And it shall be forgiven

q ver. 8-10. r Lev. 4. 23. c. 28. 15. Ezra 6. 17. 8. 35.

s Acts 3. 17, 19. 1 Tim. 1. 13. Heb. 5. 2.

well worthy of consideration:—"If my own opinion be required,—I would not be confident on so obscure a subject, but I am inclined to think that the bullock was to be offered, when the whole congregation of Israel, though in other respects retaining their own rites, and following the worship of the true God, yet led away by one common error, transgressed without knowing it, some prohibitory precept. The kid for a sin-offering, accompanied with a bullock for a burnt-offering, I apprehend to have been required when the people, neglecting their ancient rites and unmindful of the divine laws, which often happened under wicked kings, were generally seduced into strange worship. As the law seems to contemplate such a state of the nation, so perhaps it commands a holocaust to be offered in token of a return to their ancient worship and religion, and a sin-offering for the expiation of all the sins which had been committed in the substitution of idolatry for the worship of the true God. For this reason I suppose it was, and it is a circumstance which adds much probability to my opinion, that after the temple had been long shut, 2 Chr. 28 : 24. 29 : 3, the daily sacrifices discontinued, and many strange rites admitted by the people through ignorance, Hezekiah commanded bullocks to be immolated as burnt-offerings, and goats as sin-offerings for the whole nation, 2 Chr. 29 : 21–24. Thus also, the Jews who returned from Babylon into their own land, offered, after the rebuilding of the temple, and the restoration of their ancient worship, the same kinds of sacrifices for all Israel. It forms no objection, that whereas Moses commanded only one bullock and one goat, Hezekiah sacrificed seven, and the Jews who returned from exile, offered twelve of each kind of victims. This I suppose them to have done from a conviction that the smaller number was absolutely necessary, but that the larger number was better; Hezekiah choosing the number seven as an emblem of perfection; and the returned exiles fixing upon twelve in reference to the number of the tribes." Comp. Ezra 8 : 35.——¶ *According to the manner.* Heb. "According to the judgment." That is, according to the mode prescribed by the Lord, vs. 9, 10.

V. 25. *For all the congregation.* Several commentators suggest that "all the congregation" both here and in v. 26, may be rendered "every congregation," and thus the law apply to the several tribes, cities, villages, and synagogues scattered throughout the land. This may perhaps be admitted, provided only we bear in mind that the appointed sacrifice was to be offered at the temple or wherever the centre of worship might be.

V. 26. *And the stranger that sojourn-*

all the congregation of the children of Israel, and the stranger
that sojourneth among them;
seeing all the people *were* in
ignorance.
27 And if [t] any soul sin
through ignorance, then he shall
bring a she-goat of the first
year for a sin-offering.
28 And [u] the priest shall
make an atonement for the soul
that sinneth ignorantly, when
he sinneth by ignorance before
the LORD, to make an atonement for him; and it shall be
forgiven him.
29 Ye shall have one law for
him that sinneth through ignorance, *both for* him that is born
among the children of Israel,
and for the stranger [v] that sojourneth among them.
30 But the soul that doeth
aught presumptuously [w], *whether he be* born in the land, or a
stranger, the same reproacheth

t Lev. 4. 27, 28. *u* Lev. 4. 35.

v Rom. 3. 29, 30. *w* Deut. 17. 12. Ps. 19. 13. Heb. 10. 26. 2 Pet. 2. 10.

---

eth among them. Gr. "And the proselyte that is settled among you."——¶ *Seeing all the people (were) in ignorance.* Heb. "Because (it happened) to all the people in or through ignorance."

V. 27. *If any soul sin through ignorance.* That is, any person. Chald. "If one man." As in what precedes allusion is had to cases where the sin in question could be considered as that of the whole congregation, so in the present passage the sin of a single individual, acting on his sole responsibility is treated of, and the appointed sacrifice specified. Such a private person, when guilty of any mistake or neglect in the worship of God through inadvertence, ill example, or infirmity, was required, as soon as he became sensible of his offence, to bring a female goat to the priest, for a sin-offering, the penitent oblation of which would exempt him from any farther penalty.

Of Presumptuous Sins.

V. 30. *The soul that doeth (aught) presumptuously.* Heb. "Doeth with a high hand," that is, in a bold, daring, defiant manner, giving way to deliberate acts of transgression against light, conviction, and inward remonstrance, and in despite of divine authority. Gr. "Shall do any thing with a presumptuous hand." Chald. "Shall do any thing with an uncovered head," that is, openly, fearlessly, without shame, for under emotions of shame men were prone to cover their heads, as Jer. 14 : 4, "The ploughmen were ashamed, *they covered their heads.*" The original phrase, in certain connections, is capable of a good sense, equivalent to boldness, courage, magnanimity, both in heart and deportment, as when it is said of Israel that they went out of Egypt *with a high hand,* Ex. 14 : 8. Num. 33 : 3; but here it implies knowingly, purposely, and presumptuously going counter to the express ordinance of heaven in contempt of the divine majesty and authority.——¶ *The same reproacheth the Lord.* Or, Heb. "Blasphemeth." Gr. and Chald. "Provoketh to anger." The original denotes primarily verbal reproaching, or reviling, as in 2 Kings 19 : 6, 22; but is applied here to a reproaching or blaspheming by deeds, as in Ezek. 20 : 27, "In this your fathers have blasphemed me in that they have committed a trespass against me." It is a truth of sol-

the LORD; and that soul shall be
cut off from among his people.
31 Because he hath despised [x]
the word of the LORD, and hath
broken his commandment, that
soul shall utterly be cut off; his
iniquity [y] *shall be* upon him.
32 And while the children

[x] 2 Sam. 12. 9. Prov. 13. 13. Acts 13. 41. Heb. 10. 28, 29.

[y] Lev. 5. 1. Ps. 38. 4. Ezek. 18. 20. 2 Pet. 2. 21.

---

emn import, that every presumptuous sinner is a virtual blasphemer of Jehovah, even though he may never orally profane his name.——¶ *That soul shall be cut off from among his people.* Gr. "Shall be utterly destroyed." Chald. "That soul shall perish." On the peculiar import of this phrase see the Note on Gen. 17:14, where it is fully explained. The Jewish writers extend the force of the threatening into the next world. "Although we find apostates to live more than fifty years, and that they are not cut off from the life of this world, yet know that their deserts hang upon them in this world, and vengeance shall be taken upon them abundantly in the world to come."—*Rab. Menahem.* It is probable that, when there were witnesses to the fact, the offender was punished by the magistrates either by death or beating. See Note on Deut. 25:2.

V. 31. *Because he hath despised the word of the Lord.* Heb. *bâzâh, hath contemned, set at naught as vile, dishonored.* Comp. with this Prov. 13:13, "He that despiseth the word shall be destroyed; but he that feareth the commandment shall be rewarded."——¶ *Hath broken the commandment.* Heb. *hēphar, hath annulled, frustrated, made void* or *of none effect,* in opposition to establishing or confirming. It is a term usually applied to breaking the covenant with God, as Gen. 17:14. Lev. 15:44; and often in the prophets. Sometimes spoken of the law and the commandments, as Ps. 119:126. Ezra 9:14. Heb. 10:28.——¶ *That soul shall be utterly cut off.* Heb. "Shall be cut off, shall be cut off;" reduplicated for the sake of emphasis.——¶ *His iniquity shall be upon him.* Heb. "Its iniquity shall be upon it." That is, the iniquity of that soul; which however stands for the person, and is correctly enough rendered. By "iniquity" may be understood the punishment of iniquity, as in Gen. 19:15. Lev. 22:9. It is observable, however, that several of the Jewish commentators give a more interior sense. Thus Sol. Jarchi says, "its iniquity shall be in it," means, "when his iniquity is in him, and he repenteth not." Rab. Menahem also gives the following as an exposition of the ancients: "That soul shall be cut off, and the iniquity thereof with it," as if he should say, The iniquity shall cleave unto it after it is cut off, to be punished for ever, according to that (Is. 66:24), Their worm shall not die, which Jonathan (the Chaldee Paraphrast) expounds, Their soul shall not die. And our doctors have said, It shall be cut off in this world, it shall be cut off in the world to come." Jonathan's words are, "That man shall be destroyed in the world that is to come, and shall give account of his sin at the great day of judgment." Pool explains it, that his punishment shall be confined to himself, and not fall upon the congregation, as it would do if they were to neglect to cut him off. After every attempt at a true solution of the meaning of the phrase, some doubt will still remain.

The Case of the Sabbath Breaker.

V. 32. *While the children of Israel were in the wilderness.* Several of the

of Israel were in the wilderness, they found a man that gathered sticks [z] upon the sabbath-day.

33 And they that found him gathering sticks brought him unto Moses and Aaron, and unto all the congregation:

34 And they put him in ward [a], because it was not declared what should be done to him.

35 And the LORD said unto Moses, The man [b] shall be surely put to death: all the congregation shall stone [c] him with stones without the camp.

z Ex. 35. 2, 3.

a Lev. 24. 12. b Ex. 31. 14, 15. c Lev. 24. 14.

---

foregoing ordinances it was not expected would be observed during their journeyings to the promised land, but the sabbath was to be honored wherever they were; therefore it is expressly mentioned that this incident occurred "in the wilderness." It is doubtless cited as an instance of presumptuous sin; for as the law of the sabbath was plain and positive, this transgression must of course have been known and wilful. The offence, according to the purport of the original, was *gathering and binding or bundling up wood.*

V. 33. *Brought him unto Moses and Aaron, and unto all the congregation.* Not perhaps literally into the presence of the whole congregation, consisting of hundreds of thousands, but before the heads and representatives of the whole body, to which the name of the congregation was often given.

V. 34. *And they put him in ward.* Heb. *bammishmor, in keeping;* as they had previously dealt with the blasphemer, Lev. 24 : 12.——¶ *Because it was not declared what should be done to him.* Gr. "They had not judged, or determined." They knew, indeed, that the sabbath-breaker was to die (Ex. 31 : 4. 35 : 2), but by what death he should die, or whether this gathering of sticks made him obnoxious to that sentence, they were not certain. It was clear that he had done it presumptuously, but whether the act came fairly within the compass of the law, and in what precise manner it was to be dealt with, they were not fully resolved in their own minds. As this was the first offence of the kind, and as neither Moses nor the people were disposed to act precipitately in the matter, they saw fit to await a specific direction from the Lord himself.

V. 35. *And the Lord said unto Moses.* Probably in answer to the special inquiry which Moses went into the tabernacle to make, as he did in another case of difficulty mentioned before, ch. 9 : 8.——¶ *Shall stone him with stones without the camp.* Stoning was the most dreadful of all the punishments inflicted upon malefactors under the Jewish dispensation; the event recorded furnishes, therefore, a striking and solemn testimony to the sacredness and divine obligation of the sabbath law, and one which should not be lost upon us at the present day. The offence was apparently light and trivial, and for which we should be apt to suppose such a punishment entirely disproportioned; but the dignity and majesty of the divine Being against whom it is committed is to be considered, and su[ch] an example teaches how enormous th[ose] acts become, which, though not sinful in their own nature, are yet forbidden by the supreme authority of the universe. Actions ventured upon in defiance or contempt of an express divine command, draw after them a fearful

36 And [d] all the congregation brought him without the camp, and stoned him with stones, and he died; as the LORD commanded Moses.

37 And the LORD spake unto Moses, saying,

38 Speak unto the children of Israel, and bid them that they make them [e] fringes in the borders of their garments, throughout their generations, and that they put upon the fringe of the borders a riband of blue:

d Josh. 7. 25.

e Deut. 22. 12. Mat. 23. 5.

load of responsibility. See Note on Lev. 20:2 for a particular account of the manner in which this punishment was inflicted.——¶ *Without the camp.* Hence arose the custom of taking those who were to be stoned to a distance from cities and from the judgment-hall, as is remarked by Sol. Jarchi. Thus they dealt with Stephen, casting him "out of the city," and stoning him, Acts 7:58; likewise with Naboth, 1 Kings 21:13, and with the blasphemer, Lev. 24:14. This aggravated the punishment, from involving a degree of *reproach*, as is evident from the language of the apostle, Heb. 13:11–13, "For the bodies of those beasts, whose blood is brought into the sanctuary by the high priest for sin, are burned without the camp. Wherefore Jesus also, that he might sanctify the people with his own blood, suffered without the gate. Let us go forth therefore unto him without the camp, bearing his reproach." The severity of the punishment in cases of the violation of the sabbath no doubt points typically to the sad lot of those who do not keep the true spiritual sabbath, "entering into the rest of God by faith, and ceasing from their own works, as God did from his," Heb. 4:1–11.

Law respecting Fringes.

V. 38. *Bid them that they make fringes in the borders of their garments.* Heb. *tzitzith*, from *tzitz*, *a flower*, probably from the fact that the fringe was an ornamental appendage somewhat resembling a flower. The English term occurs Deut. 22:12, "Thou shalt make thee *fringes* upon the four quarters (Heb. wings) of thy vesture," but in this case the original is *gedilim*, of a somewhat different, but related purport, as it denotes the *tufts* or *tassels* which were inserted in the fringe. From the threads or thrums of a fringe hanging down from the edge of the garment somewhat like locks of hair, the original word *tzitzith* is so rendered Ezek. 8:3, "And he put forth the form of an hand, and took me by a *lock of mine head.*" It is rendered in the Gr. by κρασπεδα *kraspeda*, which occurs Mat. 23:5, where our version has "borders"—"they make broad their phylacteries and enlarge the *borders* of their garments," i. e. the fringes. "There have been various conjectures as to the object of this law. The most probable is that the 'fringe' was intended as a sort of badge or livery, by which, as well as by circumcision and by the fashion of their beards, and by their peculiar diet, the Hebrews were to be distinguished from other people. Be this as it may, much superstition came in the end to be connected with the use of these fringes. The Pharisees are severely censured by our Saviour for the ostentatious hypocrisy with which they made broad the 'borders' of their garments. Our Lord himself wore the fringe, which is commonly

39 And it shall be unto you for a fringe, that ye may look upon it, and remember all the commandments of the LORD,

called in the New Testament the 'hem or border,' and it was this part of his dress which the sick desired to touch, under the impression that the contact would make them whole. It was probably the peculiar sanctity of this part of the dress, which directed attention to it in preference, for we may be certain that Christ himself did not point it out. We think that we may thus obtain a new light on the subject which has escaped observation. In Luke 8 : 43, a woman having an issue of blood comes *behind* him, touches the 'border' of his garment, and is healed. She *afterwards* falls down at his feet and acknowledges what she has done. Hence the 'fringe,' so to call it, was not, as the modern Jews think, before exclusively, but behind also, if not wholly behind; and hence also the same fringe could scarcely have been at the bottom of the robe, as the other account supposes. We may therefore ask whether it was not in fact such an embroidered edge, of various breadth, as we now see wrought with colored worsted or silk around the opening for the neck and down the breast of the *abba*, or woollen mantle, now in use among the Arabs (see the note on Ex. 22 : 27) and which is a very ancient article of dress, and probably in use among the Jews. This border might, on the one hand, be touched by a person behind the wearer, while on the other, the part in front would be under his own eye, as the law seems to require. We would by no means make a stand upon this conjecture; but being founded on a real Oriental usage, it is at least entitled to as much attention as the others, which are not so."—*Pict. Bible.*——¶ *In the borders of their garments.* Heb. "On the wings." The *skirt, edge,* or *border* of a garment is usually called *a wing*, as Ruth 3 : 9. 1 Sam. 15 : 17. Deut. 22 : 30. Zech. 8 : 13. So the four corners of the earth are called its *four wings*, Is. 11 : 12. Ezek. 7 : 2. Job 37 : 3. The fringes were the threads left unwoven at the end of the web, on the edge of which, or just above the fringe, was put a band or lace of blue, or rather of purple color, binding the fringe, which was of the same color with the garment, and that was usually white. This band or ribbon served not only to distinguish them from other people, but when they looked down upon it they were reminded of the duty they owed to God, as a holy and consecrated nation. Such among them as laid claim to greater sanctity than others, enlarged their fringes and extended them to so great a length that they sometimes swept the ground, which made them the more noticeable, of which they were ambitious. The modern Jews wear a long tassel at each corner, consisting of eight white woollen threads, knotted with five knots like small buttons, and open and untwisted at the ends.——¶ *Riband of blue.* The blue color, the color of the firmament of heaven, with which the purple was closely allied, seems to have been deemed of peculiar sanctity, and as it was the color of the priest's robe, so it would naturally tend to put the Israelites in mind that they were a kingdom of priests, and thus bound to act in accordance with their holy designation.

V. 39. *That ye may look upon it, and remember, etc.* This appendage to their dress was appointed as a badge, a memento, by which they were constantly reminded of their peculiar relation to God, and of their obligations to walk holily and religiously before him.——

and do them; and that ye seek
not after your [f] own heart, and
your own eyes, after which ye
use to go a [g] whoring:
40 That ye may remem-
ber, and do [h] all my commandments, and be holy [i] unto your
God.
41 I [k] *am* the LORD your
God, which brought you out of
the land of Egypt, to be your
[l] God: I *am* the LORD your God.

f Deut. 29. 19. Job 31. 7. Jer. 9. 14. *g* Ezek. 6. 9. Ps. 73. 27. 106. 39. *h* Ps. 119. 4.

i Lev. 11. 44, 45. *k* Lev. 22. 33. *l* Heb. 11. 16.

¶ *That ye seek not after your own heart, etc.* Heb. *tāthoru*, from the root *toor*, which we have explained in the Note on ch. 14 : 36, where it is employed in reference to the *searching* or *exploring* the land of Canaan by the spies, and implies, as we have shown, a *turning* or *circling about* in opposition to pursuing a direct and straight-forward course. Gr. "Ye shall not turn back after your imaginations, and after (the sight of) your eyes in the things after which ye go a whoring." Chald. "Ye shall not err, or wander, after the cogitation of your heart." The Chald. term here used does not signify, says Fagius, mere cogitation, but that kind of thought which proceeds from an impious curiosity, when we do not simply believe in and cleave to the word of God, but indulge in a spirit of vain speculation and disputation, against the nature of true faith. The "seeking after their own heart and their own eyes" implies therefore a giving way to their own imaginations and inventions in the matter of worship and general obedience, and lapsing into idolatry, which is spiritual fornication and adultery.

V. 40. *That ye may remember, and do all my commandments.* The end of *remembering* is *doing;* and we have reason to be thankful for any appointed means or appliances which shall assist us in impressing our minds more deeply with our religious obligations, and keep us in the way of the actual performance of every duty. The Israelites were not to regard the wearing of these fringes as having in it any real intrinsic sanctity, but only as an instrumental and sensible help to the dulness and sluggishness of their minds in relation to the deportment which they were required, as a holy people, to observe.

CHAPTER XVI.

The Rebellion of Korah, Dathan, and Abiram.

We have, in the present chapter, an account of the most formidable conspiracy against the authority of Moses and Aaron which occurs anywhere in the compass of the sacred narrative. It took place soon after the doom of the forty years' wandering had been pronounced, and the effect of that sentence would naturally be to beget a disposition to plots and conspiracies among the people. Being distressed and uneasy, they were in a fit condition to listen to the suggestions of factious spirits. As they were doomed to die, at any rate, before entering the promised land, they would be apt to cherish a certain desperation that could easily be turned into the channel of revolt. And as the circumstances were favorable for such a schism, so the concoctors of it were the very persons among whom we might expect it to originate. We see a twofold interest at work—one against the civil supremacy of Moses, and the other against the

CHAPTER XVI.

NOW Korah[a] the son of Izhar, the son of Kohath, the son of Levi, and Dathan and Abiram the sons of Eliab, and On the son of Peleth, sons of Reuben, took *men:*

a Ex. 6. 21. c. 26. 9. Jude 11.

priestly pre-eminence of Aaron. A part of the conspirators were of the tribe of Reuben, which had been subordinated to that of Judah in the recent arrangements, and they would naturally aim to regain the precedency which they deemed their birthright. Korah, again, was a Kohathite, descended from a brother of Levi, and probably an elder brother; and his feeling seems to have been, that the priesthood should, by right of birth, have belonged to his family, and by consequence that he should himself have been high-priest. Setting himself forth, therefore, as the champion of the whole Levitical body, he might readily enlist great numbers of them in the schism; and this result would be facilitated by the local proximity of these two tribes, which would give the projectors an opportunity of conferring together in regard to their plans. The Kohathites and the Reubenites were encamped on the same side of the Tabernacle. Considering the nature of the conspiracy and the standing of the parties engaged in it, it was all-important that it should be put down by some signal and terrible judgment, and of such a judgment the history proceeds to give an impressive account. The event is celebrated by the Psalmist, Ps. 106 : 16, 17, in brief but emphatic terms: "They envied Moses also in the camp, and Aaron, the saint of the Lord. The earth opened and swallowed up Dathan, and covered the company of Abiram."

V. 1. *Now Korah the son of Izhar, etc.* Gr. "Kore," which occurs in nearly the same form, Jude 11, "the gainsaying of Core." This Korah was a Levite, and cousin-german to Moses and Aaron; for Amram, the father of Moses and Aaron, and Izhar, the father of Korah, were brothers, being the sons of Kohath, as appears from Ex. 6 : 18. ——¶ *The sons of Eliab.* This Eliab was the son of Pallu, the second son of Reuben. Ch. 26 : 7–9, Gen. 46 : 9.——¶ *On the son of Peleth.* It appears that he was a descendant of Reuben, but of what particular family we are not informed. As nothing further is said of him, as he does not appear at all in the further progress of the plot, it is not unlikely that though he entered into it in the outset, yet he subsequently withdrew, and we may hope escaped the doom of his accomplices.——¶ *Took (men).* Heb. *va-yikah,* from *lâkah, to take.* This verb is the first word of the verse, and though in the singular number, yet it evidently includes the several nominatives that follow. But Gesenius remarks it as a peculiarity of the Hebrew, that when the verb precedes it may have several nominatives, though in itself singular, whereas if it follows it will be plural. Still it is to be inferred that Korah was the prominent actor, and to him the verb would naturally have primary reference. But the main question is in regard to the true import of "took" in this connection. As "men" does not occur in the original, what was it that Korah and his associates *took?* By some it is supposed that the "and" before Dathan is superfluous, or is equivalent to "both," and that Dathan, Abiram and On are the true objects of the verb, the persons whom Korah took, that is, took into association with himself in carrying out his purposed insurrection. This view, however, we reject as doing a certain violence to the more simple and natural

2 And they rose up before Moses, with certain of the children of Israel, two hundred and fifty princes of the assembly, famous [b] in the congregation, men of renown:
3 And [c] they gathered them-

b c. 26. 9. c Ps. 103. 16.

construction of the text. If we have recourse to the ancient versions we find ourselves but little assisted, as they evince great diversity. Gr. "And Kore spoke," implying that he wrought upon others by persuasion to join his faction. Chald. "And Korah separated himself," that is, he took himself aside, he withdrew himself in a scheming, plotting manner, as did also his associates. In like manner the Syr. "And Korah dissented," that is, started an opposition. The Arab. exhibits "aggressus est," *he made an attempt*, and this we think comes very near the true sense. "He took" we understand to be here equivalent to "he undertook;" or, if the reader pleases, he may supply the word "counsel"—"he took counsel"—but the idea is substantially the same; he engaged in an enterprise, he took hold of a scheme, he adventured upon something, and to make out the complete sense, this word should be read in immediate connection with the first words of the ensuing verse,—"He (and his accomplices) undertook a project, and they rose up, etc." A similar use of the Heb. verb without an objective expressed occurs 2 Sam. 18:18, "Now Absalom in his life-time *had taken* (*lâkah*) and reared up for himself a pillar," i. e., had taken counsel, or had undertaken an enterprise with a view to erect a pillar. How could he have *taken* a pillar before erecting it, when it was no doubt constructed of stone on the spot? As to the time to which this transaction is to be referred, we have no special data on which to form an opinion. Conjecture assigns it to the period of their stay at Kadesh-barnea after their repulse by the Canaanites and Amalekites.

V. 2. *And they rose up before Moses.* Heb. *va-yâ-kumu, they rose up* rebelliously or mutinously; *they made an insurrection.* As the verb in this case follows its nominatives occurring in the preceding verse, it assumes the plural form.——¶ *With certain of the children of Israel.* Heb. "And men of the children of Israel." That is, the men whom Korah had inveigled and drawn in to be his accomplices in the plot.——¶ *Princes of the assembly.* Gr. "Leaders of the congregation."——¶ *Famous in the congregation.* Heb. "The called ones of the congregation." See this phrase explained in the Note on ch. 1 : 16. The expression is applied to Dathan and Abiram, ch. 26 : 9, where it is rendered "famous in the congregation." Gr. "The called in council." Chald. "The princes of the congregation who were called by their names in the time of council." It is clear that they were persons of so much consideration and standing in the tribes as to give a very dangerous character to the conspiracy. ——¶ *Men of renown.* Heb. "Men of name." Gr. "Men of renown." The original phrase occurs with respect to the giants, Gen. 6 : 4, where see Note.

V. 3. *And they gathered themselves together.* Heb. "Were gathered together;" the Niphal or passive form. Gr. "They rose up against." The above named company assembled in a body against Moses and Aaron as the usurpers and arbitrary dispensers of all preferment.——¶ (*Ye take*) *too much upon you.* Heb. "Much to you;" or "Enough for you." The phrase is rendered "let it suffice," in Deut. 3 : 26. Vulg. "Let it be enough for you that all the multitude consisteth of holy ones." Sol. Jar-

selves together against Moses
and against Aaron, and said unto them, *Ye take* too much upon you, seeing all [d] the congregation *are* holy, every one of
them, and the LORD [e] *is* among
them: wherefore then lift ye up
yourselves above the congregation of the LORD?
4 And when Moses heard it,
he [f] fell upon his face:
5 And he spake unto Korah
and unto all his company, saying, Even to-morrow the LORD

d Ex. 19. 6. e Ex. 29. 45. f c. 14. 5. 20. 6.

chi paraphrases the passage, "Ye have taken to yourselves greatness much more than enough."——¶ *Seeing all the congregation* (*are*) *holy*, every *one of them.* Heb. "For all the congregation, all of them, are holy." The language is emphatic, indicating that there was no adequate ground in point of sanctity for the distinction between the priesthood and the laity; consequently that he and his associates were as worthy the office of ruler and priest as Moses and Aaron. This, however, was a direct encroachment upon a divine institution, for the office of priesthood was an honor which no man was to take to himself, "but he that was called of God as was Aaron," Heb. 5:4. Under the Christian dispensation the priesthood, properly so termed, is abolished, as all Christians constitute "a holy nation, a royal priesthood;" but still it does not follow from this that all the men of the church are equally qualified to discharge the functions of leaders and teachers. This depends upon their spiritual gifts, which are the true basis of ministerial character.——¶ *The Lord is among them.* Chald. "And the majesty (Shekinah) of the Lord dwells among them." That is to say, the Lord, by the sublime symbol of his presence, dwells among the congregation at large, and not merely among the tents of Moses and Aaron and the Levites. This was in itself true, but it did not authorize them to aspire to an office which the Lord had specially appropriated to another party.——¶ *Wherefore then lift ye up yourselves above the congregation of the Lord?* As we are, in fact, upon a level, no one portion of the people standing higher in the Lord's sight than another, why do you arrogate to yourselves such a lofty superiority over your brethren? The original for "above" is the same with that rendered "against" as applied to Moses and Aaron in this verse, and carries with it, perhaps, a latent intimation that they were actually taking a stand not only *over* but *against* the mass of the people, that is, in such a way as to be *oppressive* to them.

V. 4. *Fell upon his face.* In conjunction probably with Aaron, as they had both done on a former occasion, ch. 14:5. Aware of the aggravated nature of the offence, and fearful of the tremendous judgment it would be likely to incur, they fell prostrate before God, both to deprecate his displeasure in behalf of the people, and to seek direction in what manner to proceed in this trying emergency. A Jewish commentator says upon this passage, "He was abashed, and cast down his face on the ground unto prayer, and then it was said unto him what he should say unto Korah."

V. 5. *Even to-morrow the Lord will show, etc.* Heb. "And he spake, saying, The morning, and the Lord will make known." Wait but till the morning, and the Lord will discover by manifest tokens whether you or we are in the right. The delay would also af-

will show who *are* his, and *who is* holy [g]; and will cause *him* [h] to come near unto him: even *him* whom he hath chosen will [i] he cause to come near [k] unto him.

6 This do: Take you censers, Korah, and all his company;

7 And put fire therein, and put incense in them before the LORD to-morrow: and it shall be *that* the man whom the LORD doth choose, he *shall be* holy [l]: *ye take* too much upon you [m], ye sons of Levi.

8 And Moses said unto Korah, Hear, I pray you, ye sons of Levi:

g Lev. 21. 6, etc. h Heb. 12. 14. i c. 17. 5. k Lev. 10. 3. 21. 17, 18. c. 3. 10. Ezek. 40. 46. 44. 15, 16.

l Eph. 1. 4. m Heb. 5. 4.

---

ford them time to reflect upon their course, and, as a consequence, peradventure to retrace their steps.——¶ *Will show who (are) his.* Heb. "Will make known him that is his," or, "those that are his." Gr. "The Lord knoweth (or hath known) those that are his," which precise words are quoted by Paul, 2 Tim. 2 : 17, as if having the present history in his eye: "Nevertheless, the foundation of God standeth sure, having this seal, The Lord knoweth them that are his." Chald. "Will make known him that is fit for him."——¶ *And who is holy.* Heb. "And the holy one." That is, the one who is solemnly set apart and consecrated, by divine appointment, to the sacred office of priesthood.——¶ *And will cause (him) to come near unto him.* Heb. *hikrib*, of the import of which see Note on Lev. 10 : 3. Num. 3 : 5, 6. The Gr. rendering of this verse is as follows: "God hath seen and known who are his, and who are holy, and hath brought them near to himself; even those whom he chose he hath brought near to himself." The Chald. has: "God will make known him that is right (or fit) for him, and who is holy that he may approach him, in his sight; and whomsoever he shall choose, he will apply him to his service (or, ministry)."——¶ *Cause to come near him.* That is, for the purpose of constantly ministering before him. The term has an appropriated sense, as may be seen in the Note on Lev. 10 : 3. Num. 3 : 5, 6. The two ideas of "choosing" and "bringing near" are exhibited in the parallel passage, Ps. 65 : 5, "Blessed is the man whom thou *choosest* and *causest to approach* unto thee." This latter clause of the verse is rendered negatively in the Gr. "And those whom he hath not chosen to himself, he hath not brought near to himself."

V. 6. *Take you censers.* Rendered "fire-pans," Ex. 27 : 3, where see Note. The command for them thus to take censers and burn incense in them, was in effect the same as saying, Perform the office of priests, as you see fit to deny my claim to it as a right.

V. 7. *Put fire therein, etc.* Heb. "Give fire therein and put incense on them." We give this literal rendering that it may be known that "put" in the two clauses does not represent the same word in the original.——¶ *Whom the Lord shall choose.* That is, whom the Lord shall indicate by manifest tokens to be the man of his choice.——¶ *He (shall be) holy.* That is, shall be declared to be holy, or to be officially sacred, and thus confirmed as a priest.——¶ *Before the Lord.* Before the symbol of the divine presence; with their faces turned towards the sanctuary, at the gate of which they stood.——¶ *(Ye take) too much upon you.* The same phrase with that occurring above, verse

9 *Seemeth it but* a small [n] thing unto you, that the God of Israel hath separated [o] you from the congregation of Israel, to bring you near to himself to do the service of the tabernacle of the LORD, and to stand before the congregation to minister unto them?

n ver. 13. Is. 7. 13. *o* c. 3. 41, 45. 8. 14. Deut. 10. 8.

3, which Moses here justly retorts upon them: "You accuse me of taking too much upon myself; it is precisely this charge which I bring against you; the result will show with how much justice." So Elijah retorted upon Ahab the charge of troubling Israel, 1 Kings 18:17, 18.

V. 9. (*Seemeth it but*) *a small thing unto you?* Heb. lit. "Is it small from you?" which may properly admit the construction, "Do you regard it as something less than becomes you?" Such is the force of the original form of expression, as the preposition מִ, *m*, denotes *from* rather than *to*, and *from* has in such connections the import of a comparative. He appeals to them to consider how ungrateful a part they were acting towards the Lord for the honor done them in selecting their tribe to minister at his tabernacle and serve him as his own domestics. He would have them reflect how unworthily they demeaned themselves by thus contemning the honorable post assigned them, and mutinously aspiring to an office previously bestowed upon others. How weak and foolish, moreover, was their spite at Aaron, who was but passive in the case, and appointed a superior minister with his family under him, by the Lord's special direction.——¶ *Separated you.* As the people of Israel, as a body, was separated from all other nations, and set apart as the Lord's peculium, Lev. 20:26, 1 Kings 8:53, so were the Levites separated from the mass of their brethren to be the especial attendants upon the Most High in every thing pertaining to his worship. It is perhaps in reference to this that the apostle Paul speaks of himself as "*separated* unto the gospel of God."——¶ *To bring you near to himself to do the service of the tabernacle.* Heb. "To serve the service." They were not, indeed, brought so near as the priests, but still nearer than all other men, being the constant assistants of the priests in their duties. ——¶ *To stand before the congregation.* Standing is a sign of service, and occasionally used for it, as where the sacred writer in one place, Jer. 52:12, says of Nebuzar-adan, that he "stood before the king;" in the parallel history, 2 Kings 25:8, it is said he was "a servant of the king." Accordingly the "standing" of the Levites, Neh. 12:44, is equivalent to their "serving" or "waiting," and as they are said, Deut. 10:8, to "stand before the Lord to minister unto him," so here it is said, "to stand before the congregation to minister unto them," thus acting with a twofold reference, to the Lord and to the people, as servants to both. So Josiah said to the Levites, 2 Chron. 35:3, "Serve now the Lord your God, and his people Israel." Comp. Ezek. 44:11. ——¶ *To minister unto them.* Heb. *leshârethâm.* This word, in strictness, should perhaps be rendered, "to perform their service," or, "to minister for them," as the Levites rather ministered *for* the congregation than *to* them. The service of the tabernacle was originally incumbent on the whole congregation, but the Levites were chosen by special appointment—were chosen as deputies or proxies of the whole people. In this sense they officiated *for* them.

10 And he hath brought thee near *to him*, and all thy brethren the sons of Levi with thee: and seek ye the priesthood also?
11 For which cause *both* thou and all thy company *are* gathered together against the LORD: and [p] what *is* Aaron, that ye murmur against him?
12 And Moses sent and called Dathan and Abiram, the sons of Eliab; which said, We will not come up.

p Ex. 16. 8. 1 Sam. 8. 7. Acts 5. 4. 1 Cor. 3. 5.

V. 10. *Seek ye the priesthood also?* Not content with the privileges and honors already conferred upon you, do ye aspire also to the office of the priesthood, which the Lord holds at his own disposal, and which he has otherwise bestowed? "Therefore thou and thy sons with thee shall keep your priest's office for every thing of the altar, and within the vail; and ye shall serve: I have given your priest's office unto you as a service of gift; and the stranger that cometh nigh shall be put to death." They doubtless would not *say* that this was their object, but Moses saw it was in their eye. The Chald. has, "Seek ye the great or the high priesthood?" Gr. "Seek to do the priest's office?"

V. 11. *For which cause.* Heb. *lākēn, therefore.* Implying that this is the true construction of their conduct. No other inference can be drawn from their rebellion against the Lord's chosen servants, than that it was in effect a rebellion against the Lord himself. So when the people refused Samuel's government, the Lord said, 1 Sam. 8:7, "They have not rejected thee, but they have rejected me that I should not reign over them." Comp. Luke 10:16. John 13:20.——¶ *And what is Aaron, etc.* Heb. "And Aaron, what is he?" or, "Aaron, what hath he done?" What is he more or other than the Lord has made him? What ground is there for finding fault with him when he was wholly passive in his own elevation? What wrong conduct can be laid to his charge? A similar language is employed by Paul, 1 Cor. 3:5, "Who is Paul, and who is Apollos, but ministers by whom ye believed?" Indeed, Moses himself had on the occasion of a former murmuring expostulated in like style; Ex. 16:7, 8, "What are we that ye murmur against us? Your murmurings are not against us, but against the Lord."

V. 12. *We will not come up.* The object of Moses in sending for them was undoubtedly to treat with them in a way of kindly admonition and remonstrance, and thus if possible recall them from their infatuation, and save them from the doom that he saw otherwise to impend over them. It would appear that from some reason these individuals did not present themselves with Korah before Moses, or that they retired to their tents before he had ceased from his prayer. The summons had required their attendance at the usual public place of judgment in the camp, and not upon any mountain elevation, notwithstanding the peculiar phraseology "come up." It is usual to find this language employed in reference to the going to the central place of worship or convention, wherever it might be. Thus Deut. 25:7, "And if the man like not to take his brother's wife, then let his brother's wife *go up* to the gate unto the elders, and say," etc. Ruth 4:1, "Then *went* Boaz *up* to the gate, and sat him down there." Sol. Jarchi remarks that Dathan and Abiram would not *come up* because they were destined to *go down.* The reply was full of insolence, and gives Bp. Hall occasion to

13 *Is* [q] *it* a small thing that
thou hast brought us up out of
a land that floweth with milk
and honey, to kill us in the wilderness, except thou make thyself altogether a prince [r] over us?
14 Moreover, thou hast not
brought us into a land that floweth [s] with milk and honey, or
given us inheritance of fields
and vineyards: wilt thou put
out the eyes of these men? we
will not come up.
15 And Moses was very wroth,

q ver. 9. r Ex. 2. 14. s Ex. 3. 8. Lev. 20. 24.

say, "their message was worse than their absence." It was one that showed them ripe for judgment.

V. 13. *Out of a land that floweth with milk and honey.* Whatever might have been the natural fertility and luxuriance of the land of Egypt, it certainly had not proved to *them* "a land flowing with milk and honey," but a land of hard bondage, of misery, and affliction. And then how outrageous the insult to the divine majesty thus to describe Egypt in the very terms in which God himself had often spoken of the land of promise!——¶ *To kill us in the wilderness.* Heb. "To cause us to die." That is, to bring us into circumstances which expose us to death; of which death is a very legitimate consequence, whether intended or not.——¶ *Except thou make thyself altogether a prince over us.* Heb. "That thou makest thyself a prince over us, even making thyself a prince." The doubling of the clause has the effect to intensify the charge. The implication is, that Moses, without the divine sanction, and prompted solely by his own presumption, was only, wholly, and continuously intent upon self-aggrandizement.

V. 14. *Wilt thou put out the eyes of these men?* The original is peculiarly strong; *tenakkēr*, wilt thou *dig out*, or, *bore out*, q. d. "Dost thou think so absolutely to blind us, that none of us shall discern thy craft and ambition? Thinkest thou that thou wilt be able to hoodwink us, and to lead us about at pleasure, like blind men, under pretence of bringing us to a rich and fertile country?" Alas, their language and their conduct showed that they *were* most grievously blinded by the operation of their discontented, proud, and rebellious spirits. They could not see that they were altogether in fault, while accusing Moses, and were quarrelling with their Maker in rejecting the authority of his servants. By "these men" is probably to be understood the conspirators, who would lay claim to a penetration which they seemed to think was not possessed by the congregation at large.

V. 15. *And Moses was very wroth.* The Gr. would seem to understand from this nothing more than that Moses took it heavily:—"It made him exceeding sad." But this seems not to come up to the force of the original, which implies a glowing indignation. The anger, however, excited on this occasion we do not look upon in the light of a sinful infirmity, or as the ebullition of a personal resentment on the part of Moses, but as a holy indignation stirred up in his mind in view of the indignity and insult cast upon the Lord. It was, we suppose, the working of a devout and active zeal for the Lord of hosts, similar to that which was kindled within him when he came down from the mount and found the people engaged in the worship of the golden calf, by which he was prompted to throw down and break to pieces the two tables of stone.

and said unto the LORD, Respect[t] not thou their offering: I[u] have not taken one ass from them, neither have I hurt one of them.

t Gen. 4. 5. Is. 1. 10-15. u 1 Sam. 12. 3. Acts 20. 33. 2 Cor. 7. 2.

16 And Moses said unto Korah, Be thou and all thy company before the LORD, thou, and they, and Aaron, to-morrow:

17 And take every man his censer, and put incense in them,

A truly good man will be incensed at a dishonor put upon God, when he would meekly forgive an injury done to himself.——¶ *Respect not thou their offering.* Heb. "Turn not to their offering." That is, turn not thy face towards them; bestow not thy favorable regards upon them. Chald. "Accept not with favor their oblation." It was a prayer that the Lord would treat their offering with the same want of respect that he did that of Cain as compared with that of Abel. The sin could not admit of any palliation, and therefore the sinners could not hope for any acceptance. The original for "offering" is *mincha, meat* or *meal-offering*, of which see in the Notes on Gen. 4:3. Lev. 2:1. The true reference of the term is not easily settled. One of the Rabbinical writers says it points to the incense which they were to offer on the morrow. Another explains it thus: "I know they have a part in the daily sacrifices of the congregation; let not their part be accepted before thee." This latter we think the most probable interpretation, as it seems forced to apply the term "meat or meal-offering" to the incense which they proposed to offer.——¶ *I have not taken one ass from them.* This was an appeal to the Lord on the part of Moses whether he had ever in any, even the slightest particular, abused his power, or encroached upon the rights or the property of any person. He was accused by the conspirators of usurpation, which would of course imply oppression and extortion. But as he had committed neither oppression nor extortion, he can boldly affirm his innocence of the charge of usurpation. So far was he from this, that he declares before God that he had not *taken*, i. e. received by gift or reward, even the vilest beast; much less had he appropriated any thing of the kind by violent seizure. In like manner Samuel appeals, 1 Sam. 12:3, to the people of Israel to bear witness to his integrity. "Behold, here I am; witness against me before the Lord, and before his anointed; whose ox have I taken? or whose ass have I taken? or whom have I defrauded? whom have I oppressed? or of whose hand have I received any bribe to blind mine eyes therewith? and I will restore it you." Despotic power all over the East, and from the earliest ages, has always asserted itself by imposing the most galling burdens of tribute and taxation. Comp. 1 Sam. 8:16.

V. 16. *Be thou and all thy company before the Lord.* Cause thyself to be; present thyself; an emphatic expression which receives light from what we have said on the verb "to be," in the Note on ch. 3:17. Gr. "Sanctify thy congregation, and be ye ready before the Lord." As the rebellion was rather against the Lord than against Moses, therefore he leaves the decision of the controversy to him. "Before the Lord" in this connection is equivalent to "at the door, or in the court, of the tabernacle" mentioned v. 18.

V. 17. *Two hundred and fifty censers.* It is a question how such a number of censers was obtained. As Korah and

and bring ye [v] before the LORD every man his censer, two hundred and fifty censers; thou also, and Aaron, each *of you* his censer.

18 And they took every man his censer, and put fire in them, and laid incense thereon, and stood in the door of the tabernacle of the congregation with Moses and Aaron.

19 And Korah gathered all the congregation against them

v 1 Sam. 12. 7.

others associated with him were merely Levites and not priests, they could not have belonged to them in the former capacity. The presumption therefore is, that they were among the utensils brought by the Israelites out of Egypt, of which the present number may in some way have come into the hands of Korah and his party.

V. 18. *They took every man his censer.* That is, the two hundred and fifty men exclusive of Korah, Dathan and Abiram. Korah, it would appear, was employed in mustering as many as he could gather of the congregation against Moses, v. 19, and after that, he seems to have gone to his tent, v. 24. But the making out distinctly the various items of the transaction is a matter attended with some little difficulty. Bp. Patrick even says, "it may be doubted in what way Korah perished."——¶ *Stood in the door of the tabernacle.* This was not of course the usual place where incense was to be offered, which was within the Holy Place of the Tabernacle. But as that room was not sufficiently large to contain so great a number, and as the occasion was extraordinary, the scene of the trial was transferred to the court of the Tabernacle. As this event was of such a nature as to require to be witnessed by the people in general, which it could not have been within the Tabernacle, therefore a place was chosen which would give it the utmost publicity. So Moses, on another important occasion, v. 46, 47, offered incense "in the midst of the congregation."

V. 19. *And Korah gathered all the congregation against them.* The question naturally suggested here is, what congregation is intended by these words. Had the rebellious spirit of Korah and his company infected so large a part of the whole body, that this expression can be understood of them? Did Moses and Aaron and a faithful few alone remain unmoved by this deep-laid and wide-spread conspiracy? This has been the opinion of some commentators, especially those who by "all the congregation" understand more especially the distinguished or leading men of the congregation. But we may perhaps adopt the construction of the Gr., which renders, "Collected all his congregation," meaning those who took sides with him. Or we may adopt yet another construction, which we are inclined to think comes nearer the truth than either of the others; viz.: that Korah, without any special active agency, *was the means* of gathering a multitude of the congregation together. A man who raises a disturbance in the streets of a populous city, causing hundreds to flock together to the spot to witness what is going on, may be said to gather them together, simply because he is the *occasion* of the concourse. So with Korah here. In this case, the original, *a lĕhem*, is properly rendered *to* or *upon them*, which is its literal sense. Still it is evident, from v. 41, that the number of the disaffected was large, as several thousand were slain by the plague for their mur-

unto the door of the tabernacle of the congregation: and [w] the glory of the LORD appeared unto all the congregation.

20 And the LORD spake unto Moses and unto Aaron, saying,

21 Separate [x] yourselves from among this congregation, that I may [y] consume them in a moment.

22 And they fell [z] upon their faces, and said, O God, the God [a] of the spirits of all flesh, shall

w c. 14. 10. x ver. 45. Rev. 18. 4.

y Heb. 12. 28, 29. z c. 14. 5. a c. 27. 16. Job 12. 10. Eccl. 12. 7. Is. 57. 16. Zech. 12. 1. Heb. 12. 9.

muring over the doom of Korah and his company, implying that they had previously sympathized with him in his enterprise.——¶ *The glory of the Lord appeared, etc.* The Shekinah, or the Divine Majesty, suddenly made its appearance in a visible and tremendous manner in the pillar of cloud over the sanctuary, as it did in several other cases when the emergency called for it. See v. 42. ch. 12 : 5. 14 : 10. This supernatural symbol of the Divine presence was made on these occasions to assume some new and striking phase, to which Moses gives the name of the "Glory of the Lord," and out of this appearance now issued a voice, addressing itself to Moses and Aaron, and uttering the words that follow.

V. 21. *Separate yourselves.* Heb. *hibbâdelu, be ye separated* or *divided.* The address was made to all those who were disposed to give heed to it. A discrimination was to be made, and all those who would be found on the Lord's side are here commanded to withdraw from a position where they would be in danger of sharing in the impending destruction. The phrase, "from among this congregation," goes rather to countenance the suggestion above made, that Korah and his company are especially alluded to in the terms.——¶ *That I may consume them in a moment.* Heb. "May eat or devour them." The language is fearfully emphatic, as if the judgment was just ready to burst upon the culprits, and scarcely knew how to brook delay, when yet at the same time it is evident that as wrath did not come upon Sodom till Lot and his family were removed, so here, also, was an impediment until the commanded separation should take place. His arm is withheld while the possibility of salvation for any remains.

V. 22. *And they fell upon their faces, and said, etc.* "The same tongue that prayed against the conspirators, prays for the people. Korah had so far prevailed, that he had drawn the multitude to his side. God, the avenger of treason, would have consumed them all at once. Moses and Aaron pray for the rebels. Although they were worthy of death, and nothing but death could stop their mouths, yet their merciful leaders will not buy their own peace with the loss of such enemies. Oh rare and admirable mercy! The people rise up against their governors; their governors fall on their faces to God for the people. So far are they from plotting revenge, that they will not endure God should revenge for them." *Bp. Hall.*——¶ *The God of the spirits of all flesh.* By "all flesh" is meant "all mankind," as in Gen. 6 : 13. Is. 40 : 5, 6. Ezek. 20 : 48. Joel 2 : 28. A similar phraseology occurs in Job 12 : 10, "In whose hand is the soul of every living thing, and the breath of all mankind." (Heb. "the spirit of all flesh of man.") Moses, with a beautiful propriety, gives to the Most High this title, in acknowledgment of his power to save or to destroy,

one [b] man sin, and wilt thou be wroth with all the congregation?

23 And the LORD spake unto Moses, saying,

24 Speak unto the congregation, saying, Get you up from about the tabernacle of Korah, Dathan, and Abiram.

25 And Moses rose up and went unto Dathan and Abiram; and the elders of Israel followed him.

26 And he spake unto the congregation, saying, Depart [c], I pray you, from the tents of these wicked men, and touch nothing of theirs, lest ye be consumed in all their sins.

27 So they gat up from the tabernacle of Korah, Dathan,

b Gen. 18. 32. Josh. 7. 1, etc. Rom. 5. 18.

c Gen. 19. 12, 14. Is. 52. 11. 2 Cor. 6. 17. 1 Tim. 5. 22. Rev. 18. 4.

---

as he had threatened to *consume* all Israel. It implies a strong motive to urge the divine compassion: "O God, the father and creator both of the souls and bodies of men, and who hast therefore the power of preserving as well as of destroying; deign to display that power in the exercise of mercy towards this people. Thou, the Searcher of hearts, knowest the authors of this sedition, and distinguishest them from those who have been made, through weakness and credulity, their dupes. Have mercy upon the latter!"——¶ *Shall one man sin, etc.* Alluding, of course, to Korah, the ringleader of the revolt. Gr. "If one man hath sinned." As all have not sinned, why wilt thou be angry with all?——¶ *With all the congregation.* That is, all that portion of the congregation which formed Korah's company.

V. 24. *Get you up from about the tabernacle, etc.* Heb. *mishkan*, which is here, we think, collective, equivalent to *tabernacles* or *dwellings*. Gr. "Depart from the congregation of Kore round about." It will be observed, too, that in v. 26, it is said, "Depart from the *tents* of these wicked men."

V. 25. *Moses rose up and went unto Dathan and Abiram.* Having proclaimed the preceding order first at the Tabernacle to the people that followed Korah and his party, Moses then went in person to the camp where Dathan and Abiram still persisted in remaining, after having treated so contemptuously the summons sent them. He went, accompanied by a train of elders, and gave notice to all that dwelt round about, to remove themselves and all they had from the dangerous vicinity, lest they also should share in the coming doom of the rebels.

V. 26. *Depart, I pray you, etc.* "God and Moses knew how to distinguish betwixt the heads of the faction and the train; though neither be faultless, yet the one is plagued, the other forgiven. God's vengeance, when it is at the hottest, makes differences of men. Even before common judgment there is a separation." *Bp. Hall.* It does not appear that any thing was said to Dathan and Abiram personally, but only to the congregation gathered about their tents.——¶ *Touch nothing of theirs.* As they themselves had become unclean and execrable, they accordingly communicated a kind of pollution to every thing with which they came in contact, bringing it under an anathema or curse. Accordingly every thing perished together, as we learn from v. 32. Comp. Deut. 13:16, 17.

V. 27. *The tabernacle of Korah, Dathan, and Abiram.* "Had Korah re-

and Abiram, on every side: and Dathan and Abiram came out, and stood in the door of their tents, and their wives, and their sons, and their little children.

28 And Moses said, Hereby ye [d] shall know that the LORD hath sent me to do all these works; for I *have* not *done them* of mine own mind [e].

d Ex. 3. 12. Zech. 2. 9. John 5. 36. *e* Jer. 23. 16.

---

moved his tent near to those of Dathan and Abiram? As a Kohathite, his tent could not properly be in the camp of Reuben, and still less could the tents of Reubenites be in the camp of the Levites. The present direction seems to imply that the tents were together; yet further on, we only read of Dathan and Abiram; and it does not from this chapter appear, unless by inference, that Korah's tent was swallowed up; and that it actually was not, would appear from the fact, that whereas the children of the Reubenite rebels perished with their parents, those of Korah did not. (See ch. 26 : 11. 1 Chron. 6 : 22–38, where his genealogy is reckoned.) We therefore think that Moses here merely uses the names of the leaders to describe the rebellious party; but that Korah's tent remained in the Kohathite camp, and that he was himself afterwards destroyed with those that offered incense. As a Levite aspiring to priestly functions, that is the place where we should certainly expect to find him. It is true that he is not mentioned by name among those destroyed there; and it is equally true that the present Heb. text of ch. 26 : 10, describes Korah as swallowed up with the rest. But that obscure passage is differently read in the Samaritan, which expressly says that Korah was destroyed by fire, with the men that offered incense. With this the narrative of Josephus concurs; and the Psalmist, in his rapid view of the transactions in the wilderness, only mentions the Reubenites as being swallowed up. (Psl. 106 : 17.)"—*Pict. Bible.*——¶ *Came out and stood.* Heb. "Came out standing;" implying an easy, unconcerned, and sauntering kind of air; they came out and stood in a leaning or lounging way at the door of their tents, as if to see what or whether any thing would take place. Those who were not actually partners in the conspiracy appear to have taken timely warning and fled; while the rest, with astonishing recklessness, came forth with their families and put themselves in the very jaws of destruction. "Moses had well hoped that when these rebels should see all the Israelites run from them, as from monsters, and looking affrightedly upon their tents, and should hear that fearful proclamation of vengeance against them, their hearts would have misgiven. But, lo, these bold traitors stand impudently staring in the door of their tents, as if they would out-face the revenge of God; as if Moses had never wrought a miracle before them; as if no one Israelite had ever bled for rebellion. Those that shall perish are blinded. Pride and infidelity obdure the heart and make even cowards fearless."—*Bp. Hall.*

V. 28. *Hereby ye shall know, etc.* The works to which he here especially alludes were the institution of the priesthood, the appointment of the Levites, and other matters of government; to which we may add also the ordering of Korah and his company to appear with censers on this occasion.——¶ *Not (done them) of my own mind.* Heb. *millibbi, of my own heart.* Chald. "Not of my own will, or pleasure." Gr. "Not of myself." Vulg. "That I have not

29 If these men die the common death of all men, or if they be visited after the visitation[f] of all men; *then* the LORD hath not sent me.

30 But if the LORD make a new[g] thing, and the earth open her mouth, and swallow them up, with all that *appertain* unto

f Is. 10. 3.

g Job 31. 3.

forged them of my own head." For a kindred purport of the phrase, see Num. 24:13. Ezek. 13:2. It was no device, design, or assumption of my own. I did it not from any ambitious promptings tending to my own aggrandizement, nor from any private affection or favoritism towards my brother.

V. 29. *If these men die the common death, etc.* Heb. "If according to the dying of all men, these men die." And so substantially the Gr. and the Chald. That is, if they shall die a natural death. Moses now intimates that the issue of the controversy is to be put upon what the Lord is about to do in vindication of his servants. If these men that now oppose and scandalize us shall die the common death of other men, then you are all at liberty to think of us as ill as you please. But if, on the other hand, an immediate and unheard of miracle is wrought for their destruction, by causing the earth to open her mouth and swallow them up, and all that belong to them; then you will have no excuse for refusing to acknowledge that Aaron and myself are acting as we do by a divine commission, and that the conspiracy now formed is less against us than against the Lord himself. "From the beginning of the world unto this day," says Mr. Kitto, "no man ever made so bold and noble an assertion of divine approval, or subjected his claims, in the presence of a nation, to a test so immediate and so infallible." It would, of course, have been the height of folly to have made such an appeal to God, even though conscious of his own divine appointment, and also of the sin and rebellion of the guilty parties, if he had not at the same time felt within himself that special and extraordinary impulse, by which he knew that the event would be as he predicted. And by the event he was justified.——¶ *If they be visited after the visitation of all men.* That is, if such a judgment is now seen to come upon them as is common and familiar in the world, viz. pestilence, the sword, or famine, then, indeed, you may infer that the Lord hath not sent me.

V. 30. *But if the Lord make a new thing, etc.* Heb. "*beriâh yibra, create a creature;*" that is, perform a new, unprecedented, and wonderful work, by dooming them to such a death as men never died of before. Of the import of the word *bârâ*, see Note on Gen. 1:1. It is there given as one of its leading senses to denote *the production or effectuation of something new, rare, and wonderful;* the bringing something to pass in a striking and marvellous manner. Thus in Is. 45:7, God is said to "create evil," by which is meant, however, not the evil of sin, but of judgment. Ex. 34:10, "Before all thy people I will do marvels such as have not been *done* (*nibre-u, created*), in all the earth." Is. 48:6, 7, "I have showed thee new things from this time, even hidden things, and thou didst not know them. They are *created* now, and not from the beginning." Comp. Is. 65:18.——¶ *The earth open her mouth and swallow them up.* That is, on a sudden; at a time when all is calm and still, with

them, and they go down quick into the pit; [h] then ye shall understand that these men have provoked the LORD.

31 And it came to pass, as he had made an end of speaking all these words, that the ground clave asunder that *was* under them:

32 And [i] the earth opened her mouth, and swallowed them up, and their houses, and all the

h ver. 33. Ps. 55. 15.

i c. 26. 10. 11. Deut. 11. 6. Ps. 106. 17, 18.

no premonitions of an earthquake; and in such a way, moreover, that only the guilty shall be involved, the rest being delivered.——¶ *With all that (appertain) to them.* Heb. *kol asher lâhem, all that is to them.* This the Vulg. probably correctly, refers to "things" rather than "persons:"—"All things that belong to them." The Gr. amplifies upon the original:—"Swallow them up, and their houses, and their tents, and all that belongs to them." The whole history of the divine providence shows that it has ever regarded a man's surroundings and appendages as a part, as it were, of himself.——¶ *And they go down quick into the pit.* That is, alive and active, hale and sound, not dead, as men usually are before they descend into the grave. Gr. "Shall descend alive into Hades." But upon the true import of "pit" in this connection, see Note on v. 33, below.——¶ *That these men have provoked the Lord.* Rather, perhaps, according to the Heb. "have contemptuously treated." Vulg. "Have blasphemed."

V. 31. *The ground clavè asunder, etc.* The response to the awful appeal of Moses was speedily made. He had scarce done speaking ere the earth opened, as it were, its ponderous jaws, and the guilty band with all their households and effects were precipitated into the yawning abyss. "So soon as the innocent are severed, the guilty perish; the earth cleaves and swallows up the rebels. This element was not used to such morsels. It devours the carcases of men; but bodies informed with living souls, never before. To have seen them struck dead upon the earth had been fearful; but to see the earth at once their executioner and grave, was more horrible."—*Bp. Hall.* As we have already seen, the fate of Korah himself is by the narrative left doubtful. The Psalmist speaks thus of the event, making no allusion to Korah; Ps. 106 : 17, "The earth opened, and swallowed up Dathan; and covered the company of Abiram." So in the parallel passage, Deut. 11 : 6, "And what he did unto Dathan and Abiram, the sons of Eliab, the son of Reuben; how the earth opened her mouth, and swallowed them up, and their households, and their tents, and all the substance that *was* in their possession, in the midst of all Israel."

V. 32. *And their houses.* That is, their households, a very frequent sense of "house." Chald. "The men of their houses." Moses himself thus explains it Deut. 11 : 6, "Their households, and their tents, and all the substance that was in their possession."——¶ *All the men that (appertained) unto Korah.* With the exception of his children, of whom it is expressly said, ch. 26 : 11, "Notwithstanding the children of Korah died not." Their names are enumerated 1 Chron. 6 : 22–24, and we find, moreover, several of the Psalms bearing the title, "For the sons of Korah," as Ps. 42 : 44 : 45 : 48 : 49. Indeed, it was from the stock of Korah that Samuel the prophet derived his pedi-

men that *appertained* unto Korah, and all *their* goods.
33 They, and all that *appertained* to them, went down alive
into the pit, and the earth closed
upon them: and they perished
from among the congregation.
34 And all Israel that *were*
round about them fled at the cry
of them: for they said, Lest the
earth swallow us up *also*.
35 And there came out a fire
[k] from the LORD, and consumed
the two hundred and fifty [l] men
that offered incense.

k Lev. 10. 2. c. 11. 1. l ver. 17.

gree, 1 Chron. 6:28. Some commentators have suggested that the original word for *appertained* might as properly be rendered *adhered*, which would tend to simplify the account, by restricting it to those only who were his accomplices.——¶ *And all their goods.* Or, Heb. "Substance." Gr. "Their cattle," a sense which the original undoubtedly bears, 1 Chr. 11:6. 2 Chr. 31:3. 35:7.

V. 33. *Went down alive into the pit.* Heb. שאלה *sheolâh, to Sheol,* the term which is usually rendered by the Gr. "Hades," and in English sometimes by "grave," and sometimes by "hell." Here it is unquestionably to be taken in the sense of *pit, gulf,* or *chasm in the earth,* as it would be absurd to suppose that the *houses* descended into *hell,* to say nothing of the unreasonableness of the idea that the souls of the little children were doomed to that abode, although their bodies, in the course of the divine providence, perished in the overthrow of their parents. Thus, says Theodoret, those who had marched through the sea (in safety) were swallowed up on the land.——¶ *And the earth closed upon them.* "It was a marvel that the waters opened (for Israel); it was no wonder that they shut again; for the retiring and flowing was natural. It was no less a marvel that the earth opened; but more marvel that it shut again; because it had no natural disposition to meet when it was divided. Now might Israel see, they had to do with a God that could revenge with ease."—*Bp. Hall.* The deprecatory prayer of David, Ps. 69:15, seems to allude to this terrible judgment:—"Let not the water-flood overflow me, neither let the deep (i. e. gulf) swallow me up, and let not the pit shut her mouth upon me."

V. 34. *Fled at the cry of them.* Heb. "At the voice of them." At the cry or noise they made in perishing, for we can well believe that the most heart-rending shrieks would be heard from the multitude when they found themselves being ingulfed in the opening caverns of the earth.

V. 35. *And there came out a fire from the Lord.* That is, from the divine glory enthroned in the pillar of cloud over the tabernacle, as is to be inferred from the general *usus loquendi.* As the sin was not unlike that of Nadab and Abihu, so the punishment was similar. Korah, as before remarked, was probably in this company, and perished in their destruction. This catastrophe, like the other, is celebrated by the Psalmist, Ps. 106:18, "And a fire was kindled in their company; the flames burned up the wicked."——¶ *Consumed.* Heb. "Ate up." "There were two sorts of traitors; the earth swallowed up one, the fire the other. All the elements agree to serve the vengeance of their Maker. Nadab and Abihu brought fit persons, but unfit fire to God; these Levites bring the right fire, but unwarranted persons before

36 And the LORD spake unto Moses, saying,

37 Speak unto Eleazar the son of Aaron the priest, that he take up the censers out of the burning, and scatter thou the fire yonder; for [m] they are hallowed.

38 The censers of these sinners [n] against their own souls, let them make them broad plates *for* a covering of the altar; for they offered them before the LORD, therefore they are hallowed: and they shall be a sign [o] unto the children of Israel.

m Lev. 27. 28.

n Prov. 8. 36. 20. 2. Hab. 2. 10. Ezek. 14. 8. *o* c. 17. 10.

him; fire from God consumes both. It is a dangerous thing to usurp sacred functions. The ministry will not grace the man; the man may disgrace the ministry."—*Bp. Hall.*

V. 37. *Speak unto Eleazar.* The particular grounds on which this order was given to Eleazar, it is not easy to determine with precision. The Jewish writers say it was because the Lord would not have Aaron, as a representatively holy person, run the risk of pollution by going among the dead; which is perhaps as probable a suggestion as any other——¶ *Out of the burning.* Heb. *mibbën hasserëphâh, from between or among the burning.* Gr. "From the midst of those who were burnt." That is, from among the mass of the dead bodies upon which the fire had just done such a destructive work. Burning is supposed to stand here for those who were burnt, the abstract for the concrete, as *captivity* for *captives*, Num. 21 : 1, and *poverty* for *poor*, 2 Kings, 24 : 14.——¶ *Scatter thou the fire yonder.* Whatever fire, or cinders, still remained in the smoking censers was to be hurled away at once, and to the farthest possible distance, probably to the spot where all the refuse of the camp was cast, in order to indicate that the service performed by them was rejected with the utmost loathing and detestation as profane. Gr. "As for the strange fire, scatter it there;" in which rendering we have no clue to lead us to the precise import of "there."——¶ *For they are hallowed.* Heb. *kâdëshu, they are sanctified, consecrated, hallowed;* the original being a verb and not an adjective. The reason is given in the next verse, viz.: that having once been employed, by divine command, in the holy service of the sanctuary, they were henceforth forbidden to be put to any other use.

V. 38. *The censers of these sinners against their own souls.* That is, against their own lives. Ged. "The censers of these men, who by sinning have lost their lives."——¶ *Let them make them broad plates.* Heb. "Outspreadings of plates." That is, plates beaten out and spread broad so as to cover with them the brazen altar. The original is from the same root with the word rendered "firmament," which, as we have shown in the Note on Gen. 1 : 6, involves the idea of spreading out by beating. They were to be laid on over the precious covering of brass which enveloped the brazen altar, or the altar of sacrifice, as described, Ex. 27 : 12.——¶ *They shall be a sign.* That is, a memorial to put Israel in mind of the transgression in which the fact originated, and to serve as a perpetual warning to them against repeating the offence. "Not only the Israelites in general, but also the Levites in particular, save Aaron's sons only, are counted strangers in respect of the priest's office; and this covering of the altar, with those censers of

39 And Eleazar the priest took the brazen censers, wherewith they that were burnt had offered; and they were made broad *plates for* a covering of the altar:

40 *To be* a memorial unto the children of Israel, that [p] no stranger which *is* not of the seed of Aaron come near to offer incense before the LORD; that he be not as Korah, and as his company: as the LORD said to him by the hand of Moses.

41 But, on the morrow all the congregation of the children of Israel [q] murmured against Moses and against Aaron, saying, Ye have killed the people of the LORD.

p c. 3. 10. 2 Chr. 26. 18.

q c. 14. 2. Ps. 106. 25, etc.

---

polished splendid brass, was as a looking-glass for all to behold, that none might, afterwards, like Korah, presume to the priesthood."—*Ness.* Thus Aaron's rod was kept for a *sign*, Num. 17 : 10, and God threatens, by destroying the wicked man, to make him "a sign and a proverb," Ezek. 14 : 8. "Now all these things happened unto them for ensamples; and they are written for our admonition, upon whom the ends of the world are come."—1 Cor. 10 : 11.

V. 39. *And they were made broad (plates), etc.* Heb. lit. "And they broadened them;" that is, by a process of beating expanded them into thin laminæ, adapted to serve as a covering to the altar.

V. 40. *That he be not as Korah.* This would seem to imply that Korah perished by fire with the company of two hundred and fifty who offered incense. The force of the example is drawn from the case of these men, with whom Korah is evidently classed. This confirms the suggestions offered above relative to his fate.——¶ *As the Lord said to him.* Implying that he had had fair warning. Others understand the "him" of Eleazar.

V. 41. *All the congregation murmured,* So fearful a judgment as they had just been called to witness would have been sufficient, one would suppose, to prevent the outbreak of any further murmurings or discontent. Yet how different the matter of fact! As the vessel, in its course through the deep, leaves a track of foam behind it which is a little while distinct and well defined, but soon mingles with the mass of waters and is seen no more, so was it with the judgment of heaven on this occasion, and the impression it created. It endured for the night, but discontent and rebellion came in the morning. With a unanimity that is amazing, "all the congregation"—not merely the rulers or a few intractable spirits—but the great mass of the people, gave way to groundless complaints. With tumultuous outcries and accusations, they press upon Moses and Aaron, charging them with the destruction of a multitude of their brethren, the peculiar people of the Lord; as if these atrocious transgressors had been good and holy people, and Moses and Aaron had been their persecutors. Alas, how will pride, passion, and self-will prevail to blind the understanding of men, so that they will call evil good, and good evil, and put darkness for light, and light for darkness. Especially does this hold among large bodies of men in times of public tumult. By saying, however, that they had killed them, their meaning doubtless was that they had been the means, the procuring cause, of their losing their lives, and not that they had

42 And it came to pass,
when the congregation was
gathered against Moses and
against Aaron, that they looked toward the tabernacle of the
congregation: and behold, the
cloud [r] covered it, and the glory [s] of the LORD appeared.
43 And Moses and Aaron
came before the tabernacle of
the congregation.
44 And the LORD spake unto
Moses, saying,
45 Get [t] you up from among
this congregation, that I may
consume them as in a moment.
And [u] they fell upon their faces.
46 And Moses said unto
Aaron, Take a censer, and put
fire therein from off the altar,
and put on incense, and go quick-
ly unto the congregation, and

r Ex. 40. 34. s ver. 19. t ver. 21. 24. u ver. 22. c. 20. 6.

directly slain them. Accordingly the Chald. renders, "ye have caused the death."

V. 42. *They looked toward the tabernacle.* The intimation is that they, i. e., Moses and Aaron more especially, looked imploringly in that direction, that they invoked help from the Lord in his dwelling-place, and the consequence was an immediate manifestation in their favor. That awful phenomenon termed "the glory of the Lord," shone forth, as on former occasions, with an aspect of threatening which they well understood. It was now, however, unaccompanied by any voice, but a silent judgment proceeded from it, as we learn from the effect that followed, which was the cutting off of more than 14,000 of the host by a deadly plague or stroke from the divine hand.

V. 45. *And they fell upon their faces.* Doubtless to intercede afresh for these high-handed offenders. No provocations avail to abate their charity and compassion in behalf of the people, however undeserving. A true benevolence seems unable to discover that point in the divine displeasure beyond which it is in vain to sue for mercy. It will still lift up its prayer in the very article of inflicted vengeance. Comp. 1 Chron. 21:16.

V. 46. *Take a censer and put fire therein, etc.* Incense was regularly to be offered nowhere but at the golden altar within the sanctuary; but on the present extraordinary emergency, Aaron is sent with it into the camp in order to stay the plague, by making an atonement for the people; the natural effect of which would be to afford them a convincing proof of the sanctity and authority which should henceforth pertain to his ministry. "God might have stayed the plague without the intervention of Aaron; but in this time of discontent, it pleased him to afford another convincing testimony that the high-priest was acting in his sacred office by his appointment and under his direction. They must have been hardened indeed who could doubt the authority under which the high-priest acted, after such a striking evidence of the Lord's respect to his official intervention."—*Kitto.* The Jewish writers say on this passage that Moses intended to warn Aaron lest perchance he should err through haste, and offer strange fire, as Nadab and Abihu had done, as also those who had recently perished. They remark, too, that "the incense which caused death when it was not in the hand of the priest, giveth life when it *is* in the hand of the priest."——¶ *Make an atonement.* That is, by acting as a mediator or interceder on behalf of the

make an atonement for them; for there is [v] wrath gone out from the LORD; the plague is begun.

47 And Aaron took, as Moses commanded, and ran into the midst of the congregation; and, behold, the plague [w] was begun among the people: and he put on incense [x], and made an atonement for the people.

48 And he stood between [y] the dead and the living; and the plague was [z] stayed.

49 Now they that died in the plague were fourteen thousand and seven hundred, beside them that died about the matter of Korah.

50 And Aaron returned unto Moses, unto the door of the tabernacle of the congregation: and the plague was stayed.

v Lev. 10. 6. c. 11. 33. 18. 5. 1 Chr. 27. 24. w Ps. 106. 29. x Deut. 33. 10.

y Heb. 7. 24, 25. z 1 Chr. 21. 26, 27.

---

people. There is nothing of an expiatory kind implied in the use of the term in this connection.——¶ *The plague is begun.* The Heb. *negeph* from *nâgaph to strike, to smite,* is a term of general import denoting any severe stroke or infliction from the divine hand. Our English word *plague* is derived from the Latin *plaga,* and that from the Gr. πληγη, *plēgē,* in both which languages it is used to signify *a stroke, a blow, a stripe, a wound.* By an extension of the import of the word it is made to denote a *pestilence* or some other *fatal disease,* which would naturally be regarded as an extraordinary scourge proceeding directly from the Lord. This is probably to be considered its sense in the present connection. The Chald. renders it "the death." It is impossible to elicit from the term any more definite import. As to the fact itself, we know not how Moses became possessed of it so as to be able to announce it, though it is altogether probable it was conveyed to his mind by a divine monition. In proportion as we are faithful and familiar with God, so much the earlier do we discern his judgments in the earth. We become, as it were, of his council.

V. 47. *And Aaron took as Moses commanded.* Aaron was as full of anxiety for the people as his brother. He instantly did as he was commanded. He ran into the midst of the congregation, fearless of their wrath, fearless of the contagion of the plague; he put the incense upon the sacred fire in the censer, and made an atonement with it for the people; and he stood between the living and the dead; and the plague was stayed.——¶ *Ran into the midst of the congregation.* The spirit evinced both by Aaron and Moses, on this occasion, was pre-eminently worthy of such distinguished servants of heaven. Insulted and opposed as they had been, taunted and falsely accused, they have no ill will or resentment, they seek no revenge for themselves, nor feel gratification at the punishment of their factious and rebellious people. On the contrary, they suffer long and are kind. They count not their own lives dear unto themselves if so be that they may save the lives of these offenders. This is the conduct of men who are taught and governed by the laws of heaven.

V. 48. *And he stood between the dead and the living.* Thus interposing between the infected and the uninfected portions of the camp, and exposing himself to the ravages of the plague in behalf of the people. "As one that would part a fray, he thrusts himself under the strokes of God, and puts it to

CHAPTER XVII.

AND the LORD spake unto Moses, saying,
2 Speak unto the children of Israel, and take of every one of them a rod [a] according to the house of *their* fathers, of all

a Ezek. 37. 16.

the choice of the revenger whether he will smite him or forbear the rest; he stands boldly between the living and the dead, as one that will either die with them or have them live with him; the sight of fourteen thousand carcases dismayed him not; he that before feared the threats of the people now fears not the strokes of God."—*Bp. Hall.* How striking a type of the intervention of our Lord do we recognize in the conduct of Aaron on this occasion. Our great and compassionate High-Priest, moved by the contemplation of our danger, not only at the hazard of life, but in the sure prospect of death, hastened into our midst to make atonement for us.

> "With pitying eyes the Prince of Peace
> Beheld our helpless grief;
> He saw, and oh, amazing love,
> He ran to our relief."

CHAPTER XVII.

The Budding and Blossoming of Aaron's Rod.

V. 1. *And the Lord spake unto Moses, etc.* At what particular time we are not informed, but probably within a short period after the plague above described had ceased. It is reasonable to infer that the miracle here recorded took place while the minds of the people were yet in an excited state, in consequence of the poisonous insinuations of Korah and his associates, who had so recently perished in their presumption. Every divine judgment executed upon transgressors has a merciful intention towards survivors. The design is to inspire a salutary fear, and thus to prevent the commission of similar iniquities. The present chapter affords an instance strikingly in point. The Lord is pleased, as here recorded, to put the appointment of his priests to another proof, and to work another miracle, that he might effectually silence all future murmurings on the score of the authority claimed by Moses and Aaron. The test was unequivocally decisive.

V. 2. *Take of every one of them a rod according to the house of their fathers.* Heb. "Take of them a rod, a rod, for (or according to) every father's house." The duplication is a Hebraism of common occurrence, carrying with it a distributive sense. Gr. "Take of them a rod (or staff), a rod according to the houses of their patriarchal families." Chald. "Receive from them a rod each throughout the houses of (their) fathers." It is evident from what follows that the requisition was, not a rod from each individual Israelite, but one from each tribe; and this was to be presented in the name of the leading man or "prince" of each tribe. The order here given seems to imply that it was not the subordinate Levites alone who aspired to the priesthood, for in that case we cannot well see why there should not have been two rods instead of twelve, one for Aaron and one for his opponents. But by all the tribes being required to contribute a rod, it would appear that all would put in a claim to the dignity, according to what is said, ch. 16 : 3, "Ye take too much upon you, seeing that all the congregation are holy, every one of them." The decision, therefore,

their princes according to the house of their fathers, twelve rods: write thou every man's name upon his rod.

3 And thou shalt write Aaron's name upon the rod of Levi: for one rod *shall be* for the head of the house of their fathers.

4 And thou shalt lay them up in the tabernacle of the con-

---

was to be final for the whole host. The original word for "rod" (*matteh*) is for the most part used to denote a *staff, stick, walking-stick*, or *wand*, rather than a *green rod, branch*, or *bough*. It would seem, from Num. 21:18, that the princes of the tribes carried staves in their hands, as a kind of *baton*, that should serve as a badge of authority. "The rods or staves were doubtless official ensigns of the authority with which the heads of tribes were invested. Hence the Scripture frequently uses the word 'rod' as equivalent to 'sceptre;' and indeed the more modern use of sceptres is derived from this ancient custom. These staves were of course dry, and had probably been for years in use; and that such should blossom and bear fruit again, is such a moral impossibility, that the ancient heathen used to swear by their rods or sceptres with a view to that circumstance. Thus Achilles, in Homer, when enraged against Agamemnon, says:

'But hearken. I shall swear a solemn oath.
By this sceptre, which shall never bud,
Nor boughs bring forth, as once; which having left
Its stock on the high mountains, at what time
The woodman's axe lopt off its foliage green,
And stript its bark, shall never grow again;—
By this I swear,' etc. COWPER.

The king Latinus, in Virgil, confirms, by a similar oath, his covenant with Æneas. To preclude mistake or imposition in the present transaction, the name of each tribe was inscribed on the rod of its chief; and the question being to try the right to the priesthood, this method of settling the point seems to indicate that other tribes (probably that of Reuben in particular) had thought their claims, *as tribes*, as good or better than those of Levi."—*Pict. Bible.*——¶ *Write thou every man's name upon his rod.* In what manner the writing was executed we have no means of determining with any certainty. It may have been by some kind of incision on the surface, or possibly by some sort of label attached to the several rods. By some means a signature was affixed that should serve to identify the rods to the owners.

V. 3. *Thou shalt write Aaron's name upon the rod of Levi.* This preference was given to Aaron, because that, by being invested with the office of high-priest, he was made prince of that tribe, or "head of the house of their fathers." Moreover, if Levi's name had been on the rod, it would have left the controversy undecided as between Aaron and the Levites.

V. 4. *And thou shalt lay them up.* Heb. "Thou shalt cause them to rest." ——¶ *Tabernacle of the congregation.* Heb. *beohel moëd, tent of meeting.*—— ¶ *Before the testimony.* That is, before the Ark wherein were deposited the tables of the Law, called "the Testimony." See Notes on Ex. 25:16. Above was the Mercy-Seat, where the divine Glory resided. To lay the rods "before the testimony" was to lay them before the divine Presence and Majesty, who intended thereby to determine the present controversy.——¶ *Where I will*

gregation, before the testimony,
where [b] I will meet with you.
5 And it shall come to pass,
that the man's rod, whom I shall
choose [c], shall blossom: and I
will make to cease from me the
murmurings of the children of
Israel, whereby [d] they murmur
against you.

6 And Moses spake unto the
children of Israel; and every
one of their princes gave him a
rod apiece, for each prince one, according to their fathers' houses,
even twelve rods: and the rod
of Aaron *was* among their rods.
7 And Moses laid up the rods
before the LORD in the tabernacle [e] of witness.

b Ex. 25. 22. 29. 42, 43. 30. 36. *c* c. 16. 5. *d* c. 16. 11.

e Ex. 38. 21. Acts 7. 44.

meet you. Heb. *ivvâëd*, from *yâad, to appoint a meeting*, and in the Niphal or passive, *to be gathered together.* This is the form in which it occurs in the present connection, and, as such, is remarkable, as it represents the Lord as being *acted upon* and *drawn* into convention by the force of his own self-assumed obligations, or by his fidelity to his covenant engagements, which are thus represented as operating as if by an external influence. This is the reason why the Tabernacle was called *the tent of meeting*, or of *congregation*, a phrase which is usually understood simply of men's meeting together, or congregating; whereas, in fact, the Lord gave the appellation to the Tabernacle on the express ground of *his* meeting there with his people in the person of their representative Moses. See Note on Ex. 29:42. 30:36. It is to be observed, however, that the import here is that of the Lord's *habitual presence*—"where I am accustomed to meet with you." Four manuscripts, and several of the ancient versions, here exhibit *lekâ, with thee*, instead of *lâkem, with you.* But the latter is probably correct, being confirmed by Ex. 29:42, 43, where the like phraseology occurs. But it is still to be borne in mind that the Lord neither met then with the people, nor with Aaron, any otherwise than through Moses as a representative medium.

V. 5. *The man's rod whom I shall choose.* Heb. "The man (as to) whom I shall have complacency in him." This is not essentially different from "choose," but it preserves the prepositional usage "in him," which is quite common with the original verb.——¶ *Shall blossom.* This would have been better rendered "shall bud," as is the case in v. 8, where there is a marked distinction indicated between *budding, blossoming,* and *yielding fruit.* The original *yiphra* here is the word there that answers to *bud.*——¶ *Will make to cease from me, etc.* The Heb. is used elsewhere in reference to the *ceasing* or *assuaging* of waters, Gen. 8:1, and also of wrath, Est. 2:1. It is here applied to the murmurings of the people, which were like raging waters. It will be observed how strikingly the Lord identifies himself with his people: "I will make to cease from *me* the murmurings whereby they murmur against *you.*"

V. 6. *The rod of Aaron was among their rods.* The Vulg. has here, "And there were twelve rods besides the rod of Aaron," supposing that the tribe of Joseph was divided into two—Ephraim and Manasseh—which would make twelve besides that of Levi. But this is unwarranted by the original. The probability is much stronger that there were only twelve and not thirteen rods.

V. 7. *Before the Lord in the taber-*

8 And it came to pass, that on the morrow, Moses went into the tabernacle of witness; and, behold, the rod[f] of Aaron for the house of Levi was budded, and brought forth buds, and bloomed blossoms, and yielded almonds.

9 And Moses brought out all the rods from before the LORD unto all the children of Israel: and they looked, and took every man his rod.

10 And the LORD said unto Moses, Bring Aaron's rod again before the testimony, to be

f Ps. 110. 2. Ezek. 19. 12, 14.

---

nacle of witness. The inference is, that the rods were deposited in the Most Holy Place in the presence of the divine Glory, whither Moses alone had ordinary access. There it was kept according to the statement of the apostle, Heb. 9 : 3, 4.

V. 8. *Was budded, and brought forth buds, and bloomed blossoms, and yielded almonds.* Gr. and Targ. Jon. "Nuts." The miracle consisted in the sudden vegetation of the rod, and that in different degrees. It would seem that in some places of the rod tender buds were seen just emerging from the surface; in others the buds were fully developed; in others, again, they had blossomed, and those blossoms, in other parts, had ripened into fruit, the fruit of the almond-tree. On the name and peculiar properties of the almond, see Note on Ex. 25 : 33. It is a tree that blossoms and bears fruit earlier than other trees, and hence its appellation, *shâkëd,* from *shâkad, to make haste, to be in a hurry,* and thence to *awake early, to be vigilant, to watch.* That this effect should have been produced in a single night upon Aaron's rod, while all the rest were as dry as before, could not but be looked upon with amazement, and prove an incontestable evidence of the Lord's designation. "It could not but be a great comfort unto Aaron to see his rod thus miraculously flourishing; to see this wonderful testimony of God's favor and election. Sure he could not but think, Who am I, O God, that thou shouldst choose me out of all the tribes of Israel! My weakness hath been more worthy of the rod of correction, than my rod hath been worthy of these blossoms. How hast thou magnified me in the sight of all thy people! How able art thou to uphold my imbecility by the rod of thy support! How able art thou to defend me with the rod of thy power, who hast thus brought fruit out of the rod of my profession!"—*Bp. Hall.*

V. 9. *And Moses brought out all the rods—unto all the children of Israel.* It would plainly be all-important that no suspicion of fraud should attach at all to the transaction. We may suppose, therefore, that as the rods were to be deposited "in the tabernacle of the congregation," or in the sacred precincts, they were sealed up in one receptacle, the princes, or others authorized by them, watching it through the night to see that no dishonesty was practised. Certainly, they were not in Moses's custody; for "on the morrow Moses *went to* the Tabernacle of witness to examine them." No charge of unfair dealing could be brought against him, and he submits the rods openly to the view of the parties interested, who took them into their hands, and, by close inspection, satisfied themselves of their identity.

V. 10. *Bring Aaron's rod again before the testimony.* That is, return, restore it, after sufficient examination, to the place where it was deposited before the ark of the testimony.——¶ *To be*

kept [g] for a token against the
rebels; and thou shalt quite
take away their murmurings
from me, that they die not.
11 And Moses did *so:* as the
LORD commanded him, so did he.
12 And the children of Israel spake unto Moses, saying,
Behold, we die, we perish [h], we
all perish.
13 Whosoever [i] cometh any
thing [k] near unto the tabernacle
of the LORD shall die: shall we
be consumed with dying?

g Heb. 9. 4.

h Ps. 90. 7. Is. 57. 16. *i* c. 1. 51, 53. 18. 4, 7. *k* Eph. 2. 13. Heb. 10. 19–22.

kept for a token. Heb. "For a keeping, or reservation." As a specimen of the manna was preserved in the golden pot within the Most Holy Place of the sanctuary, "for a keeping," Ex. 16 : 33, that subsequent generations might see the bread which their fathers ate in the wilderness, so this rod was kept in the same place "for a reservation" and "for a sign," that all that lived afterwards might be aware of the confirmation of the priesthood in Aaron's line. ——¶ *For a token against the rebels.* Heb. "For a sign to the sons of rebellion." Gr. "A sign for the children of the disobedient." This appellation is given to the Israelites from the fact, that they were so much given to rebellion that they might be said to be born of it as of a parent. This is equivalent to the testimony of Moses, Deut. 9 : 24, "Ye have been rebellious against the Lord from the day that I knew you." The use of "sons" in the sense of *subjects of certain qualities* is quite common in holy writ, as Ps. 89 : 22, "Son of wickedness;" Prov. 31 : 5, "Sons of affliction" (marg.); Deut. 13 : 13, "Sons of Belial;" and also 1 Sam. 2 : 12; Eph. 2 : 2, "Sons of disobedience." Comp. Eph. 5 : 6. Mat. 11 : 19. 1 Pet. 1 : 14. ——¶ *Thou shalt quite take away their murmurings, etc.* Heb. *tekel, thou shalt end, finish, do utterly away with.* Gr. "Let their murmuring cease from me, and they shall not die." "Take away from me" is literally according to the original, "take away from upon me."

V. 12. *Behold, we die, we perish, we all perish.* Heb. *gâvanu, we expire.* The term signifies not so precisely *to die*, as to be brought into that state of *painful suffocation* which is very likely to end in death. "We give up the ghost."—*Ains.* A miracle of mercy seems to have extorted from them the confession which the previous miracles of judgment had failed to do. We take the words as implying not an unjust complaint or the outbreak of a still remaining discontent, but an humble acknowledgment of their just deserts and of the imminent peril from which they had barely escaped. The Chald. paraphrases the words thus: "Behold, the sword hath killed some of us, and behold, the earth hath swallowed some of us, and behold, some of us are dead with the pestilence." The Targ. Jon. thus: "Behold, some of us are consumed with flaming fire, and some of us are swallowed up into the earth; behold, we think as did they, so we all of us shall perish." They virtually confess that, by reason of their rebellion, they were as good as dead, and that they would certainly incur that doom should they hereafter offend. Their language shows how much more efficacious is the mercy than the tokens of the divine wrath to touch the conscience and awaken the emotions of godly sorrow and repentance for sin.

V. 13. *Whosoever cometh any thing near, etc.* The following is the literal rendering of the verse: "Every one

CHAPTER XVIII.

AND the LORD said unto Aaron, Thou, and thy sons, and thy father's house with thee, shall bear [a] the iniquity of the

[a] Ex. 28. 38. Is. 53. 6, 11. 1 Pet. 2. 24.

that cometh near, every one that cometh near unto the tabernacle of Jehovah shall die; shall we be consumed in expiring, or giving up the ghost?" Our translators have aimed to indicate the repetition, in the commencement of the verse, by inserting the words "any thing," which answers somewhat to the import of the duplicated clause, hinting at the prohibition of *any degree* of approach. The doubling of words and phrase has often the effect, in Hebrew, of giving greater emphasis and intensity to the expression.——¶ *Shall we be consumed with dying?* Will the Lord proceed with us in this course of unsparing justice? Will he show us no mercy till all the people, doomed to die one after another, are cut off? "The name of Aaron was not more plainly written in that rod than the sin of Israel was in the fruit of it; and how much Israel finds their rebellion beaten with this rod, appears in their present relenting and complaint: "Behold, we are dead, we perish."—*Bp. Hall.*

CHAPTER XVIII.

The special Charge assigned to the Priests and the Levites.

V. 1. *And the Lord said unto Moses, etc.* The recent manifestations recorded in the two preceding chapters, had operated so effectually upon the congregation as to fill them with a kind of panic consternation in view of the danger of approaching the Tabernacle, or dealing in any way with the sanctities of worship. The divine benignity designs, in the present chapter, to reassure their confidence, and at the same time to impress Aaron himself with a deep and abiding sense of the responsibility that rested upon him in the discharge of the duties of that sacred office which had been so signally confirmed to him by the miraculous tokens of the Lord's appointment. These indications might tend to puff him up with a conceit of his own importance, and therefore he is here reminded of the burden laid upon him and the duty required of him as a priest. The consequence would naturally be that instead of being made proud of his preferment, he would receive the honors of his office with reverence and holy awe, being made aware of the danger arising from any default in his service. When men are invested with authority, their responsibility rises in proportion. It is a law running through the whole providential economy of heaven, that to whom much has been given, from them much is required.——¶ *Thy father's house.* That is, the house or posterity of Levi, who was father to all the priests and Levites.——¶ *Shall bear the iniquity of the sanctuary.* That is, shall bear the punishment for all the iniquity that is done in the sanctuary, in which term is embraced the courtyard, and the sacred precincts generally. Chald. "Shall propitiate over the sins of the sanctuary." Arab. "Shall make expiation for the faults of the holy things." If the sanctuary should be profaned by the intrusion of strangers or the unclean, the priests and the Levites were to be held answerable for the offence, to whose negligence it was owing. Jarchi: "Upon you will I bring the punishment of the strangers that shall

sanctuary: and thou and thy sons with thee shall bear the iniquity of your priesthood.

2 And thy brethren also of the tribe of Levi, the tribe of thy father, bring thou with thee, that they may be joined [b] unto thee, and minister [c] unto thee: but thou and [d] thy sons with

b Gen. 29. 34. c c. 3. 6, 7. d c. 3. 10, etc.

sin concerning the sanctified things that are delivered unto you." See Note on ch. 1:51.——¶ *Shall bear the iniquity of your priesthood.* Shall be responsible for whatever iniquity might be committed in connection with the discharge of the priestly functions. This charge is more fully amplified in the ensuing verse. Rab. Menahem: "By this admonition was signified, that the priests should not intermeddle with the service of the Levites, nor the Levites with the service of the priests." All this would tend to calm the apprehensions of the people, who were afraid they should die for every error committed in their approaches to the sanctuary, and it would serve also to extinguish any degree of envy they might cherish in respect to the priestly dignity, when they saw with how much peril its possession and exercise was attended.

V. 2. *The tribe of Levi, the tribe of thy father.* The original here exhibits two different words for tribe, *matteh* (*the tribe*) *of Levi*, and *shebet* (*the tribe*) *of thy father;* of which the former signifies *a staff*, the latter *a rod*, and both of them being occasionally used to denote *a tribe* or *kindred*, on the same principle on which any distinguishing badge or ensign is in our own and other languages employed to signify the persons or bodies by whom it is borne. ——¶ *That they may be joined unto thee.* Heb. *yillâvu*, from the root *lâvâh*, signifying *to join, to couple, to associate.* From this root comes the name *Levi*, the reason of which was assigned by his mother at his birth, Gen. 29:34, "Now this time will my husband *be joined* unto me." And the term here employed displays a peculiar paranomasia, or play upon words, equivalent to "may be *Levited*," i. e. adjoined to or associated with the priests. They shall conjointly perform the sacred office, but the priests shall be principal, the Levites their associates or assistants. Gr. *prostethetosan, let them be added.* This Gr. word as the rendering of the Heb. *lâvâh* occurs several times in the Old Testament, and is thence transferred to the New. The following passages especially receive illustrative light from the usage now adverted to. Is. 14:1, "And the stranger *shall be joined* (*nilvâh*, Gr. *prostethesetai*) with them." Is. 56:3, "Neither let the son of the stranger *that hath joined himself* (*hannilveh*, Gr. *proskeimenos*) to the Lord speak, saying," etc. Comp. Is. 56:6. Jer. 50:5, "Come and let us *join ourselves* (*nilvu*) to the Lord in a perpetual covenant." Esth. 9:27, "Upon all *such as joined themselves* (*hannilvim*, Gr. *prostetheimenois*) unto them." Acts 2:41, 47, "And the same day there were *added unto them* (Gr. *prosetethesan*) about three thousand souls." Acts 2:47, "And the Lord *added* (Gr. *prosetithei*) unto the church daily such as should be saved." Acts 5:14, "And believers *were* the more *added* (*prosetithento*) to the Lord." Acts 11:24, "And much people *was added* (Gr. *prosetethe*) unto the Lord." These heathen converts, brought into the Christian church by the preaching of the apostles, were the "strangers" pointed at by the prophets of the old economy as those who were

thee *shall minister* before the tabernacle of witness.

3 And they shall keep thy charge, and the charge of all the tabernacle: only they [e] shall not come nigh the vessels of the sanctuary and the altar, that neither they, nor ye also, die.

4 And they shall be joined unto thee, and keep the charge of the tabernacle of the congregation, for all the service of the

e c. 16. 40.

---

to be *Levitically adjoined* or *added* to the covenant people in the latter day. Their accession to the church and its divine Head was represented by the adjunction of the Levites to the priestly order under the Jewish dispensation. The following passage may be cited in this connection as a parallelism of striking character:—Is. 66 : 21, "I will also take of them for priests and Levites, saith the Lord." The prophet is here speaking of the accession of heathen converts at a future day of the church. ——¶ *And minister unto thee.* Heb. *vesharithuka*, lit. *shall minister thee*, i. e. to thee; although in the original, both here and elsewhere the preposition *to* or *for*, which properly pertains to the word, is wanting. Gr. *leitourgeitosan*, *let them liturgize* for thee. Comp. Num. 3 : 6. 8 : 26. Deut. 10 : 8. 18 : 6, 7. 1 Sam. 3 : 1. 2 Chron. 29 : 11.——¶ *Before the tabernacle of witness.* Heb. "Before the tent of the testimony." Before the Most Holy Place in which the ark stood. The common priests, but not the Levites, ministered before, i. e. on the outside of, but not within, this inner room, which was separated from the outer by a vail. It was only the high priest who penetrated beyond this vail. The office of the Levites was to assist in killing the sacrifices, taking the blood, and giving it to the priests for sprinkling, and in general performing all the more menial parts of the requisite service about the Tabernacle and its court. The priests served at the altar and in the Holy Place.

V. 3. *They shall keep the charge.* Or, Heb. "Observe thine observation, thy custody." See the Note on ch. 3 : 7, where this phraseology is explained. ——¶ *And the charge of all the tabernacle.* Aaron is here commanded to make a strict discrimination between the priestly and the Levitical orders; the Levites having nothing to do but to be keepers and carriers of the Tabernacle and its utensils. Upon any movement of the camp, they were not allowed so much as to handle or touch the ark, altar, table, or candlestick, but only to take them from the priests when they had packed them. The priests, on the other hand, were to use the Levites as ministers, and by their constant care and admonitions were to prevent all others from incurring the divine displeasure, on account of profane intrusions into so holy a function.——¶ *That neither they nor ye also die.* They for so doing, and you for suffering it.

V. 4. *And they shall be joined unto thee.* Heb. *nilvu*, that is, shall be adjoined *Levitically*—the same term with that previously used in a similar connection. A Levite was an *adjunct.* They were to be considered as an *appended portion* of that general body of men who were devoted to the special service of God in the work of the sanctuary.——¶ *For all the service of the tent.* That is, for the heaviest part of the service, called their *burden*, and mentioned particularly ch. 4 : 3, 4, and throughout the rest of that chapter. This is the peculiar import of the ori-

tabernacle: and a stranger shall
not come nigh unto you.
5 And ye shall keep the
charge of the sanctuary, and
the charge of the [f] altar; that
there be no wrath [g] any more
upon the children of Israel.
6 And I, behold, I have
taken your brethren the Levites from among the children
of Israel; to you *they are* [h]
given *as* a gift for the LORD, to
do the service of the tabernacle
of the congregation.
7 Therefore thou [i] and thy
sons with thee shall keep your
priest's office for every thing of
the altar, and within [k] the vail;
and ye shall serve: I have given
your priest's office *unto you as*

f Ex. 30. 7, etc. Lev. 24. 3. *g* c. 16. 46. *h* c. 8. 19. *i* ver. 5. *k* Heb. 9. 3, 6.

---

ginal *abodâh* from the root *âbăd, to serve,* denoting the more menial kind of services such as pertained especially to bondmen.——¶ *A stranger.* Even any one of the Israelites who was not a Levite was counted a stranger in this relation; and as to the functions of the priests, the Levites themselves fell into the category of strangers, v. 7. See Note on ch. 3:10.

V. 5. *Ye shall keep the charge of the sanctuary.* Heb. "Of the holy, or holiness." Gr. "Of the holies;" the same term as that employed by the apostle, Heb. 9:2, 3, in reference to the *first tabernacle,* i. e. the first or outer room of the tabernacle wherein was contained the Candlestick, the Table, and the Shew-bread. The inner room, by way of contradistinction, was called the Holy of holies, or the Holiest of all. To "keep the charge of the tabernacle" was to exercise continual care night and day that all things were kept pure and uncorrupted, and administered strictly according to the divine will.——¶ *That there be no wrath any more, etc.* That by constant care and vigilance all occasions of wrath might be precluded. "The preventing of sin is the preventing of wrath; and the mischief sin has done, should be a warning to us for the future, to watch against it both in ourselves and others."—*Henry.*

V. 6. *Have taken your brethren the Levites.* See ch. 3:12, 41, 45. 8:6, 16, 18, with the Notes. The Levites are here denominated "brethren," that the priests might not be prompted to despise or disparage them by reason of the inferior capacity in which they served. On the contrary, they were required to treat them with kindness and brotherly affection.——¶ *From among the children of Israel.* Heb. "From out of the midst."——¶ *To you (they are) given (as) a gift for the Lord.* Though directly assigned to you as servitors and assistants, yet let it not be overlooked that this gift is to redound ultimately to the Lord, to whom you are yourselves given as ministers.

V. 7. *Keep your priest's office for every thing of the altar and within the vail.* Keep or preserve it to yourselves, discharging its functions, and allow no other person to invade it. This you are to do with a twofold reference to the altar of burnt offerings, where the sacrifices are to be performed, the blood sprinkled, etc.; and also to all that is to be done, whether within the outer or the inner vail, as, for instance, burning incense, putting on the shew-bread, and lighting the lamps.——¶ *And ye shall serve.* "Not, 'Ye shall rule;' it was never intended that they should lord it over God's heritage, but 'Ye shall serve God and the congregation.'

a service of gift: and the stranger that cometh nigh shall be put to death.

Note, The priesthood is a service. 'If any desire the office of a bishop, he desireth a good work.' Ministers must remember that they are *ministers*, that is, *servants;* of whom it is required that they be humble, diligent, and faithful."—*Henry.*——¶ *A service of gift.* That is, a service freely given you, and to be regarded as a favor and a privilege, imparting at the same time a corresponding duty and service. The priest's office, viewed as a "gift," was a privilege, and as a "service," a work, according to the language of the apostle, 1 Tim. 3:1, "If a man desire the office of a bishop, he desireth a good *work.*" The Jewish writers explain the clause thus: "I have given it unto you by gift, that none should say, Ye are come into it of yourselves," which is true as far as it goes, but comprises not the whole sense. It is a declaration clearing the incumbents of the sin of usurpation. ——¶ *The stranger.* That is, any Israelite, Levite, or whosoever were not of the seed of Aaron. See Note on ch. 3:10.

Provision for the Maintenance of the Priests and the Levites.

V. 8. *Behold, I also have given, etc.* The general line of duty, both for priests and Levites, having been above prescribed, the Lord now provides for their maintenance, which was to be derived from certain parts of the votive and free-will offerings that came upon the altar. They had the skins of almost all the sacrifices, and they had a considerable share of the meat-offerings, sin-offerings, etc. In addition to this, they had a money stipend also, as they were entitled to the price of what was redeemed, as the first-born of man, and of those beasts which could not be offered in sacrifice. The various first-fruits were also appropriated to them, together with the tithes of the produce of the land; so that they were, on the whole, amply provided for. On this head, the following remarks of Michaelis (*Laws of Moses*, p. 1, § 52) will be seen to have a peculiar pertinence: "If we would duly understand the genius of the Mosaic polity, and be able, without idle wonder, to account for the rich revenues of the priests and Levites, we must learn to entertain of these two descriptions of persons ideas completely opposite to those which commonly prevail. For if we look upon them in no other point of view than that of ministers of religion, their revenues cannot but appear exorbitant beyond all bounds. A tribe, including no more than 22,000 males, and, of course, not above 12,000 arrived at man's estate, received the tithes of 600,000 Israelites; consequently each individual Levite, without having to deduct seed and charges of husbandry, had as much as five Israelites reaped from their fields or gained from their cattle. A tribe, which did not make the *fifteenth* part of the people, enjoyed one *tenth* of the whole produce of the lands, and many other privileges besides. For mere ministers at the altar, mere clergymen, this would have been far too much. Guides to happiness we certainly should have cheaper; nor are they requisite in so great a multitude. It will, however, probably be granted me that *for the whole body of literati*, that is, for the ministers of religion, the judges, the scribes, and keepers of the genealogical registers, and the mathematicians employed in the service of the police, the revenues of the Levites, considerable as they may ap-

8 And the LORD spake unto Aaron, Behold, I also have given thee the charge of mine heave-

offerings[l] of all the hallowed things of the children of Israel; unto thee have I given them, by reason of the anointing[m],

l Lev. 7. 32. c. 5. 9.

m Ex. 29. 29. 40. 13, 15.

pear, were by no means too great." It is, however, to be observed in this connection, that the Levitical tribe cannot justly be compared with the preachers of the Christian dispensation. "We nowhere find," says Michaelis, "that Moses mentions, even *en passant*, any such profession as that of our clergymen, or that he instituted preaching on the Sabbath. The circumstance of the priests and Levites having their abode fixed in forty-eight distinct cities of their own, altogether incapacitated them from performing the duties of the clergy in regard to religious instruction, and what we call *the cure of souls:* for what more absurd could be imagined, than our having cities in which several hundred preachers dwelt together, while not one lived in our other cities, or was dispersed through the country. A clerical class of men was wanting in the constitution of the Mosaic church and state. A body of *doctors*, properly so called, did not exist among the Jews until after the Babylonish captivity, when the pressing emergencies of the church required its establishment; as the people, from the change of their language and manners, could no longer understand their ancient law without the aid of expounders. With all this, however, the Levites were in so far ministers of religion as they performed holy ceremonies, copied the law, and, in doubtful cases, explained it. To them the original of the law was committed, Deut. 31 : 9; they were to be its guardians, and take care to make correct transcripts of it. Printing was yet for many ages unknown; and an order of learned clerks (*clerici*), that is, of *scribes*, was very necessary for the preservation of books. The king had to take his copy of the law from theirs, Deut. 17 : 18. They were bound, at the end of every seven years, to read over the law in the hearing of all the people, Deut. 31 : 10–13; and even to be so conversant in it that they could, at least when questioned, give instructions concerning religion. In so far, therefore, were they a Spirituality, and, exactly according to the ideas of the middle ages, *clerks*, that is, people who could handle the pen, and who transcribed books of importance. All these circumstances taken together, rendered the Levites a class highly important and useful to the state; and it was not unreasonable that, as a *learned noblesse*, destined to discharge such grave duties, they should have enjoyed considerable revenues."

These abundant revenues thus provided, would have the effect of giving them respectability in the eyes of the people, while they would enable them to devote themselves the more entirely to their ministry without the danger of diversion or interruption from the pressure of worldly cares. The principle of this provision is very distinctly recognized by the apostle, 1 Cor. 9 : 13, 14, "Do ye not know that they which minister about holy things live of the things of the temple? and they which wait at the altar are partakers with the altar? Even so hath the Lord ordained that they which preach the gospel should live of the gospel." The fact that the priests and Levites lived thus in the main upon the sacrifices about which they were employed, seems to point to that spiritual sustenance which the Lord's ministerial servants find in the

and unto thy sons, by an ordinance for ever.

9 This shall be thine of the most holy things, *reserved* from the fire: Every oblation of theirs, every[n] meat-offering of theirs, and every sin-offering[o] of theirs, and every trespass-offering[p] of theirs, which they shall render unto me, *shall be* most holy for thee and for thy sons.

10 In[q] the most holy *place* shalt thou eat it; every male

n Lev. 2. 2, 3. 10. 12, 13. o Lev. 6. 25, 26. p Lev. 7. 7. 14. 13. q Lev. 6. 16, etc.

duties of their calling, and which gives occasion to Henry to remark, that "God's work is its own wages, and his service carries its own recompense along with it. Even in keeping God's commandments there is great reward. The present pleasures of religion are part of its pay."——¶ *The charge of mine heave-offerings.* Heb. "The keeping, or observation, of mine heave-offerings." Called a *charge* or *keeping*, because they were to be carefully received and reverently and devoutly used as gifts from the Lord. They are therefore called holy things (Chald. "separated things"), and were to be eaten (some of them) in the holy place, and by clean persons only, as v. 9, 10, 11. ——¶ *By reason of the anointing.* Implying that it was not so much on the ground of their personal merits that they had these revenues assigned them, but on the score of their office; by being anointed with the holy oil they were consecrated to the priestly office. Thus, Lev. 7 : 35, after defining the portion of the offerings which was to the priests, "This is the portion of the anointing of Aaron, and of the anointing of his sons, out of the offerings of the Lord made by fire."

V. 9. *This shall be thine of the most holy things.* Heb. "Of the holiness of holinesses." Gr. "The hallowed, or sanctified, holy" things. Of the distinction between most holy and holy things, see Note on Lev. 2 : 3.——¶ (*Reserved*) *from the fire.* That is, such sacrifices, or such parts of sacrifices, as were not burnt in the fire. Chald. "Left, or remaining, from the fire." These, however, did not include all the most holy things allotted to the priests, for they were entitled to the twelve loaves taken off from the table of show-bread every Sabbath.——¶ *Every oblation of theirs.* Heb. *kol korbanâm, all their korbans,* or *gifts.* This appears to be a general term embracing all the particulars that follow, q. d. every oblation of theirs, to wit, every meat-offering, every sin-offering, etc.——¶ *Which they shall render unto me.* Or, Heb. "Which they shall return, or restore, unto me." These words seem to refer to the clause immediately foregoing, that is, they allude to the compensation which was to be made to the Lord for a trespass committed, a ram of atonement being usually prescribed in that case, as appears from Num. 5 : 8 compared with Lev. 6 : 2–6. All such offerings are said to be "most holy" to Aaron and his sons, because they were specially set apart for them and to be used by none else.

V. 10. *In the most holy (place) shalt thou eat it.* Heb. "Holy of holies, or holiness of holinesses." This is the term usually employed to denote the inner recess or room of the Tabernacle in contradistinction from the outer, called "the holy place." But here it evidently has another import, as the most holy place of the Tabernacle was never used as a place for eating. It

shall eat it: it shall be holy unto thee.

11 And this *is* thine: the heave-offering [r] of their gift, with all the wave-offerings of the children of Israel: I have given them unto thee [s], and to thy sons, and to thy daughters with thee, by a statute for ever: every one that is [t] clean in thy house shall eat of it.

12 All the best of the oil,

r ver. 8. s Deut. 18. 3. t Lev. 22. 3.

here denotes the court of the priests, where there were places for this use, and which is here called "most holy," not in an absolute, but in a comparative sense, as this in respect to the outer court, and much more in respect to the whole camp of Israel, was a most holy place, as not being accessible for this purpose, but to a holy and separated class of persons. Moreover, it might properly be so termed from its being the most holy of all the places appointed for the eating of holy things, of which some might be eaten in any clean place in the camp (Lev. 10:14), or in their own houses. That this is the true interpretation appears from Lev. 6:16, where it is said of the unleavened bread, "It shall be eaten in the holy place; in the court of the tabernacle of the congregation shall they eat it." See Note *in loc.* Pool remarks, "As the *most holy* place is sometimes called simply *holy*, so it is not strange if a *holy* place be called *most holy*, especially this place which was near to the altar of burnt-offerings, which is called *most holy*, and made all that touched it holy, Ex. 29:37." It appears that there were chambers for similar uses in the temple, Neh. 13:5, 9. Compare also what is said, Ezek. 42:13, respecting the spiritual temple that was to distinguish the latter days. "Then said he unto me, The north chambers and the south chambers, which are before the separate place, they be holy chambers, where the priests that approach unto the Lord shall eat the most holy things: there shall they lay the most holy things, and the meat-offering, and the sin-offering, and the trespass-offering; for the place *is* holy."——¶ *Every male shall eat it.* Restricted to males, because the wives and daughters of priests are elsewhere forbidden to eat of the most holy things, as they did of the simply holy and common things. See v. 11, 13, 19. Lev. 6:18, 29. 7:6. Under the Gospel, all such restriction is done away; "there is neither male nor female; all are one in Christ Jesus." Gal. 3:28.——¶ *It shall be holy unto thee.* Not lawful for any one else. Vulg. "Consecrated to thee."

V. 11. *And this is thine.* The writer here passes on to the recital of the lesser or lighter holy things, which might be eaten by the priests with their sons and daughters, and male and female servants, and that, too, without the sanctuary.——¶ *The heave-offering of their gift, etc.* That is, the right shoulder and the heave-breast of their peace-offerings, for these were to be given to the priests, as also the right shoulder of the ram of atonement, mentioned ch. 6:19, 20. Comp. Lev. 7:11, 12, 14, 30–34.

V. 12. *All the best of the oil.* Heb. "All the fat of the new oil." Chald. "All the best." Gr. "All the first-fruits." This is an Hebraism, whereby "fat" is often used for what is good or for the *best* of any thing. Comp. Gen. 27:28. 45:18. Deut. 32:14. Ps. 81:17. It is equivalent to our phraseology when

and all the best of the wine, and of the wheat, the first-fruits [u] of them which they shall offer unto the LORD, them have I given thee.

u Ex. 23. 19. Deut. 18. 4. Neh. 10. 35, 36.

13 *And* whatsoever is first ripe in the land, which they shall bring unto the LORD, shall be thine: every one that is clean in thine house shall eat *of* it.

---

we speak of the best part as the *cream* of any thing. Maimonides says accordingly of the heave-offerings, "They heave not up any but the fairest." The things here mentioned were allotted for the sustenance of the priests. Some of the first-fruits of their land were brought to the Lord at their great feasts, as a sheaf of barley at the feast of the passover or unleavened bread, ch. 23 : 10, and two loaves of new wheat at the feast of Pentecost, ch. 23 : 17, and the first of their wine and oil at the feast of tabernacles. But these were brought in the name of all the inhabitants of the land in general. Besides these, therefore, particular individuals were to bring of their own corn and fruits the first-fruits to the Lord as prescribed in several places, Ex. 22 : 29. 23 : 19, concerning which no other directions are given but that they should be, as here intimated, of the first and the best, the precise quantity being left to the free impulse of the donor, who would naturally give according as the divine Providence had blessed him in his basket and his store.

V. 13. *Whatsoever is first ripe in the land.* That is, not only the first-fruits of the oil and wine and wheat above mentioned, but the first-fruits of all other grains, and all fruit-trees, etc. Upon this part of the Mosaic institute we give in this connection the substance of what Michaelis remarks on the subject (*Laws of Moses*, § 193). "Firstlings and first-fruits constituted a very considerable portion of the salary of the priests. Ever since the exodus from Egypt, the first-born of every creature was consecrated to God in remembrance of the terrible judgment which accompanied that event. But the following distinctions were to be observed: Beasts which might be offered in sacrifice (that is, oxen, sheep and goats) could not be redeemed. Their blood must be sprinkled on the altar, and their fat consumed upon it; while their flesh belonged to the priest, who used it as his share of the sacrifice, v. 17, 18. All other creatures, which could not be offered as victims on the altar, such as human beings and unclean beasts, might be redeemed. In the case of a first-born son this was an incumbent duty on his parents; but in the case of unclean beasts, such as asses, camels, horses, etc., it remained optional to the owners to redeem them or not as they pleased. The redemption of a child took place when it was a month old, v. 16; if it died sooner, the parents were not obliged to redeem it. It died, as it were, to God and to the priest, to whom it previously belonged. As to the child that was to be redeemed, the priest was to put a value upon it; and as all children were not of the same value, it would seem that a weakly child, and likewise the child of very poor parents, were estimated at a lower rate; but the father had always to give *something* as a recognition of the Lord's right to the first-born. Only there was a fixed tax, beyond which the priest was never to go, viz., five shekels, v. 16. The redemption-money belonged to the priest, v. 15. Unclean beasts were redeemed

14 Every [v] thing devoted in
Israel shall be thine.
15 Every [w] thing that openeth
the matrix in all flesh, which
they bring unto the LORD, *whether it be* of men or beasts, shall be
thine : nevertheless the first-
born of man shalt thou surely
redeem [x], and the firstling of
unclean beasts shalt thou redeem.
16 And those that are to be
redeemed, from a month old
shalt thou redeem, according to

v Lev. 27. 28. w Ex. 13. 2. 22. 29. x Ex. 13. 13. 34. 20.

by giving a sheep or a goat instead of them; and if the owner did not choose to do so, he was obliged to break their necks, Ex. 13 : 12, 13, where see Notes. The first-fruits were given to the priest after the harvest and the vintage, from corn, must, oil, and likewise from the first baked bread of the new crop, ch. 15 : 20, and from the wool of the sheep when shorn, Deut. 18 : 4. This, however, was a gift, the greatness of which depended entirely on the giver's pleasure. These first-fruits came not to the altar; they belonged merely to the priest; and hence it was lawful to use honey and leaven along with them. Lev. 2 : 11. Of another class of firstlings, see Deut. 12 : 6. 14 : 23. 15 : 19–23, and the accompanying Notes.

V. 14. *Every thing devoted.* Heb. *'herem,* on which see Note on Lev. 27 : 28. A thing devoted was something dedicated to God by vow or otherwise. Some things were devoted absolutely, and provided it was any thing that might be eaten or consumed by use, it went to the priest; but such things as vessels or treasures of gold and silver were dedicated to the uses of the sanctuary, and could not be otherwise appropriated.

V. 15. *Every thing that openeth the matrix.* Heb. "Every opener, or opening, of the womb." Gr. "Every thing that openeth every matrix (or womb)." See Note on Ex. 13 : 2, where it is shown that the *first-born* are intended, and these it appears from Deut. 15 : 19. Ex. 34 : 19, were to be males.—The Notes upon various parallel passages referred to in the margin will be found to contain an explanation of many particulars on which we cannot here dwell.

V. 16. *Those that are to be redeemed.* That is, of men, but not the unclean beasts mentioned in the preceding verse, for these were to be redeemed by a lamb, Ex. 13 : 13, and that after they were eight days old, Ex. 22 : 30. "Redemption of the first-born is one of the rites which is still practised among the Jews. According to Leo of Modena, it is performed in the following manner: —When the child is thirty days old, the father sends for one of the descendants of Aaron: several persons being assembled on the occasion, the father brings a cup containing several pieces of gold and silver coin. The priest then takes the child into his arms, and addressing himself to the mother, says: Is this thy son?—MOTHER. Yes.—PRIEST. Hast thou never had another child, male or female, a miscarriage or untimely birth? —MOTHER. No.—PRIEST. This being the case, this child, as first-born, belongs to me. Then, turning to the father, he says: If it be thy desire to have this child, thou must redeem it.—FATHER. I present thee with this gold and silver for this purpose.—PRIEST. Thou dost wish, therefore, to redeem the child?—FATHER. I do wish so to do. —The priest then, turning himself to the assembly, says: Very well; this child, as first-born, is mine, as it is

thine estimation[y], for the money of five[z] shekels, after the shekel of the sanctuary, which[a] *is* twenty gerahs.

17 But the firstling[b] of a cow, or the firstling of a sheep, or the firstling of a goat, thou shalt not redeem; they *are* holy: thou shalt sprinkle[c] their blood upon the altar, and shalt burn their fat *for* an offering made by fire, for a sweet savour unto the LORD.

18 And the flesh of them shall be thine, as[d] the wave-breast and as the right shoulder are thine.

19 All[e] the heave-offerings of the holy things, which the children of Israel offer unto the LORD, have I given thee, and thy sons and thy daughters with thee, by a statute for ever: it *is* a[f] covenant of salt for ever before the LORD unto thee, and to thy seed with thee.

y Lev. 27. 2, 6. *z* c. 3. 47. *a* Ezek. 45. 12. *b* Deut. 15. 19. *c* Ex. 29. 16. Lev. 3. 2, 5. Heb. 12. 24.

d Ex. 29. 26, 28. Lev. 7. 34. *e* ver. 11. *f* Lev. 2. 13. 2 Chr. 13. 5.

written in Bemidbar, (Num. 18 : 16,) Thou shalt redeem the first-born of a month old for five shekels, but I shall content myself with this in exchange. He then takes two gold crowns, or thereabouts, and returns the child to his parents."—*A. Clarke.*——¶ *According to thine estimation, for the money of five shekels.* Better, "According to thine estimation, even the money (or amount) of five shekels." That is, according to the estimation or valuation prescribed for thee, and which is to be of universal application. The sum was fixed at this number, and was to be uniform whether the case were that of a rich or a poor man.

V. 17. *The firstling of a cow, etc.* In all which cases a *male* is to be understood, as otherwise it was not sanctified or given to the priest.——¶ *Shalt not redeem.* Thou mayest not give the value of it, or any other for it, but the beast itself was to be given; neither might the owner use or derive any profit from it, from the wool, or any thing pertaining to it, Deut. 15 : 19.

V. 19. *It is a covenant of salt for ever.* That is, a firm, stable, incorruptible covenant, salt being an emblem of perpetuity. In like manner the kingdom over Israel was given to David and to his sons "by a covenant of salt," 2 Chr. 13 : 5, where the Gr. has "an everlasting covenant." See Note on Lev. 2 : 13. "It is generally agreed that this denotes a perpetual and incorruptible covenant, with a particular allusion to the preserving properties of salt, which has, in different countries, been very commonly held, on that account, as an emblem of incorruptibility and permanence, of fidelity and friendship. It also seems that there is a particular reference here to some use of salt in the act of contracting the covenant; and what this use was, is rather variously understood. Some think, that, as with all sacrifices salt was offered, a covenant of salt means one confirmed by solemn sacrifices. Others are of opinion that it contains an allusion to the fact that covenants were generally confirmed by the parties eating together—an act to which the use of salt was a necessary appendage. We are inclined to combine both ideas, and to say, that the phrase alludes generally to such a custom as in common use, and more particularly to the specific covenant in view, in which we may safely, from general analogy, understand, that salt

20 And the LORD spake unto Aaron, Thou [g] shalt have no inheritance in their land, neither shalt thou have any part among them: I [h] *am* thy part, and thine

[g] c. 26. 62.

[h] Deut. 10. 9. 12. 12. 14. 27, 29. 18. 1, 2. Josh. 13. 14, 33. 14. 3. 18. 7. Ps. 16. 5. Ezek. 44. 28.

was offered on the altar with the Lord's portion, and that the other contracting party ate the remainder with salt. Thus both parties ate the salt of the covenant; for whatever was offered on the altar was, in a certain sense, considered as the Lord's meat. We deduce this interpretation from the fact that in the East it is the act of eating salt together which constitutes the inviolability of an engagement. And this selection of salt is, in our apprehension, not exclusively or principally with a reference to its peculiar properties, but because salt, being generally mixed with all kinds of food, does practically constitute a fair representation of the whole act of eating. Hence a man will say he has *eaten salt* with you, when he has partaken of any kind of food; and he will also say that he has *eaten* with you, when haste or any other circumstance prevents him from doing more than tasting salt. We have been the more desirous to explain this matter, because travellers have generally stated the oriental practice in such a way as to convey the impression that the act of eating salt as a pledge or token of engagement, was something different from, and more solemn than, the act of eating in a general way together. But the principle is really the same in both; or rather, salt is the part, colloquially or practically, taken for the whole. Thus understood, the act of "eating salt" is considered to imply, even without any explanation to that effect, that the parties will be faithful to each other and will not act to each other's prejudice. This is strictly incumbent on the person who eats the salt of another. In peculiar cases and emergencies this "covenant of salt," is entered into with a distinct understanding and declaration of its intention. Among the Desert Arabs and other uncivilized people, a covenant thus ratified is rendered, by usage and the sentiment of honor, far more inviolable than those engagements to which they have been solemnly sworn: and to such an extent does this feeling operate that the unintentional eating with, or what belonged to, a person against whom aggressive designs were entertained, is quite sufficient not only to secure him from offensive measures, but to ensure him protection from those who otherwise would have plundered or slain him without pity."—*Pict. Bible.*

V. 20. *Thou shalt have no inheritance in their land.* The words are addressed to Aaron as if he were personally regarded in this appointment, but he is evidently to be considered as the representative of his order and his tribe. He himself died before entering the promised land, consequently the words have respect to his posterity. They were to have no inheritance in the land appropriated to their brethren of the other tribes ("*their* land"). By which is meant that they were not to have a distinct and separate allotment of territory, as had each of the other tribes, though they had several cities, with the adjacent suburbs, appropriated to their use. These cities, however, they did not properly possess as their own, as an inheritance. They held them of the other tribes, within whose bounds they were situated. It is not difficult to assign adequate reasons for this law. (1.) The Lord had made ample provision for their support in the tithes, first-fruits, oblations, etc. which were

inheritance, among the children of Israel.

21 And, behold, I have given the children of Levi all the

set apart to them for that purpose. (2.) He would have them free from worldly encumbrances and cares, that they might devote themselves more entirely to the service of God in the functions prescribed them. (3.) The ends aimed at in the institution of such an order required that when not serving at the sanctuary they should be dispersed among the people, to whom they would serve as a bond of union. (4.) Their sequestration from secular interests, and their entire dependence upon the special providence of the Lord, would afford a striking specimen of a heavenly life, and tend to call off the minds of the nation at large from placing too great a value upon earthly things. (5.) The arrangement would tend also to strengthen the ties of charity and brotherly kindness between them and the other tribes, the Levites ministering to those tribes in spiritual things, and they to them in temporal things.——¶ *Neither shalt thou have part among them.* It is reasonable to conclude that these words do not mean precisely the same with those in the preceding clause. There is doubtless some distinction to be understood between "inheritance" and "portion." The original, *'hêlek*, here rendered *portion*, is indeed in some cases spoken of a part or portion of land, as Josh. 15: 13. 19:9. Yet for the most part it is applied to the part, portion, or share of the spoils taken from a conquered enemy; and so it might here be properly understood of the spoils obtained in the wars with the Canaanites, which were of great value, but which were forbidden to the sons of Levi, because the Lord himself was to be their part and portion. Of these spoils Joshua says, ch. 22:8, "Return with much riches unto your tents, and with very much cattle, with silver, and with gold, and with brass, and with iron, and with very much raiment: divide the spoil of your enemies with your brethren." But in this division the Levites were to have no share, the Lord himself and the holy things of his service having been appointed their portion. They were called to war another kind of warfare in the Lord's sanctuary, as appears from ch. 4:23, where see Note. The Hebrew writers say on this head, "All the tribe of Levi are warned that they have no inheritance in the land of Canaan; likewise they are warned that they take no part of the spoil at the time when they conquer the cities."——¶ *I am thy part and thine inheritance.* As Israel was a peculiar people, and not to be numbered among the nations; so Levi was a peculiar tribe, and not to be settled as the rest of the tribes, but in all respects distinguished from them. "A good reason is given why they must have 'no inheritance in the land,' for, says God, 'I am thy part and thine inheritance.' Note. Those that have God for their Inheritance and their Portion for ever, ought to look with a holy indifference and contempt upon the inheritances of the world, and not covet their portion in it. The Levites shall have no inheritance, and yet they shall live very comfortably and plentifully—to teach us that Providence has various ways of supporting those that live in a dependence upon it; the fowls reap not, and yet are fed; the lilies spin not, and yet are clothed; the Levites have no inheritance in Israel, and yet live better than any other tribe."—*Henry.*

V. 21. *And, behold, I have given all the tenth.* He now announces the provision specifically made for the Levites,

tenth[i] in Israel for an inheritance, for their service which they serve, *even* the service of the tabernacle of the congregation.

22 Neither must the children of Israel henceforth come nigh the tabernacle of the congregation, lest they bear sin, and die[k].

23 But[l] the Levites shall do the service of the tabernacle of the congregation, and they shall bear their iniquity. *It shall be* a statute for ever throughout your generations, that among the children of Israel they have no inheritance.

24 But the tithes[m] of the children of Israel, which they offer

i Lev. 27. 30, 32. k c. 1. 51.

l c. 3. 7. m ver. 21. Neh. 10. 37. 12. 44. Mal. 3. 8-10. Heb. 7. 5-9.

---

as he had before that made for the priests. "The covenant of salt for ever," says Chazkuni, "was to the Levites also." Though the smallest of all the tribes, yet they were to have a tenth part of all the products of the land, without the trouble and expense of ploughing and sowing. But the details of the provision will appear in what follows.——¶ *For their service which they serve.* That is, as a compensation for their services, the specific nature of which is more fully declared in ch. 4.

Vs. 22, 23. *Neither must the children of Israel henceforth come nigh.* That is, so nigh as to do any act appropriate to the priests or Levites, as had been attempted by Korah and his company. ——¶ *Lest they bear sin and die.* Heb. "Lest they bear sin to die." That is, incur guilt to such a degree as to expose them to die. Gr. "To bear a deadly, or death-bringing sin." "This order seems set in opposition to that concerning the priests and Levites, that they should have "no inheritance in Israel," to show how God dispenses his favors variously. The Levites have the honor of attending the Tabernacle, which is denied to the Israelite; but then the Israelites have the honor of inheritances in Canaan, which is denied the Levites; thus each is kept from either envying or despising the other, and both have reason to rejoice in their lot. The Israelites must not "come nigh the tabernacle," but then the Levites must have "no inheritance in the land;" if ministers expect that people should keep in their sphere, and not intermeddle with sacred offices, let them keep in theirs, and not entangle themselves in secular affairs."—*Henry.*——¶ *They shall bear their iniquity.* That is, they shall bear the punishment of their own iniquity if they transgress, and that of the people if they suffer them to transgress. Thus Sol. Jarchi:—"They, the Levites, shall bear the iniquity of the Israelites, for it is their duty to warn strangers of coming near to them." It was upon this ground that the priests withstood king Uzziah, when he would have burnt incense to the Lord, 2 Chron. 26:17, 18.

V. 24. *Which they offer* (*as*) *an heave-offering.* Heb. "Which they heave up." Gr. and Chald. "Which they separate unto the Lord." It is not probably to be understood that they were actually heaved up or waved before the Lord, but they were virtually so dealt with by being consecrated and set apart to divinely appointed uses. The words contain essentially an admonition to the people, that as it was the express will of Jehovah that the Levites should have no determinate

as an heave-offering unto the LORD, I have given to the Levites to inherit: therefore I have said unto them, Among the children of Israel they shall have no inheritance.

25 And the LORD spake unto Moses, saying,

26 Thus speak unto the Levites, and say unto them, When ye take of the children of Israel the tithes which I have given you from them for your inheritance, then ye shall offer up an heave-offering of it for the LORD, *even* a tenth *part* [n] of the tithe.

27 And *this* your heave-offering shall be reckoned unto you, as though [o] *it were* the corn of the threshing-floor, and as the fulness of the wine-press.

28 Thus ye also shall offer an heave-offering unto the LORD of all your tithes which ye receive of the children of Israel, and ye shall give thereof the LORD's heave-offering to Aaron the priest.

n Neh. 10. 38. *o* ver. 30.

---

portion of land, but should be subsisted upon the tithes of the yearly product of the land, so the people were not to grudge them their due, but were to pay it as an offering to God the supreme Proprietor, who had bestowed it upon them as truly and as completely as he had the lands upon the other tribes.

V. 26. *A tenth (part) of the tithe.* Or, "the tithe of the tithes," as it is rendered Neh. 10 : 38. A divine order is here communicated through Moses, requiring that, as the whole nation paid an annual tenth to the Levites, so they also in gratitude to the Lord and as a token of their subserviency to the priests, should regularly pay a tenth of that tithe to the priesthood, who received, therefore, one hundredth part of the produce of the lands and herds. "The Levites were to give God his dues out of the tithes, as well as the Israelites out of their increase. They were God's tenants, and rent was expected from them, nor were they exempted by their office. Thus now, ministers must be charitable out of what they receive; and the more freely they have received, the more freely they must give, and be examples of liberality."—*Henry.*——¶ *Ye shall offer up an heave-offering of it for the Lord.* That is, they were to look upon this tribute in the light of an offering or oblation to the Most High, who, if they rendered it punctually and heartily, would accept it as favorably as he did the tithes of the whole nation paid to them. The language is pregnant in meaning, teaching us that whatever we bestow upon the Lord's people, out of sincere regard to his will, is bestowed upon him, who will never be unmindful of our benefactions. Literal heave-offerings are not now required of us, but prayers and praises lifted up to God, or the heart lifted up in them, will be regarded as a virtual equivalent.

V. 27. *Shall be reckoned unto you, etc.* That is, though this tithe thus paid was not the fruit of their ground, nor of their own labor, as were the tithes of other Israelites, yet being such as they had, and being cordially offered, it would be as readily accepted as if it were, and should be accredited to them as such.

V. 28. *To Aaron the priest.* Not so much to Aaron in person, as to Aaron the head and representative of his tribe. His successors in the high-priesthood were to enjoy the benefit of this law,

29 Out of all your gifts ye
shall offer every heave-offering
of the LORD, of all the best
thereof, *even* the hallowed part
thereof, out of it.
30 Therefore thou shalt say
unto them, When ye have heaved
the best thereof from it, then [p] it
shall be counted unto the Levites as the increase of the
threshing-floor, and as the increase of the wine-press.
31 And ye shall eat it in
every place, ye and your households: for it *is* your reward [q] for
your service in the tabernacle
of the congregation.
32 And ye shall bear [r] no sin
by reason of it, when ye have
heaved from it the best of it:

p ver. 27.

q Mat. 10. 10. Luke 10. 7. 1 Cor. 9. 13. 2 Cor. 12. 13. 1 Tim. 5. 18. r Lev. 19, 8. 22. 16.

together with the inferior priests connected with him.

V. 29. *Out of all your gifts, etc.* That is, out of the various gifts bestowed, by the divine appointment, upon the priestly order, embracing not only the tenth of their tithes, but the tenth also of other things, as of their own grounds, the suburbs and fields given to the Levites by the ordinance, Num. 35 : 4.——¶ *Ye shall offer every heave-offering of the Lord.* Heb. *tarimu terumah, shall heave an heave-offering.* This was to be actually presented to the priest, but being done by the Lord's order, and in his name, it is accounted as an offering made to the Lord himself.——¶ *Of all the best thereof.* Not perhaps that all the tithe was to be taken out of the very best part of the crop, and none out of the more inferior; but that it should consist of the best as well as of the worst; or, in other words, that the people should pay to the Levites, and the Levites to the priests, as good of every thing as they retained for themselves.——¶ *Even the hallowed part thereof out of it.* Heb. *eth migdesho, its consecration,* or that part which was especially consecrated by being set apart and devoted to a holy use.

V. 30. *It shall be counted unto the Levites, etc.* That is, that when they had thus complied with the divine injunction, and first paid the priests their appropriate tithes, they might use the remainder as freely as any man in Israel could use the corn or the wine of his own land when he had paid the prescribed tithes.

V. 31. *Ye shall eat it in every place.* They might have the enjoyment of it with their families in their own houses, or any where else that might seem good to them, provided the place were clean. The tithes were thus distinguished from the other holy things allotted to the priests, which, being offered at the altar, were to be eaten only in the holy place; but the tithes, though a species of offering to the Lord, yet not being presented at the altar, might be eaten any where; provided only the priestly dues were previously paid out of them.

V. 32. *Ye shall bear no sin by reason of it.* Ye shall not incur guilt, nor suffer punishment by eating it with your households. This, however, they would do, if they heaved not, or separated a tenth part of the best of it, as above commanded. Their "heaving" or offering from it its best portion would prevent its being an occasion of iniquity, and consequently of penalty.——¶ *Neither shall ye pollute, etc.* A general warning, both to priests and Levites, that the holy things of the people be not profaned by them, nor be suffered to be profaned by others.

neither shall ye pollute [s] the holy things of the children of Israel, lest ye die.

s Lev. 22. 2, 15. Mal. 1. 7. 1 Cor. 11. 27, 29.

CHAPTER XIX.

AND the LORD spake unto Moses and unto Aaron, saying,

CHAPTER XIX.

The Ordinance of the Red Heifer.

The sudden death of so many Israelites as had fallen under the stroke of the recent judgments, had put great numbers of their friends and relatives into a state of legal uncleanness, which made them incapable of approaching the Tabernacle for divine worship, and which was one ground of the extreme consternation expressed by them, ch. 17 : 12, 13. To relieve their minds of undue apprehension on this score, the Lord here enacts a standing ceremony for the purification of all such kinds of uncleanness, the performance of which should render them again capable of being admitted to public worship. The ordinance enjoined was one of the most onerous of all that mass of observances which was imposed upon the Jews, and of which it is said by the apostle Peter that they constituted "a yoke which neither they nor their fathers were able to bear." This kind of defilement which was to be remedied was as light and venial as could well be conceived; it implied no moral guilt whatever; nor could it possibly in some cases be avoided; yet it rendered a person unclean seven days; and every thing that he touched was also made unclean; and every person who might, however inadvertently, come in contact with any thing that had been touched by him, was also made unclean. Moreover, if any person that had contracted this ceremonial defilement concealed it, or refused to submit to the prescribed form of purification, he was to be cut off from the Lord's people. Add to this, that the rite was of such a nature that even in applying it there was a continual liability to the contraction of fresh defilement. The priest who officiated, the man that burnt the heifer, he that gathered up the ashes, he that prepared, he that sprinkled, and even he that touched the water—all became unclean. Who, then, can wonder that the nation of Israel should have groaned under the yoke of ceremonies in their own land almost as much as they did under the yoke of bondage in the land of Egypt! Who can be surprised that they should have longed for the coming of the promised Messiah, who was to deliver them from such an oppressive burden! As to the reasons which governed the appointment of this peculiar rite, we are aware that the learned have endeavored to show that it pointed, by way of contravention, to some of the superstitions of the heathen world around them, especially the Egyptians. Spencer, in his great work on "The Laws of the Hebrews," goes elaborately into this argument, and incidentally throws valuable light upon many features of the ordinance. He shows that while the Egyptians sacrificed red bulls and oxen, red heifers or cows were never offered by them upon their altars, but held sacred to Isis. So in various other particulars, he would trace an express design to counteract the ideas of the Egyptians in regard to sacrificial worship. The reader will find this view of the subject satisfactorily unfolded in Mr. Kitto's Notes on this chapter. Without denying *in toto* the soundness of the theory, we content ourselves with deducing from the language of Paul (Heb. 9 : 11–15) a typical and spiritual design in the ordinance, the various

2 This *is* the ordinance of the law which the LORD hath commanded, saying, Speak unto the children of Israel, that they

items of which will be elucidated as we proceed. In like manner, we make comparatively little account of considerations of a *sanitary* nature, which are so much insisted upon by Michaelis and his school. Admitting that the dangers of defilement from dead bodies would tend directly to secure their speedy interment, and thus promote the general health and comfort of the living, yet we can see an ulterior reason for the enactment drawn directly from the adaptation of natural death to shadow forth spiritual death, and of the defiling effects of the former to represent the deadly pollutions of the latter. In fact, but for some such design and import as this—some moral and interior significance terminating in Christ, as the substance of all the Levitical shadows—we could not but regard these institutions as little worthy of the wisdom in which they originated. Apart from such a design, the temple of Jerusalem could scarcely be regarded in any other light than as a gigantic slaughter-house, sending forth continual streams of the blood of bullocks and goats. But when viewed in the light of New Testament teachings, every thing is consistent, rational, instructive, and worthy its divine Author. In the present rite we may safely consider the burning of the heifer as representing the excruciating sufferings of Christ, its ashes the permanent merit of his sacrifice, the running or living water the power and grace of his Holy Spirit, called the water of life and the laver of regeneration, while the mixture of the two together fitly represents the inseparable union which exists between the justification and the sanctification of a sinner. But we proceed to the details.

V. 2. *This (is) the ordinance of the law.* Heb. *hukkath hattorâh, statute, constitution, prescript,* or *ordinance.* Gr. *diastolē tou nomou, the distinction of the law.* Vulg. "This is the observance of the victim," i. e., this is the rule to be observed respecting the victim. There seems to be a reference to some law previously given, and in ch. 8 : 7, we find mention made of "water of purifying," but hitherto we have had no intimation of the mode of preparing it. This is done in the chapter before us. Drusius, on this passage, gives several extracts from Jewish writers, who intimate that the expression "ordinance, or statute, of the law" implies something mystical. Thus, Rab. Moses Gerundensis, while excusing himself from giving a reason for this precept, says: "We who, by reason of our sins, are contaminated in this captivity, do not know the cleansing of holiness (nor shall we) until the Spirit comes upon us from on high, and God shall pour clean water upon us, and we shall be cleansed. Amen. God grant it may come to pass in our days." Rab. Solomon says: "The words are no other than the decrees of a king, given without any reason," i. e., of which no distinct reason is given why they should be observed. Rab. David, on the 119th Ps., says: "Statutes are precepts of which the reason is not laid open." The "statute of the law," therefore, implies a command given by divine authority, the grounds or reasons of which are not disclosed, but which is still obeyed because God wills that it shall be. In respect to the Jews, this may probably hold good, for the typical import of the prescribed rite no doubt escaped their penetration. That which is now unfolded to us was a secret hidden from them.——¶ *That they bring unto thee.*

bring thee a red heifer without spot, wherein [a] *is* no blemish, *and* upon which [b] never came yoke.

a Ex. 12. 5. Mal. 1. 13, 14. 1 Pet. 1. 19.

b Deut. 21. 3. 1 Sam. 6. 7.

Heb. "That they take unto thee;" that is, that they take and bring. See, for a similar phraseology, Gen. 15 : 9. Ex. 25 : 2. Lev. 24 : 2. This was to be done as a common act, or as the common charge of the people, for whose common benefit the rite was appointed.——¶ *That they bring thee a red heifer.* Heb. *pârâh*, the fem. of *par, a young bullock*, usually understood to be two or three years old, from which the age of the heifer here spoken of is supposed to be about the same. The Hebrew canons say, "It is commanded that the red heifer be of the third or fourth year, and it may be older." As a general fact, male animals only were allowable for sacrifice, but a female is here commanded to be offered, though not upon the altar like the usual sacrifices. The reason suggested for this by Spencer is, that the ancient Egyptians were accustomed to sacrifice a bull to Typhon so perfectly red that not a hair of another color was to be found on him, in direct and designed opposition to which a female of the same species and the same color was here commanded to be offered. We find the solution rather in the fact, that all the feminine, as well as the masculine, virtues are to be recognized as centring in the Lord Christ, the great Sacrifice. This animal was to be of a *red* color with a reference to its typical bearings, although Josephus explains the original by a term (*xanthos*) signifying a *deep or ruddy yellow*, and Michaelis renders it by *gelb-brauner, yellowish-brown.* Whatever were the peculiar hue, *red* no doubt predominated, and it was all over of one color. The language of the apostle, Heb. 9 : 11–13, makes it evident that the sacrifice pointed to Christ, whose perfect sacrifice solves this hieroglyph of the desert: "If the blood of bulls and goats, *and the ashes of an heifer sprinkling the unclean*, sanctifieth to the purifying of the flesh; how much more shall the blood of Christ—purge your conscience from dead works to serve the living God." As *blood*, therefore, is pointed at in the representative, the "red" color of the sacrifice is recognized at once as most appropriate to the aim.——¶ *Without spot.* Heb. *temimâh, perfect.* Gr. *amomon, without blemish.* This was to be the character of all the sacrifices, Lev. 12, but in the present instance the Jewish writers refer the issue to the color, implying that which is *perfectly red* without the least admixture of any other color, for "if it have but two hairs black it is unlawful." The Targ. Jon. paraphrases thus: "Speak unto the children of Israel that they take unto thee a red cow two years old, in which there is not the least mark or spot of white hair, on which a bull never rose, which has never done work or felt the goad." This, however, is not the genuine sense of the expression, which implies *general faultlessness* in the animal offered, both in respect to soundness of condition and integrity of form. To this sense we adhere, as the adequate authority for any thing beyond it is wanting. It is only the idea that something antagonistic to Egyptian notions is involved in the institute, that has suggested any other than the usual meaning. As this sacrifice was in an especial manner appointed for purification or expiation, it seems to have been proper that the color should typify the blood of Christ shed in his passion as well as that of the sacrifices generally; and as the flagrancy of sin, requiring a

3 And ye shall give her unto Eleazar the priest, that he may bring her forth without [c] the

c Lev. 4. 12, 21. 16. 27. Heb. 13. 11.

bloody expiation, causes it to be described as of the color of *scarlet* and *crimson*, Is. 1 : 18, so we may combine all these references together in the true purport of the red color of the victim.——¶ *Wherein is no blemish.* Heb. *moom.* The general law on this head is thus delivered Lev. 22 : 21, 22. "And whosoever offereth a sacrifice of peace offerings unto the Lord to accomplish his vow, or a freewill offering in beeves or sheep, it shall be perfect (Heb. *tâmin*) to be accepted; there shall be no blemish (Heb. *moom*) therein. Blind, or broken, or maimed, or having a wen, or scurvy, or scabbed, ye shall not offer these unto the Lord, nor make an offering by fire of them upon the altar unto the Lord." As compared with the previous term "perfect," it is merely an expansion of the same idea; it is not essentially different. It is, perhaps, simply a specification of several particulars to which the general idea of *perfectness* or *soundness* stands opposed. "All blemishes," says Maimonides, "which disable the holy things, disable this heifer. . . . For whatsoever maketh holy things unlawful for the altar, maketh the heifer unlawful." Thus it is said of our Lord, the great antitype, that "he offered himself *without spot* unto God.——¶ *Upon which never came yoke.* Which had never been employed in ploughing the ground, or in any other work; for heifers, as well as bullocks, were trained to the plough in the East. See Judg. 14 : 18, and Hos. 10 : 11. But an unworked heifer or bullock was the only one that was allowable as a victim for sacrifice. "Among most of the pagan nations of antiquity also, an animal which had been employed in any labor or for any common purpose, was not considered a proper sacrifice to the gods. This, as Dr. Adam Clarke remarks, is one of many usages in matters of sacrifice in which the identity of the heathen practice with that of the Hebrews seems to indicate the common patriarchal origin of both. We cannot too frequently repeat that, in this as in many other things, the Hebrew legislator is not to be considered as originating usages and institutions, but as modifying and improving, so as to render fit for adoption those already in existence. Homer has several passages in allusion to the practice in question; and the following from Virgil (Georg. iv. 550) may be quoted:

'From his herd he culls,
For slaughter, four the fairest of his bulls;
Four heifers from his female stock he took,
All fair, and *all unknowing of the yoke.*'"

DRYDEN.

—*Kitto.*

The typical reference here is probably to the fact, that the Saviour was free from the bondage of sin and corruption, and free from any prior obligation to interpose in our behalf, and undergo what he did in the work of our redemption. Every thing of this nature was divinely spontaneous.

V. 3. *Unto Eleazar the priest.* The victim was to be brought, in the name of the whole congregation, to Moses, as the preceding verse directs, and then Moses and Aaron were to deliver her to Eleazar. The reason of this is supposed to have been, that the officiating priest on such occasions became unclean until evening, v. 7. As there was but one high priest, this, in his case, would be attended with considerable inconvenience, and yet as the rite was one of special importance and solemnity, it was not to be intrusted to an ordinary priest, and was therefore committed to

camp, and *one* shall slay her before his face.

4 And Eleazar the priest shall take of her blood with

Eleazar as next in rank to Aaron. The agency of the priest in the matter pointed typically to the fact, that our redemption and purification is the work of Christ's priesthood, who indeed may be viewed as both priest and sacrifice. We may here remark, moreover, that the reason assigned by the fathers Augustin and Cyril for the heifer's being consigned to Eleazar "was to imply, that our Lord's sacrifice of himself was to be at a distance in the succession of the priesthood;" and that Eleazar here "represented that whole sanctified body which Peter styles 'a chosen generation, a royal priesthood, an holy nation, a peculiar people,' to whom Christ was given by God the Father, for sanctification and deliverance."——¶ *That he may bring.* Or, Heb. "That one may bring." Gr. "They shall bring;" and so in the ensuing clause, "they shall slay." This is a phraseology equivalent to "she shall be brought;" "she shall be slain." It implies that Eleazar did not do it in person, but that some other one did it under his direction. This is evident from its being said that the heifer was slain "before his face," which indicates that some other person did it. But the word "bring" is no more definite as to its nominative than "slay." Nothing, however, is more usual in Scripture than to speak of one as the doer of a thing which he merely directs, orders, or commands. Thus, when it is said, Mark 15:45, that Pilate gave the body of Christ to Joseph, we are told by Matthew, ch. 27:58, that he "commanded the body to be delivered."——¶ *Without the camp.* As something exceedingly unclean by reason of its being ceremonially laden with the sins of the people; and whatever was unclean was to be removed from the camp, ch. 5:2, 3. In this respect the sacrifice of the red heifer differed from the ordinary sacrifices, which were offered upon the altar in the midst of the camp. It thus became a more suitable representative of Christ. "For the bodies of those beasts, whose blood is brought into the sanctuary by the high priest for sin, are burned without the camp. Wherefore Jesus also, that he might sanctify the people with his own blood, suffered without the gate." This was the place where malefactors also suffered, Lev. 24:14, with whom our Lord was reckoned. As a general rule, the greater the degree of impurity laid upon any sacrifice, the farther was it removed from the sanctuary in the offering. Witness the scape-goat, which was not so much as burnt, but banished into the wilderness, nobody knew whither. The Jewish writers inform us, that after the building of Solomon's temple, the blood of the red heifer was sprinkled without the city on the Mount of Olives, where also the blood of the antitype, our divine Saviour, was shed, when "his sweat was, as it were, great drops of blood falling to the ground." From this point also, from which the prospect was directly into the door or entrance of the Tabernacle, the edifice facing the east. In this straight line towards the sanctuary the blood was sprinkled. In strictness of speech, the red heifer was not a *sacrifice*, though designed to answer somewhat the purpose of one, by effecting a legal purification of the people from their greatest defilement.

V. 4. *Shall take of her blood, and sprinkle, etc.* The Jews maintain that in the sprinkling of the blood consisted the very essence of an expiatory sacri-

his finger, and [d] sprinkle of her blood directly before the tabernacle of the congregation seven times.

5 And *one* shall burn the heifer in his sight; her [e] skin, and her flesh, and her blood, with her dung, shall he burn:

6 And the priest shall take cedar [f] wood, and hyssop, and

d Lev. 4. 6. 16. 14, 19. Heb. 9. 13. 12. 24.

e Ex. 29. 14. f Lev. 14. 4, 6, 49.

fice, and its being done "seven times" signified the thoroughness and completeness of the effect produced by the application of the Redeemer's blood, that "blood of sprinkling," which "cleanseth from all sin." As the "finger of God," Luke 11 : 20, is interchanged with "spirit of God," Mat. 12 : 28, we may properly consider the term "finger" as indicative of the divine power exerted in the application of that spiritual virtue which is denoted by the act of sprinkling.——¶ *Directly before the tabernacle, etc.* That is, directly towards the front part, or door, of the Tabernacle. The priest was to stand at a distance, without the precincts of the sacred edifice, and dipping his finger in the basin containing the blood he was to sprinkle it before him in the direction of the Tabernacle. This he was to do seven times in succession. The defilement he contracted would not allow of his coming near to the holy tent, and yet he must turn and act *towards* it. The Hebrew canons say, "If he sprinkled (the blood) and not towards the sanctuary, it was unlawful; likewise if he did slay or burn her, and not over against the sanctuary, it was unlawful."

V. 5. *And (one) shall burn the heifer in his sight.* That is, some one shall burn her in Eleazar's sight; or Eleazar shall cause her to be burnt before his eyes; for it is clear, from v. 8, that some assistant performed the task of burning; whence the Targ. Jon. "And the priest shall burn."

V. 6. *Cedar wood, and hyssop, and scarlet.* That is, scarlet wool. The precise design of the use of these articles in connection with the present ceremony, it is difficult to determine. Some of the older commentators suppose that the odorous properties of the cedar and the hyssop were intended to correct the foul smell arising from the burning entrails of the victim. But this will not apply to the scarlet wool, and therefore it is probably safer to rest in the conclusion, that for some reasons not perfectly known to us, these articles were peculiarly adapted to represent some features of the process of purification. The apostle, Heb. 9 : 19, mentions scarlet wool and hyssop as used by Moses himself, when he sprinkled the book of the covenant, etc., with the blood of the sacrifice, and therefore they may have been burnt with the ashes of the heifer, and thus mingled with the water of purification to denote their cleansing virtue. "The ashes, the hyssop, the scarlet wool, and the clear water," says Priestley, "all bore some relation to *cleansing*, and therefore were emblematical of purification. This virtue is by all the ancients ascribed to hyssop. Besides, as it consisted of small leaves, it was adapted to retain a quantity of the liquor in which it was immersed for the purpose of sprinkling. A handful of wool might be used to wipe any thing with, and the red or purple color, being costly, would make it more respected. The same instrument, viz., a bunch of hyssop tied with a red woollen thread to a stick of cedar, was also used in the ceremony of cleansing a leper, Lev. 14 : 4." It is quite possible that the three things were formed into an

scarlet, and cast *it* into the
midst of the burning of the
heifer.
7 Then the priest shall wash
his [g] clothes, and he shall bathe
his flesh in water, and afterward
he shall come into the camp,
and the priest shall be unclean
until the even.
8 And he that burneth her
shall wash his clothes in water,
and bathe his flesh in water,
and shall be unclean until the
even.
9 And a man *that is* clean

g Lev. 11. 25. 15. 5.

---

aspergillum, or instrument for sprinkling, and that this was cast into the burning mass with the typical purpose above mentioned. We have not, at any rate, any more satisfactory solution of the problem to offer.

V. 7. *The priest shall wash his clothes.* A well known sign of purification, which was prescribed also for him that burnt the heifer, v. 8, for him that gathered the ashes, v. 10, and for him that sprinkled the water of separation, v. 21. The order for a twofold bathing—of the clothes and the flesh—will be observed. Upon this Augustin remarks: "This washing of the garments and the body—what is it but the cleansing of our faculties external and internal?" Eleazar does not appear to have been employed, either in killing or burning the heifer, and yet, having touched her blood, he became unclean. It is evident from the whole, that there was no natural or necessary connection between the sprinkling of the ashes of the heifer upon a person, and the cleansing him from sin. It was simply the divine appointment that gave efficacy to the act. So far was it from being able of itself to cleanse from sin, that the very observance of the rite rendered every person unclean that was engaged in it, and laid them under a necessity of washing both their bodies and their clothes, in order to the requisite purification. All this showed clearly enough that the ordinance had in itself no purifying power, inasmuch as those who prepared for the purifying of others were themselves polluted by the preparation. It might seem strange that the same thing should pollute those that were clean, and yet purify those that were unclean. But in fact all the sacrifices which were offered for sin were looked upon as unclean, for the reason that the sins of men were putatively laid upon them, as our sins were upon Christ, who is therefore said to be "made sin for us." The suggestion seems not unreasonable, that the sin of the priests and others who procured the death of Christ is prefigured by this transaction. "All that had a hand in putting Christ to death contracted guilt thereby; his betrayer, his persecutors, his judge, his executioner, all did what they did with wicked hands, though it was 'by the determinate counsel and foreknowledge of God;' yet some of them were, and all might have been, cleansed by the virtue of that same blood which they had brought themselves under the guilt of."—*Henry.*

V. 9. *A man that is clean.* The whole being thoroughly burnt, the ashes were to be gathered up by a person who was under no legal defilement—for no unclean person must touch a sacrifice—then sifted clean, and carefully laid up in some suitable place without the camp as a permanent ingredient of the purification-water designed for cleansing all persons who had contracted the specified kind of legal defilement. As a very small quantity of the ashes would be

shall gather up the ashes [h] of the heifer, and lay *them* up without the camp in a clean place, and it shall be kept for the congregation of the children of Israel, for [i] a water of separation: it *is* a purification for sin.

10 And he that gathereth the ashes of the heifer shall

h Heb. 9 13.

i ver. 13. 20, 21. c. 31. 23.

sufficient to mingle with the water, it could be distributed thence, in after times, to any part of the nation which might have occasion for it; to which, however, an alternative supposition to this is that of Henry, who suggests that one place would serve for keeping these ashes in as long as Israel was so closely encamped; yet that afterwards, when they came to Canaan, some of them might be kept in every town, as there would be frequent occasion for the use of them. This small quantity, however, wherever kept, sufficed for the whole nation, and for many generations. The Jews say that the red heifer was killed only nine times during the entire continuance of their national polity. The durable nature of these ashes made them a fit emblem of the great and perpetual propitiation of our Lord Jesus Christ, who "offered himself once for all."——¶ *Without the camp.* To denote that they who would participate in the benefits of our Lord's death must "Go forth unto him without the camp bearing his reproach." Heb. 13 : 13. ——¶ *It shall be kept for the congregation, etc.* Heb. "It shall be to the congregation of the children of Israel for a keeping, or reservation." See a similar phraseology respecting the manna. Ex. 16 : 32, 33.——¶ *For a water of separation.* That is, water to be sprinkled for separation, or on such as are separated from the congregation on account of uncleanness. Comp. v. 13. The original term, *niddâh*, which properly signifies *separation* or *removal for uncleanness*, is sometimes figuratively used for *uncleanness* itself, which is to be done away, as 2 Chron. 29 : 5. Ezra 9 : 11, where it is rendered *filthiness.* For this reason the water which cleanses it is called *the water of separation*, rendered in the Chald. and Gr. *the water of sprinkling*, in accordance with which the blood of Christ is called *the blood of sprinkling*, Heb. 11 : 14, from its purifying the conscience from dead works. Heb. 9 : 13, 14.——¶ *It is a purification for sin.* Heb. "It is a sin." This term is often used to denote a sin-offering, or an expiatory sacrifice, and though the red heifer was not strictly such, yet it had in it something of that nature, as being possessed of a purifying property; and it may also in some sense be termed a *sin-offering*, inasmuch as the victim, like the great sin-offering on the day of atonement, was burnt without the camp, and its blood sprinkled seven times towards the sanctuary, though not shed at the altar. The word is here applied to the water which purified sin, v. 12. Gr. "It is a sanctification, or purification." These two names, applied to the "water of separation," are subsequently used by the prophet, Zech. 13 : 1, in announcing the grace of Christ in the Gospel: "In that day there shall be a fountain opened to the house of David and to the inhabitants of Jerusalem *for sin* (Heb. *lehattath*) and *for uncleanness* (Heb. *leniddah*);" i. e., for a *purification for sin* and for a water of *separation for uncleanness.*

V. 10. *Shall wash his clothes.* The case here supposed is parallel to that in

wash his clothes, and be unclean until the even: and it shall be unto the children of Israel, and unto the stranger that sojourneth among them, for a statute for ever.

11 He [k] that toucheth the dead body of any man shall be unclean seven days.

12 He [l] shall purify himself with it on the third day, and

k Lev. 21. 1. c. 5. 2. 9. 6, 10. Lam. 4. 14. Hag. 2. 13. l c. 31. 19.

Lev. 6 : 27, "When there is sprinkled of the blood thereof upon any garment, thou shalt wash that whereon it was sprinkled in the holy place." So here, he that gathered up the ashes was to wash his clothes, for some of the ashes could hardly fail to light upon him.—— ¶ *The stranger that sojourneth.* By this is meant a *proselyte,* and not any *stranger* whatever. Gr. "The proselytes that are adjoined."

V. 11. *He that toucheth the dead body of any man.* Heb. "He that toucheth the dead of any soul of man." That is, the corpse of any man. The term "soul" is used here as elsewhere for *dead body.* See Note on Lev. 19 : 28; also on Num. 6 : 6. He that touched a dead beast was unclean till the evening only of the same day; but whoever came in contact with a dead human body was to be unclean for seven days, during which time he was not allowed to come into the sanctuary, nor to touch any holy thing, nor to be in the Lord's camp, to which the city of Jerusalem corresponded in after times, and was therefore called "the holy city." Comp. Lev. 7 : 19, 21. Neh. 11 : 1, 18. Mat. 4 : 5. Usages somewhat similar are at this day not uncommon in the East. "All who attend a funeral procession, or ceremony, become *unclean,* and before they return to their houses must wash their persons and their clothes. Neither those in the sacred office, nor of any other caste, can, under these circumstances, attend to any religious ceremonies. They cannot marry, nor be present at any festivity, nor touch a sacred book. A person, on hearing of the death of a son or other relative, immediately becomes unclean. The Brahmins are unclean twelve days; those of the royal family, sixteen days; the merchants, twenty-two; and all other castes thirty-two days."—*Roberts.* The ordinance has an air of great severity when it is considered that taking care of the dead, stripping, washing, shrouding, carrying out, and burying them, was not only a pious duty to them, but a good office to the living. Yet none of these acts could be performed without contracting defilement, thus denoting that the pollutions of sin mix with and cleave to our best services. If we seek the reason why contact with a corpse was made such a defiling thing, we can only answer, that the revolting and polluting effects of natural death are due to the power of spiritual death. This works a ruin to the soul similar to that which death achieves in the body, and this enactment of the ceremonial law would have us look upon the one as the measure and representation of the other. Since the Lord's advent the power of death has been weakened, it is viewed in a new light, it is divested of its terrors, and therefore dead bodies are no more defiling. Thanks be to Him who hath enabled us to say, "O grave, where is thy victory?"

V. 12. *Shall purify himself with it.* Heb. *yith hattâ bo, shall purify himself with* or *in it.* That is, the water of separation. Chald. "He shall sprinkle." Gr. "He shall be purified." The original denotes an action that is re-

on the seventh day he shall be clean; but if he purify not himself the third day, then the seventh day he shall not be clean.

13 Whosoever toucheth the

flected back upon the agent. In its true purport it signifies to *purify from sin*, whence the Dutch Annotations render *to unsin one's self*, an nncouth but still expressive term. The remarks of Adam Clarke on this expression are worthy of notice. "*Yith hatta bo*, literally, *he shall sin himself with it.* This Hebrew form of speech is common enough among us in other matters. Thus *to fleece*, and *to skin*, do not signify to *add a fleece*, or *a skin*, but to take one away; therefore, *to sin himself*, in the Hebrew idiom, is not to *add* sin, but to take it away, *to purify*." The phraseology implies that this outward uncleanness represented the pollution of the soul by reason of sin, and the purification here commanded may in like manner have denoted "repentance from dead works," and "faith towards God," which "purifies the heart." Heb. 6:1. Acts 15:9. On a close inspection of the original, and comparing the passage with v. 19, we are constrained to doubt whether our version conveys the true sense. From that it would appear that if the unclean purified himself on the third day he would become clean on the seventh without any farther purification; but this is scarcely accordant with v. 19, which implies that he must purify himself again on the seventh day. The genuine rendering of the clause we think to be the following:—"He that shall purify himself with it, on the third day, and on the seventh day, shall be clean." The ancient versions for the most part confirm this rendering. Gr. "He shall be purified on the third, and on the seventh day, then shall he be clean: but if he be not purified on the third, and on the seventh day, he shall not be clean." Vulg. "He shall be sprinkled with this water on the third day, and on the seventh, and so shall be cleansed." Arab. "And he shall expiate himself thereby on the third day, and on the seventh, and shall be cleansed; and unless he shall have expiated himself on both these days, he shall not be cleansed." The third day's purification may be considered as pointing to the resurrection of Christ on that day, by which we are spiritually cleansed or sanctified. That on the seventh day is calculated to teach us that our purification in this life is gradual, and not perfected till we come to that eternal sabbath with which the seventh day corresponds.——¶ *But if he purify not himself the third day, etc.* Here again the rendering is to be amended to make the clause consistent with the foregoing:—"But if he purify himself on the third day and on the seventh day, he shall not be clean." This is the literal version, and the same with that given by Ainsworth, the most accurate of translators. The two clauses are evidently designed to be exactly antithetical to each other, and the rendering of the one requires to be modified to agree with v. 19, so also does the other. The days were reckoned, we may suppose, *from* the last time of his touching or coming near the dead body; for he would not begin the days of his cleansing, while he was still under a necessity of repeating the pollution; but when the dead body was buried, so that there was no further occasion of meddling with it, then he began to reckon his days. The above is the very reasonable suggestion of Henry.

V. 13. *Whosoever toucheth the dead body, etc.* The law as above given, is

dead body of any man that is
dead, and purifieth not himself,
defileth [m] the tabernacle of the
LORD: and that soul shall be
cut off from Israel: because
the water [n] of separation was
not sprinkled upon him, he shall
be unclean; his uncleanness [o] *is*
yet upon him.
14 This *is* the law when a
man dieth in a tent; All that
come into the tent, and all that
is in the tent, shall be unclean
seven days.
15 And every open vessel [p],
which hath no covering bound
upon it, *is* unclean.
16 And whosoever toucheth
one that is slain with a sword in
the open fields, or a dead body,

m Lev. 15. 31. *n* ver. 9. c. 8. 7. *o* Lev. 7. 20. 22. 3.

p Lev. 11. 32.

---

very explicit, that every Israelite who touched the dead body of a man, woman, or child, was to consider himself in a state of defilement for a whole week, and could be cleansed in no other way than by being sprinkled with this sacred water, which was to be done twice, viz. upon the third, and again upon the seventh day; nor could he be restored if he omitted either of these sprinklings. In the present verse it is enacted that if any person whatever, thus defiled, should presume knowingly and wilfully to approach the Tabernacle—and so the Temple afterwards—till he were duly cleansed, he should be sentenced to death as a profaner of God's worship. The subsequent application of the purifying water should have no effect to avert the threatened penalty. This is clearly the import of "defiling the tabernacle of the Lord;" and penetrating beyond the letter to the spirit, it is easy to perceive a new emphasis in the apostolic declaration:—"If any man defile the temple of God, him shall God destroy; for the temple of God is holy, which temple are ye." A person who allows himself in any corrupting course of conduct, whereby his body as well as his soul is injured, is so far guilty of defiling the Lord's tabernacle or temple.——¶ *That soul shall be cut off from Israel.* Chald. "That man shall be destroyed;" implying of course that he came presumptuously; otherwise, as for instance if it were done ignorantly, he was to bring a sacrifice. Lev. 5:3–6, 17, 18.

V. 14. *When a man dieth in a tent.* Tents were their habitations in the wilderness when this law was delivered. But the inference is fair that the same ordinance was to hold good when they came to live in houses at a subsequent period; although Michaelis thinks we are not authorized to extend the inference any farther than to the *apartment* in which the death might occur.——¶ *All that come into the tent, etc.* That is, every person coming into the tent while the dead body lay there, or before the tent was purified, as well as they who were in it when the person died, should be rendered unclean. In like manner all the goods or furniture, especially vessels, were made unclean, except those that were covered, so as not to be exposed to the polluting effect of the atmosphere.

V. 16. *One slain with a sword in the open fields, etc.* Heb. "In the face of the field," that is, in the open field, where there was no tent, and where pollution could be contracted only by touching.——¶ *Slain with a sword.* Or with any other instrument by which a violent death might be inflicted. Comp. Num. 31:19.——¶ *Or a dead body.* That is, the body of one not

or a bone of a man, or a grave, shall be unclean seven days.

17 And for an unclean *person* they shall take of the ashes of the burnt heifer of purification for sin, and running water shall be put thereto in a vessel;

slain by violence, but who falls down dead by apoplexy, or any other sudden stroke. Vulg. "The corpse of a man that was slain, or that died of himself."——¶ *A bone of a man.* A bone taken out of a grave, or lying unburied on the surface of the earth. It is probably in allusion to the defiling effect of dead men's bones that the order is given by the prophet, Ezek. 39:15, "And the passengers that pass through the land, when any seeth a man's bone, then shall he set up a sign by it, till the buriers have buried it in the valley of Hamon-gog." The Hebrew writers say that the blood also of a dead man defiles as does the corpse itself, but as long as life remains it is clean.——¶ *Or a grave.* In which the dead have been deposited, and which has thence acquired a communicable defilement. The natural effect of this law would be to oblige the Israelites to keep the abodes of the dead at a considerable distance from those of the living. They could never, therefore, have knowingly built houses or cities on sepulchral grounds; indeed, as a matter of fact, we learn that their burying-places were always without the precincts of their towns. Consequently, it is said of the dead, that they were "carried out," i. e. carried out, not only of the house, but of the village or city, to the neighboring cemetery. The remarks of Michaelis in this connection (*Laws of Moses*, § 215) are very apropos:—"With us, on the contrary, in our very churches, to the great injury of men's health and lives, there are often burial-places; a practice first introduced from superstition, and still kept up from pride, fashion, and avarice. How important this effect of the law must have been, may be judged from the consequences of our contrary practice of thus burying in churches. The graves frequently emit very noxious *effluvia*, particularly when imperfectly covered, or when the water runs through them. On other occasions, the mischief is more insidious and slow in its progress, and does not betray itself by the smell; but still the diseases of the dead infect the living; for infection bursts forth at once with increased violence when graves are opened, and begin to emit the poisonous vapors that have been long pent up in them." The same effects are liable to follow from converting church-yards into burying-grounds, which practice, however, is now happily being more and more done away. All the different contacts here mentioned put an Israelite under a condition of legal impurity for a week's time. This was a species of ceremonial quarantine prescribed with a view to show the effects of that internal moral or spiritual pollution which is so destructive in its own nature to one's own soul, and so charged with contagious influence towards others.

V. 17. *And for an unclean (person) they shall take, etc.* That is, there shall be taken by some clean person in order to the purifying of one unclean.——¶ *Of the ashes of the burnt heifer for the purification of sin.* Heb. "Of the dust of the burning of the sin." The rendering of the established version, though sufficiently correct as to the sense, is quite paraphrastic. The ashes of the burnt heifer are here called *'hatta, sin*, which shows that they had in them the virtue of a sin-offering, v. 9.——¶ *Running water shall be put thereto.*

18 And a clean person shall take hyssop[q], and dip *it* in the water, and sprinkle *it* upon the tent, and upon all the vessels, and upon the persons that were there, and upon him that touched a bone, or one slain, or one dead, or a grave:
19 And the clean *person* shall sprinkle upon the unclean on the third day, and on the seventh day; and on[r] the seventh day he shall purify himself, and wash his clothes, and bathe himself in water, and shall be clean at even.
20 But the man that shall be unclean, and shall not purify himself, that soul shall be cut off from among the congregation,

q Ps. 51. 7.

r Lev. 14. 9.

Heb. "Living water." See Notes on Gen. 26:19. Lev. 14:5. Chald. "Springing, or welling water."

V. 18. *A clean person shall take hyssop.* By which is not necessarily meant a priest, but any person legally clean, as any such person might slay the heifer and burn her. Yet it is to be presumed that this office was generally performed by a priest, Lev. 13. Of the use of hyssop in sprinklings, see Lev. 14:4, 6, 7, 49, 50. The tent and its contents, both animate and inanimate, were to be thus sprinkled to purify them from the taint communicated.

V. 19. *The clean person shall sprinkle, etc.* This explains more distinctly what was rather obscurely delivered, v. 12. Patrick suggests that the term "unclean" in this connection embraces both persons and things; but the original, being in the singular, would seem to imply more properly persons only. ——¶ *On the seventh day he shall purify himself.* The true interpretation of this clause is not altogether obvious. The original phrase rendered "shall purify himself" is *'hitteo, shall purify him,* whereas the Hebrew for *purify himself* is uniformly *yithhattâ*, in the Hithpael or reflexive form. We would propose the following therefore as the genuine rendering of the verse: "And the clean (person) shall sprinkle upon the unclean on the third day, and on the seventh day: and he shall (fully and effectually) purify him on the seventh day; and he (the purified) shall wash his clothes, and bathe himself in water, and shall be clean at even." We submit this rendering to the judgment of those who are competent to decide upon its probability. It rests mainly upon the fact, that the original term, in the Pict form, nowhere else in the whole Scripture has any other than an active and transitive signification. We find also that Vatablus gives this rendering, and scarce any biblical authority weighs with us higher than his. Of the ancient versions the Gr. and the Vulg. conform rather to the established English; but the Chald., Syr., Sam., and Arab. expressly confirm our proposed rendering, of which, however, we were not aware till we had settled in our own minds upon what we regard as the true sense.

V. 20. *The man that shall be unclean, etc.* The standing law on the subject of defilements is, that every person or thing coming in contact with a dead body becomes unclean for a day. Even the person that purifies with the sacred water one thus defiled comes into the same condition for that day; and whatever Israelite, rendered impure by such contacts, should presumptuously approach the public worship of the sanctuary, before being cleansed in the

because he hath defiled [s] the sanctuary of the LORD: the water of separation hath not been sprinkled upon him; he *is* unclean.

21 And it shall be a perpetual statute unto them, that he that sprinkleth the water of separation shall wash his clothes; and he that toucheth the water of separation shall be unclean until even.

22 And whatsoever [t] the unclean *person* toucheth shall be unclean; and [u] the soul that toucheth *it* shall be unclean until even.

CHAPTER XX.

THEN [a] came the children of Israel, *even* the whole con-

s ver. 13. t Hag. 2. 13. u Lev. 15. 5. a c. 33. 36.

---

manner here prescribed, was to be summarily cut off as a contemner of a sacred rite instituted by the Lord himself, and replete with a divine significancy.——¶ *Hath defiled the sanctuary of the Lord.* By coming into it without the due purification; for if such were shut out of the camp, ch. 5 : 2, how much more out of the sanctuary? Accordingly, at a later period, 2 Chron. 23 : 19, porters were stationed at the gates of the temple, "that none which was unclean in any thing should enter in."

V. 21. *Shall wash his clothes.* Being accounted unclean simply from having had to do with the water of separation, which had a contrary effect upon the clean and the unclean, purifying the one and defiling the other, just as the heat of the sun melts wax and hardens clay.——¶ *Shall be unclean until even.* That his clothes were also to be washed may be fairly inferred from what goes before. The Jewish writers say that uncleanness till evening is implied in the former clause of the verse, and the washing of the garments in the latter, though not expressed. It is obvious that the mere staying *till even* could have no purifying effect without some rite of cleansing.

V. 22. *And whatsoever.* Heb. *kol, all,* i. e., whatsoever or whomsoever, implying both persons and things.——¶ *The unclean.* By this is not meant the person made unclean by touching the purification-water, but the primary unclean person spoken of all along in this chapter; the person who was defiled by touching a dead body.——¶ *The soul that toucheth (it) shall be unclean until even.* In the case of the one, the uncleanness was to continue for seven days, and in that of the other, only till evening of the same day. It is to be observed that, not only he whom the unclean person touched, but he also who touched the unclean, whether person or thing, became unclean till evening, and was required to wash his clothes for his cleansing.

CHAPTER XX.

Arrival the Second Time at Kadesh.

V. 1. *Then came the children of Israel, etc.* In point of chronology we pass over a wide chasm in making the transition from the preceding to the present chapter. No less than thirty-eight years elapsed between their first and second arrival at Kadesh, for with Kitto we take it that there was but one place of that name, although this supposition requires that the generally received location of Kadesh be changed to a point considerably farther south. But, on this head, we must refer the reader

gregation, into the desert of Zin in the first month: and the people

to the various authorities which treat at length of the topographical argument, as we prefer to devote our space to other departments of elucidation. We will give, however, the pith of Mr. Kitto's remarks upon the subject, with the intimation, that in his extended note on the present passage in the "Pictorial Bible," and in the article "Kadesh," in his "Biblical Cyclopædia," will be found condensed the substance of all that is most valuable on the subject. "We conclude that there is but one Kadesh mentioned in Scripture; and that the difficulties which have seemed to require that there should be a second, or even a third, place of this name, may be easily and effectually obviated by altering the position commonly assigned to Kadesh-Barnea—that is, the Kadesh from which the spies were sent in the fifteenth ch., and from which the desert wanderings commenced. We are at perfect liberty to make such alteration, because nothing whatever is distinctly known of such a place, and its position has been entirely fixed according to conjectural probability. But being once fixed, it has generally been received and reasoned upon as a truth; and it has been thought better to create another Kadesh, to meet the difficulties which this location occasioned, than to disturb old maps and old topographical doctrines. Kadesh is usually placed within or close upon the southern frontier of Palestine, and about midway between the Mediterranean and the Dead Sea. This location would seem in itself improbable, without any strong counter reasons; for we do not find that a hostile people, when not prepared for immediate action, confront themselves directly with their enemies, but encamp at some considerable distance, and send scouts and spies to reconnoitre the country; nor is it by any means likely that they would have remained so long at Kadesh, as they seem to have done at their first visit, if they had been in the very face of their enemies, as they must have been in the assigned position. We should, therefore, on this ground alone, be inclined to place Kadesh more to the south or south-east than this. Besides, if this were Kadesh, how could it be described as on the border of Edom, since the Edomites did not, till some centuries later, occupy the country to the south of Canaan, and were at this time confined to the region of Seir? Moreover, from a Kadesh so far north, they were not likely to send to the king without moving down towards the place where they hoped to obtain permission to cross Mount Seir; particularly as, by so moving, they would at the same time be making progress towards the point which the refusal of the Edomites would oblige them to pass, and which they actually did pass. Therefore, the stay of the host at Kadesh, waiting for the king's answer, seems to imply that Kadesh was so near as not to make it worth their while to move till they knew the result of their application to him. Further, we read in ch. 33:36, after an enumeration of distances of evidently no very great length, that in the present instance the removal to Kadesh was from Ezion-geber at the head of the Gulf of Akaba, the distance between which and the Kadesh of the map is about one hundred and twenty miles; and this is the consideration which has chiefly influenced those who determined that there must have been two places of this name; and we must confess that, while thinking over the other reasons we have stated, we were inclined to consider them as leading to that conclu-

abode in Kadesh; and [b] Miriam died there, and was buried there.

b Ex. 15. 20.

sion, and that the second Kadesh must have been very near Mount Hor. . . . But we think all difficulties are sufficiently met by placing the single Kadesh neither close to the border of Canaan nor close to Mount Hor, but at a middle point between them, on the western border of the Wady-el-Ghor, which is the northern half of the Desert of Zin—say in or about lat. 30° 5′, at nearly an equal distance between Mount Hor and the Kadesh-Barnea of the maps. This spot will be on or in the Desert of Zin, not too near to Canaan, nor too distant for Mount Hor and the capital of Edom."—*Pict. Bible.* At this place, then, we find the Israelites re-encamped, after the lapse of thirty-eight years from the time it had been occupied by their fathers, when just upon the point of invading Canaan. Of the events which had occurred in that time no record is left, though eighteen stations are recited in ch. 33, at which they halted and remained for a longer or shorter time. It is no doubt the popular impression that they roved about in a compact mass, without any special employment or object, except to be kept out of Canaan; and were miraculously supplied with food from heaven, until all above twenty years of age, when they came out of Egypt, had been gradually wasted away, and an entirely new generation had come up in their place. But we think it may justly be doubted whether this impression is correct. We question whether there was any thing more vague and objectless in their mode of life than distinguishes nomade races in general. The region over which they wandered is indeed termed a "desert," or "wilderness," but it was not such in our idea of the term, but simply a tract of unclaimed country, destitute for the most part of settled habitations, though still marked by numerous posts, villages, and cities, of which the names of several that lay in the track of the Israelites are expressly given, ch. 33:16–36. The country called Arabia is believed even now to sustain a population of at least eight or ten millions. It is in many parts abundantly fertile in wheat, millet, rice, and a great variety of vegetables and fruits, and this holds more especially of the tract round about Mount Sinai and the region termed "El Ghor." From a remote antiquity even down to the present day these tracts have been traversed by the Bedouin tribes, whose manner of life exhibits no doubt a very correct image of that of the Israelites during their wanderings there. With their herds and beasts of burden, these unsettled hordes pass from place to place as led by the prospect of water and pasture; being entire strangers to the arts, objects, and employments of civilized life. The previous habits of the Israelites, not only in Egypt but in Canaan, made it easy for them to fall into the nomadic life, and we suppose they did, in fact, *become inhabitants of the desert for the time being*, though still enjoying the tokens of the divine presence and guidance, and distinguished by their prerogatives, rites, and institutions from all other people. In this capacity they would naturally change their locality from time to time, like the Bedouins of all ages, but still cherishing the hope of eventually becoming possessors of the land of promise. Meantime they are not to be conceived as dwelling, in their intervals of repose, in a compact camp, which the nature of the country forbade to such an immense multitude, amounting to a population half as large again as that of the city of London, but as expatiating in bands, here and there, over the adjacent country, still having the Tabernacle as the centre and the rendezvous to which they would return. It is at least certain, that we must not attribute to the sons of Israel our own ideas of living or journeying, for every thing with them was formed on a different model from what it is with us. A very important process of discipline was to be accomplished by their abode in the desert, which could be effected nowhere else, and as it had been foretold that the far greater portion of the congregation should be consumed before entering the land of promise, the divine Providence so ordered things that a long series of years should be consumed in bringing about the designed results. It is to be borne in mind, therefore, that the congregation, at this time, was composed of the children of the generation that had come out of Egypt, their fathers having, one after another, dropped off, though the events recorded in the present chapter show that the perverse spirit of the fathers still lived in the bosoms of their descendants, and that the deeds of their fathers they would do.——¶ *(Even) the whole congregation.* However they had hitherto become separated into roaming or straggling detachments, yet now they all came in one solid compact mass into the desert of Zin, and the station of Kadesh, which they had left upwards of thirty-eight years before. They came hither at this time from Ezion-geber, which is a port on the "shore of the Red Sea," as we learn from 1 Kings 9 : 26. This part of their wandering is also thus alluded to by Jephthah, Judg. 11 : 16, "But when Israel came up from Egypt, and walked through the wilderness unto the Red Sea, and came to Kadesh, etc."——¶ *Into the desert of Zin.* This is a region of the peninsula, quite different from that called, Ex. 16 : 1, by nearly the same name (Sin), which was in the immediate vicinity of the Red Sea, while this lay on the confines of Edom (Idumea). Its precise locality is to be fixed by the considerations that determine the site of Kadesh, on which see Note above. Between Hazeroth, Num. 12 : 16, and the portion of the wilderness of Zin, in which they were now encamped, there had occurred eighteen stations, as enumerated ch. 33 : 18–36.——¶ *In the first month.* That is, of the fortieth year after they had left the land of Egypt, as appears from Num. 33 : 38, compared with v. 28 of this ch., and Deut. 2 : 1–7. This, therefore, was the last year of Israel's sojourn in the wilderness, and during the course of it Miriam, Aaron, and Moses, all died. ——¶ *And the people abode in Kadesh.* The time of their stay in this place it appears, from comparing ch. 33 : 38, was about four months, as on the first day of the fifth month Aaron died at Mount Hor, whither they had previously removed.——¶ *Miriam died.* Heb. *Mir-yâm, bitterness.* Gr. *Mariam.* Josephus, *Mariamne.* She was the sister of Moses and Aaron, and supposed to be the same that watched her infant brother when exposed on the Nile; in which case she was probably ten or twelve years old at the time, Ex. 2 : 4, sq. When the Israelites left Egypt she naturally became the leading woman among them, and therefore it is written, Mic. 6 : 4, "I sent before thee Moses, and Aaron, and Miriam." She is called "a prophetess," Ex. 15 : 20, and after the passage of the Red Sea she led the music, dance, and song, with which the women celebrated their deliverance. She died and was buried at the station Kadesh, four months before her brother Aaron, and eleven months before Moses; and Eusebius says that

2 And [c] there was no water for the congregation: and [d] they gathered themselves together against Moses and against Aaron.

c Ex. 17. 1, etc. d c. 16. 42.

her sepulchre was to be seen there in his day. She was probably near a hundred and thirty years old.

The People Murmur for Water. The Sin of Moses.

V. 2. *There was no water.* This most necessary gift of divine Providence was withheld from the people for a little season during their abode in this place; probably as a trial of their faith, and that it might be known whether the present generation resembled their fathers, who had perished in the wilderness. The event showed that their moral paternity was as unquestionable as their natural. Bp. Patrick and several of the elder commentators suppose that hitherto the host of Israel had been supplied with water from the stream that had continued to flow from the rock Rephidim, formerly smitten by Moses, and which had followed them during all their forty years' sojourn in the wilderness, Ex. 17 : 4. But this we must regard as a mere idle Rabbinical conceit, unsustained by any authority whatever. The apostle says, indeed, 1 Cor. 10 : 4, that "they drank of that spiritual Rock that followed them: and that Rock was Christ;" but this surely refers not to a supply of literal or natural water. A spiritual rock must give forth spiritual water, and as the rock is expressly said to have been Christ, the water must have been the communication of his Holy Spirit, constituting their spiritual drink. The note of Bloomfield on this passage of the apostle is very clear and satisfactory. "The meaning is, that Christ, who is typified by that rock, every where accompanied and went with them, supplying (spiritual) water miraculously furnished; which, as it never failed them, might be said popularly to *follow* them, as Christ who supplied it did." The general sense is, says Mr. Holden, that "the Israelites had the same spiritual advantages and privileges offered to them *typically*, which are offered to us really." The congregation were no doubt supplied with water from such springs as they met with in their journeyings. At the present day, water, though not plenty in the Arabian desert, still is by no means utterly wanting, and the inhabitants, with their cattle and flocks, are continually passing over it from place to place. We have no intimation that water, like their food, was usually furnished to the Israelites miraculously. At the spot where they were now encamped there was, for some reason, a scarcity, although we read of nothing of the kind on the former occasion, when they were there. But the wells and fountains of the East have not always a constant supply of water.——¶ *They gathered themselves together against Moses and against Aaron.* As the fathers, under a similar destitution, rebelled against their leaders at Rephidim, so do the children here; as the fathers then "chode" with Moses and murmured at his bringing them out of Egypt, so did the children here; as Moses then cried unto the Lord by reason of the outrage of the people, so he and Aaron here fall down before the Lord; as the Lord then promised and gave them water out of the rock, so also here; and so in regard to the rod, the manifestation of the divine glory and other points, the coincidences in the two cases are very striking. The present was a new outbreak of that characteristic perversity, which though

3 And the people chode with Moses, and spake, saying, Would [e] God that we had died when our brethren died before the LORD!

4 And why have ye brought up the congregation of the

[e] c. 14. 2, etc.

---

occasionally suppressed by severe judgments, seems never to have been effectually subdued. But while they thus proved themselves the children of their fathers, we should not forget that our waywardness proves equally that we are *their* children in moral relationship, and that the deeds of our fathers we continue to do.

V. 3. *And the people chode with Moses.* Heb. *yâreb*, *contended*, from a root signifying to *strive*, *contend*, *litigate*, especially by bitter and reproachful words. Gr. "The people reviled Moses." At a season like this, when he might more justly have looked for their sympathy and condolence, he is beset and aggrieved by reproaches and accusations for which he had given not the least occasion.——¶ *Would God that we had died, etc.* Heb. "Oh, that we had given up the ghost (expired) in our brethren's giving up the ghost (expiring) before the Lord." Gr. "Oh, that we had perished in the destruction of our brethren before the Lord." It is not unlikely that they refer to the plague, the destructive ravages of which are mentioned, ch. 16 : 49, and which, above other judgments, is supposed to come more immediately from the hand of the Lord, as appears from the language of David, 2 Sam. 24 : 14, 15. They preferred this to perishing by hunger and thirst, which would seem to be countenanced by the words of the prophet, Lam. 4 : 9, "They that be slain with the sword are better than they that be slain with hunger: for these pine away stricken through for want of the fruits of the field." For this reason, it is supposed, that they employ the term for *giving up the ghost* as implying an easier kind of death than that by the sword, or hunger, or thirst, or death by any other violent means. The Hebrew writers explain the original for *giving up the ghost* to denote a death without pain or protracted sickness. It is evident that in the simple sensation of thirst there was no sin, but in the language in which they gave vent to their impatience there was great and grievous sin against God, as well as gross ingratitude in view of past mercies. They wish they had died with the seditious band of rebels who had conspired against God, and whom yet here they dignify with the name of "brethren." Now surely as one can die but once, the death would have been substantially the same whether they died on account of a failure of springs of water or by being smitten down by pestilence. But it was base ingratitude for men who had frequently experienced such signal deliverances at the hands of the Lord thus to murmur against Him, in upbraiding his servants, because their wants were not immediately supplied. Yet thus it is that "the foolishness of man perverteth his way, and his heart fretteth against the Lord."

V. 4. *Why have ye brought up, etc.* Vulg. "Why have ye brought out the church of the Lord into the wilderness, etc." They proceed to expostulate with Moses for bringing them out of the land of Egypt, which they would fain represent as stocked with every luxury, into a wilderness, dry, barren, and desolate; as though Moses and Aaron had acted in this matter from their own impulse without divine direction.——¶ *That we*

Lord into this wilderness, that we and our cattle should die there?

5 And wherefore have ye made us to come up out of Egypt, to bring us in unto this evil place? it[f] *is* no place of seed, or of figs, or of vines, or of pomegranates; neither *is* there any water to drink.

6 And Moses and Aaron went from the presence of the assembly unto the door of the tabernacle of the congregation, and they fell upon their faces; and the glory of the Lord appeared unto them.

7 And the Lord spake unto Moses, saying,

8 Take the rod, and gather thou the assembly together, thou and Aaron thy brother, and speak ye unto the rock before

f c. 16. 14.

---

and our cattle should die there. Gr. "To kill us and our children."

V. 5. *It is no place of seed, or of figs, etc.* No place in which to sow seeds, to plant vines or fig-trees, or any thing of the kind. On the contrary, they had been led into a wilderness which was "a land of deserts and of pits, a land of drought, and of the shadow of death, a land that no man passed through, and where no man dwelt."

V. 6. *And Moses and Aaron went, etc.* Instead of turning upon the people in a recriminating tone, and denouncing divine judgments against them, they have immediate recourse to the appointed meeting-place, where the Lord was to be sought, and there humbly prostrate themselves before his face, deprecating the displeasure which the murmurings of Israel had provoked. So striking was the contrast between the conduct of the leaders and the conduct of the led! The people sinned; but Moses and Aaron prayed. These saviours of Israel, these typical daysmen between Israel and their God, now stand in the breach, as they had often done before, and avert the due penalty. Happy for the congregation that the Lord had not left the camp, or Moses and Aaron ceased their functions!——¶ *The glory of the Lord appeared unto them.* This phenomenon in the cloudy pillar had often occurred before on special emergencies, as a token of the Lord's special presence, of his cognizance of what was transpiring, and of his purpose in some way to interpose in vindication of his own glory. See Notes on Ex. 16:10. Num. 14:10. 16:19, 42.

V. 8. *Take the rod, etc.* Doubtless the same rod with which he had wrought the miracles in Egypt, and by which the rock of Rephidim had been smitten on a former occasion. Some expositors favor the idea of its being the rod that budded and blossomed, from the fact that it is said to have been taken "from before the Lord," or out of the tabernacle, where it appears, from ch. 17:10, that Aaron's rod was laid up as a testimony. But the presumption is that the rod of Moses, the instrument of such signal displays of the divine power, was also carefully preserved within the precincts of the Tabernacle, and ready to be employed whenever the fit occasion should occur. In v. 11, it is called "his" rod, and although the matter will always be subject to doubt, yet the congruity of circumstances determines us to the adoption of the opinion above expressed.——¶ *Speak ye unto the rock before their eyes.* Here, indeed, we read no express command to smite the rock, but simply to take the rod in hand

their eyes; and it shall give
forth his water, and thou shalt
bring forth to them water out
of the rock[g]: so thou shalt
give the congregation and their
beasts drink.
9 And Moses took the rod
from before the LORD, as he
commanded him.
10 And Moses and Aaron
gathered the congregation together
before the rock: and he
said unto them, Hear now, ye
rebels[h]; must we fetch you
water out of this rock?

g ver. 11. Neh. 9. 15. Ps. 78. 15, 16. 105. 41. 114. 8. Is. 43. 20. 48. 21.

h Ps. 106. 33.

---

as a symbol of the divine power, and then to address the rock; but as it is difficult to conjecture for what purpose the rod was to be taken unless it was to be used, the presumption is that it *was* intended to be used either in smiting or waving, in conjunction with the words to be uttered. Yet as it is evident that Moses sinned in some way in the transaction, the precise nature of his offence will be considered in the ensuing note.

V. 10. *Hear now, ye rebels.* Hitherto, in following the march of Israel through the wilderness, we have been called to deplore the iniquity of the *people.* The scene, in a single instance, is now changed; and, instead of regarding the *rulers* of the host as men "more sinned against than sinning," we behold Moses and Aaron, the prophet and the priest, overpowered by temptation and falling into sin. "Hear now, ye rebels." No such language of rebuke entered into the commission with which Moses was now intrusted, and therefore it was wholly unwarranted. He was commanded to speak to the rock, and not to the people; and though they undoubtedly deserved censure, and were acting the part of rebels, yet it was not his duty now to upbraid them therewith. His reproachful appellation did not belie them, but it was unworthy of him, and injurious to his spiritual state. The words evince an undue excitement, impatience, irritation, and indignation in one form where, as a pattern of meekness, we had a right to expect rather a calm dignity and placid confidence in God than a tone of rashness and petulance.——¶ *Must we fetch water out of this rock?* Heb. "Shall we from this rock bring forth water for you?" It is evident from what follows that some degree of sinful doubt and distrust is couched in this language; and this sense is not badly conveyed by the paraphrase of Bp. Hall: "Hear now, ye rebels; Is it likely that we shall fetch water out of this hard rock to satisfy your thirst? This we are required to do; but is this a thing possible to be done?" The use of the word "must," in our version, does not seem warranted by the original, and conveys a shade of meaning which obscures the genuine import of the passage. As it now reads, the main implication is that of a kind of arrogant self-sufficiency, as if *they*, by some power or virtue of their own, were to perform the miracle. This, we apprehend, would be doing injustice to Moses and Aaron, although their proceeding was not free from blame. They did not probably so much claim the ability to bring forth water themselves, as cherish a doubt whether the Lord would do it in behalf of such gross offenders. Therefore they speak distrustfully, and they may have discovered in other ways an uncertainty in their own minds whether water would come forth or not. This was a prominent part of the offence which they soon learned

11 And Moses lifted up his hand, and with his rod he smote the rock twice: and the [i] water came out abundantly: and the congregation drank, and their beasts *also*.

12 And the LORD spake unto Moses and Aaron, Because [k] ye

i Ex. 17. 6. Deut. 8. 15. 1 Cor. 10. 4.

k c. 27. 14. Deut. 3. 26. 32. 51.

was to cost them so dear. Vulg. "He said to them, Hear, ye rebellious and incredulous, can we bring you forth water out of this rock?"

V. 11. *Smote the rock twice.* Showing hereby the passionate excitement to which he was wrought up. He was not expressly commanded to smite the rock even once; yet he does it twice.

V. 12. *Because ye believed me not, to sanctify me, etc.* Chald. "Ye believed not in my Word." That is, ye have not believed in me with that practical faith which would have led you to sanctify, or, in other words, to honor and glorify me in the eyes of this people. To this sense inclines the Arab. "In like manner as ye have not made them to believe in *me*, nor have sanctified me before the sons of Israel, so I also will not introduce this rabble into the region promised them." Moses alone is spoken of in this transaction, although it is evident that Aaron is regarded as sharing the blame. He was present, and, considering the office he bore, sanctioned by his silence whatever was wrong in the proceedings of Moses. On such an occasion it behooved him to speak if a wrong against the Lord's honor were committed, as there plainly was. This, their sin, is therefore called a "rebellion against the mouth of the Lord," Num. 27 : 14, and a "transgression" or "trespass," Deut. 32 : 51, which word, the Jewish writers remark, properly implies *falsity*, as in Lev. 6 : 2, it is joined with *false-denial*, and John says, 1 John 5 : 10, "He that believeth not God hath made him a liar." The unbelief here charged upon Moses and Aaron was not, we suppose, so much a positive mental incredulity settled and cherished in their own minds in regard to the divine power and goodness, as a temporary wavering growing out of the heat and perturbation of spirit which the conduct of the multitude had excited. They consequently failed to *act* in their usual consistent and obedient manner, and failing in this, they failed to produce the proper impression upon the minds of the people, of fear and reverence towards the God of Israel. It is, however, to be remarked, that the real character of the sin of Moses and Aaron on this occasion has been a matter of much debate among the learned. Our most definite information respecting it is contained, Ps. 106 : 32, 33, "They angered him also at the waters of strife, so that it went ill with Moses for their sakes: because they provoked his spirit, so that he spake unadvisedly with his lips." Here it is obvious that the precise transgression charged upon Moses is provocation of spirit and "speaking unadvisedly with his lips." It is not so much any thing that he *did*, as what he *said*, and the *spirit* from which he said it. We are inclined, therefore, with Saurin (*Dissert.* 62d), not to place the main offence in the striking of the rock, though he doubtless erred in striking it *twice*, but in the impatient and exasperated state of mind under which he acted, and in the corresponding rash and intemperate language which he uttered. It was not a *cordial* and *punctilious* obedience which he rendered to the divine

believed me not, to sanctify *l* me in the eyes of the children of Israel, therefore ye shall not

l Lev. 10. 3. Ezek. 36. 23. 1 Pet. 3. 15.

command. Consequently, he failed to "sanctify the Lord of hosts" in the eyes of the people, i. e., to act in such a manner in their presence as to impress upon them the idea that He was to be exactly obeyed in every injunction and the most implicit faith reposed in his word. This, therefore, was an aggravated offence on the part of Moses and Aaron. They should have remembered that Nadab and Abihu had been devoured by fire before the Lord for irreverently offering common fire in their censers, instead of the fire that was burning on the altar; and that the Lord had said on that occasion, "I will be sanctified in them that come nigh unto me, and before all the people will I be glorified," Lev. 10:3, on which see Note. The remarks of Calvin, in this connection, are confirmatory of the view now suggested. "If it be asked in what respect Moses transgressed, the origin of his transgression was unbelief, for it is not allowable, when this particular form of sin is specified in the answer of God, to imagine that it was any thing else. In asking whether he should fetch water out of the rock, he seems to reject as impossible and absurd what God had promised to do. He inquires whether he shall fetch water out of the rock, whereas he ought to have recollected that this had already (on a former occasion) been granted him. It became him, then, confidently to assert that God had again promised the same thing, rather than to speak with hesitation. Others think that he sinned, because he was not contented with a single blow, but smote the rock twice. And this did arise, perhaps, from distrust. But the origin of the fault was, that he did not simply embrace God's promise, and strenuously discharge the duty assigned to him as an evidence of his faith. Although, therefore, his smiting the rock twice might have been a token of his want of confidence, still it was only an aggravation of the evil, and not its origin or cause. Thus, then, we must always come back to this, that Moses did not give God the glory, because he rather considered what the people had deserved, than estimated the power of God according to his word."—*Harm. of Pent.*——¶ *Therefore ye shall not bring, etc.* To the judgment of human reason this might appear, perhaps, to have been a sentence of undue severity. Considering that these venerable men had been for forty years faithful and indefatigable in the Lord's service, and that this was, in respect to Moses at least, the first open offence of which they were guilty, we should have hoped that they might have been spared the heavy punishment now denounced. Shall one apparently venial offence avail to exclude them hopelessly from the land of promise, to which they had looked forward with such ardent desire and assured expectation? But we are soon silenced with the unanswerable question, "Shall not the Judge of all the earth do right?" We are very incompetent to determine what it becomes the Divine Majesty to do. But we learn elsewhere in the Word that the Lord marks with especial severity the sins of those who in knowledge, official station, and high prerogative, are elevated to a rank nearest himself, and deals with them according to their greater responsibility. "Because you only have I known of all the nations of the earth, therefore will I punish your iniquities." Whoever may escape, the Lord will not fail to punish the provocations of his

bring this congregation into the land which I have given them.

13 This *is* the water of Meribah; because the children of

own "near ones," his own servants and children. We do not learn that Moses and Aaron, for their conduct on this occasion, were shut out of the kingdom of heaven; but they were debarred from entering into the land of Canaan, which represented heaven, and were thus called to suffer an affliction and a grievance which weighed very heavily upon them. This is evident from the manner in which Moses speaks of it in Deut. 3 : 23–27, "And I besought the Lord at that time, saying, O Lord God, thou hast begun to show thy servant thy greatness and thy mighty hand: for what God is there in heaven or in earth that can do according to thy works, and according to thy might? I pray thee, let me go over and see the good land that is beyond Jordan, that goodly mountain, and Lebanon. But the Lord was wroth with me for your sakes, and would not hear me: and the Lord said unto me, Let it suffice thee; speak no more unto me of this matter. Get thee up into the top of Pisgah, and lift up thine eyes westward, and northward, and southward, and eastward, and behold it with thine eyes: for thou shalt not go over this Jordan." And according to the sentence so was the execution, as Aaron died shortly after in Mount Hor, and Moses on Mount Nebo, after having surveyed the country with his eyes. Thus was fulfilled the words of the Psalmist in regard to Moses and Aaron, Ps. 99: "Thou wast a God who forgavest them, though thou tookest vengeance of their inventions." Probably, however, we are not to look upon this dispensation wholly in the light of a judgment. One of the ancient fathers suggests that had Moses lived to conduct the people into the promised land, and triumphantly to establish them in it, his memory might have been so cherished by his countrymen that it might have led them at last to a species of deification. To this we may add the typical considerations, which no doubt availed in the divine counsels. Moses represented the law, or the Levitical system, which is of itself unable to bring the soul into the kingdom of heaven, inasmuch as by its deeds shall no flesh be justified. Its function is to lead the soul, in its preliminary desert wanderings, before it reaches the place of the heavenly Canaan entered by regeneration. It was fitting, therefore, that Moses, the representative of the law, should give way to a successor in office whose typical functions should more nearly accord with the facts shadowed forth. Joshua, therefore, called "Jesus," Acts 7 : 47. Heb. 4 : 8, was appointed for the purpose, and he, as a lively type of Christ, supplied Moses' "lack of service" in this respect.

V. 13. *This is the water of Meribah.* Heb. "This is the water of strife, contention, or altercation." Gr. "Of contradiction." The same name, originating in the same cause, had been previously bestowed upon the locality of Rephidim, where the former miracle had occurred, Ex. 17 : 7. But this place is sufficiently distinguished from that, being called, Deut. 32 : 51, "The waters of Meribah-Kadesh in the wilderness of Zin." It may be remarked, however, that Hengstenberg, in replying to some of the German critics who would maintain the identity of the transaction recorded here and in Ex. 17, denies that Meribah, in this connection, is to be considered as a proper name, but should be simply rendered, "These are the waters of strife." "The assertion is false, that the place received both times the same

Israel strove with the LORD, and he was sanctified [m] in them.

m Ezek. 20. 41.

14 And [n] Moses sent messengers from Kadesh unto the king

n Judg. 11. 16, 17.

name. The first place obtained the names of Massah and Meribah; the second those of Kadesh and En Mishpat, Gen. 14:7. The occasion of the error lies in Num. 20:13, 'This is the *water of strife* (*më meribah*), because the children of Israel *strove* (*râbu*) with the Lord, and he was sanctified in them.' Not a word is said here about giving the name *Meribah* to the place. Elsewhere only the *waters of strife* at Kadesh are spoken of. That the author uses the expression *waters of strife* is intentional. The repetition of the designation, which, on the former occasion, became a proper name, here serves as an allusion to it, and therefore sets in a more conspicuous light the unbelief of the people and of their leader."—*Gen. of Pent.*, vol. ii. p. 310. The usage of the sacred writers favors, we think, this construction. Thus, Ps. 95:8, "Harden not your hearts as in the *provocation* (*meribah*), and as in the day of *temptation* (*massah*) in the wilderness." So Deut. 32:51, "Because ye trespassed against me among the children of Israel at the waters of *Meribah-Kadesh* (*meribath Kadesh, strife of Kadesh*), in the wilderness of Zin." Here we find *Meribah* in the construct state (*meribath*), which, though common with appellatives, is very unusual with proper names, except in the case of words which are found in the construct state only. Still this point must always be held with some degree of diffidence.——¶ *Strove with the Lord.* They strove with the Lord by striving with Moses and Aaron, his servants. Comp. Ex. 16:8. Gr. "Reviled before the Lord."——¶ *And he was sanctified in them.* That is, although Moses and Aaron had failed to sanctify him by faith and obedience, yet he took the matter of his vindication and glorification into his own hands, and sanctified himself by punishing his friends and favorites, and demonstrating in the eyes of the congregation his omnipotence, veracity, and clemency

A Passage through the Land of Edom sought and refused.

V. 14. *Moses sent messengers from Kadesh.* It is generally supposed that this was done under a special divine direction, to be recognized in the tenor of what is recorded, Deut. 2:1–6. Upon reference to that passage, it does not appear that the present message was expressly commanded, although general directions are given as to the deportment the Israelites were to observe in passing through the Edomite territory. It is, therefore, only by inference that a divine order is made out for sending messengers to the ruler of that country. It may have been so, but it is not distinctly affirmed. The relative position of the land of Edom to the region of Kadesh, where they were now encamped, and to the most direct route to the country of Canaan, must be ascertained from the maps, of which Prof. Robinson's are probably the most accurate. It extended along the southern boundary of Canaan, from the Dead Sea to the eastern arm of the Red Sea, on the east of the deep and dreary valley which reaches from the one sea to the other. It is a mountainous region, to which also the appellation of *Seir*, or *Mount Seir*, is occasionally given. The word *Seir* means *hairy* (being thus synonymous with Esau), and when applied to a country may signify *rugged, jagged, mountainous*, and so says Jo-

of Edom, Thus saith [o] thy brother Israel, Thou knowest all the travail that hath befallen us;

[o] Deut. 2. 4.

sephus: "Esau named the country 'Roughness' from his own hairy roughness." It was formerly called the country of the *Horim*, i. e., cave-dwellers (Troglodytes) from *hōr, a cave.* The famous city of Petra, which was in the territory of Edom, was composed of dwellings excavated in the solid rock. This region the Lord had prophetically assigned to Esau, and He would not have him disturbed in the possession of it. It is at present wholly occupied by various tribes of Bedouin Arabs. Moses being now ordered to decamp and set forward toward the land of Canaan, and the straightest route thither leading directly through the domains of Edom, he is prompted to despatch delegates to the prince of that country to solicit a free passage through it, which he does upon consideration of the near affinity subsisting between the two nations, and upon the pledge of keeping the common thoroughfare, without deviating to the right hand or the left, without invading or injuring any one's property, and without asking either food or drink, except upon condition of punctually paying for it.——¶ *Thus saith thy brother Israel.* Israel is the collective name of the whole nation descended from Jacob, who was called by that name; and in like manner we find both Esau and Edom used to denote the national posterity of Esau. See Obad. v. 1, 6, 10. Mal. 1:1–4. The Lord would have the brotherly relation cheerfully acknowledged on the part of his people, as they both looked to a common ancestor in Isaac, and both inherited the rite of circumcision, which would naturally be a bond of fraternal connection. By this respectful and affectionate appeal they would win their way to his heart, and obtain the object of their suit. They acted herein in the spirit of the precept, Deut. 23:7, "Thou shalt not abhor an Edomite, for he is thy brother." But as this might not prevail, they are commanded to urge other considerations.——¶ *Thou knowest all the travail that hath befallen us.* Heb. *kol hattelâah asher metzâthenu, all the wearisome-molestation that hath found us.* The same phrase occurs, Ex. 18:8, "And Moses told his father-in-law all that the Lord had done unto Pharaoh, and to the Egyptians for Israel's sake, *and all the travail that had come upon them* by the way." See Note *in loc.* This language was well calculated to conciliate the mind of Edom, for we must consider the prince as fairly representing the people, or as an organ of their sentiments. The words made an appeal to the ordinary feelings of humanity; for nature itself dictates sympathy and aid to the wretched who are unjustly oppressed. In this view he says that the afflictions which they had endured were notorious, viz., that as sojourners in Egypt they had been tyrannically harassed and oppressed. As he takes it for granted that they were no strangers to what had happened to them, the inference is obvious that the marvellous events which had marked the deliverance of Israel from Egypt were widely bruited and well known throughout the peninsula, as one tribe had communicated the news to another, and we cannot but wonder that the evidence of the divine protection in their behalf should not have overawed the minds of those who were predisposed to treat them ill. Such an effect in general had been predicted upon the overthrow of Pharaoh, Ex. 15:14, 15, "The people shall hear, and

15 How our fathers went down[p] into Egypt, and we have dwelt[q] in Egypt a long time; and the Egyptians vexed us and our fathers:

16 And when[r] we cried unto

p Gen. 46. 6. q Ex. 12. 40. r Ex. 2. 23.

be afraid: sorrow shall take hold on the inhabitants of Palestine. Then the dukes of Edom shall be amazed; the mighty men of Moab, trembling shall take hold upon them; all the inhabitants of Canaan shall melt away." But they were hardened to their own detriment, as we learn from their subsequent history.

V. 15. *The Egyptians vexed us and our fathers.* By thus recapitulating their sufferings in Egypt, and reciting the Lord's merciful interpositions in their behalf, they wove an argument well calculated to work upon the minds of those they addressed. They would give them to understand that however cruelly they had been treated, and however low they had been brought, yet the Lord had adopted them into his favor, and therefore they might justly challenge the favor of their fellow-men. It would be a great outrage to deny assistance or courtesy to those to whose kind regards the Lord had recommended them by his example; on the contrary, it would be eminently for their interest to ingratiate themselves with those who had so high an interest in heaven, and it would be at their peril if they offered them harm. "It is our wisdom and duty to be kind to those whom God is pleased to own, and to take his people for our people."—*Henry.*

V. 16. *When we cried unto the Lord, etc.* The fair inference from this would be that the Edomites themselves were bound to be imitators of God, who had been merciful in delivering his people. How could they hope for mercy or favor for themselves, if they withheld it from the needy? Their cry to heaven was no doubt marred by many imperfections, but the Lord heard it, and what could have a more powerful effect in commending their cause?——¶ *And sent an angel.* It is remarkable that upon this passage even Dr. Priestley himself says, "This *Angel* was evidently no other than the Supreme Being himself, manifesting his presence by a luminous cloud. No other intelligent being had been introduced." This is the true explanation, though we may well doubt whether Priestley would have admitted the relation of this angel to Christ, which we have endeavored to establish in our Notes on Ex. 3 : 2. 13 : 21. He was obviously no other than the "Angel of the Covenant," Christ Jesus, who first appeared to Abraham, Gen. 12 : 1. Acts 7 : 2, then to Moses at the burning bush, and subsequently in the cloudy pillar, who in fact led Moses and the people out of Egypt, and conducted them through the wilderness, Ex. 14 : 19. 23 : 20. 33 : 14. Some of the Rabbinical critics suppose Moses himself to be intended, from the circumstance that the title "angel" or "messenger" is sometimes bestowed upon the prophets, 2 Chr. 36 : 16. Hag. 1 : 13. But this construction is very improbable, as Moses would scarcely refer to himself in this connection, or if he did, would he do it in such a dark and enigmatical manner. A supernatural being is plainly intended, and as the attributes predicated of him do not suit the nature of any creature, however exalted, we are forced to the conclusion that it was no other than Jehovah himself, who thus saw fit to anticipate,

the LORD, he heard [s] our voice, and sent [t] an angel, and hath brought us forth out of Egypt; and, behold, we *are* in Kadesh, a city in the uttermost of thy border:

17 Let [u] us pass, I pray thee, through thy country: we will not pass through the fields, or through the vineyards, neither will we drink *of* the water of the wells: we will go by the king's *high*-way, we will not turn to the right hand nor to the left, until we have passed thy borders.

s Ex. 3. 7. *t* Ex. 3. 2. 14. 19. 23. 20. 33. 2. *u* c. 21. 22. Deut. 2. 27.

---

in this form of theophany, his subsequent tabernacling in the flesh. But we have already treated this subject so fully in our Notes above referred to, on Exodus, that we need not here enlarge upon it. If it be objected that God could not properly be said to "send himself" in the form of an angel, we would say in reply, that the same objection holds good also against the idea of "sending himself" in the "likeness of sinful flesh" for the redemption of the world, as to which the testimony of the New Testament is clear beyond dispute.

V. 17. *Let us pass, I pray thee, through thy country.* A civil and reasonable request preferred simply because the route through Edom was the nearest to the land of Canaan, to which they were destined. They had, indeed, been assured of being put in possession of the land of promise, and as the Lord who had promised was the universal Proprietor of all things, they might have forced their way despite of all opposition; yet He who is infinite equity and wisdom combined would not have their good evil spoken of, or wrong done to any under the plea of the divine guidance. In making this request they not only avoid the appearance of evil, but they virtually acknowledge that the children of Esau had obtained their possession by a similar right to that whereby the land of Canaan had been secured to the posterity of Jacob. If they desired, therefore, to enjoy their own inheritance, they were not to interfere with that which had been prophetically assigned to Esau. The course pursued was entirely in accordance with a just appreciation of the divine counsels in this respect, and it set a noble example of waiving a claim that might have been violently enforced, because the interests of righteousness and peace dictated such a policy. The request, however, was churlishly denied, and their course was accordingly altered. Deut. 2:8, "They turned and passed by the way of Moab." Comp. Judg. 11:17, 18.——¶ *We will not pass through the fields, etc.* They would relieve the Edomites, as far as possible, from any apprehensions arising from the passage of so large a host through their territory, and therefore assure them they had no hostile intentions, that they would not in any way molest the inhabitants, that they would keep themselves to the common public highway, and instead of committing the least depredation, would not even ask a drink of water for themselves or their cattle without paying for it—a stipulation of no small importance in the case of so large a multitude, and in a country where the inhabitants depend, during the greater part of the year, upon the water which may be collected in the season when rain falls.—"We will not drink of the water of the wells:—if I, and my cattle, drink of thy water, then

18 And Edom said unto him, Thou shalt not pass by me, lest I come out against thee with the sword.

19 And the children of Israel said unto him, We will go by the high-way: and [v] if I and my

[v] Deut. 2. 6, 28.

will I *pay for it.*"—This is always expected; and though Edom *might* in friendship have let his brother Israel drink *gratis,* had he recollected their consanguinity, yet Israel did not insist on such accommodation. How strange would it sound in England, if a person in travelling, should propose to pay for drinking water from the wells by the roadside! Nevertheless, still stronger is the expression, Lam. 5 : 4; 'We have drank *our own water* for money:' we bought it of our foreign rulers; although we were the natural proprietors of the wells which furnished it."—*Taylor in Calmet.*

V. 18. *Thou shalt not pass by me.* Heb. "Shall not pass in me," i. e. through me, by which is meant through my land and people, with which he identified himself. Their courteous and respectful application was therefore answered by a surly negative, not only refusing the desired passage, but threatening to oppose them by force of arms if they made the attempt. The consequences of this refusal we describe in the words of Mr. Kitto: "They were therefore to retrace their steps to the head of the eastern gulf of the Red Sea, where the land of Edom ended, and passing round the extremity of the chain of mountains, which constituted the chief part of that realm, put themselves on the eastern border of that territory, and so proceed northward to the region east of the Dead Sea. A reference to any map of this district, will show that the mountains of Edom extended along the eastern side of that broad valley (the Arabah), which lies between the Dead Sea and the gulf of Akabah. It is down this valley that they seem to have proceeded on their retrogressive movement. On the way they encamped at Mosera, which seems to have been at or near the present Wady Mûsa, in which lie the ruins of Petra, the city whose marvellous excavations have only within the present century been brought to light, and which have since formed the theme of many able pencils and eloquent pens. The encampment must, we apprehend, have been in the neighborhood of the mouth of this valley, and in presence of Mount Hor."—*Daily Bible Illus.*

V. 19. *We will go by the high-way.* Heb. *mesillâh,* from the root *sâlal, to raise, cast,* or *throw up,* as an embankment, a terrace, a causeway. The primary import is that of an elevated pathway, a thoroughfare, such as were often made for military purposes. The epithet "high," which in v. 17, is in Italic, is here called for by the literal sense of the original. The Gr. renders it, "Let us pass through along the mountains."——¶ *Then I will pay for it.* Heb. "I will give the price thereof." This was according to the divine direction, Deut. 2 : 6, 7, "Ye shall buy meat of them for money, that ye may eat; and ye shall also buy water of them for money, that ye may drink. For the Lord thy God hath blessed thee in all the works of thy hand: he knoweth thy walking through this great wilderness: these forty years the Lord thy God hath been with thee; thou hast lacked nothing." The Lord's blessing them is added as a reason, lest the people should be grieved at spending their money, of which they could be supposed to have but little, in buying meat and drink. There are, however, two

cattle drink of thy water, then I will pay for it; I will only, without *doing* any thing *else*, go through on my feet.

20 And he said, Thou [w] shalt not go through. And Edom came out [x] against him with

w Judg. 11. 17. x Obad. 10-15.

considerations involved; first, that they were so enriched by God's bounty, that they were fully supplied with the means of buying food; and, secondly, that they must not doubt that he would relieve their necessity by miracle, if required, since he had thus far provided for them without suffering them to want any thing. If it be asked how the Lord could say, that he had blessed the work of their hands, when they had no commerce with other nations by which to make the smallest gains whatever, we may suggest in reply, that we know not that their isolation was so absolute that they had no traffic whatever with the neighboring tribes; but however this may be, and however they were sustained gratuitously in the desert, without expending even a single penny in buying shoe-latchets, yet their cattle had increased, and doubtless during their long stays at particular stations, they had not passed the time idly, but had employed themselves in the fabrication of various articles which would naturally turn to account when occasions like the present arose.——¶ *I will only, without (doing) any thing (else), go through on my feet.* Heb. *raq aïn dâbâr*, lit. *only no word*, of which the import is not very clear, though "word" is often used for "thing," and our present version may be correct. The Chald. renders, "Provided only there shall be no mischief or evil, I will pass through on my feet." That is, in case there shall be no impediment or harm on your part, there shall be none on ours. Gr. "Grant but this; it is a small matter; let us march through along the mountain." Vulg. "There shall be no difficulty in the price, only let us pass speedily." Arab. "There is nothing (i. e. nothing evil intended); I will only pass through on my feet." On the whole we find nothing preferable to our present English version.

V. 20. *Thou shalt not go through, etc.* He still persists in his refusal, which is now followed by an act of hostile invasion. Instead of allowing them water, they would have shed their blood; instead of giving them passage through their land, they would have swept them from the face of the wilderness. How naturally does this recall the persecutions of Esau! He that was born after the flesh still persecuted him that was born after the Spirit, each acting in his representative capacity. And so is it to this day. It marks the hostility of the world to the church, which we see everywhere exemplified. Their conduct on this occasion, however, though not immediately punished, was yet remembered, and in due time met with a fit retribution. The main burden of the prophecy of Obadiah is the judgments denounced against Edom, and these are referred primarily to his cruel treatment of his brother Israel in the day of his emergency. "The pride of thy heart hath deceived thee, thou that dwellest in the clefts of the rock, whose habitation is high; that saith in his heart, Who shall bring me down to the ground? Though thou exalt thyself as the eagle, and though thou set thy nest among the stars, thence will I bring thee down, saith the Lord. . . . How are the things of Esau searched out! how are his hidden things sought up!

much people, and with a strong hand.

21 Thus Edom refused to give Israel passage through his border: wherefore Israel turned away from him.

22 And [y] the children of Israel, *even* the whole congregation, journeyed from Kadesh, and came unto mount Hor.

y c. 33. 37.

. . . For thy violence against thy brother Jacob, shame shall cover thee, and thou shalt be cut off for ever."

V. 21. *Wherefore Israel turned away from him.* They turned away, not as cowards, but as those whom the Lord had laid under a prohibition not to fight, Deut. 2:5. He could, of course, with infinite ease, have made a passage through Edom, He who had led Israel through the deep, who had scattered the forces of Amalek, and who had hitherto borne his people as on eagles' wings. But the faith and patience of that people were still further to be tried, and the day of vengeance to Edom to be yet longer delayed. "They could not err who were under the direction of an infallible guide. Though they turned another way circuitously, yet still it was the right way, a way determined in the plan of heaven, and pointed out by the covenant Angel. Their march became obstructed, yet the Lord's purposes were not interrupted; it was not through Edom, but by the wilderness of Moab, that they were to go. Could we look at the purpose of God and compare it with the course of his providence, we should see that in all the windings and conflicts of the wilderness, as well where an enemy obstructs, as where a friend opens our way, the path is right."—*Seaton.* Israel, by divine commandment, turned away, and compassed the land of Edom upon its southern and eastern borders, and it appears from Deut. 2:28, 29, that there was so much relaxation of the purpose declared by the prince, that he consented to furnish Israel with needed provisions, both in meat and drink, for their money.

The Israelites journey to Mount Hor, where Aaron dies.

V. 22. *Came unto Mount Hor.* Heb. *hōr hâhâr, to Hor the mountain;* the original word frequently implying *a mountainous range*, as was no doubt the case with this locality in the first instance, although the name has since become appropriated to one particular mountain, of which the modern designation is *Jebel Haroun*, or *Mount Aaron.* It is situated in Arabia Petræa, on the confines of Idumea, forming a part of the Mountain of Seir or Edom, of which it is the most conspicuous in the whole range. It stands about midway betweed the Dead Sea and the Ælanitic Gulf. It has been supposed questionable whether this be really the Mount Hor on which Aaron died, but from its height and the commanding manner in which it rises among the surrounding rocks, it seems not unlikely to have been the scene chosen for that event. To this may be added that Josephus affirms Mount Hor to have been near Petra; and near *that* place there is certainly no mountain which can contest the distinction with the one now in view. Without, however, deciding upon its claims, we refer the reader to the travels of Stephens, Robinson, Stanley, Martineau, and others, for all that desirable information in the department of topography, which we could only give by transcribing their words. As

23 And the LORD spake unto Moses and Aaron in mount Hor, by the coast of the land of Edom, saying,

24 Aaron shall be gathered [z] unto his people: for he shall not enter into the land which I have

z Gen. 25. 8. Deut. 32. 50.

to the apparent discrepancy between this passage and the statement, Deut. 10:6, see Note on the latter place.

V. 23. *By the coast of the land of Edom.* That is, by the *border*, in which sense the word *coast* frequently occurs in the Scriptures. In ch. 33:37, the journey hither is thus described, "And they removed from Kadesh and pitched in Mount Hor, *in the edge of the land of Edom.*" The southern extremity of Edom we suppose to be indicated.

V. 24. *Aaron shall be gathered unto his people.* That is, shall die and be buried, and his soul, i. e., himself, shall be gathered among "the spirits of just men made perfect." Gr. *prostethētō, let (Aaron) be added.* "Gathering" is a term frequently employed in reference to the removal of men by death, as in v. 26, and Is. 57:1, "Merciful men are *taken away* (Heb. *gathered*), none considering that the righteous is *taken away* (Heb. *gathered*) from the evil to come." That is, they are gathered and housed in heaven, as a shepherd gathers and folds his sheep when the storm is coming. So also, Ps. 104:29, "Thou *takest away* (Heb. *gatherest*) their breath, they die, and return to their dust." The "people" to whom he was to be gathered or adjoined, were his ancestors who had gone to the spiritual world before him, as is said of David, Acts 13:36, "For David, after he had served his own generation by the will of God, fell on sleep, and *was laid unto his fathers* (Gr. *prosetethē, was added*, or *gathered*)." This is the usual Gr. rendering of the Hebrew phrase for being gathered unto one's fathers, viz., *prosetethē*, which is here infelicitously translated "laid unto," which fixes the idea rather upon the body than the soul, contrary to what is the case with the original. Judg. 2:10, "And all that generation were gathered unto their fathers." (Gr. *prosetethēsan, were added.*) On the other hand, David prays, Ps. 26:9, "Gather not my soul with sinners." See Note on Gen. 25:8.——¶ *He shall not enter, etc.* The sternness of the divine interdict is not at all relaxed by the affecting circumstances of the occasion. The sentence previously passed must go into execution, that the Lord's veracity suffer not, and that the people might know that he never threatens in vain. They could not but realize that they themselves were the original procuring causes of the doom of exclusion which had befallen their leaders, whose spirits their perverseness had "angered at the waters of strife," and thus provoked them to sin; and when even so sacred personages as Moses and Aaron could not escape, how clearly would they perceive that God was not to be trifled with, and that it was a stretch of divine forbearance that they were spared, when they so richly deserved to suffer. ——¶ *Because ye rebelled against my word, etc.* Heb. "Against my mouth." The singular number is here exchanged for the plural, that they might be reminded that they had shared in a common guilt and were now to be associated in punishment. In respect to Aaron, the sentence implied that by reason of the transgression of which he had been guilty, he could no longer enjoy the honor of typically representing the Messiah who was to come, and who was to be the great High Priest of the

given unto the children of Israel, because ye rebelled[a] against my word at the water of Meribah.

a ver. 12.

25 Take Aaron and Eleazar his son, and bring them up unto mount Hor:

26 And strip Aaron of his

spiritual Israel. This office was now to be transferred to his son, who was to be clothed with his father's pontifical robes, which were the proper *insignia* of the priestly dignity. As the priesthood of Aaron pointed to the sacerdotal supremacy of Christ, who was to be in all things head over the Church, therefore it was ordered that the transaction should occur on the head or top of a mountain, which would most fittingly shadow forth that supremacy.

V. 26. *Strip Aaron of his garments, and put them upon Eleazar his son.* Implying thereby that Eleazar was to be invested with the attributes or prerogatives of his father's office. These were undoubtedly his priestly robes, and the inference is fair that he had put them on for this particular purpose before leaving the camp and ascending the mountain. "A transfer of office, from the circumstance of *putting the clothes* of the late possessor on the person intended to succeed him, was called *investing* or *investment* (*clothing*), as removing a person from an office was called *divesting* or *unclothing.* Among the Catholics, and in the Church of England, the same method is used in degrading ecclesiastics. Hence such a degradation is termed by the common people *stripping a man of his gown.*"—*Adam Clarke.* Those "garments of holiness" which Moses had formerly put upon him for "honor and for glory," Ex. 28 : 2, at the time of his consecration to the priesthood, he is now to divest him of, or, as the Targ. Jon. expresses it, to "strip" him of the honorable garments of the priesthood. This act, of taking off of official garments and putting them upon another, was symbolical of the transfer of the office itself. Thus, Is. 22 : 15–21, "Thus saith the Lord God of hosts, Go, get thee unto this treasurer, even unto Shebna, which is over the house, and say, . . . And I will drive thee from thy station, and from thy state shall he pull thee down. And it shall come to pass in that day, that I will call my servant Eliakim, the son of Hilkiah: And I will clothe him with thy robe, and strengthen him with thy girdle, and I will commit thy government into his hand: and he shall be a father to the inhabitants of Jerusalem, and to the house of Judah." In the present case the implication was manifest, not only that the priesthood then existing was to yield to one more perfect, but that a dying priest was to yield to one that should live for ever. Had it not been designed to set forth some great truth like this, Aaron would not have attired himself for death as though about to enter into the holy of holies. Perhaps one lesson intended to be taught was, that he was not to enter that blissful abode which the holy of holies represented, as a priest, but as a man. There all external and adventitious distinctions cease, all official appendages fall away, and the internal character alone determines the final allotment. The garments of priests, the robes of princes, and the rags of beggars, are all equally worthless in themselves when the shroud of dissolution is to take their place, and when even this avails not to cover the spirit, which appears naked before its Judge, and is assigned its destiny according to its dominant qual-

garments, and put them upon Eleazar his son: and Aaron shall be gathered *unto his people*, and shall die there.

27 And Moses did as the LORD commanded: and they went up into mount Hor, in the sight of all the congregation.

---

ities and deeds. But the pre-eminence of Christ over all earthly priests, and the perpetuity and stability of his dispensation over the weakness and imperfection of that which preceded, is the grand truth which the divine wisdom would teach by the circumstances of Aaron's demise. "They truly," says the apostle, Heb. 7:23, 24, "were many priests, because they were not suffered to continue by reason of death; but this man, because he continueth ever, hath an unchangeable priesthood."

"Their priesthood ran through several hands,
For mortal was their race;
Thy never-changing office stands,
Eternal as thy days."

It was not consistent with God's typical designs that either Aaron or Moses should live to bring the tribes to rest; that was assigned to another. But Christ has power to bring in the church to the promised possession; for he has, by virtue of his everlasting merits, already entered, now to appear in the presence of God for us.——¶ *Put them upon Eleazar his son.* The man dies, but not the priest. The transfer is made while Aaron can be conscious of it, and receive comfort from it. The robes are taken from him when living, and not when dead. This was in accordance with an oracle uttered long afterwards, Jer. 33:17, "Neither shall the priests, the Levites, want a man before me to offer burnt-offerings, and to kindle meat-offerings, and to do sacrifice continually." We may well suppose it was cheering to the departing saint to know that the priestly function would not cease with him, but that it should continue in his posterity through all ages till He should come who was to be "a priest for ever after the order of Melchizedek;" who should be the true Eleazar (i. e., *the help of God*), "made not after the law of a carnal commandment, but after the power of an endless life." Aaron's perception may have been vague and dim of all that was embraced in the compass of the divine counsels on this head, but it would no doubt tend to relieve the bitterness of death to be assured that his own removal would cause no break in the chain of proposed blessings to the church.——¶ *Aaron shall be gathered (to his people).* The closing words are in italics to indicate that in the original it is said simply that Aaron should "be gathered," a phrase equivalent to being taken away by death, as before remarked, v. 24.——¶ *Shall die there.* Heb. "Shall be a corpse there." This is, perhaps, simply exegetical of the preceding clause, unless we suppose that the former has more especial reference to the soul, and the latter to the body; implying that while his lifeless remains were lying before them, his freed spirit was rejoicing in the society of the spirits of his fathers who had preceded him in the race of mortality.

V. 27. *And they went up into Mount Hor in the sight of all the congregation.* A special publicity was designed to be given to this solemn event, in order that the great body of the people might have every assurance that the succession was ordered by the Lord himself. They might otherwise have been prompted, from ill will to Aaron's family, to take the election into their own hands, and in their perverseness have

28 And [b] Moses stripped Aaron of his garments, and put them upon Eleazar his son: and Aaron died there in the top of the mount: and

b c. 33. 38, etc.

made choice of one from another tribe. Or they might possibly have repudiated the priesthood altogether. To guard against any contingency of this kind, and to provide effectually that this sacred office should not perish with its first incumbent, the Lord took into his own hands the appointment of a successor, and so ordered the circumstances that the congregation should be profoundly impressed with the divine arrangement; for it is doubtless to be supposed that they were made acquainted with the object for which he ascended the mountain. As to Aaron himself, the whole tenor of the narrative would imply that he went up to the summit of the holy mount with unfaltering step, and composed himself to die with as much serenity as if he were but laying himself down upon his bed to sleep. There is no intimation but that he was in perfect health at the time, though he had reached the very extended term of one hundred and twenty-three years. It was not in the waste of age, or through decays of sickness, or by a sudden stroke, that he was to pass away from among men, but at the call of heaven. As there is a place where to die, as well as a time when to die, both of which are in the divine appointment, so to both these the high-priest of Israel was now brought. He had reached his last stage in the wilderness, beyond which he could not pass. He had finished his priestly functions, he had made his last offering, he had left the sanctuary on earth, never again to enter it or to minister before the Lord. Many eyes were doubtless upon him as he went forth, eager to catch the last glimpse of his receding person, their many hearts invoking many blessings. Father, son, and brother went up together, and this was the last of their intercourse on earth. What passed on the way is not said, but we may well believe their conversation savored of heaven, and was serious, holy, and pleasant. In such circumstances, when the brightest scenes of earth fade away from the view, and the heart sickens at worldly thoughts, nothing but divine manifestations and the spiritual realities of another life, can possibly sustain the soul. These supports we cannot doubt that Aaron enjoyed as he went up the mount to die; for, to him, dying was ascending, as it will be to all the Lord's people, whatever be the circumstances of their departure. Some die in seclusion, unnoticed and unknown; some die embosomed in a circle of sorrowing friends. Yet it matters little where the saints depart, whether on a mount or in a vale, except as symbolical or typical considerations give one place a preference over another. Both Aaron and Moses died on a mountainous elevation, and we may not question that some rich significancy was veiled under the fact. In frequent cases recorded in Scripture things of a very important and memorable nature are said to have occurred on mountains, with which we are prone to connect what is conspicuous, remarkable, and involving high and heavenly mysteries. Our Lord died on Mount Calvary and ascended from the Mount of Olives, and in this respect the departure of his forerunners conformed to his.

V. 28. *Aaron died there in the top of the mount.* "This mountain is of important Scriptural interest; for, arrived at this spot, Aaron, in obedience to his recent doom, was commanded to

Moses and Eleazar came down from the mount.

29 And when all the congregation saw that Aaron was dead, they mourned for Aaron thirty days, *even* all the house of Israel.

CHAPTER XXI.

AND *when* king Arad [a] the Canaanite, which dwelt in the south, heard tell that Israel

a c. 33. 40. Judg. 1. 16.

---

go up to this mount, and die. He was to be accompanied by his brother and his eldest son, who were to divest him of his priestly robes, to receive his dying sigh, and to deposit his remains safely in this high place. The spot was probably selected, not only to impress the Israelites with the solemnity of the occasion, but to enable the dying pontiff to give one last look over the camp of Israel, surrounding, in goodly rows, the tabernacle of God; to survey the scene of his long pilgrimage; and to catch a distant glimpse of the utmost borders of the promised land, before stepping across the boundary between this world and the world to come. There is no doubt whatever about the mountain which was the scene of this transaction. Even local tradition has preserved the memory of this event, the mountain itself bears the name of Aaron (Harun); and upon the top an old Moslem tomb stands to his honor, which is much visited by Mohammedan pilgrims, few of whom quit the place without sacrificing a sheep in honor of the Jewish saint."—*Daily Bible Illus.*

V. 29. *When all the congregation saw that Aaron was dead.* Heb. "Had expired or given up the ghost." *Seeing* is here, as elsewhere, used for *perceiving* or *taking cognizance.* They would *know* the fact by the verbal relation of Moses and Aaron, by the circumstance of Aaron's not returning with them, and also by seeing Eleazar arrayed in the priestly garments of his father. In like manner "Jacob *saw* (i. e. *knew*) there was corn in Egypt," when he *heard* thereof. So the people "*saw* the voices," Ex. 20 : 18, and various parallel places. See Notes on Gen. 42 : 1. Ex. 20 : 18.——¶ *They mourned for Aaron thirty days.* Heb. *yibku, they wept or bewailed* Aaron. How characteristic this of the instability and fickleness of all human regards, whether of love or hate! How prone is our fallen nature to reverse its judgment, and its treatment of good men when they have ceased to be numbered with the living! The people of Israel, during Aaron's lifetime, had frequently sought to stone him; they had murmured against him and raised great tumults in order to cast him down from the dignity in which God had placed him. Now that he is dead, they forget their malignity and envy, and pour out their lamentations over his decease. But mourning in itself is an honorable testimonial to departed worth, and Calvin well remarks, that "if the utility of this custom be corrupted by its abuse, it is not just that what is right in itself should be blamed for the fault of men." The same period of mourning was allotted also to Moses, Deut. 34 : 8.

CHAPTER XXI.

Israel assaulted by a Canaanitish King. The Result.

V. 1. *And (when) king Arad the Canaanite, etc.* Or, Heb. "The Canaanite, king of Arad." This is the prevalent rendering of the versionists ancient and modern, and is that which the original seems most to favor. Precisely the same

ame by the way[b] of the spies; then he fought against Israel, and took *some* of them prisoners.

b c. 13. 21.

ɔrm in the Heb. is rendered, Josh. 12: 4, "King of Arad;" while in Num. 33: :0, it appears as here, "King Arad the Canaanite." We derive an important hint as to the locality in question, from Judg. 1:16; "And the children of the Kenite, Moses' father-in-law, went up out of the city of palm-trees with the children of Judah, unto the wilderness of Judah, *which lieth on the south of Arad*," i. e., in the south parts of the tribe of Judah about the city Arad. Arad, therefore, was the name of a city on the southernmost borders of Canaan, which Eusebius and Jerome place about twenty Roman miles from Hebron, equal to about eight hours with camels. Prof. Robinson observed a place in about the same locality, on the route from Petra to Hebron, called "Tell Arad," which he thinks may with great probability be regarded as the site of the ancient city here spoken of. The Israelites were now advancing northwards, though still hovering about the south-eastern border of Edom, when this petty potentate of Canaan, getting intelligence of their movements and thinking it good policy to keep the war at a distance, marched forth from his own territory in considerable force, determined to dispute their further progress. His assault was at first partially successful, but we learn that he subsequently paid dear for his victory. "The trials of a wilderness state terminate only with our journey. Fears within and fightings without, are often the lot of the Church on earth. The time of the promise was not far off, yet they must conflict for possession. It might be thought, that as the church approached nearer and nearer to the land of promise, difficulties would lessen, and that peaceful and unopposed possession would be gained. Instead of this trials have multiplied, and just when in reach of home more than at any period before."—*Seaton.* So with the Christian in his journey towards heaven. Instead of finding himself released from combat, his faith and patience are exercised by new forms of temptation, new battles with new enemies have to be fought, and he at length settles down in the assurance that there is "no discharge in that war," till he has crossed the Jordan of death, and sat himself down in peace in the Canaan beyond.——¶ *Heard tell that Israel came by the way of the spies.* Heb. *derek hâathârim*, in regard to the true purport of which versions and commentators greatly differ. The Chald., Syr. and Vulg. render with our translators "the way of the spies," understanding thereby the way into Canaan travelled by the spies whom Moses had sent many years before to explore the land. But it is objected to this interpretation that the original word for *spies* is properly *târim*, from *toor, to traverse*, also *to spy out, to examine, to explore*, whence the normal form would be *hattârim* instead of *athârim*, which comes analogically from *âthar*, although this verb nowhere occurs. For this reason many critics are disposed to concur with the Sept. and the Arab., which renders it as a proper name, "by the way of Atharim," notwithstanding we have nowhere else the least intimation of the existence of any place of this name. For ourselves we incline to adhere to the established rendering. The Israelites, it is true, were now at a quite remote distance from the southern limits of Canaan when the spies had entered, but they were advancing in that general direction,

2 And Israel vowed [c] a vow unto the LORD, and said, If thou wilt indeed deliver this people into my hand, then I will utterly [d] destroy their cities.

c Gen. 28. 20. Judg. 11. 30.

d Lev. 27. 28. Deut. 13. 15.

---

and the king of Arad may have naturally supposed that they designed to enter the country through some passage which, from the circumstance alluded to, had perhaps in the mean time acquired the name of "the way of the spies." The use of the article suggests an appellative import to the original word, instead of its being a proper name, and Drusius has shown that the addition of the prosthetic א — *a* (אתרים *athârim*) is paralleled by אזרוע *ezroa*, for זרוע *zeroa, arm*, and other similar usages. The evidence, on the whole, predominates in our view in favor of the usual English version of the phrase. ——¶ *And took* (*some*) *of them prisoners.* Heb. "Took captive of them a captivity." The abstract is here used for the concrete as in ch. 31 : 12, "And they brought the *captives* (Heb. *the captivity*), and the prey, and the spoil, etc." Judg. 5 : 12, "Arise, Barak, and lead thy *captivity captive.*" Comp. Ps. 68 : 19. 2 Chron. 28 : 5. Thus we have *poverty* for a company of poor people, 2 Kings 24 : 14; *spoil* for a people spoiled, Am. 5 : 9; *thanks* for those who gave thanks, Neh. 12 : 31, and so in numerous other instances. The discomfiture which Israel now experienced was permitted of the Lord, not only to be a snare to the victors, but also to serve as a salutary lesson to the chosen people, to teach them their own intrinsic weakness and their constant dependence on the divine sufficiency for success in their warfare. The reverse, therefore, now met with would be an exercise of faith and a spur to fortitude. But although success may for a while attend the enemies of the Lord's church, it cannot be lasting. His servants may be temporarily "made prisoners," yet they are always "prisoners of hope," and the time of release, the year of jubilee, will come, when liberty is proclaimed to the "captives," and the opening of the prison to them that are bound.

V. 2. *Israel vowed a vow unto the Lord.* This implied a calling upon the Lord for his help, and religiously promising to *devote* to him their enemies and all their substance. See Note on Gen. 28 : 20. It does not appear that God had thus far openly and explicitly commanded the cities of Canaan to be utterly destroyed, yet it is a fair inference that the purpose now expressed was acceptable to him, as it fell in with his general design in regard to those nations. He had resolved upon their destruction, and he had appointed the Israelites to execute the sentence. It would seem, therefore, if it was right for them, as the Lord's ministers, to do this work, it was right to vow to do it; and we learn from the sequel that they were enabled to accomplish the object of their vow, while no hint of the divine disapproval is anywhere to be met with. "The Lord hearkened to the voice of Israel, and delivered up the Canaanites." The vow, then, did not originate in inconsiderate zeal, but virtually in the divine determination. Hence it was not idly spoken, but was founded on the Lord's word, which is always the grand rule for vowing rightly. It may be conceded, that it was allowable for them to spare the cities which they wished to occupy themselves; but it was also allowable to devote them as an offering of first-fruits to God, as we are elsewhere informed, in regard to

3 And the LORD hearkened[e] to the voice of Israel, and delivered up the Canaanites; and

e Ps. 22. 4, 5.

the city of Jericho, Josh. 6 : 21.——¶ *I will utterly destroy their cities.* Heb. *ha haramti*, from the root *'hâram, to devote* or *doom, to devote to destruction.* Gr. "Anathematize." From the same root is derived the word *hormah*, implying destruction accompanied by anathema, as if the place so called were devoted to the curse of God. Under the operation of this kind of *devotement* persons were to die, and property to be confiscated to the Lord, Lev. 27 : 28, 29. See Note on Judg. 11 : 30. Thus when Jericho was devoted, the people and the beasts were killed, the city burnt, and the goods made over to the Lord's treasury, Josh. 6 : 17–24. The vow, therefore, was a promise that they would reserve none of the captured possessions of the king to their own use, but would devote it all to destruction, which was the nature of the vow called *Herem.* This gives Calvin occasion to remark, "Praiseworthy indeed was their magnanimity in refusing to avail themselves of a comfortable home, by destroying the cities which they should acquire by the right of war."

V. 3. *The Lord hearkened to the voice of Israel.* Chald. "Received the prayer of Israel." This implies, undoubtedly, an approval of their vow, although, as we shall see, the execution of it was postponed to a future day.——¶ *And they utterly destroyed them and their cities.* Heb. *yaharëm, devoted to destruction,* from the before-mentioned root *'hâram.* A cursory reading would lead to the impression that this defeat and destruction of the Canaanitish king and his cities occurred immediately upon the assault mentioned in the first verse. But this impression will be apt to be corrected by reference to a map of the region in question, and to the course of events as recorded in the ensuing history. The locality assigned to Arad, as we have seen, is in the tribe of Judah, in the southern part of Canaan. The position of Israel, at this time, was in the vicinity of Mount Hor, far to the southeast, with the mountainous tract of Edom and other hostile tribes interposed. If they at once pushed on and destroyed the cities of Arad, they must have passed the mountain range lying in their way, have actually entered the land of Canaan, and after achieving their conquests fallen back to the neighborhood of Mount Hor, where the Tabernacle was now pitched, from thence to resume their circuitous route round the head of the Dead Sea, and the country of Moab. All this appears in the highest degree improbable. If there had been at this time such a triumphant inroad into the land of Canaan, we should find some intimation of it elsewhere. But no such intimation occurs, and we therefore infer that the events mentioned in this verse did not take place till after their arrival in Canaan under Joshua, when the conquest of Arad was effected and their vow executed. In Josh. 12 : 14, we find the "king of Arad" mentioned among the kings "which Joshua and the children of Israel smote," after taking possession of the land of promise. From the following allusion, Judg. 1 : 17, we infer that Arad was also called "Zephath." "And Judah went with Simeon his brother, and they slew the Canaanites that inhabited Zephath, and utterly destroyed it. And the name of the city was called Hormah." It seems fair to conclude, from the name thenceforth given to the city, that not only were Arad and Zephath identical, but that now was the time when the vow men-

they utterly destroyed them and their cities: and he called the name of the place Hormah.

4 And [f] they journeyed from mount Hor by the way of the Red Sea, to compass the land [g] of Edom: and the soul of the

f c. 20. 22. 33. 41. *g* Judg. 11. 18.

tioned in the present connection was fulfilled. It is probable that no very serious efforts were made at this time to chastise the temerity of this rash but puny chieftain, who had probably with a mere clan of his followers, fallen upon some straggling parties of Israel, and taken them captive without making any impression whatever upon the main host. The prisoners may have been soon recovered, and the marauders repulsed for the time, when the congregation pursued its journey regardless of the interruption. But as they showed a malicious intent, and may possibly have perpetrated some cruelties, it was proper their assault should be remembered and punished at another time. This they vowed to do at the present time, but the execution of the vow was delayed till they could take their enemies in hand in earnest. In like manner the punishment of Amalek was delayed till the time of Saul and Samuel. The record of the fact, as contained in the verse before us, was probably added by another hand long after the period of Moses.——¶ *He called the name of the place Hormah.* That is, *utter destruction*, the name being designed as a memorial of the doom to which it was subjected. Gr. "Anathema." The expression "he called" is virtually impersonal, equivalent to "one called," or "it was called."

The Journeying of the People from Mount Hor. A fresh Murmuring against Moses.

V. 4. *Journeyed from Mount Hor by the way of the Red Sea.* Their course was southwardly to the head of the Red Sea, through the Wady-el-Arabah, and from thence they branched off to the east through the Wady Ithm, as it is now called, and by that route compassed the extreme south-eastern border of Edom, which it is plain from 1 Kings 9 : 20, extended quite to the head of the Arabian Gulf. From this they would reach the high *plateau* of the great eastern desert, along which they passed, with the mountains of Edom and Moab on their left, between them and the Dead Sea.——¶ *The soul of the people was much discouraged because of the way.* Heb. *tiktzar, was shortened or straitened*, applied originally to such things as are shortened by cutting, as wood, corn, grass, or any kind of harvest; and thence, secondarily, to the mind under the influence of such passions and emotions as cause a shortness of breath, as grief, sorrow, anger, impatience, etc.; whereas, on the contrary, one who is cool, calm, dispassionate, patient, is longsuffering (Heb. *long of anger*). Gr. "The people became small (i. e., faint, feeble) of soul, or lost courage." See for illustration by parallel usage, ch. 11 : 23. Is. 37 : 27. Judg. 16 : 16. Zech. 11 : 28. See also Note on Ex. 6 : 9, where the phrase is fully explained. From the following remarks of Kitto, upon the peculiarities of the region they were now called to traverse, it would appear that there was enough in the hardships of the way to elicit the complaints of the natural man. "In pursuing the course which had been marked out for them, the Hebrew host traversed southward the arid, hot, and sandy Arabah, and passing by the head of the eastern gulf of the Red Sea,

people was much discouraged because of the way.
5 And the people spake
[h] against God, and against Moses, Wherefore [i] have ye brought

[h] Ps. 78. 19. [i] Ex. 16. 3. 17. 3.

gained the equally desolate region constituting the desert *east* of the mountains of Edom. "This Wady-el-Araba is undoubtedly the 'way of the Red Sea' of the text; and the discouragement which the Israelites felt 'because of the way' may be accounted for no less by the naturally depressing influence of the obligation of going so far about to their destination, which they had hoped to reach by a shorter and more pleasant route, than by the naturally cheerless aspect of the country which they were traversing. The Wady-el-Araba, although a natural road to the countries north and north-west of the Red Sea, is yet as sterile as the desert, although the small bushy tufts, which grow here and there in the sand, retain for some time a little of the verdure which they receive during the rainy season. It is indeed in some respects worse than the common desert, being, to an extent beyond the latitude of Mount Hor, an expanse of shifting sand, of which the surface is broken by innumerable undulations and low hills. This sand appears to have been brought from the shores of the Red Sea by the southerly winds. The few travellers who have visited this region reiterate the complaints of the Israelites as to the scarcity of water in this district. Indeed when we consider the general want of water in the Arabian deserts, and the vast quantity which the Hebrew host must have required, there is less cause to wonder at their frequent complaints on the subject than that they were enabled, for so many years, to subsist in a collective body in regions thus consumed with drought. It is our firm conviction that they must utterly have perished long before but for the miraculous supplies which, on occasions of emergency, were granted to them."—*Pict. Bible.* As nothing is more trying than to be put back when, after a long and toilsome travel, one has almost reached the point of his destination, so here we can readily account for, though we cannot excuse, the murmurings and complaints to which the people now gave vent. Still we cannot doubt that their discouragement arose more from the inward frame of their spirits than from any external cause. But this was not the first time they had experienced toilsome marches or the privations of a wilderness life. They had long known fatigue, want, and danger in their journey; but had not the Lord continually encircled them with his protection, and supplied them by his providence? Trying as their situation was, their encouragements far exceeded their discouragements; and so will it ever be found by the faithful, that in every condition of Providence they have more cause for thankfulness than for complaint; and that their mercies vastly surpass their judgments. "He that will pass to the promised land, must neither stand upon length of way, nor difficulty. Every way hath its inconveniences; the nearest path hath more danger, the furthest hath more pain; either or both must be overcome, if ever we will enter the rest of God."—*Bp. Hall.*

V. 5. *The people spake against God, and against Moses.* Chald. "The people murmured before the Lord, and contended with Moses." So also v. 7. From some allusions elsewhere bearing upon this part of their history, it would appear that under the title God, our Lord and Saviour Jesus Christ is to be especially recognized. He was the Angel of God's

us up out of Egypt to die in
the wilderness? for *there is* no
bread, neither *is* [k] *there any*
water: and our soul loatheth
this light bread.
6 And [l] the LORD sent fiery

k Ps. 68. 6. c. 11. 6.

l Deut. 8. 15. 1 Cor. 10. 9.

face or presence, in whom was all the infallible virtue of the divine name, Ex. 23:20, 21. Is. 63:5. In accordance with this the apostle says, 1 Cor. 10:9, "Neither let us tempt Christ, as some of them also tempted, and were destroyed of serpents." Their unbelieving hearts here find murmuring tongues. They show themselves herein lineal descendants of the generation whose carcases had fallen in the wilderness. Nothing could be more heinous in view of all the circumstances. To speak against the servant was a great offence; but to speak against the Master himself was a still greater. But the mind, once thrown off its balance by the power of sharp or long continued temptation, is prone to go even the length of "charging God foolishly" rather than of bowing submissively and saying, "I was dumb, and opened not my mouth; for thou didst it."——¶ *For (there is) no bread, neither (is there any) water.* How strangely does excited feeling discolor and distort the objects at which it looks! The fretful impatience of the people renders them incapable of seeing and acknowledging the truth of their condition. They cannot admit that they are supplied with either bread or water. The bread which the Lord gave them from heaven is not worthy the name. "As an angry child casts away that which is given him, because he hath not that he would, so these foolish Israelites; their bread is light, and their water unsatisfying, because their way displeased them. Was ever people fed with such bread, or such water? Twice hath the very rock yielded them water, and every day the heaven affords them bread. Did any one soul amongst them miscarry, either for hunger or thirst? But no bread will answer for them, save that which the earth yields; no water but that from the natural wells or rivers."—*Bp. Hall.*——¶ *Our soul loatheth this light bread.* Heb. *kelokēl*, from a root signifying primarily *to be light*, and thence *to account light, vain, vile, contemptible.* Here, as the radicals are doubled, the meaning is intensified, and the idea conveyed is that of bread which is regarded as *exceedingly vile and despicable.* Chald. "This manna the light food." Gr. "This vain, or empty bread;" i. e., bread unsubstantial, innutritive, and worthless. This was not only a wicked disparagement of the natural gift which the Lord bestowed upon them from heaven, but it was a virtual turning away with loathing from that spiritual or heavenly manna which we are taught to recognize in the Lord, the Saviour, whose own words authenticate this interpretation. See John 6:48–51. Comp. Ps. 78:23, 24. "This manna rained upon them from heaven was both corporeal and spiritual food for them, a figure of the 'hidden manna' with which Christ feedeth his people unto life eternal. Rev. 2:17. So the contempt thereof was the contempt of Christ and his grace; and into this sin do all they fall that loathe and leave Christ and his gospel for the momentary pleasures of life."—*Ainsworth.*

The Plague of Serpents and the Remedy.

V. 6. *The Lord sent fiery serpents among the people.* Heb. *hannehâshim hasserâphim*, lit. *the serpents the seraphim*, i. e. as generally interpreted

serpents among the people, and they bit the people; and much people of Israel died.

---

fiery or *burning serpents*, from *sâraph*, *to burn*, whether so called from their glowing, fiery color, or from the intense and excruciating heat and thirst produced by their bite, or finally from the red and inflamed appearance of the skin of those who had been bitten. The original term is a substantive, and not an adjective, as it is rendered in our version. It denotes some class of the serpent tribe which were ordinarily somewhat abundant in that region, although now probably miraculously multiplied to answer a special end of the divine providence. The popular idea has for some cause invested these serpents with wings; but there is nothing in the original to warrant it. The epithet is simply "fiery," not "fiery flying" serpents. The prophet Isaiah, ch. 14:29. 30:6, makes mention of "fiery flying serpents," but even in this case it is supposed that the epithet "flying" was given from their power of *leaping* to a considerable distance in passing from tree to tree. Chald. "Burning serpents." Gr. "Deadly serpents." Syr. "Direful serpents." Arab. "Serpents of burning bites." Bochart, Michaelis, and others have undertaken to identify the species, but as all attempts of this kind can lead only to conjectural results, we shall waive them entirely, confining our remarks to points capable of being satisfactorily illustrated. The most important lessons to be derived from the narrative are of a practical nature, and these do not depend upon the *kind* of serpent alluded to. In Deut. 8:15, it is said of the region through which the Israelites wandered, probably with a reference to this particular part, "The great and terrible wilderness wherein were fiery serpents, and scorpions, and drought, where there was no water." "This description," says Mr. Kitto, "answers, to this day, with remarkable precision to these desert regions, and particularly to that part, about the head of the gulf of Akaba, where the Israelites now were. Scorpions abound in all the desert, and are particularly common here, and they inflict a wound scarcely less *burning* than the serpents of the same region. As to the serpents, both Burckhardt and Laborde bear witness to the extraordinary numbers which are found about the head of the gulf; but it is to be regretted that neither of these travellers speaks particularly of the species. Burckhardt, who at the time of making this observation did himself not see much of the head of the gulf, and was only on the western coast, nearly opposite the spot where the Israelites appear to have been thus visited, says:—'Ayd told me that serpents are very common in these parts; that the fishermen were much afraid of them, and extinguished their fires in the evening before they went to sleep, because the light was known to attract them. As serpents then are so numerous on this side, they are probably not deficient towards the head of the gulf on its opposite shore, where it appears that the Israelites passed when they journeyed from Mount Hor, by the way of the Red Sea, to compass the land of Edom, and when the 'Lord sent fiery serpents among the people.' ('Tour in the Peninsula of Sinai,' p. 499.) . . . . It would thus appear that no creation of serpents for this occasion was required, but that they were collected perhaps in extraordinary numbers, and endued probably with a stronger propensity than usual to assault all persons who fell in their way, until it pleased

7 Therefore [m] the people came
to Moses, and said, We have sinned, for we have spoken [n] against
the LORD, and against thee; pray
[o] unto the LORD, that he take

m Ps. 78. 34. n ver. 5.

o Ex. 8. 8, 28. Deut. 9. 20, 26. 1 Sam. 12. 19. 1 K. 13. 6. Job 42. 8, 10. Jer. 15. 1. Acts 8. 24. James 5. 16.

God, through an agency which would have been wholly inoperative but through Him, to heal those who had been wounded and were dying of their wounds."—*Pict. Bible.* The evidence, then, is conclusive, that the route of Israel lay over a region infested by venomous serpents, and it must be ascribed to the protecting care of the divine providence that they had not hitherto received harm from this source. But the time had now come when they had justly rendered themselves obnoxious to the plague, and when we may conceive the Lord as saying, "I will command the serpent, and he shall bite them," Am. 9 : 3.——¶ *And they bit the people; and much people of Israel died.* The remark of one of the Jewish writers in this connection, as to a certain analogy between their sin and their punishment is worthy of being repeated. This sin, he observes, was a virtual calumniation of the divine providence; but calumny is at once suggestive of the bite of a serpent. Ps. 140 : 3, "They have sharpened their tongues like a serpent; adders' poison is under their lips." Comp. Eccl. 10 : 11. Ps. 58 : 4. Jer. 8 : 17. The divine protection being now withdrawn, these ministers of the Lord's displeasure were sent to do their work of death amidst the guilty congregation. They inflicted upon them their terrible bites. Being surcharged with poison, the effects produced made the wretched sufferer feel as though the current of his blood was changed into tides of fire in his veins, causing the anguish of intolerable fever and thirst. Life was corrupted at the fountain; the blood ran polluted from the heart, and spread its defilement over the whole frame, until the victim sank beneath his malady; "and much people of Israel died." In this we behold a most striking similitude with the deadly agency of that "old serpent" who aimed at the life of man from the beginning, and whose venom has slain so many thousands of our race. The fatal fang of these serpents of the desert was but an emblem of the far more fearful wound inflicted by the serpent of Eden. "The sting of death is sin," and this is a sting which entails perdition to both body and soul. And as no unguent or medicine, no appliance of human device could heal the bite of the fiery serpents that now wrought such devastation in the camp of Israel, so the remedy for the moral poison which has corrupted the life of the soul can be supplied by the Lord alone. His alone it is to administer the balm of Gilead, for he alone is the physician there. But he will order his interposition in such a manner that it shall be appreciated and sought for before it is enjoyed.

V. 7. *We have sinned, etc.* In the extremity that was now upon them, what could the people do? It was in vain that antidotes were sought, and as to arming themselves against the danger, this was impossible, for they were assailed on every side, and the assaults were irresistible. The course pursued was the only right and reasonable one. They apply themselves to him, who alone was able to deliver. They humble themselves before God, and entreat Moses to intercede for them. If the Lord had not mercy on them, they must all perish. The very first step in conciliating the forfeited favor of heaven is the penitent confession of our

away the serpents from us. And Moses prayed [p] for the people.

p Ps. 106. 23.

8 And the LORD said unto Moses, Make thee a fiery ser-

offences, for "he that confesseth and forsaketh sin shall find mercy." Such had been the people's course on former occasions, and always with a happy result, and to this fact we have allusion Ps. 78 : 34, "When he slew them, then they sought him; and they returned and inquired early after God." Past experience prompts them to the same course now, and with like results; for though the plague was not immediately removed, yet an effectual antidote was graciously provided.——¶ *Pray unto the Lord, that he take away the serpents from us.* Heb. "And let him take away the serpent from us," col. sing. for plur. as in multitudinous instances elsewhere. "They had spoken against God and Moses, and now they humbly speak to Moses, that he would pray to God for them. Now the people are glad to seek to Moses unbidden. Ever heretofore they have been wont to be sued to and entreated for without their own entreaty; now their misery makes them importunate; there needs no solicitor where there is sense of smart. It were pity men should want affliction, since it sends them to their prayers and confessions. All the persuasions of Moses could not do that which the serpents have done for him."—*Bp. Hall.* They seem to be conscious of their own unworthiness, and therefore crave the intercession of one who they believed had more power with God than themselves. "How soon is their tone altered! They who had just before quarrelled with Moses as their worst enemy, now make their court to him as their best friend, and choose him as their advocate with God. Afflictions often change men's sentiments concerning God's people, teach them to value those prayers, which at a former period they had scorned."—*Henry.*——¶ *And Moses prayed for the people.* Heb. *yithpallēl*, in the Hithpael or reflexive form, implying that he interposed himself and prayed as a mediator. The meekness, patience, and forgiving spirit of Moses appeared conspicuous on this occasion. Though so often the subject of their reproaches and provocations, yet upon the slightest evidence of repentance and amendment, he turns with a parental yearning towards them, and virtually says in the language of Samuel on a like occasion, 1 Sam. 12 : 19, 23, "As for me, God forbid that I should sin against the Lord in ceasing to pray for you; but I will teach you the good and the right way."

V. 8. *Make thee a fiery serpent.* This is expressed in the Heb. by a single word *sârâph, sâraph*, or *burner*, rendered by the Gr. *a serpent.* As appears from the following verse it was a "serpent of brass," i. e., the brazen image of a serpent, which was now to be constructed, and elevated as a signal in the sight of the congregation. The material ordered was no doubt well adapted to represent the fiery quality of the serpents, as it is said of the cherubim seen in Ezekiel's vision, ch. 1 : 7, that "they sparkled like burning brass." This will be seen to be still more apropos if we bear in mind, the brass of the Scriptures is supposed to have been really copper, the livid hue of which comes still nearer to that of poisonous serpents. Such was the device of the divine wisdom and goodness. Misery here gives occasion for mercy. A remedy is pointed out equal and suitable to the disease. Had the serpents been merely removed, accord-

pent, and set it upon a pole: and it shall come to pass, that every one that is bitten, when he looketh upon it, shall live.

ing to the prayer of the people, yet that would not have healed the wounded. A remedy was to be provided that should also recover the dying, and save the living. Such a remedy is provided in the brazen serpent now ordered to be set up. Its efficacy as a means of healing was not inherent in itself. Obviously there was nothing in the representative semblance that could possibly tend to effect a cure. Its potency in this respect was due entirely to the divine appointment. This fact is thus wisely recognized and discoursed upon in the apocryphal book, entitled "The Wisdom of Solomon," ch. 16:5–8, "For when the horrible fierceness of beasts came upon them, they perished with the stings of crooked serpents. But they were troubled for a small season, that they might be admonished, having a sign of salvation, to put them in remembrance of the commandment of thy law. For he that turned himself toward it, was not saved by the thing that he saw, but by thee that art the Saviour of all. And in this thou madest thine enemies confess, that it is thou who deliverest from all evil."——¶ *And set it upon a pole.* Heb. נס *nës*, signifying properly a *banner-staff.* It is often used in the Prophets and Psalms in the sense of an *ensign* or *banner*, as a signal for the assembling of the people, and which, with a view to its being more conspicuous, was frequently erected on the summit of a hill. So it may be presumed in the present case, that the standard-pole, surmounted by the appointed symbol, was elevated in some position which made it visible to the greatest extent throughout the camp. The object of this appointment is announced in what follows.——¶ *Every one that is bitten, when he looketh upon it, shall live.* Targ. Jon. "He shall look upon it and live, if his heart be intent upon the name of the Word of the Lord." It is evident, to the most superficial glance, that the remedy, viewed in itself, was entirely inadequate to the effect to be produced. As Bp. Hall well remarks, "A serpent of brass could no more heal than sting them. What could a serpent of cold brass prevail against a living and fiery serpent?" Yet although neither Moses nor the wounded Israelites had any suitable conceptions of the full import of the divine ordination here recorded, still with the light afforded to us in regard to its typical bearings, we can recognize a wonderful adaptedness in the measure to the ends to be attained by it. The healing of the body was designed to be an emblem of the healing of the soul, and as this moral cure was to be compassed by means such as human reason would never have devised, so it was fitting that the symbolical recovery should be effected by a process equally strange, extraordinary, and incredible. If a resort had been ordered to the virtues of herbs or balsams, the divine power would have been apt to have been lost sight of in the natural properties and operations of the remedies. Had the serpents been removed at the solicitation of the people, the mercy of heaven would indeed have been conspicuous, but no intimation would have been given of that hatred of sin and that delight in holiness which were figuratively displayed in the suspension on the pole, corresponding to the Saviour's suspension on the cross. The representation, or typical relation, between the lifting up of the serpent in the wilderness and the lifting up of Christ upon the cross is expressly affirmed by our Lord himself, John 3 : 14, 15, and it is therefore proper, in order to make the narrative more impressive, that we should collect and array before our minds all the points of coincidence between the two events. Among these the following are the most striking: (1.) The disease in both cases is similar. Both parties of sufferers are bitten of serpents—the one by natural serpents inhabiting the desert, and armed with poisonous tooth; the other by that Old Serpent, the Devil, called also a Great Red Dragon. Sin is the biting of this deadly serpent, who may be called "fiery," as his temptations are termed "fiery darts," whose influence *inflames* all the evil passions and lusts, and who brings his subjects at last to a fiery perdition. Through his conquest the poison of sin rankles in our whole constitution; the body and the soul are affected by it; the body being the victim of disease, and the soul of depravity. (2.) In both cases the remedy was divinely prescribed, and no other could be of any avail. (3.) The cure prescribed was, in both instances, of a nature very unlikely to be effectual. The sight of a lifeless serpent of metal, working as an antidote to the mortal poison of one alive, how incredible and absurd would it appear to human reason! So our salvation by the cross of Christ is "to the Jews a stumbling-block, and to the Greeks foolishness." Yet how mighty the efficacy of the remedy as flowing from the divine appointment! The believing Israelite hears, even in his dying agonies, the proclamation of deliverance, lifts up his drooping head, looks, and is healed. The perishing sinner hears the voice of the Son of God, saying, "Look unto me, and be ye saved, all the ends of the earth," and turns towards him an eye of faith. This suggests another point of resemblance, viz., (4.) That it was solely by a *look* that the effect was produced. There was nothing else required of the bitten Israelites. They were not to look at the aggravations of their wounds, or to attempt partially to heal themselves by the application of some other remedy in conjunction with this. Nor were they to do any thing either to merit or to increase its efficacy. They were simply to look upon the serpent as God's ordinance for recovery. In like manner, it is by renouncing every other dependence, and simply looking to the Lord as lifted up for our salvation that we experience the benefits of his saving mercy. "Whosoever believeth in him shall not perish, but shall have everlasting life." (5.) That which cured was shaped in the likeness of that which wounded. So our divine Saviour, though perfectly free from sin himself, yet was he "made in the likeness of sinful flesh." (6.) The mercy bestowed was in both cases provided when it was least expected. The Israelites had just been murmuring against a merciful Providence which had led and supplied them for many years in their wearisome march through the wilderness. They had quarrelled with Moses and with the Lord on the ostensible ground that they were not furnished with a due supply of bread and water, though one miracle after another had been wrought to satisfy both their hunger and their thirst. Yet on the very heels of these provocations, when they had more reason to expect severer judgments than fresh mercies, the Most High comes forward with this amazing device for their deliverance from the miseries which they had brought upon themselves. So when we, by our iniquities, had utterly forfeited every favor at the Lord's hands, and condign punishment was all we could reasonably anticipate, the cloud,

9 And Moses made a serpent[q] of brass, and put it upon a pole: and it came to pass, that if a

q 2 K. 18. 4. John 3. 14, 15.

apparently surcharged with wrath, broke in mercy over our heads, and the divine Saviour was lifted up "that he might draw all men unto him."

These points of similitude might be still further multiplied, but those already cited will be sufficient for our purpose, the scope of which may be summed up in the words of Henry: "The brazen serpent's being lifted up would not cure, if it was not looked upon. If any pored on their wound, and would not look up to the brazen serpent, they inevitably died. If they slighted this method of cure, and had recourse to natural medicines, and trusted to them, they justly perished. So, if sinners either despise Christ's righteousness, or despair of benefit by it, their wound will, without doubt, be fatal. Whoever looked up to this healing sign, though from the outermost part of the camp, though with a weak and weeping eye, was certainly healed. So, whosoever believes in Christ, though as yet but weak in faith, shall not perish."

V. 9. *Moses made a serpent of brass, and put it upon a pole, etc.* The leader of Israel here shows himself, as usual, the obedient servant of God. He consults not with flesh and blood, nor yields to the suggestions of carnal wisdom. He is not staggered by the strangeness of the command. He stays not to reason whether it were likely that a piece of brass should remedy a deadly bite, or whether a dead thing should be made a medium of life. Having received the command, he knows that nothing remains for him but to obey, and this he does with promptitude and fidelity.——¶ *If a serpent had bitten any man, etc.* So richly laden is this portion of the sacred story with instruction, that we are prompted to dwell somewhat more at length upon the various particulars that challenge our attention. It is clear that the serpents were not removed according to the prayer recorded v. 7, for they still continued to bite the people; but the divine mercy provided an antidote which should be efficacious in the midst of the bites, and thus evince how far superior was the divine power to save to the power of the enemy to destroy. So when Paul besought the Lord thrice to remove from him the thorn in the flesh, he did not obtain the precise favor sought, but he received an assurance which was abundantly equivalent, "My grace shall be sufficient for thee." So in the present case death was arrested, and life and health restored, notwithstanding the plague continued. Let us pause for a moment on the scene that the pencil of inspiration depicts before us. An Israelite has been bitten. A darting pain shoots through his system, and a deadly sickness and faintness comes upon him, soon to be succeeded by a burning heat which seems to consume his very vitals. His whirling brain is racked with ineffable torture, and as the poison approaches nearer and yet nearer to the fountain of life, he looks wildly around for aid that none can render. He is just ready to yield to hopeless despair, when the voice of mercy is heard, "LOOK AND LIVE." The eye of the poor sufferer, already glazed in death, is feebly turned to the blessed object, and how rich is the reward! One glimpse is LIFE. The fever subsides, the inflammation leaves the blood, the convulsions cease, the action of the pulse returns, the pain dies away, the whole frame is conscious of renovation. It is the work of a few

serpent had bitten any man, when he beheld the serpent of brass, he lived.

10 And the children of Israel set forward, and pitched in Oboth[r].

r c. 33. 43, 44.

---

moments only; the cure is perfected; the sufferer is well. Those lately marked for death, and almost numbered with the dead, take their places again among the living. The man resumes his outdoor occupations, and the woman her domestic employments, whilst the child returns to its play. Many who were given up as lost are now found again; they come flocking by hundreds and thousands to their tents, and as fathers, mothers, brothers, sisters, and children rush into each other's arms, the general mourning is turned to dancing, and the camp becomes one scene of tumultuous and grateful joy. How all this finds its counterpart in the case of the sin-slain soul looking up to him who was elevated upon the cross for our salvation, will be easily perceived from what we have already said upon the typical scope of the transaction.

We remark in addition, as to the final disposal of the brazen serpent, that it seems not improbable that whether the camp was subsequently molested in the same manner or not, still the sacred symbol was carried with them in their after journeyings, and set up whenever they encamped as a preservative against a recurrence of the danger; and that when they settled in Canaan, they fixed it somewhere within the borders of the land. This is fairly to be inferred from the fact, that in the history of Hezekiah, 2 Kings 18:4, we read that the brazen serpent was preserved, doubtless as a memorial of the miracle here recorded, till his time, when, in consequence of its having become an object of idolatry, he caused it to be destroyed. It is to be presumed, therefore, that if it had been kept for so long a period, it was laid up at Jerusalem or some other part of the land of Canaan, for we cannot suppose that the people of Israel went so far off as this station into the wilderness, to burn incense to it, as we find they did in the passage referred to. "He removed the high places, and brake the images, and cut down the groves, and brake in pieces the serpent that Moses had made; for unto those days the children of Israel did burn incense to it: and he called it Nehushtan." The term "Nehushtan" is a diminutive from Heb. *nehosheth, brass*, and implies a certain degree of contempt; as if he had said, "Whatever of honor or reverence may have pertained to this symbol in ancient times, it is intrinsically but *a mere piece of brass, a brazen bauble*, and so long as you are disposed to idolize it, it is proper it should be called by a name that suitably expresses its quality." Types are no farther valuable than as they lead to the spiritual mysteries of Christ. They are perverted from their end when viewed as clothed with peculiar sanctity apart from the substance which they represented. The propensity to a superstitious veneration of the relics of antiquity has been apparent in all ages, and in the idolatrous regard that finally sprung up for this significant emblem we may recognize perhaps a foreshadowing of that excessive reverence for the bare *cross* which has for ages distinguished the Roman Catholic church.

The Route of the Children of Israel along the Borders of Moab, in their farther progress towards the Land of Canaan.

V. 10. *The children of Israel set forward.* Heb. "Broke up," as explained

11 And they journeyed from Oboth, and pitched at Ije-abarim, in the wilderness which *is* before Moab, toward the sun-rising.

in the Note on ch. 2 : 9.——¶ *And pitched in Oboth.* The meaning of the original is *bottles*, i. e., sacks or vessels made of skins for holding water. As it is evident, from v. 16, that names were sometimes given to stations founded upon some features of the place, or upon some incident there occurring, we deem it altogether probable that this was the case in the present instance; that the station was named from the supply of water with which they were now enabled to provide themselves. As all these wanderings of Israel in the desert represent the diversified states of Christians in the progress of their regeneration, a pious reflection is here naturally suggested, viz., that as they who had so often experienced thirst in the desert, and had thus known the preciousness of water, would, upon leaving a place, be careful to carry away with them their vessels full; so believers should endeavor to keep their vessels full to serve them for those seasons when the springs should become comparatively dry. They will be of use as long as they sojourn in the wilderness. Ere long their journey will be ended, when the weary pilgrims will come to the rest and be led to the living fountains of waters. Meantime let them not throw away their vessels or neglect the means of spiritual reviving. Happy they who carry with them water for the way; whose memory, understanding, and heart, filled with the Lord's heavenly treasure, become like a well of water springing up to everlasting life. It appears, from ch. 33 : 41, 42, that after leaving Mount Hor their first encampment was at Zalmonah, and the second at Punon, both which are here omitted. As Zalmonah is derived from *tzelem, image*, it is supposed that it was at that station that the plague of the serpents occurred, and that the erection of the image of a serpent was designed to be commemorated in the name given to the place. As to their route henceforward, it is difficult to trace it in detail, but we know in general that from a point near the head of the Gulf of Akabah, they proceeded through some mountain pass, to the east, probably the Wady Ithm, and, rounding the south-eastern borders of Edom, emerged on to the great plains which are traversed by the Syrian pilgrims going south to Mecca, and others going north to Damascus. The course of the Israelites would have been mainly to the north, along the eastern frontiers of Moab, whose territory lay between their route and the eastern shore of the Dead Sea. This route they would naturally follow till they reached the point a little beyond the northern extremity of that Sea, whence they were to turn westward to cross the Jordan. Reference to the best modern maps of this region, as, for instance, those of Robinson, Stanley, or Kiepert, will supply all that is wanting in our verbal description. Of the several stations mentioned in this connection, the precise locality is matter of conjecture; and therefore the older maps conveniently place them at about equal distances from each other, which may be correct, or may not. Happily nothing of moment depends upon the ascertainment of their exact position.

V. 11. *Pitched at Ije-Abarim.* That is, *at the heaps of the fords*, as the original implies; referring, perhaps, to some heaps of stones that had for some reason been piled up at certain fording-places across which lay their route. Chald. "Close by the ford of the pas-

12 From thence they removed, and pitched in the valley of Zared[s].

13 From thence they removed, and pitched on the other side of[t] Arnon, which *is* in the wilderness that cometh out of the coasts of the Amorites: for Arnon *is* the border of Moab, between Moab and the Amorites.

14 Wherefore it is said in the book of the wars of the LORD, What he did in the Red Sea, and in the brooks of Arnon,

s Deut. 2. 13. t c. 22. 36. Judg. 11. 18.

sengers."——¶ *In the wilderness before Moab, toward the sun-rising.* That is, to the east of the country of Moab, which lay between the small rivers Arnon and Jabbok, as its northern and southern boundaries.

V. 12. *Pitched in the valley of Zared.* Heb. *benâ'hal, in the valley*, elsewhere rendered *river*, and implying a valley which, in a rainy season, was liable to become the bed of a stream. The same word occurs, Deut. 2:13, where Moses is recounting the events of this part of their journey, "Now rise up, said I, and get you over the *brook* (*na'hal*) Zared; and we went over the *brook* (*na'hal*) Zared." It is hardly practicable at present to identify this locality, though both Kitto and Robinson incline to regard it as the same with a considerable stream now called Ahsa, or Ahsy, which empties into the south-eastern corner of the Dead Sea. It favors this supposition, that the Ahsy is not only the largest river south of the Arnon, but is the first the Israelites would meet with in coming from the direction of the Elanitic Gulf, as they did.

V. 13. *Pitched on the other side of Arnon.* This river formed the southern boundary of the Israelitish tribes dwelling on the eastern side of the Jordan, and separating their territory from the land of Moab. It is now known under the name of Wady Modjeb. It rises in the mountains of Gilead, whence it pursues a circuitous course of about eighty miles to the Dead Sea. It flows in a rocky bed, and in several places in a channel so deep and precipitous as to appear inaccessible; yet along this channel, winding among huge fragments of rock, lies the most frequented road, and, not being far from Dibon, probably that taken by the Israelites. The stream is almost dried up in summer; but large masses of rock, torn from the banks, and deposited high above the usual channel, evince its fulness and impetuosity in the rainy season. Burckhardt, and Irby and Mangles have given the fullest account of this river.

V. 14. *Wherefore it is said in the book of the wars of the Lord, etc.* We here encounter one of the most impenetrably obscure passages in the whole compass of Holy Writ. The voluminous labors of commentators of all periods still leave the meaning of the sacred writer enveloped in doubt. We shall not enter into a discussion of the various senses that have been put upon the words, but simply state what appears to us, on the whole, most probable. The passage is evidently a quotation, but the source from which it is derived it is impossible clearly to determine. The term rendered "book" may signify *narrative* or *rehearsal*, and refer either to some writing of the Amorites recounting in poetical style the victories of Sihon their king, or some document originating with the Israelites, but long since lost, like other works to which we find occasional allu-

15 And at the stream of the brooks that goeth down to the dwelling of Ar [u], and lieth upon the border of Moab.

u Deut. 2. 18, 29.

---

sion in the canonical Scriptures. The passage may thus be presented in its most literal form:

"Wherefore it is said in the book (or narrative) of the wars of the Lord:

'Vaheb in a whirlwind,
And the brooks of Arnon;
And the lowlands of the streams
Which turn to the dwelling of Ar,
And incline to the border of Moab.'"

From the impossibility of eliciting a coherent sense from these words, we infer that it is a fragmentary extract from some pre-existing work which is here introduced apart from its connections both preceding and succeeding, and therefore leaving us without an adequate clue to its meaning. "What he did in the Red Sea" is given in our English version as a translation of the original *eth vaheb besuphah,* for which the marginal reading exhibits "Vaheb in Supha," as if both were proper names, but about which nothing definite was known. By some violence *vaheb* may be converted into a verb with the import of *doing* or *acting*, and as the common Heb. term for *Red Sea* is *suph*, or rather *yam suph*, our translators have rendered it "What he did in the Red Sea," wherein they follow the Chaldee, which renders it in the same manner. But the original is not *suph*, but *suphah, a violent storm or whirlwind,* and may here imply the desolating character of the divine judgments, as recorded in the ancient documents referred to—judgments, perhaps, inflicted upon the Moabites by Sihon, king of the Amorites, vs. 28, 29. Wars, we know, are often represented under the figure of fire, tempest, whirlwind, etc. Thus, Am. 1:14, "I will kindle a fire in the wall of Rabbah, and it shall devour the palaces thereof, with shouting in the day of battle, with a tempest in the day of the whirlwind." Is. 29:6, "Thou shalt be visited of the Lord of hosts with thunder, and with earthquake, and great noise, with storm and tempest, and the flame of devouring fire." Is. 66:15, "The Lord will come with fire, and with his chariots like a whirlwind." Comp. Neh. 1:3. Is. 5:28. Jer. 4:13. Thus, too, the Gr. "The war of the Lord hath set Zoob on fire," where "Zoob" is intended to answer to "Vaheb," but corrupted by the translators mistaking V (ו) for Z (ז). From vs. 28, 29, of this chapter, it appears that Arnon as well as Heshbon, formerly the possession of Moab, had some time previous been wrested from that people by Sihon, king of the Amorites, and, being now in their hands, it was lawful for the Israelites to capture it, as it was said to them, Deut. 2:24, "Rise up and take your journey, and pass over the river Arnon: behold, I have given into thine hand Sihon the Amorite, king of Heshbon, and his land: begin to possess it, and contend with him in battle." Towards the Moabites, on the other hand, they were to engage in no acts of hostility, Deut. 2:9. On the whole, therefore, we deem it most probable, that Moses is here quoting some history or poem of the Amorites, with a view to determine the extent of the country of which, by his victory over them, he had become master. He adduces the lines to show, that this people had, in their wars with the Moabites, pushed their southern boundary as far as the river Arnon; and accordingly, as far as this, the Israelites might now maintain a claim against

16 And from thence *they went* to [v] Beer: that *is* the well whereof the LORD [w] spake unto Moses, Gather the people together, and I will give them water.

17 Then Israel sang [x] this

v Judg. 9. 21. w c. 20. 8. x Ex. 15. 1. Judg. 5. 1. Ps. 106. 12.

the people of Moab, whom they did not propose to disturb in their own possessions. Ar was a city of Moab, v. 28. By "lying (Heb. leaning) upon the border of Moab," is meant being conterminous with it.

V. 16. *From thence (they went) to Beer.* Heb. "To the well," that is, to the place distinguished by the digging of a well, and the obtaining thence a fresh supply of water. The name "Beer" does not occur among the names of the stations mentioned, ch. 33.——¶ *Whereof the Lord spake unto Moses.* The want of water had no doubt begun to be experienced by the host; but, unlike their deportment in former instances, we now read of no murmurings or complaints. The Lord, therefore, had compassion upon them, and brought them to a well of water to encourage them to wait upon him in the patience of hope, assured that he would ever care for them so long as they calmly put their trust in him. "They that seek the Lord shall not want any good thing." It is implied that a promise was given, at least to Moses, that their wants in this respect should be supplied; but when this promise was given, whether before they came to the place, or at the time, does not appear from the narrative. But we may with confidence say, that the well of Beer was a spring previously ordained to afford refreshment to the "church in the wilderness." The Lord knew the spot, though they themselves were ignorant of it; and so in the matter of our salvation, the divine beneficence anticipates our own conscious wants. He "prevents us with the blessings of goodness."——¶ *Gather the people together, and I will give them water.* In obedience to the divine direction, they are convened on the very spot where the water is to burst forth, and yet know it not till Moses points it out to them. They are gathered in expectation and desire, looking for the fulfilment of the promise. The princes surround it with their staves, but as yet no well is seen, no water appears; the dry and sandy surface indicates no treasure beneath. But throughout the whole of their journey, their supplies had been furnished them contrary to all appearances. As from the smitten flinty rock a flowing stream broke forth, so from the parched soil, when pierced, a fountain, not before expected, arose. So in the spiritual experience of the church, while passing on to its Canaan in heaven, is the prophetic declaration verified, "in the wilderness shall waters break forth, and springs in the desert." The cheering truths of the Word are suddenly opened to them in the midst of spiritual death and desolation, and they are enabled to sing of the Lord's mercies as did Israel on this occasion.

V. 17. *Then Israel sang this song.* Being wrought up to a kind of transport of grateful joy on account of the unexpected kindness of the Lord in supplying their wants, they burst forth into a song of celebration, a poetical apostrophe, making memorable ever after this oasis in the desert. Analogous is the language of the prophet, Is. 12:3, 4, "Therefore with joy shall ye draw water out of the wells of salvation. And in that day shall ye say, Praise the Lord, call upon his name,

song, Spring up, O well; sing ye unto it:
18 The princes digged the well, the nobles of the people digged it, by the *direction of* the lawgiver [y], with their staves. And from the wilderness *they went* to Mattanah:
19 And from Mattanah to

y Deut. 33. 4. Is. 33. 22.

---

declare his doings among the people, make mention that his name is exalted."——¶ *Spring up, O well; sing ye unto it.* Or, Heb. "Ascend, O well." It would appear, from the ensuing verse, that the people were gathered to a certain appointed spot, around which stood the princes or heads of the tribes, together with Moses, their "law-giver," with their staves in their hands, and that, at a given signal, they struck them into the earth, when the hidden waters forthwith gushed forth as they did from the rock when smitten by the rod of Moses. As they had now demeaned themselves properly, abstaining from all murmuring and complaint, the whole people are, through their princes, admitted to share in the honor of working the miracle; whereas, formerly, their rebellious conduct rendered them unworthy, and therefore the honor was restricted to Moses.——¶ *Sing ye unto it.* Heb. "Answer ye unto it." The original term "answer" is employed to denote that kind of alternative or responsive singing, of which a specimen occurred in the case of Miriam and the children of Israel at the Red Sea, Ex. 15 : 20, 21, "And Miriam the prophetess, the sister of Aaron, took a timbrel in her hand: and all the women went out after her, with timbrels, and with dances. And Miriam answered them, Sing ye to the Lord, for he hath triumphed gloriously: the horse and his rider hath he thrown into the sea." So also, 1 Sam. 18 : 6, 7, "And it came to pass as they came, when David was returned from the slaughter of the Philistine, that the women came out of all the cities of Israel, singing and dancing, to meet king Saul, with tabrets, with joy, and with instruments of music. And the women answered one another as they played, and said, Saul hath slain his thousands, and David his ten thousands." Again, Ps. 147 : 7, "Sing (Heb. answer) unto the Lord with thanksgiving." The suggestion of Ainsworth strikes us as probable, viz., that the order of the words may be properly transposed, so as to read, "Answer (or sing) ye unto it, Spring up, O well." A transposition very similar occurs, Is. 27 : 2, "In that day sing ye (Heb. answer ye) unto her, A vineyard of red wine." These two clauses change places in the original.

V. 18. *The princes digged the well, etc.* Heb. "The well, the princes digged it:" or, "O well, which the princes digged, which the nobles delved." The import of the two original words is very nearly the same. The act of digging is no doubt literally implied by them, but it is palpable that staves are not the proper implements for digging, and therefore we take the expression to be poetical or hyperbolical, the effect of striking their staves into the sandy soil having been the same as if they had actually dug a well with spades and pickaxes.——¶ *From the wilderness (they went) to Mattanah.* The verb indicating their journeying is omitted, both here and in other places in the connection, and the general style is somewhat peculiar, as if the poetical cast of the preceding verses was still continued. Neither this nor the other names occurring in this context are

Nahaliel: and from Nahaliel to Bamoth:

20 And from Bamoth *in* the valley, that *is* in the country of Moab, to the top of Pisgah, which looketh [z] toward Jeshimon.

21 And [a] Israel sent messen-

z c. 23. 28. a Deut. 2. 26, 27. Judg. 11. 19, 20.

---

found in the catalogue of stations given in ch. 33. The reasons of this, together with a great many minor points of criticism growing out of the text, we forbear to enlarge upon, as we despair of attaining to certainty respecting them.

V. 20. *From Bamoth (in) the valley.* Rather, *to* the valley, as the construction seems to require, which is the same with that in the preceding verse, where there is nothing in the original to answer to the word "to." As to the precise locality it is in vain to think at this day of identifying it. Chazkuni, a Jewish writer, says it is the same with what is called, ch. 33 : 49, "Abel-shittim in the plains of Moab."——¶ *To the top of Pisgah.* Heb. "The head of Pisgah." The preposition "to" is wanting in the Hebrew, and some would render it literally, "And from Bamoth (to) the valley which is the field of Moab, the head of Pisgah." But, as Rosenmuller remarks, a strange sense is made by "a valley which is in the field (or country) of Moab, the head of Pisgah." His suggestion is, that it denotes a general acclivity commencing in the low grounds of Moab, and terminating in the mountain summit known as Pisgah, which is apparently the same with Mount Nebo, both mountains being assigned as the place where Moses died. But we shall hereafter have occasion to consider the topography of these mountains more fully.——¶ *Which looketh toward Jeshimon.* Or, Heb. "And it standeth out, or projecteth, before the face (or in front of) the wilderness;" implying a kind of promontory, from which, on one side, an extensive view of the wilderness they had passed was afforded, while on another, the eye could reach along the valley of the Jordan, and to the promised region beyond. Jeshimon is rendered "wilderness" in repeated instances. See Deut. 32 : 10. Ps. 68 : 7. 78 : 40. The Chald. understands this entire context of the flowing of the water of the well, v. 16, along the route of the Israelites. "And from (the place) where it was given unto them, it descended with them to the valleys; and from the valleys it ascended with them to the high places; and from the high places to the valley that is in the field of Moab, etc."

Messengers sent to Sihon, King of the Amorites.

V. 21. *Israel sent messengers.* This is attributed to Moses, Deut. 2 : 26, but the same act is often ascribed interchangeably to an individual, or to a multitude in whose name he acts. The place from which these messengers were dispatched was Kedemoth, from *Kedem, east,* the eastern territory. It seems to have had its name given to it by a city which subsequently fell to the tribe of Reuben, Josh. 13 : 18, situated near the river Arnon, which constituted the boundary between the kingdom of the Ammonites and the Moabites. In thus dispatching messengers to the Amoritish king, he pursued the same friendly policy as he had before towards the king of Edom, of whom he civilly requested a free passage through his dominions, at the same time offering every reasonable pledge to abstain from all molestation

gers unto Sihon king of the Amorites, saying,

22 Let [b] me pass through thy

b c. 20. 17.

of himself or his subjects. The occasion which suggested this measure we recognize in the Lord's words, Deut. 2: 24, "Rise ye up, take your journey, and pass over the river Arnon: behold, I have given into thy hand Sihon the Amorite, king of Heshbon, and his land: begin to possess it, and contend with him in battle." The result we read in what follows.

V. 22. *Let me pass through, etc.* Gr. "Let us pass through." The singular is often used for the plural, where a special unity is implied in the collective body. It has occurred to some as a difficulty, that Moses should have sent such an embassy and offered terms of peace, when at the same time the Israelites had been commanded to destroy them and take possession of their country; as it seems altogether inconsistent to offer conditions of peace when war has been actually determined upon. But the supposed inconsistency is founded on the presumption that the sole design of sending the messengers was to induce Sihon to grant the favor desired. This presumption, however, is not well sustained, as the Most High may have had other ends to answer in directing or secretly prompting the message to be sent. On parallel grounds it might be objected, that the message to Pharaoh to let Israel go was inconsistent with the previous declaration that he would not let him go. In either case the event was of course fully known to Omniscience, but it was entirely proper for Him to adopt a course which would more fully disclose the latent iniquity and obstinacy of the rebellious king, and thus make the justice of his punishment more obvious. The divine wisdom would so order things that all occasion should be cut off of remonstrance or complaint, importing that he had not been honorably or fairly dealt with. It is to be remarked, moreover, that Sihon did not stand on the same footing with the rest of the Canaanites. His territory was originally a possession of the Moabites. Otherwise this embassy of peace would not have been sent to him. A similar mission to the Canaanites on the west side of the Jordan, would have been a practical denial of the divine promises. There such language as, "*If* thou wilt let me pass, *then* I will do thee no harm," would have been totally out of place, because the relation of that people to the purposes of heaven was altogether different. In the present case, all excuse was to be taken away from one who could voluntarily provoke to war a people that declared themselves willing to be at peace with him. We therefore rest in the language of holy writ respecting this event, Deut. 2: 30, "But Sihon, king of Heshbon, would not let us pass by him, for the Lord thy God hardened his spirit, and he made his heart obstinate, that he might deliver him into thy hand." The way is opened for him by which, if so disposed, he can escape his fate. His deliverance is placed in his own hands, and if he will fling it away and blindly rush upon destruction, the consequences are his own. The Lord hardens only by his *permissive* providence, never by any positive act. In the allusion to this incident, Judg. 11: 19, we read that "Israel said unto him, Let us pass, we pray thee, through thy land unto my place." We know too little of the geography of the region to judge of what they would have gained by passing through the territory of the Amorites, or what would have been their precise route in

land: we will not turn into the fields, or into the vineyards; we will not drink *of* the waters of the well: *but* we will go along by the king's *high*-way, until we be past thy borders.

23 And Sihon would not suffer Israel to pass through his border; but [c] Sihon gathered all his people together, and went out against Israel into the wilderness: and he came to Jahaz, and fought against Israel.

24 And [d] Israel smote him

c Deut. 29. 7. d Josh. 12. 1, 2. 24. 8.

---

so doing, but it would seem that their aim was to avoid the necessity of continuing so far to the east and the north before turning westward to the fords of the Jordan.——¶ *We will not drink (of) the waters of the well.* Gr. "Of thy well;" that is, of any of thy wells; collective singular for plural, as in multitudes of other instances. Of course no particular well is intended.——¶ *By the king's (high) way.* See Note on ch. 20:17. It is literally "the king's way," there being nothing in the original to answer to the epithet "high." It undoubtedly denotes the most open and public thoroughfare. The parallel passage, Deut. 2:27, is worded somewhat differently; "I will go along by the way, by the way," i. e. I will keep constantly in the way without turning aside from it.

V. 23. *And Sihon would not suffer Israel to pass through his border.* Heb. "Sihon gave not (granted not) Israel to pass through," etc. The reason of this refusal is more explicitly stated in the recital of the circumstances by Jephthah, Judg. 11:19, 20, "And Israel sent messengers unto Sihon king of the Amorites, the king of Heshbon; and Israel said unto him, Let us pass, we pray thee, through thy land unto my place. But Sihon trusted not Israel to pass through his coast: but Sihon gathered all his people together, and pitched in Jahaz, and fought against Israel." From this it appears that he was actuated by distrust, being ready, no doubt, to impute to others the motives by which he was conscious he would himself be governed in the same circumstances. Men that know themselves to be unworthy of confidence are usually the first to withhold it from others.——¶ *Gathered all his people together, and went out against Israel.* This haughty prince contented not himself with a bare denial of the request of Israel. Worse than the Edomites on a former occasion, he not only refused them passage, but mustered his forces and, passing out of his own border, he went forth into the wilderness to attack the advancing host. As this was done without the least provocation on the part of Israel, he could not but encounter his own ruin in thus assaulting them. He little thought of the power he was contending with in this rash onset. "The enemies of God's church are often infatuated in those very counsels which they think most wisely taken."—*Henry.*

V. 24. *Israel smote him with the edge of the sword.* The most important practical inference to be drawn from this is suggested by the parallel passage in Judg. 11:21, "And the Lord God of Israel delivered Sihon and all his people into the hand of Israel, and they smote them: so Israel possessed all the land of the Amorites, the inhabitants of that country." So also Deut. 2:32, 33, "Then Sihon came out against us, he and all his people, to fight at Jahaz. And the Lord our God delivered him before us; and we smote him, with the edge of the sword, and possessed his land from Arnon unto Jabbok, even unto the children of Ammon: for the border of the children of Ammon *was* strong.

---

and his sons, and all his people." This ascribes the glory of the victory to the proper source. As it was the Most High who, to punish these guilty nations, ordered Israel to destroy them, so it was *his* power, and not their own, that obtained for them the victory. And in like manner, both in the Psalms and the Prophets, all occasion for Israel's glorying in his own prowess, is cut off. Ps. 135 : 10, 11, "Who smote great nations and slew mighty kings; Sihon king of the Amorites, and Og king of Bashan, and all the kingdoms of Canaan." Comp. 136 : 17–21. So also Amos 2 : 9, "Yet destroyed I the Amorite before them, whose height was like the height of the cedars, and he was strong as the oaks; yet I destroyed his fruit from above, and his roots from beneath." It was now that those judicial exterminating wars commenced which were undertaken by the Israelites at the express command of God, and which they were to continue to wage, until all the guilty nations of Canaan were cut off. As they approached the Jordan, their conflicts with their enemies became more severe and their victories more signal. So the Christian, as he nears the Jordan of death, is often called to record a similar experience. As his spiritual enemies then redouble their assaults upon him, greater conquests are vouchsafed him. That he may be the better prepared for heaven, faith grows stronger, hope becomes brighter, love increases in ardor, and therefore Satan is more effectually trodden under foot. Thus the Christian goes on conquering and to conquer, till at length his last enemy, death, is vanquished, and he stands on Zion waving the palm-branch of victory.——¶ *Possessed his land from Arnon unto Jabbok.* The Amorites formed one of the devoted nations whose land God had promised to Abraham and his seed, which promise was to be fulfilled when "the iniquity of the Amorites should come to the full," Gen. 15 : 16. This time had now arrived, and the victory which the Israelites were enabled to achieve over them put them in possession of their lands, while the virtue of the divine promise, made ages before, enabled them to keep possession. This conquest is therefore justified against the Amorites, who had also been the aggressors and provoked the war, so that by the laws of nations they were justly deprived of their territory. The Jabbok is one of the streams which traverse the country east of the Jordan, and which, after a nearly westerly course, falls into that river about thirty miles below the Lake of Tiberias. It is mentioned in Scripture as the boundary between the kingdom of Sihon and that of Og king of Bashan; and it appears subsequently to have formed the boundary between the tribe of Reuben and the half tribe of Manasseh.——¶ *For the border of the children of Ammon was strong.* It is not clear whether this is stated as a reason of the Israelites' not pushing on their conquests farther into the country of the Ammonites, or as a reason why Sihon had not gained upon the country of the Ammonites as he had upon that of the Moabites. Owing to the defences furnished by the river, or by the strongholds and fastnesses of the mountains, the borders of the Ammonitish territory were practically inaccessible. This seems on the whole the most probable construction, as the Israelites were expressly forbid-

25 And Israel took all these cities: and Israel dwelt in all the cities of the Amorites, in Heshbon, and in all the villages thereof.

26 For Heshbon[e] *was* the city of Sihon the king of the Amorites, who had fought against the former king of Moab, and taken

e Cant. 7. 4. Is. 15. 4.

den, Deut. 3:8, to meddle with the Ammonites. In respect to this latter people we may remark, that the boundaries between them and the Moabites appear never to have been well defined or distinctly preserved. Moab was east of the Dead Sea; and Ammon north of Moab and east of the lower part of Jordan. But cities about Heshbon and eastward from the mouth of the Jordan are sometimes enumerated among the cities of Moab; at others as belonging to Ammon.

V. 25. *And Israel took all these cities.* How complete was the conquest on this occasion we learn from the parallel recital, Deut. 2:32–35, "Then Sihon came out against us, he and all his people, to fight at Jahaz. And the Lord our God delivered him before us; and we smote him, and his sons, and all his people. And we took all his cities at that time, and utterly destroyed the men, and the women, and the little ones, of every city; we left none to remain: only the cattle we took for a prey unto ourselves, and the spoil of the cities which we took."——¶ *And in all the villages thereof.* Heb. "In all the daughters thereof." This is in accordance with the usage which terms chief cities *mothers;* the adjacent towns and villages would then naturally receive the denomination of *daughters.* 2 Sam. 20: 19, "Thou seekest to destroy a city and a mother in Israel," where the Gr. renders, "Thou seekest to destroy a city and a mother-city (metropolis) in Israel." Comp. Ezek. 16:44–53. The villages (daughters) here spoken of are alluded to Deut. 3:5, under the appellation of "unwalled towns." Israel's dwelling in these cities and towns showed that they had not devoted them to destruction by anathema, as in that case they would not have been at liberty to occupy them.

V. 26. *For Heshbon (was) the city of Sihon, etc.* Sihon, after wresting this part of their country from the hands of the Moabites, had made Heshbon the seat of his kingdom. This place was situated in the southern district of the Israelitish territory beyond the Jordan, parallel with, and twenty-one miles east of, the point where the Jordan enters the Dead Sea, and nearly midway between the rivers Jabbok and Arnon. It originally belonged to the Moabites; but when the Israelites searched this region, it was found to be in the possession of the Amorites, from whom it was taken by Moses, and became eventually a Levitical city in the tribe of Reuben; but being on the confines of Gad, is sometimes assigned to the latter tribe. At the present day it is known by its ancient name of Heshbon, in the slightly modified form of *Hesbun.* The ruins of a considerable town still exist, covering the sides of an insulated hill, but not a single edifice is left entire. It was formerly noted for its pools of water, Cant. 7:4, but no remains of these of any consequence are now to be seen.——¶ *Who had fought against the former king of Moab, and taken all his land out of his hand, even unto Arnon.* It is not to be inferred with any certainty that the Sihon whom the Israelites now vanquished was the same with him who had dispossessed the Moabites. It was probably some one of his ancestors called by the same name.

all his land out of his hand, even unto Arnon.

27 Wherefore they that speak in proverbs[f] say, Come into Heshbon, let the city of Sihon be built and prepared:

28 For[g] there is a fire gone out of Heshbon, a flame from

f Hab. 2. 6.

g Jer. 48. 45, 46.

This is confirmed by the Gr., which renders, "that heretofore, or formerly, was king of Moab." It was usual in the East for royal titles to be perpetuated, as Abimelech in Palestine, Pharaoh in Egypt, etc. The design of alluding in this connection to the incidents mentioned is to vindicate the seizure recorded against any claims that might be urged on the part of the Moabites, who had formerly been the proprietors of the country. Moses here furnishes the ground of the plea which was made by Jephthah 260 years afterwards, when Israel's title was questioned, Judg. 11: 23, 24. The position assumed is, that Israel did not take it out of the hands of the Moabites, who had previously lost it to the Amorites; and having taken it from the Amorites they were under no obligation to restore it to the Moabites, whose title was long since extinguished. Without, therefore, transgressing the divine command relative to distressing or disturbing Moab, they had still come in possession of what was once his territory.

V. 27. *Wherefore they that speak in proverbs, say, etc.* Heb. *hammoshelim*, *parabolists*, or those who deal in parables. Gr. "Enigmatists, or those who deal in riddles." The original term is applied occasionally to the Hebrew prophets, who delivered their messages in a parabolical style, as Ezek. 17:2. 20:49, but doubtless denotes in this connection those bards or rhapsodists who delivered historical events to posterity in a poetical style, with the adornments of figure and allegory. This was the more frequent form of national annals in the early ages of the world, and the probability is, that the present is a quotation from some Amorite war-poem, originally written to celebrate their victory over the Moabites. These poems, becoming familiar in the lips of the people, would in process of time be quoted like proverbs or common sayings, for which the appropriate Heb. term is *meshallim*, from *mâshal*, *to utter a comparison* or *proverb*, *to speak in parables*.——¶ *Come into Heshbon.* This is doubtless to be regarded as a kind of summons or appeal by which the victorious Amorites would encourage one another to flock to and repair the captive and ruined city of Heshbon, and make it the seat of their own princes.

V. 28. *For there is a fire gone out of Heshbon, etc.* The strain commenced in the preceding verse is here continued. The tide of victory which had set in from the centre and mother city would soon spread and overrun the whole extent of the Moabitish territory. The "fire" and "flame" here spoken of denote the ravages of war. See Is. 47:14. Dan. 11:33. Amos 1:7, 10, 12, 14. Obad. 1:18. Ps. 78:63. Chald. "A strong east wind like fire, and warriors like a flame." Jerus. Targ. "A people strong and burning like fire, and warriors like a flame of fire."——¶ *From the city of Sihon.* That is, from the city which had now become Sihon's. It is worthy of notice, that in the predictions of Jeremiah against Moab, the language of the prophet bears a close analogy to that of the canticle here quoted. Jer. 48:45, 46, "They that fled stood under the shadow of Heshbon because of the force: but a fire shall come forth out of Heshbon, and a

the city of Sihon: it hath consumed Ar [h] of Moab, *and* the lords of the high places of Arnon.

29 Woe to thee, Moab! thou art undone, O people of Chemosh [i]: he hath given his sons that escaped, and his daughters, into captivity unto Sihon king of the Amorites.

30 We have shot at them: Heshbon is perished even unto

h Deut. 2. 9, 18. Is. 15. 1, 2.

i Judg. 11. 24. 2 K. 23. 13.

---

flame from the midst of Sihon, and shall devour the corner of Moab, and the crown of the head of the tumultuous ones. Wo be unto thee, O Moab! the people of Chemosh perisheth: for thy sons are taken captives, and thy daughters captives."——¶ *Hath consumed Ar of Moab.* Heb. "Hath eaten up or devoured." That is, the war hath destroyed the people, the inhabitants, of Ar, rather than the city itself, for the city remained still at a much later period the possession of the Moabites, Deut. 2:9, 18, 29. Jer. 15:1. Jeremiah, instead of "Ar of Moab," has "the corner of Moab," which may be equivalent to *chief place*, or *principal dignity* of Moab, as the corner of a room, according to oriental ideas and usages, is the most honorable position, and occupied by great personages.——¶ *Lords of the high places of Arnon.* Or, Heb. "Masters (patrons) of the high places." Chald. "The Chemarims (or priests) which served in the God's-house (or temple) of the high place of Arnon." Gr. "The pillars of Arnon."

V. 29. *O people of Chemosh.* Chald. "O people that serve Chemosh." Chemosh was the idol-god, or "abomination" (1 Kings 11:7) of the Moabites, considered to be the same as Baal-Peor, and thus referred to by Milton:

"Next *Chemosh*, th' obscene dread of Moab's sons,
Peor his other name, when he enticed
Israel in Sittim, on their march from Nile,
To do him wanton rites, which cost them woe."

His worshippers are here exulted over as having been betrayed or abandoned by their deity, who had shown himself incapable of protecting his sons or his daughters, i. e., his most devoted worshippers, against the conquering arms of their enemies. The following parallel allusions may be cited in this connection, Jer. 48:13, "Moab shall be ashamed of Chemosh, as the house of Israel was ashamed of Beth-el their confidence." Is. 16:12, "And it shall come to pass when it is seen that Moab is weary on the high place, that he shall come to his sanctuary to pray; but he shall not prevail." So Jephthah, speaking in the language of idolaters, who make their gods dispensers of good and evil to their votaries, says, Judg. 11:24, "Will not thou possess that which Chemosh thy god giveth thee to possess?"

V. 30. *We have shot at them.* Heb. *vannirâm âbad Heshboon ad Dibon*, of which it is extremely difficult to determine the true sense. The radical word *nir*, a *light*, or *lamp*, seems to be invoked in *vannirâm*, which would in that case bring out the rendering preferred by Ainsworth, Horsley, and others, viz., "their light (or lamp) has perished (or been taken away) from Heshbon unto Dibon," that is, from one extremity of the land to another. By *lamp*, in this connection, the old versionists understand *seed, heir, succession*, intimating that the line of rulers is entirely cut off. This would seem to be confirmed by the language of the Lord through Abijah,

Dibon[k], and we have laid them waste even unto Nophah, which *reacheth* even unto Medeba.

31 Thus Israel dwelt in the land of the Amorites.

32 And Moses sent to spy

k Jer. 48. 18, 22.

1 Kings 11 : 36, "And unto his son will I give one tribe, that David my servant may have a light always before me in Jerusalem, the city which I have chosen me to put my name there." So also, 1 Kings 15 : 4, "Nevertheless, for David's sake did the Lord his God give him a lamp in Jerusalem, to set up his son after him, and to establish Jerusalem." As this strikes us as on the whole the most probable construction, we waive the recital of any others, which may be found in abundance in Rosenmuller.——¶ *Unto Dibon.* This name, it appears, is still preserved in a ruined town called *Diban*, about three miles north of the Arnon. This, with other towns of this district, was originally assigned to the tribe of Gad (ch. 32 : 3, 33, 34), but it is afterwards found in the possession of Reuben. ——¶ *Unto Medeba.* "This name is preserved in that of 'Madeba,' applied to a large ruined town about six miles south-east from Heshbon. In Is. 15 : 2, its name is connected with Mount Nebo : 'Moab shall howl over Nebo and over Medeba.' By which we are probably to understand that this was, in the time of the prophet, the principal town of this rich district. 'Madeba' was built upon a round hill, and is now most completely ruined. There are many remains of the walls of private houses, constructed with blocks of silex; but not a single edifice is standing. On the west side of the town may be seen the remains of a temple, built with large stones, and apparently of great antiquity. A part of its eastern wall remains; and at the entrance to one of the courts stand two Doric columns, which have the peculiarity of being thicker in the centre than at either extremity : a circumstance which Burckhardt, to whom Scripture geography owes the discovery of this site, never elsewhere observed in Syria. There is no spring or river near this town; but the large tank or reservoir of hewn stone still remains, which appears to have secured the inhabitants a supply of water."—*Pict. Bible.*

V. 31. *Thus Israel dwelt in the land of the Amorites.* Gr. "In all the cities of the Amorites." This region having been formerly wrested from the Moabites by the Amorites, and having now been taken from the latter by the Israelites, they entered at once upon the occupancy of it, according to what we read, ch. 32 : 33, 34, etc., "And Moses gave unto them, even to the children of Gad, and to the children of Reuben, and unto half the tribe of Manasseh the son of Joseph, the kingdom of Sihon king of the Amorites, and the kingdom of Og king of Bashan, the land, with the cities thereof in the coasts, even the cities of the country round about."

V. 32. *And Moses sent to spy out Jaazer.* This is supposed to be identical with the modern *Szyr*, about fifteen miles from Heshbon. The region was esteemed so excellent for pasture-ground that the children of Reuben and Gad, who had extensive herds of cattle, came to Moses with a special request that he would allot it to them. See ch. 32 : 1–5. This will account for Jaazer's being particularly specified when it had been said just before in general terms, that "Israel dwelt in

out [l] Jaazer; and they took the villages thereof, and drove out the Amorites that *were* there.

33 And [m] they turned and went up by the way of Bashan:

l c. 32. 1.

m Deut. 3. 1, etc.

the land of the Amorites."——¶ *The villages thereof.* Heb. "The daughters thereof." See Note on v. 25.

Encounter with Og, King of Bashan.

V. 33. *And they turned and went up by the way of Bashan.* We insert from Kitto an interesting sketch of the region thus denominated. "The beautiful kingdom of Og, on the east of Jordan, extended from the river Jabbok on the south to Mount Hermon on the north. It comprehended three districts, all famous in the Bible for their exuberant fertility and their general excellence. Of these Argob was in the north; Bashan, properly so called, in the middle; and Gilead in the south. Part of Gilead, however, which lay south of the Jabbok, was not included in the kingdom of Bashan. But Argob may seem to be only a district of Bashan; whence the whole of Og's kingdom may be said to consist of all Bashan, and the greater part of Gilead. Or, indeed, it may be that Bashan was the general name for the whole, and Argob and Gilead only of particular districts—the former a small district in the north, and the latter a large one in the south. Parts of this country have been well described by Mr. Buckingham. He crossed the Jordan about ten miles above Jericho, and proceeded north-west to Jerash; consequently, till he came to the Jabbok (Zerka), his journey lay through that part of Gilead which was south of that river, and which had belonged to the Amorites. After ascending two ranges of barren hills, 'we found ourselves on plains of nearly as high a level as the summits of the hills themselves, and certainly 800 feet at least above the level of the Jordan. The character of the country, too, was quite different from any thing I had seen in Palestine. . . . We were now in a land of extraordinary richness, abounding with the most beautiful prospects, clothed with thick forests, varied with verdant slopes, and possessing extensive plains of a fine red soil, now covered with thistles, as the best proof of its fertility, and yielding in nothing to the celebrated plains of Zabulon and Esdraelon, in Galilee and Samaria.' ('Palestine,' vol. ii. p. 104, 8vo. edit.) This continued to be the character of Gilead south of the Jabbok. After passing that river, the travellers entered that part of Gilead which formed the south portion of the kingdom of Bashan: "We ascended the steep on the south side of the Zerka (the Jabbok), and on reaching its summit, came again on a beautiful plain, of an elevated level. . . . We continued our way over this elevated tract, continuing to behold, with surprise and admiration, a beautiful country on all sides of us; its plains covered with a very fertile soil, its hills clothed with forests, at every new turn presenting the most magnificent landscapes that could be imagined. Among the trees the oak was frequently seen, and we know that this territory produced them of old." (Is. 2:13. Ezek. 27:6. Zech. 11:2.) . . . "Some learned commentators, indeed, believing that no oaks grew in this supposed desert region, have translated the word by *alders*, to prevent the appearance of inaccuracy in the inspired writers. The expression of *the fat bulls of Bashan*, which occurs more than once in the Scriptures, seemed to us equally incon-

and Og the king of Bashan went out against them, he and all his people to the battle of Edrei.

---

sistent, as applied to a country generally thought to be a desert, in common with the whole tract that is laid down in our modern maps as such, between the Jordan and the Euphrates; but we could now fully comprehend not only that the bulls of this luxuriant country might be proverbially fat, but that its possessors, too, might be a race renowned for strength and comeliness of person." ('Travels,' vol. i. p. 113–14.) Continuing the journey in a north-westerly direction—"The general face of this region improved as we advanced farther in it, and every new direction of our path opened upon us views which charmed us by their grandeur and their beauty. Lofty mountains gave an outline of most magnificent character; flowing beds of secondary hills softened the romantic wildness of the picture; gentle slopes, clothed with wood, gave a rich variety of tints, hardly to be imitated by the pencil; deep valleys, filled with murmuring streams and verdant meadows, offered all the luxuriance of cultivation; and herds and flocks gave life and animation to scenes as grand, as beautiful, and as highly picturesque, as the taste or genius of a Claude could either invent or desire." (Vol. i. p. 117–18.) The travellers returned from Jerash to the Jordan by a more northerly route. In the first part of the journey, the beautiful wooded scenery of the south was still continued. Mr. Buckingham says: "Mr. Bankes, who had seen the whole of England, the greater part of Italy and France, and almost every province of Spain and Portugal, frequently remarked that, in all his travels, he had met with nothing equal to it, excepting only in some parts of the latter country, Entre Minho and Duoro, to which he could alone compare it. It is certain that we were perpetually exclaiming, 'How rich!' 'How picturesque!' 'How magnificent!' 'How beautiful!' and that we both conceived the scenery around to be quite worth all the hazard and privation of a journey to the eastward of Jordan." It is true that, in prosecuting their route to the Jordan, the travellers met with much austere and barren land; but that the general character of the northern part of Og's kingdom coincides in a great degree with this account of the southern portion, we can gather even from the brief and inanimate indications of Burckhardt, who traversed the more northern parts of Bashan and Argob, and speaks frequently of desert fields covered with the richest pasturage, and than which artificial meadows could not be finer; and describes the soil, where cultivated, as affording the richest crops of wheat and barley. Upon the whole, the regions of Bashan and of Gilead, even now, after ages of neglect and desolation, bear witness to the accuracy of the frequent allusions to their fertility and beauty, which occur in the Sacred books. For the knowledge of this we are entirely indebted to modern research, as the region beyond Jordan has only ceased to be an unknown land within the present century."—*Pict. Bible.*——¶ *And Og the king of Bashan went out against them.* It would naturally have been supposed that the fate of the neighboring kings of Edom and the Amorites would have operated as a warning to this proud potentate, but it seems to have been lost upon him, and he accordingly courts his own destruction by resisting the march of Israel. A more particular account is given of this passage in the history in Deut. 3:

34 And the LORD said unto Moses, Fear him not: for I have delivered him into thy hand, and all his people, and his land; and thou shalt do to him as thou didst unto Sihon king of the Amorites, which dwelt at Heshbon.

35 So[n] they smote him, and his sons, and all his people, until there was none left him alive: and they possessed his land.

n Deut. 29. 7. Josh. 13. 12. Ps. 135. 10, 11. 136. 20.

CHAPTER XXII.

AND[a] the children of Israel set forward, and pitched in the plains of Moab, on this side Jordan *by* Jericho.

a c. 33. 48.

11, etc., from which it appears that Og was personally a man of gigantic dimensions, and probably for that reason prompted to rely much on his individual prowess. But it proved unavailing.

V. 34. *Fear him not. I have delivered him into thy hand.* So strong and absolute is the assurance of conquest that they might consider it as in effect already achieved. "I *have* delivered," etc.

V. 35. *So they smote him, etc.* The contest ended as it could no otherwise end with those who fight against the Lord. Had a peaceable passage been allowed to Israel, and only the kindness due to strangers shown them, these trans-Jordanic tribes would doubtless have been exempted from the slaughter and devastations to which their obstinacy subjected them. But the measure of their iniquity was full, and in the infatuation of hardened sinners they rushed headlong upon their destruction. The description given in the parallel history of Deuteronomy of this royal giant, and of the fortified places the people inhabited, magnify the conquest obtained. "Threescore cities fenced with high walls, gates, and bars, besides unwalled towns a great many." The most impregnable fortresses, whether of nature or art, give way at once to the breath of Omnipotence. The Most High makes men feel that all refuges fail them, and that nothing secures from his stroke, when once he goes forth to contend with his armies. And what are the strongholds of sin and Satan when assailed by the weapons of the Gospel? "Many high places, fortresses of spiritual wickedness, have become the conquests of truth. Many citadels in the dominion of darkness, even principalities and powers, once under the control of the god of this world, have yielded to the subduing sword of the Spirit. Gigantic forms of wickedness, like the king of Bashan, have lain breathless at the feet of our all-conquering Redeemer."—*Seaton.*

CHAPTER XXII.

Encampment in the Plains of Moab. Balaam sent for by Balak to curse the chosen People.

V. 1. *The children of Israel set forward.* Heb. *yissu, broke up.* The station of the Israelites prior to the present removal is thus indicated, ch. 33: 48, "And they departed from the mountains of Abarim, and pitched in the plains of Moab, by Jordan near Jericho." Abarim was the name of a chain of mountains forming or belonging to the mountainous district east of the Dead Sea and the lower Jordan. It presents many distinct masses and elevations, commanding extensive views of the country west of the river. From one of the highest of these, called Mount Nebo, Moses surveyed the Promised Land before he died. From the manner in which the names Abarim, Nebo, and Pisgah are connected, Deut. 32 : 49. 34 : 1, it would seem that Nebo was a mountain of the Abarim chain, and that Pisgah was the highest and most commanding peak of that mountain. The loftiest mountain of the neighborhood is Mount Attarous, about ten miles north of the Arnon; and travellers have been disposed to identify it with Mount Nebo. But Prof. Robinson was unable to fix upon any special locality answering to the description given in the sacred narrative. As, however, he did not cross the Jordan, his inability to identify the spot is not surprising. Other travellers, who may succeed in getting on the precise track of the Israelites, will be likely to be more fortunate. But if the particular locality should never be determined, it will be of no special consequence, as it is certain that there are several points in the vicinity from whence the venerable leader of Israel might have surveyed the inspiring scenery upon which he was not permitted to enter. It would seem that the Israelites, in their conquests of the country of the Amorites which had formerly belonged to the Moabites, had proceeded considerably farther north than the parallel of the ford of the Jordan, and from hence returned southward before bending their course eastward towards the place where they were to cross that river.——¶ *Pitched in the plains of Moab.* Heb. *bearboth Moab, in campestribus Moab, in the champaign country of Moab.* This phrase denotes that region of the country of Moab which bordered upon the Jordan, and is now called *El Ghor,* of which an ample account will be found in Robinson and other oriental travellers. The "plains of Moab" are formed by a narrow strip of land scarcely six miles in breadth, lying along the eastern bank of the Jordan, opposite to the plains of Jericho. The Dead Sea lies to the south of it, Mount Pisgah somewhere on the southeast, and the mountains on the east; and towards the north, losing its specific name, this plain continues as "the valley of the Jordan," even to the Sea of Tiberias. This side formed part of the territory which had formerly been taken by the Amorites from Moab; but, as usual in such cases, it still retained the name of the former possessors. It is probable the phrase was designed to include more than the mere narrow strip along the course of the river, although how much more it is difficult to say. It appears that there are several passes from the valley of the Jordan to the table-lands of Moab, and that when these are attained, the eye is refreshed with the view of undulating downs, clothed with rich grass throughout, and in the northern parts with magnificent forests of sycamore, beech, terebinth, ilex, and enormous fig-trees. Such was the general face of the country to which the Israelites had now arrived, but the central point of their encampment was undoubtedly in the valley of the Ghor, termed the *arboth Moab,* or *plains of Moab.* Here they remained for several months, even till the death of Moses, encamping "from Beth-jesimoth unto Abel-shittim," ch. 33 : 49. This station became in fact the theatre of all the events recorded from this point of the history onwards to the end of Deuteronomy and the beginning of Joshua. These events embraced the deliverance from the curse of Balaam; the mustering for the inheritance of Canaan; the victory over the Midianites; the additional enact-

2 And Balak[b], the son of Zippor, saw all that Israel had done to the Amorites.

b Judg. 11. 25.

3 And [c] Moab was sore afraid of the people, because they *were* many: and Moab was distress-

c Ex. 15. 15. Deut. 2. 25.

ment of various divine ordinances, especially the repetition and enforcement of the whole Law, and the renewal of the covenant between God and the people by the hand of Moses—all which matters form the subject of the remainder of this book, and of the book of Deuteronomy which follows. In reference to this series of events the Lord says unto their posterity by the prophet, Mic. 6:5, "O my people, remember now what Balak king of Moab consulted, and what Balaam the son of Beor answered him from Shittim unto Gilgal; that ye may know the righteousness of the Lord." That is, remember the many gracious providential incidents that occurred between Shittim, where they now were, and Gilgal where they were circumcised by Joshua, Josh. 5:2–9.——¶ *On this side Jordan* (*by*) *Jericho.* Heb. *mëëber, leyardën,* lit. *from across to the Jordan,* an expression variously interpreted, but implying in general *at the passage of the Jordan.* It is to be rendered *on this side* or *on that side,* according to the position of the speaker. Here the general consent of interpreters renders it *on this side,* from which the inference is fairly drawn, that the author of the book, at the time of writing, was on the east of the Jordan, which is virtually the same as saying that it was written by Moses, prior to the entrance of the Israelites into Canaan.

V. 2. *And Balak the son of Zippor saw all that Israel had done to the Amorites.* That is, considered, pondered, viewed in its consequences. The genuine force of the original does not require that he should have been an eye-witness of all that Israel had done to the Amorites, though he may have been. But if he were, he looked upon it with an evil eye, and could not appropriate to himself the words of the wise man, Prov. 24:32, "Then I saw and considered it well: I looked upon it, and received instruction."

V. 3. *Moab was sore afraid of the people because they* (*were*) *many.* The trepidation of Moab on this occasion was in truth groundless, for Israel had received express orders not to molest that people on their way, Deut. 2:9. But there was evidently a secret hostility in the mind of Balak, which was doubtless shared in by his people, prompting him to oppose their farther progress. But, in order to justify his course, he must adduce to himself some plausible ground for the contemplated opposition, and this he does on the plea that they are undoubtedly intending evil against him. "Thus it is common," says Henry, "for those that design mischief, to pretend that mischief is designed against them; and their groundless jealousies must be the color of their causeless malice. They hear of the triumphs of Israel over the Amorites, and think their own house is in danger when their neighbor's is on fire." Notwithstanding that in destroying the Amorites they had done the Moabites a service, for they had released them from the yoke of their oppressors, yet, being smitten with a kind of panic terror, and cherishing an innate aversion to the favored people, they persuade themselves that a nation so numerous and mighty, which had already conquered two powerful kings, would not scruple to push on their advantages, and, if possible, vanquish all

ed because of the children of Israel.

4 And Moab said unto the elders of Midian, Now shall this company lick up all *that*

d c. 31. 8. Josh. 13. 21, 22.

before them. This, however, was in accordance with "the prophecy which went before upon them," Ex. 15:15, "Then the dukes of Edom shall be amazed, the mighty men of Moab, trembling shall take hold upon them." Thus it is said also of the beginning of their victories, Deut. 2:25, "This day will I begin to put the dread of thee, and the fear of thee, upon the nations, that are under the whole heaven, who shall hear report of thee, and shall tremble, and be in anguish because of thee."——¶ *Moab was distressed because of the children of Israel.* Heb. *yâkâtz*, implying both the idea of *chagrin* and *abhorrence.* They were prompted by a peculiar kind of *loathing* towards the Israelites, as were the Israelites themselves in regard to the manna, ch. 21:5, where the word in the original is the same. See also the Note on Ex. 1:12, where the import of the term is fully illustrated. Gr. "Moab was incensed," the original word being the same with that Heb. 3:10, "Wherefore I was *grieved* with that generation." The "distress" here predicated of Moab was evidently self-procured, for the command given to Israel, Deut. 2:9, was, "*Distress not* the Moabites, neither contend with them in battle." They had therefore only themselves to blame for their trouble.

V. 4. *And Moab said unto the elders of Midian, etc.* Gr. "The senate, or eldership, of Madiam." The elders in those ancient countries were the senators who managed the affairs of state, and were thence called "princes," v. 8. The Midian here spoken of is undoubtedly to be regarded as a different region from that where Moses found refuge when he fled from Egypt, and whose priest or sheikh was Jethro, who became the father-in-law of the future law-giver of Israel. These people dwelt about the eastern arm of the Red Sea, which was at too great a distance from the territories of Moab to allow of their being referred to in the present connection. The Midianites here mentioned, though probably descended from Abraham and Keturah, were a people of nomade or semi-nomade habits, occupying the country east and south-east of the Moabites, who, as we have seen, were seated on the east of the Dead Sea. They pastured their flocks in the unsettled country beyond the Moabites, with whom they seem to have been on the most friendly terms, and on whose borders were situated those "cities and goodly castles which they possessed." Num. 31:10. They seem also to have shared with the Moabites in a deep-rooted hostility to the Israelites, as in conjunction with them they designedly enticed the Israelites to idolatry, as we read in the sequel to the present narrative. It was this class of Midianites who, at a subsequent period, harassed the chosen people to such a degree that Gideon was raised up as a divinely endowed champion and deliverer of his people, and enabled to achieve a signal and final triumph over these marauders, from which they never afterwards recovered. The communication was no doubt made by messengers sent for the purpose, and though the precise purport of the message is not stated, yet the sequel makes it evident that they united in the scheme of engaging Balaam to come and exercise his magical skill in banning or cursing the chosen people, as it is said, v. 7, that "the elders of Moab and the elders of Midian departed

are round about us, as the ox licketh up the grass of the field. And Balak, the son of Zippor, *was* king of the Moabites at that time.

5 He sent[e] messengers, there-

e Deut. 23. 4. Josh. 24. 9. Neh. 13. 1, 2. Mic. 6. 5.

---

with the rewards of divination in their hands."——¶ *Now shall this company lick up all (that are) round about us, etc.* Heb. *yelahaku hakkâhol eth kol sebebothënu, the congregation shall lick up all our surroundings.* An analogous mode of speech still prevails in the East. "A native gentleman, who had many people depending upon him, says, 'Yes, they are all grazing upon me. If I am not careful, they will soon graze up all I have.' Of people who have got all they can out of one rich man, and who are seeking after another, 'Yes, yes, they have done grazing there, and are now looking out for another place.' 'These bulls are grazing in every direction.'"—*Roberts.* The root of the Heb. verb is *lâhak*, from which our English *lick* is evidently derived. The import is that of *devouring* or *consuming*, as a fire that consumes is said to *lick up*, 1 Kings 18 : 38. Here, however, the metaphor is taken from the feeding of cattle, of which Buffon, in his "Natural History," says, "The horse eats day and night, slowly, but almost continually; the ox or beeve, on the contrary, *eats quick, and takes in a little time all the nourishment he wants;* after which he ceases to eat, and lies down to chew the cud." The policy of Moab is first to inoculate Midian with his own fear, which he does by assuring him that this mighty host, without some concerted resistance on the part of the exposed nations and tribes, will sweep the whole of them from the face of the ground, with the same ease that the grazing ox causes the grass to disappear in the pasture. The actual conduct of Israel had already effectually disproved the justice of this charge. They had, of their own accord, turned aside into a circuitous route in order to avoid doing them injury. This forbearance would have delivered them from all apprehension, had not their own malignity prompted them to entertain foul suspicions; for why had not the Israelites made a direct attack upon their territories, but that they designed to obey the divine command and leave them totally unharmed? The representation of Balak, however, takes effect, and the two peoples agree to act together in the emergency which is now upon them.

V. 5. *He sent messengers therefore, etc.* The despatching the messengers is here attributed solely to Balak, doubtless because he was principal in the affair, but it is evident, from v. 7, that the Midianites shared in the delegation.——¶ *Unto Balaam the son of Beor.* Heb. בלעם *Bilâm*, from *bâla, to consume, to destroy,* and *âm, people,* equivalent to *destroyer of the people.* The name was probably borne by Balaam as a dreaded charmer and conjurer, though given to him, we may suppose, according to Oriental custom, at a later period, when the fact indicated by it had become well known. This import of the name is confirmed by Rev. 2 : 6, 14, 15, where mention is made of the Nicolaitans as holding the same doctrines with the Balaamites, and Nicolaitans is a name signifying etymologically *conquerors or destroyers of the people.* There is no evidence from Church history of the existence of any such heretical sect as the Nicolaitans, and therefore there need be no hesitation in taking the denomination mystically or symbolically as denoting false teachers of a certain type, just as

fore, unto Balaam the son of Beor, to Pethor, which *is* by the river of the land of the children of his people, to call him,

---

the name of Jezebel occurs, Rev. 2 : 20, not as a historical but as a symbolical designation. It is used simply to denote a class of persons who inculcated the most abominable doctrines, and therefore were fitly denominated by the name of a woman who had proved the vilest and most detestable of her sex.——¶ *The son of Beor.* There would be nothing to call for special remark in regard to the parentage of Balaam, were it not that the apostle Peter, 2 Pet. 2 : 15, calls him "Balaam the son of Bosor." This may be explained either on the ground of a transmutation of letters with a view to soften the sound of the original Hebrew letters, of which Ainsworth (*in loc.*) has given a number of analogous instances; or with Grotius, we may suppose "Bosor" is another mode of writing "Pethor," and that Peter does not intend to say that Balaam was the son of Bosor, but that he was of the city or place "Bosor," inasmuch as the original Gr. phrase is elliptical, "the son" being omitted.——¶ *To Pethor.* Heb. *pethorâh,* having the local particle at the close indicating the direction *to which* or *towards.* As the name is beyond question derived from the radical *pâthor, to interpret,* some of the ancient versions have rendered it by *soothsayer,* as the Vulg., while the Syriac represents it by *expounder* or *augur.* The probability is, that it is the name of a place so called from the fact of its being a chief resort of men devoted to occult arts, or professing to *interpret* the will of the gods. The precise location of the place is of course unknown to geography, and we are obliged to content ourselves with the bare intimation that it was situated in Mesopotamia. ——¶ *Which is by the river of the land of the children of his people.* One is conscious at once of something peculiar in the phraseology of this clause, that prompts the inquiry whether it is accurately translated from the original. Judging from the diversity of renderings, this may be justly doubted. Our version follows, perhaps, the current of authorities, which is always entitled to special weight with an interpreter, though not an absolute criterion of truth. The Hebrew is capable of being translated thus: "He sent messengers unto Balaam the son of Beor to Pethor (which is by the river), the land of the children (sons) of his people." The parenthesis is inserted simply to show the connection. "The river" is here emphatic, denoting the Euphrates, which is several times so termed in the Scriptures. The purport on this construction, would be, that Balak sent messengers to Balaam, who resided at Pethor, on the Euphrates, a country distinguished as the dwelling-place of "the children of his people," by which we may perhaps understand *the stock of his peculiar kind of people, a class composed of persons similar to himself,* i. e., soothsayers and reputed prophets, who were prone to rendezvous and concentrate themselves about particular districts. As this sense of the words has not been previously suggested, the reader will probably share in the hesitation of the author in adopting it. The Vulg. has the following: "He sent therefore messengers to Balaam the son of Beor, a soothsayer, who dwelt by the river of the land of the children of Ammon." This reading depends upon a substitution of the Heb. *benë Ammon, children of Ammon,* instead of *benë ammo, children of his people,* for which it is said there is authority in some of the ancient manuscripts, as

saying, Behold, there is a people come out from Egypt: behold, they cover the face of the earth, and they abide over against me.

also in the Syriac and Samaritan versions. The change is favored by Mr. Kitto (Note *in loc.*). But our proposed construction renders the reading unnecessary, to which we may add, that there is no evidence of the territory of the Ammonites ever having extended to the Euphrates. Yet that Balaam came from Mesopotamia (Aram), through which runs the Euphrates, is expressly affirmed, ch. 23:7. We are on the whole strongly persuaded of the correctness of the above interpretation.——¶ *To call him, saying, etc.* The signal success of the Israelites in conquering all the opposing powers with whom they came in conflict, had impressed the king and people of Moab with the conviction that it was vain to contend with them by force of arms, while they so manifestly enjoyed the blessing and protection of the Divine Power. They must, therefore, have recourse to some other policy than that of open warfare, and they concluded that if, in accordance with the ideas then prevalent among ancient nations, they could lay upon them the anathema or ban of some powerful magician, they might be shorn of their strength, and having become as weak as other men, might be made an easy prey to their adversaries; for even among the heathen there was a latent conviction, that the removal of God's blessing was the exhaustion of the strength and heroism of a people. The general belief on which their policy was founded is thus alluded to by Mr. Kitto: "Their procedure, in seeking to lay the armies of Israel under a curse, that their own arms might be successful against them, is a strange notion to us. But it is not so in the East. Even at the present day, the pagan Orientals, in their wars, have always their magicians with them to curse their enemies, and to mutter incantations for their destruction. Sometimes they secretly convey a potent charm among the opposing troops, to ensure their destruction. In our own war with the Burmese, the generals of that nation had several magicians with them, who were much engaged in cursing our troops; but as they did not succeed, a number of witches were brought for the same purpose. We may, indeed, trace it as a very ancient opinion, among all people, that the maledictions and the blessings, the charms, the incantations, and the devotements of men, who were believed to be inspired by a superior spirit, good or evil, had the most marked effects not only upon individuals but upon regions and entire nations, and even upon cattle and upon the fruits of the field." In Balaam they were well assured of finding an instrument suited to their purpose, and accordingly they resolve to enlist him in their service. His character will develope itself as the narrative proceeds.——¶ *Behold they cover.* Heb. *kissâh, it covereth,* the collective people being spoken of as one—a frequent idiom in Hebrew.——¶ *The face of the earth.* Heb. "The eye of the earth." See the phrase fully explained in the Note on Ex. 10:5.——¶ *They abide over against me.* Heb. "He is sitting over against me." The subject is still the "people" spoken of above, which in the original is singular, and, consequently, the predicates all along are singular, with still a plural import. The various items of grievance here mentioned were intended to form a plea or an argument which should avail with Balaam. By saying that they were a people that had come out of Egypt,

6 Come now, therefore, I pray thee, curse[f] me this people, for they *are* too mighty for me: peradventure I shall prevail, *that* we may smite them, and

f c. 23. 7.

he would intimate that, being strangers, they had no right to invade the land; the fact that they covered the face of the earth, was an indication of their great numbers, by reason of which they had prevailed over the Amorites and shown themselves irresistible in ordinary warfare; while their abiding over against Moab was a sure sign, that they meditated an early invasion of that territory. In all this there is no intimation of the fact, of which the Moabites as descendants of Abraham could not well have been ignorant, that the Lord had of old promised the land of Canaan to Israel, Gen. 15:18; or that the sins of the Canaanites should grow to that pitch of enormity that the land should spew them out, Lev. 18:24, 25; or how Israel, in their progress, had religiously abstained from harming either Moab or Edom, Deut. 2:4, 8, 9, 13, warring only with the devoted nations. All these facts were ignored in the message, and the proposed resistance put solely on the ground of the *presumed hostile intentions* of the chosen people. Even supposing there had been no special divine appointments in the case, how much worse was it for the Israelites to expel the Canaanites, than it was for these very Moabites, Edomites, and Ammonites to combine and drive out the Emims, Horims, and Zamzummims, and possess their lands and cities, as they were now doing? Deut. 2:9–21. But men have not the same eyes with which to look upon their own faults, and those of their neighbors.

V. 6. *Come now therefore, I pray thee, curse me this people.* Although a prophetic malediction might be supposed to have some efficacy when uttered at ever so great a distance, yet it is clear that Balak imagined that the prophet's personal presence, when his senses as well as his thoughts could act, would be attended with deeper interest, more vehemency of spirit, and, consequently, with more intensity of influence. This was on the principle that "the eye affects the heart," and it seems to be recognized in the case of Elisha when he cursed the mocking children, 2 Kings 2:24, "And he turned back and *looked on them*, and cursed them in the name of the Lord." So when Balaam had arrived, it is said, v. 41, that "Balak took Balaam, and brought him up into the high places of Baal, that thence he might see the utmost part of the people." The more he saw of them, the more he would be likely to be affected by the sight, and the more he was affected the greater would be the efficacy infused from that affection into the words he might utter. "It was," as Calvin remarks, "to the credit of Balak that he recognized an overruling Providence, whose favorable regards he would conciliate and secure, as the only basis of the success which he promised himself in the undertaking. He places his confidence of victory, not in his own sufficiency, but in the auspices of a superior power. But in seeking the interposition of this power by indirect and circuitous ways, he in fact departs still further from him. He desires deliverance from danger, but the means fixed upon are of his own device, and therefore fruitless. When he would purchase incantations from a mercenary prophet, and bind the Most High down to his own corrupt inventions, he could not but array the divine Providence against him." As to the widely extended and long established

that I may drive them out of the land: for I wot that he whom thou blessest *is* blessed, and he whom thou cursest is cursed.

---

belief relative to the potency of charms, exorcisms, and anathemas, we are inclined to think there is some foundation for it in the truth of things, provided it be borne in mind that no such influence can reach the truly good who, by a devout, believing, obedient, and holy life, put themselves under the protection of Omnipotence. Of all such the constrained words of Balaam himself must ever hold true, "Surely there is no enchantment against Jacob, neither is there any divination against Israel." But in the case of the wicked towards the wicked, we are inclined to believe that an exceedingly evil and malignant spirit may concentrate itself in a curse that shall have more or less power to harm, and therefore that the traditions, prevalent to a degree among all nations, of the power of "the evil eye" and of inward imprecations, do not rest upon a basis of mere idle superstition. But it is, of course, among heathen peoples, destitute of the light of revelation, that we are to look for these manifestations of the effects of infernal agency, for it is among them that the sway of evil spirits is more free and rampant. At any rate, the facts related of the marvellous powers of conjurers, wizards, necromancers, etc., evinced among many barbarous nations, when sifted and divested of the ordinary large measure of fiction, would seem to be in many instances such as to challenge a rational credence. However this may be, there is no doubt that both Balak and Balaam were well aware that a peculiar potency attached to a divine curse, and that nothing would be more efficacious to weaken and annihilate the strength of Israel than to bend the divine purpose so as to make that people subject to such an execration, for "they that are cursed of Him shall be cut off," Ps. 37 : 22. This, however, they were powerless to effect.——¶ *They (are) too mighty for me.* Heb. "It (the people) is mightier than I." That is, both in number and strength, and therefore too formidable for me to cope with. This was, in respect to Israel, a fulfilment of the promise made to Abraham, that he should become, in his seed, "a mighty nation," as indeed had been verified at an earlier period, inasmuch as in the land of their affliction, "he made them mightier than their enemies." Ps. 105 : 4. Balak's conscious inability to match them in a fair field prompts him to resort to magical imprecations.——¶ *I wot that he whom thou blessest (is) blessed, and he whom thou cursest is cursed.* Every thing bespeaks the infatuated and corrupt mind of this Moabitish king. He is convicted out of his own lips of being a man of violence and wrong. Why should he desire to smite the Israelites, who had done him no harm? And if he thought that Balaam could bless as well as curse whom he pleased, why did he not choose a blessing for himself rather than a curse for Israel? Why not desire to be himself protected from the injury which he feared, rather than to have power to injure those who had as yet done him no wrong? But this is the nature of envy, jealousy, and uncharitableness the world over. Men seek to exalt themselves by depressing their rivals, and not by the legitimate operation of their own superior excellence. A true Christian, while he seeks, from good ends, to promote himself in whatever position the Divine Providence has placed them, will not knowingly disparage others in so doing; but a thoroughly malignant and envious

7 And the elders of Moab, and the elders of Midian, departed with the rewards [g] of divination in their hand; and they came unto Balaam, and spake unto him the words of Balak.

8 And he said unto them, Lodge here this night, and I will bring you word again, as

g 1 Sam. 9. 7, 8. Mic. 3. 11. Jude 11.

---

nature will be sure to seek its own triumph through the degradation of others.

V. 7. *With the rewards of divination in their hand.* Heb. "(With) divinations in their hands." But the idea is no doubt correctly expressed in our version, *rewards of divination,* which is equivalent to the *wages or fees of soothsaying.* The words of the apostle, 2 Pet. 2 : 15, confirm this sense of the phrase, as he calls it "the wages of unrighteousness." Targ. Jon. "The fruits of divinations sealed in their hands." A similar idiom appears 2 Sam. 4 : 10, "Who thought I would have given him a *reward for his tidings,*" where the Heb. is simply *besorâh, tidings.* But the sense requires the established rendering. So also, Job 7 : 2, "work" is used for the "reward of work," and "sin" often for the "punishment of sin." Some commentators have suggested that, as it was usual for those who consulted prophets and seers to bring a present with them, 1 Sam. 9 : 7, 8, it cannot be fairly inferred that the intention was to corrupt him, but merely to comply with a universal custom. The testimony, however, of both Peter and Jude, that he "loved the wages of unrighteousness," and "ran greedily after error for reward," is decisive that the passion of covetousness was rankling in his heart, and this is abundantly evinced in the sequel. Compare this with what the Lord says by the prophet, Mic. 3 : 10–12, respecting the discharge of sacred offices from venal motives: "They build up Zion with blood, and Jerusalem with iniquity. The heads thereof judge for reward, and the priests thereof teach for hire, and the prophets thereof divine for money : yet will they lean upon the Lord, and say, Is not the Lord among us? none evil can come upon us. Therefore, shall Zion for your sake be ploughed as a field, and Jerusalem shall become heaps, and the mountain of the house as the high places of the forest." It is worthy of remark, that while all manner of wizards, conjurers, and witches are ready to engage to help others to the possession of great riches, they never rely upon these means, but upon the fees received from their dupes, to enrich themselves.

V. 8. *Lodge here this night, and I will bring you word again, as the Lord shall speak unto me.* His object in this invitation was undoubtedly to secure the night season for consulting the Most High, and receiving such communications as he should be pleased to make. "O God, who shall give me this care to obey thee that seemeth to be in this man!—that I may say nothing, think nothing, do nothing, without consulting with thee." —*Bp. Babington.* It was the divine wont to speak to the prophets by dreams and visions of the night, Num. 12 : 6. Job 4 : 13. 33 : 14, 15. Jer. 23 : 25, 28. But the question here arises, whether Balaam knew that the Israelites were under the especial divine care and providence—that they were a people whom the Lord had marvellously distinguished by the tokens of his favor—and whom he was now conducting by his own hand to a land long since promised? We think he must

the Lord shall speak unto me: And the princes of Moab abode with Balaam.

---

have known this, for the things in question had not been transacted in a corner. But if he did know them, here was the point, at the very outset of the communication, where he should have taken his stand. He should have told the messengers that this people was blessed, and that it was vain and impious to think of cursing them. He should have sent back his advice to the king of Moab, to let them pass safely and without molestation, and even to court their friendship by rendering them service. But his requesting them to stay betrayed an anxiety on his part to get over the obstacles, if possible, which stood in the way of his receiving the proffered rewards. Instead of this, he should not even have entertained them for a night. Had not the ruling passion of his mind been accordant with their wishes, he would have left the men to find lodging where they could, and have had nothing more to do with them. But he would tamper with temptation. He would try an experiment on the divine forbearance, the result of which he promised to report to the messengers in the morning. This the Gr. renders, "I will answer you the things which the Lord shall speak unto me." This, we think, is to be regarded as an honest declaration on the part of Balaam at the time, though the leaven was secretly at work in his mind which prompted him, when the morning came, to fall short of the exact truth in his statement. But we see no reason to doubt that he possessed a certain degree of the knowledge of the true God, here denominated "Jehovah," and that hitherto he had been comparatively a sincere worshipper of Him, and had acquired an extensive reputation as one who had near access to the Deity and great power and prevalence with him as a prophet. Long prior to the selection of the Jewish people as the special depositories of the divine truth, there was undoubtedly a wide-spread knowledge of the Most High which obtained among what are termed the Gentile nations, though it was continually becoming more and more dim and confused, till it finally became extinguished in the midnight of idolatry. Hengstenberg, in his elaborate essay on the "History of Balaam and his Prophecies," appended to his "Genuineness of Daniel," thus remarks on this question, "Whence Balaam had obtained what he possessed of the knowledge and fear of God." While inclined himself to the opinion that Balaam's acknowledgment of the true God had been derived from the knowledge of the God of Israel, which had been widely diffused in the Mosaic age, from the covenanted people, among the surrounding heathen nations, he thus alludes to another theory on the subject, according to which, "the religious state of Balaam is to be regarded as one excited and developed on heathen soil, by the traditions from monotheistic antiquity, and, indeed, by isolated sounds from the revelations to the patriarchs, which had resounded into the heathen world, and had not then entirely died away. This opinion is the general one." And then, after observing that it was held by Buddeus and Benzel among the earlier writers, cites Tholuck among the later as espousing the same view. In fact, the latter writer, in a parallel drawn between Balaam and Melchizedek, remarks: "Appearances such as these serve to confirm the belief, that a purer worship preceded idolatry and natural religion with all nations, but which was already

9 And God came unto Balaam, and said, What men *are* these with thee?

10 And Balaam said unto God, Balak the son of Zippor, king of Moab, hath sent unto me, *saying*,

11 Behold, *there is* a people come out of Egypt, which covereth the face of the earth: come now, curse me them; peradventure I shall be able to overcome them, and drive them out.

---

at the time of Abraham extinguished among the greater part of mankind." Some portion of the lingering relics of this ancient faith we suppose still to have survived in Mesopotamia, the native country of Abraham, and the place of Jacob's sojourn, and now found its principal representative in the person of Balaam. At the same time we are ready to admit, with Hengstenberg, that the marvellous manifestations of the divine omnipotence in behalf of Israel must have produced a powerful sensation throughout the surrounding nations, in which Balaam probably shared. But we nevertheless are persuaded that independent of this, he was, to a certain degree, a worshipper of the true God.

V. 9. *And God came unto Balaam, and said, etc.* God is said to "come" to men when he imparts to them special communications or revelations; and this he does for the most part, as here, in the night season, when he can converse with them by the medium of dreams and visions. Thus he "came to Abimelech in a dream by night," Gen. 20:3. So he "came also to Laban the Syrian, in a dream by night," Gen. 31:14. For purposes of his own glory, and the good of his people, he has often seen fit to reveal his counsels, and even impart the gifts of knowledge and understanding in his word to those who were inwardly estranged from him.——¶ *What men are these with thee?* No one acquainted with the peculiar diction of Holy Writ will suppose that God required to be informed respecting the messengers or their errand, any more than he sought for new information when he asked Adam in Paradise, "Where art thou?"—or Cain, "Where is thy brother Abel?"—or Hagar, Sarah's maid, "Whence comest thou, and whither goest thou?"—or Abraham, "Where is Sarah thy wife?"—or Hezekiah, upon receiving the Babylonish ambassadors, "Whence are these men? What said they? What have they seen in thy house? etc." The interrogation proceeded of course from the purpose of eliciting from Balaam himself the character of the men and the object of their errand. "I have ever seen that God loves to take occasion of proceeding with us from ourselves, rather than from his own immediate prescience."—*Bp. Hall.* The language is evidently that of rebuke, as when it was said to our sinning first parent, "Where art thou, Adam?" It is tacitly assumed that he could not answer the question without bringing himself into an attitude where he would have reason to be overwhelmed with a sense of his own perverseness. What apology could he offer—professed prophet as he was, of the true Jehovah—for being found in such equivocal company?

V. 11. *Come now, curse me them.* Heb. *kâbâh*, a different word from that occurring v. 6, and there rendered "curse," though of equivalent import as appears from the use of both terms ch. 23:7, 8. It properly denotes *a pricking, piercing*, or *striking through*, with evil, reproachful, and blasphemous speeches. See the Note on Lev. 24:11,

12 And God said unto Balaam, Thou shalt not go with them; thou shalt not curse the people: for [h] they *are* blessed.
13 And Balaam rose up in the morning, and said unto the princes of Balak, Get you into your land: for the LORD refuseth [i] to give me leave to go with you.

h Gen. 22. 16–18. Deut. 33. 29.

i Deut. 23. 5.

where the word is more fully explained. "The blasphemer, Lev. 24 : 11, did, as it were, *strike through* that sacred and tremendous name of *Jehovah;* and here Balak grows upon Balaam, not only with stronger assaults in his more honorable ambassadors and highest preferments, but also with his demands of deeper performances. Balaam must do more work for more wages. He must now not only curse Israel lightly, but he must strike them through with his curses, and utterly devote them to destruction."—*Ness.* It will be observed that Balaam in reply gives a perfectly correct statement of the matter of fact, and yet we wonder how he dared to do it. He knew, in all probability, that it was God's own people that he was now asked to curse, and yet he was in treaty with the enemies of that people, and consequently with the enemies of the God of that people. Notwithstanding all this, and notwithstanding he shows no resentment that they should have attempted to seduce him from his allegiance, he coolly recites to the Most High the object of the visit of the messengers rather with the composure of a martyr than with the terror of a traitor. But in his answer to the deputies, v. 13, he is not quite so scrupulously exact.

V. 12. *Thou shalt not go with them, etc.* Here was a positive command coupled with plain and direct information relative to the lot of the chosen people, which should have removed every doubt from the mind of Balaam, and become at once the imperative law of his conduct. "Thou shalt not go with them; thou shalt not curse the people; for they are blessed." The tenor of the covenant with Abraham ran thus, "I will curse him that curseth thee." This made it not only fruitless, but perilous, to attempt to curse them. Balaam's own welfare was therefore consulted in the prohibition, which not only forbade him to go with the messengers for the purpose, but even to attempt to curse them at a distance. The reason was—"they are blessed," and the gifts and callings of God are without repentance. When once the blessing was pronounced upon Jacob, Esau could not avail to reverse it:—"I have blessed him; yea, and he shall be blessed." Israel had, indeed, often provoked the Lord by their sins in the wilderness, but he would not suffer their enemies to curse them. He made them heirs of the blessedness pertaining to those "whose iniquities are forgiven, and whose sins are covered." Accordingly, the people are subsequently reminded of this signal instance of the divine favor, Deut. 23 : 5, "Nevertheless, the Lord thy God would not hearken unto Balaam; but the Lord thy God turned the curse into a blessing unto thee, because the Lord thy God loved thee."

V. 13. *Get you into your own land; for the Lord refuseth to give me leave to go with you.* This was true, but not the whole truth. The divine prohibition, v. 12, consisted of two parts, one forbidding him *to go*, the other forbidding him *to curse.* The latter he sup-

14 And the princes of Moab rose up, and they went unto Balak, and said, Balaam refuseth to come with us.

15 And Balak sent yet again princes, more, and more honourable than they.

16 And they came to Balaam, and said to him, Thus saith Balak the son of Zippor, Let nothing, I pray thee, hinder thee from coming unto me:

---

presses, and dwells only on the former. He admits that the Lord had interdicted his going with them, but says not a word of his being strictly commanded not to curse them, inasmuch as it would be wicked and dangerous both for him and them to seek to Israel's harm, for that they were blessed. He evidently softened the terms of his response, so as to indicate that his heart was really with them, and that he would intrinsically like to go. He virtually says, "God does not give me leave to go. I wish he would give me leave; but as he does not, I cannot gratify or enrich myself by the attempt to oblige your master." "Those are a fair mark for Satan's temptation that speak diminishingly of divine prohibitions, as if they amounted to no more than the denial of a permission, and as if to go *against God's law* were only to go *without his leave.*"—*Henry.*

V. 14. *Balaam refuseth to come with us.* Here is a farther instance of the propensity of unprincipled men to *minify* instead of *magnify* the Lord's word. Balaam told the princes less than God spake to him, and now they relate less to Balak than Balaam told them. All the account they give of it is, "Balaam refuseth to come with us;" intimating that he only wanted more solicitation and higher proffers. They left him to infer that the refusal was wholly the act of Balaam himself, keeping back the fact that God had expressly forbidden the prophet's compliance with their invitation. As the matter was reported to Balak, it is not at all surprising that he should have sent again.

V. 15. *Balak sent yet again princes more, and more honorable than they.* By fitting out and dispatching a more numerous retinue, composed of more honorable and imposing personages, he determines to assault his cupidity more vigorously. From all that he could learn he was persuaded that Balaam "had his price," and he would not run the risk of losing his services by underbidding. He therefore bids still higher in this second mission, and therein shows an example of persistency in an evil cause which might well be imitated by the advocates of a good one. "O that we could be so importunate for our good, as wicked men are for the compassing of their own designs! A denial doth but whet the desires of vehement suitors. Why are we faint in spiritual things, when we are not denied, but delayed?"—*Bp. Hall.*

V. 16. *Let nothing, I pray thee, hinder thee from coming unto me.* Heb. "Be not kept back, or withholden, from coming." Gr. "I pray thee, delay not (or, slack not) to come unto me," the same word in the original with that which occurs Acts 9:38, where the disciples send to Peter "desiring that he would not *delay* to come unto them." It imports that Balaam should not suffer himself, either by the repugnance of his own will, or from any other cause, to be prevented from compliance with Balak's urgent entreaties. Importunity is therefore added to unlimited proffers.

17 For I will promote thee unto very great honour, and I will do whatsoever thou sayest unto me: come [k] therefore, I pray thee, curse me this people.
18 And Balaam answered and said unto the servants of Balak, If [l] Balak would give me his house full of silver and gold, I [m] cannot go beyond the word of the LORD my God, to do less or more.
19 Now therefore, I pray you, tarry ye also here this night, that I may know what the LORD will say unto me more.

k ver. 6. l c. 24. 13. m 1 K. 22. 14. c. 23. 26. 24. 13.

He appeals to the vanity and ambition, as well as the covetousness, of the prophet. Under the influence of the powerful motives presented he would have Balaam manfully break through every impediment and hasten to a closure with his offers.

V. 17. *I will promote thee unto very great honor, etc.* Heb. "Honoring I will honor thee very much." Gr. "I will honorably honor thee." It is natural for those who put a great value themselves upon worldly honors and dignities to suppose that others are not proof against their seductions. The experience of all ages has shown that they are few indeed who are not assailable from this quarter, and the sequel shows that Balaam formed no exception to the general rule.

V. 18. *If Balak would give me his house full of silver and gold, etc.* The answer of Balaam thus far was truly noble, and worthy of being prompted by a better spirit. But the effect of it is utterly spoilt by what follows, wherein he invites them to tarry over night. He had nothing more to do than to cut the matter short at once and dismiss them without farther ceremony. But the sequel shows that under a seeming resistance to the temptation there was a real yielding to it.——¶ *I cannot go beyond the word of the Lord my God.* Heb. "Beyond the mouth of the Lord." Chald. "Beyond the decree of the Word of the Lord." Vulg. "I cannot alter the word of the Lord my God." His emphatic appropriation of Jehovah as his God is no doubt to be regarded as proof of his possessing a knowledge of the true object of worship, to whose will he did not dare to go directly counter, notwithstanding his heart was hankering for the lucre which Balak held out before his eyes. He was now obviously involved in a struggle between his convictions and his corruptions. He *knew*, indeed, that the wealth of this world, all its gold and silver, was as nothing compared with the favor of God, and probably for a moment persuaded himself that he would act according to his convictions. But alas, how soon does he waver! In the next sentence he manifests clearly that he loves the wages of unrighteousness, and is in hopes that some way may open by which he can compass the secret desire of his soul without at the same time forfeiting his title to the divine regards. "Balaam here becomes the graphical picture of a covetous and ambitious hypocrite, *pre*tending one thing, and *in*tending another. Oh how shy he here seems! By no means must he dare to act any thing against the revealed will of God, no, not for a housefull, when with all his heart he would have done it for an handful, of gold and silver."—*Ness.*——¶ *To do less or more.* Heb. "Little or great," equivalent to any thing at all.

V. 19. *That I may know what the*

20 And [n] God came unto Balaam at night, and said unto him, If the men come to call thee, rise up, *and* go with them; but

n ver. 9.

Lord will say unto me more. But what "more" could he wish or expect to receive from the Lord? Did he fashion to himself a god after his own heart, and imagine that he also was to be moved from his purpose by the gifts and promises of Balak? Did he think that God was a man that he should lie, or the son of man that he should repent? Did he hope to obtain from him permission to curse a people which had been so long and so conspicuously the object of his covenant care, and whom he had so emphatically pronounced "blessed?" What could more decidedly prove what Peter calls "the *madness* of the prophet" than his thus tampering with the Moabitish emissaries? Why did he not repel their proposal as did Peter that of Simon Magus, "Thy money perish with thee." Why did he not dismiss them as did our blessed Lord the tempter who "showed him all the kingdoms of the world, and the glory of them, and said unto him, All these things will I give thee if thou wilt fall down and worship me." The answer was instant and decisive, "Get thee hence, Satan; for it is written, Thou shalt worship the Lord thy God, and him only shalt thou serve." Alas, the canker of covetousness was even then eating into the vitals of his soul.

V. 20. *If the men come to call thee, etc.* But the men had already come, and had called or invited him to go with them, and there is no reason to suppose that any *additional* call was anticipated. Therefore the preferable rendering undoubtedly is, "since, seeing that, inasmuch as, the men are come." This is often the force of the Heb. *im, if.* It is what is termed the *concessive* sense of the particle.——¶ *Rise up, (and) go with them.* This permission, when viewed in contrast with the express prohibition, v. 12, may well be conceived to constitute a stumbling-block in the way of the ordinary reader of the Bible. It has surely the air of marked inconsistency to forbid the prophet's going in one sentence, and then allow it in another. But if the internal state of the man's heart be viewed in connection with the laws of the divine providence, we shall obtain the key to the solution of the mystery. Lured by the prospect of the rewards, Balaam's heart was set upon going; and as the divine wisdom, in its procedures with men, allows them always to act in freedom, so here it is permitted Balaam to go, seeing he was so fully bent upon it. His telling him to go was, we suppose, *merely the Lord's providential permission put into words.* It was the virtual language of his dealing with the mercenary prophet. We read in the following paragraph a strikingly analogous incident, 1 Kings 22 : 19–23, "And he said, Hear thou therefore the word of the Lord: I saw the Lord sitting on his throne, and all the host of heaven standing by him on his right hand and on his left. And the Lord said, Who shall persuade Ahab, that he may go up and fall at Ramoth-gilead? And one said on this manner, and another said on that manner. And there came forth a spirit, and stood before the Lord, and said, I will persuade him. And the Lord said unto him, Wherewith? And he said, I will go forth, and I will be a lying spirit in the mouth of all his prophets. And he said, Thou shalt persuade him, and prevail also: go forth and do so. **Now** therefore, behold, the Lord hath **put a**

yet [o] the word which I shall say unto thee, that shalt thou do.

21 And Balaam rose up in the morning, and saddled his ass, and went with the princes of Moab.

o v. 35. c. 23. 12

lying spirit in the mouth of all these thy prophets, and the Lord hath spoken evil concerning thee." The Lord is here pleased to attribute to himself, or to his agency, what he *permits* to be done with an evil intent. In no other sense could he be said to put a lying spirit into the mouth of prophets. It is no unusual thing for the Most High to act on this principle with men as free moral agents. Thus Ps. 81 : 11, 12, "But my people would not hearken to my voice; and Israel would none of me. So I gave them up unto their own heart's lust: and they walked in their own counsels." When men refuse to hearken to the Lord's voice, they are not to be surprised if he leaves them to themselves to rush into the open jaws of destruction. "As God sometimes denies the prayers of his people in love, so sometimes he grants the desires of the wicked in wrath."—*Henry*.——¶ *The word which I shall say unto thee, that shalt thou do.* It would, no doubt, appear at first blush that a more natural expression would be, "The word which I shall say unto thee, that shalt thou *speak*." But the original for "word" often denotes "thing," as we have shown in the Note on Gen. 15 : 1. The idea therefore is, that Balaam's whole *course of procedure* was to be so overruled that the Lord's counsel should stand, and every purpose of his will should be accomplished. We regard the words rather as a prediction than a command. It is as if the Most High had said, "Inasmuch as the messengers are so importunate with thee, and thou so earnest with me; since thou wilt take no denial, nor yield to my behest, then go; go forward; follow thine own course; do as I perceive thou art determined to do; yet know that I will bridle thy tongue, and constrain thee to utter the promptings not of thine own pleasure, but of mine." This, though a mere concession to the prophet's waywardness, and not implying the least particle of approbation, Balaam yet took as a *quasi* allowance of the Divine providence, and proceeded accordingly to act upon it. The event showed how dangerous is the licence men may sometimes obtain when they *beg leave to sin.*

V. 21. *Balaam rose up in the morning and saddled his ass.* The idea attached to this phrase by a European or an American will be very apt to be erroneous. There were not, in those days, in the East any proper saddles. This is a later invention for riding on horseback, and it is not even now, among the Orientals, generally applied to asses. The saddling of asses, mentioned in Scripture, probably consisted merely in placing upon their backs thick cloths, or mats. "Something of the same kind," says Mr. Kitto, "or pieces of rug, felt, carpet, or cloth, are still in general use—although a kind of pad is now frequently to be seen upon asses in the large towns of Egypt, Syria, and Arabia—especially among those let out for hire. Such town asses have also bridles, and sometimes stirrups, none of which, any more than the pad, do we remember to have noticed on asses upon actual journeys, and we have known asses travel continuously on journeys quite as long as that now undertaken by Balaam, and that by persons whose position in life quite enabled them to ride a horse or mule had they so chosen. It would not be at all extraordinary, even now, that a person, expecting to be laden with riches and

22 And God's anger was kindled because he went: and [p] the angel of the LORD stood in the way for an adversary against him. Now he was riding upon his ass, and his two servants *were* with him.

p Ex. 4. 24.

honors, should ride upon an ass—still less in an age and country where no other mode of conveyance, except that of riding upon camels, appears to have been known." In ancient times the ass was a far more valuable animal than the horse is now, and probably far more beautiful than the specimens with which we are familiar. Hence we read, "The kings that ride on white asses." Balaam evidently caught greedily at the verbal permission to go, hoping, no doubt, that as God had gone thus far, he would bend still farther to his wishes, and allow him to gratify Balak, and thus secure his rewards. Accordingly he waited for no summons in the morning, but was in all haste to set forth, being as eager to go as they were to take him with them.

V. 22. *And God's anger was kindled because he went.* But how, we are prompted to ask, could God's anger be kindled at his going, when he had given him permission to go? It may be replied, that God was angry at his *desire* to go when he had forbidden him; angry at the *motive* from which he went; and angry at the *spirit* of malediction which, against his better knowledge, he bore in his bosom in acceding to the message. Arab. "The Lord's anger was kindled against him because he had gone under the influence of the cupidity of gain." It is not to be supposed that the Lord's permission of sin is inconsistent with his anger against it, when the divine anger is rightly understood.——¶ *The angel of the Lord stood in the way for an adversary against him.* Heb. *lesâtân lo, for a satan to him.* This name, when applied to an adversary to the Lord's people, is usually equivalent to the appellation *Devil*, Job 1 : 6. Mat. 4 : 10. Rev. 12 : 9; but being here synonymous with an adversary to the wicked and a defender of the church, it is applied to a holy angel, or rather to the Lord of angels, as the original *Malak-Yehovah* imports. In v. 35 this angel speaks as the Most High himself, "Go with the men; but only the word that I shall speak unto thee, that shalt thou speak." We may, therefore, properly infer that the term indicates no other than the personage elsewhere called the "angel who redeemed Jacob from all evil," Gen. 48 : 16, and who now came to redeem Jacob's children from the curse meditated against them. It was the same angel who was sent before Israel to keep them in the way, Ex. 23 : 20, 21, the angel of the covenant, in whom was the name or quality of Jehovah. In all these manifestations we suppose there was a created mediatory angel present, but that he was so fully seized and possessed by the Divine Spirit speaking through him, that his own selfhood was put temporarily in abeyance, and he knew not for the time but that he was Jehovah himself, and therefore speaks in his name. His own self-consciousness was merged in that of the Supreme himself. On any other ground it is difficult to conceive why the term "Angel" should be applied to the Deity. "This angel was an *adversary* to Balaam, because Balaam counted him an adversary; otherwise those are really our best friends, and we are so to reckon them, that stop our progress in a sinful way."—*Henry.*——¶ *His two servants were with him.* Heb. "Two of his young men." It would appear

23 And the ass saw [q] the angel of the LORD standing in the way, and his sword drawn in his

q 2 K. 6. 17. Dan. 10. 7. Acts 22. 9. 1 Cor. 1. 27–29.

that at the time of this rencontre with the heavenly messenger, both the servants of Balaam and probably the emissaries of Balak were either behind or before the prophet, and that he was holding on his way alone. At any rate, there is no intimation in the text that even his servants were privy to the transaction recorded.

The Miracle of the Ass Speaking.

V. 23. *And the ass saw the angel of the Lord standing in the way, etc.* That portion of the sacred narrative upon which we now enter has ever been regarded as fraught with difficulties to the commentator. The grand point of the problem is to determine the precise nature of the event here recorded, whether it took place in reality according to the letter of the history, or whether it occurred in vision; or, in other words, whether it were *objective* or *subjective*—whether the words ascribed to the ass really proceeded from her and were audible to the external ear of Balaam, or whether the whole scene was transacted in his own mind in that state of ecstasy or trance into which the prophets were usually brought when Divine communications were made to them. We shall aim to present, in as brief a compass as possible, a compendious view of the arguments urged on either side, leaving it to the reader to assign to each its proper degree of weight.

(1.) It is held by the advocates of the literal sense that in an historical book, and in a narrative bearing an historical character, the incidents recorded are to be assumed as having literally occurred, so long as no intimation is given to the contrary.

To this it is replied, that there are unquestionably numerous instances in the Scriptures where such transitions from one style of narrative to another are made, when, at the same time, the reader is not expressly advertised of the fact. But all writing supposes some exercise of discernment on the part of the reader, and some capacity of inferring, from significant circumstances, what is not distinctly announced. Unless when attention is specially called to the circumstance, the common reader will be somewhat surprised to find how often the sacred writers slide, from a narrative of real incidents in the natural world, into the relation of a vision or dream, and that, too, in such a manner as to require the reader to infer a transition from the altered character of the occurrences described. Thus it is said of Abraham, Gen. 15 : 1, that the word of the Lord came to him in a vision, and yet it cannot be doubted that the *following* circumstances belong to the vision, though the language is that of plain historical narrative. For v. 5, Abraham is led into the open air, and pointed to the stars of heaven; while, on the contrary, according to v. 12, the sun is only near setting. Then in the *daytime* Abraham sees the stars, which is only possible in vision. In like manner, we think there can be no reasonable doubt, that Abraham's entertaining the three angels, Gen. 18 : 1–8, was done in vision; as otherwise we seem to be forced to the conclusion that they, for the time being, assumed material bodies, bodies capable of eating and drinking material food—a theory encompassed with difficulties all but insuperable. So also we read, Jer. 13 : 1–7, that Jeremiah was commanded to go to the river Euphrates and hide his

hand: and the ass turned aside out of the way, and went into the field: and Balaam smote the ass, to turn her into the way.

girdle there in a hole of the rock. Yet the prophet was then in the land of Canaan, hundreds of miles from the Euphrates. Thus again, Ezekiel, when in the land of Babylon, ch. 8 : 1–12, was ordered to dig a hole in the wall at Jerusalem, and then shown the abominations committed by the house of Judah, which, of course, must have transpired in a vision. In a vision, moreover, we suppose that Hosea took "a wife of whoredoms" according to the divine command, Hos. 1 : 2, although this is not intimated in the sense of the letter. Into the same category comes also the sight (Heb. *mareh*) of the burning bush by Moses, Ex. 3 : 2, and the voice addressed to Samuel in the temple, 1 Sam. 3 : 1. "The word of the Lord," it is said, "was precious in those days; there was no open vision;" according to which the occurrence had no doubt the character of a *vision*. It is said also, v. 15, that "Samuel feared to show Eli the *vision*" (Heb. *mareh*). But the word *mareh* is always used of internal visions and sights. In the New Testament we meet with some striking parallel cases, where a manifestation, apparently external and objective, is yet really internal and subjective. Thus in John 12 : 28, 29, the Evangelist speaks of a voice which came from heaven in a manner that would indicate a perfectly audible external and articulate voice, and yet it is plain, from what follows, that it was addressed to the inner sense of certain individuals present, while to the outward ear of others it seemed only as a vague hollow noise. To those alone who were capable of the opening of an internal sense were the precise words intelligible; while the multitude hear only a sound without meaning. Such, also, was the case in Paul's conversion, Acts 9 : 3–8. There is not a word in the narrative itself to indicate that the incident was to him internal or subjective, yet upon comparing ch. 9 : 7, with ch. 22 : 9, we are forced inevitably to that conclusion. Finally, we should not judge from the mere sense of the letter, that the women, who visited our Lord's sepulchre early in the morning, Luke 24 : 14, saw the two angels clothed in white with any other than their natural eyes, and yet it is indubitable that it was by the sudden opening of their spiritual eyes that they were favored with the vision. These instances, it is thought, are sufficient to warrant the conclusion, that the prevailing historical character of a narrative like the present does not militate with the fact of its being at the same time the record of a transaction occurring within the domain of the spiritual world. Yet neither on the other hand do they necessitate a spiritual construction. There is a presumptive and *prima facie* evidence in favor of the historical sense, unless some paramount reason can be adduced for rejecting it. Even though the subjective view *might* be intrinsically admissible, still the opposite view may be the most probable.

(2.) It is maintained that Peter, 2 Pet. 2 : 15, 16, speaks of the incident as an external one:—"Which have forsaken the right way, and are gone astray, following the way of Balaam the son of Bosor, who loved the wages of unrighteousness; but was rebuked for his iniquity: the dumb ass, speaking with man's voice, forbade the madness of the prophet."

To this it is answered, that the mere quotation of a passage like this from the Old Testament does not necessarily establish the sense of the latter as the true sense. The writer takes it as he finds it, and as the latter alone conveys the lesson which he wishes to teach, he neither affirms nor denies as to any other sense. Yet, on the other hand, as the literal sense is the most obvious sense, and such as would strike the mass of readers as the true one, so Peter may have been prompted to cite it as having that sense, and which it is impossible to show to be erroneous.

Various other considerations might be adduced bearing upon the points above stated, but we pass them by to exhibit a little more distinctly the positive grounds on which Hengstenberg and others rely to establish the subjectivity of the incident.

(1.) Visions and dreams are designated in Num. 12 : 6, as the ordinary mode of divine communication to the prophets, and as Balaam belonged to this class of men, and the speaking of the ass to communications from God, who is expressly said to have "opened the mouth of the ass," we are authorized, it is said, to assume that the present was a case of subjective or visionary revelation.

(2.) Balaam, in the introduction to his third and fourth prophecies, ch. 24: 3, 4, 15, 16, speaks of himself as "the man which heard the words of God, which saw the vision of the Almighty, falling into a trance, but having his eyes open." It is maintained, that the reference in this passage is especially to the incident here recorded. It was on this occasion that he fell into a trance, and in that state had his spiritual eyes opened to perceive and read the lessons which the Lord designed in this way to impart to him. The visions of the Almighty were usually accorded in a state of prophetic ecstasy. The presumption therefore is, that if such a man as Balaam, a seer by profession, sees and hears in his own proper sphere, what he thus hears and sees is spiritual instead of natural. If the contrary is maintained, it should be clearly established. The advocates of the strictly historical theory reply to this, that there is none but mere conjectural ground for affirming that the passage cited refers to the miraculous event under consideration. Viewed in its relations to the context it appears to have a much more natural reference to the state into which he was brought when uttering the inspired prophecies recorded in the subsequent chapters.

(3.) It cannot well be doubted that the appearance of the angel immediately preceding the speaking of the ass was an appearance addressed not to the outward, but to the inward senses. But if the appearance of the angel was designed for the spiritual eye of Balaam, then we may reasonably suppose also that the voice of the ass was intended for his spiritual ear. That such was the fact, it is supposed, may be concluded from the circumstance of his not seeing the angel as soon as the ass saw him. But why should not he and the animal have seen him simultaneously if he actually appeared on the natural plane like any other external object? To this, however, it is an obvious reply, that admitting there was a spiritual or internal perception of the angel, it does not follow that the vocal utterances of the ass were heard by any other than the natural ear. A miracle, on any ground, must be admitted in the case, and taking this for granted, there is no difficulty in conceiving that divine power may have caused articulate sounds to proceed from the thorax of the animal that could be heard by the outward ear as readily as his natural bray.

(4.) The declaration that "God opened the eyes of Balaam" goes far to establish the internal or subjective character of the miracle. The eyes here opened were the eyes of the mind, not of the body. There is no intimation of physical blindness, and therefore the words can only properly be compared with such as the following:—2 Kings 6 : 17, "And Elisha prayed, and said, Lord, I pray thee, open his eyes, that he may see. And the Lord opened the eyes of the young man; and he saw: and behold, the mountain was full of horses and chariots of fire round about Elisha." Ps. 119 : 18, "Open thou mine eyes, that I may behold wondrous things out of thy law." On this head it is readily granted that there was a supernatural couching of Balaam's vision to enable him to see the angel standing in menacing attitude before him, but it is denied that we can justly argue from this that there was *any thing more* of a miraculous influence exerted upon Balaam. So far as a "vision" is predicated of the prophet, it seems to have been confined to this single feature of the transaction. Nor is it to be doubted that the same power which opened Balaam's eyes to the perception of the angel may also have opened the eyes of the ass to the view of the same object.

(5.) The fact that Balaam expresses no astonishment at the occurrence argues strongly in favor of its internal character. What could take place more astounding, as an external event, than for a man to find himself addressed by a dumb beast in a moving remonstrance against his cruelty,—"What have I done unto thee, that thou hast smitten me these three times?" Should we not suppose he would have been struck speechless himself at thus hearing articulate speech proceeding apparently from the organs of the beast on which he rode? Yet he expresses not the least particle of surprise, but in a fit of petulancy, as if chiding an old cross-grained servant, exclaims, "Because thou hast mocked me; I would there were a sword in mine hand, for now would I kill thee." This would seem to be far enough from the language of a man whose attention has just been arrested by a prodigy so overwhelmingly marvellous. He answers as coolly as if such an altercation, carried on by blows on one side and complaints on the other, had been a matter of frequent occurrence. It cannot be denied that there is considerable force in this suggestion, though it cannot be regarded as absolutely decisive. It is not the wont of Holy Writ to describe the emotions experienced by parties witnessing marvellous or miraculous events. We cannot recall any one instance where this is done, and therefore feel that the force of the present objection, if not entirely annulled, is at least greatly weakened.

(6.) The current of Jewish interpretation, it is said, is in favor of the visionary character of the transaction. To this purpose the following remark is quoted from Maimonides:—"In whatever connection we find it written in Scripture that an angel spoke with any one, or that any thing was revealed to any one by God, you are to know that this is to be no otherwise understood than as having been done in a dream or a prophetic vision." To this it is replied, that the solution is admitted where a simple theophany, or a vision of angels is concerned. An ecstatic state is granted to have occurred to Balaam so far as relates to the rencontre with the angel. He was undoubtedly seen with the eyes of the mind, and not of the body; but when we go beyond this, and claim that the other incidents of the journey were visionary or subjective, it is contended that the evidence is insufficient to establish the position. It is scarcely possible to resist the conviction that the prophet actually saddled and mounted the ass, and proceeded on his journey like any other traveller—that he passed through just such localities as are described—that the animal thrust herself against the wall in affright, thereby crushing Balaam's foot—and that then, and not till then, did any of the incidents become visionary. But at that particular crisis the angel was revealed to the spiritual eyes of Balaam, and the visionary or ecstatic state continued as long as the interview lasted with the angelic personage. Otherwise, it appears impossible to define the limits between the external or historical and the subjective. Where is the line of demarcation? What part of the narrative is natural, and what supernatural? It would seem, therefore, the safest and soundest position, to hold that all the incidents actually occurred on the natural plane with the single exception of the prophet's seeing and conversing with the angel.

V. 23. *And his sword drawn in his hand.* The import of "sword" as a symbol is that of opposition or antagonism, amounting in many cases to what is usually understood by wrath or vengeance. Thus David, 1 Chron. 21: 16, beheld the angel that plagued Israel "with a drawn sword in his hand." Joshua, in like manner, saw the angel of the Lord similarly armed, Josh. 5: 13, 14, when he appeared to him as "captain of the Lord's host," and about to execute judgment against the Canaanites. The appearance of the angel thus accoutred in the present instance carried with it the implication, that if the prophet presumed to pronounce a curse upon the people whom the Lord had blessed, it would be regarded as virtually declaring war against God and his holy angels, who would assuredly fight against him. "Balaam went with a purpose to curse Israel, and afterwards to have them killed with the sword. His curses would have been like "the piercings of a sword;" he had "whetted his tongue as a sword," and bent his arrow "even a bitter word;" and the Lord to reward him according to his works sendeth out a sword against him."—*Ainsworth.* But for the present Balaam was so blinded by his cupidity, that he saw not the formidable opponent who confronted him in his way. Little cause had he now to boast of his visions, when his ass saw more than he did. How many have God and the angels of God against them, who do not see it! So, on the other hand, the righteous are surrounded like Elijah and Elisha with chariots of fire and horses of fire for their protection, though like the servant of the latter they may require the couching of their spiritual eyes in order to see it. "What a comfort is this to all that wish well to the Israel of God, that he never suffers wicked men to form any attempt against them, without sending his holy angels forth to break this attempt, and secure his little ones."—*Henry.*——¶ *The ass turned aside out of the way, etc.* It might without impropriety here have been said to Balaam in the language of Job, "Ask now the beasts and they shall teach thee," for his folly was here reproved by the action of the ass, as it was afterwards by her words. Inasmuch as Balaam's own way was perverse before the Lord, as he had forsaken the right way and gone astray, 2 Pet. 2:15, so we may properly recognize a representation of this in the turning aside of the ass, which should have given her rider a useful hint, notwithstanding the animal was prompted to the movement by a sufficient cause. "The ass knows his owner," sees his danger, and avoids it, but Balaam

24 But the angel of the LORD stood in a path of the vineyards, a wall *being* on this side, and a wall on that side.
25 And when the ass saw the angel of the LORD, she thrust herself unto the wall, and crushed Balaam's foot against the wall: and he smote her again.
26 And the angel of the LORD went further, and stood in a narrow place, where *was* no way to

---

"does not know, does not consider," and therefore virtually rushes on to destruction, v. 33.——¶ *And went into the field.* "In the East the roads are like bridle-paths across commons, and even through cultivated grounds are wholly unenclosed, except when they pass through gardens and plantations in the neighborhood of towns."—*Pict. Bible.* Mr. Kitto suggests in the same connection, that the ass, after the first view of the angel, turned aside from one of these bridle-paths into the wide fields through which it passed. Balaam then forced her back by blows into the road. But presently they came to a place where a deviation from the road was not possible, seeing it was confined by vineyard walls on the right hand and on the left. This fact he regards as an intimation, that they were approaching a town or village, and that the Moabite lords had gone on ahead to prepare a place for the diviner's reception. As the ass was gradually compelled into narrower and narrower straits, so it was with Balaam himself, and so it is with all men who imitate his perverse example in turning aside from the straightforward path, and roam abroad in the open fields or byways of disobedience.——¶ *And Balaam smote the ass, to turn her into the way.* Gr. "Smote the ass with his rod, or staff," taken doubtless from v. 27. The perverseness of Balaam was equal to that of the beast, and equally deserving of chastisement.

V. 24. *The angel of the Lord stood in a path of the vineyards.* Heb. *be-mishol, in a very narrow pass.* The walls of two adjoining vineyards here stood so near to each other that an extremely narrow passage was all that remained between them, and the ass therefore could not diverge into the fields, as she had done before. If she attempted to move either way, in consequence of her advance being opposed, she must necessarily be brought in collision with the wall on one side or the other.

V. 25. *She thrust herself against the wall, and crushed Balaam's foot against the wall.* The original word for "thrust" and "crushed" is here the same (*lâhatz*), only one is in the passive or reflexive form, and the other in the active—lit. "She was violently pressed against the wall, and violently pressed Balaam's foot against the wall." The word occurs, 2 Kings 6:32, where the king's messenger, who was sent to take away Elisha's head, was "pressed (or crushed) in the door," though rendered in our version "held fast." "The children of God have the angels to keep them in all their ways, and to bear them up, 'lest they dash their foot against a stone,' but Balaam, tempting the Lord, hath his angel to withstand him, whereby his foot is crushed against the wall; yet maketh he no good use thereof."—*Ainsworth.* Physical disasters may befall the best of men, but the occurrence of such incidents is always calculated to prompt the inquiry within us, whether our way is right in his sight or not.

V. 26. *Where was no way to turn either to the right hand or to the left.* The

turn either to the right hand or
to the left.
27 And when the ass saw the
angel of the LORD, she fell down
under Balaam: and Balaam's
anger was kindled, and he smote
the ass with a staff.
28 And the LORD opened[r] the
mouth of the ass; and she said

r 2 Pet. 2. 16.

road-way, it seems, continued to grow more and more compressed and narrow, till at length it passed between walls so near together that any degree of turning was impossible. Here again the opposing angel took his station, and for the third time arrested the progress of the ass and his rider—emblematical, as we have before remarked, of the gradual course of the Divine providence in hedging up the way of wicked men, and causing them to fall before him. "Fear, and the pit, and the snare shall be upon thee. He that fleeth from the fear, shall fall into the pit; and he that getteth up out of the pit, shall be taken in the snare." Jer. 48:43, 44.

V. 27. *And when the ass saw the angel of the Lord, she fell down under Balaam.* It is said to have been an old Pythagorean maxim, "Go not in the way where an ass has fallen down," something of evil omen being thereby implied. But for the deplorable hardness of Balaam's heart, he must have been struck and confounded by so extraordinary an incident as the ass' falling to the ground, as she was not usually restive, nor had she ever before served him thus. But he was too intent upon the attainment of his ends to consider the circumstance in its true light, and also to be aware that the falling of the ass had been the means of saving his life from the sword of the angel.——¶ *And Balaam's anger was kindled, and he smote the ass with a staff.* "Thus they who by wilful sin are running headlong into perdition, are angry at those who would prevent their ruin."—*Henry.*

V. 28. *The Lord opened the mouth of the ass.* The precise nature of the miracle here recorded it is not easy to define. From the simple letter we should infer that the vocal sounds were formed by the pulmonary organs of the animal, nor can we affirm that such was not the fact. Yet, on the other hand, they may have been caused by a direct act of divine power, and made to produce upon the auditory nerve of Balaam the same effect as if they had issued from the organs of the ass. But certain it is, that the ass *understood* nothing that was uttered. Articulate sounds with men are caused by the action of the mind operating upon the lungs, and are, in fact, thought speaking. Not so with the brute animal. He is not capable of that kind of thought which shapes itself into words, and, therefore, if he speaks, his lungs must be mechanically moved by a foreign power, or the speaking must proceed apparently from the animal, but really from Omnipotence. The difference, however, between the two modes of construing the record is rather formal than real. A miracle is to be affirmed in either case, and on either view the credit of the Holy Volume, as an inspired book, is abundantly sustained.——¶ *What have I done unto thee, that thou hast smitten me these three times?* The simple pathos of this appeal would seem capable of softening the obduracy and disarming the rage of Balaam, whose *madness* was thus powerfully and affectingly rebuked. But one whose folly would not be amended by *braying* in a mortar, Prov.

unto Balaam, What have I done
unto thee, that thou hast smitten me these three times?
29 And Balaam said unto the
ass, Because thou hast mocked
me: I would there were a sword
in mine hand, [s] for now would I
kill thee.

30 And the ass said unto
Balaam, *Am* not I thine ass,
upon which thou hast ridden
ever since *I was* thine unto
this day? was I ever wont to
do so unto thee? And he said,
Nay.
31 Then the LORD opened [t] the

s Ps. 12. 10.

t Gen. 21. 19. 2 K. 6. 17. Luke 24. 16, 31.

27:22, would be little likely to be wrought upon by the intelligent and articulate *braying* of the ass.

V. 29. *Because thou hast mocked me.* He could see the alleged mockery of the ass toward him, but could not realize his own mockery of God, who had so solemnly charged him as to the conduct he was to observe in this emergency.——¶ *For now I would kill thee.* This might properly have reminded him of his impotency in regard to any injury he would have inflicted upon Israel. His will would not be seconded by his ability. Another practical lesson to be drawn from this item of the narrative is suggested by the old commentator Ness: "The ass had turned out of the literal highway for saving her own life, and the life of her master, yet did he smite her, and would have killed her for so doing: Whereas himself had turned out of the metaphorical way of the Lord, and followed his own crooked ways with a purpose to destroy the lives of God's people; therefore he deserved more to be smitten, yea, and killed, than his ass."

V. 30. *Upon which thou hast ridden ever since (I was) thine unto this day.* The phrase in the original is somewhat indefinite, being made up of the particle for "since" and the suffix "thou" or "thine"—lit. "since thou," i. e., since thou wast a rider. Gr. "From thy youth." Chald. "Since thou hast been." Sam. "From thy beginning." Vulg. "Am not I thy beast on which thou hast been always accustomed to ride until this present day?" The import probably is, that he was the only animal on which Balaam had ridden since the time that he began to ride at all, or, in other words, from his youth. He was his familiar hack; and as he had now done three times what he had never done before, he had at least the right to claim of Balaam that he should attribute it to some extraordinary cause. See a parallel usage, Gen. 48:15, where the same Heb. term is rendered "all my life long." Gr. "From my youth."——¶ *Was I ever wont to do so unto thee?* Heb. "Have I accustoming been accustomed?" As the ass was of course incapable of understanding Balaam, or of making any such remonstrance as this, the words are to be considered as the Lord's own rebuke, apparently uttered by the dumb beast, of the harshness and cruelty of Balaam. It clearly involved the implication, that when the creatures over whom the Lord has given us dominion, depart from their wonted obedience, it is to be presumed that there is some good reason for it, and that reason is to be sought in ourselves. To forbear to make the inquiry is to give evidence of astonishing hardness of heart and blindness of mind.——¶ *And he said, Nay.* Thus confessing to the justice of the ass's plea. Even with all his perverseness he could not withstand the reasonableness of the expostulation.

V. 31. *Then the Lord opened the eyes*

eyes of Balaam, and he saw the angel of the LORD standing in the way, and his sword drawn in his hand: and he bowed [u] down his head, and fell flat on his face.

[u] Ex. 34. 8.

of Balaam, and he saw the angel, etc. Or, Heb. "Uncovered the eyes," as if by the removal of a veil. That is, the eyes of his spirit, for angels and divine theophanies are never seen by the natural eye. He had, no doubt, the use of outward vision before, but here was a supernatural couching of the internal eye which revealed to him a divine antagonist confronting him in his way. The reproving aspect of the august personage before him was rendered still more terrible by the drawn sword in his hand, the symbol of opposition and warfare. The prophet was apparently going forward in accordance with a divine dictation, yet in truth in contrariety to the will of God. A conditional permission he had construed unconditionally, and notwithstanding he had been so solemnly assured that Israel was *blessed*, and was *to be blessed*, still he was going with a desire and a purpose to *curse* them. In order to awaken him to a sense of his wickedness, the Lord sent an angel, or rather appeared as an angel, to stop him in his presumptuous course. It is thus that the Most High often interposes to arrest the progress of sinners, and prevent the commission of iniquity. Not that he manifests himself *precisely in this way*, but as his resources are infinite, he has innumerable methods of putting forth providential hindrances in the way of the perpetration of evil on the part of rash or heedless transgressors. How many, by the approach of some unexpected person, or by some suggestion of their own minds, are deterred from theft, robbery, burglary, adultery, or murder. It only requires that the eyes of our understandings should be opened to see under what obligations of gratitude we are laid by these seasonable and saving interpositions, however unwelcome they may be at the time. "Lo all these things worketh God often times with man, to bring back his soul from the pit, that he may be enlightened with the light of the living." "When our eyes are opened, we shall see what danger we are in in a sinful way; and how much it was for our advantage to be crossed in it, and what fools we were to quarrel with our crosses, which helped to save our lives." —*Henry.*——¶ *And he bowed down his head, and fell flat on his face.* The original is here marked by a certain degree of ambiguity, so that we are left in doubt whether it is intended to be said that Balaam fell down upon his own face, or that he prostrated himself before the face or person of the angel, as is clearly understood by the Greek. The usage of the Hebrew will admit of either rendering, but it would require an extended display of that usage to determine the question to the satisfaction of the reader. This we shall waive for the present, simply remarking that, as far as we have investigated the diction of the sacred writers, the evidence preponderates to our mind in favor of the Greek version, viz., that he humbled himself before the face of the angel. So also the Vulg. "Adoravit eum pronus in terram," *adored him* (*falling*) *prone to the ground.* It would seem that Balaam recognized in the heavenly visitant a proper object of the profoundest worship, which we know that angels are not. From the tenor of the narrative it is to be inferred, also, that Balaam had at this time dismounted from the ass, which he had probably done when she laid down under him, v. 27.

32 And the angel of the LORD said unto him, Wherefore hast thou smitten thine ass [v] these three times? behold, I went out to withstand thee, because *thy* [w] way is perverse [x] before me:

v Ps. 145. 9. w 2 Pet. 2. 14. x Prov. 14. 2. 28. 18.

V. 32. *Wherefore hast thou smitten thine ass, etc.* The Angel-Jehovah here opens his rebuke of the prophet by charging upon him his abusive treatment of the beast on which he rode. He is determined to show himself the avenger of the wrongs of the brute creation, over which man was appointed to rule, but not to tyrannize. But this was not the only lesson which Balaam was bound to learn from this incident. If the laws of mercy forbade him to treat thus cruelly the simple ass, and that without adequate cause, how much more was he forbidden to smite innocent men with the scourge or curse of his tongue, when the Lord had declared himself their patron-protector. The proper inference, moreover, to be drawn by Balaam was, that he had much more reason to smite upon his own breast, and to condemn himself, than to have bestowed his blows upon the ass.——¶ *I went out to withstand thee.* Heb. "To be a satan to thee," as in v. 22, on which see Note. The language conveys the idea, that if men, by their perverseness and disobedience, will act a *satanic* part towards God, he also will repay them in kind, and act a *satanic* part, or what shall seem such, towards them. "If ye walk contrary to me, I also will walk contrary to you." "In what case are the wicked, that have God's angels for their opposites! How deplorable and desperate is their estate! God they have made their enemy, angels they cannot call their friends, devils labor to destroy them, the world cannot save them; whither should they run for refuge? 'They shall keep us in our ways;' out of the way it is their charge to oppose us, as it is to preserve us in the way. Nor is this more a terror to the ungodly, than to the righteous a comfort. For if an angel would keep even a Balaam from sinning, how much more careful are all those glorious powers to prevent the miscarriages of God's children! From how many falls and bruises have they saved us! In how many inclinations to evil have they turned us, either by removing occasions, or by secretly casting in good motions! We sin too often, and should catch many more falls, if those holy guardians did not uphold us."—*Adams.*——¶ *Because (thy) way is perverse before me.* Heb. *yârat hadderek lenegdi, the way is rash, precipitate, perilous before me.* We have given a diversity of renderings to the original in order to make sure, if possible, of embracing the true one among them, as the term *yârat* is one of the most dubious in the whole compass of the Hebrew vocabulary. The lexicographal authorities of the highest class assign severally the different meanings we have specified, and we know of no critic who has ventured to pronounce with confidence that any one of them is correct to the exclusion of the others. Our English translation probably conveys the true idea as well as any single word that could be adopted. The ancient versions afford us but little help in the emergency, as in some of them the text is probably corrupt, and in others the equivalent term is quite as obscure as the original. Gr. "Thy way is not seemly before me." Chald. "It is manifest before me that thou wouldst go in a way contrary to me. Syr. "Behold,

33 And the ass saw me, and turned from me these three times: unless she had turned from me, surely now also I had slain thee, and saved her alive.

34 And Balaam said unto the angel of the LORD, I [y] have sinned; for I knew not that thou stoodest in the way against

y 1 Sam. 15. 24, 30. 26. 21.

I have come out that I might be an adversary to thee, since thou hast directed thy way against me." Sam. "Because evil is thy way before me." The import is, Thy purpose and intent in going this journey is contrary to my will as before made known to thee, v. 12. The apostle Jude calls it "the error of Balaam," and Peter speaks of it as "forsaking the right way and going astray." It is observable that the angel speaks in the language of supremacy, as having the most absolute right to command. "Thy way is perverse before ME," as if it were the Lord himself who utters the words, which we doubt not is the fact.

V. 33. *The ass saw me and turned from me, etc.* Heb. "Turned at my face or presence." So also in the ensuing clause.——¶ *Unless she had turned from me, surely now also I had slain thee, etc.* How penetrating and cutting the purport in itself of this language to Balaam we can easily conceive, though the sequel evinces that its impression was very slight and transient upon his mind. So in thousands of cases, if the eyes of thoughtless transgressors were not, as it were, hermetically sealed—if Satan had not so completely blinded them by his delusive arts—they would perceive and acknowledge the fearful perils to which they have been exposed, and the infinite mercy by which they have been spared. Who shall tell how often it might have been said concerning each of us, "Truly, as the Lord liveth, and as thy soul liveth, there is but a step between thee and death." Who shall recite to us those manifold gracious but unseen providences which have saved us from sin and punishment, because the Lord was not willing that we should perish, but would that we should come to repentance and live.

V. 34. *I have sinned.* A confession is at length extorted from Balaam, but it covers not the whole ground of his offence. He confesses that he had done wrong in abusing his beast, and perhaps would go so far as to acknowledge a fault in setting out upon the journey at all, but the covetous prompting and the malicious design against the chosen people he does not confess. While the Lord's hand was stretched out against him, and his wrath impending, he could say he had sinned, and profess a willingness to return home, but in all this there was merely the working of a servile and compulsory fear, that trembled at the thought of punishment, and of that only. He intimates that his treatment of the ass was owing solely to his ignorance that the angel stood in the way against him, but it was the underlying reason why the angel was there to withstand him at all that ought to have been the subject-matter of his confession. Indeed, we may recognize, perhaps, a slight acknowledgment on this score, as otherwise it is not perfectly obvious why he should confess to having sinned, inasmuch as he would not be apt to plead guilty to not having seen the angel standing in the way, were it not that he was aware that he *ought* to have seen him, and that he would have seen him but for the sin-blinded state of his mind. There seems

me: now therefore, if it displease thee, I[z] will get me back again.

35 And the angel of the LORD said unto Balaam, Go[a] with the men: but[b] only the word that I

z Job 34. 31, 32.

a Is. 47. 12. b ver. 20.

to have been an under-current of consciousness that the non-perception of his divine antagonist reflected directly upon the obtuseness of his moral vision.——¶ *Now, therefore, if it displease thee, I will get me back again.* Heb. "If (it be) evil in thine eyes." Gr. "If it please thee not." This has somewhat the air of a proper retraction, but it does not meet the demands of the case; rather it betrays a lurking hypocrisy in the spirit of the speaker. He is ready to return if his proceeding onward should *displease* God. But what room was there for an "if" in the case, when the divine will had been so clearly made known to him? The cherishing of the least doubt on the subject, or putting the case at all hypothetically, showed that his heart still went after its covetousness, and that he was extremely loth to abandon the expedition. It was a mere *feigned* willingness which he professed. He was inwardly desirous of going, but if necessity constrained him he would turn back, making, at the same time, a virtue of this necessity.

V. 35. *Go with the men.* Here again the Lord "chooses the delusions" of the infatuated prophet. He has no more complacency in his course than he had in the former instance, v. 20. But the same principle dictates his acquiescence now that did then. Seeing him bent upon pursuing his chosen way, he is represented as saying to him in words what he says to him in his providential permission, "Go; and take the consequences." Such is Jarchi's interpretation;—"Go with the men, for thy portion is with them, and thine end is to perish out of the world." Thus it is that the Most High sometimes grants the wicked desires of men's hearts, while the concession is a token of anger and not of mercy. He answers them "according to the idols set up in their own hearts," Ezek. 14: 3, 4. One may be allowed, in a way of evil, to prevail, as it were, against God, and against his own soul, little dreaming what a price he pays at length for his triumph. The case thus recorded fitly represents the spiritual condition of the man whom the Lord's gracious providence has checked by some wholesome restraint, by the rebuke of sickness, or affliction, or the voice of conscience, that he might turn from the way of death; but who after the first terror has passed away, and the heavy hand of his God is removed, lapses again into evil, gives way to his besetting sin, and rushes onward in the career of transgression. In respect to Balaam, we are ready perhaps to wonder that he was not stricken down as well as withstood on this occasion; but as Adams (on 2 Pet. 2:15) remarks, "He spares Balaam, because he had more to do with him: that tongue shall get him honor in Moab, which meant there to dishonor him. God sees it more for his glory to fetch good out of evil, than to suffer no evil at all. He could soon rid the world of bad members, but then he should lose the praise of working good by evil instruments."——¶ *But only the word that I shall speak unto thee, that thou shalt speak.* This may as properly be understood as a prediction, as a precept; implying that whatever the bias of his spirit might prompt him to utter, he would still find himself under a superior con-

shall speak unto thee, that thou
shalt speak. So Balaam went
with the princes of Balak.
36 And when Balak heard
that Balaam was come, he went
out to meet him unto a city of
Moab, which *is* in the border
of Arnon, which *is* in the utmost coast.
37 And Balak said unto Balaam, Did I not earnestly send
unto thee to call thee? where-

---

trol which it would be impossible to resist. His going to Balak is permitted, but by the circumstance of the ass's speaking as with man's mouth, he is taught that he is himself to be merely the *mouth* of God; not speaking his own words, but such as should be put into his mouth; even as the words of the animal had been put into her mouth. Indeed, the whole miraculous incident seems to have been ordered with the design of showing that Balaam was as truly an involuntary instrument in uttering his blessings upon Israel as was the ass in uttering articulate words against its own nature.

V. 36. *He went out to meet him, etc.* That is, he went out with a cavalcade to meet and welcome him in a style of princely magnificence. In like manner, though with less pomp, Moses went out to meet his father-in-law, Ex. 18:7, Joseph to meet Israel his father, Gen. 26:29, and the kings of Sodom and of Salem to meet Abraham, Gen. 14:17, 18. Heb. 7:1. Although we cannot now determine the point from which Balak started, yet it is to be inferred from the localities mentioned, that he travelled to a very considerable distance, even to Ar, on the border of Arnon, which was the boundary between Moab and the Amorites, ch. 21: 13, 26. The respect shown to the hireling prophet on this occasion evinces the spirit of those who are devoted to superstition without a sincere fear of God. They are cringing to their false prophets; they load them with flatteries and favors, and come but little short of worshipping them. But they will have it understood that these prophets must be obsequious to their wishes; they must favor their schemes of pride, ambition, avarice, lust, or oppression, or they are soon made to feel that their services are not required. We may see from this instance, also, how much stronger with some are the bonds of self-interest than those of neighborly or brotherly affection. These Moabites, instead of meeting their brother Israel with bread and water in the way, when they came out of Egypt, would fain meet them in hostile array and repel them from their borders; and yet the king himself does not hesitate to go forth to the extreme limit of his kingdom to meet this mercenary soothsayer, whom he had hired to curse the chosen people. We have no ground to wonder at the malediction pronounced against that nation, Deut. 23:3–6.

V. 37. *Did I not earnestly send unto thee?* Heb. "Sending, did I not send unto thee?" He is at a loss, like all men clothed with power and wealth, and accustomed to have their will regarded as law, and their inducements considered as irresistible, to conceive why his solicitation should not have taken effect at once.——¶ *Am I not able, indeed, to promote thee to honor?* Heb. *kabbedĕkâ, to make thee heavy*, a term employed elsewhere to signify that moral weight which arises from the bestowment upon one of riches and honor. In this case, however, it is clear that whatever were Balak's boast of his ability, it amounted to nothing,

fore camest thou not unto me? am I not able indeed to promote [c] thee to honour?

38 And Balaam said unto Balak, Lo, I am come unto thee: have I now any power at all to say any thing? the word [d] that God putteth in my mouth, that shall I speak.

39 And Balaam went with Balak, and they came unto Kirjath-huzoth.

40 And Balak offered oxen and sheep, and sent to Balaam,

c ver. 17. c. 24. 11. Ps. 75. 6. John 5. 44.

d ver. 18.

as he finally sent away Balaam in disgrace, because he was withheld by a divine power from cursing the people whom the Lord had blessed. "They both looked for promotion, either from the other; and he that said, 'Am I not able to promote thee?' insinuates a confession withal, Thou art able to promote me. Two would be raised, and both by the downfall of a third."—*Adams.*

V. 38. *Have I any power at all to say any thing?* Heb. "Having ability am I able." The word for "ability" or "power" is repeated in the original to make the intimation more emphatic. This is in some degree expressed by the phrase "at all" in our version. The purport of Balaam's reply is this: "I am come, indeed, in compliance with your request, and in reality should be glad to act in accordance with your wishes; but I must forewarn you that I am under a mysterious constraint, and can speak only what the Lord shall be pleased to put into my mouth. Therefore be not surprised if the whole affair should prove a failure." The words contain a virtual excuse or apology, uttered in anticipation, and designed to avert the king's displeasure in case the attempt should prove abortive. How clearly did the Most High in this vindicate his character as the Lord that "frustrateth the tokens of the liars, and maketh diviners mad; that turneth wise men backward, and maketh their knowledge foolish." Is. 44:25.

V. 39. *They came to Kirjath-Huzoth.* Heb. "The city of streets." It probably denotes the city to which the party returned, and in that case we may suppose it with probability to have been the city of the royal residence, and perhaps at no great distance from where the Israelites were now encamped.

V. 40. *And Balak offered oxen and sheep.* The offering of these beasts on this occasion had nothing to do with the subsequent oblations and invocations of Balak and Balaam as related in the following chapters. This was evidently merely a sacrifice of thanksgiving to the gods of Moab for the safe arrival of the welcome guest, who is treated with a feast upon the sacrifice. It was doubtless something similar to the feast mentioned ch. 25:2, of which it is said, "they called the people of Israel unto the sacrifices of their gods; and the people did eat and bowed down to their gods." Of such a feast was Balaam, a professed worshipper of the true God, invited to partake, and from aught that appears, accepted the invitation. According to the principles laid down by Paul, 1 Cor. 10:18–21, this was but another step in the career of evil in which he had embarked;—"Behold Israel after the flesh: are not they which eat of the sacrifices, partakers of the altar? What say I then? that the idol is any thing, or that which is offered in sacrifice to idols is any thing? But I say, that the things which the Gentiles sacrifice, they sacrifice, to

and to the princes that *were*
with him.

41 And it came to pass on
the morrow, that Balak took
Balaam, and brought him up
into the high [e] places of Baal,
that thence he might see the
utmost *part* of the people.

CHAPTER XXIII.

AND Balaam said unto Balak,
[a] Build me here seven al-

e Deut. 12. 2.

a ver. 29.

devils, and not to God: and I would not that ye should have fellowship with devils. Ye cannot drink the cup of the Lord, and the cup of devils: ye cannot be partakers of the Lord's table, and of the table of devils."——¶ *And sent to Balaam and to the princes.* That is, sent portions of the meat of sacrifice to Balaam and his friends where they were lodged. It does not mean that he sent for them to attend at the feast itself. Vulg. "And when Balak had killed oxen and sheep, he sent presents to Balaam, and to the princes that were with him."

V. 41. *Brought him up to the high places of Baal.* Heb. *bâmoth Baal,* i. e., the consecrated high places of Baal. Gr. "The pillars (or monuments) of Baal." Chald. "The high places of his Fear," i. e., of the god of his fear. Targ. Jon. "The fear of Peor," i. e., the object of the idolatrous fear. Baal, having the import of *Lord, Master,* or *Patron,* was the name given by many nations in that part of Asia to the idols worshipped on high places, hills, or mountains. Wherever employed it signified the sun, and with the Moabites was but another name for *Chemosh,* their presiding deity. Balak made choice of an elevated position, both because such places were chiefly used for the purpose of sacrificing to the gods, and from such a place Balaam could have a more distinct view of the camp of the Israelites, which was thought to be a matter of peculiar importance, as giving additional efficacy to the curse uttered.

CHAPTER XXIII.

Balak's First Sacrifice.

V. 1. *Build me here seven altars.* A peculiar sanctity did indeed attach to the number seven among the Jews, but we nowhere read of seven altars in the appointed worship of that people. As they acknowledged but one God, so they had but one altar. Hence the erection of seven, by Balaam's order, savored seemingly of the tricks of magic and incantation. The more charitable conjectures of some expositors would refer it, however, to a desire to propitiate the God of the Jews, who had created the world within seven days, and had otherwise signalized this number. This we are inclined to regard as the correct solution of the incident, as otherwise we cannot so well account for the language in v. 3, "peradventure the Lord (Jehovah) will come to me," which implies, we think, that he designed to address his worship to the true God. Yet his conduct was marred as usual by gross inconsistency. His impiety is here evinced by the fact that instead of dissuading Balak from his wicked purpose by citing the authority of God, who had forbidden him to curse Israel, he unites with him in endeavoring to effect this iniquitous end, and that, too, under color of religious service, building altars and offering sacrifices, as if the unchangeable Jehovah could be wrought upon by such ceremonies. Alas, how soon had he forgotten the oracle of God, the sword

tars, and prepare me here seven
oxen and seven rams.
2 And Balak did as Balaam
had spoken; and Balak and
Balaam offered [b] on *every* altar
a bullock and a ram.
3 And Balaam said unto Balak, [c] Stand by thy burnt-offering, and I will go: peradventure
the LORD will come to meet me,
and whatsoever he showeth me,
I will tell thee. And he went
to an high place.
4 And [d] God met Balaam:

b ver. 14, 30. *c* ver. 15. *d* ver. 16.

---

of the Angel, and the dangers he had so narrowly escaped in the way, and how eagerly was he now "running after the error" of his evil heart, making good the saying of the prophet, "Let favor be shown to the wicked, yet will he not learn righteousness."

V. 2. *And Balak did as Balaam had spoken.* It may doubtless be presumed that Balaam had used his best efforts to convince Balak of the necessity of directing his worship to the God of Israel, if they would succeed in their scheme of malediction; and yet how astounding that they should not have seen the absurdity of endeavoring to engage the Most High to go counter to his own counsels and attributes!

V. 3. *Stand by thy burnt-offering.* Heb. "Cause thyself to stand," i. e., present thyself here in a devout attitude before the Lord, and retain thy position without attempting to follow me in my retirement. Offerers were wont to stand by their sacrifices while burning, and thus present themselves to the Lord, who had first respect to the offerer and then to his gift, Gen. 4: 4, 5. Accordingly Balak and his princes were to stand there, if so be God would have respect to their persons.——¶ *Peradventure the Lord will come to meet me.* Gr. "If perhaps the Lord will appear."——¶ *I will go.* That is, will go by myself into some private place, where I can perform those additional secret rites which are necessary to complete success. This may be inferred from ch. 24:1, "And when Balaam saw that it pleased the Lord to bless Israel, he went not, as at other times, *to seek for enchantments*, etc.——¶ *And he went to an high place.* Heb. *va-yëlek shephi*, of which the true sense is not easily ascertained. "Solitary," or "to a solitary place;" "a valley;" "a cliff of a rock;" "a bare hill," are the various renderings ascribed to it by critics and lexicographers. Chald. "He went alone." Gr. "He went straight forward." Vulg. "When he was gone with speed." A satisfactory choice from among these conflicting senses is scarcely possible, but as the current of authority inclines to the signification of "hill" or "summit," we, on the whole, abide in that as the most probable. Hengstenberg, with much confidence, adopts "bare hill" as the rendering, as the verb *shâphâh*, from which *shephi* is derived, has for its primary signification *to plane or smooth off*. The altars were probably erected on a summit or summits shaded with trees, which intercepted the prospect; the hill to which Balaam went may be supposed to have been a bare or naked eminence, giving him an unobstructed view of the neighboring regions. Prof. Lee translates it, "An elevated and conspicuous place, having an extensive view."

V. 4. *And God met Balaam.* Gr. "God appeared to Balaam." Chald. "The Word from before the Lord met (or came unto) Balaam." Sam. "The Angel of God found Balaam." The

and he said unto him, I have
prepared seven altars, and I
have offered upon *every* altar a
bullock and a ram.
5 And the LORD put [e] a word
in Balaam's mouth, and said,

e c. 22. 35. Deut. 18. 18. Jer. 1. 9.

Return unto Balak, and thus
thou shalt speak.
6 And he returned unto him;
and, lo, he stood by his burnt-sacrifice, he, and all the princes
of Moab.
7 And he took up his para-

"meeting" was probably by a visible manifestation in the form of an angel, as on a former occasion. Although Balaam now sought the Lord, both from wrong motives and in wrong methods, so far as enchantments were employed, yet he was pleased to meet him and put a word in his mouth, in which he acted with a view to the good of his people, rather than to the personal gratification of the prophet. "But will God meet with a sorcerer? Will he make a prophet of a magician? O man, who shall prescribe God what instruments he shall use! He knows how to employ, not only saints and angels, but wicked men, beasts, devils, to his own glory. He that puts words into the mouth of the ass, puts words into the mouth of Balaam: the words do but pass from him; they are not polluted, because they are not his."—*Bp. Hall.*——¶ *I have prepared, etc.* Heb. "I have set in order." Balaam here recites his doings before the Lord, as if he did not know how many altars he had made, and how many sacrifices he had offered, or as if he would be pleased with such a magnificent show of devotion. Well might the reproof have now been addressed to Balaam which was afterwards given to Saul: "Hath the Lord as much delight in sacrifices and offerings, as in obeying the voice of the Lord: behold, to obey is better than sacrifice, and to hearken than the fat of lambs." So again, Prov. 21 : 3, "To do justice and judgment is more acceptable to the Lord than sacrifice."

V. 5. *And the Lord put a word in Balaam's mouth.* Paying no attention to Balaam's pompous parade of his hypocritical worship, which was in fact an abomination to him, Prov. 15 : 8, he sends him back with a burden of blessing instead of cursing, though contrary to his own and to Balak's desire. "The preparations of the heart in man, and the answer of the tongue, is from the Lord." "This speaks comfort to God's witnesses, whom at any time he calls out to speak for him; if God put a word into the mouth of Balaam, who would have defied God and Israel, surely he will not be wanting to those who desire to glorify God and edify his people by their testimony; but 'it shall be given them in that same hour what they should speak.'"—*Henry.*

Balaam's first Prophecy.

V. 7. *And he took up his parable.* Heb. *mâshâl, comparison, similitude.* The term is applied to any kind of allegorical or figurative speech of a more solemn and weighty import than usual. Under this head come such sayings as the proverbs and apophthegms of wise men, and such prophetical utterances as those here recorded, of which the style is somewhat elevated and majestic. We do not find it, however, a designation of prophecy in general, but only of that species which partakes of the sententious and oracular. Targ. Jon. "He took up the parable of his prophecy." By "taking up" is denoted uttering or pronouncing in a

ble[f], and said, Balak the king of Moab hath brought me from Aram, out of the mountains of the east, *saying*, Come, curse[g] me Jacob, and come, defy[h] Israel.

8 How[i] shall I curse, whom God hath not cursed? or how shall I defy, *whom* the LORD hath not defied?

9 For from the top of the rocks I see him, and from the hills I behold him: lo, the peo-

f ver. 18. c. 24. 3, 15, 23. Job 27. 1. 29. 1. Ps. 78. 2. Ezek. 17. 2. Mic. 2. 4. Hab. 2. 6. Mat. 13. 33, 35. *g* Prov. 26. 2. *h* 1 Sam. 17. 10.

i Is. 47. 12, 13.

somewhat elevated tone of voice, such as would be calculated to command particular attention.——¶ *Hath brought me from Aram.* That is, *Aram-Naharaim, Aram of the two rivers* (Tigris and Euphrates), to which answers the ancient *Mesopotamia*, or *region between the rivers.* Gr. "Balak the king of Moab, hath sent for me from Mesopotamia." Targ. Jon. "Balak hath sent for me from Aram, which is by Euphrates." Comp. Deut. 23:4, "They hired against thee Balaam the son of Beor, of Pethor of Mesopotamia, to curse thee." This region is for the most part flat, but the northern part of it is mountainous, and from that quarter came Balaam, as he here declares that he was called out of "the *mountains* of the east."——¶ *Defy Israel.* Heb. *zoamâh*, implying to execrate with violent threats and indignant rage—a word of peculiar intensity of meaning. It occurs Dan. 11:30, "Therefore shall he be grieved, and return, and *have indignation* against the holy covenant." Hengstenberg remarks, "The sense of *being angry* will appear quite appropriate to this passage, if it be considered that the curse can only be the result of the most violent inward excitement against the object of it, and that any one would strive, before pronouncing it, to arouse himself to rage in every way, upon the intensity of which the efficacy of the curse depended."

V. 8. *How shall I curse whom God hath not cursed, etc.* I am required, says Balaam, to *curse* Israel, but how *can* I, when God, the true author and sole lord of blessing and cursing, does not curse, but blesses him? This was honestly acknowledging that his tongue was tied, so that he could utter nothing except as he was prompted by a divine impulse. The fundamental import of the declaration is, that as God hath not cursed, so Balaam cannot. Blessed are they whom the Lord himself will not curse, and upon whom he pronounces a blessing, even in the presence of them that *would* curse. This is the privilege of all the Israel of God, and of every single believer in Christ. To every secret or open enemy the Lord says, "Thou shalt not curse whom I have blessed." This was a clear demonstration of the vanity of the compliment paid him by Balak, "I wot that he whom thou blessest is blessed, and he whom thou cursest is cursed."

V. 9. *From the top of the rocks I see him, etc.* His elevated position on the rocks gave him a commanding view of the encampment of Israel, but the words have a reach of meaning beyond what was embraced in the mere external vision. Though as seen from the great distance at which he stood they must have been diminished to a dwarf-like size, yet they portended something great and formidable. In the spirit of prophecy he sees far more in the people of God than struck the outward eye. In fact, we are no doubt to consider that Balaam's ecstatic vision through-

ple shall dwell alone[k], and shall[l] not be reckoned among the nations.

k Deut. 33. 28. *l* Ex. 33. 16. Ezra 9. 2. Eph. 2. 14.

out was not merely corporeal, but that with the seeing of the bodily eye there was combined the penetration of the spiritual eye which pierces into the depths and essences of invisible things. This is evident from the subsequent prophecy, ch. 24:5, when, with open eyes he depicts the loveliness of the tents of Israel in a manner which shows that the outward beholding is introduced only as a basis for the inward. ——¶ *The people shall dwell alone, etc.* Heb. *lebâdâd yishkon, shall dwell,* or *tabernacle, alone,* the root from which comes *Shekinah.* The original term for "alone" is closely related in signification to the Heb. *bâteh,* implying *safety, security,* and both ideas are to be included in the present rendering. The word "for" (*ki*) in the commencement of this verse is no doubt to be regarded as a connective between what precedes and what follows:—"How shall I curse or defy the people whom God hath not cursed or defied, *for,* beholding as I do with interior vision the vast congregation, I perceive that their destiny is to dwell as an isolated race, separate from all other nations, and enjoying the peculiar auspices of heaven both temporal and spiritual." Here was a declaration of their present blessedness, and a remarkable prophecy of their future condition, to the fulfilment of which all history bears witness. It has uniformly been their great peculiarity, and now, after the lapse of three thousand years "the people still dwell alone, and are not reckoned among the nations." Other nations have passed away, or been melted down into one common mass, while the race of Israel has remained distinguished by indubitable marks of national character, and by special peculiarities of feature, manners, and laws. Their knowledge and worship of the true God has ever formed a broad line of demarcation between them and the various peoples that have been sunk in ignorance and idolatry. They are now indeed, for their sins, and especially for their rejection of Christ, scattered over the earth, yet they dwell alone; they do not amalgamate with other nations; they are not reckoned among them. Their own strongly marked peculiarities, and the prejudices and antipathies of Christians, Mohammedans, and Pagans, still keep them unmingled with those among whom they sojourn, and in many cases deprive them of participation in the common privileges of citizenship. Even in their captivities their peculiarities as a people have remained unshaken. While other nations, when vanquished and dispersed, have become incorporated with their victors, and been assimilated to the people among whom they have dwelt; the Jews in every country are a distinct people, and are living witnesses to the truth of this prophecy. But "how," as Bp. Newton inquires, "could Balaam, upon a distant view only of a people, whom he had never seen or known before, have discovered the genius and manners, not only of the people then living, but of their posterity to the latest generations?" Surely nothing short of a divine inspiration could have opened their character and destiny to his view. But his words are not to be understood of the literal Israel only. They are equally true of that spiritual body which Israel after the flesh represented. The members of the Lord's true Christian church also dwell alone. Owing to the influence of the principles by which they are governed, and to the hatred and opposition of the world of the un-

10 Who [m] can count the dust of Jacob, and the number of the fourth *part* of Israel? Let me

m Gen. 13. 16.

godly, they are inevitably separated from them. Denying ungodliness and worldly lusts, renouncing all sinful pleasures, gains, and glories, they are marked by a holy singularity, and are reckoned as a distinct and separate people. All this is to be considered as entering into the purport of this inspired prediction, and we are to recognize the spiritual as well as the literal fulfilment throughout.——¶ *Shall not be reckoned among the nations.* Or, Heb. "Shall not reckon itself," which is a well-known and very frequent usage of the Hithpael conjugation (*yithhashshâb*). However it might be in the estimate of others, yet this holy singularity should be fully asserted to the consciousness of the chosen people, both the external and the internal. This conscious isolation expresses itself appropriately in the language of the apostle, "We know that we are of God, and the whole world lieth in wickedness," 1 John 5:19.

V. 10. *Who can count the dust of Israel, etc.* Heb. "Who counteth?" Chald. "Who is able to count?" The "dust of Jacob" is evidently the seed of Jacob multiplied according to the promise, Gen. 28:14, to a number which could only be compared to the dust of the earth, whence Geddes renders it, "Who shall count the dust-like seed of Jacob?" Of the ancient versions the Gr. has, "Who hath exactly calculated the seed of Jacob?" Chald. "Who can count the little ones of the house of Jacob, of whom it was said that they shall be multiplied as the dust of the earth?" Yet as there seems to be no good reason for supposing that Balaam was acquainted with this promise, we cannot well resist the conclusion that the language was put into his mouth by a divine suggestion wholly independent of his own intelligence and his own will. The words embody a prophetic intimation of the vast physical increase of the Israelitish people, but we apprehend that the spiritual seed is the principal theme of the prediction, those numbers of the true people of God which have been gathered together into his Chuch through all ages, and of which the sum is continually swelling. We think it has respect to that "great multitude, which no man can number, of all nations, and kindreds, and people, and tongues, which stand before the throne and before the Lamb, clothed with white robes and palms in their hands."——¶ *And the number of the fourth (part) of Israel.* Or, "Of a quarter," as also in the Chald. "Of one of the four camps of Israel," in allusion to the fourfold division of the tribes in the order of encampment, as described ch. 2, having the Tabernacle in the midst. It was equivalent to saying, How vast is already the number of this favored people, when even in their present condition one department of their camp looks like a whole nation! But how much more immense shall be the increase of their spiritual seed in after times!——¶ *Let me die the death of the righteous, and let my last end be like his!* Heb. "Let my soul die;" a Hebrew phrase in which the soul is put for the person, whether I, thou, or he, as the case may be. We find it said of Rachel, Gen. 35:18, that "it came to pass *as her soul was in departing*," an expression equivalent to *death.* So also Samson says, Judg. 16:30, "Let my soul die with the Philistines." So likewise, when the Lord is said to swear by his soul, Jer. 51:14, the meaning is, that he swears by himself. The original term for "righteous" is ישרים *yeshâ-*

die the death [n] of the righteous, and let my last end be like his!

n Ps. 37. 37. Prov. 14. 32. 2 Cor. 5. 1.

11 And Balak said unto Balaam, What hast thou done unto

rim, from a root implying *rectitude, probity, integrity*. Its first three letters correspond with the first three in *Israel* (ישראל), to which Hengstenberg and others suppose it alludes. It is doubtless equivalent also to "Jeshurun," Deut. 32 : 15, signifying *upright* or *righteous*. He would intimate, by applying the word *upright* to Israel, that he regarded their lot as superior in distinction and privilege to that of all other people, and therefore would wish to have his own identical with it. Chald. "Let my soul die the death of the just men thereof," i. e., of the people of Israel. As if he had said, They are a people not only happy in this life above other nations, and therefore beyond the reach of my curses, but they have this peculiar privilege, that they are happy after death. Their happiness begins where the happiness of others ends; and I therefore heartily wish that my soul may have its portion with theirs when I die. But, alas, the sequel shows how vain was the wish. Refusing to live the life of the righteous, and intent upon the wages of iniquity, he perished at last by the sword of Israel, being found among their enemies, ch. 31 : 8. Josh. 13 : 22. The spirit of prophecy, however, undoubtedly refers to the favored lot of the *true* as well as of the *typical* Israelites, for an ungodly Jew can no more be saved than an ungodly heathen. Looking onward to the future lot of the spiritual Israel, he saw them distinguished from the rest of the world, and however they might be involved in the calamities of the wicked *here*, yet he beheld them translated at death to a state of endless blessedness and peace; and therefore he desired that the death which they died he might die also. Gr. "Let my soul die with the souls of just men."——¶ *And let my last end be like his.* Heb. *aharithi, my hereafter*, lit. *my afterhood.* Gr. "Let my seed be like their seed," i. e. my posterity. This is usually understood as the expression of a wish on the part of Balaam that his *last end*, or *closing scene*, might be like that of the righteous. This idea we may properly include in the import of the term, but from dominant usage we incline to give it a more extended sense, as equivalent to *his general or entire future, the whole sequel of his lot, both in this world and the next.* This idea of *simple futurity* will be found to be the prevailing sense of the term in the sacred writers, and this brings it sufficiently into parallelism with the preceding clause. Viewed in this light, the words convey the virtual desire of every man, even the most abandoned, who is capable of appreciating the contrasted lot of the righteous and the wicked. Who is there that lives under the light of the Gospel but feels an inward persuasion that God will put a radical difference between these two classes? However much the worldly or vicious man may hate the *persons* of the righteous, he envies their *state*, and inwardly cherishes the thought, "If I were now to die, I should be glad to be found in their lot." But vain is the hope of any man to *die the death* of the righteous if he will not *live his life;* or that he shall attain to his *end* without walking in his *way;*

"'O let me die his death!' the prophet cries,
'Then live his life,' the sacred word replies."

V. 11. *I took thee to curse mine enemies.* Heb. *lâkahtikâ*, I received thee.

me? I [o] took thee to curse mine
enemies, and, behold, thou hast
blessed *them* altogether.
12 And he answered and
said, [p] Must I not take heed to
speak that which the LORD hath
put in my mouth?
13 And Balak said unto him,
Come, I pray thee, with me unto [q] another place, from whence

o c. 22. 11. p c. 22. 38. q 1 K. 20. 23.

Gr. and Vulg. "I have called thee." Chald. "I have led thee." This allusion, we think, is to his first sending for Balaam and his subsequent reception of him in his territories. The words express the vexation of the king at the abortive attempts of Balaam to inflict his curses upon Israel. It is as if he had said, "What an impotent prophet, what a sad hireling, art thou! I took thee for one who would do the work for which my wages paid thee; and now how grievously hast thou failed me! Instead of cursing, thou hast altogether blessed them." Heb. "Blessing thou hast blessed them." Notwithstanding all his pompous parade of altars and sacrifices, as if he would devoutly wait for such an answer as God should send him, yet when the result failed to answer his expectations, he was wrought into a passion against Balaam, as if he were the sole cause of the disappointment. "Sometimes God makes the enemies of his church a vexation one to another, while He that sits in the heavens laughs at them, and the efforts of their impotent malice."—*Henry*.

V. 12. *Must I not take heed to speak that, etc.* Or, Heb. "Shall I not observe to speak?" Although the proud king, in the preceding verse, reproaches Balaam as though he had fairly purchased the authority to control his utterances as he pleased, yet the prophet here represses his arrogance by pleading the divine command, and assuring him that he could announce only what the Lord had put into his mouth. It is clear, however, from the whole narrative, that the inclination of his heart was towards Balak and his rewards, and that if he had been left to himself, he would have yielded without reserve to the wishes of his royal employer. But being inwardly withheld from cursing, he speaks as if he would make a virtue of his obedience to the necessity laid upon him, which probably went to deepen the self-deception that he was all along practising upon himself.

V. 13. *Come, I pray thee, with me unto another place, etc.* Balaam having now declared to Balak the reason of his failure, the infatuated king strangely imagines that the locality was in fault, and that the Most High would be more propitious to him in another situation, and would look more graciously upon fresh sacrifices. He therefore proposes to him to shift his position, with a view to gain a better prospect of the objects of his anathemas, as if a change of place with man could produce a change of purpose in God! The proposal implies a confidence in some magical power exercised by the eye, as if this organ contributed somewhat to the efficacy of the imprecation. That the clear, fixed gaze of the enchanter had a decided effect upon his art, is the unequivocal testimony of ancient writers who have described the superstitions of their age. Balak accordingly determines, if possible, to bring him to such a stand-point on the mountains that he shall not be dismayed by a view of the whole body of the people *en masse*, but shall see only such a portion of them as shall be most favorable to the effect of his malediction.

thou mayest see them: thou
shalt see but the uttermost part
of them, and shalt not see them
all: and curse me them from
thence.
14 And he brought him into
the field of Zophim, to the top
of Pisgah, and built [r] seven altars, and offered [s] a bullock and
a ram on *every* altar.
15 And he said unto Balak,
Stand here by thy burnt-offering, while I meet *the LORD*
yonder.

16 And the LORD met Ba-
laam, and put [t] a word in his
mouth, and said, Go again unto
Balak, and say thus.
17 And when he came to
him, behold, he stood by his
burnt-offering, and the princes
of Moab with him. And Balak
said unto him, What [u] hath the
LORD spoken?
18 And he took up his parable, and said, Rise [v] up, Balak,
and hear; hearken unto me,
thou son of Zippor:

r ver. 12. s Is. 1. 11.

t ver. 5. u 1 Sam. 3. 17. Jer. 37. 17. v Judg. 3. 20.

Balaam's Second Parable.

V. 14. *Brought him into the field of Zophim.* That is, to the field of the *spies* or *watchers*. Gr. "He took him to a watch-tower of the field." It was probably some lofty position commanding a wide view of the adjacent country, and such as was usually chosen for a place of espial by those appointed to watch the approach of enemies.——¶ *To the top of Pisgah.* Gr. "To the top of the quarried (rock)." Chald. "To the top of the hill;" both versions understanding the original as a common instead of a proper name. As the Hebrew term has the article, there is perhaps some ground for this opinion, and for the rendering "top (head) of the hill," but it is now impossible to determine the minutiæ of the topography of this region. Hengstenberg, in the Geographical Appendix to his treatise on the History of Balaam, has treated the subject more fully than any other one.

V. 15. *While I meet (the Lord) yonder.* The words supplied are evidently to be understood, as may be inferred from the similar passage, v. 3. Gr. "I will go to inquire of God." The phrase "going to meet" was probably technical with prophets and diviners. The next verse shows that "the Lord" is to be understood.

V. 18. *Rise up, Balak, and hear.* This can hardly be understood of the bodily position, for it seems, v. 17, that he was then standing by his burnt-offering. It is to be conceived rather as having reference to a mental erection or attentiveness. Hengstenberg well remarks: "He calls upon the king to rise mentally, as the importance of the prophecy he was about to utter demanded. This 'Rise up' is applicable not to Balak only, but to all who approach the holy Scripture. Whoever would understand God's Word, must free himself from his natural sloth and mental dissipation—must gird himself up and collect his mental powers." Such an internal state would, however, ordinarily express itself by suitable outward gestures; the words are therefore equivalent to an intimation that he should hearken with every token of becoming reverence to a message brought from God, even as Ehud, Judg. 3:20, told Eglon that he had brought him such a message; it is said that "he arose out of his seat."——¶ *Hearken unto me, thou son of Zippor.* The words

19 God [w] is not a man, that he should lie; neither the son of man, that he should repent: hath he said, and shall he not do *it?* or hath [x] he spoken, and shall he not make it good?

w 1 Sam. 15. 29. Ps. 89. 35. Rom. 11. 29. Tit. 1. 2. Heb. 6. 18. James 1. 17.

x 1 Chr. 17. 17. Mic. 7. 20.

---

of Balaam are all along marked by the equivalent parallelisms, or *hemistichs*, so peculiar to Hebrew poetry. There is usually some shade of difference in the meaning of the two clauses, while the substantial purport is the same. The authoritative tone which Balaam here assumes, in commanding Balak's attention, is to be referred to the same general afflatus or impulse under which he speaks throughout. The words are a fit preface to the solemn enunciation that follows, which, in point of style, rises to the highest pitch of sublimity and grandeur.

V. 19. *God is not a man that he should lie, etc.* The rendering of the Chald. is here peculiar: "The word of God is not like the speeches of the sons of man, (for) the sons of man do say and lie." The language implies a virtual reproach, as much as to say, "Wouldst thou make God a liar?" No more fearful mistake is made than when we judge the Lord from ourselves. Men change their minds, and therefore break their word; they lie, because they repent. But God does neither. He never changes his mind, and therefore never recalls his promises. His very name, "Jehovah," implies the unchangeable as well as the eternal. "He is of one mind; and who can turn him?" This immutability makes it "impossible for him to lie," and consequently he can never swerve from his purpose of preservation and benediction towards his people.——¶ *Neither the son of man, that he should repent.* A parallel testimony we find borne by Samuel before Saul, 1 Sam. 15:29, "The strength of Israel will not lie nor repent; for he is not a man that he should repent." The Scripture, indeed, occasionally predicates repentance of the Most High, but the scope of the context will make it plain in such cases, that it is the language of *apparent* rather than of *real* truth, and that nothing more is meant by it than that a change takes place in the mode of his dealings with his creatures in view of a corresponding change in their deportment towards him. The principle is clearly developed in the following passage from Jer. 18:7–10, "At what instant I shall speak concerning a nation, and concerning a kingdom, to pluck up, and to pull down, and to destroy it: if that nation against whom I have pronounced, turn from their evil, I will repent of the evil that I thought to do unto them. And at what instant I shall speak concerning a nation, and concerning a kingdom, to build and to plant it: if it do evil in my sight, that it obey not my voice, then I will repent of the good, wherewith I said I would benefit them." But all this is to be understood in perfect consistency with the essential truth, that in him "there is no variableness, nor shadow of turning." All such language is a mere adaptation to our feeble modes of conceiving divine things.——¶ *Hath he spoken, and shall he not make it good?* Heb. "Shall he not cause it to stand?" that is, confirm it. Chald. "And all his words shall be confirmed." Gr. "Shall he speak, and shall he not continue?" that is, constantly perform what he hath spoken. A comparison of the following passages will show the relation

20 Behold, I have received *commandment* to bless, and he [y]hath blessed; and I cannot [z]reverse it.

21 He [a]hath not beheld iniquity in Jacob, neither hath he

y c. 22. 12. z John 10. 28, 29. Rom. 8.38, 39.

a Ps. 103. 12. Is. 1. 18. 38. 17. Mic. 7. 19. Rom. 4. 7, 8. 8. 1.

between *confirming* and *continuing.* Deut. 27 : 26, "Cursed be he that *confirmeth not* all the words of this law to do them." Gal. 3 : 10, "For it is written, Cursed is every one that *continueth not* in all things which are written in the book of the law to do them." The words convey a universal truth, although it is not improbable that they were spoken with a more specific reference to what the Lord had declared through Balaam in his first promise, and the substance of which is recited in the ensuing verse. The causes which operate to make men fail in accomplishing their intentions or promises can have no place with Jehovah. He is indeed said in Scripture to repent when he withholds his punishments on the repentance of men, or when he revokes the mercies which they have abused. But his purposes are irrevocable by himself, and unalterable by others. Whatever of mercy or of judgment he hath declared to any man or people, neither men nor devils can hinder, for being unchangeable on earth himself, he cannot but be immutably true to his word.

V. 20. *I have received* (*commandment*) *to bless.* The word supplied is evidently required by the sense, and the Hebrew usage furnishes frequent instances of similar omissions, which are easily supplied from the scope of the passage. Thus, 1 Chron. 18 : 6, "Then David put in Syria-Damascus," which is expressed in full in the parallel passage, 2 Sam. 8 : 6, "Then David put *garrisons* in Syria of Damascus."——¶ *And I cannot reverse it.* Or, Heb. "I shall not turn it away, or turn it back." Chald. "And I shall not turn my blessing from them." Our version, however, conveys the correct sense. Balaam *would not* reverse the divine decree because he *could not;* and what he says of himself holds true of all others and in all ages. The divine purposes insure to the members of the true church the performance of the divine promises. Not an iota of all that the Lord hath said shall fail. No power in heaven, earth, or hell, can avail to turn aside the Most High from his fixed purpose of bestowing the blessings of eternal life upon his genuine people. Is. 14 : 27, "For the Lord of hosts hath purposed, and who shall disannul it? and his hand is stretched out, and who shall turn it back?" How cheering the thought amidst the mutabilities of life —"Jesus Christ, the same yesterday, to-day, and forever!" How great the consolation to the Lord's followers, that none can reverse what he has said; none turn the blessing into a curse!

V. 21. *He hath not beheld iniquity in Jacob, neither hath he seen perverseness in Israel.* Heb. *âven, iniquity,* a term of large import, denoting all the various kinds of sin or iniquity which cause pain, sorrow, and misery, and applied in particular to idolatry, as it is rendered 1 Sam. 15 : 23, while in Is. 66 : 3, it is rendered *an idol.* So also Chald. "I see that there are none who worship idols in the house of Jacob, nor any servants of trouble and vanity in Israel." Vulg. "There is no idol in Jacob, neither is there any image-God to be seen in Israel." When applied thus to idolatry it involves the accessory idea of *nothingness* and *vanity* as predicable

seen perverseness in Israel: the LORD [b] his God *is* with him, and the shout [c] of a king *is* among them.

b Ex. 29. 45, 46. 33. 16. Ps. 46. 11.

c Ps. 118. 15.

thereof; and when Paul says, 1 Cor. 8:4, "an idol is *nothing* in the world," the allusion is undoubtedly to the term *âven, vanity,* occurring in this and other connections. The Gr. has, "There shall be no calamity in Jacob, nor shall misery be seen in Israel." Some degree of ambiguity will still adhere to the words, preventing us from defining the exact shade of meaning, but from dominant usage in respect to both the original terms for "iniquity" and "perverseness" (*âven* and *âmal*) it is evident that the idea of *idolatrous worship* does enter into their import, although the authority for the present rendering cannot be fairly questioned. The purport, then, of the passage, we take to be, that God had not seen in Israel that degree of *iniquity* and *perverseness* which should be a sufficient ground for inflicting upon them a curse, which was Balaam's desire and Balak's design. But as we know the Lord *did* see, in the literal Israel, the grossest outbreaks of wickedness and rebellion—as he says expressly Ex. 32:9, "I have seen this people, and, behold, it is a stiff-necked people;" and again, Am. 3:2, "You only have I known of all the families of the earth; therefore I will punish you for all your iniquities"—we are naturally prompted to look beyond the representing to the represented body, and recognize the truth of the declaration in its reference to the spiritual instead of the natural Israel. As predicated of his true church in subsequent times, indeed in all times, the Lord may be said not to see iniquity or perverseness in it, because he does not see it to punish it, or to permit it to prevent their salvation. It means that he does not so see their sins as to be provoked thereby utterly to forsake, curse, and destroy them. In this sense God is said *not to see* sins, as elsewhere he is said to *forget* them, Is. 43:25. Jer. 31:24; and to *cover* them, Ps. 32:1, which keeps them out of sight, and so out of mind; to *blot them out,* Ps. 51:1, 9; and to *cast them behind his back,* Is. 38:17, or *into the depth of the sea,* Mic. 7:19. And so parents are sometimes said *not to know* or *not to see* those sins in their children which they do not so take notice of as to chastise them. Other interpretations more or less plausible have been proposed by commentators, but we forbear to state them, as the above answers sufficiently the demands of the text, and strikes us as far the most probable.——¶ *The Lord his God is with him.* Chald. "The Word of the Lord their God is for their help." These words point directly to the source of their peculiar blessedness. It was from the divine presence dwelling in the midst of them, sustaining and protecting them. This prerogative was a sign of the gracious state of those to whom it pertained, as otherwise the privilege of communion with Him could not have been enjoyed, according to the intimation 1 John 1:6, 7. So also Ex. 33:3, "For I will not go up in the midst of thee; for thou art a stiff-necked people, lest I consume thee in the way." The Lord was indeed symbolically and typically *with* the Israelites in the wilderness and in Canaan, but the fulness of the declaration is to be realized only in that Israel which is after the spirit and not after the flesh.——¶ *And the shout of a king (is) among them.* Heb. "In him," i. e. in Jacob or Israel, spoken of collectively. The original term for "shout" (*teruath*) is used to denote the

22 God [d] brought them out of Egypt: he hath [e] as it were the strength of an unicorn.

d c. 24. 8. e Deut. 33. 17. Ps. 92. 10.

alarm-sound made by the silver trumpets described ch. 10:5, 6, on which see Note. It is employed also to denote a shouting of joy and exultation, as when a king or conqueror returns in triumph from war, and his coming is hailed with jubilant acclamations on the part of the people. "When people pass along the road, if they hear a great noise of joy or triumph, they say, 'This is like the shout of a king.' 'What a noise there was in your village last evening! Why, it was like the shout of a king.'"—*Roberts.* It implies, in its ulterior reference, that the Lord's true people should be victorious in their divine Head over all enemies, and that at the last day, "at the voice of the archangel and the trump of God," they should be triumphantly put in possession of their glorious and eternal inheritance.

V. 22. *God brought them out of Egypt.* Heb. "Is bringing them," implying a continuous act. We learn from ch. 22:5, that Balak sent word to Balaam, "Behold, there is a people come out from Egypt." This would seem to imply that in his view they had come forth from Egypt of their own motion. But Balaam now informs him that such is not the fact; that they were brought out by the hand of God himself, and that he was still bringing them; that he had not relinquished his guiding and guardian care towards them; and consequently that, to endeavor to oppose them, to contend with them, or to visit them with imprecations, would be no less than a foolish fighting with God—a vain conflict of weakness against Omnipotence. Viewed in this light the use of the Participle in the present connection is peculiarly significant. "The fruitlessness of his undertakings against Israel is here proved to Balak, not from the fact that God had brought them out of Egypt, but that he is bringing them out. The idea is, whoever has God for a leader or companion on his way, the world with all its power can do nothing against him."—*Hengstenberg.*——¶ *He hath as it were the strength of an unicorn.* Gr. "The glory of an unicorn." The "he" in this passage we take to refer to Israel, and not to God, although Ains worth recognizes an allusion to both, the Most High as the head of his people possessing this strength in himself, and then imparting it to them, according to the words of the Psalmist, Ps. 68:35, "The God of Israel is he that giveth strength and power unto his people." For the natural history of the Unicorn, or the animal so denominated, see Bochart, Paxton, Robinson's Calmet, Kitto's Bib. Cyclopædia, Bush's Script. Illustrations, etc., where the subject is fully discussed. This animal, whatever it were, is noted in Scripture mainly for the potency of its *horn,* wherefore the Psalmist says, "Mine horn shalt thou exalt like the horn of an unicorn." It thence became an ordinary symbol of strength, and especially of the prowess of a people against their enemies, as in what Moses says of Joseph, Deut. 33:17, "His glory is like the firstling of his bullock, and his horns are like the horns of unicorns: with them he shall push the people together to the ends of the earth." In this sense Balaam here speaks of Israel, as also in the parallel passage, ch. 24:8, "God brought him forth out of Egypt; he hath as it were the strength of an unicorn: he shall eat up the na-

23 Surely *there is* no enchantment against Jacob, neither *is* *there* any divination against Israel: according to this time it

tions his enemies, and shall break their bones, and pierce them through with his arrows." The pertinence of the comparison will be more obvious upon reference to the character which Job, ch. 39 : 9–12, gives of this animal, "Will the unicorn be willing to serve thee, or abide by thy crib? Canst thou bind the unicorn with his band in the furrow? or will he harrow the valleys after thee? Wilt thou trust him, because his strength is great? or wilt thou leave thy labor to him? Wilt thou believe him, that he will bring home thy seed, and gather it into thy barn?" In like manner it is latently implied that as the unicorn spurns the dominion of man, and refuses to be tamed or to be serviceable to him in any way, so Israel should be endowed with strength to vanquish their enemies, while they are vanquished of none, and are subject to none. In this, as in the other parts of the prophecy, that which is spoken of the literal Israel is subordinate to that which is predicated of the spiritual.

V. 23. *Surely (there is) no enchantment against Jacob, neither (is there) any divination against Israel.* Or, Heb. "For there is no augury in Jacob, nor divination in Israel;" i. e-, none practised. According to this rendering, the present verse assigns a reason for the use of the similitude in the preceding. It is there asserted that God led Israel out of Egypt, and that in consequence they were armed with a power inexhaustible and invincible. How does this appear? The verse before us answers—*because*, or *for*, Israel is not to resort to the arts of soothsaying and augury in order to acquire a knowledge of the divine will, but God clearly reveals to them, at all times, what he does, and what, accordingly, his people are to do. This is the construction which Hengstenberg puts upon the passage, and in which, on the whole, we are constrained to concur, although always disposed, when possible, to abide by our present version. That version makes the purport of the language to be, that no such magical arts as Balaam had resorted to would be of any avail against Israel, inasmuch as they were constantly under the powerful protection of heaven, which would be certain to render the machinations of their enemies utterly abortive. This is indeed in itself true, and would make a very appropriate sense if adequately sanctioned by philology. But it is a serious objection to it, (1.) That the original words *nahash* and *gesem* do not properly signify *witchcraft* and *enchantment*, but *augury* and *divination*. (2.) That the Heb. for "*against* Jacob" and "*against* Israel" is precisely the same with that rendered "*in* Jacob" and "*in* Israel," v. 21. The preposition ב = *b*, *in*, occurs in both cases, and although instances may be adduced when it is properly rendered *against*, yet we can hardly suppose that precisely the same expression in the same context would require to be rendered in any other than the same manner. The ancient versions exhibit, as usual in difficult cases, a diversity of rendering. Gr. "For there is no augury used in Jacob, nor divination in Israel." Chald. "For auguries are not acceptable in the house of Jacob, nor does the multitude of the house of Israel will that there should be divinations." Vulg. "There is no soothsaying in Jacob, nor divination in Israel." Syr. "For there is no omen against Jacob, neither divination against Israel." Arab. "Neither is there any augury which shall harm the

shall be said of Jacob and of Israel, What [f] hath God wrought!

24 Behold, the people shall rise up [g] as a great lion, and lift

f Ps. 31. 19.

g Gen. 49. 9. Mic. 5. 8.

progeny of Jacob, nor Pythonic art which shall avail against the stock of Israel." From this it appears that these versions are about equally divided in their support of the two modes of rendering; but we rest in our reasons for giving a preference to the former. ——¶ *According to this time it shall be said, etc.* Heb. "According to the time." It is extremely difficult to affix a precise idea to these words. Ainsworth gives as an alternative rendering, "Even at this time it shall be said;" i. e., not hereafter only, but even now, it shall be said by me, who am to prophesy concerning this people, What great things God hath wrought, and will work for them. Rosenmuller's construction is not very different: "As at this time, i. e., about this time, as likewise hereafter it shall be said, How great things hath God wrought! equivalent to saying, Not only these, but many more wonderful things will God perform in behalf of Israel." Others, again, take the Heb. term to signify about this time next year; as it does Gen. 18 : 10, where see Note. So Chazkuni, a Jewish writer, "The next year after they had gone over Jordan, about the time (or, this time) it shall be said concerning Jacob and Israel; how many (great) works hath the holy blessed God wrought for them." Dathius renders it, "The time is at hand when it shall be said, etc." Calvin paraphrases it thus: "God shall henceforth perform mighty works for the defence of his people, which should be related with admiration. Balaam would say, that great should be the progress of God's grace, the beginnings only of which then appeared; in short, he declares that henceforth memorable should be the performances of God in behalf of his people which should supply abundant subjects for history." We may, perhaps, safely suppose the import to be that *on all occasions* there should be ample ground for saying of Jacob and Israel, what hath God wrought in their behalf. The ancient versions afford no material assistance in this case, but such as they are we give them. Gr. "In due season it shall be told to Jacob and to Israel what God will execute." Vulg. "In their times it shall be told to Jacob and to Israel what God hath wrought." Chald. "In time it shall be told to Jacob and Israel, what God hath wrought." Sam. "As at this time it shall be said to Jacob and Israel, what hath God done." Syr. "In a like time it shall be said to Jacob and Israel, what shall God work?" Arab. "And it shall be said unto them, what so great things hath the (All) Powerful done?"

V. 24. *Behold the people shall rise up as a great lion.* Heb. "As a courageous lion." Here the blessing which was bestowed specifically upon the tribe of Judah, Gen. 49 : 9, is applied to the whole nation of Israel collectively: "Judah is a lion's whelp; from the prey, my son, thou art gone up: he stooped down, he couched as a lion, and as an old lion; who shall rouse him up?" But this blessing reaches on and expends itself on the Christian church, with whom is the victorious presence of Christ, "the Lion of the tribe of Judah."——¶ *And lift himself up as a young lion.* Emblematic of strength, courage, and majesty. In the primary sense this phrase and the "rising up" in the former clause, may be conceived as pointing to the bold and valorous onset which Israel should make upon their enemies the Canaan-

up himself as a young lion: he
shall not lie down [h] until he eat
of the prey, and drink the blood
of the slain.
25 And Balak said unto Balaam, Neither curse them at all,
nor bless them at all.
26 But Balaam answered [i]
and said unto Balak, Told not
I thee, saying, All that the
LORD speaketh that I must do?

27 And Balak said unto Balaam, Come, I pray thee, I will
bring thee unto another place:
peradventure it will please God
that thou mayest curse me them
from thence.
28 And Balak brought Balaam unto the top of Peor, that
looketh toward Jeshimon.
29 And Balaam said unto
Balak, Build me here seven al-

h Gen. 49. 27. i ver. 12. 13.

ites, the record of which is contained in the book of Joshua. But beyond this we recognize also the easy triumphs of the spiritual Israel over their various enemies, Satan, sin, and the world, which are all leagued against them, but which are destined inevitably to be overcome. The language of the final clause is to be interpreted to the same effect.

V. 25. *Neither curse them at all, nor bless them at all.* Heb. "Neither cursing curse him, nor blessing bless him." The impatience and vexation of Balak breaks out uncontrollably in these words. Since Balaam will not say what he would have him, he wishes him to say nothing. If he could procure no evil to be done to Israel, he would at least debar them from the reception of any good.

V. 26. *Told I not thee, saying, etc.* The groundwork of Balak's reproach was the consideration, that Balaam, by his very coming, had laid himself under an obligation, at least, to do nothing against the interest of the king. To this Balaam replies by appealing to the declaration made on his first arrival, that he could only utter what was put into his lips. He is willing to own himself overruled, although he does not confess that he would have been very willing to comply with Balak's order if he had been able.

V. 27. *Peradventure it will please God, etc.* Heb. "Peradventure it will be right in the eyes of God." If Balak, in uttering these words, had any thought of the true God in his mind, the absurdity as well as the impiety of the suggestion is astounding. To think that the Most High could be prevailed upon to turn from his purpose of blessing, and *be pleased* to curse his people, was the height of delusion, and making the Lord to be "a God who hath pleasure in wickedness." But it is possible that Balak, by the term "God," had mental reference to some other deity, in which case we cannot so much wonder at the crudeness of his apprehensions.

V. 28. *And Balak brought Balaam unto the top of Peor.* Gr. "Phogor." Chald. "To the top of the high place of Peor." It was the name of a mountain in Moab where the people of that country used to sacrifice to their idol *Baal*. It was hence called *Baal-Peor*, ch. 25:2, 3, 18, and they seem there to have had a temple called *Beth-peor*, or *the house of Peor*, near which was a city of the same name, that the Israelites took from king Sihon, and afterwards gave for a possession to the tribe of Reuben, Deut. 3:29. Josh. 13:15, 20. ——¶ *That looketh toward Jeshimon.* That is, towards the desert so named. See Note on ch. 21:20. This wilderness, according to ch. 24:1, compared

tars, and prepare me here seven
bullocks and seven rams.
30 And Balak did as Balaam
had said, and offered a bullock
and a ram on *every* altar.

CHAPTER XXIV.

AND when Balaam saw that it pleased the LORD to bless Israel, he went not, as at other times, to seek for enchantments,

---

with v. 2, is situated at the northern extremity of the Dead Sea, and is the same tract which is elsewhere called Arboth Moab, or *fields* or *plains of Moab*, respecting which see Note on ch. 22 : 1. We are led to the same conclusion by the words "that looketh toward the wilderness," since they are not probably to be understood so much as a general geographical remark, as indicative of the suitableness of the place for Balak's object. A high peak or pinnacle like that of Peor could not properly be said to command one single view, but rather an extended prospect in every direction; but as it was important for Balaam to have a distinct view of the Israelites in order to give efficacy to his curses, it is therefore intimated that such a view was especially to be obtained from the station now chosen. That this wilderness is denoted Jeshimon is moreover inferrible from the fact that we find a place situated in it, to which the Israelitish camp reached from Gilgal, bearing the name of Beth-jeshimoth, ch. 33 : 48, 49. If, then, the Jeshimon here mentioned denotes the Arabah of the northern extremity of the Dead Sea, then by the clause, "that looketh toward the wilderness," the position of Peor is determined with tolerable exactness. It must have stood somewhat to the eastward overlooking the "plains of Moab." This appears also from Deut. 3 : 29, "So we abode in the valley over against Baal-peor." So likewise Deut. 4 : 45, 46, "These are the testimonies, etc. . . . which Moses spake unto the children of Israel . . . on this side Jordan, in the valley over against Beth-peor;" from which it appears, that when the Israelites were encamped in the plains, Beth-peor was situated in the immediate vicinity above them and looking down on the encampment below.

CHAPTER XXIV.

Continuation of Balaam's Prophecy as relating to Israel.

V. 1. *When Balaam saw that it pleased the Lord to bless Israel.* Heb. "That it was good in the eyes of Jehovah." The Most High always esteems it *good* to abide by his purposes and promises. This fact respecting the Lord it is said that Balaam "saw," by which we are to understand that he became assured of it from the internal consciousness of being overruled in his utterance by a superior power which he could not resist.——¶ *He went not, as at other times, to seek for enchantments.* Heb. "Not at (this) time as the time (before)." Gr. "According to his custom." Seeing there was no likelihood of obtaining leave from God to curse his people, he resolves no more to seek for enchantments, but sets his face towards the wilderness, that is, towards the place where Israel lay encamped, apparently giving himself up to the influence which had proved too strong for his wicked will, and perhaps disposed in his own mind to make a virtue of the necessity that he felt laid upon him. His object in retiring on the former occasions, while Balak was left standing by his altars, was not expressly stated, but here we are informed in effect that it was to practise in

but he set his face toward the wilderness.

2 And Balaam lift up his eyes, and he saw Israel abiding

private those cabalistic and magical arts which were common to sorcerers, and which he was in hopes might have made him master of his impious purpose, wherein, however, he was disappointed. These devices he now abandoned, because he saw they were fruitless, although his heart was in reality no better than before, as we infer from the sequel of the narrative. The original word for "enchantments" (*nehâshim*) is closely related to the Heb. term for *serpent* (*nahash*) and the relation between the ideas conveyed by *serpent* and *divination* or *augury* is undoubtedly recognized in more places than one in the original Scriptures. The literal rendering in the present instance is "to meet enchantment or magic-omens." The phrase undoubtedly implies the meeting, or seeking an interview with the Lord, for the purpose of making him propitious to his design by certain ceremonies of a cryptic or mysterious nature known as *divinations* or *auguries.*——¶ *He set his face toward the wilderness.* Heb. *el hammidbar*, the usual term to denote the dreary desert through which Israel had wandered after leaving Egypt, but implying in this connection a region which could only be *comparatively* denominated a desert or wilderness, as they were encamped in the valley of the Jordan, while Balaam was beholding them from the heights above. It appears from the occasional usage of the term, that any large and extensive tract of champaign country, even though it may happen to have villages in it, is called in the Scripture *wilderness.* It would seem, however, that both the Chaldee and Jerusalem paraphrases were somewhat misled by the use of the term *midbar*, and supposed that Balaam turned his face in the direction of the wilderness from which they had recently emerged, as is to be inferred from their interpretation. Chald. "He set his face towards the calf that Israel had made in the wilderness," implying, perhaps, that a people guilty of such a flagrant iniquity might properly be the subjects of a curse. But this supposes that Balaam knew of their transgression, which might have been the fact, or might not. Targ. Jerus. "He set his face toward the wilderness, and remembered concerning them the work of the calf, and would have cursed Israel." Finding all his previous incantations of no effect whatever, he resolves to abandon them, and utter what was put into his mouth. It was moreover wisely ordered in providence that the august and glorious predictions that follow respecting the Messiah and the Lord's church should not be preceded by magical rites, which would in some degree have weakened their credit or tarnished their lustre.

V. 2. *Saw Israel abiding* (*in his tents*). Heb. *shokën*, the root of *Shekinah.* See Note on Ex. 29 : 45. The addition in italics, "in his tents," is very proper, as the allusion is to that mode of habitation. Indeed, the Tabernacle, the special residence of the Shekinah, was a movable tent, though of peculiar and unique structure. Gr. "Saw Israel encamped by tribes." The order prescribed for the disposition of the several tribes was always observed during their encampment, and this exact and beautiful order seems to have made a profound impression upon the spirit of Balaam, as may be inferred from his language in vs. 5–7.——¶ *And the Spirit of God came upon him.* Chald. "The spirit of prophecy from before the Lord

in his tents according to their tribes; and [a] the Spirit of God came upon him.

3 And he took up his parable, and said, Balaam the son of Beor hath said, and the

a 1 Sam. 10. 10.

rested upon him." This Sol. Jarchi intimates was with a view to keep him from cursing Israel. It evidently implies a strong compulsory influence emanating from the Lord himself, and overruling and restraining him from uttering the anathemas which he had conceived in his heart, and inspiring him to see and to foretell future events. The phrase imports a divine impulse or afflatus which was often imparted to men independent of their moral character. It was a species of possession or inspiration for the time being, and those who were subjects of it "spake as they were moved by the Holy Ghost." Thus, it is said ch. 11:26, "The Spirit rested upon them, and they prophesied." So also v. 29 of the same chapter, "Would God that all the Lord's people were prophets, and that the Lord would put his Spirit upon them." In like manner the Spirit of God came upon Saul, converting him temporarily into a new man, but not making any permanent change in his character, 1 Sam. 19:19–23. "'Tis sometimes said, 'The Lord came to Balaam' as he did to Abimelech, Gen. 20:3, and to Laban, Gen. 31:24; but 'tis never said 'The word of the Lord' came to him, as to Jeremiah, Jer. 1:4, and to the rest of God's prophets. God never vouchsafed his 'word' to any but to his prophets, of whom 'tis said always, that 'the word of the Lord came to them.'"—*Ness.* The remarks of Calvin on this incident are very appropriate. "It is said 'the Spirit of God was upon him,' not as if it had begun to inspire him at that particular moment when he cast his eyes upon the camp of Israel; but because it prompted him to look in that direction, in order that the impulse of prophecy might be stronger in him, as respecting a thing actually before his eyes. But after the Spirit had thus affected his senses, or at any rate had prepared them to be fit instruments for the execution of his office, it then also directed his tongue to prophesy; but in an extraordinary manner, so that a divine majesty shone forth in the sudden change, as if he were transformed into a new man. In a word, 'the Spirit of God was upon him,' showing by manifest token that He was the author of his address, and that Balaam did not speak of his own natural intelligence. To the same intent it is said that 'he took up his parable,' because the character of his address was marked with unusual grandeur and magnificent brilliancy." Dr. Chalmers also speaks in a similar vein of this prophecy. "He is made the involuntary instrument of further revelations; and what he now utters when the Spirit of God came upon him, is in the very highest style and strain of lofty inspiration. We cannot fix on any portion of Scripture that bears a nobler or more sustained elevation than these effusions poured forth by Balaam from the mountains, as he looked down on the tents of Israel stretched out in full and far perspective before him."—*Bib. Readings in loc.* Still the rhetorical or poetical merit of the utterance is comparatively of very little consequence when viewed in relation to its spiritual import.

V. 3. *Balaam the son of Beor hath said.* Heb. *neum bilam, the saying, affirmation, averment of Balaam.* The term is applied for the most part to divine oracles or declarations, which are

man whose eyes are open hath said;

4 He hath said, which heard the words of God, which saw

"faithful sayings," worthy of all confidence and acceptation. It is of very emphatic import, and its use in this exordium is no doubt to be referred to the Spirit who spake through Balaam, and thus put a seal upon the prophecy as a truly divine revelation. The Most High was greatly magnified in thus ratifying his blessing upon his people through Balaam, a sorcerer and corrupt prophet who fain would have cursed them. And this circumstance, tending so much to the divine glory, Balaam himself is made an instrument of proclaiming. He is virtually made to say, Even the man whose power to curse was so much relied on, and who leaned so strongly to compliance with Balak's suit—even he must and will affirm it, and vigorously stand to it, that Israel shall be blessed. The language of David, 2 Sam. 23 : 1, 2, is strikingly analogous, as the same word which occurs there also conveys clearly the intimation that what he said is not said from himself, but from the inspiration of the Lord's Spirit, though uttered by his organs. "Now these be the last words of David. David the son of Jesse said, and the man who was raised up on high, the anointed of the God of Jacob, and the sweet psalmist of Israel, said, The Spirit of the Lord spake by me, and his word was in my tongue."——¶ *The man whose eyes are open hath said.* Heb. *shethum haäyin, opened of eye.* The margin of our version gives, "Who had his eyes shut (but now opened);" from which it would naturally be inferred that there was a degree of ambiguity in the original. This is the fact, as commentators are very much divided between "open" and "shut" as the true rendering. A satisfactory decision between the claims of the two is not easy. The Chald. has "The man who sees fairly (pulchre)." Gr. "The truly seeing man." Syr. "The man whose eye is disclosed, or laid open (retectus)." Vulg. "The man whose eye is stopped up (obturatus)." The original (*shethum*) occurs only here and v. 15, and Hengstenberg and others take it as the original form of the word, which was afterwards softened into *sâtham,* a word of not unfrequent occurrence, and signifying *to close, to shut.* But Drusius, on the other hand, and from him Rosenmuller, refer *shethum* to the Chald. *shâtham, to perforate,* and hence *to open,* which is favored by some of the ancient versions, as the Syr. Sam. and Arab. We incline, on the whole, to embrace both senses, on the ground that an ecstatic or trance state is described, in which, as is well known, the external sight is closed while the internal is opened. Glassius, in his "Sacred Philology," gives a multitude of examples from the Hebrew Scriptures in which the same word conveys directly contrary meanings. In the Gr. of the New Testament the same peculiarity occasionally obtains. Thus, Mat. 6 : 2, "Verily I say unto you they have their reward;" where the original (*apechomai*) has both a negative and affirmative sense, implying that in having their reward they have it not, since in seeking applause of men they lose that higher and better blessing which comes from God only.

V. 4. *He hath said which heard the words of God.* Heb. *neum, the assured saying,*—the same form of expression with that occurring v. 3, and implying a degree of emphasis and asseveration such as pertains to a divine oracle rather than to a human utterance. "The words of God" is in the original "the

the vision of the Almighty, falling *into a trance*, but having his eyes open:

sayings of God," which the Chald. renders "The word from before the Lord," and the Gr. "The oracles of the Strong," i. e., of the Almighty, with reference to the Hebrew name of God, which is here *El*, signifying *strong* or *mighty*.——¶ *Which saw the vision of the Almighty*. Heb. *Shaddai, the All-sufficient*. The "vision of the Almighty" is probably to be understood of the vision, that is, the prophetic perception, vouchsafed by the Almighty, as this is the general import of the term. Otherwise it might be understood of the vision of the divine appearance in person, which is supposed, indeed, by some to have been the case in the manifestation of the Angel-Jehovah to the prophet during his journey. But the usage of the original is so uniform in respect to that kind of vision which was granted to the prophets in their ecstatic states, that we feel shut up to that interpretation.——¶ *Falling* (*into a trance*). The words "into a trance," it will be observed, are supplied in our version, their equivalents not occurring in the original. This gives occasion to a twofold diversity of rendering. One class of expositors, agreeing with our translators, understand it of his falling into a trance-state on the occasion mentioned ch. 22, while on his way to Moab. Another takes the term "falling" as having reference to the frequent effect of the prophetic influx, which was to cause the subjects of it to *fall down* prostrate to the earth, as was the case with Saul, 1 Sam. 19 : 24. Compare also Gen. 15 : 12. Dan. 8 : 17, 18. Rev. 1 : 17. Ezek. 1 : 28. 3 : 23. 43 : 3. 44 : 4. "The word," says Hengstenberg, "indicates the force of the afflatus which, like an armed man, comes upon the seer and strikes him down." But he judiciously observes of this afflatus, that "it assumed such a violent character, prostrating both soul and body, only where it found an unripe (or unadapted) state. The falling down is mentioned only of such a class of persons as Balaam, Saul, and the prophetic scholars. In a Samuel we can hardly imagine such violent appearances. The more the mind, in its ordinary consciousness, is penetrated by the Spirit, the less necessary is it for the Spirit to set itself against it in a hostile attitude, by its extraordinary manifestations; it then only comes to its own, to what is homogeneous." He does not accordingly consider the instances of Abraham, Ezekiel, Daniel, and John, as altogether parallel with the present, inasmuch as in them "the falling down did not proceed from the influences of the Spirit forcibly pressing down the natural life, but from an overpowering impression of the glory of the person beheld, an impression of terror and reverence." We conclude, therefore, on the whole, that what Balaam intended was to affirm of himself that his case was marked by this characteristic of a true prophet, that the illapse of the Divine Spirit upon him, when it came, was so powerful as to cause him habitually to fall to the ground; while, at the same time, we see nothing to forbid the idea that he had a collateral reference to the incidents of his journey, one of which was the falling into a trance, although it is not this kind of "falling" which is here immediately indicated by the use of the term. But he was doubtless during some part of this journey under the influence of a trance; and we have, in a former Note, referred to this passage as affording to some commentators a

5 How goodly are thy tents, O Jacob, *and* thy tabernacles, O Israel!

6 As the valleys are they spread forth, as gardens by [b] the river's side, as the trees of lign-

b Ps. 1. 3. Jer. 17. 8.

strong incidental proof that the miracle recorded ch. 22, was subjective rather than objective—a conclusion, however, which we do not indorse except in a qualified sense. Gr. "Who in sleep hath seen a vision of God." Chald. "Who seeth a vision from before the face of the Almighty, falling down and it is revealed unto him." Vulg. "He that hath beheld the vision of the Almighty, he that falleth, and so his eyes are opened." Syr. "Who sees the visions of God, and when he is prostrate (or cast down) then his eyes are opened." As a general fact, the ancient versions render by a term signifying *falling*, but the term itself having no allusion to *falling into a trance*.——¶ *But having his eyes open.* Heb. "Uncovered, or unveiled." Chald. "And it was revealed unto him." A close relation between the "falling" and the "opening of the eyes" is no doubt intended to be conveyed, and which is clearly indicated by the Vulg. and Syr. versions as given above; and we know that, psychologically, the ecstatic state is accompanied with a special opening of the interior vision which reveals marvellous things of the spiritual world to the soul.

V. 5. *How goodly are thy tents, O Jacob, etc.* Heb. "How good!" but the original term has frequently the import of that *good* which is recognized in beauty, joy, delight, etc. The expression is here prompted by a spiritual perception of the moral order and beauty of the church as represented by the regular and imposing arrangement of the tents of Israel as they lay encamped on the plains of Moab. He had just before, with open outward eye, beheld the chosen people abiding in their tents according to their tribes, and this external view is a kind of substratum on which the spiritual beholding develops itself. In other words, he is carried onwards in spirit from the shadow to the substance, and sees the spiritual Israel arrayed in a glory and symmetry corresponding with that of the literal. "Tents" and "tabernacles" are not unfrequently spoken of in the Divine word as the habitations of the Israelites in Canaan, although even in these cases we may perceive an adumbration of the Christian Church in its external order. Ainsworth remarks that the original word for tabernacles implies *vicinity* or *nearness*, and therefore points to the communion of the Church with its Divine Lord and with one another; and the passage is expounded by Targ. Jon. as follows: "The tabernacle of the congregation which is set among you, and your tabernacles which are round about it, O house of Israel." As to the distinction implied in the two names of the father of the twelve tribes, it may be sufficient to suggest, that Jacob is the name of the Church in respect to its own intrinsic infirmity, in allusion to which it is said, Is. 41 : 14, "Fear not, thou worm Jacob," and Am. 7 : 25, "By whom shall Jacob arise, for he is small," while Israel is its name derived from its power and prevailing with God and man. See Note on Gen. 32 : 28.

V. 6. *As the valleys are they spread forth.* The sentiment contained in the preceding verse is here farther amplified; the loveliness of the tents of Israel being exhibited in a succession

aloes which the LORD hath planted, *and* as [c] cedar trees beside the waters.

7 He shall pour the water out of his buckets, and his seed *shall be* in many waters, and his

c Ps. 92. 12-14.

of comparisons. First, they are spread out like valleys, implying both length and breadth, and conveying an idea of the large extent of Israel's habitations. The original *nahal* denotes primarily *a brook;* then *a valley,* through which a brook runs. That here the latter meaning is intended, as our translators have taken it, is to be obviously inferred from the following comparisons, in which the tents of Israel are not compared to waters, but to objects by the side of waters, such as gardens, trees, etc. The scenery wrought into the picture is such as would be most charming to an Oriental eye, and such as would stand in most marked contrast with the wild, barren, rocky, and dreary desert through which Israel had passed, and in which they had so long abode. Here the images are those of fertility and beauty, and thus in accordance with the frequent strains of prophecy, setting forth under similar figures, the future prosperity, abundance, and universal welfare of the spiritual church. The best commentary on the passage is doubtless to bring it into juxtaposition with parallel passages, as to which there can be no question that they involve an ulterior reference to the Christian Church. "A garden inclosed is my sister, my spouse; a spring shut up, a fountain sealed. Thy plants are an orchard of pomegranates, with pleasant fruits; camphire, with spikenard, spikenard and saffron; calamus and cinnamon, with all trees of frankincense; myrrh and aloes, with all the chief spices: a fountain of gardens, a well of living waters, and streams from Lebanon. Awake, O north wind; and come, thou south; blow upon my garden, that the spices thereof may flow out. Let my beloved come into his garden, and eat his pleasant fruits." Is. 58:11, "And the Lord shall guide thee continually, and satisfy thy soul in drought, and make fat thy bones; and thou shalt be like a watered garden, and like a spring of water, whose waters fail not." Ps. 65:9, "Thou visitest the earth and waterest it: thou greatly enrichest it with the river of God, which is full of water." Ps. 46:4, "There is a river, the streams whereof shall make glad the city of God, the holy place of the tabernacles of the Most High." This river is the Lord's divine truth embodied in his Word which ministers sustentation, comfort, and refreshment to his people, of whom it is written, Jer. 31:12, "Their soul shall be as a watered garden, and they shall not sorrow any more at all." It was therefore the state of the church in its prosperous periods represented by these significant images, to which the words of Balaam are to be applied.——¶ *Trees of lign-aloes.* Heb. *ahalim,* a term denoting some kind of odoriferous tree, but the precise species of which is not at present known with certainty, but supposed to be the *Agollocham,* which ancient writers say was burnt for the sake of the odorous fumes it produced. It belonged probably to the cone-bearing family, inasmuch as the word in Heb. is composed of the same letters as *ohalim, tents,* and these trees, it is said, from their shape, resemble, when growing together, an encampment of tents.

V. 7. *He shall pour the water out of his buckets.* Or, Heb. "Water shall flow out of his buckets." That is, he

king shall be higher than Agag, and his kingdom shall be exalted.

---

shall be an instrument and a medium of imparting an abundance of spiritual blessings to others. As thirsty plants or fields are refreshed and fertilized by copious irrigation, so shall the barren moral wastes be beautified by the agency of the sons of the church. The idea is substantially the same with that expressed by the prophet, Is. 12 : 3, where the pouring out, or the abundant supply, of the Spirit of Truth is hinted at, and it is said, "With joy shall ye draw water out of the wells of salvation." It is an intimation directly the opposite to that of the woman of Samaria, who said to our Lord, the true "fountain of Israel," "Sir, thou hast nothing to draw with (no bucket), and the well is deep; from whence then hast thou that living water?" It is the prerogative of the spiritual Israel to supply the waters of salvation to those who are destitute. "Out of Zion shall go forth the law, and the word of the Lord from Jerusalem." But as the church is embodied in the Lord who is its life, its all in all, so it is no contradiction to what we have now said to recognize him as the grand dispenser of the waters of life to a thirsty world.——¶ *His seed (shall be) in many waters.* The primary idea conveyed to the mind of an oriental by this language would probably be very nearly the same with that received from the kindred words of the prophet, Is. 32 : 20, "Blessed are they that sow beside all waters, that send forth thither the feet of the ox and the ass." "This," says Sir John Chardin, "exactly answers the manner of sowing rice; for they sow it upon the water; and before sowing, while the earth is covered with water, they cause the ground to be trodden by oxen, horses, and asses, who go mid-leg deep; and this is the way of preparing the ground for sowing." This then is doubtless the image couched under the letter of the text, but the spirit gives us a richer meaning grafted on the literal sense. The effusion of water, mentioned in the preceding clause, denotes the impartation of that scriptural or doctrinal truth which goes to prepare the mind for a fructifying process, as water which irrigates and saturates the earth prepares it for bringing forth an abundant crop of the grain sown. The "seed in many waters," or the seed-corn sown in moist, watery, and fruitful fields, points to that higher spiritual element which is implanted in the instructed mind, and results in the production of the fruits of a holy life; for fruits are from seeds, and seeds are fruitful in proportion as the ground in which they are sown is well watered. The water and the seeds, therefore, denote different degrees of divine influence.——¶ *And his king shall be higher than Agag.* Our divine Lord and Saviour Jesus Christ is undoubtedly here intended to be designated, by the spirit of prophecy, under the title of "his king." Of him it is said, Ps. 89 : 28, that "he is higher than the kings of the earth;" and one of these kings, or perhaps rather a line of kings, is here specified under the name of "Agag." This was the name of the king of the Amalekites, who were subdued by Saul, king of Israel, 1 Sam. 15 : 8. But it is supposed that the name was common to the Amalekite kings, like Pharaoh in Egypt, Abimelech in Philistia, and Cesar in Rome. The nation of the Amalekites was at this time powerful and formidable, as may be inferred from their bold assault upon a people so numerous as the Israelites, and from the declaration, v. 20,

8 God brought him forth out of Egypt; he hath as it were the strength of an unicorn: he shall eat up the nations his enemies, and shall break [d] their bones, and pierce [e] *them* through with his arrows.

d Ps. 2. 9. e Ps. 45. 5.

---

that they were "the first of the nations." This was probably the reason why they were specified in preference to any other. He announces that the King of Israel should be the greatest of kings, inasmuch as no greater than Agag was then known. Some think the words refer to Saul, the first king of Israel, who subdued the Amalekites and took Agag captive, to wit, that Israel, in Saul its king, should be thus paramount to Agag. But we are forced from the general analogy of the predictions to recognize an ulterior reach of import in the passage, embracing an intimation of the triumphs of the Messiah and his kingdom over every opposing power, even down to the final consummation. Among the ancient versions the Gr. has "And a kingdom greater than Gog's shall be raised up." Sam. "And his king shall be exalted above Gog." Symmachus, according to Grotius, renders in a similar way. The other versions have "Agog." Simonis (*Onomasticon*, § II. c. 6.) by comparing the Arab. and Pers. *oog, to be high, lofty, sublime,* deduces a like meaning for *Agag*, so that to be higher than Agag is to be higher than the highest. Simonis refers also to the same root the Germ. *hoch, high,* the proper name *Hugo, Ogyges,* and *gigas, giant.* As *Gog* seems to have relation to the same root, we incline to the opinion that Agag may here be taken as of equivalent import with Gog, and thus stand as a mystical denomination for that formidable hostile power predicted by Ezekiel, 38 : 2. 39 : 1, and John, Rev. 20 : 8, as among the last grand enemies of the church. "As *Gog* in Scripture seems to mean the enemies of God's people, the promises here may imply that the true worshippers of the Most High shall ultimately have dominion over their enemies."—*A. Clarke.*——¶ *His kingdom shall be exalted.* That is, in Saul, in David, in Solomon, and pre-eminently in Christ, in whom the kingdom culminated to its highest glory, Is. 2 : 2. Dan. 2 : 44. Rev. 11 : 15.

V. 8. *God brought him forth out of Egypt.* These words are here repeated from ch. 23 : 22, and the purport in both places is, that as it was the Most High himself, their divine vindicator, guide, and king, who with a strong arm brought them forth out of Egypt, so that same God would make them victorious over all their enemies, so that consequently every form of opposition would be vain. This would constitute an appeal to Balak to halt in the dangerous path in which he was treading.——¶ *He hath as it were the strength of an unicorn.* The comparison is here also repeated and amplified from ch. 23 : 22, as giving a reason for the previous intimation respecting the final victory of Israel.——¶ *Shall break their bones.* Gr. "Shall unmarrow (or eat out the marrow) of their fat (bones);" rendered by Thomson, "shall exhaust their fatness." It implies such an effectual weakening of their forces and resources that they should never be able to recover.——¶ *Pierce them through with his arrows.* Gr. "Shoot through the enemy with his arrows." Arrows are often mentioned among the weapons of war, and that there are spiritual as well as physical arrows is clear from the words of the Psalmist, Ps. 45 : 6,

9 He couched, he lay down as [f] a lion, and as a great lion: who shall stir him up? Blessed [g] *is* he that blesseth thee, and cursed *is* he that curseth thee.
10 And Balak's anger was kindled against Balaam, and he smote his hands together: and Balak said unto Balaam, I called thee to curse mine enemies, and, behold [h], thou hast altogether blessed *them* these three times.
11 Therefore now flee thou to thy place: I thought to promote thee unto great honour; but, lo, the LORD hath kept thee back from honour.

f c. 23. 4. *g* Gen. 12. 3. *h* Neh. 13. 2.

"Thine arrows are sharp in the heart of the King's enemies." These arrows are the words of Christ penetrating the hearts of rebellious men. Comp. Ps. 64:4. Here, as elsewhere, what is primarily applied to Israel or the church, holds good mainly of Him who is the essential life and personality of the church.

V. 9. *He couched, he lay down as a lion, etc.* This verse, as well as the 24th of the former chapter, refers primarily to the entire course of conquest of Israel over their enemies the Canaanites, and their subsequent perfect and quiet possession of the land promised; but ultimately to that career of spiritual victories achieved by the *true* Israel, in their own persons and in the person of their head, over the numerous adversaries they should encounter, and to that peaceful rest and repose which should follow.——¶ *Blessed (is) he that blesseth thee, etc.* It is observable that the Lord here puts into the mouth of Balaam the same language with that which Isaac applies to Jacob in closing his benediction, Gen. 27:29, and with which also God crowns Abraham, the father of the faithful, Gen. 12:3. The Lord herein confirms the assurance of his favor to the righteous and their seed forever, and gives them to understand how profound and permanent shall be the peace of the church after her warfare is accomplished.

Balak's angry Rebuke of Balaam.

V. 10. *And Balak's anger was kindled against Balaam.* This unexpected termination of the affair exhausted the last remains of the patience of Balak, and led to mutual recriminations between himself and the hireling prophet. His predictions on this occasion had the air of a voluntary benediction pronounced upon a hated people, and nothing is so repugnant to the feelings of wicked men as the assured prosperity of the righteous.——¶ *Smote his hands together.* Heb. "Clapped the palms of his hands"—a token of indignation, and at the same time of contempt. Thus, Job 17:23, "Men shall *clap their hands at him*, and shall hiss him out of his place." Lam. 2:15, "All that pass by the way *clap their hands at thee*, and wag their heads." He proceeds to charge Balaam with putting upon him a base affront and an intolerable cheat. Though he had called the prophet to curse his enemies, yet he had virtually shown himself in league with them, although by his altars, and sacrifices, and other rites, he had made him believe that he would certainly curse them; instead of which he had three times blessed them, and that too in a very plenary and emphatic manner.

V. 11. *Therefore flee now to thy place.* Heb. "Flee for thyself," i. e. get thee gone without delay. Hie or hasten to

12 And Balaam said unto
Balak, Spake I not also to thy
messengers which thou sentest
unto me, saying,
13 If Balak would give me
his house full of silver and gold,
I cannot go beyond the commandment of the LORD, to do
either good or bad of mine own
mind; *but* what the LORD saith,
that will I speak?
14 And now, behold, I go
unto my people: come *therefore, and* I will advertise thee

---

thine own land or city (thy place), if thou wouldst get beyond the sphere of my resentment and contempt.——¶ *The Lord hath kept thee back from honor.* Gr. "The Lord hath deprived thee of honor." The God with whom you profess to be so familiar, and to whom you render such a dutiful obedience, has now rewarded you as you might have expected. He has deprived you of the best post in my court for the service you have done him. Thus it is that they who appear to be losers by obeying God rather than man, are apt to be rebuked by the worldly-minded as having foolishly thrown away the highest proffered advantages. We cannot, indeed, say much for the motives by which Balaam was governed in yielding compliance to the Divine impulse, but we can still affirm, that if he had been voluntary and sincere in his obedience, whatever honor he lost thereby at the hands of Balak, it would have been more than made up to him by that remunerating Providence which never forgets its own promises to those who devoutly trust in it. Prov. 11:18, "The wicked worketh a deceitful work; but to him that soweth righteousness shall be a sure reward."

V. 12. *Spake I not also, etc.* Balaam makes the best of his case in vindicating himself from the charges alleged against him. He excuses the disappointment by referring to the restraining and constraining power of the Most High, who had irresistibly controlled his utterance. He pleads, moreover, that he could not be charged with deception, inasmuch as he had told him from the outset what he must depend upon. He had forewarned him of the contingency which had now actually occurred, and therefore it would be unjust to lay upon him the blame of what he could not help, of an inability which he had expressly announced as possible.——¶ *I cannot go beyond the commandment of the Lord.* Heb. "Beyond the mouth of the Lord." Gr. "Cannot transgress the word of the Lord;" implying not only the divine decree, but the divine dictate within the prophet's bosom, which he would fain have suppressed if he could. But he indicates that he was bound by the power of the Spirit to declare, even against his own will, whatever revelation he received.——¶ *To do either good or bad of mine own mind.* Heb. "Out of mine own heart." The word "heart" is here contrasted with the operation of the Lord's Spirit, as impostors are said to speak "out of their own heart," when they falsely use the name of God to cover their own inventions. Being under a divine prompting, he did not feel at liberty to speak "of his own heart."

V. 14. *I will advertise thee what this people shall do, etc.* The original term here translated "advertise," i. e., inform, usually signifies *to counsel, to advise,* and some have supposed it was on this occasion that Balaam gave the infamous counsel mentioned ch. 31:16, by which Israel was seduced into a fatal transgression with the Midianitish

what this people shall do to thy
people in the latter days.
15 And he took up his parable, and said, Balaam the son
of Beor hath said, and the man
whose eyes are open hath said;
16 He hath said, which heard
the words of God, and knew the
knowledge of the Most High,
which saw the vision of the
Almighty, falling *into a trance*,
but having his eyes open:
17 I [i] shall see him, but not

i Rev. 1. 7.

women. The Vulg. renders it, "I will give thee counsel what thy people shall do to this people in the latter days;" where it will be observed that instead of "what this people shall do to thy people," we read, "what thy people shall do to this people." Chald. "I will counsel thee what thou shalt do; and I will show thee what the people shall do." And the Jerus. Targ. still more explicitly, "I will advise thee what thou shalt do to this people; make them to sin; otherwise thou shalt not have dominion over them; but this people shall not domineer over thy people in the latter end of days." But the weight of evidence is in favor of the present rendering, to wit, that he would inform Balak, in the exercise of his prophetic gift, what the people of Israel should eventually do to the people of Moab, whom, for the present, they were not to disturb, but in respect to whom we learn that in a subsequent age, in the reign of David, the prediction went into accomplishment, 2 Sam. 8:2, "And he smote Moab, and measured them with a line, casting them down to the ground; even with two lines measured he to put to death, and with one full line to keep alive. And so the Moabites became David's servants, and brought gifts." Again, in Jer. 48, there is an extended prophecy of Moab's destruction, with a promise of the returning of their captivity "in the latter days."——¶ *In the latter days.* Heb. lit. "In the afterhood of days," a phrase imputing the time to come, whether that be more or less remote. Here doubtless it has an extended reach of meaning, embracing the era of the Messiah and his New Testament Church, when the spiritual Israel should waste away the spiritual Moab.

Balaam's Final Prophecy.

V. 15. *Took up his parable.* That is, began to prophecy, but in a dark and mystic strain. Thus the Psalmist, Ps. 78:2, "I will open my mouth in a parable; I will utter dark sayings of old."

V. 16. *And knew the knowledge of the Most High.* Chald. "Knowing knowledge from before the Most High," i. e., knowledge made known to him by revelation from God. This clause is additional to what we have in v. 4. Baalhatturim here remarks, "He saith this because he would reveal the days of Christ."

V. 17. *I shall see him, but not now, etc.* The prevailing consent of commentators here determines in favor of rendering the verbs in the present instead of the future, "I see him, but not now; I behold him, but not nigh." A similar change of tenses is of frequent occurrence in Hebrew. The idea is, that he had a view in dim perspective of the event or the personage which constituted the main theme of his prophecy. As if he should say, "The person of whom I am now prophesying does not at present exist among the Israelites, nor shall he appear in this generation. His manifestation is reserved

now; I shall behold him, but not nigh: there shall come a Star [k] out of Jacob, and a Scep-

k Rev. 22. 16.

to after-times." He sees him not *now*, for he is rapt in spirit out of the present into the future, to the "end of the days," and *there* he sees him. He beholds him not *nigh*, for a great distance lies between the *seer* and the *seen*. His vision of Him is therefore like that of Abraham, who saw Christ's day afar off, John 8 : 56. Chald. "I shall see him, but not now; I shall behold him, but he is not near." Gr. "I will point to him, but not now; I will bless him, but he draws not near." This is extremely paraphrastic, but the import seems to be, that, taking Israel for the subject of the prediction, whatever had been promised him should be fulfilled, though not immediately; that he would in due time accumulate blessings upon him by prophetic announcement, although the time was not yet at hand. Neither these, however, nor the other versions throw much light upon the passage. A special difficulty is to determine whether the suffix to the verbs should be translated "him" or "it;" understanding by "it" the general subject of the prediction. On this point the original is doubtful, and the versions vary. The Arab. however countenances the latter: "I see it, and it is not yet in existence; I behold it, and it is not yet nigh at hand." But the decision is not intrinsically of much importance, as, if Israel be meant, it is Israel advanced to the height of his destiny, and viewed in conjunction with his Lord and Head. If the reference be to Christ, then we must assent to the remark of Calmet, to wit, that Balaam, under a divine impulse, points to the Messiah just as if the whole previous discourse had contemplated him, though he had not been expressly named, but was to be recognized from the main drift of the oracle. This strikes us as on the whole extremely probable, since the Messiah would form the prominent figure in the prophetic picture.——¶ *There shall come a star out of Jacob, etc.* Heb. *dârak*, which has the import of *stepping onward, coming forth, proceeding*, and sometimes of *walking in a stately manner*, like a king. From *dârak*, as a root, comes the derivative *derek, a way.* It is however, on the whole, an unusual word to bear the signification of *coming*, and doubtless involves an interior recondite sense in the present connection. What that sense is, we think, may be ascertained by bringing the passage into parallelism with the evangelical history of Christ's birth, which we hold to be a perfectly legitimate mode of treating it. On that occasion we learn that a mysterious Star appeared to the Wise Men of the East, and guided their steps to the stable in Bethlehem where the Saviour was born. This was the *moving, proceeding*, or *going forth* of the Star which the prophet now beheld in anticipative vision. "They departed, and lo the star which they saw in the east, *went before them*, till it came and stood over where the young child was." A star has always been regarded in the East as a symbol of distinction, as the herald of any great and glorious birth among men, and this fact enables us to perceive the connecting link between seeing a star and concluding, as the wise men did, that a "King of the Jews" was born. It is no objection to this that the Star seen by Balaam was a symbol of Christ himself, whereas that seen by the Wise Men was a mere concomitant of his birth. In either case the Star was the ensign of an august personage, and Hengstenberg remarks that "it is not simply a

tre[l] shall rise out of Israel, and shall smite the corners of Moab, and destroy all the children of Sheth.

l Ps. 110. 2.

literal star that is meant by Balaam. He uses the 'star' metaphorically, as is customary among all nations, to designate a great and illustrious ruler." Nor is the objection to the proposed parallelism of any weight, that the Star prophetically seen by Balaam is said to "come out of Jacob," whereas that seen by the Magi appeared first in the Eastern world remote from Judea, the birth-place of the Saviour. It is sufficient that He who was represented by the Star did originate, as to his earthly humanity, in the midst of the nation collectively denominated "Jacob," and nothing in the local relations or aspects of the Star will avail to weaken the force of the symbolical coincidence to which we have alluded. The language describing the prophetic imagery sets before us a *star proceeding*, and such a star marshalled the way of the Wise Men to the birth-place of our Lord. Can we doubt then that, viewed in this light, the Star of the Eastern Magi stands in the closest relation to the star which Balaam saw in spirit, especially when our Lord expressly speaks of himself, Rev. 22 : 16, as "the root and offspring of David, the bright and morning Star." This view is confirmed by the fact, that the Jews understood this prophecy as referring to the Messiah or Christ. The false Christ who, under Hadrian, took up arms against Rome, gave himself out as the Messiah whom Balaam had foretold, and assumed the name of *Bar-chocab*, or the *Son of the Star*, for the purpose of placing himself in nearer connection with that prophecy, although after being slain in battle the Jews, finding themselves deceived, called him *Bar-coziba*, *the son of a lie.* We are well aware of the dissenting opinions of many of the modern German critics, as it regards the designed application of this oracle to the stellar phenomenon which distinguished our Lord's nativity, or even to the Lord himself; but we deem it not expedient to advert to them, as the above interpretation is satisfactory to us, and will probably commend itself to those who are prepared to believe that the Sacred Volume has proceeded from an intelligence which "sees the end from the beginning." So also in regard to a secondary application both of the Star and the Sceptre to David. As we see no evidence of any such intended application, we pass it by without remark. To the "Sceptre" we assign substantially the same symbolical significance as to the Star. They differ only as Jacob differs from Israel, which is merely in certain phases of representative import. The original may be rendered literally *a rod* or *a staff*, and denotes a badge or emblem of government. Gr. "A man shall rise out of Israel." Chald. "Messiah (or Christ) shall be anointed of the house of Israel," i. e., shall assume the sovereign power. As David and other kings bore the sceptre as an ensign of power, so it is said of Christ, that he should have a *rod* or *sceptre.* Ps. 45 : 7, "The sceptre of thy kingdom is a right sceptre." Heb. 1 : 8, "Thou shalt rule them with a rod (or sceptre) of iron." The emblem of regal authority and supremacy, becomes him who is King of Zion and the Prince of Peace. But his kingdom is not of this world. He received it not by any earthly appointment. It is not an outward and visible kingdom, but a kingdom established in men's hearts, and its sceptre is swayed over the thoughts and emotions of the soul, softening, subduing, and sweetly controlling them. His kingdom is a government of religious and heavenly influence, a system of righteousness, and peace, and joy in the Holy Ghost. To this kingdom, established near thirty centuries after the days of Balaam, does the immense reach of this prophecy extend.——¶ *Shall smite the corners of Moab.* Chald. "Shall kill the princes of Moab." Gr. "Shall crush the chieftains of Moab." These renderings, we think, afford a clue to the genuine sense, though the relation between "corners" and "princes" or "chieftains" may require some explanation. Such an explanation is afforded by the Oriental ideas and usages in regard to "corners." Sitting in a corner is with them a stately attitude, and is expressive of superiority. "The divans at Aleppo," says Russell, "are formed in the following manner: Across the upper end and along the sides of the room is fixed a wooden platform, four feet broad and six inches high; upon this are laid cotton mattresses exactly of the same breadth, and over these a cover of broadcloth, trimmed with gold lace and fringes hanging over the ground. A number of large oblong cushions stuffed hard with cotton, and faced with flowered velvet, are then ranged in the platform close to the wall. The two upper *corners* of the divan are furnished also with softer cushions half the size of the others, which are laid upon a square fine mattress, spread over those of cloth, both being faced with brocade. *The corners, in this manner distinguished, are held to be the places of honor, and a great man never offers to resign them to persons of inferior rank.*" Mr. Hogg, in his "Visit to Damascus," speaks to the same effect. "Round three sides of the room was a broad scarlet divan, supplied with cushions of gold brocade, resting against the walls. *The corners were distinguished as places of honor* by a square of crimson and gold silk, with a cushion of the same color and materials at the back of each." "Corners," therefore, in this connection we take for *those who occupy them*, that is, dignitaries or princes, so that "smiting the corners of Moab" is, in reality, abolishing the power and predominance of Moab, viewed as the symbol of a spiritual power adverse to the interests of the Lord's kingdom, and a multiplicity of passages may be adduced in which it is obvious that *Moab* has this mystic significance, as we know is the case with Egypt, Babylon, Edom, and other countries spoken of in Scripture.——¶ *Destroy all the children of Sheth.* Heb. *karkor kol benë Shëth,* a clause respecting the purport of which the greatest diversity of opinion prevails. In regard to *karkor*, there is a wavering between the sense of *destroy, lay waste, devastate,* and *unwall* or *demolish the walls* of a fortress or city, although the difference is so slight that it is of little consequence which we adopt. The other term, *Shëth*, is of more difficult solution. The more ancient interpretation is to understand it of the "children of Seth," the son of Adam, which, in this relation, would be equivalent to the whole human race; for the posterity of Cain and Adam's other sons all perished in the deluge, the line of Seth only having been preserved in Noah and his family. Chald. "He shall have dominion over all the sons of men." Gr. "He shall spoil all the sons of Seth." Vulg. "He shall waste all the sons of Seth." So also in substance the Syr. and Arab. The Sam. is peculiar: "He shall transfix the foolish of Moab, and the crown of the head of all the sons of Seth." But to this it may be objected that it does not appear obvious why mankind

18 And Edom [m] shall be a possession, Seir also shall be a possession for his enemies; and Israel shall do valiantly.

m Ps. 60. 8-12.

at large should be named, not after Adam, their first progenitor, nor after Noah, their second, but after Seth, who stands between the two. So also we perceive the harshness of the intimation, that the predicted King of Israel should *destroy* the race of men instead of exercising benignity towards them, and therefore the Syriac and Chaldee soften it to the expression that he shall *subdue* all the sons of Sheth, and *rule over* all the sons of men. But to the whole of this mode of exposition Hengstenberg replies that the context does not allow of it. "Balaam speaks first, v. 17, of Moab; v. 18, of Edom; and shall he here between them abruptly make the whole human race the subject of his prophecy? The parallel, moreover, between Edom and Seir, v. 18, leads us to think that the sons of Seth are nearly, if not entirely, identical with Moab." The Jerus. Targ. translates it "the sons of the East," the Moabites lying east of Judea. Rabbi Nathan says that *Sheth* is the name of a city in the border of Moab, while Grotius apprehends *Sheth* to be the name of some distinguished king among that people. Pool, who is generally judicious, conjectures that "it is the name of some then eminent, but now unknown place or prince in Moab, there being innumerable instances of such places or persons sometime famous, but now utterly lost as to all monuments or remembrances of them." According to Hengstenberg, Verschuir, a German critic, is entitled to the credit of having established the correct interpretation. He suggests that the original שת *Shĕth* is contracted from שאת *sheeth*, a derivative from שאה *shâăh*, which occurs, Lam. 3 : 47, in parallelism with *shĕber*, *destruction*, and is synonymous with שאון *shâon*, *tumult*. The term implies, therefore, a people restless, tumultuous, and addicted by their continual incursions, vexations, and contests, to creating annoyances to others, which he supposes to apply with peculiar pertinency to the Moabites. It is supposed to be a confirmation of this interpretion, that Jeremiah, ch. 48 : 45, where he imitates this passage, exhibits the following parallelism:

"A fire shall come forth out of Heshbon,
And a flame from the midst of Sihon,
And shall devour the corner of Moab,
And the crown of the head of the *tumultuous ones* (שאון *sons of tumult*)."

Additional support would appear to be given by the allusion to this passage in Amos 2 : 2.

"But I will send a fire upon Moab,
And it shall devour the palaces of Kirioth,
And Moab shall die with *tumult*,
With shouting, and with the sound of the trumpet."

As in many other cases, the opinion of Hengstenberg appears to us to be here too confidently expressed, yet in the absence of any assured exposition of our own, we submit it to the reader for what it is worth. The passage is one of those which we think will hereafter receive the light of a clearer elucidation than has yet been shed upon it.

V. 18. *And Edom shall be a possession.* This was primarily fulfilled in David, of whom it is said, 2 Sam. 8 : 14, that "he put garrisons in Edom; throughout all Edom he put garrisons, and all they of Edom became David's servants." So also David himself in two of his psalms, Ps. 60 : 8. 108 : 9, mentions together his conquest of Moab and

19 Out of Jacob shall come he that shall have dominion, and shall destroy him that remaineth of the city.

Edom, as they are also joined together in this prophecy; "Moab is my wash-pot, over Edom will I cast out my shoe." But the ulterior reference of this prophecy to Christ and his victory over a spiritual Edom is evident from Is. 63: 1-6, "Who is this that cometh from Edom, with dyed garments from Bozrah?" etc.——¶ *Seir also shall be a possession for his enemies.* That is, shall be or become a possession of Israel. Seir is the name of the mountain, or mountainous region, where Esau dwelt, Gen. 36 : 7, 8, for which reason the Gr. renders it, "And Esau his enemy shall be a possession (or inheritance)." Edom and Seir are here used on the principle of parallellism so common in Hebrew poetry. They differ not more than Jacob and Israel.——¶ *Israel shall do valiantly.* Heb. *oseh hâyil, shall do valiantness,* or *valiant acts,* a phrase of somewhat ambiguous import, as it is sometimes to be understood of the achievement of valiant deeds in war and the obtaining of victory, 1 Sam. 14 : 48, and sometimes of the acquisition of wealth, as Ezek. 28 : 4. With Gesenius, we see nothing to prevent the embracing of both senses in the present passage. Chald. "And Israel shall be prospered in substance." The fact here asserted of Israel corresponds with the import of his name, as having power and prevailing with God and with men, Gen. 32 : 28, and David, after vanquishing the Edomites, celebrated thus the truth of this promise, Ps. 60 : 12, "Through God we shall do valiantly; for he it is that shall tread down our enemies." But the scope of the prophecy looks to a future period far beyond that of David. "Since Edom here is only to be considered as the representative of the powers of the world hostile to the kingdom of God, and Israel continues to exist in the Church of the New Testament, so the consummation of the fulfilment is to be looked for in the times when the conflict of the kingdom of God with the world will be completed by the victory of the former." —*Hengstenberg.*

V. 19. *Out of Jacob shall come he that shall have dominion.* This is little more than a repetition of the announcement, v. 17, under the figure of the "Star" and the "Sceptre." The verb in the original has no subject expressed, but it is easily supplied from the tenor of the context. It is observable, however, that our translators have here relaxed somewhat of their usual scrupulousness in regard to Italics, according to which they should have rendered:—"Out of Jacob *shall come he* that shall have dominion." The Lord the Messiah is evidently the personage intended, and thus has it been understood from the earliest periods by the Jews. Thus Chald. "And there shall descend one from the house of Jacob and shall destroy him who escapes from the city of the peoples." Targ. Jon. "And a ruler shall rise up out of the house of Jacob." So Sol. Jarchi, "And yet there shall be another ruler out of Jacob, and he shall destroy him that remaineth of the city. Of the King Christ he speaketh thus, of whom it is said (Ps. 72 : 8), 'He shall have dominion from sea to sea.'"——¶ *Shall destroy him that remaineth of the city.* A clause of extreme obscurity. Eusebius says, "Who can this be but the divine *Logos,* the Messiah, foretold by the prophets; who did indeed destroy that which remained of the city, i. e. of the city of Jerusalem, which in the conclusion forfeited and lost its polity and its inhabitants." Calvin gives another

20 And when he looked on Amalek, he took up his parable, and said, Amalek *was* the first of the nations; but his latter end *shall be*, that he perish for ever.

---

turn to the expression :—"He shall destroy him that remaineth of the cities, i. e. all enemies whom he shall find incorrigible." As the closing scenes of prophecy in the Revelation present to view two cities in antagonism with each other, to wit, Babylon and the New Jerusalem, one of which is to be utterly destroyed, it may be that it is to this catastrophe that the Spirit alludes, implying that every lingering inmate should perish in the city's overthrow. It is worthy of notice that Edom, as a prophetical or mystical denomination, has long been understood by the Jews to apply to Rome. Ainsworth cites as parallel the following from the prophet Obadiah, v. 18, "And the house of Jacob shall be a fire, and the house of Joseph a flame, and the house of Esau for stubble, and they shall kindle in them, and devour them ; and there shall not be any remaining of the house of Esau; for the Lord hath spoken it."

V. 20. *When he looked on Amalek.* Heb. "And he looked upon Amalek." That is, looked with the eyes of his mind; fixed his mental vision and regards upon. He saw the Amalekites, as he saw the Star out of Jacob, in prophetic contemplation. The hypothesis of Rosenmuller and others, that there was at the same time an outward beholding of the Amalekites, is destitute of all probability. We have no evidence that any portion of that people was located within the present range of Balaam's vision. But as the outward sight of Israel was effective in eliciting a blessing upon them, so the mental survey of this devoted nation was potent also to prompt a judgment and a curse.——¶ *Amalek* (*was*) *the first of the nations.* Or, Heb. "The beginning of the nations," in allusion at once to the antiquity of their origin and to the pre-eminence which they attained, as may be inferred from what is said of them Gen. 14 : 7, and from their daring assault upon the chosen people during their march in the wilderness, Ex. 17 : 8–16. The sense of *beginning* is specially supported by the contrast of *end* in the next clause. It is not necessary to interpret this expression as implying the absolute priority of the Amalekites among the nations of the earth, but simply that of all the adjacent *heathen* races with which Israel came in contact, no one was more conspicuous than this, which dated back at least to the time of Abraham. We think, too, that *their own estimate of themselves* may be properly included in the import of the phrase, and that Calvin's remark is well-founded :—"Poor and unsatisfactory is the view of some commentators, who think that Amalek is called 'the first of the nations,' because they first took up arms against Israel, and encountered them in order to prevent their advance. Rather is the pride of Amalek indirectly rebuked, because they claimed superiority for themselves over other nations, and this on the score of their antiquity, as if they had been created together with the sun and moon. There is, then, a pointed comparison between this noble origin, and the slaughter which awaited them at their end."——¶ *His latter end* (*shall be*) *that he perish for ever.* Our present version seems to fail in giving the exact sense of the original, although it is extremely difficult, by a merely literal rendering to make the Hebrew intelligible. The term for "perish" is in fact a present participle

21 And he looked on the Kenites[n], and took up his parable, and said, Strong is thy dwelling-place, and thou puttest thy nest in a rock.
22 Nevertheless the Kenite

n Gen. 15. 19.

equivalent to "the perishing one;" so that the true version would be something like this:—"His end shall be (shall reach, extend) to the perishing one." "*The perishing one*," says Hengstenberg, "was, as it were, an ideal to whom, or to whose condition, the end of Amalek reached." We would submit, however, whether the personage be not real rather than ideal, and be not to be recognized in that "Man of Sin," or Antichrist, who is at last to "go into perdition," and with whose doom that of the spiritual Amalek is to be synchronical.

V. 21. *And he looked on the Kenites, etc.* We here again encounter a dubious passage. It is difficult to determine precisely what people is meant by the Kenites. There is mention in the Old Testament of a twofold people by this name, one of which may be termed Canaanitish, the other Midianitish. Of the former, see Gen. 15 : 19, where they are enumerated among the Kenizzites, Hittites, Perizzites, etc., which were afterwards devoted to destruction, although we do not subsequently find the Kenites expressly mentioned. The other branch was intimately associated with the Midianites. Jethro, the father-in-law of Moses, is called, Ex. 3 : 1, "the priest of Midian," and in Judg. 1 : 16, "the Kenite." Of these Kenites a part followed Israel; but the greater part, we may presume, remained among the Midianites and Amalekites, and that to these last the prophecy applies, inasmuch as its tone of announcement is severe and threatening. That portion of the Kenite race with which the family of Jethro is identified, appears always to have lived in friendly relations with Israel, and thus were not regarded as obnoxious to the prophetic curse. It is the Canaanitish tribe of Kenites who fall under the anathema.——¶ *Thou puttest thy nest in a rock.* There is in this and the next verse a striking *paranomasia*, or *play upon words*, which cannot well be preserved in a translation. The Heb. *Kēn*, *Kenite*, is also the word for *nest*, and the Kenites are in effect *nestlers*, as if it were said, "Looking towards the *Nestler*, he said, Although thy *nest* thou hast fixed in a rock," as eagles, ravens, and other birds of prey are wont to do. Under this figurative mode of speech there is perhaps an allusion to their fixing their strong habitations among the Amalekites, with whom they appear to have dwelt, 1 Sam. 15 : 6, "And Saul said unto the Kenites, Go, depart, get you down from among the Amalekites, lest I destroy you with them," etc. A designed analogy is also traced by commentators between this passage and the following paragraph from the prophet Obadiah, vs. 3, 4, "The pride of thine heart hath deceived thee, thou that dwellest in the clefts of the rock, whose habitation is high; that saith in his heart, Who shall bring me down to the ground? Though thou exalt thyself as the eagle, and though thou set thy nest among the stars, thence will I bring thee down, saith the Lord."

V. 22. *Nevertheless the Kenite shall be wasted, etc.* Heb. *Kain*, a word varying slightly from the original as it occurs elsewhere in this connection, but probably rendered correctly, and designating the name of the founder of the Kenites. This name is employed to denote the nation his descendants. This people appear to have thought, by reason of

shall be wasted until Asshur
shall carry thee away captive.
23 And he took up his parable, and said, Alas, who [o] shall
live when God doeth this!
24 And ships [p] *shall come*

o Mal. 3. 2. p Dan. 11. 30.

---

their high and scarcely accessible dwelling-place, they were secure from every danger. The Spirit of prophecy here grants them the distinction of which they boast, but assures them that it will not be sufficient to ward off from them the doom which their hostility against Israel, the people of the Lord, would bring upon them. This doom is, that they shall be gradually wasted, and finally carried captive to Babylon by the Assyrians. Their lot, in this respect, seems to have been milder than that of Amalek, as that people was to be utterly destroyed, whereas the Kenites were to be carried captive. That such was their fate there is no reason to doubt, as we find some of them mentioned among the Jews after their return from captivity, 1 Chron. 2:55. Ashur, in this connection, is equivalent to Assyrians.

V. 23. *Alas, who shall live when God doeth this?* Heb. "When God putteth or disposeth this." The general idea is plainly that of extreme distress and tribulation. Who, amidst the impending general destruction, shall preserve his life? Who shall be accounted worthy to escape? Chald. "Woe to the sinners who shall live when God doeth these things." It would be a momentous crisis in human affairs, and as the period to which this train of prophecies reaches is that of the grand consummation mentioned by our Lord in the Gospels, therefore his words come into striking parallelism with those of Balaam:—Mat. 24:21, 22, "For then shall be great tribulation, such as was not since the beginning of the world to this time, no, nor ever shall be. And except those days should be shortened, there should no flesh be saved: but for the elect's sake those days shall be shortened."

V. 24. *And ships (shall come) from the coast of Chittim, etc.* Heb. "From the hand of Chittim," i. e. from the side. Expositors have gone into considerable diversity of opinion relative to the people denominated *Chittim*, but as it would involve us in extended ethnographical discussion to follow them in their various researches, we shall content ourselves with stating what we conceive the most probable general conclusion, viz. that Chittim is a name of large signification, similar to Levant, applied to the islands and coasts of the Mediterranean, in a loose sense, without definitely fixing the particular part. Chittim was the son of Javan, who was one of the sons of Japhet, Gen. 10:5. From him descended a people who inhabited Greece, or "the isles of the Gentiles," Gen. 10:5, from whence a colony was transplanted into Italy. The term Chittim, therefore, sometimes denotes Greece in a large sense, especially as including Macedonia, 1 Mac. 1:1 and 3:5, and sometimes Italy, Dan. 11:30, whence the Vulg. here renders by "Romanos," *Romans*. The countries beyond the seas were not so well known to the Israelites as to enable them clearly to distinguish them, and therefore the name primarily applied to Greece, and also to the island of Cyprus, is occasionally transferred to Italy. In the present passage we see no valid reason to prevent our adopting both senses, as each nation successively acted its part in fulfilling the terms of the

from the coast of Chittim, and shall afflict [q] Asshur, and shall afflict Eber [r], and he also shall perish for ever.

q Gen. 10. 4.

r Gen. 10. 21, 25.

prophecy. Indeed, we may sum up the drift of the oracles here given, vs. 23, 24, in the following compendious paraphrase:—How wondrous and amazing will be the revolutions, desolations, and afflictions that shall mark the succession of worldly empires, till they shall all, one after another, pass away in their turn, and give place to the one spiritual, universal, and eternal kingdom of the Messiah, the divine King of Israel! As the Assyrian and Persian monarchies shall first domineer over a great part of the known world, leading into captivity God's own people the Israelites; so shall there afterward arise from the descendants of Japhet, by Chittim the son of Javan, a second monarchy, viz. that of the Greeks or Macedonians under Alexander, that shall completely break the Persian or Babylonian power. From the same source, the race of Chittim, by colonies transplanted by ships to Italy, shall arise still another monarchy, the Roman, which shall conquer all before it, lay waste the country of the Israelites or Hebrews, and drive them into a final dispersion. Yet eventually shall this last and most formidable monarchy be dissolved, Rome itself with all its idolatry, pomp, and superstition, be destroyed, and thus a way made for spreading the religion, and establishing the kingdom of the Messiah over all kindreds, and nations, and tongues.—In these few verses is condensed the substance of Daniel's predictions of the four great empires and their successor, the spiritual kingdom of the Lord, which was to supersede them all. ——¶ *And shall afflict Ashur.* Ashur, according to general usage, denotes the descendants of Ashur, or the Assyrians. The prophecy was fulfilled primarily in the conquest of Alexander, who overthrew the Persian empire that then held in subjection the Chaldeans and Assyrians.——¶ *And shall afflict Eber.* This, like Ashur, is no doubt to be understood as a collective name for the posterity of Eber (or Heber), of whom it is said, Gen. 10 : 21, that "Shem was the father of all the children of Eber," and as Abraham was directly descended from Eber, and in him the nation of Israel, so we gather that the power denoted by Chittim should oppress and afflict the Jews, which was done by the Seleucidæ, the successors of Alexander, and especially by Antiochus Epiphanes, and also by the Romans, who not only subdued and oppressed them, but eventually "took away their place and nation," and dispersed them over the face of the earth. As the intimation in this oracle is of rather a sinister import as compared with the usual style of blessing which Balaam is prompted to employ towards the chosen people, there seems to be a designed change of terms that shall serve to discriminate between the fortunes of the literal and the spiritual Israel. The spiritual Israel, or the church, is never called "Eber," but generally "Israel" or "Jacob," and here the spirit of prophecy has probably designed to teach us that a destiny was predicated of the Jews as a nation, which would not hold good of the church which they typically represented.——¶ *And he also shall perish forever.* The phraseology here is the same with that in the final clause of v. 20, on which we have already remarked. The original has nothing to answer to "forever," and the undoubted import is that of some subject, some "perishing one," entirely independent of that which goes

25 And Balaam rose up, and went and returned to his place: and Balak also went his way.

---

before, but with which that is in some way compared, or to be associated. He or they shall perish, even as shall the perishing one. The allusion is to some devoted power, some power emphatically doomed, which though wholly unknown to Balaam, was well known to the spirit of prophecy speaking through him, and which, in our view, is no other than the Man of Sin, or the Antichrist of the last times. "Thus Balaam, as he began with the blessing of Israel, endeth with the destruction of their enemies; God by his mouth confirming the promises made unto Abraham and to his seed forever, the accomplishment of all which is in Christ."—*Ainsworth.*

V. 25. *And Balaam rose up, and went and returned to his place.* There is an apparent contradiction between this passage, which seems to say that Balaam, after fulfilling his mission, immediately, and without tarrying on the road, returned and reached his home in safety, and Num. 31 : 8, 16 (comp. Josh. 13 : 22), according to which Balaam was killed by the Israelites in the war which they undertook against the Midianites, as a righteous punishment for the counsel given to that people with a view to lead Israel into sin. In the solution of this difficulty, which has been long since remarked, some have supposed that Balaam returned home, but made a second journey to the Midianites, though it is no easy matter to find sufficient time for this double journey. A far preferable mode of reconciling the apparent discrepancy is to understand the words in an *inchoative* sense, implying that he started with the *purpose* of returning home, but was detained by the Midianites. For instances of this phraseology see Ex. 8 : 18. Num. 14 : 40. This construction is favored by the fact that the original *shoob* properly signifies *to turn from, to turn back,* while the reaching the object aimed at is not included in the meaning of the word itself. So in like manner, Gen. 18 : 33, "And the Lord went his way as soon as he had left communing with Abraham; and Abraham returned back to his place," where not so much the *arrival* as the *direction* is meant; he set out on his return. They parted each one his own way. So here also the parallelism leads us to suppose that not the *end*, but the *direction*, the *course*, is intended. Whether he *reached* the end of his journey or not, is indifferent to the object which the inspired historian had in view in relating the incidents. He could let him journey without troubling himself how it fared with him, and what he did further. This is intimated in the sequel quite incidentally. The writer began with telling how Balak had sent for the prophet in order to destroy Israel, and he closes his narrative with simply telling how the parting took place without the object being attained.

CHAPTER XXV.

The Israelites, at their last Station in the Wilderness, seduced to Idolatry with the Moabites and Midianites by the Counsel of Balaam.

We have seen thus far the fruitless attempts of Balak and Balaam to curse the people whom God had blessed. Their attempts had recoiled upon their own heads, and their disappointment had not only resulted in deep chagrin on the part of each, but also in mutual dissatisfaction with each other. Balak had obtained no aid against the people

CHAPTER XXV.

AND Israel abode in Shittim [a], and the people began to commit whoredom [b] with the daughters of Moab.

a c. 33. 49. Mic. 6. 5.

b c. 31. 16. 1 Cor. 10. 8.

whom he feared, and Balaam had lost the wealth and honors which he coveted. The failure in this respect he would fain make good if possible. He saw that the favor of God was with the Israelites, and he knew that while they were possessed of it they would be invincible. He perceived that the only way to prevail against them was to cause them to forfeit that favor. If he could lead them to sin against the Lord, then they would be deserted by their strength, Balak would be able to overcome them, and he should reap his reward. With diabolical malice and cunning, therefore, he puts Balak and his people upon a plan for corrupting them, and the success of the scheme and its consequences are detailed in the course of the present chapter.

V. 1. *And Israel abode in Shittim.* This was the name given to some part of the tract called "the plains of Moab," lying on the borders of the Jordan where they were now encamped. It is termed *Abel-Shittim*, ch. 33 : 48, 49, and as "Abel" signifies *mourning*, it is probable the name was given it from the lamentation made over the transgressors who were cut off for their grievous offence at this place. It is no unusual thing with the Hebrew writers to omit the first part of compound names. Thus Judg. 3 : 3, *Hermon* for *Baal-Hermon;* 1 Chron. 4 : 29, *Tholad* for *Ethtolad;* Josh. 19 : 4, *Nimrim* for *Beth-Nimrim;* Ps. 66 : 3, *Salem* for *Jerusalem.* The original *Shittim* means *Acacias*, probably from their growing abundantly in this vicinity, and Keil (on Jos. 2 : 1) renders *Abel-Shittim* by *Acacia-Meadows.* Its true location appears to have been in the Arboth-Moab (*plains of Moab*) at the foot of the mountainous range of Abarim, and immediately under Nebo opposite to Jericho. Hence it is to be looked for near the point at which the Wady Hesban enters the plains of Moab, probably to the south of this Wady. According to Josephus, the town of Abila was afterwards built on the site previously occupied by Shittim, in a country abounding with date-bearing trees, sixty stadia from the Jordan. In this place Israel abode (Heb. "sat") until after the death of Moses, consequently until every thing related in the book of Deuteronomy had transpired. It was from hence, too, that Joshua took his departure, Josh. 2 : 1, when the host passed over to Gilgal. Of this period of their history the chosen people are reminded by the prophet, Mic. 6 : 5, "O my people, remember now what Balak king of Moab consulted, and what Balaam the son of Beor answered him from Shittim unto Gilgal; that ye may know the righteousness of the Lord."——¶ *The people began to commit whoredom with the daughters of Moab.* Or, Heb. "Profaned, or profanely began, etc." The idea of *profanation* is undoubtedly included in the original term. The prompters to this iniquity are said to have been "the daughters of Moab," but to them are to be added the daughters of Midian, as appears from vs. 6, 17, 18. The sin here predicted of "the people" is not to be understood of the whole body of them, but only of a portion, and these all met with a condign punishment, as we learn from the sequel. The iniquity in which Israel now became involved was plainly instigated by Balaam, of

2 And[c] they called the people unto the sacrifices of their gods: and the people did eat, and bowed[d] down to their gods.

c Ex. 34. 15, 16. d Ex. 20. 5.

whom it is said, Rev. 2:14, "But I have a few things against thee, because thou hast there them that hold the doctrine of Balaam, who taught Balak to cast a stumbling-block before the children of Israel, to eat things sacrificed unto idols, and to commit fornication." It was the more aggravated from the fact that the Lord had borne with them so long and had conducted them so far, as they were now in fact just upon the borders and in full sight of the land of promise. The lapses of Christians as they near the end of their pilgrimage and are in full view of heaven, have a peculiar enormity, which should cause them to be shunned with the most profound abhorrence and awful dread.

V. 2. *And they called the people, etc.* As the verb in the original is here in the feminine, it implies that the *calling* or *invitation* was given by these daughters of Moab, who no doubt exerted various fascinating arts to inveigle the sons of the covenant into their snares. ——¶ *Unto the sacrifices of their gods.* Or, Heb. "Of their god." Gr. and Chald. "Of their idols," meaning Baal-Peor, as we learn from v. 3. Baal-Peor is probably the localized title of a general heathen deity worshipped in various ancient countries, but here deriving his appellation from the name of a mountain, mentioned ch. 23:28, just as Jupiter, among the Greeks, was called *Jupiter Olympus*, from the name of a mountain specially dedicated to him. He was worshipped with the most obscene and revolting rites, so that the learned have conceived him to be identical with the Priapus of the Greeks and Romans. Whether this were so or not is not very important, as the moral bearings of this transaction claim our first attention. It evinces clearly that our most formidable enemies are evermore within and not without us. Lusts inwardly cherished are more to be dreaded than external foes; for here we perceive that what the curse of Balaam could not effect was brought about by their own corruptions. The charms and incantations of infernal magic do not work so much mischief as the seductive arts and blandishments of siren females, who beguile to idolatry by yielding to licentiousness. Still the weight of our condemnation must fall upon the unprincipled fathers, brothers and husbands of the miserable women who had doubtless been pressed in the first instance, against their better instincts, into complicity with this nefarious scheme.——¶ *And the people did eat, and bowed down to their gods.* The act of eating in common carries with it an implication of the parties being closely conjoined together, and when this is done over the sacrifices offered in religious worship, it implies a unanimity of views and feelings which could not be supposed to exist, without downright profanation, between the worshippers of the true God and the votaries of idols. Now against this aggravated iniquity the chosen people had been especially warned on a former occasion. Ex. 34:12–16. "Take heed to thyself lest thou make a covenant with the inhabitants of the land whither thou goest, lest it be for a snare in the midst of thee; but ye shall destroy their altars, break their images, and cut down their groves: for thou shalt worship no other god: for the Lord, whose name is Jealous, is a jealous God: lest thou make a covenant with the inhabitants

3 And Israel joined [e] himself unto Baal-peor: and the anger of the LORD was kindled against Israel.

e Josh. 22. 17. Ps. 106. 28, 29. Hos. 9 10.

---

of the land, and they go a whoring after their gods, and do sacrifice unto their gods, and one call thee, and thou eat of his sacrifice; and thou take of their daughters unto thy sons, and their daughters go a whoring after their gods, and make thy sons go a whoring after their gods." This strain of prohibition would seem to have been intended for just such a case as the present, yet it is grossly disregarded, and the fearful moral guilt of a mixed, polluted, and prostituted worship incurred. The subject will be better appreciated by adducing the reasonings of Paul in relation to this species of profanation, 1 Cor. 10:16–21, "The cup of blessing which we bless, is it not the communion of the blood of Christ? the bread which we break, is it not the communion of the body of Christ? For we, being many, are one bread, and one body; for we are all partakers of that one bread. Behold Israel after the flesh; are not they which eat of the sacrifices partakers of the altar? What say I then? that the idol is any thing? or that which is offered in sacrifice to idols is any thing? But I say, that the things which the Gentiles sacrifice, they sacrifice to devils and not to God: and I would not that ye should have fellowship with devils. Ye cannot drink the cup of the Lord, and the cup of devils: ye cannot be partakers of the Lord's table, and of the table of devils." Here the general idea is plainly, that by partaking of the sacrifices offered upon any altar, we do in fact partake of the altar, and by partaking of the altar we own, communicate with, and worship the god of the altar, Mal. 1:7. For as "swearing by the altar" is swearing "by him" whose altar it is, Matt. 23:20, so having communion with the altar is having communion with him whose altar it is. "Bowing down to their gods" is, in effect, uniting in the worship of idols, as "gods" is rendered both in the Gr. and the Chald. The Psalmist, in a significant allusion to this event, says, Ps. 106:28, "They joined themselves also unto Baal-peor, and ate the sacrifices of the dead," so called not only because the idol itself was a dead thing, opposed to the true and living God, but because the sacrifices were offered in honor of some distinguished personage who was deified after death, somewhat after the fashion of the canonization of saints in the Romish Church.

V. 3. *Israel joined himself to Baal-Peor.* Heb. "Was joined, coupled, or yoked." Vulg. "Israel was initiated to Beelphegor." Gr. "Israel was consecrated to Beelphegor." Chald. "Israel was conjoined to the worshippers of Baal-Peor." Syr. and Arab. "Israel cleaved closely to Beel-Pheor." It is probably to this peculiar phrase that Paul alludes, 2 Cor. 6:14, "Be ye not *unequally yoked* with unbelievers." As two kinds of animals were not to be yoked together in ploughing, so neither were Christians and Heathen to be associated in the sacred acts of worship. The expression is highly significant, and as Baal, *lord*, has somewhat of a *marital* import, we recognize an indirect allusion to that holy union into which the Most High had entered with his people, and which they are here accused of violating, and of *joining, coupling,* and *yoking* themselves in impious alliance with his enemies. "Hence, therefore," says Calvin, "this general instruction may be gathered, that when

4 And the LORD said unto Moses, [f] Take all the heads of the people, and hang them up before the LORD against the sun, that the fierce [g] anger of the LORD may be turned away from Israel.

5 And Moses said unto the judges of Israel, Slay [h] ye every

f Deut. 13. 6-9. g Deut. 13. 17. h Ex. 32. 27.

we turn aside from pure religion, we in a manner *connect ourselves* with idols, so as to *coalesce in one body* with them, and conspire to renounce the true God." ——¶ *The anger of the Lord was kindled against Israel.* Thus paralleled in the language of the Psalmist, Ps. 106 : 29, "They provoked him to anger with their inventions; and the plague brake in upon them."

V. 4. *Take all the heads of the people, etc.* It is not entirely clear how this is to be understood. From the wording of our English version it would appear that they regarded the "heads of the people" as denoting the chief actors in the transgression, and that they were the ones who were commanded to be hung. And so the words are construed by a large proportion of commentators, both ancient and modern. But they are capable of another, and perhaps, on the whole, a preferable sense, by which the clause "take all the heads of the people," means to take them for assistants in carrying out the sentence of judgment now enjoined. In this case the word "them" in the next clause refers not to the "heads of the people," but to those who had joined themselves to Baal-Peor. The Hebrew affords abundant examples of similar usage in regard to relatives and antecedents, and the suggestion is evidently favored by the next verse, where the "judges of Israel" appear to be the same persons with the "heads of the people." So also Chald. "Take the princes of the people, sit in judgment, and slay him who shall be worthy of death." The following is the version of Geddes: "Take all the chiefs of the people with thee; and let them slay those men who have worn the badges of Baal-Peor; and hang them up before the Lord until sunsetting." Bp. Patrick, while he thinks the other to be the most natural sense, yet remarks, that "it must be acknowledged that there is a great current of interpreters which runs the other way," and to this current we confess ourselves to belong. ——¶ *Hang them up before the Lord.* Heb. "To or for the Lord;" i. e., as an offering to his just displeasure, as a token of his retributive justice. Gr. "Make a public example of them, for the Lord, against the sun." It is to be understood that the victims were first stoned to death, and then hung up in this open exposed manner, in the light of day, for hanging alive was never practised among the people of Israel. Crucifixion was not a Jewish, but a Roman punishment. Hanging, however, subsequent to stoning, was considered as a special mark of the divine malediction, as appears from Deut. 21 : 23, "He that is hanged is accursed of God," i. e., his being hung is a sign of his being accursed, or, as Jerome remarks (on Gal. 3 : 13), "He was not accursed because he was hanged, but he was hanged because he was accursed."

V. 5. *Slay ye every one his men.* That is, the men under his special jurisdiction, as they were distributed in Ex. 18 : 25. Aben Ezra and Sol. Jarchi understand by the language, that the heads of the people, divided into several courts of judgment, should examine and ascertain who had been guilty

one his men that were joined unto Baal-peor.
6 And, behold, one of the
children of Israel came, and
brought unto his brethren a
Midianitish woman, in the sight
of Moses, and in the sight of all
the congregation of the children
of Israel, who *were* weeping[i] *be-*
fore the door of the tabernacle
of the congregation.
7 And when Phinehas[k] the
son of Eleazar, the son of Aaron
the priest, saw *it*, he rose up
from among the congregation,
and took a javelin in his hand:
8 And he went after the man
of Israel into the tent, and thrust

i Joel 2. 17.

k Ps. 106. 30.

of idolatry, and then put them to death, as here commanded. It is supposed that the judicial system suggested by Jethro was continued all the time they were in the wilderness, and that it was their duty to find out the guilty in their several departments or divisions. This explains the phrase, "Slay ye every one *his* men." They were the men for whom each of the judges were severally, in a sense, responsible from their falling under their supervision.

The Outrage so signally avenged by Phinehas, and his consequent Reward.

V. 6. *Behold, one of the children of Israel came, and brought unto his brethren, etc.* Heb. "Brought near to his brethren;" i. e. brought near in the sight of his brethren. This is the only sense in which she was brought to them, implying a peculiarly open, public, and shameless proceeding on the part of the offenders. It was done not only in the sight of the brethren of the culprit, but of Moses also, and of a large portion of the congregation who were at that time collected at the door of the Tabernacle weeping and mourning over the fearful transgression. It is not improbable, in fact, that the judgment had even then begun, and what must have been the enormity of introducing a paramour, in these circumstances, into an Israelitish tent, in open defiance of every restraint of decency and religion!

V. 8. *He went after the man of Israel into the tent, etc.* Heb. *el hakkubâh, into the recess.* The original word here rendered "tent" is not the term (*ohel*) usually employed for that purpose. Rosenmuller remarks, that it is equivalent to the Arab. *kubbah* or *kobbah*, and with the article *alkobbah*, from which is derived the Spanish *alcoba* and *alcova*, Eng. *alcove*, denoting an interior chamber appropriated to sleeping. Into this retired room the offenders were followed by Phinehas, and both transfixed by a single stroke of his javelin. The way of transgressors is hard, and their end sometimes strikingly awful. Though all are not cut off by the stroke of exemplary justice, yet the close of a sinful and impenitent life must be destruction, whether through the gradual decays of nature, the waste of sickness, or the sudden seizure of death. The act on the part of Phinehas seems to have been prompted by a sudden impulse of holy zeal, which received, indeed, the divine approbation, although it is not to be regarded as a precedent in ordinary cases. Sudden emergencies warrant extraordinary expedients. As a priest, it was not the office of Phinehas to punish crime, but in this instance, while all others held back, he was no doubt moved by a divine inspiration to enter

both of them through, the man of Israel, and the woman through her belly. So the plague was stayed from the children of Israel.

9 And those [l] that died in the plague were twenty and four thousand.

l Deut. 4. 3. 1 Cor. 10. 8.

upon the work of vengeance. "If any private person should in his preposterous zeal take upon himself to punish a similar crime, in vain will he boast of being an imitator of Phinehas, unless he shall be thoroughly assured of the command of God. In order that our zeal may be approved of God, it must be tempered by spiritual prudence, and directed by His authority; in a word, the Holy Spirit must go before, and dictate what is right."—*Calvin.* But while the *act* of Phinehas would be unjustifiable in those who had received no such commission, either from God or man, yet *the spirit from which it proceeded* would be commendable, in whomsoever it were found. We *ought* to be filled with zeal for God's honor. We *ought* to feel indignation against sin. We *ought* to be penetrated with compassion towards those who are seduced into dangerous courses by the evil acts of others. We *ought* to be ready to assist the civil magistrate in the suppression of iniquity.——¶ *So the plague was stayed from the children of Israel.* Heb. *hammaggëphâh, the stroke.* This is usually understood to denote a pestilence which the Lord had caused to break forth on this occasion, and to rage with destructive violence. But as nothing has been previously said of any such pestilence, and as the term is elsewhere applied to a slaughter by the sword, 1 Sam. 4:17, we see no good reason to doubt that it is here used in reference to the execution of the judgment commanded above, vs. 4, 5, which now reached its climax in the fearful act of Phinehas towards the culprits slain by his hand. To this event in the history the Psalmist alludes as follows, Ps. 106: 29, 30, "Thus they provoked him to anger with their inventions: and the plague brake in upon them. Then stood up Phinehas, and executed judgment: and so the plague was stayed." The original word for "plague" is here the same with that before us, and we see no evidence of any other "plague" than that of the slaughter recorded by the historian.

V. 9. *Twenty and four thousand.* The number here specified affords a fearful indication of the ravages of the divine judgment, but it has greatly tasked the ingenuity of commentators to reconcile with it the statement of Paul, 1 Cor. 10:8, "Neither let us commit fornication, as some of them committed, and fell in one day *three and twenty thousand.*" The solution usually given depends upon the assumed distinction between the number of those who fell by the plague and those who fell by the sword of the judges. Moses, it is supposed, in the 24,000, comprehends all that perished both by the sword and the pestilence, whereas Paul refers only to the latter. But as we see no evidence of the occurrence of any plague on this occasion, so we are compelled to reject this explanation. In our view Paul had no design to specify the precise number. He had in his mind the fact of a tremendous judgment inflicted on the Israelites for a particular sin, but whether it were exactly 23,000 or 24,000 he might not have recollected at the moment, and as the precise specification was not important for the moral lesson which it was calculated to teach, instead of arresting his pen and turning to the inspired volume to certify himself on the

10 And the LORD spake unto
Moses, saying,
11 Phinehas the son of Eleazar, the son of Aaron the priest, hath turned [m] my wrath away from the children of Israel, (while he was zealous for my sake among them,) that I consumed not the children of Israel in my jealousy [n].
12 Wherefore say, Behold, I give unto him [o] my covenant of peace:
13 And he shall have it, and his seed after him, *even* the cov-

m Ps. 106. 23. John 3. 36.

n Ex. 20. 5. Deut. 32. 16, 21. 1 K. 14. 22. Ps. 78. 58. Ezek. 16. 38. Zeph. 1. 18. 3. 8. o Mal. 2. 4, 5.

point, he set down the number of 23,000 as being at least the number slain, without assuming to give it with absolute accuracy. Now if the assertion of Moses was true, that 24,000 perished on this occasion, the assertion of Paul is likewise true that 23,000 perished, and the assertion of the less number does not deny that of the greater. As, then, it cannot be shown that there is any thing intrinsically false in Paul's statement, why not be content with it as it stands without striving to bring it to a perfect tally with Moses?—especially when the only ground on which this is attempted to be done is a gratuitous assumption utterly incapable of proof? We are persuaded it will be forever a futile attempt to maintain that the Holy Spirit, speaking through Paul, *designed* to state the *exact* number of the victims who fell under the judgment now visited upon the people, for this would bring him in conflict with his own declaration made through the Old Testament writer.

Vs. 10, 11. *The Lord spake unto Moses, etc.* The Most High here announces to Moses that it was his pleasure that the whole nation should know how much they owed to the heroic act of retribution—this courageous and well-timed zeal—on the part of Phinehas, inasmuch as by vindicating the divine honor he had staid the hand of justice from striking and consuming the whole mass of a congregation so corrupted.——¶ *While he was zealous for my sake among them.* Or, Heb. "He was jealous with my jealousy." See Note on ch. 5:14, where the import of the original term for "zeal" is fully unfolded. The meaning is, that in thus vindicating the divine honor he showed that he could no more tolerate this forbidden connection of the chosen people with an idolatrous race than a man would suffer his wife to prostitute herself to strangers. In this sense the Lord himself is said to be "jealous," Ex. 20:5. The term conveys an allusion to the conjugal relation which the Lord sustained to his people.

V. 12. *Behold, I give unto him my covenant of peace.* Heb. *berithi shâlom*, implying an abundant prosperity, comprising multitudinous forms of happiness and comfort. Such is the import of the original term for "peace;" so that this promised "covenant of peace" is nothing more than the divine stipulation that his lot should be crowned with a fulness of blessings, both temporal and spiritual. So the Lord says of Levi, Mal. 2:5, "My covenant was with him of life and peace; and I gave them to him for the fear wherewith he feared me, etc." The Targ. Jon. renders thus: "Behold, I decree unto him my covenant of peace, and I will make him the messenger of my covenant, and he shall live forever to preach the Gospel of redemption in the end of days."

V. 13. *Even the covenant of an everlasting priesthood.* As if he should say,

enant of an [p] everlasting priesthood; because he was [q] zealous for his God, and made an [r] atonement for the children of Israel.

14 Now the name of the Israelite that was slain, *even* that was slain with the Midianitish woman, *was* Zimri the son of Salu, a prince of a chief house among the Simeonites.

15 And the name of the Midianitish woman that was slain *was* Cozbi, the daughter of Zur [s]; he *was* head over a people, *and* of a chief house in Midian.

p Ex. 40. 15. q Ps. 69. 9. r Heb. 2. 17. s c. 31. 8. Josh. 13. 21.

Let Phinehas know that by way of reward for so noble and pure an example of religious zeal, a zeal not prompted by private passion, by hasty, uncharitable, or ungovernable resentment, but by a solid and earnest regard to the honor of the divine majesty, the love of truth, and the highest welfare of his brethren, his family shall, in direct line from him, be honored with the privilege of a long succession in the high-priesthood; and though this succession may be temporarily interrupted, yet it shall return again to his posterity, and remain with them even to the passing away of the dispensation now instituted. He was indeed already entitled to the office, and had actually held it since the death of Aaron; but it is now confirmed to him as a birthright, and ordained to run down in his family, and doubtless in the eldest son, instead of being transferred to some other branch of Aaron's descendants. The interruption spoken of occurred when the priesthood passed from the family of Phinehas to that of Ithamar, where it remained about 150 years, Eli being one of his descendants, but it was restored again in the person of Zadok, 1 Chron. 6 : 50, and thence continued in the family, as far as is known, down to the close of the Jewish economy. The "everlasting priesthood" belongs properly to Christ, and it would seem that the promise made to Phinehas, as a type of Christ, glides imperceptibly into that which receives its fulfilment in him who was made "a priest forever after the order of Melchisedek."——¶ *And made an atonement for the children of Israel.* Heb. "Atoned upon (or for) the children of Israel." That is, made reconciliation, pacified, propitiated. Thus Moses, in addressing the Israelites after the great crime which they had committed in worshipping the golden calf, says, Ex. 32 : 30, 32, "Ye have sinned a great sin; and now I will go up unto the Lord; peradventure *I will make an atonement for* your sins." So again, in respect to the rebellion of Korah, Num. 16 : 46, 48, "And Aaron took as Moses commanded, and ran into the midst of the congregation; and, behold, the plague was begun among the people: and he put on incense, and *made an atonement* for the people. And he stood between the dead and the living; and the plague was stayed." So the Psalmist makes honorary mention of this act of Phinehas, Ps. 106 : 30, "Then stood up Phinehas and executed judgment, and so the plague was stayed."

Vs. 14, 15. *Now the name of the Israelite, etc.* The names and the pedigree of the offending parties are here particularly cited, both in order to consign their character to deeper infamy in after ages, and to do higher honor to Phinehas, who, in this transaction, regarded not the rank or dignity of the transgressors. These, it appears, were of high condition on both sides, yet

16 And the LORD spake unto Moses, saying,
17 Vex [t] the Midianites, and smite them:
18 For they vex you [u] with their wiles, wherewith they have beguiled you, in the matter of Peor, and in the matter of Cozbi, the daughter of a prince of Midian, their sister, which was slain [v] in the day of the plague, for Peor's sake.

CHAPTER XXVI.

AND it came to pass, after the plague, that the LORD spake

t c. 31. 2. u c. 31. 16. Rev. 2. 14. v ver. 8.

---

their standing gave them no exemption when the stroke of retribution fell. The passage before us is a testimony that the Lord would give publicity to the sin as a warning to others, that the most exalted sphere in life will protect no one from the just consequences of his crimes.

V. 17. *Vex the Midianites and smite them.* Heb. "Straighten, distress." Gr. "Treat as enemies." The divine justice having visited deserved punishment upon his own people, now decrees vengeance against his and their enemies, although the actual execution of it was delayed till after the numbering of the people and the occurrence of various other events recorded in the next five chapters. The infliction of this vengeance was to be the last public act of Moses, as it is said, ch. 31:2, "Avenge the children of Israel of the Midianites; afterward shalt thou be gathered unto thy people." Judgment often begins at the house of God, but it does not end there. Accordingly the Lord says, by the prophet, Jer. 25:29, "For lo, I begin to bring evil on the city which is called by my name, and should ye be utterly unpunished? Ye shall not be unpunished: for I will call for a sword upon all the inhabitants of the earth, saith the Lord of hosts." The judgment is here denounced against the Midianites rather than against the Moabites, because the Midianites, in this particular instance, seem to have taken the lead in the conspiracy suggested by Balaam. Balak had turned away the wicked prophet in disgrace, but the Midianites, in all probability, retained him in the midst of them, as it was amongst them that he was slain, ch. 31:8. We cannot mistake in accounting those our greatest enemies who would entice us into sin, and though we are never to indulge in a vindictive spirit, yet we may be and ought to be moved by a righteous indignation against whatever tends to effect a separation between us and our heavenly Father.

V. 18. *For they vex you with their wiles, etc.* Heb. "Distress you," the same word occurring in the preceding verse, but denoting here, not war, but a resort to the arts of subtlety and deceit. This was a peculiar source of vexation to them, whence Henry well remarks, that "whatever draws us to sin should be a vexation to us, as a thorn in the flesh."

CHAPTER XXVI.

A new Census taken in the Plains of Moab.

V. 1. *It came to pass after the plague, etc.* After the *slaughter* of the 24,000 who fell by the sword of the judges as stated ch. 25:9, as this is the undoubted sense of the word "plague" in this connection. We may properly recog-

unto Moses, and unto Eleazar the
son of Aaron the priest, saying,
2 Take [a] the sum of all the
congregation of the children of
Israel, from twenty years old
and upward, throughout their

a Ex. 30. 12. 38. 25, 26. c. 1. 2, 3.

father's house, all that are able
to go to war in Israel.
3 And Moses and Eleazar
the priest spake with them in
the plains [b] of Moab, by Jordan
near Jericho, saying,

b ver. 63. c. 35. 1.

---

nize a moral as well as a historical significancy in the command to number the people afresh. It was a token of the Lord's special regard for those who survived and had cleaved to him in the midst of a wide-spread defection. Deut. 4 : 3, 4, "Your eyes have seen what the Lord did because of Baal-peor: for all the men that followed Baal-peor, the Lord thy God hath destroyed them from among you. But ye that did cleave unto the Lord your God are alive every one of you this day." The Hebrew writers, in a somewhat pious vein, illustrate it "by the similitude of a shepherd, who, when a wolf has gotten among his flock, and worried some of them, he counteth them to know the number of those that are left." Again, "As when they came out of Egypt and were delivered to Moses, they were delivered to him by tale (Ex. 38 : 26), so now when Moses was ready to die, and to deliver his flock again, he delivered them by tale."—*Sol. Jarchi.* A farther reason for the measure may be found in the divine determination to make good the promise to Abraham, to multiply his seed as the stars of heaven, notwithstanding it might seem to be countervailed by the fearful diminution in their numbers caused by the sweeping judgments which their sins had incurred. "This was the reason why the people was numbered immediately after the plague, in order that it might be more conspicuous that God had marvellously provided lest any diminution should appear after the recent loss of so many men."—*Calvin.* The whole generation existing thirty-eight years before, with the exception only of Caleb and Joshua, had been wasted away, and as the promised land was now about to be distributed to their descendants, which would be facilitated by a new census, one is accordingly ordered. The matter was intrusted to the charge of Eleazar, who was now, since the death of Aaron, high priest. As Aaron had performed this office in conjunction with Moses on a former occasion, ch. 1 : 3, so Eleazar is called to do it now. He also united with Joshua afterwards, Josh. 14 : 1, in dividing the land among the people.

V. 2. *Take the sum of all the congregation.* Heb. "Take the head." On the import of this expression see Note on ch. 1 : 2. Chald. "Take the count, or the sum." This was the third census of which we have an account in the sacred narrative. The particular terms occurring in this verse will be found explained in the Notes on ch. 1 : 2, 3.

V. 3. *Moses and Eleazar the priest spake with them, etc.* The purport of this and the following verse, particularly as expressed in the original, is not very clear, since the command given in v. 2 to Eleazar, appears here to be given to some other party intimated by "them," which, as it stands, is of very indefinite reference. The clue to the sense would seem to be given by the Targ. Jon. "Spake unto the princes, and said to number them (the people)." According to this the order was given

4 *Take the sum of the people*,
from twenty years old and upward; as the LORD commanded
Moses, and the children of Israel, which went forth out of
the land of Egypt.
5 Reuben[c], the eldest son of
Israel: the children of Reuben;
Hanoch, *of whom cometh* the
family of the Hanochites: of
Pallu, the family of the Palluites:
6 Of Hesron, the family of
the Hesronites: of Carmi, the
family of the Carmites.
7 These *are* the families of
the Reubenites; and they that
were numbered of them were
forty and three thousand and
seven hundred and thirty.
8 And the sons of Pallu;
Eliab.
9 And the sons of Eliab;
Nemuel, and Dathan, and Abiram. This *is that* Dathan and
Abiram *which were* famous in
the congregation, who strove[d]
against Moses and against Aaron
in the company of Korah, when
they strove against the LORD.
10 And the earth opened her
mouth, and swallowed them up
together with Korah, when that
company died, what time the fire

c Gen. 46. 8.

d c. 16. 1, etc.

to the chiefs of the tribes, who acted as assistants to Moses and Aaron in the former numbering.

V. 4. (*Take the sum of the people*). These words are wanting in the original, but are evidently implied in the general tenor of the command, and therefore properly inserted.——¶ *As the Lord commanded, etc.* Implying that they were now to proceed according to the directions given them by the Lord himself on the occasion of the former numbering, ch. 1 : 1–4. This favors the construction above suggested.

V. 5–7. *Reuben, the eldest son of Israel, etc.* The enumeration begins with Reuben the eldest-born, as it did also in the former instance, ch. 1 : 5, 20. Four families are here enumerated to Reuben, as we read also Gen. 46 : 9. 1 Chron. 5 : 3.——¶ *Hanoch (of whom cometh) the Hanochites.* Heb. "The Hanochite," sing. for the plur. as elsewhere throughout this chapter. The phraseology of the original identifies the descendants of Hanoch with Hanoch himself, which is according to a frequent Scriptural usage. So likewise with the other three families of this tribe. The census now made shows that the tribe had decreased by near three thousand men. But whole households had perished in the preceding judgments, as is evident from v. 9. ——¶ *Forty and three thousand and seven hundred and thirty.* The Reubenites, at the last numbering, gave a total of 46,500; their decrease consequently, up to this time, was 2,720, which may be accounted for, at least in part, by the ravages of the divine judgment in consequence of Korah's conspiracy.

V. 9. *Famous in the congregation.* Heb. "The called, the summoned." See Note on ch. 1 : 16, where the term is fully explained. Comp. also ch. 16 : 1, 2, etc.——¶ *Strove.* Gr. "Made insurrection against." Chald. "Gathered themselves together against." These strove against Moses and Aaron in the striving of Korah's company against the Lord.

V. 10. *Together with Korah.* These words, taken as they read, would seem to import that Korah was swallowed up

devoured two hundred and fifty
men; and [e] they became a sign.
11 Notwithstanding, the children[f] of Korah died not.
12 The sons of Simeon after
their families: of Nemuel[g], the
family of the Nemuelites: of
Jamin, the family of the Jaminites: of Jachin[h], the family of
the Jachinites:
13 Of Zerah[i], the family of
the Zarhites: of Shaul, the family of the Shaulites.

e c. 16. 38. 1 Cor. 10. 6. 2 Pet. 2. 6. f Ex. 6. 24. g Gen. 46. 10. Ex. 6. 16. *Jemuel.* h 1 Chr. 4. 24. *Jarib.* i Gen. 46. 10. *Zohar.*

with Dathan and Abiram—contrary to the conclusion stated in our Note on ch. 16:32. But it is palpable that the language of the verse before us is somewhat confused in the present rendering, as it is not clear whether the sacred writer meant to say that Korah's company perished by the opening of the earth, or by the fire; and therefore we do not hesitate, with Patrick, Poole, Geddes, Boothroyd, and others, to propose another translation conformed substantially to the Samaritan, which reads thus: "And the earth opened its mouth, and swallowed them up, and when this company died a fire devoured Korah and two hundred and fifty men." The original will admit, we think without violence, of the following version: "And the earth opened her mouth, and swallowed them up (i. e., Dathan and Abiram with their immediate associates, ch. 16:32), and as for Korah (he perished) in the dying of that company, at the time the fire devoured two hundred and fifty men." This is not a forced construction, and it agrees well with Ps. 106:17, 18, "The earth opened and swallowed up Dathan, and covered the company of Abiram." Here it is plain that Korah is not included. Josephus says to the same effect, "This fire was very bright, and had a terrible flame, such as is kindled at the command of God; by whose irruption on them, all the company, *and Korah himself*, were destroyed." But whichever be the construction adopted, the moral lesson conveyed by the event is the same, and the allusion is here made to these conspirators to affix a new brand of infamy to their names. ——¶ *And they became a sign.* Heb. "They became for an ensign, or banner." That is, they were made an example of; they were made a monument of the Lord's righteous displeasure against those who would wrong his ministers, and a warning to all posterity not to walk in their steps. The fittest commentary on the words is the language of Paul, 1 Cor. 10:11, "Now all these things happened unto them for ensamples; and they are written for our admonition upon whom the ends of the world are come." What is here said of the persons of the rebels is in ch. 16:38, 40, said of their censors, that they were to be "a sign unto the children of Israel," and "a memorial that no stranger, which is not of the seed of Aaron, come near to offer incense before the Lord; that he be not as Korah and his company, etc."

V. 11. *The children of Korah died not.* His immediate sons were Assir, Elkanah, and Abiasaph, Ex. 6:24. These with their posterity lived and served officially in Israel, as their genealogy is reckoned, 1 Chron. 6:22, 28, and frequent honorable mention is made of the sons of Korah, both in the Psalms and elsewhere. It is reasonably to be supposed that they were not with Korah, when he met his fate, being engaged in ministering at the Tabernacle,

14 These *are* the families of the Simeonites, twenty and two thousand and two hundred.

15 The children of Gad, after their families: of Zephon[k], the family of the Zephonites: of Haggi, the family of the Haggites: of Shuni, the family of the Shunites;

16 Of Ozni[l], the family of the Oznites: of Eri, the family of the Erites:

17 Of Arod[m], the family of the Arodites: of Areli, the family of the Arelites.

18 These *are* the families of the children of Gad, according to those that were numbered of them, forty thousand and five hundred.

19 The sons of Judah[n] *were* Er and Onan: and Er and Onan died in the land of Canaan.

20 And the sons of Judah after their families were: of Shelah, the family of the Shelanites; of Pharez, the family of the Pharzites: of Zerah, the family of the Zarhites.

21 And the sons of Pharez were; of Hezron, the family of the Hezronites: of Hamul, the family of the Hamulites.

22 These *are* the families of Judah according to those that were numbered of them, threescore and sixteen thousand and five hundred.

23 *Of* the sons of Issachar after their families: *of* Tola, the family of the Tolaites: of Pua, the family of the Punites.

24 Of Jashub, the family of the Jashubites: of Shimron, the family of the Shimronites.

25 These *are* the families of Issachar according to those that were numbered of them, threescore and four thousand and three hundred.

26 *Of* the sons of Zebulun[p] after their families: of Sered, the family of the Sardites: of Elon, the family of the Elonites: of Jahleel, the family of the Jahleelites.

27 These *are* the families of the Zebulunites, according to those that were numbered of them, threescore thousand and five hundred.

28 The sons of Joseph[q], after their families, *were* Manasseh and Ephraim.

29 Of the sons of Manasseh: of[r] Machir, the family of the Machirites: and Machir begat Gilead: of Gilead *come* the family of the Gileadites.

k Gen. 46. 16. *Ziphion.* l Gen. 46. 16. *Ezbon.* m Gen. 46. 16. *Arodi.* n Gen. 38. 2-10. 1 Chr. 2. 3, etc.

o Gen. 46. 13. 1 Chr. 7. 1. p Gen. 46. 14 q Gen. 46. 20. r Josh. 17. 1. 1 Chr. 7. 14, 15.

---

or that they did not consent to their father's rebellion, or having at first enlisted in it, were afterwards induced to repent and abandon the enterprise upon the warning appeal given by Moses, ch. 16 : 5. See Notes on ch. 16 : 5, 31–35.

V. 14. *These are the families of the Simeonites.* That is, the families which remained, for it appears from Gen. 46 : 10. Ex. 6 : 15, that there was another family, that of Ohad; but this had doubtless become extinct in the wilderness, and is therefore omitted here.——¶ *Twenty and two thousand and two hundred.* A great diminution in number, since at the former census they

30 These *are* the sons of Gilead: *of* Jeezer, the family of the Jeezerites: of Helek, the family of the Helekites:

31 And *of* Asriel, the family of the Asrielites: and *of* Shechem, the family of the Shechemites:

32 And *of* Shemida, the family of the Shemidaites: and *of* Hepher, the family of the Hepherites:

33 And Zelophehad[s] the son of Hepher had no sons, but daughters; and the names of the daughters of Zelophehad *were* Mahlah, and Noah, Hoglah, Milcah, and Tirzah.

34 These *are* the families of Manasseh, and those that were numbered of them, fifty and two thousand and seven hundred.

35 These *are* the sons of Ephraim after their families: of Shuthelah, the family of the Shuthalhites: of Becher[t], the family of the Bachrites: of Tahan, the family of the Tahanites.

36 And these *are* the sons of Shuthelah: of Eran, the family of the Eranites.

37 These *are* the families of the sons of Ephraim, according to those that were numbered of them, thirty and two thousand and five hundred. These *are* the sons of Joseph after their families.

38 The sons of Benjamin[u] after their families: of Bela, the family of the Belaites: of Ashbel, the family of the Ashbelites: of Ahiram[v], the family of the Ahiramites:

39 Of Shupham[w], the family of the Shuphamites: of Hupham, the family of the Huphamites.

40 And the sons of Bela were[x] Ard of Naaman: *of Ard*, the family of the Ardites: *and* of Naaman, the family of the Naamites:

41 These *are* the sons of Benjamin, after their families: and they that were numbered of them *were* forty and five thousand and six hundred.

42 These[y] *are* the sons of Dan, after their families: of Shuham, the family of the Shuhamites. These *are* the families of Dan after their families.

43 All the families of the Shuhamites, according to those that were numbered of them,

s c. 27. 1. 36. 11. *t* 1 Chr. 7. 20. *Bered.*

u Gen. 46. 21. 1 Chr. 7. 6. *v* Gen. 46. 21. *Ehi.* 1 Chr. 8. 1. *Aharah.* *w* Gen. 46. 21. *Muppim and Huppim.* *x* 1 Chr. 8. 3. *Addar.* *y* Gen. 46. 23.

---

amounted to 59,300, ch. 1 : 23. The difference, therefore, amounts to no less than 30,100, more than half their original number. Their guilty participation in the sin brought about by the evil counsels of Balaam "in the matter of Peor," is probably to be regarded as the procuring cause of this remarkable decrease. Zimri was "a prince of a chief house among the Simeonites," and it is presumable that large numbers of his tribe joined with him in the wicked revolt and fell in the punishment that ensued. It is probably to this circumstance also that we are to refer the fact, that Moses, in blessing the tribes, Deut. 33, makes no mention of Simeon.—In the subsequent parts of

were threescore and four thousand and four hundred.
44 *Of* the children of Asher[z],
after their families: of Jimna,
the family of the Jimnites: of
Jesui, the family of the Jesu-
ites: of Beriah, the family of
the Beriites.
45 Of the sons of Beriah:
of Heber, the family of the He-
berites: of Malchiel, the family
of the Malchielites.
46 And the name of the
daughter of Asher *was* Sarah.
47 These *are* the families
of the sons of Asher, according to those that were numbered of them, *who were* fifty
and three thousand and four
hundred.
48 *Of* the sons of Naphtali[a],
after their families: of Jahzeel,
the family of the Jahzeelites:
of Guni, the family of the Gun-
ites:
49 Of Jezer, the family of
the Jezerites: of Shillem[b], the
family of the Shillemites.
50 These *are* the families of
Naphtali, according to their families: and they that were numbered of them *were* forty and
five thousand and four hundred.
51 These[c] *were* the numbered of the children of Israel,
six hundred thousand, and a
thousand seven hundred and
thirty.
52 And the LORD spake unto
Moses, saying,

z Gen. 46. 17. 1 Chr. 7. 30.

a Gen. 46. 24. 1 Chr. 7. 13. b 1 Chr. 7. 13. *Shallum.* c c. 1. 46.

this chapter to v. 51, there is nothing especially requiring remark, though various details of names, genealogies, etc., may be found treated by other commentators.

V. 51. *Six hundred thousand and a thousand seven hundred and thirty.* The sum total of the former census was 603,550, which number, compared with the present, shows a decrease in thirty-eight years of 1820, exclusive of the Levites, who were numbered apart. So great was the divine beneficence, and such the Lord's faithfulness to his promises, that notwithstanding all the former generation above twenty years of age had passed off the stage, yet so fast had he multiplied their posterity, that in that space of time their numbers had nearly kept good.

The following comparative statement will show how much some of the tribes had *increased*, and others had *diminished*, since the enumeration in ch. 1:

	Ch. xxvi.	Ch. i.	
Reuben..	43,730,	46,500,	2,770 *decrease.*
Simeon..	22,200,	59,300,	37,100 *decrease.*
Gad.....	40,500,	45,650,	5,150 *decrease.*
Judah...	76,500,	74,600,	1,900 increase.
Issachar.	64,300,	54,400,	9,900 increase.
Zebulon..	60,500,	57,400,	3,100 increase.
Manasseh	52,700,	32,200,	20,500 increase.
Ephraim	32,500,	40,500,	8,000 *decrease.*
Benjamin	45,600,	35,400,	10,200 increase.
Dan......	64,400,	62,700,	1,700 increase.
Asher....	53,400,	41,500,	11,900 increase.
Naphtali	45,400,	53,400,	8,000 *decrease.*
Total..	601,730,	603,550,	1,820 *decrease* on the whole in 38 years.

Decrease in all............61,020
Increase in all.............59,200

Here it is to be observed that though there was an *increase* in seven tribes of not less than 74,800 men, yet so great was the *decrease* in the other five tribes, that the balance against the present census is 1,820, as appears above.

53 Unto [d] these the land shall be divided for an inheritance, according to the number of names.

54 To [e] many thou shalt give the more inheritance, and to few thou shalt give the less inheritance: to every one shall his inheritance be given according to those that were numbered of him.

55 Notwithstanding the land shall be divided by lot: according to the names of the tribes of their fathers shall they inherit.

d Josh. 11. 23. 14. 1. e c. 33. 54.

Division of the Land by Lot.

V. 53. *Unto these the land shall be divided, etc.* Heb. "Apportioned." The enrolment of the names in the census-register was a preliminary step equivalent to a profession of their being heirs of the promises, just as those are partakers of the kingdom of heaven, whose names are written in the Lamb's book of life. To all such the declaration here made is a comforting assurance, since it virtually put the promised land into their present possession. The demonstrative pronoun is used emphatically to preclude the apprehension that they were longer to be put off, or that their posterity and not themselves were to be made the actual inheritors.——¶ *According to the number of names.* That is, according to the number of the persons registered under each family. According as these were numerous or otherwise, the portion assigned was to be large or small. Comp. ch. 33 : 54.

V. 54. *To many thou shalt give the more inheritance, and to few thou shalt give the less inheritance.* Heb. "To many thou shalt multiply his inheritance, and to few thou shalt diminish his inheritance." Thus, Sol. Jarchi, "To the tribes which had the greater multitudes they gave the greater portion, though the portions were not equal; for, lo, every tribe had his portion according to his multitude." This reminds us of the rule prescribed to the Israelites in gathering the manna, Ex. 16 : 16–18, "This is the thing which the Lord hath commanded, Gather of it every man according to his eating: an omer for every man according to the number of your persons, take ye every man for them which are in his tents. And the children of Israel did so, and gathered, some more, some less. And when they did mete it with an omer, he that gathered much had nothing over, and he that gathered little had no lack: they gathered every man according to his eating."

V. 55. *Notwithstanding the land shall be divided by lot.* These lots would seem to have been cast only for the tribes, and not for the families, for to them the distribution was evidently to be governed by the rule laid down v. 54. Yet in case any lot was too large for the tribe, it appears that there was nothing to prevent their giving up a part of their right to others, as we learn was the case with Judah, which relinquished a portion of its territory to Simeon and Dan. It is easy to conceive that without some mode of appeal to the Supreme Arbiter the burden of responsibility in regard to the several allotments would have been very heavy, and probably led to charges of partiality or prejudice; for which reason the lot seems to have been ordained, "the whole disposing of which is of the Lord."——¶ *According to the names of the tribes of their fathers.* This gives countenance to the

56 According to the lot shall
the possession thereof be divided
between many and few.
57 And[f] these *are* they that
were numbered of the Levites,
after their families: of Gershon,
the family of the Gershonites:
of Kohath, the family of the
Kohathites: of Merari, the family of the Merarites.
58 These *are* the families of
the Levites: the family of the
Libnites, the family of the Hebronites, the family of the Mahlites, the family of the Mushites,
the family of the Korathites:
and Kohath begat Amram.
59 And the name of Amram's
wife *was* Jochebed[g], the daughter of Levi, whom *her mother*

f Gen. 46. 11. Ex. 6. 16-19. 1 Chr. 6. 1, 16.

g Ex. 2. 1, 2. 6. 20.

idea that the lot had reference only to the inheritance of the tribes and not of the subordinate families. In being cast they probably bore the names of each tribe or each patriarch. It is, however, to be observed, that only nine and a half lots were to be assigned on the west of the Jordan, as two and a half tribes had chosen their inheritance on the east of that river, ch. 34:13-15.

V. 56. *According to the lot shall the possession, etc.* That is, the portion or share which shall fall by lot to each tribe, shall be distributed to the several families in such proportions as their numbers shall require. The precise mode in which the lots were drawn is not known with any certainty.

The Numbering of the Levites.

V. 57. *These (are) they that were numbered of the Levites.* The Levitical families are here numbered by themselves, because they were not to have a distinct share of the land, although they were to be provided with 48 cities and their suburbs for habitations. It is to be observed, however, that they are not enumerated with the same precision as the other tribes, some families being here wholly omitted. Comp. Ex. 6:17-19. The register was now made under the three branches of that tribe, specified ch. 3:17, 18, etc., from one of which descended Moses and Aaron, and Aaron's sons the priests. There were four of these, but two of them, Nadab and Abihu, were cut off by the hand of heaven for their impiety, and yet the Lord so ordered it, that they were preserved and increased in their posterity so as to afford a sufficient number for the discharge of the priestly functions.

V. 58. *The family of the Korathites.* Or, more properly *Korhites,* from Korah the son of Izhar, the son of Kohath, the son of Levi, ch. 16:1. Korah himself died in the rebellion, but his children were exempted from his fate, and are therefore here reckoned for a family in the fourth generation from Levi, which is one degree farther than the other families extend. Upon comparing Ex. 6:17, we find two sons of Gershon mentioned, viz. Libni and Shimi, yet here the former is enumerated and the latter omitted. Then also Kohath has four sons, Amram, and Izhar, and Hebron, and Uzziel, yet here Uzziel is wholly omitted, nor is Izhar named otherwise than impliedly in his sons the Korathites.

V. 59. *The name of Amram's wife was Jochebed, etc.* We give upon this passage the note of Calvin (Harm. of Pent.) which will be seen to be altogether appropriate. "Why Moses should expressly state the name of his mother, contrary to the usual custom of Scripture, does not clearly appear;

bare to Levi in Egypt: and she
bare unto Amram, Aaron, and
Moses, and Miriam, their sister.
60 And unto Aaron [h] was born
Nadab, and Abihu, Eleazar, and
Ithamar.
61 And [i] Nadab and Abihu
died, when they offered strange
fire before the LORD.
62 And [k] those that were numbered of them were twenty and
three thousand, all males, from
a month old and upward: for
[l] they were not numbered among
the children of Israel, because
there was no inheritance [m] given
them among the children of
Israel.

h c. 3. 2. i Lev. 10. 1. 2. c. 3. 4. 1 Chr. 24. 2. k c. 3. 39. l c. 1. 49. m c. 18. 20-24. Deut. 10. 9. Josh. 13. 14, 33. 14. 3.

63 These *are* they that were
numbered by Moses and Eleazar the priest, who numbered
the children of Israel in [n] the
plains of Moab, by Jordan *near*
Jericho.
64 But among these [o] there
was not a man of them whom
Moses and Aaron the priest numbered, when they numbered the
children of Israel in the wilderness of Sinai:
65 For the LORD had said [p] of
them, They shall surely die in
the wilderness. And there was
not left a man of them, save Caleb the son of Jephunneh, and
Joshua the son of Nun.

n ver. 3. o Deut. 4. 3, 4. p c. 14. 28-30. 1 Cor. 10. 5, 6. Jude 5.

for it is not likely that he did this as a distinction to his own family, because he at the same time shows how he himself, as well as his children, was deprived of the honor of the priesthood, in which there is no appearance of ambition. It is more probable, if the word *daughter* is literally taken, that he did not conceal a disgraceful circumstance, in order to extol more highly the indulgence of God; for in this case, Moses and Aaron sprang of an incestuous marriage, since Amram their father must have married his aunt, which natural modesty forbids. It will then be rather an ingenuous confession of family dishonor, than an ambitious boast."

V. 60. *Unto Aaron was born Nadab and Abihu, etc.* Here the names of Moses' children, Gershon and Eleazar, are again omitted, and only those of Aaron mentioned. But a reason for this may be suggested in the fact, that the sudden death of two of his sons seemed in itself to endanger the perpetuity of the high-priesthood, which, according to the divine order, appeared to depend on their life. With this view Moses cites the history of the sad event in order that the Lord's wonderful providence might be more clearly perceived in the preservation of this sacred class, with which the well being of the whole church was so intimately connected. To which we may add, that the renewed mention of their fate and its occasion would administer a wholesome admonition to the priests of all degrees diligently to beware of wilful sacrilege, as also of error and negligence in their ministrations.

V. 62. *Twenty and three thousand.* The former census exhibited 22,000 as the total of this tribe; so that their increase in the wilderness was 1000 males, ch. 3 : 39.

V. 64. *Among these there was not a man, etc.* This is stated in order to show how punctual the Most High had been in executing the threatening so

CHAPTER XXVII.

THEN came the daughters of [a] Zelophehad, the son of Hepher, the son of Gilead, the son of Machir, the son of Manasseh, of the families of Manasseh the son of Joseph: and these *are* the names of his daughters; Mahlah, Noah, and Hoglah, and Milcah, and Tirzah.

2 And they stood before Moses, and before Eleazar the priest, and before the princes and all the congregation, *by* the

a c. 26. 33. 36. 1-11. Josh. 17. 3.

---

emphatically pronounced against the murmurers of a former generation, ch. 14:23, 28, 29. Of the vast total of upwards of 600,000 then enumerated, Caleb and Joshua alone had their names registered in the present census. This, however, is to be understood with a peculiar qualification. It is evident from Josh. 14:1. 22:13, that both Eleazar and Phinehas did actually enter into the promised land. How is this consistent with the statement here made? We reply that the sentence of exclusion applied to the other tribes which were enumerated on two former occasions, and in which the Levites were not embraced. We do not read that they had any share in the transaction which brought the divine denunciation upon the mass of the people. This tribe did not, like the others, send a spy into Canaan, nor does it appear that it concurred in the general murmuring which the report of the spies occasioned.

CHAPTER XXVII.

The Case of Zelophehad's Daughters claiming an Inheritance.

V. 1. *Then came the daughters of Zelophehad, etc.* Heb. "Then came near, or approached." Targ. Jon. "Then came near to the place of judgment." In the late census of the Israelitish families, ch. 26:33, mention is made of Zelophehad, son of Hepher, of the tribe of Manasseh, who died without male issue, having five daughters as his only heirs. These women, hearing that the land of Canaan was to be divided amongst the heads of the tribes and the families mentioned in that census, were at once filled with apprehension that being females, they were to be excluded from all inheritance in the lands and estates of the country, and, consequently, that the name and family of the Hepherites would be extinguished in Israel. They accordingly determined to make a representation of their case to Moses, in a full court of the high-priests and judges, assembled with him at the door of the Tabernacle. "This peculiar case gave occasion for the discovery of exemplary piety in these daughters, who had faith to believe that Canaan would be actually possessed, and grace enough to desire a share in the inheritance. It is a mercy when under no consideration sons or daughters are satisfied to resign a portion among the Lord's people, their part in the heavenly Canaan. Reader! the inheritance is dividing; the time is now for the settlement of titles and the decision of interests. Have you no concern for a clear and indisputable case, a satisfactory claim? If not, the daughters of Zelophehad reproach your indifference."—*Seaton.*

V. 2. *Stood before—all the congregation.* This is not to be understood in its literal sense, for such a gathering of the whole host of the people at the door

door of the tabernacle of the
congregation, saying,
3 Our father died [b] in the wilderness, and he was not in the
company of them that gathered
[c] themselves together against the
LORD in the company of Korah;
but died in his own [d] sin, and
had no sons.
4 Why should the name of
our father be done away from
among his family, because he
hath no son? Give [e] unto us,
therefore, a possession among
the brethren of our father.
5 And Moses [f] brought their
cause before the LORD.
6 And the LORD spake unto
Moses, saying,
7 The daughters of Zelophehad speak right: thou [g] shalt
surely give them a possession
of an inheritance among their
father's brethren; and thou shalt

b c. 14. 35. 26. 64, 65. *c* c. 16. 1, 2. *d* Ezek. 18. 4. John 8. 21, 24. Rom. 6. 23.

e Josh. 17. 4. *f* Ex. 18. 15, 19. Job 23. 4. *g* c. 36. 2.

of the Tabernacle was impossible. "All the congregation" here undoubtedly denotes the seventy elders, representatives of the congregation, mentioned ch. 11:24, who are elsewhere called *kol hâ-ëdâh, the whole congregation*, and sometimes simply *ëdâh*, the *congregation*. See Note on ch. 10:7.

V. 3. *But died in his own sin.* That is, for his own sin, and that only. He had not engaged in any conspiracy or rebellion like Korah, and thus been instrumental in drawing other men into sin. Targ. Jon. "Nor did he cause others to sin." His daughters hereby express the hope that, as their father had not participated in any act of rebellion or mutiny, or been in any way a disturber of the public peace, and had died chargeable only with the common iniquities of mankind, they might not be deprived of their just rights and privileges, and see their family extinct, but might have their share with the rest, and that the male children they might subsequently have, though begotten by fathers belonging to other families of the same tribe, should enjoy their inheritance under the name of Hepherites. See ch. 36:3–10. "They distinguish his private sin from any public crime, which should have caused him to deserve to be disinherited. At the same time, they hold fast to the principle dictated by the common feelings of religion, that death is the wages of sin." —*Calvin.* They were happy in being able to make this plea on the ground of the good character of their father, and it is happy for any one when the testimony can be borne of him, that whatever were his own personal infirmities or transgressions, he was not accessory to the ruin of others by involving them in sin. "Here we may see what a comfort, what a credit and glory, honest parents be to their children. They leave a good name behind them, making their children bold to speak of them; when others must hang their heads and blush either to mention them themselves, or to hear them spoken of by others."—*Bp. Babington.*

V. 5. *Moses brought their cause before the Lord.* Heb. "Brought near their judgment." It would seem from this that the case was considered too difficult for the judges to decide, being without precedent and involving important consequences, and therefore was referred to the Lord, as was Moses' wont in all doubtful matters.

V. 7–11. *The daughters of Zelophehad speak right.* The divine response de-

cause the inheritance of their father to pass unto them.

8 And thou shalt speak unto the children of Israel, saying, If a man die, and have no son, then ye shall cause his inheritance to pass unto his daughter.

9 And if he have no daughter, then ye shall give his inheritance unto his brethren.

10 And if he have no brethren, then ye shall give his inheritance unto his father's brethren.

11 And if his father have no brethren, then ye shall give his inheritance unto his kinsman that is next to him of his family, and he shall possess it: and it shall be unto the children of Israel a statute [h] of judgment; as the LORD commanded Moses.

12 And the LORD said unto Moses, Get thee [i] up into this

h c. 35. 29. *i* c. 33. 47. Deut. 3. 27. 32. 49. 34. 1.

---

clares the suit of these women to be just and equitable, and orders it to be accorded to them. At the same time, he takes occasion to graft upon this particular case a general law, to wit, that if any Israelite died without male children, his daughters were to inherit his land; that in default of direct heirs in the female line, it was to go to his brothers; if he left no brothers, to his father's brothers; and, failing that relationship, then to his nearest collateral kinsman, always keeping to the relations nearest in blood.—We find some further particulars respecting the case of Zelophehad's daughters in the last chapter, to the Notes on which the reader is referred.

Moses' Death announced to him.

V. 12. *Get thee up into this mount Abarim.* Abarim, as we have already remarked, ch. 23 : 14, was the name of a somewhat extensive chain of mountains on the east of the Dead Sea, among the principal distinct elevations or peaks of which was Nebo or Pisgah. It does not appear that the Lord designed Moses should *now* ascend the mount specified, for his compliance with the command is not here mentioned. Indeed, we are obliged to confess to some degree of difficulty in adjusting the chronological relations of the incident here referred to The order of events as described in this part of the history is the punishment of the people on account of their sin in the matter of Midian, the numbering of the people, the application of the daughters of Zelophehad, the command to ascend the mountain, and the appointment of Joshua as his successor. From the third chapter of Deuteronomy it would appear that this command to ascend the mountain was given after he had delivered his special charge to the tribes of Reuben and Gad, which in the book of Numbers occurred at a somewhat later date than that we are now considering. Again, in Deut. 32, we learn that Moses had uttered his inspired and prophetic song, when, "in that self-same day the Lord spake unto Moses, saying, Get thee up into this mountain Abarim, unto mount Nebo," etc. But from Deut. 34 : 1–4, it appears that the final blessing upon the tribes was pronounced before he went up from the plains of Moab to the mountain of Nebo. It is not indeed probable that any great length of time intervened between these several events, but we naturally feel a desire to fix, if possible, their precise order. This, in the present instance, it is not possible to do, and occasionally in other cases in the

mount Abarim, and see the land
which I have given unto the
children of Israel.
13 And when thou hast seen
it, thou also shalt be gathered[k]
unto thy people, as [l] Aaron thy
brother was gathered.
14 For [m] ye rebelled against
my commandment in the desert
of Zin, in the strife of the congregation, to sanctify me at the
water before their eyes: that *is*
the water of Meribah [n] in Kadesh in the wilderness of Zin.
15 And Moses spake unto
the LORD, saying,
16 Let the LORD, the God [o] of
the spirits of all flesh, set [p] a man
over the congregation,
17 Which may go out [q] before

k c. 20. 24. 31. 2. *l* c. 20. 28. Deut. 10. 6. *m* c. 20. 10–12.

n Ex. 17. 7. *o* c. 16. 22. Heb. 12. 9. *p* Jer. 3. 15. *q* Deut. 31. 2. 1 Sam. 8. 20. 18. 13. 2 Chr. 1. 10. John 10. 9.

Sacred Volume we find transpositions and dislocations in the record which have given occasion of cavil to skeptical critics, while at the same time nothing could be clearly indicated as militating with the intrinsic truth of the narrative, or implying any greater lack of order than might reasonably be expected in documents of such extreme antiquity.——¶ *See the land which I have given unto the children of Israel.* As this is the intimation of a privilege which was not actually enjoyed till some time afterwards, we defer our remarks upon it till we reach the period of its occurrence, Deut. 34 : 1–4.

V. 16. *Let the Lord, the God of the spirits of all flesh.* Gr. "Let the Lord, the God of the spirits and of all flesh." So also ch. 16 : 22. The phraseology implies not only that God is the original Creator of all men's souls or spirits, Eccles. 12 : 7. Zech. 12 : 1, but that he is also the divine Bestower of the various spiritual gifts of grace, knowledge, etc., which are termed "spirits," 1 Cor. 14 : 12, "Even so ye, forasmuch as ye are zealous of *spiritual gifts* (Gr. *of spirits*), seek that ye may excel," etc. The burden of Moses' prayer on this occasion is, that the Lord would set a man over the congregation who should be abundantly furnished with those spiritual endowments that should best qualify him for the office. As these gifts and graces were to come from the Lord alone, therefore he addresses him as the "God of the spirits of all flesh," that is, the God who so works upon and endows the spirits of men as to render them most competent for the functions he assigns them.——¶ *Set a man over, etc.* Heb. *yiphkod, visit over*, i. e. constitute, appoint, make to preside over. See Note on ch. 1 : 3. The conduct of Moses, in view of the intimation now given him, is eminently worthy his general character. Instead of giving way to vain regrets, striving to turn the Most High from his purpose, he forgets himself, and makes the welfare of the people his great concern. His absorbing anxiety is, that they may not be deprived of the services of a competent leader—that they may not be left as sheep without a shepherd. We have but to compare this with his whole previous career to see that the same unselfishness of spirit, the same zeal for the honor of God, the same devoted concern for the well-being of the people, which had marked his course hitherto, shine conspicuous on this occasion, confirming his title to rank high among the excellent of the earth.

V. 17. *Which may go out before them, and which may go in before them.* That is, who may guide and govern them

them, and which may go in before them, and which may lead them out, and which may bring them in; that the congregation of the LORD be not as sheep [r] which have no shepherd.

18 And the LORD said unto Moses, Take thee Joshua the son of Nun, a man in [s] whom *is* the spirit, and lay [t] thine hand upon him:

19 And set him before Eleazar the priest, and before all the congregation; and give him [u] a charge in their sight.

r 1 K. 22. 17. Zech. 10. 2. Mat. 9. 36. 1 Pet. 2. 25.

s Gen. 41. 38. Judg. 3. 10. 11. 29. 1 Sam. 16. 13, 18. Dan. 5. 14. Acts 6. 3. t Deut. 34. 9. Acts 6. 6. u Deut. 31. 7.

---

both at home and abroad, in times of peace and of war, and who may undertake the charge of defending them from their enemies; for under this phrase of "going out and coming in before them, of leading them out and bringing them in," all the offices of the supreme magistracy are comprised. Hence Moses, when on the point of resigning the government, uses this language of himself, Deut. 31:2, "I can no more go out and come in." The similitude is taken from the case of shepherds, whose custom it is to go out and in before their flocks, to lead them forth to their pastures, and then to bring them home again to their folds.

Inauguration of Joshua.

V. 18. *A man in whom is the spirit* That is, the Spirit of God, as manifested in the gifts and graces with which he was endowed. Thus, Deut. 34:9, "And Joshua the son of Nun was full of the spirit of wisdom; for Moses had laid his hands upon him." In this respect he was an evident type of Him to whom the Lord "gave not the Spirit by measure."——¶ *Lay thine hand upon him.* Heb. *sâmaktâ, lean* or *impose thine hand upon him,* i. e. thine hands, v. 23, and as it is rendered in the Gr. "Thou shalt lay thine hands upon him." By this ceremony of the imposition of hands was signified the transfer of the office of leader of Israel from Moses to Joshua, and the communication of the requisite spiritual gifts and endowments for its right discharge. A similar ceremony obtained subsequently in the primitive Christian church when men were separated and set apart for the discharge of special holy functions. See 1 Tim. 4:14.

V. 19. *Set him before Eleazar the priest, and before all the congregation.* The relation which he was to sustain to the high-priest and to the congregation, made it fitting that this act of inauguration or consecration should be performed in the presence of all the people, that they might thus signify their devout reception of their new leader, as designated and appointed for them of the Lord himself.——¶ *Give him a charge in their sight.* Heb. "Thou shalt command him." We read the purport of this charge, Deut. 31:7, 8. "And Moses called unto Joshua, and said unto him in the sight of all Israel, Be strong and of a good courage: for thou must go with this people unto the land which the Lord hath sworn unto their fathers to give them; and thou shalt cause them to inherit it. And the Lord, he it is that doth go before thee; he will be with thee, he will not fail thee, neither forsake thee: fear not, neither be dismayed." In addition to this the Lord himself gave Joshua a charge in the Tabernacle, Deut. 31:14, of which it is said, v. 23, "And he (the Lord) gave Joshua the son of Nun a charge, and

20 And [v] thou shalt put *some*
of thine honour upon him, that
all the congregation of the children of Israel may be [w] obedient.
21 And he shall stand before
Eleazar the priest, who shall
ask [x] *counsel* for him, after the
judgment of [y] Urim before the
LORD: at his word shall they go
out, and at his word they shall
come in, *both* he, and all the
children of Israel with him,
even all the congregation.
22 And Moses did as the
LORD commanded him: and he
took Joshua, and set him before
Eleazar the priest, and before
all the congregation.
23 And he laid his hands upon him, and gave him a charge,
as the LORD commanded [z] by
the hand of Moses.

v 2 K. 2. 9, 15. *w* Josh. 1. 16, 17. *x* Judg. 20. 18, etc. 1 Sam. 22. 10. 23. 9. 30. 7. *y* Ex. 28. 3.

z ver. 19.

said, Be strong and of a good courage; for thou shalt bring the children of Israel into the land which I sware unto them; and I will be with thee." The charge thus given tended at once to confirm the authority of Joshua, and to bind him more solemnly to the discharge of his duties. As Moses also gave him his instructions in the name of God, he would be exempt from the imputation of mercenary motives, while Joshua would be strengthened in faith and diligence.

V. 20. *Thou shalt put* (*some*) *of thine honor upon him.* Heb. "Thou shalt give of thine honor, majesty, or glory, upon him." The inserted word "some" is perhaps implied, though not absolutely necessary. The spiritual gifts and endowments conferred upon Moses rendered him honorable in the sight of the people, and the communication of these gifts to Joshua was *apparently* a divesting of himself of a portion of them, and putting them upon his successor. In like manner, it is said, of the seventy elders chosen to assist Moses in the government of Israel, ch. 11:17, that God would take of the spirit which was upon him and put it upon them. Joshua was not, indeed, to have the full measure of Moses' gifts, but a certain portion of them, so that the pre-eminence of Moses should remain unimpaired. Of him alone could it be said, that "there arose not a prophet since in Israel like unto Moses." The purport of the command is, regard Joshua no longer henceforth as a servant, but as a brother and an equal, united in joint commission with thyself, and entitled to the ensigns and evidences of thine own authority, whatever they may be.

V. 21. *He shall stand before Eleazar the priest, etc.* Notwithstanding his high position as head of the Israelitish host, he shall still be required to render a suitable deference to the priest, and upon all proper occasions to present himself before him, and avail himself of his counsels and intercessions. By the priest's "asking counsel for him after the judgment of Urim," is meant that he should assume the Ephod, in which was the breastplate, whereunto were affixed the Urim and Thummim, the medium of oracular responses from the Lord. On this subject we refer the reader to our Note on Ex. 28:30, where it is treated at length. From 1 Sam. 23:6, we learn that when Saul would have consulted the Lord by Urim, he answered him not.

CHAPTER XXVIII.

AND the Lord spake unto Moses, saying,
2 Command the children of Israel, and say unto them, My offering, *and* my bread for my sacrifices made by fire *for*[a] a sweet savour unto me, shall ye observe to offer unto me in their due season.

a Lev. 3. 11.

CHAPTER XXVIII.

The stated Sacrifices re-enjoined.

V. 2. *Command the children of Israel, and say unto them, etc.* The people having now been numbered, a leader in the place of Moses appointed, and orders for the distribution of the land given, the Most High is pleased to re-enact the ordinances touching the stated oblations to be made upon his altar in the order of daily, weekly, monthly, and annual. The regular routine of sacrifices and services pertaining to the Tabernacle had doubtless been very much interrupted, if not wholly omitted, during the last thirty-eight years while wandering to and fro in an unsettled state through the desert, and as the generation now living was mostly unborn when the ritual system was at first given from Mount Sinai, it seemed proper to enjoin anew the observance of the sacred rites, that they might have no excuse for neglecting the punctilious performance of them when fully established in the land of Canaan. They were now, moreover, about entering upon a career of war, and as they might be tempted to regard this as a species of dispensation from the regular offering of the appointed sacrifices, the Lord is particular to repeat his injunctions on this score mainly in the form in which they were given in Exodus and Leviticus, but with here and there new explanations and amplifications as occasion seemed to demand. It is deemed probable that these directions were delivered in the eighth month of the last year of their travels in the wilderness.——¶ *My offering (and) my bread, etc.* Rather according to the Heb. "My offering, (even) my bread," as the conjunction "and" is wanting in the original. "Offering" is moreover there expressed by "korban," equivalent to *gift*, of which we have formerly given a full explication. See especially Note on Lev. 1 : 2. The following is the literal rendering of the whole verse: "Command the children of Israel, and say unto them, Mine oblation, my bread for my fire-(offerings), the savor of my rest, ye shall observe to offer unto me in their due season."——¶ *My bread for my sacrifices, etc.* Chald. "The bread ordained for my oblations." Under the term "bread" is included all kinds of food, even the flesh itself, or the fat of sacrifices, as is remarked in the Note on Lev. 3 : 11.——¶ *A sweet savor unto me.* Heb. "The savor of my rest." Implying that the savor or odor of sacrifices had the effect of quieting or pacifying the divine displeasure, and causing the services of the people to be acceptable to him. Gr. "For a savor of sweetness." Chald. "To be accepted with favor."——¶ *In their due season.* Heb. "In his appointed time." At the season especially appointed and prescribed by the Lord himself. Gr. "In my feasts;" as the original word for "appointed time" is used also for a *solemn feast* appointed by God. See Lev. 23 : 2, with the Note. Every sacrifice is here limited to its specified season, so that if it were passed over the omission was not to be attempted to be

3 And thou shalt say unto them, This *is* [b] the offering made by fire which ye shall offer unto the LORD; two lambs of the first year without spot, day by day, *for* a continual burnt-offering.

4 The one lamb shalt thou offer in the morning, and the other lamb shalt thou offer at [c] even;

5 And a tenth *part* of an ephah of flour for a meat-offering [d], mingled [e] with the fourth *part* of an hin of beaten oil.

6 *It is* a continual burnt-offering, which was ordained in mount Sinai for a sweet savour, a sacrifice made by fire unto the LORD.

7 And the drink-offering

b Ex. 29. 38. c Ex. 12. 6. d Lev. 2. 1. c. 15. 4. e Ex. 29. 40, etc.

---

supplied by that oblation being offered at another day or time, as it is said v. 10, "The burnt-offering of the sabbath in or on his sabbath." Hence the Jewish saying, "If the time be past, the oblation is past." On the same ground Jeroboam, 1 Kings 12 : 32, 33, who kept the feast of the seventh month "in the eighth month," is virtually rebuked for it, in its being said that he did this "in the month which he had devised of his own heart." The general purport of the passage is therefore very explicit, that that which the Lord calls his food or bread is to be rendered to him with the utmost regularity in its appointed season, so that without violence we may say, that as we are to call upon him for our daily bread, he in like manner says to us, "Give me day by day my daily bread."

The Daily Offering.

V. 3. *Two lambs of the first year, etc.* This is the daily sacrifice of two choice and perfect lambs, one for the morning and one for the evening, making an offering which was upon no account to be intermitted, whatever additional sacrifices might at any time be offered. It is therefore called the "continual burnt-offering," of which a full account is given in the Notes on Ex. 29 : 38–45, where it will be seen that the continued manifestation of the divine presence was made dependent upon the *regularity* with which this daily service was performed. So in our private and domestic devotions, if we are remiss, inconstant, and irregular, allowing trifling or inadequate occasions to break in upon the fixed routine of worship, we shall be very certain to forfeit and lose the tokens of the Lord's presence with us, and bring leanness into our souls.

V. 4. *The one lamb shalt thou offer in the morning.* Heb. "Shalt thou make;" a sacrificial term implying all that was necessarily involved in the act of oblation, such as killing the victim, sprinkling its blood, cutting it in pieces, laying and burning it on the altar, etc., as indicated Lev. 1.——¶ *At even.* Heb. "Between the two evenings." That is, in the afternoon, as will be seen explained at length in the Note on Ex. 12 : 6. It pointed typically to the Lord's being offered in his crucifixion at the same hour. Comp. John 19 : 14. Matt. 27 : 46, 50.

V. 5–8. *Ordained in Mount Sinai.* The order respecting the two lambs is repeated with little variation from Ex. 29, but he speaks more respecting the concomitants of flour and wine, which are the bread and the beverage of the divine meal partaken from off the altar as from a table. The reference of this ordinance back to Mount Sinai, the scene of

thereof *shall be* the fourth *part*
of an hin for the one lamb: in
the holy *place* shalt thou cause
the strong wine to be poured
unto the LORD *for* a drink-offering.
8 And the other lamb shalt
thou offer at even: as the meat-offering
of the morning, and as
the drink-offering thereof, thou
shalt offer *it*, a sacrifice made
by fire, of a sweet savour unto
the LORD.
9 And on the sabbath-day
two lambs of the first year without
spot, and two tenth deals of
flour *for* a meat-offering, mingled
with oil, and the drink-offering
thereof.
10 *This is* the burnt-offering
of every sabbath[f], beside the
continual burnt-offering, and his
drink-offering.
11 And in the beginning[g] of
your months ye shall offer a
burnt-offering[h] unto the LORD;
two young bullocks, and one
ram, seven lambs of the first
year without spot;
12 And three tenth deals of
flour *for* a meat-offering, mingled
with oil, for one bullock;

f Ezek. 46. 4. *g* c. 10. 10. 1 Chr. 23. 31. 2 Chr. 2. 4. Neh. 10. 33. Is. 1. 13, 14. Ezek. 45. 17. Col. 2. 16. *h* c. 15. 3–11.

---

so much sanctity, would commend it the more to their devout observance. To each of the lambs was to be annexed, as bread and drink requisite to the furniture of a table, about three quarts of the finest flour, about a quart of pure oil for mixing with the flour, and as much, we may suppose, of the strongest wine, to be poured upon the fire along with the rest. The action of the fire upon these materials was the Lord's consuming them, as one and the principal party to the feast.——¶ *Strong wine.* "The richest and most generous, and best-bodied wine they could get. Though it was to be poured out upon the altar, and not drunk (they might therefore be ready to think the worst would serve to be so thrown away), yet God requires the strongest, to teach us to serve God with the best we have."—*Henry.*

The Sabbath, or Weekly Offering.

Vs. 9, 10. *And on the Sabbath day two lambs, etc.* The special feature of the Sabbath or weekly offering is the duplication of the lambs. This appears, from comparing vs. 9 and 10, from which it is evident that the two lambs here spoken of were over and above "the continual burnt-offering." This suggests to us the propriety of doubling our devotions on the Sabbath.

Offering on the New Moons.

Vs. 11–15. *In the beginning of your months ye shall offer, etc.* The third stated sacrifice was monthly, being offered on the first day of every month. This is not, indeed, included in the list of solemn feasts enumerated Lev. 23, yet we find there was a celebration of this kind to which special allusion is made, Num. 10:10, and which was distinguished by extraordinary sacrifices, by abstinence from servile labor, Am. 8:5, by the sounding of trumpets, and by sacred assemblies, 2 Kings, 4:23. The design of this commemoration undoubtedly was not only to teach the chosen people that all the separate portions of time, whether days, weeks, months or years, were to be consecrated to the Lord as in reality his, and

and two tenth deals of flour *for*
a meat-offering, mingled with
oil, for one ram;
13 And a several tenth deal
of flour mingled with oil, *for* a
meat-offering unto one lamb;
for a burnt offering of a sweet
savour, a sacrifice made by fire
unto the LORD.
14 And their drink-offerings
shall be half an hin of wine unto
a bullock, and the third *part* of
an hin unto a ram, and a fourth
part of an hin unto a lamb: this
is the burnt-offering of every
month throughout the months
of the year.
15 And [i] one kid of the goats
for a sin-offering unto the LORD
shall be offered, beside [k] the continual burnt-offering, and his
drink-offering.
16 And in the fourteenth [l] day
of the first month *is* the passover of the LORD.
17 And in the fifteenth day
of this month *is* the feast: sev-
en days shall unleavened bread
be eaten.
18 In the first day *shall be*
an holy convocation; ye shall
do no manner of servile work
therein.
19 But ye shall offer a sacrifice made by fire, *for* a burnt-
offering unto the LORD; two
young bullocks, and one ram,
and seven lambs of the first
year: they shall be unto you
without [m] blemish:
20 And their meat-offering
shall be of flour mingled with
oil: three tenth deals shall ye
offer for a bullock, and two
tenth deals for a ram.
21 A several tenth deal shalt

i c. 15. 24. *k* ver. 11. *l* ch. 9. 3. Ex. 12. 6, 18. Lev. 23. 5, 6. Ezek. 45. 21.

m ver. 31. Lev. 22. 20. c. 29. 8. Deut. 15. 21. Mal. 1. 13, 14. 1 Pet. 1. 19.

---

to be devoted to his service, but also to guard them against that form of idolatry which prevailed among the Gentiles, viz., worshipping the new moon upon its appearance, with various profane rites. By a sacrifice and service directed to the true God, the only proper object of worship, their minds would be led away from these perversions and centred upon the only suitable theme. The offering on this occasion consisted of two young bullocks, a ram, and seven lambs, of the choicest quality on the score of fat and fairness. The meal and drink-offering annexed to each was to be proportionate, viz., each bullock to have three times the quantity allotted to a lamb; the ram to have double that quantity; and so accordingly for the wine and oil. There was on this day also added a kid for a sin or expiation sacrifice, having a special typical reference to the great redemption-offering of Him in whom these legal shadows all pass into substance.

The Passover Offering.

Vs. 16–25. *In the fourteenth day of the first month, etc.* The fourth stated and national sacrifice was annual, the great Passover festival, with the feast of unleavened bread annexed to it. But as the origin, design, and mode of observance of this institution have already been largely considered in the Notes on Ex. 12 : 3–20. Lev. 23 : 5–8, we shall waive any further explanation in this connection.

thou offer for every lamb, throughout the seven lambs:

22 And one goat [n] *for* a sin-offering, to make an atonement for you.

23 Ye shall offer these beside the burnt-offering in the morning, which *is* for a continual burnt-offering.

24 After this manner ye shall offer daily, throughout the seven days, the meat of the sacrifice made by fire, of a sweet savour unto the LORD: it shall be offered beside the continual burnt-offering, and his drink-offering.

25 And on the seventh day ye shall have an holy convocation; ye shall do no servile work.

26 Also in [o] the day of the first-fruits, when ye bring a new meat-offering unto the LORD, after your weeks *be out*, ye shall have an holy convocation; ye shall do no servile work:

27 But ye shall offer the burnt-offering for a sweet savour unto the LORD; two young bullocks, one ram, seven lambs of the first year;

28 And their meat-offering of flour mingled with oil, three tenth deals unto one bullock, two tenth deals unto one ram;

29 A several tenth deal unto one lamb, throughout the seven lambs;

30 *And* one kid of the goats, to make an atonement for you.

31 Ye shall offer *them* beside the continual burnt-offering, and his meat-offering (they shall be unto you without blemish [p],) and their drink-offerings.

n ver. 15. o Ex. 23. 16. 34. 22. Lev. 23. 10, etc. Deut. 16. 10. Acts 2. 1.

p ver. 19.

CHAPTER XXIX.

AND in the seventh month, on the first *day* of the month, ye shall have an holy convocation: ye shall do no servile work; it [a] is a day of blowing the trumpets unto you.

a Lev. 23. 24. Ps. 81. 3, 4.

The Offering of the First-Fruits.

Vs. 26–31. *Also in the day of the first-fruits, etc.* The fifth of these stated offerings was also annual, being that of the harvest festival, when the first-fruits of the corn were to be offered. This festival was twofold, first, the barley harvest first-fruit, beginning at the Passover, and then, at the end of seven weeks, the wheat harvest festival called the Feast of Weeks, or Pentecost. This has also been previously treated at length. See Notes on Lev. 23: 15–22.

CHAPTER XXIX.

The Particulars of the three remaining National and Stated Sacrifices.—The Offering at the Feast of Trumpets.

V. 1. *In the seventh month, on the first (day) of the month, etc.* The month here spoken of is the month *Tisri*, the *seventh* month of their ecclesiastical year, but the *first* of their civil year, answering to our *September*. The present was, therefore, a kind of New Year's festival, although invested with the sanctity of the Sabbath so far

2 And ye shall offer a burnt-
offering for a sweet savour unto
the LORD, one young bullock,
one ram, *and* seven lambs of the
first year without blemish:
3 And their meat-offering
shall be of flour mingled with
oil, three tenth deals for a bullock, *and* two tenth deals for a
ram,
4 And one tenth deal for
one lamb, throughout the seven
lambs;
5 And one kid of the goats
for a sin-offering, to make an
atonement for you:
6 Beside the [b] burnt-offering
of the month, and his meat-
offering, and [c] the daily burnt-
offering, and his meat-offering,
and their drink-offerings, according [d] unto their manner, for
a sweet savour, a sacrifice made
by fire unto the LORD.
7 And [e] ye shall have on the
tenth *day* of this seventh month

b c. 28. 11. *c* c. 28. 3. Heb. 10. 1. *d* c. 15. 11, 12. Ezra 3. 4. 1 Cor. 14. 40. *e* Lev. 16. 29 23. 27.

as servile work was concerned, all which was strictly prohibited. One of its principal features was its being ushered in with the blowing of trumpets, which took place all over the land, and of which we have given a full account in the Note on Lev. 23 : 24. The special design and import of the blowing of trumpets on this occasion, not being stated in Scripture, has given rise to numerous conjectures with the Jewish and other expositors, which we cannot afford space to recount. It may perhaps be sufficient to suggest that the day, being new-year's day, was celebrated by the blowing of trumpets for much the same reason that that day is celebrated in modern times by the ringing of bells, firing of ordnance, large and small, and various other noises, as if simply to usher in the day with tokens of public rejoicing. The sound of the trumpets may have served at the same time as a shadow of the future preaching of good and joyful news of the Gospel, for we think it beyond question that the general typical purport of trumpet-sounding, under the old economy, was evangelization.

Vs. 2–6. *Ye shall offer a burnt-offering, etc.* As the Feast of Trumpets fell in with the New Moon sacrifice, appointed ch. 28 : 11, 12, and a large offering was prescribed for *that* occasion, but one bullock is now ordered to be killed. But as two were to be slain at *every* new moon, there were, of course, three to be sacrificed at the Trumpet Festival, added to which were two rams and fourteen lambs for burnt-offerings, and two goats for a sin-offering, besides the two lambs for the daily oblation. The tenor of the command suggests that stated ordinary religious exercises are not to be superseded by extraordinary. Our private devotions cannot well be set aside by an increase of public services, whether on the Sabbath or at other times. Let not the morning or the evening sacrifice be intermitted.——¶ *According unto their manner.* Heb. "According to their judgment." That is, according to their prescribed order and regular observance—a frequent sense of the original word for "judgment."

Offerings for the Day of Atonement.

Vs. 7–11. *Ye shall have on the tenth (day) of this seventh month, etc.* This was the day of atonement, as fixed by Lev. 23 : 27, "Also on the tenth day of

an holy convocation; and ye shall afflict [f] your souls: ye shall not do any work *therein:*

8 But ye shall offer a burnt-offering unto the LORD *for* a sweet savour; one young bullock, one ram, *and* seven lambs of the first year; they [g] shall be unto you without blemish.

9 And their meat-offering *shall be of* flour mingled with oil, three tenth deals to a bullock, *and* two tenth deals to one ram,

10 A several tenth deal for one lamb, throughout the seven lambs:

11 One kid of the goats *for* a sin-offering, beside the [h] sin-offering of atonement, and the continual burnt-offering, and the meat-offering of it, and their drink-offerings.

12 And [i] on the fifteenth day of the seventh month ye shall have an holy convocation; ye shall do no servile work, and ye shall keep a feast unto the LORD seven days:

13 And [k] ye shall offer a burnt-offering, a sacrifice made by fire, of a sweet savour unto the LORD; thirteen young bullocks, two rams, *and* fourteen lambs of the first year; they shall be without blemish:

14 And their meat-offering *shall be of* flour mingled with oil, three tenth deals unto every bullock of the thirteen bullocks, two tenth deals to each ram of the two rams,

15 And a several tenth deal to each lamb of the fourteen lambs;

16 And one kid of the goats *for* a sin-offering, beside the continual burnt-offering, his meat-offering, and his drink-offering.

f Ps. 35. 13. Is. 58. 5. g c. 28. 19. h Lev. 16. 3, etc. i Lev. 23. 34. Deut. 16. 13. Ezek. 45. 25.

k Ezra 3. 4.

this seventh month there shall be a day of atonement: it shall be an holy convocation unto you; and ye shall afflict your souls, and offer an offering made by fire unto the Lord." The whole round of ceremonies connected with the observance of this institute will be found detailed at length in the elaborate Notes on Lev. 16:5–34. It was to be a day of special humiliation, fasting, and prayer, hence called, Acts 27:9, by way of eminence "the fast." It was a season for "afflicting their souls," that is, doing violence to their sensual nature by fasting and abstinence, which, when rightly observed, tends to develope the inward graces of the spirit, and bring the entire man into a better state.——¶ *One kid of the goats (for) a sin-offering, etc.* This, it appears, was *beside* the "sin-offering of the atonement," and implied that even in our humiliation and repentance so many defects and infirmities mingle, that we have need of that virtue which was signified by the sin-offering to make them acceptable. "We have need," says Henry, "of an interest in a sacrifice to expiate the guilt even of that part of our holy things. Though we must not repent that we have repented, yet we must repent that we have not repented better."

Offering for the Feast of Tabernacles.

Vs. 12–34. *On the fifteenth day of the seventh month, etc.* On this day com-

17 And on the second day
ye shall offer twelve young bullocks, two rams, fourteen lambs
of the first year, without spot:
18 And their meat-offering,
and their drink-offerings, for the
bullocks, for the rams, and for
the lambs, *shall be* according to
their number, after the manner[l].
19 And one kid of the goats
for a sin-offering; beside the
continual burnt-offering, and the
meat-offering thereof, and their
drink-offerings.
20 And on the third day
eleven bullocks, two rams, fourteen lambs of the first year without blemish;
21 And their meat-offering,
and their drink-offerings, for the
bullocks, for the rams, and for
the lambs, *shall be* according to
their number, after the manner:
22 And one goat *for* a sin-
offering; beside the continual
burnt-offering, and his meat-
offering, and his drink-offering[m].
23 And on the fourth day ten
bullocks, two rams, *and* fourteen
lambs of the first year without
blemish:
24 Their meat-offering, and
their drink-offerings, for the
bullocks, for the rams, and for
the lambs, *shall be* according to
their number, after the manner:
25 And one kid of the goats
for a sin-offering; beside the
continual burnt-offering, his
meat-offering, and his drink-
offering.
26 And on the fifth day nine
bullocks, two rams, *and* fourteen
lambs of the first year without
spot:
27 And their meat-offering,
and their drink-offerings, for the
bullocks, for the rams, and for
the lambs, *shall be* according to
their number, after the manner:
28 And one goat *for* a sin-
offering; beside the continual
burnt-offering, and his meat-
offering, and his drink-offering.
29 And on the sixth day
eight bullocks, two rams, *and*
fourteen lambs of the first year
without blemish:
30 And their meat-offering,
and their drink-offerings, for the
bullocks, for the rams, and for
the lambs, *shall be* according
to their number, after the manner:
31 And one goat *for* a sin-
offering; beside the continual

l ver. 3, 4, 9, 10. c. 15. 12. 28. 7, 14. *m* Ps. 16. 4. Joel. 1. 9, 13. 2. 14.

menced the Feast of Tabernacles, or Booths, commemorative of their sojourn in the wilderness. It was held at a season of the year when they had gathered in their corn and wine, and had seen the blessing of God in all their increase, and in all the works of their hands, Deut. 16 : 13, 15, and when their hearts, enlarged by a grateful sense of the divine mercies, would prompt a more liberal bestowment of offerings for the Lord's altar. On other festivals *two bullocks* sufficed; but here are no less than *thirteen* prescribed; and so they continued to be offered seven days successively, decreasing by one bullock every day, till on the seventh day only *seven* were offered, which in all made seventy bullocks. The rams also were in double the usual proportion. This

burnt-offering, his meat-offering, and his drink-offering.
32 And on the seventh day
seven bullocks, two rams, *and*
fourteen lambs of the first year,
without blemish:
33 And their meat-offering,
and their drink-offerings, for the
bullocks, for the rams, and for
the lambs, *shall be* according to
their number, after the manner:
34 And one goat *for* a sin-
offering; beside the continual
burnt-offering, his meat-offering,
and his drink-offering.
35 On the eighth [n] day ye
shall have a solemn assembly;
ye shall do no servile work
therein:
36 But ye shall offer a burnt-
offering, a sacrifice made by fire,
of a sweet savour unto the LORD;
one bullock, one ram, seven lambs
of the first year without blemish:
37 Their meat-offering, and
their drink-offerings, for the
bullock, for the ram, and for
the lambs, *shall be* according to
their number, after the manner:
38 And one goat *for* a sin-
offering; beside the continual
burnt-offering, and his meat-offering, and his drink-offering.

n Lev. 23. 36. John 7. 37.

---

was intrinsically a heavy draft upon the resources of the people, but easier to be borne at this season than any other; for it was now a time of leisure and plenty; their barns being full; their presses bursting forth with new wine; and their hearts overflowing with joy and thankfulness towards the Divine Donor for all the blessings of the harvest. On the reasons of this daily diminution of the number of the bullocks, Calvin remarks: "I confess it is not clear to me; and it is better to confess my ignorance than by too subtle speculations to vanish into mere smoke." But in regard to this point the suggestion of Scott is worthy of consideration: "The decrease of the number of bullocks sacrificed on the several days of the feast, until on the last and great day only one was offered, is the most observable circumstance in this law. The reason is not evident, unless it be intimated that the Mosaic institution would gradually wax old, and at length vanish away when the promised Messiah came." To this we are disposed to add the explanation proposed by Ainsworth:—"By this diminishing of one bullock every day, the Holy Ghost might teach their duty to grow in grace and increase in sanctification; that their sins decreasing, the number of their sacrifices (whereby atonement was made for their sins) should also decrease daily."

Vs. 35–38. *On the eighth day ye shall have a solemn assembly.* The eighth and last day, though the crown of all the rest, and called by the evangelist, John 7:37, "the last day, that great day of the feast," and notwithstanding it was to be regarded as a kind of Sabbath, on the score of strict abstinence from labor and the performance of solemn religious duties, was yet distinguished by a less number of sacrifices than any of the preceding, viz., one bullock, one ram, seven lambs, with the kid for a sin-offering; as if the design were to impress the minds of his people with a conviction, that it was not by a multitude of sacrifices that the blessings of eternal life were to be secured, and that eventually these shadowy rites would come to an end, while

39 These *things* ye shall do unto the LORD in your set[o] feasts, beside your vows[p], and your freewill-offerings, for your burnt-offerings, and for your meat-offerings, and for your drink-offerings, and for your peace-offerings.

40 And Moses told the children of Israel, according to all that the LORD commanded Moses.

o Lev. 23. 2, etc. 1 Chr. 23. 31. 2 Chr. 31. 3. Ezra 3. 5. Neh. 10. 33. Is. 1. 14. p Lev. 7. 11, 16. 22. 21, 23. Deut. 12. 6.

CHAPTER XXX.

AND Moses spake unto the heads[a] of the tribes concerning the children of Israel, saying, This *is* the thing which the LORD hath commanded.

2 If a man vow[b] a vow unto the LORD, or swear[c] an oath to bind his soul with a bond; he shall not break his word, he

a c. 1. 4-16. b Lev. 27. 2. Deut. 23. 21. Judg. 11. 35, 36. Ps. 15. 4. Ecc. 5. 4. c Lev. 5. 4. Matt. 5. 33. 14. 7-9. Acts 23. 14.

---

something far more substantial and durable would come in their place. It was on this occasion, also, that the Saviour called the people from their carnal observances, and bade them come unto him that they might drink the waters of eternal life. John 7 : 37.

V. 39. *Beside your vows, etc.* The preceding commands covered the general ground of the duty of the people as a body, but room was still to be left for the operation of private devotedness and generosity in the way of glorifying God by vows, free-will offerings, etc., as their spirits might move them. On the distinction between vows and voluntary offerings, see Note on Lev. 7 : 16.

CHAPTER XXX.

General Instruction in regard to the Obligation of Vows and Oaths.

V. 1. *Moses spake unto the heads of the tribes, etc.* It is easily conceivable that under the influence of the fervent zeal inspired by the festivals enjoined in the preceding chapter, there would be prompted many of those voluntary gifts and services which are alluded to ch. 29 : 30. In regard to such votive offerings, Moses is here commanded to impart instruction to the mass of the people through their appointed head-men or chiefs, who are variously denominated "the heads of the people," "the chief of all the people," "the princes of Israel, the princes of all the tribes," "the elders of Israel," "the council, the princes and elders," etc. Some have supposed that a particular case of doubt relative to this subject had been propounded to Moses, and that in answering it he took occasion to deliver the rules, contained in this chapter, covering substantially the whole ground, and serving as a directory to the nation in all the various cases that might occur in future ages. On the subject of vows, see Notes on Lev. 27 : 2-13.

V. 2. *If a man vow a vow unto the Lord, etc.* "Vow" is represented by a Hebrew word (*neder*) which signifies *to promise*, and may therefore be defined as a religious promise made to God, either of a positive kind, whereby a person engages to do or perform something; or negative, whereby he binds himself to abstain from doing or performing something. Here it is implied that if a man of mature years, being wholly at his own disposal, shall assume the responsibility of a voluntary vow, whether it be a simple promise made to the Lord, or a vow confirmed by the solemnity of an oath, he is to deem himself

shall do [d] according to all that proceedeth out of his mouth.

d Job 22. 27. Ps. 22. 25. 50. 14. 66. 13, 14. 116. 14, 18. Nah. 1. 15.

3 If a woman also vow a vow unto the LORD, and bind *herself* by a bond, *being* in her father's house in her youth;

sacredly bound to keep his word, and to "do according to all that proceedeth out of his mouth." So also, Deut. 23 : 21, "When thou shalt vow a vow unto thy God, thou shalt not slack to pay it." The principle of the precept is otherwise well expressed, "It is better not to vow than to vow and not to pay." It is assumed, however, that the object vowed is in itself lawful, for a vow by which one engages to do what is intrinsically wrong cannot properly bind the conscience. Such was the vow of Herod to the daughter of Herodias, and such the vow of the forty men, Acts 23 : 21, who had "bound themselves with an oath that they would neither eat nor drink till they had killed Paul."——¶ *Shall not break his word.* Heb. "Shall profane his word." That is, shall not, by violating it, show a disregard of its sacred binding character, but shall religiously and scrupulously observe it. A similar phraseology occurs in regard to the covenant, Ps. 55 : 20, "He hath broken (Heb. profaned) his covenant." The sanctity of a vow arises from its "binding the soul with a bond." It has a peculiar force from its voluntary nature, inasmuch as it was not binding before it was assumed. Take, for instance, the case of the temperance pledge. A man may conceive that total abstinence is not in itself absolutely and universally obligatory, and yet if he has once "taken the pledge," he is solemnly bound to keep it, and could not break it without undermining the very foundations of morality in his own soul. The greatest caution and circumspection should be observed in making vows, but when made they should be held sacred when lawful, no matter at what inconvenience. It is mentioned as one of the traits of a good man, Ps. 15 : 4, that "he sweareth to his own hurt, and changeth not."——¶ *All that proceedeth out of his mouth.* It would seem to have been essential to the validity of a vow that it should be actually uttered with the mouth, and not merely made in the heart. Thus, Ps. 66 : 13, 14, "I will go into thy house with burnt-offerings; I will pay thee my vows, which my lips have uttered, and my mouth hath spoken when I was in trouble." If a person merely made a vow in his heart, without letting it pass his lips, it would have been apt to be regarded as only a resolution to vow, and not a vow itself. This would have tended to beget great anxiety in conscientious people, inasmuch as if a vow made in the heart were valid, it would often be difficult to determine whether what was thought of was a bare intention or a genuine vow. It would appear, therefore, that here, just as in a civil contract with our neighbor, words, *uttered* words, were necessary to prevent all uncertainty and make the vow acceptable as such.

V. 3. *If a woman also vow a vow unto the Lord, etc.* The case is evidently that of a woman who is under authority, and not entirely at her own disposal. The law here is, that the vows of such shall not stand if disallowed by those under whose authority she is. By analogy the same rule is no doubt to be extended to the case of minors and servants, who have no just right to will away or dispose of what does not prop-

4 And her father hear her
vow, and her bond wherewith
she hath bound her soul, and
her father shall hold his peace
at her; then all her vows shall
stand, and every bond wherewith she hath bound her soul
shall stand.
5 But if her father disallow
her in the day that he heareth;
not any of her vows, or of her
bonds, wherewith she hath
bound her soul, shall stand:
and the LORD shall forgive her,
because her father disallowed
her.

6 And if she had at all an
husband, when she vowed, or
uttered aught out of her lips,
wherewith she bound her soul;
7 And her husband heard *it*,
and held his peace at her in the
day that he heard *it;* then her
vows shall stand, and her bonds
wherewith she bound her soul
shall stand.
8 But if her husband [e] disallowed her on the day that he
heard *it;* then he shall make
her vow which she vowed, and
that which she uttered with her

e Gen. 3. 16. 1 Cor. 7. 4. 14. 34. Eph. 5. 22, 24.

erly belong to them. Young women, while abiding at home under the parental roof, were especially interdicted these rash vows, and the spirit of the law would seem to strike at the practice in Catholic countries, of young females devoting themselves, by voluntary vows, to a life of seclusion and celibacy; and also at all the arts of priests and others to inveigle them into this surrender.

V. 4. *And her father hear her vow, etc.* This states a case where her vow shall stand. Though the father may not by words reprove the course of his daughter, yet if he is cognizant of it, and keeps silence, he virtually consents to it, and her conscience therefore remains bound. We gather, as a fair inference from this, that any one having the power to check an evil in its bud, and neglecting to do it, is really chargeable with it. His connivance is a kind of tacit approbation.

V. 5. *If her father disallow her in the day that he heareth.* That is, whether on the day that she vowed, or whether on some subsequent day, when it first came to his ears. His disallowance was to vacate her vow, and if her conscience were made uneasy on that account, she was to know that the Lord would forgive her sinful rashness in vowing, or dispense her from the obligation of her vow. There is great homage ordained here to the rightful authority of those who should bear rule over a household. But a more important remark is that of Calvin on the passage:—"The expression is remarkable, 'And the Lord shall forgive her,' whereby Moses gently reproves the foolish thoughtlessness of the girl; and soon afterwards the same thing is spoken of married women. And surely their rashness is worthy of reprehension, if, unmindful of their condition, they, as it were, shake off the yoke, and hastily commit themselves. God therefore hints that they are not without blame; but lest they should be tormented by secret remorse, He removes every scruple, declaring that He will forgive, if the performance of the vow shall have been prevented in any other quarter."

Vs. 6–8. *If she had at all an husband.* This brings up the case of married women, who are forbidden to assume upon them a vow of any importance without their husband's consent. His

lips, wherewith she bound her
soul, of none effect: and the
LORD shall forgive her.
9 But every vow of a widow,
and of her that is divorced,
wherewith they have bound
their souls, shall stand against
her.
10 And if she vowed in her
husband's house, or bound her
soul by a bond with an oath;
11 And her husband heard
it, and held his peace at her,
and disallowed her not; then
all her vows shall stand, and
every vow wherewith she bound
her soul shall stand.
12 But if her husband hath
utterly made them void on the
day he heard *them; then* whatsoever proceedeth out of her
lips concerning her vows, or
concerning the bond of her soul,
shall not stand; her husband
[f] hath made them void, and the
LORD [g] shall forgive her.
13 Every vow and every
binding oath to afflict the soul,
her husband may establish it,
or her husband may make it
void.
14 But if her husband altogether hold his peace at her,

f 1 Cor. 11. 3. *g* ver. 5. 8. c. 15. 25, 28.

---

concurrence with it at the outset shall render it obligatory and irreversible on her part, while his refusal shall make it null and void.——¶ *On the day that he heard (it).* Arab. "On whatsoever day he shall at length have heard of it."

V. 9. *Every vow of a widow, etc.* This is another instance of the application of the law to persons who are at their own disposal, and can act in the premises as they please. The vows of widows and parties divorced were to stand good against them.

Vs. 10–13. *If she vowed in her husband's house, etc.* As this cannot well be supposed a bare repetition of the law given vs. 6–8, the probability is, that it contemplates the case of widows and wives divorced. That is to say, if the vow of such widow or divorced wife were made during the husband's life, but not then performed, the obligation to fulfil in her widowhood or state of divorcement shall depend upon his consent to it or refusal of it at the first making, when she was under his power and authority. His voice in these cases binds or looses the wife. Married women might be sometimes very forward to make large vows of what they would do if ever they again became free, and yet being free might make light of performing their vows on the plea that they were uttered when they were under the power of their husbands. To prevent this, the present law seems added, enacting that in case a woman vowed in her husband's house, and he held his peace (v. 11), then all her vows should stand, even after his death, or after she is made free by divorce. Another supposition is, that the widow or divorced woman may have returned to her father's house (Lev. 22:13), and he, supposing himself to have recovered his original power over her, might presume to disannul her vows, as though she had been married. The present injunction would guard against such a contingency. The dependence of vs. 10–13 upon v. 9, seems strongly to confirm this interpretation.

Vs. 14, 15. *If her husband altogether hold his peace, etc.* The husband was to have it in his power to "establish or

from day to day; then he establisheth all her vows, or all her bonds, which *are* upon her: he confirmeth them, because he held his peace at her in the day that he heard *them*.

15 But if he shall any ways make them void, after that he hath heard *them*; then he shall bear her iniquity.

16 These *are* the statutes which the LORD commanded Moses between a man and his wife; between the father and his daughter, *being yet* in her youth in her father's house.

CHAPTER XXXI.

AND the LORD spake unto Moses, saying,

2 Avenge [a] the children of Israel of the Midianites: afterward shalt thou be gathered [b] unto thy people.

a c. 25. 17. b c. 27. 13.

---

make void" the vows of his wife, but in case of his tacit or explicit consent to the religious vow of his wife—and so in like manner of the father towards his daughter—once freely given at the first making of the vow, should give it sanction and make it irreversible. He, in fact, thus made the vow his own, and was not at liberty to retract it. His silence at the time was to be fairly interpreted as consent, and if he attempted to recall that consent, or to hinder the due performance of the vow, then he was "to bear her iniquity," that is, the Lord would punish *him*, not *her*, for a gross breach of faith. "Hence we learn," says Jarchi, "that he which is a cause of scandal or offence unto his neighbor, shall come in his stead into all punishments."

V. 16. *These (are) the statutes which the Lord commanded Moses, etc.* That is, these statutes were ordained for the preservation of order, for the good of families, for the peace and tranquillity of all parties. It is altogether probable that some differences had arisen in families in regard to these matters, and that the immediate aim of the laws here enacted was to settle the power of husbands over their wives, and of parents over their children, while they were young and abode in the family.

CHAPTER XXXI.

The War against the Midianites.

V. 1. *The Lord spake unto Moses, etc.* The command had before been given, ch. 25:17, that Israel should "vex the Midianites, and smite them," but for some reason the execution of the command was then deferred for a season, or the writer has not followed the precise order of events, as the various orders relative to numbering the people, declaring the law of female inheritance, appointing Joshua as Moses' successor, prescribing the sacrifices, etc., intervene between the issuing of the command for the invasion of Midian and its accomplishment. But nothing is more usual than such breaks and translocations in the sacred narrative, and as all the facts intended are really recorded, it is not of so much moment that the precise order of the facts should be punctiliously observed.

V. 2. *Avenge the children of Israel of the Midianites.* Heb. "Avenge the vengeance of the children of Israel;" a Hebraistic form of expression, carrying with it a peculiar emphasis. Gr. "Avenge the cause of the children of Israel on the Midianites." Vulg. "Revenge first the children of Israel on the

3 And Moses spake unto the people, saying, Arm some of yourselves unto the war, and let them go against the Midianites, and avenge the LORD of Midian.

4 Of every tribe a thousand, throughout all the tribes of

Midianites." The people of Israel were not hereby commanded to enter upon this work with vindictive feelings, but as the instruments of a just retribution upon a guilty race who had incurred the divine displeasure by "the wiles wherewith they had beguiled Israel in the matter of Peor," ch. 25 : 18. By the wicked advice of Baalam, and with an express and diabolical intention of depriving them of Jehovah's protection, they had attempted to seduce the Israelites to idolatry and its obscene orgies. The consequence was that 24,000 of the chosen people fell victims to their own temerity. But were *they* thus to be punished, and should the prime instigators of the horrible wickedness escape with impunity? By no means. The Lord accordingly here ordains vengeance to be executed upon the transgressors. He does it, as the Lord supreme, to whom vengeance and recompense belong, and who would not have men avenge themselves. It is therefore a measure which cannot be brought into precedent as justifying a similar war without a like commission, for the Hebrews in this matter were merely the executioners of a judicial sentence. This event the Lord determined should be brought about prior to the death of Moses, that he might have, as it were, a last token of the divine care for the welfare of his people. This he was to witness and then be "gathered unto his people." There is nothing said in this connection of the Moabites, for the reason, doubtless, that the Midianites had entertained Balaam after his departure from Balak, and that they had been chief in concocting the conspiracy which had occasioned so much disaster to Israel, and which was now about to recoil upon themselves. Add to this, that in the present sparing of Moab regard was probably had to the memory of Lot, the founder of their race; although at a subsequent period they also paid the penalty of their offences.——¶ *Gathered unto thy people.* See Note ch. 20 : 24. Gen. 25 : 8. "God sometimes removes useful men when we think they could ill be spared; but this ought to satisfy us, that they are never removed till they have done the work which was appointed them." —*Henry.*

V. 3. *Avenge the Lord of Midian.* The whole clause, literally rendered from the Hebrew, reads thus: "And let them be against (or upon) Midian to render (or give) the vengeance of Jehovah upon Midian." The phrase "giving vengeance" is parallel in the Gr. of 2 Thess. 1 : 8, "*Taking* (Gr. *giving*) *vengeance* upon all them that know not God, etc." The reader will observe that whereas God says, v. 2, "Avenge *the children of Israel* of the Midianites," here Moses says, "Avenge *the Lord* of Midian," implying that while the Lord marks his tender concern for the welfare of his people, they, on the other hand, show a paramount concern for the glory of their God; to *that* they will be prompted to subordinate every interest of their own. Jarchi: "He who arrays himself against Israel is regarded the same as if he arrayed himself against the Lord."

V. 4. *Of every tribe a thousand.* Twelve thousand in all, comparatively a small force to contend with a whole nation, the multitudes of which may be inferred from the abundance of spoils

Israel, shall ye send to the
war.

5 So there were delivered out
of the thousands of Israel, a
thousand of *every* tribe, twelve
thousand armed for war.

6 And Moses sent them to
the war, a thousand of *every*
tribe, them and Phinehas the
son of Eleazar the priest, to the
war, with the holy instruments,
and the trumpets to [c] blow, in
his hand.

7 And they warred against
the Midianites, as the LORD
commanded Moses; and [d] they
slew all the males.

8 And [e] they slew the kings
of Midian, beside the rest of
them that were slain; *namely*,

c c. 10. 9. d Deut. 20. 13. Judg. 21. 11 1 K. 11. 15, 16. e Josh. 13. 21, 22.

---

taken, and from the slaughter of five kings who fell on this occasion, v. 8. An hundred thousand fighting men would have been but a sixth part of the disposable force which might have been employed in this enterprise had infinite wisdom seen fit, but as the Most High determined that the glory should not be referred to the number of those engaged in achieving the victory, he no doubt prescribed to Moses the amount of men to be detailed for the service, and these were to be taken in equal proportion from all the tribes, that one tribe might not vaunt itself over another in view of the result, but that all the glory might be ascribed to the Lord alone. "There is no restraint to the Lord to save by many or by few." 1 Sam. 14:6.

V. 6. *And Phinehas the son of Eleazar the priest.* The capacity in which Phinehas was to go was not, we presume, that of general or leader of the expedition, which would more naturally devolve on Joshua, but as a general encourager of the host, and especially as overseer of the Levites, to whose care was intrusted "the holy instruments and the trumpets," which latter were always to be blown upon occasions like the present, when war was to be engaged in. Yet the precise import of "holy instruments (Heb. instruments or vessels of holiness)," in this connection, it is not easy to determine. Some have understood the ark of the covenant and its appurtenances, and some the Urim and Thummim; but the probable construction, we think, is that of Le Clerc, who would translate "and" by "even," and have *instruments* stand in apposition with *trumpets*; "with the holy instruments *even* the trumpets to blow, etc." This, as we have often remarked before, is a very usual sense of the Heb. word for "and." As to the suggestion of Spencer and others, founded upon the Chald. version, that the Urim and Thummim were included in the instruments, this is less likely from the fact, that these articles, with the Golden Plate or Pectoral, were properly in the hands of Eleazar the High Priest and not of Phinehas, ch. 27:21. 20:26.

V. 8. *Slew the kings of Midian.* The title "kings" is doubtless here to be taken in quite a limited sense. In the parallel passage, Josh. 13:21, they are called "dukes of Sihon," importing the same as vassals or tributaries. After the death of Sihon they probably rose somewhat in the scale of dignity and were thence called "kings," but the true idea is that of petty chieftains. One of the five, viz., Zur, was the father of Cozbi, the Midianitess, killed by Phinehas, ch. 25:15.——¶ *Balaam also, the son of Beor, they slew with the sword.* However this miserable man may have

Evi, and Rekem, and Zur, and
Hur, and Reba, five kings of
Midian: Balaam also, the son
of Beor, they slew with the
sword.
9 And the children of Israel
took *all* the women of Midian
captives, and their little ones,
and took the spoil of all their
cattle, and all their flocks, and
all their goods.
10 And they [f] burnt all their
cities wherein they dwelt, and
all their goodly castles, with
fire.
11 And they took all the
spoil [g] and all the prey, *both* of
men and of beasts.
12 And they brought the
captives, and the prey, and the
spoil, unto Moses and Eleazar
the priest, and unto the congregation of the children of Israel,
unto the camp at the plains [h] of
Moab, which *are* by Jordan
near Jericho.

f Josh. 6. 24. Rev. 18. 8.

g Deut. 20. 14. Josh. 8. 2. *h* c. 22. 1.

found his way into the ranks of the Midianites, yet here he is, and here a condign punishment meets him. Having virtually taken the sword by being instrumental in bringing Midian into armed hostility against Israel, he perishes by the sword. The language of Ezekiel, ch. 32 : 28, finds in him a fit application: "Yea, thou shalt be broken in the midst of the uncircumcised, and shalt lie with them that are slain with the sword." He falls in the judgment which he has provoked, and leaves his name as "a by-word and a hissing" to all future generations. We wind up all further allusions to him in the following remarks of Mr. Kitto: "According to the view which we take of Balaam's character, it is not so peculiar as it seems. Separated from the external accidents of time, of country, and position—we may go into the streets, and find a Balaam in every third man we meet. He belonged to that still numerous class who theoretically know God, and who actually do fear him—but the love and fear of whom are not the governing and regulating principles of their minds. They are convinced, but not converted. They can prize and strongly desire the privileges of God's elect—they long to "die the death of the righteous," but are unwilling to live their life. They would serve God; but they must serve mammon also; and in the strife between the two contending influences, their lives are made bitter and their deaths perilous."

V. 9. *Took the spoil of all their cattle, etc.* Rather, Heb. "took as spoil," i. e., plundered, pillaged, "all their cattle, and all their flocks, etc." "Taking the spoil *of* cattle, flocks, etc.," is not a very intelligible English phrase.

V. 10. *Burnt all their cities, etc.* The destruction of these places would deprive the Israelites of all plea for taking possession of them as a kind of nestling-places where they could abide, instead of encountering the hardship of conquering Canaan.

V. 11. *Took all the spoil and all the prey.* The former implies such things pertaining to men and women as were usually taken in war, as garments, gold, silver, provisions, etc., while the latter is applied more especially to beasts and cattle. These, together with the captive women, were brought to the rulers and the congregation to learn what disposal should be made of them by divine direction.

13 And Moses and Eleazar the priest, and all the princes of the congregation, went forth to meet them without the camp.

14 And Moses was wroth with the officers of the host, *with* the captains over thousands, and captains over hundreds, which came from the battle.

15 And Moses said unto them, Have ye saved all the women [i] alive?

16 Behold, these [k] caused the children of Israel, through the counsel [l] of Balaam, to commit trespass against the LORD in the matter of Peor, and there was a plague among [m] the congregation of the LORD.

17 Now therefore [n] kill every male among the little ones, and kill every woman that hath known man by lying with him.

i Deut. 20. 13. 1 Sam. 15. 3.

k c. 25. 1–3. l 2 Pet. 2. 15. Rev. 2. 14. m c. 25. 9. n Judg. 21. 11.

V. 13. *Went forth to meet them without the camp.* Somewhat as Melchisedek, king and priest, went forth to meet Abraham after the slaughter of the kings, Gen. 14:18–14, so does Moses, the "king in Jeshurun," Eleazar the priest, and the princes now go forth to meet Abraham's children returning from the slaughter of the kings of Midian. The object was to congratulate the host upon its victory, and to make the triumphal procession more imposing. They were to do this "without the camp," inasmuch as they had become polluted by shedding blood and coming in contact with dead bodies, and must therefore undergo a process of purification before they could be received into the camp, v. 19, 20. ch. 5: 2, 3. 19:11–13.

Vs. 14–17. *Moses was wroth with the officers of the host.* Heb. *al pekudë hehäyil, with the visitors of the force.* Gr. "With the bishops of the host." These, however, are immediately explained as the *captains* of the thousands and hundreds which came from the battle. The wrath of Moses on this occasion was not excited by any provocation that was personal to himself. In his own cause he was uniformly meek and gentle; but when the Lord's honor or glory was at stake, he was filled with a holy zeal which passed easily into indignation towards the offenders. The occasion of his anger now was the sparing the females instead of putting them to death. We do not, indeed, read that an express command had been given them to this effect, but it was doubtless implied in the general order to avenge Israel of the Midianites; for as the women had been the principal instruments of seducing the people into sin in the worship of Peor, it was fair to infer that they were not to be spared. "God had put to death the adulterers of Israel by the plague, and now it was fit that the adulteresses of Midian, especially since they had been the tempters, should be put to death by the sword."—*Henry.* The sentence passed was no doubt severe in the extreme and abhorrent to our benevolent feelings, but God is the supreme arbiter of the lot of all men, and may remove them out of the world in any manner that he sees fit. If this is done by pestilence or earthquake, by shipwreck, famine, in deadly battle, wasting disease, or old age, no one complains. Why should there be complaint if, in the capacity of supreme judge and governor, he expressly *orders* a portion of his creatures to be put to death for crimes committed which can-

18 But all the women-children, that have not known a man by lying with him, keep alive for yourselves.

19 And do ye abide without the camp seven days: whosoever [o] hath killed any person, and whosoever hath touched any slain, purify *both* yourselves and your captives on the third day, and on the seventh day.

20 And purify all *your* raiment, and all that is made of skins, and all work of goats' *hair*, and all things made of wood.

21 And Eleazar the priest said unto the men of war which

o c. 5. 2. 19. 11, etc.

---

not but be admitted in the circumstances to be worthy of death? Is he to be any more accused of harshness than if they were taken away in what is termed "the course of nature," in which we are equally bound to recognize a providential agency? It is to be remembered that in all probability these very women, some or all of them, had been concerned in the abomination of Peor, and that if they were spared alive the same revolting and criminal scenes would be in danger of being enacted over again, and thus a new plague or judgment inflicted upon the people. To an eye that could take in the whole from the end to the beginning, it would undoubtedly appear that this was a procedure of kindness and mercy rather than of cruelty, and the confession extorted, "Just and true are all thy ways, thou King of saints."

V. 18. *But all the women-children, etc.* The policy which originated this order contemplated, we may presume, the rearing up of these Midianitish girls and maidens, either to be disposed of by sale to other nations, to be employed as servants, or, in case they became proselytes, to marry them as ordained, Deut. 21 : 11–14. The Jewish writers have many conceits as to the manner in which the discrimination here spoken of was to be made, but it is sufficient to suggest that the age alone would be a sufficient criterion, and there was probably no other.

Vs. 19, 20. *Yourselves and your captives.* As we cannot well suppose that the heathen nations would contract defilement from the dead, or otherwise become subject to legal uncleanness, the obligation to be purified on this occasion arose from their having come so fully into the possession of the Israelites as to constitute, as it were, a part of them. Accordingly Jarchi here remarks: "'Yourselves and your captivity;' not that heathens do receive uncleanness, and need to be sprinkled; but as you, the children of the covenant, so your captives also which come into the covenant, and are unclean, have need to be sprinkled."——¶ *All that is made of skins, etc.* Travellers inform us that among the common furniture of the Arabs at the present day are hair sacks, and trunks, and baskets covered with skins, great wooden bowls, hand-mills, and pitchers. It is to articles of this kind, which were doubtless in use among the ancient Israelites, that the injunction in the present passage refers. They were all to be cleansed in water.

Vs. 21–24. *This is the ordinance of the law, etc.* This order was given by Eleazar, the high-priest, to the people, but it may be supposed that it was first communicated to him by Moses. It was to be henceforth a standing law to the Israelitish soldiery, that all who had been in a battle, whether they had actually slain an enemy and touched

went to the battle, This *is* the
ordinance of the law which the
LORD commanded Moses;
22 Only the gold, and the
silver, the brass, the iron, the
tin, and the lead,
23 Every thing that may
abide the fire, ye shall make *it*
go through the fire, and it shall
be clean; nevertheless it shall
be purified[p] with the water of
separation: and all that abideth
not the fire ye shall make go
through the water.
24 And[q] ye shall wash your
clothes on the seventh day, and
ye shall be clean, and afterward
ye shall come into the camp.
25 And the LORD spake unto
Moses, saying,

p c. 19. 9, 17. q Lev. 11. 25.

26 Take the sum of the prey
that was taken, *both* of man and
of beast, thou, and Eleazar the
priest, and the chief fathers of
the congregation;
27 And divide[r] the prey into
two parts; between them that
took the war upon them, who
went out to battle, and between
all the congregation:
28 And levy a tribute[s] unto
the LORD of the men of war
which went out to battle: one
[t] soul of five hundred, *both* of
the persons, and of the beeves,
and of the asses, and of the
sheep:
29 Take *it* of their half, and
give *it* unto Eleazar the priest,

r Josh. 22. 8. 1 Sam. 30. 24. Ps. 68. 12. s Gen. 14. 20. Josh. 6. 19. 2 Sam. 8. 11, 12. Prov. 3. 9, 10. t ver. 30. 47. c. 18. 26.

his body or not, should be obliged thus to purify themselves; and moreover, that all kind of spoil which would endure the fire, as hard metals, gold, silver, etc., should be cleansed by fire, and then sprinkled with the *purification water* (ch. 19:1, 2, etc.); while such things as could be washed with water should undergo that process.

The Law of the Division of the Spoil.

Vs. 25–27. *Take the sum of the prey, etc.* Heb. "The head of the prey." See Note on ch. 1:2. The soldiery having been thus commanded to cleanse themselves preparatory to re-entering the camp, an order is now given relative to an equitable division of the spoil. Of this the whole amount was to be divided into two equal parts, one of which was to be distributed among the 12,000 who had been engaged in the expedition; the other half among the rest of the Israelites, as being all concerned in the common cause. David, we find, at a later period enacted a similar law, although under somewhat different circumstances. 1 Sam. 30:24, 25, "For who will hearken unto you in this matter? but as his part is that goeth down to the battle, so shall his part be that tarrieth by the stuff: they shall part alike. And it was so from that day forward, that he made it a statute and an ordinance for Israel unto this day." To prevent all partial dealing, the distribution was committed to the management of the heads of the several tribes in concert with the high-priest.

Vs. 28, 29. *And levy a tribute, etc.* This was another feature of the division. Out of the half that fell to the lot of the soldiers was to be deducted a five hundredth part of every kind of spoil, as an offering to God, in acknowledgment of him as sovereign owner of all, and the author of all their success; and

for an heave offering of the
Lord.
30 And of the children of Israel's half, thou shalt take[u] one
portion of fifty, of the persons, of the beeves, of the asses, and of the flocks, of all manner of beasts, and give[v] them unto the Levites, which[w] keep the charge of the tabernacle of the Lord.
31 And Moses and Eleazar the priest did as the Lord commanded Moses.
32 And the booty, *being* the rest of the prey which the men of war had caught, was six hundred thousand and seventy thousand and five thousand sheep,
33 And threescore and twelve thousand beeves,
34 And threescore and one thousand asses,
35 And thirty and two thousand persons in all, of women that had not known man by lying with him.
36 And the half, *which was* the portion of them that went out to war, was in number three hundred thousand and seven and thirty thousand and five hundred sheep:
37 And the Lord's tribute of the sheep was six hundred and threescore and fifteen.
38 And the beeves *were* thirty and six thousand; of which the Lord's tribute *was* threescore and twelve.
39 And the asses *were* thirty thousand and five hundred; of which the Lord's tribute *was* threescore and one.
40 And the persons *were* sixteen thousand; of which the Lord's tribute *was* thirty and two persons.
41 And Moses gave the tribute, *which was* the Lord's heave-offering, unto Eleazar the priest; as[x] the Lord commanded Moses.
42 And of the children of Israel's half, which Moses divided from the men that warred,
43 (Now the half *that per-*

u ver. 42, 47. *v* 1 Cor. 9. 13, 14. *w* c. 3. 7, etc. *x* c. 18. 8, 19.

---

this was to be presented as an heave-offering to the priests.

Vs. 30, 31. *Of the children of Israel's half, etc.* In like manner, out of the half belonging to the whole body of the people, who had not shared in the dangers and hardships of the war, a much larger proportion was to be deducted from each article of spoil, viz., a fiftieth part to be presented to the Levites, the other branch of the ministry, as a religious acknowledgment of the same purport with the preceding. In this it was designed that whatever the Lord's ministers had for their maintenance in his service should be given to them in such a manner as if it were offered to himself. The far greater number of the Levites made it proper that in the partition their portion should be much greater than that of the priests. The Levites had one part in fifty, the priests one in five hundred, equivalent to a tithe, according to the rule laid down ch. 18:21–28.

Vs. 32–47. *The booty, (being) the rest of the prey, etc.* That is, deducting the "spoils," strictly so called, the clothes, armor, and valuables of the enemy, together with the movables and money,

tained unto the congregation
was three hundred thousand and
thirty thousand *and* seven thousand and five hundred sheep,
44 And thirty and six thousand beeves,
45 And thirty thousand asses
and five hundred,
46 And sixteen thousand persons;)
47 Even [y] of the children of
Israel's half, Moses took one portion of fifty, *both* of man and of
beast, and gave them unto the
Levites, which kept the charge
of the tabernacle of the LORD;
as the LORD commanded Moses.

y ver. 30.

48 And the officers which
were over thousands of the host,
the captains of thousands, and
captains of hundreds, came near
unto Moses:
49 And they said unto Moses,
Thy servants have taken the
sum of the men of war which
are under our charge, and there
lacketh not one man of us.
50 We have therefore brought
an oblation for the LORD, what
every man hath gotten, of jewels of gold, chains, and bracelets,
rings, ear-rings, and tablets, to
make [z] an atonement for our
souls before the LORD.

z Ex. 30. 12, 16.

---

which were not divided in common, but belonged individually to the captors; also whatever persons had been slain since their return, and whatever cattle may have been killed for eating on the way; the rest or residue, which was to be divided, amounted to totals as follows:

Sheep, 675,000....	The soldiers,	337,500;	therefrom to the Lord...	675.
	The people,	337,500;	therefrom to the Levites.	6,750.
Beeves, 72,000....	The soldiers,	36,000;	therefrom to the Lord...	72.
	The people,	36,000;	therefrom to the Levites.	720.
Asses, 61,000....	The soldiers,	30,500;	therefrom to the Lord...	61.
	The people,	30,500;	therefrom to the Levites.	610.
Persons, 32,000.....	The soldiers,	16,000;	therefrom to the Lord....	32.
	The people,	16,000;	therefrom to the Levites.	320.

Vs. 48–50. *The officers which were over the thousands, etc.* The officers, upon their return from the war, made a muster of the soldiery to see what numbers they had lost, and found, to their joy and surprise, that not a single man was missing of the whole twelve thousand! This was probably a victory without a parallel in all history, and could never have been accomplished without the Lord's special intervention. This signal token of the Lord's favor would tend to minister encouragement and confidence to them in all future emergencies, and they seem to have been sensible of their obligations from the feelings now evinced; for they unanimously resolved, out of the spoil which they had taken, such as gold, jewels, bracelets, etc., which they were not required to divide with the congregation, to make a free-will offering to the Lord, for the service of the Tabernacle. So in aftertimes both the Tabernacle and the Temple were enriched with the spoils taken from the enemies of Israel. 2 Sam. 8:11, 12. 1 Chron. 26:26, 27. "We should never take any thing to ourselves in war or trade, which we cannot in faith consecrate a part of to

51 And Moses and Eleazar the priest took the gold of them, *even* all wrought jewels.

52 And all the gold of the offering that they offered up to the LORD, of the captains of thousands, and of the captains of hundreds, was sixteen thousand seven hundred and fifty shekels.

53 (*For* the men of war had [a] taken spoil, every man for himself.)

54 And Moses and Eleazar the priest took the gold of the captains of thousands and of hundreds, and brought it into the tabernacle of the congregation, *for* [b] a memorial for the children of Israel before the LORD.

a Deut. 20. 14. *b* Ex. 30. 16.

CHAPTER XXXII.

NOW the children of Reuben, and the children of Gad, had a very great multitude of cattle: and when they saw the land of Jazer [a], and the land of Gilead [b], that, behold, the place *was* a place [c] for cattle;

2 The children of Gad and the children of Reuben, came and spake unto Moses, and to Eleazar the priest, and unto the princes of the congregation, saying,

3 Ataroth, and Dibon,[d], and Jazer, and Nimrah [e], and Heshbon [f], and Elealeh, and Shebam [g], and Nebo, and Beon [h],

a c. 21. 32. ver. 35. *Jaazer.* Josh. 13. 25. 2 Sam. 24. 5. Is. 16. 8, 9. *b* Jer. 50. 19. Mic. 7. 4. *c* Gen. 13. 2, 5. 47. 4. *d* Is. 15. 2, 4. *e* ver. 36. *Beth-nimrah.* *f* Judg. 11 26. *g* ver. 38. *Shibmah.* *h* ver. 38. *Baal-meon.*

God, who "hates robbery for burnt-offering;" but when God has remarkably preserved and succeeded us, he expects we should make some particular return of gratitude to him."—*Henry.* ——¶ *To make an atonement for our souls.* That is, to make an acknowledgment to God for the preservation of their lives; as also perhaps to offer a kind of expiation for sparing the women and whatever other miscarriages they may have been guilty of in the conduct of the war.

Vs. 51–54. *Moses and Eleazar the priest took the gold, etc.* In doing which we may well suppose they commended the piety and gratitude of the offerers. The oblation was delivered to be employed in the service for which it was intended. It amounted to a vast sum, that is to say, 16,750 shekels, which, reduced to our coin, would fall little short of $140,000. The offering was henceforth laid up in the Tabernacle as a monument both of the singular mercy of God in the preservation of the army in this war, and of the pious gratitude of those who had been its principal conductors.

CHAPTER XXXII.

Reuben and Gad request an Inheritance on the East of Jordan.

Vs. 1–5. *The children of Reuben and the children of Gad had a very great multitude of cattle, etc.* A large portion of the territory recently taken from the two Amorite kings, Sihon and Og, was distinguished for the fertility of its soil and its adaptedness to the purpose of breeding and grazing cattle. This fact gave this region peculiar attractions in the eyes of Reuben and Gad, who, of all the tribes, had the greatest abundance of stock, and were most devoted to its cultivation. The greater

4 *Even* the country[i] which the LORD smote before the congregation of Israel, *is* a land for cattle, and thy servants have cattle:

i c. 21. 24, 34.

5 Wherefore, said they, if we have found grace in thy sight, let this land be given unto thy servants for a possession, *and* bring us not over Jordan.

---

part of this territory is in modern times called the "Belka," and the Bedouins say of it, "Thou canst not find a country like the Belka." Buckingham bears the strongest testimony to the picturesque beauty, the fine climate, and exuberant fertility of this part of the country east of the Jordan, and seems to have no hesitation in declaring it far superior to any part of the country *west* of the Jordan, through which he had travelled.—(*Travels among the Arab Tribes*, p. 141.) The heads of these tribes, therefore, came to Moses and Eleazar, preferring a petition that this region, so well adapted to their favorite pursuit, might be conferred upon them instead of their being required to pass over the river and receive their allotment with their brethren within the bounds of Canaan. Their motives in making this proposition, though they appeared at first somewhat questionable to Moses, yet were subsequently so explained as to remove, in great measure, his anxiety, and to redound to the credit of their fealty and fidelity. At the same time, it is not improbable that there was a larger admixture of worldly prompting in the request than they themselves imagined. The lot that befell these tribes in a subsequent age, 1 Chron. 5:25. 2 Kings, 15:29, gives great countenance to the following pithy but quaint remarks of the old commentator Ness on the passage:—"'Tis not at all unlikely that these two tribes were too much engaged in their affections to that portion of land, as Lot's mind was too much set upon the plains of Sodom; for as *he* was soon after carried away captive by the four kings, so those here are noted to have been the first that were carried away captive out of this very land who were the first of all the tribes that had this land assigned to them for their inheritance: strong affections cause strong afflictions; if we love over-much, we shall be sure to grieve over-much. When God sees us set upon it to have this or that, have it we may, but with an after-reckoning that may dissweeten it with a witness." There is nothing here said of Manasseh, though it appears, from v. 33, that half that tribe were included in the assignment.—Of Jazer, see ch. 21:32, with Note.—The land of Gilead (Gr. Galaad) was famous not only for its rich pasturage, but also for its aromatic gums, from which different kinds of balsams were made, alluded to in Scripture as the "balm of Gilead."——¶ *A place for cattle.* A place favorable to the rearing and feeding of cattle, that is, of flocks and herds. Wherefore when the Lord promises to feed his people with spiritual food, he draws the imagery from the feeding of cattle in these fertile regions. Mic. 7:14, "Feed thy people with thy rod, the flock of thine heritage, which dwell solitarily in the wood, in the midst of Carmel: let them feed in Bashan and Gilead, as in the days of old." Jer. 50:19, "And I will bring Israel again to his habitation, and he shall feed on Carmel and Bashan, and his soul shall be satisfied upon mount Ephraim and Gilead." As to the various localities mentioned in this connection, it will be sufficient to refer the reader to Kitto's

6 And Moses said unto the
children of Gad, and to the
children of Reuben, Shall your
brethren go to war, and shall ye
sit here?
7 And wherefore discourage
ye the heart of the children of
Israel from going over into the
land which the LORD hath given
them?
8 Thus did your fathers, when
[k] I sent them from Kadesh-barnea to see the land.
9 For when they went up unto the valley of Eshcol, and saw
the land, they discouraged the
heart of the children of Israel,
that they should not go into the
land which the LORD had given
them.
10 And [l] the LORD's anger
was kindled the same time, and
he sware, saying,
11 Surely none of the men
that came up out of Egypt, from
twenty years old and upward,
shall see the land which I sware
unto Abraham, unto Isaac, and
unto Jacob; because [m] they have
not wholly followed me;
12 Save Caleb the son of
Jephunneh the Kenezite, and
Joshua the son of Nun; for they
have wholly followed the LORD.
13 And the LORD's anger was
kindled against Israel, and he
made them [n] wander in the wilderness forty years, until [o] all the
generation that had done evil in
the sight of the LORD was consumed.
14 And, behold, ye are risen
up in your fathers' stead, an increase [p] of sinful men, to aug-
ment [q] yet the fierce anger of the
LORD toward Israel.
15 For if [r] ye turn away from
after him, he will yet again
leave [s] them in the wilderness,
and ye shall destroy all this
people.

k c. 13. 3–26. Deut. 1. 22. *l* c. 14. 11, 29. Deut. 1. 35.

m c. 14. 24, 30. Josh. 14. 8, 9. *n* c. 14. 33–35. *o* c. 26. 64, 65. 1 Cor. 10. 5. Heb. 3. 16–19. *p* Ps. 78. 57. *q* Neh. 13. 18. Is. 65. 6, 7. *r* Deut. 30. 17. Josh. 22. 16, 18. 2 Chr. 7. 19. 15. 2. *s* c. 14. 35.

edition of the Bible, where all the accessible information respecting them is embodied.——¶ *The country which the Lord smote before the congregation.* Implying, perhaps, that the Lord had caused it to be smitten or subjugated, in order that it might be taken as a possession and deemed a part of the promised land though not within the Jordan. This construction was not unnatural, for the country had previously belonged to Sihon, king of the Amorites, and the land of the Amorites was promised to Abraham, Gen. 15 : 16, 21.

Vs. 6–15. *Shall your brethren go to war, and shall ye sit here?* It cannot be denied that there was ground for Moses' suspicions. The request appeared to proceed from selfishness, worldliness, and unbelief. It looked as if they were willing to let their brethren go and fight their way among the Canaanites, and get possession of whatever they could; but as to the land which was already subdued, and which was of the richest quality, that they would fain have allotted to themselves without any further trouble. The land moreover was not within the precincts of Canaan proper, and to settle down so far from the house of God and the ordinances of religion seemed to argue a culpable indifference to their spiritual as compared with their temporal wel-

16 And they came near unto him, and said, We will build sheep-folds here for our cattle, and cities for our little ones;

17 But we [t] ourselves will go ready armed before the children of Israel, until we have brought them unto their place: and our little ones shall dwell in the fenced cities, because of the inhabitants of the land.

18 We [u] will not return unto our houses, until the children of Israel have inherited every man his inheritance:

19 For we will not inherit with them on yonder side Jordan, or forward; because [v] our inheritance is fallen to us on this side Jordan eastward.

t Josh. 4. 12, 13. u Josh. 22. 4. v ver. 33. Josh. 13. 8.

20 And [w] Moses said unto them, If ye will do this thing, if ye will go armed before the LORD to war,

21 And will go all of you armed over Jordan before the LORD, until he hath driven out his enemies from before him,

22 And the land be subdued [x] before the LORD; then afterward [y] ye shall return, and be guiltless before the LORD, and before Israel; and this land shall be your possession before the LORD.

23 But if ye will not do so, behold, ye have sinned against the LORD: and be sure your sin [z] will find you out.

w Deut. 3. 18, etc. Josh. 1. 14, etc. 4. 12, 13. x Josh. 18. 1. y Josh. 22. 4, 9. z Gen. 4. 7. 44. 16. Ps. 90. 8. 139. 11. Prov. 13. 21. Is. 59. 12. 1 Cor. 4. 5.

fare. Again, it had the air of shrinking from the toils and dangers, and the sanguinary scenes which might have to be encountered in conquering the land of the Canaanites. Such was the construction which Moses was led to put upon the proposed measure, and which drew from him an earnest remonstrance. He set before them what he conceived to be the pernicious tendency of their example; that it was calculated to discourage the rest of their brethren; and then reminds them that they would thereby be acting the part of their predecessors the spies, who had so grievously disheartened the congregation by their fears, and had thereby excited the divine displeasure to that degree, that that generation, for their mutinous and distrustful spirit, were excluded from the land of promise. He exhorts them, therefore, to beware of the same spirit lest the same disastrous consequences should ensue, and the people be left to perish in the wilderness.

Vs. 16–27. *They came near unto him and said, etc.* The two tribes in question, speaking through their appointed organs, neither acknowledge nor deny the charge now made, nor do they evince a disposition to take the least offence at it. On the contrary, with a view to give the utmost satisfaction to Moses, they voluntarily engaged to accompany their brethren in arms, and even to go before them to battle, continuing with them till the whole land should be subdued, and every tribe be put in possession of its destined inheritance. This was fair and equitable; and Moses readily acquiesced in the proposal, warning them, however, that if ever they should recede from their purpose, and violate their engagement, "their sin should surely find them out," and be visited upon them. In considering the proffer

24 Build [a] you cities for your little ones, and folds for your sheep; and do that which hath proceeded out of your mouth.

25 And the children of Gad, and the children of Reuben, spake unto Moses, saying, Thy [b] servants will do as my lord commandeth.

26 Our little ones, our wives, our flocks, and all our cattle, shall be there in the cities of Gilead;

27 But [c] thy servants will pass over, every man armed for war, before the LORD to battle, as my lord saith.

28 So concerning them Moses commanded Eleazar the priest, and Joshua the son of Nun, and the chief fathers of the tribes of the children of Israel:

29 And [d] Moses said unto them, If the children of Gad, and the children of Reuben, will pass with you over Jordan, every man armed to battle, before the LORD, and the land shall be subdued before you, then ye shall give them the land of Gilead for a possession.

30 But if they will not pass over with you armed, they shall have possessions among you in the land of Canaan.

31 And the children of Gad, and the children of Reuben, answered, saying, As the LORD hath said unto thy servants, so will we do.

32 We will pass over armed before the LORD into the land of Canaan, that the possession of our inheritance on this side Jordan *may be* ours.

a ver. 16, 34, etc. b Josh. 1, 13, 14. c John 4, 12. d ver. 20.

---

of these tribes it is not necessary to suppose that the whole even of their fighting men were to be included in it. It would be necessary that a portion of them should remain behind to till the ground and to guard the flocks, children, and women. Accordingly we read that only about 40,000 of the two tribes and a half went over armed, whereas their whole number was about 100,000.——¶ *On yonder side Jordan, or forward.* That is, we will not inherit with them on the opposite side of the Jordan, in the near vicinity of the river, nor yet further on, or further inland, in the more central regions of the country.——¶ *If ye will go armed before the Lord.* That is, before the Ark of the Covenant, the special symbol of the Lord's presence. The three tribes of Reuben, Gad, and Simeon, marched immediately before the Sanctuary, ch. 2:10, 14. 10:18, so that Moses requires of them only to occupy their usual place when they went to war against the Canaanites.——¶ *Your sin will find you out.* That is, the punishment of your sin will sooner or later overtake you. Gr. "Ye shall know your sins, when evils fall upon you."

Vs. 28–33. *Concerning them Moses commanded, etc.* The measure was not, therefore, actually carried out in Moses' lifetime, but was left in charge to Eleazar and Joshua, and the fathers of the tribes, to be accomplished for them in case they adhered faithfully to the terms of their engagement.——¶ *Shall give them the land of Gilead, etc.* This appears to have been the name given in a broad sense to the whole country east of the Jordan.——¶ *But if they*

33 And [e] Moses gave unto
them, *even* to the children of
Gad, and to the children of
Reuben, and unto half the tribe
of Manasseh the son of Joseph,
[f] the kingdom of Sihon king of
the Amorites, and the kingdom
of Og king of Bashan, the land,
with the cities thereof in the
coasts, *even* the cities of the
country round about.
34 And the children of Gad
built Dibon [g], and Ataroth, and
Aroer [h],

35 And Atroth, Shopham,
and [i] Jaazer, and Jogbehah,
36 And Beth-nimrah [k], and
Beth-haran, fenced [l] cities; and
folds for sheep.
37 And the children of Reuben built Heshbon [m], and Elealeh, and Kirjathaim,
38 And Nebo [n], and Baal-meon [o], (their names being changed,)
and Shibmah: and gave other
[p] names unto the cities which
they builded.
39 And the children of Ma-

e Deut. 3. 12-17. 29. 8. Josh. 12. 6. f c. 21. 24, 33. g c. 33. 45, 46. h Deut. 2. 36.

i ver. 1. 3. *Jazer.* k ver. 3. *Nimrah.* l ver. 24. m c. 21. 27. n Is. 46. 1. o c. 22. 41. p ver. 3. Ex. 23. 13. Josh. 23. 7.

will not pass, etc. Then you shall compel them so to do, and assign them, according to lot, their portion in the land of Canaan. Gr. "Then you shall drive before you their cattle, and wives, and possessions, into the land of Canaan; and they shall have, etc."——¶ *Moses gave unto them, etc.* That is, gave prospectively; indicated a purpose to give, just as the Lord is said to have given the land of Canaan to his people before they had taken possession of it.

Vs. 34–42. *And the children of Gad built Dibon, etc.* That is, repaired, renewed, fortified—a frequent sense of the original rendered "to build."——¶ (*Their names being changed.*) When they had rebuilt and fortified certain cities they changed the old names by which they were known and gave them new ones. The design of this was to break up all idolatrous associations, and efface its relics from among the chosen people. Thus Nebo and Baal-meon, for instance, were the names of idol gods worshipped among the former inhabitants, as Isaiah says, ch. 41 : 6, "Bel boweth down, and Nebo stoopeth," and these names were to be abolished in accordance with the spirit of the law, Ex. 23 : 13, "Make no mention of the names of other gods, neither let it be heard out of thy mouth." This, however, does not prevent but that the Scriptures should occasionally call these places by their old names. So Sol. Jarchi, "They were idolatrous names, and the Amorites had called their cities by the names of their idols; but the sons of Reuben turned their name to other names." Thus Nobah took Kenath, v. 42, and subsequently called it by his own name.——¶ *The children of Machir, the son of Manasseh, went to Gilead and took it, etc.* Or, Heb. "Had gone," alluding to some time previous, while they were invading the territory of the Amorites. The clause is, perhaps, here inserted to show the reason why Moses gave this part of the land to the tribe of Manasseh, to wit, because they had formerly won it by their swords.——¶ *Moses gave Gilead unto Machir.* That is, to the family or posterity of Machir, for Machir himself, being the son of Manasseh, must have been long dead.——¶ *The villages thereof.* Heb. "The daughters thereof;" on which phraseology see Note on ch. 21 : 25.

chir, the son of Manasseh, went
to Gilead, and took it, and dispossessed the Amorite which
was in it.
40 And Moses gave Gilead[q]
unto Machir the son of Manasseh; and he dwelt therein.
41 And Jair, the son of Manasseh, went and took the small
towns thereof, and called them
Havoth-jair[r].
42 And Nobah went and took
Kenath, and the villages thereof,
and called it Nobah, after his
own name.

CHAPTER XXXIII.

THESE *are* the journeys of the children of Israel, which

q Josh. 13. 29-31.

r Judg. 10. 4.

CHAPTER XXXIII.

Journeyings of the Children of Israel.

The present chapter is mainly devoted to an account of the various stages and stations, the encampments and removals, of the children of Israel on their march through the wilderness, embracing the time from their departure from Egypt to their entrance into Canaan. This was intrinsically a very memorable part of their history, and divine wisdom saw fit that Moses should write and transmit to posterity a journal of their extraordinary travels. In executing this order he recapitulates the principal stopping-places on their long journey, amounting to forty-two in number, occasionally reciting the important events that occurred here and there at different points in their progress. Many of these stations can now be determined with sufficient accuracy; others cannot. The route from Egypt to Sinai is well defined, so also, for the most part, is that from Mount Hor, where Aaron died, to the banks of the Jordan, where they crossed into Canaan. But the intermediate stages between these extremes are exceedingly difficult to be identified, as this part of their course lay through the wilder and more trackless portion of the desert, in which they were no doubt led back and forth, crossing and re-crossing their path, as the prospects of water and pasturage dictated, though they never moved independent of the guiding pillar. It was, perhaps, designed that their route should be thus mazy and labyrinthian, in order to represent more adequately those early stages of religious experience in which the soul is led, like the blind, by a way which it knows not. While the principles of the regenerate or spiritual life are slowly forming into a definite order, the experience is somewhat confused and chaotic, and the soul's progress appears to be now onward and now retrograde, though it is still, on the whole, holding on its way to the heavenly Canaan. This way becomes clearer and clearer as the end of the course is neared, till at length the weary pilgrim is planted in the land of promise.

There are doubtless many points of useful annotation in the chapter before us, but as these points are principally topographical, and as they are treated at length in various commentaries, biblical cyclopedias, and books of travels, and as our proposed limits will not allow the requisite enlargement for dwelling upon all the questions in detail, we shall waive all extended discussion, reserving our contracted remaining space for remarks and expositions which will not so easily be found elsewhere.

V. 1. *These are the journeys, etc.* Heb. "The removings, or breakings-up;"

went forth out of the land of
Egypt with their armies, under
the hand of Moses and Aaron.
2 And Moses wrote their goings out according to their journeys, by the commandment of
the LORD: and these *are* their
journeys according to their goings out.
3 And they departed [a] from
Rameses in the first month, on
the fifteenth [b] day of the first
month: on the morrow after the
passover, the children of Israel
went out with [c] an high hand in
the sight of all the Egyptians.
4 (For the Egyptians buried
all *their* first-born, which [d] the
LORD had smitten among them:

a Ex. 12. 37. *b* Ex. 13. 4. *c* Ex. 14. 8. *d* Ex. 12. 29.

upon their gods [e] also the LORD
executed judgments.)
5 And the children of Israel
removed from [f] Rameses, and
pitched in Succoth.
6 And [g] they departed from
Succoth, and pitched in Etham,
which *is* in the edge of the wilderness.
7 And [h] they removed from
Etham, and turned again unto
Pi-hahiroth, which *is* before
Baal-zephon: and they pitched
before Migdol.
8 And they departed from
before Pi-hahiroth, and passed
[i] through the midst of the sea
into the wilderness, and went

e Ex. 12. 12. 18. 11. Is. 19. 1. Rev. 12. 7–9. *f* Ex. 12. 37. *g* Ex. 13. 20. *h* Ex. 14. 2, 9. *i* Ex. 14. 22. 15. 22, 23.

---

i. e., in their migrations from place to place at the indications of the divine signal. These movements were typical of the then unsettled state of the church, as whatever holds good of the individual of the church holds good also of the church in its collective capacity. This ambulatory state of the church under Moses or the Law, is strikingly contrasted by the prophet Isaiah with its settled and abiding condition under Christ or the Gospel, where "we which have believed do enter into rest." "Look upon Zion, the city of our solemnities: thine eyes shall see Jerusalem a quiet habitation, a tabernacle that shall not be taken down; not one of the stakes thereof shall ever be removed, neither shall any of the cords thereof be broken." Is. 33 : 20.

V. 2. *By the commandment of the Lord.* This may refer either to the writing by Moses, or to the journeyings by the people, which were directed by the Lord himself. The accentuation of the Hebrew favors rather the latter construction, though in all probability Moses was prompted also by a divine suggestion to keep a diary or journal, in which were to be inserted the various stations at which they encamped, and all the memorable occurrences of their way.

V. 4. *For the Egyptians buried all (their) first-born, etc.* The Egyptians would naturally be thrown into the utmost consternation by the death of their first-born, and this, together with the duty of embalming and burying their dead, would so occupy and absorb them that it would effectually prevent their pursuing the Israelites. They had leisure, therefore, to depart with every thing belonging to them. In what precise manner the divine judgment was visited upon the gods of Egypt, we are not informed. Being probably idols, they may have been broken to pieces like Dagon before the ark.

Vs. 5–15. *And the children of Israel*

three days' journey in the wilderness of Etham, and pitched in Marah.

9 And they removed from Marah, and came [k] unto Elim: and in Elim *were* twelve fountains of water, and threescore and ten palm-trees; and they pitched there.

10 And they removed from Elim, and encamped by the Red Sea.

11 And [l] they removed from the Red Sea, and encamped in the wilderness of Sin.

12 And they took their journey out of the wilderness of Sin, and encamped in Dophkah.

13 And they departed from Dophkah, and encamped in Alush.

14 And they removed from Alush, and encamped [m] at Rephidim, where was no water for the people to drink.

15 And they departed from Rephidim, and pitched in the wilderness [n] of Sinai.

16 And they removed from the desert of Sinai, and pitched at Kibroth-hattaavah [o].

17 And they departed from Kibroth-hattaavah, and [p] encamped at Hazeroth.

18 And they departed from Hazeroth, and pitched in Rithmah [q].

19 And they departed from Rithmah, and pitched at Rimmon-parez.

20 And they departed from Rimmon-parez, and pitched in Libnah.

21 And they removed from Libnah, and pitched at Rissah.

22 And they journeyed from Rissah, and pitched in Kehelathah.

23 And they went from Kehelathah, and pitched in mount Shapher.

24 And they removed from mount Shapher, and encamped in Haradah.

25 And they removed from Haradah, and pitched in Makheloth.

26 And they removed from Makheloth, and encamped at Tahath.

27 And they departed from Tahath, and pitched at Tarah.

28 And they removed from Tarah, and pitched in Mithcah.

29 And they went from Mithcah, and pitched in Hashmonah.

30 And they departed from Hashmonah, and encamped at Moseroth [r].

31 And they departed from Moseroth, and pitched in Bene-jaakan.

32 And they removed from Bene-jaakan [s], and encamped at Hor-hagidgad [t].

k Ex. 15. 27. *l* Ex. 16. 1. *m* Ex. 17. 1. 19. 2. *n* Ex. 16. 1. 19. 1, 2. *o* c. 11. 34. *p* c. 11. 35. *q* c. 12. 16.

r Deut. 10. 6. *Mosera.* *s* 1 Chr. 1. 42. *t* Deut. 10. 7. *Gudgodah.*

---

removed, etc. For an account of all these places, see the Notes on the parallel history in Exodus, chs. 13–17.

Vs. 16–49. *They removed from the desert of Sinai, etc.* The various questions pertaining to the localities here mentioned will be found ably and amply discussed in Kitto's Notes on this chapter, and to them we refer the reader.

33 And they went from Hor-hagidgad, and pitched in Jotbathah [u].

34 And they removed from Jotbathah, and encamped at Ebronah.

35 And they departed from Ebronah, and [v] encamped at Ezion-gaber.

36 And they removed from Ezion-gaber, and pitched in the wilderness [w] of Zin, which *is* Kadesh.

37 And [x] they removed from Kadesh, and pitched in mount Hor, in the edge of the land of Edom.

38 And [y] Aaron the priest went up into mount Hor, at the commandment of the LORD, and died there, in the fortieth year after the children of Israel were come out of the land of Egypt, in the first *day* of the fifth month.

39 And Aaron *was* an hundred and twenty and three years old when he died in mount Hor.

40 And king Arad [z] the Canaanite, which dwelt in the south in the land of Canaan, heard of the coming of the children of Israel.

u Deut. 10. 7. *Jotbath.* *v* Deut. 2. 8. 1 K. 9. 26. *Ezion-geber.* 1 K. 22. 48. *w* c. 20. 1. 27. 14. *x* c. 20. 22, 23. 21. 4. *y* c. 20. 25–28. Deut. 10. 6. 32. 50. *z* c. 21. 1, etc.

41 And they departed from mount Hor [a], and pitched in Zalmonah.

42 And they departed from Zalmonah, and pitched in Punon.

43 And they departed from Punon, and pitched in Oboth [b].

44 And they departed from Oboth, and pitched in Ije-abarim [c], in the border of Moab.

45 And they departed from Iim, and pitched in Dibon-gad [d].

46 And they removed from Dibon-gad, and encamped in Almon-diblathaim [e].

47 And they removed from Almon-diblathaim, and [f] pitched in the mountains of Abarim, before Nebo.

48 And they departed from the mountains of Abarim, and [g] pitched in the plains of Moab, by Jordan *near* Jericho.

49 And they pitched by Jordan, from Beth-jesimoth *even* unto Abel-shittim in [h] the plains of Moab.

50 And the LORD spake unto Moses in the plains of Moab by Jordan *near* Jericho, saying,

a c. 21. 4. *b* c. 21. 10. *c* c. 21. 11. *d* c. 32. 34. *e* Jer. 28. 42. Ezek. 6. 14. *f* Deut. 32. 49. *g* c. 22. 1. *h* c. 25. 1. Josh. 2. 1.

A Charge respecting the Treatment of the Inhabitants of Canaan.

Vs. 50–56. *And the Lord spake unto Moses, etc.* The isolation of the children of Israel hitherto in the wilderness had doubtless preserved them from the infection of idolatry, but as they were now about to be ushered into Canaan, where they would come in contact with the evil in its most tempting forms, the Most High sees fit to give them a solemn charge respecting the utter extirpation of the nations, from the danger that was to be apprehended. Looking upon themselves as the instruments of a just Providence in punishing in these nations a long career of iniquity and vice of the most aggravated type, they were

51 Speak unto the children of Israel, and say unto them, When [i] ye are passed over Jordan, into the land of Canaan;

52 Then [k] ye shall drive out all the inhabitants of the land from before you, and destroy all their pictures, and destroy all their molten images, and quite pluck down all their high places.

53 And ye shall dispossess *the inhabitants of* the land, and dwell therein: for I have given you the land to possess it.

54 And [l] ye shall divide the land by lot for an inheritance among your families; *and* to the more ye shall give the more inheritance, and to the fewer ye shall give the less inheritance: every man's *inheritance* shall be in the place where his lot falleth; according to the tribes of your fathers ye shall inherit.

55 But [m] if ye will not drive out the inhabitants of the land from before you; then it shall come to pass, that those which ye let remain of them *shall be* pricks in your eyes, and thorns in your sides, and shall vex you in the land wherein ye dwell.

56 Moreover, it shall come to pass, *that* I shall do unto you, as I thought to do unto them.

i Deut. 9. 1. Josh. 3. 17. *k* Ex. 23, 24, 33. 34. 13. Deut. 7. 2, 5. 12. 3. Josh. 11. 11. Judg. 2. 2. *l* c. 26. 53-55.

m Ex. 23. 33. Josh. 23. 12, 13. Judg. 1. 21-36. Ps. 106. 34-36. Ezek. 28. 24.

---

to engage with the utmost zeal in invading and expelling them, nor to cease from the attempt till sooner or later they had driven and rooted them all out, destroying all their idols, pictures (painted images), statues, altars, groves, chapels, and every other relic of their idolatrous worship, sweeping the whole country, as it were, clean of its abominations, and thus to render it a fit habitation for a nation of devout worshippers of the true God. As the land became thus gradually conquered and fell into the possession of the victors, it was to be equitably divided among the tribes according to the directions before given (ch. 26). Finally, they were informed and assured that in case they failed in executing this order, and through sloth, cowardice or negligence, ceased to inflict upon the devoted nations the judgments denounced, they would be made to feel the sad effects of their remissness in the corruption of their manners, in the curse of slavery and captivity brought upon them by the very people they should have destroyed, and in all kinds of plagues and infestations which should justly follow such gross disobedience to the divine mandates. "The righteous God would turn that wheel upon the Israelites which was to have crushed the Canaanites. 'I shall do unto you as I thought to do unto them.' It was intended that the Canaanites should be dispossessed; but if the Israelites fell in with them and learned their ways, *they* should be dispossessed, for God's displeasure would justly be greater against them than against the Canaanites themselves. Let us hear this and fear. If we do not drive sin out, sin will drive us out; if we be not the death of our lusts, our lusts will be the death of our souls."—*Henry*.

CHAPTER XXXIV.

AND the LORD spake unto Moses, saying,
2 Command the children of Israel, and say unto them, When ye come into the land of Canaan, (this *is* the land that shall fall unto you for an inheritance, *even* the land of Canaan, with the coasts thereof,)
3 Then [a] your south quarter shall be from the wilderness of Zin, along by the coast of Edom; and your south border shall be the outmost coast of the salt sea [b] eastward.

a Josh. 15. 1, etc. Ezek. 47. 13, etc. b Gen. 14. 3.

CHAPTER XXXIV.

The Boundaries of the Land of Canaan defined.

V. 1. The Lord having in the previous chapter given the Israelites a strict charge respecting their treatment of the conquered nations, proceeds in the present to fix and determine the boundaries of the land promised ages before to Abraham and his seed. This measure would distinctly inform them to what extent they were to go in possessing themselves of the territory of the Canaanites, without encroaching upon ground to which they had no title. It would, moreover, tend to encourage them in their invasion of the land, and to aid them essentially in the subsequent distribution of it. There is but little difficulty in following the general outline of the boundaries, though the southern is somewhat complicated. But a good map of Canaan will afford more assistance to the reader than the most minute verbal description. To such a map we shall, therefore, refer the biblical student, reserving to ourselves only such occasional remarks as the incidentals of the text may suggest.

V. 2. *This is the land that shall fall unto you.* That is, by lot or by line, as is evident from the parallel phraseology, Ps. 78 : 55, "And divided them an inheritance by line." Heb. "Made them fall by inheritance of line." So also, Ps. 16 : 6, "The lines are fallen unto me in pleasant places; yea, I have a goodly heritage." So John 17 : 5, "And there fell ten portions to Manasseh;" i. e., Heb. "ten lines."——¶ *(Even) the land of Canaan with the coasts thereof.* That is, with the borders thereof; or, Heb. according to the borders thereof. There does not appear to have been any special reason for enclosing a part of this verse in a parenthesis, especially if it be rendered, as the original will admit, "Say unto them that ye are coming into or about entering the land of Canaan; this (i. e., the country about to be described) is the land that is to fall to you as an inheritance, even the land of Canaan according to its boundaries;" by which is meant the boundaries just about to be defined.

V. 3. *Your south quarter shall be, etc.* Here commences the southern line of boundary. The order of proceeding is from east to west for the southern line; from the south to the north for the western; from the west to the east for the north; and from the north to the south for the east. "The outmost coast of the salt sea (the Dead Sea) eastward," is equivalent to the *extremity* of the Dead Sea, implying that the boundary line should begin at the extreme easterly corner of that body of water and thence run mainly eastward to the Mediterranean, though

4 And your border shall turn
from the south to the ascent of
Akrabbim, and pass on to Zin:
and the going forth thereof shall
be from the south to [c] Kadesh-
barnea, and shall go on to Hazar-
addar, and pass on to Azmon.
5 And the border shall fetch
a compass from Azmon unto the
river of Egypt [d], and the goings
out of it shall be at the sea.
6 And *as for* the western
border, you shall even have the
great sea for a border: this shall
be your west border.
7 And this shall be your north
border: from the great sea ye
shall point out for you mount
[e] Hor:
8 From mount Hor ye shall
point out *your border* unto the
entrance of Hamath [f]: and the
goings forth of the border shall
be to [g] Zedad:

c c. 13. 26. 32. 8. d Gen. 15. 18. 1 K. 8. 65. Is. 27. 12.

e c. 33. 37. f c. 13. 21. 2 K. 14. 25. Ezek. 47. 16. g Ezek. 47. 15.

---

still, as it afterwards appears, by a very circuitous route.

Vs. 4, 5. *Your border shall turn from the south, etc.* Heb. *minnegeb*, lit. *from the south*, but implying here and elsewhere *southwardly* or *in a southern direction.* The line commencing at the southern extremity of the Dead Sea seems to have extended some way in a southerly direction, so as to embrace Kadesh-barnea, and thence to have veered to the west till it fell in with the "river of Egypt," doubtless at its mouth, whence it terminated in the Great or Mediterranean Sea. But it is difficult to identify the stream called "the river of Egypt," whether it were the Nile or a smaller stream falling into the Mediterranean near Gaza. We incline strongly to the former opinion for the reasons given in the Note on Gen. 15:18, to which the reader is referred. According to this view the southern boundary of Canaan extended from the extremity of the Dead Sea to the eastern or Pelusiac branch of the Nile. We know not, indeed, that the actual possessions of the Israelites ever embraced the whole of this region, but it was covered by the terms of the divine donation, and they would have been fully authorized to enter upon it.——¶ *The ascent of Akrabbim.* Heb. *maaleh akrabbim, the hill of scorpions*, supposed to be so called from the abundance of scorpions found there.——¶ *From the south to Kadesh-barnea.* That is, southerly to Kadesh-barnea, as above. The position of Hazar-addar and Azmon is unknown.

V. 6. *The great sea for a border.* The Mediterranean; so called in contradistinction to the Sea of Tiberias and the Dead Sea, which, though called "seas," were in fact but a larger kind of lakes.

V. 7. *Mount Hor.* Not the Mount Hor where Aaron died, which lay to the south of Canaan towards Edom, while this was situated in the opposite direction to the north, forming probably a conspicuous peak in the Lebanon chain. The original is *hor hâhâr*, lit. *Hor the mountain*, or *Hor* the mountainous range, implying some eminent or lofty elevation to the north of Canaan, and which we can nowhere else look for than in the range of Anti-Libanus.

V. 8. *Unto the entrance of Hamath.* The defile or pass in the mountains at Hamath, by which *entrance* was generally made from the north into the land of Canaan.

9 And the border shall go on
to Ziphron, and the goings out
of it shall be at Hazar-enan[h]:
this shall be your north border.
10 And ye shall point out
your east border from Hazar-
enan to Shepham :
11 And the coast shall go
down from Shepham to Riblah[i],
on the east side of Ain ; and the
border shall descend, and shall
reach unto the side of the sea
of Chinnereth[k] eastward.
12 And the border shall go
down to Jordan, and the goings
out of it shall be at the salt sea :
this shall be your land, with the
coasts thereof round about.
13 And Moses commanded
the children of Israel, saying,
This *is* the land which ye shall
inherit by lot[l], which the LORD
commanded to give unto the nine
tribes, and to the half tribe :
14 For[m] the tribe of the children of Reuben according to the
house of their fathers, and the
tribe of the children of Gad according to the house of their
fathers, have received *their inheritance;* and half the tribe
of Manasseh have received their
inheritance :
15 The two tribes and the
half tribe have received their
inheritance on this side Jordan
near Jericho eastward, toward
the sun-rising.

h Ezek. 47. 17. *i* 2 K. 23. 33. Jer. 39. 5, 6. 19. 35. Luke 5. 1. *k* Deut. 3. 17. Josh. 11. 2. *l* ver. 1. Josh. 14. 2. *m* c. 32. 23.

Vs. 9–12. *The border shall go to Ziphron, etc.* For the remaining boundaries of the land we refer the reader to the maps and the biblical gazetteers which are now generally available, and which, with the Notes of Mr. Kitto, will afford all desirable information.——¶ *And the coast shall go down from Shepham to Riblah, on the east of Ain.* "Ain" signifies *a fountain*, and the hypothesis of Boothroyd, Geddes, and others, that this was the fountain or source of the Jordan, is, we think, very probable. We are inclined also to adopt Geddes' rendering of the first clause of the verse, "And from Shepham to Riblah, the boundary shall descend to the east side of the source (of the Jordan)."——¶ *Unto the side of the sea of Chinnereth eastward.* The sea of Chinnereth is the lake of Gennesaret, or sea of Tiberias. The "eastward" in this connection is probably equivalent to "to the eastern side or shore."——¶ *The border shall go down to Jordan.* Boothroyd renders this verse far preferably thus: "And the boundary shall go along the Jordan (downwards), and its termination shall be at the salt sea; this shall be your land with its surrounding boundaries." The determination of the sense in all this chapter, so far as it treats of the boundaries of the promised land, depends very much upon the genuine meaning of the prepositions employed, and this has been much more satisfactorily settled by the labors of modern critics and commentators than it could have been in the state in which Hebrew exegesis was at the time our present English translation was made.

Vs. 13–15. *This is the land which ye shall inherit, etc.* The several boundaries of the land having been thus defined, the Lord now repeats that this is the land promised centuries ago to faithful Abraham, and which his posterity were to inherit by lot. As the two tribes of Reuben and Gad and the

16 And the Lord spake unto
Moses, saying,
17 These *are* the names of
the men which shall divide the
land unto you; [n] Eleazar the
priest, and Joshua the son of
Nun.
18 And ye shall take one
prince [o] of every tribe, to divide
the land by inheritance.
19 And the names of the men
are these: of the tribe of Judah,
Caleb the son of Jephunneh.
20 And of the tribe of the
children of Simeon, Shemuel the
son of Ammihud.
21 Of the tribe of Benjamin,
Elidad the son of Chislon.
22 And the prince of the
tribe of the children of Dan,
Bukki the son of Jogli.
23 The prince of the children
of Joseph, for the tribe of the
children of Manasseh, Hanniel
the son of Ephod.
24 And the prince of the
tribe of the children of Ephraim,
Kemuel the son of Shiphtan.
25 And the prince of the
tribe of the children of Zebulun,
Elizaphan the son of Parnach.
26 And the prince of the
tribe of the children of Issachar,
Paltiel the son of Azzan.
27 And the prince of the
tribe of the children of Asher,
Ahihud the son of Shelomi.
28 And the prince of the
tribe of the children of Naphtali, Pedahel the son of Ammihud.
29 These [p] *are they* whom the
Lord commanded to divide the
inheritance unto the children of
Israel in the land of Canaan.

CHAPTER XXXV.

AND the Lord spake unto Moses in the plains of Moab,
by Jordan *near* Jericho, saying,
2 Command [a] the children of

n Josh. 14. 1. 19. 51. *o* c. 1. 4–16.

p ver. 18. *a* Josh. 14. 3, 4. 21. 2, etc. Ezek. 45. 1, etc. 48. 8, etc.

half tribe of Manasseh had already received their portion on the other side the Jordan, only nine tribes and a half remained to be provided for, and how this was done we are informed in the verses immediately following.

Vs. 17–29. *These are the names of the men, etc.* That the division of the land might be more solemn, orderly and authoritative, the Lord here commands that the management of it should be intrusted to the hands of Eleazar, the high-priest, Joshua, the general-in-chief, and a prince, i. e., a principal officer or sheihk, chosen out of each tribe as its representative in the transaction. It is observable that the tribes are nowhere else enumerated in the order in which they here occur, but as it is precisely the order in which their allotments fell to them in the distribution of the land, the order was no doubt prescribed with reference to this fact.

CHAPTER XXXV.

Levitical Cities appointed.

V. 2. *Command the children of Israel that they give unto the Levites, etc.* As the Levites were formed into a distinct body from the rest of the nation, having no inheritance of fields or farms as-

Israel, that they give unto the Levites, of the inheritance of their possession, cities to dwell in; and ye shall give *also* unto the Levites suburbs for the cities round about them.

3 And the cities shall they have to dwell in; and the suburbs of them shall be for their cattle, and for their goods, and for all their beasts.

4 And the suburbs [b] of the cities, which ye shall give unto

b 2 Chr. 11. 14.

---

signed them, the Lord here orders that provision should be made for their dwelling in fixed residences in towns with such a portion of ground, under the name of "suburbs," as would serve them at least for the subsistence of their flocks and herds, even if their tithes were sufficient to support themselves and their families. But apart from all considerations of support, the ordinance was a very beneficent one, as their dispersion through the several tribes, instead of being congregated at one place, would tend to a more equal diffusion of the salutary influences which their order was calculated to exert upon the people at large. The patriarch's prophecy, Gen. 49:7, "I will divide them in Jacob, and scatter them in Israel," was thus turned to a blessing, as every city in which they dwelt would be a focal centre of instruction, a school or university, where the Law would be studied and taught, and where the morals of the Levites themselves would be better preserved than if they were indiscriminately mixed with the mass of the population. "These cities, therefore," as Calvin remarks, "were like lamps, shining into the very furthest corners of the land. They were also like watch-towers, in which they might keep guard, so as to drive away impiety from the borders of the holy land. Hence was the light of heavenly doctrine diffused; hence was the seed of life scattered; hence were the examples to be sought of holiness and universal integrity." Moses was accordingly directed in the distribution of the land to set apart forty-eight cities, each with a sufficient space of suburb for necessary grazing-ground for the habitations of the Levites, which cities were to be contributed by the several tribes in proportion to the extent of their respective districts.——¶ *Suburbs.* Heb. *migrosh*, from the root *gârash*, signifying *to drive out, cast out, expel, etc.* Hence the noun has the import of some place in the neighborhood of a city whither rubbish was *cast out*, or cattle *driven*, or, as others suppose, a place *excluded* from the precincts of the city. Chald. "A breathing-space." The Gr. has, in this connection, three several renderings of the Heb. term: *proasteia*, lying *before the city; aphorismata, separated from the city;* and *homora, confines* or *limits.* The English word "suburbs" probably comes as near to an exact rendering as any single term that can be found, yet it is probable it would not have conveyed precisely the same idea to the mind of an Israelite with their own Hebrew term.

V. 3. *For their goods.* Heb. *rekusham, their acquisitions, possessions, substance*, sometimes applied to cattle, but understood by some of the elder commentators to denote stables, outhouses, or storehouses, for laying up the food on which the cattle were to be subsisted. If this be not the import, the distinction intended between this and the other two terms is not obvious.

V. 4. *A thousand cubits round about.* The mention of two thousand cubits in

the Levites, *shall reach* from the wall of the city and outward, a thousand cubits round about.

5 And ye shall measure from without the city on the east side two thousand cubits, and on the south side two thousand cubits, and on the west side two thousand cubits, and on the north side two thousand cubits; and the city *shall be* in the midst: this shall be to them the suburbs of the cities.

6 And among the cities which

---

the next verse creates some difficulty in the construction of this passage. The simplest solution seems to be that of Rosenmuller, viz., that the 1000 cubits was measured outward at right angles to the wall of the city, while the 2000 denotes the outside measurement parallel to the wall, as in the subjoined diagram:

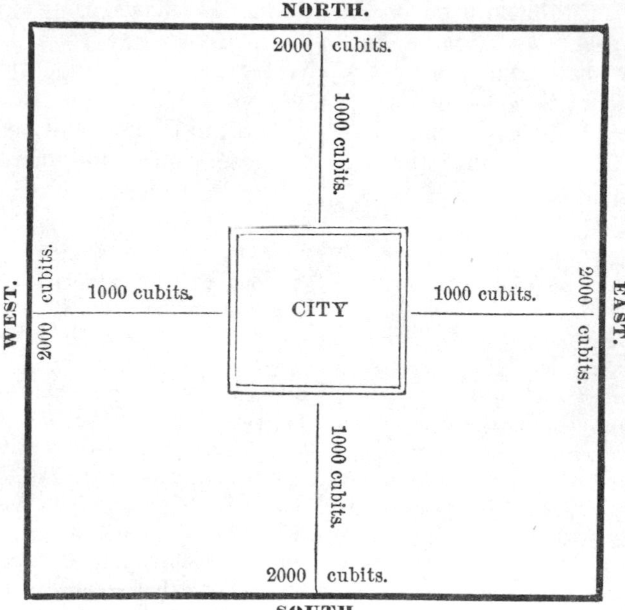

We incline to this solution from the fact that the latter measurement of 2000 cubits was to be made *without* (Heb. *mihootz*) the city, which was undoubtedly in some way different from the preceding. It is proper, however, to state that the Jewish authorities generally accord with Maimonides, who says, "The suburbs of the cities are expressed in the Law to be 3000 cubits on every side from the wall of the city and outwards. The first thousand cubits are the suburbs, and the 2000 which they measured without the suburbs were for fields and vineyards." After all, we must leave the point encompassed with some degree of uncertainty.

Six of the Levitical Cities appointed for Cities of Refuge.

Vs. 6–8. *Among the cities which ye shall give, etc.* Out of the whole number of forty-eight cities which were thus to be appropriated to the Levites

ye shall give unto the Levites, *there shall be* six cities [c] for refuge, which ye shall appoint for the man-slayer, that he may flee thither: and to them ye shall add forty and two cities.

7 *So* all the cities which ye shall give to the Levites *shall be* forty and eight [d] cities: them *shall ye give* with their suburbs.

8 And the cities which ye shall give *shall be* of the possession [e] of the children of Israel: from [f] *them that have* many ye shall give many; but from *them that have* few ye shall give few: every one shall give of his cities unto the Levites according to his inheritance which he inheriteth.

9 And the LORD spake unto Moses, saying,

10 Speak unto the children of Israel, and say unto them, When [g] ye be come over Jordan into the land of Canaan;

11 Then [h] ye shall appoint you cities to be cities of refuge for you; that the slayer may flee thither, which killeth any person at unawares.

12 And they shall be unto you cities for refuge from the avenger [i]; that the man-slayer die not, until he stand before the congregation in judgment.

c ver. 13, 14. Deut. 4. 41–43. Josh. 20. 2, 9. 21. 3, 13, etc. Ps. 62. 7, 8. Heb. 6. 18. *d* Josh. 21. 41. *e* Josh. 21. 3. *f* c. 26. 54.

g Deut. 19. 2. Josh, 20. 2. *h* Ex. 21. 13 *i* Deut. 19. 6. Josh. 20. 3–6.

(under whom the priests are included), six were to be set apart as cities of refuge or asylums, to which any person who had accidentally, or by chance-medley, killed another, might immediately repair, and take sanctuary in the manner just about to be described.——¶ *Cities for refuge.* Heb. *miklat, of gathering,* or *retention,* because the man-slayer was there *gathered* or *detained.* Gr. "A place of flight and exile." Chald. "A place of deliverance and preservation." These cities were to be assigned out of the portions of the several tribes, more out of some, and fewer out of others, according to the extent of the territory allotted to each.

General Law respecting Homicide.

Vs. 9–14. *The Lord spake unto Moses, saying, etc.* As the law here given was one fraught with most important consequences to the parties concerned and to the welfare of the nation at large, it is enounced with minute particularity that it might be distinctly understood.——¶ *At unawares.* Heb. *bishgâgâh, by error,* i. e., *ignorantly, unadvisedly, unintentionally.* See Note on Josh. 20 : 3.——¶ *For refuge from the avenger.* That is, from the avenger of blood, the next of kin, or the *Goël,* as he is termed in the East, where the institution of blood-revenge has always been rigorously observed. Of this law of *Goelism* we have already treated at some length in the Notes on Gen. 9 : 5. Josh. 20 : 3, to which we refer the reader, as also to what will be said further upon it in our remarks on Deut. 19 : 4–13.——¶ *Until he stand before the congregation in judgment.* The man who had been guilty of involuntary homicide was to flee to the nearest city of refuge, where his case was stated to the elders at the gates or entrance to the city. He was then received and retained there till sent for and taken home to the place where the act was commit-

13 And of these cities which ye shall give, six [k] cities shall ye have for refuge.

14 Ye shall give three [l] cities on this side Jordan, and three cities shall ye give in the land of Canaan, *which* shall be cities of refuge.

15 These six cities shall be a refuge *both* for the children of Israel, and for the stranger [m], and for the sojourner among them; that every one that killeth any person unawares may flee thither.

16 And [n] if he smite him with an instrument of iron so that he die, he *is* a murderer: the murderer shall surely be put to death.

17 And if he smite him with throwing a stone, wherewith he may die, and he die, he *is* a murderer: the murderer shall surely be put to death.

18 Or *if* he smite him with an hand-weapon of wood, wherewith he may die, and he die, he *is* a murderer: the murderer shall surely be put to death.

19 The [o] revenger of blood himself shall slay the murderer: when he meeteth him, he shall slay him.

20 But if he thrust him of hatred [p], or hurl at him by laying [q] of wait, that he die;

21 Or in enmity smite him with his hand, that he die; he that smote *him* shall surely be

k ver. 6. *l* Deut. 4. 41. Josh. 20. 8. *m* c. 15. 16. Lev. 24. 22. *n* Ex. 21. 12–14. Lev. 24. 17. Deut. 19. 11, 12.

o ver. 21 24, 27. Deut. 19. 6, 12. Josh. 20. 3, 5. *p* Gen. 4. 5, 8. 2 Sam. 3. 27. 20. 10. 1 K. 2. 31, 32. Prov. 26. 24. *q* Ex. 21. 14. Deut. 19. 11.

---

ted, and there it was that he "stood before the congregation." If found worthy of death upon his trial, he was delivered over to the avenger of blood to be put to death; if otherwise, he was returned to the city of refuge, where he lived in a kind of durance and exile until the death of the high-priest, when he was fully released and permitted to live where he pleased.

V. 15. *These six cities shall be a refuge, etc.* The privileges of this institution were to be extended equally to all the inhabitants of the Holy Land, whether Israelites or proselytes in whole or in part, in fine, to all who were not absolute heathen and idolaters. These six cities are specified in Josh. 20, and an inspection of the map will show how wisely those places were chosen so as to make a city of refuge easy of access from all parts of the land. The roads leading to these cities were to be kept in good repair; no hillock was left, no river or stream was allowed over which there was not a bridge; the road was to be at least two-and-thirty cubits broad, and every kind of obstruction was to be removed that might hurt his foot or hinder his speed. At every turning or branching of roads, posts were erected bearing the words, REFUGE! REFUGE! to guide the fugitive in his flight; so benign and considerate was the provision made for the benefit of the accidental slayer of his fellow-man.

Discriminations of Manslaughter and Murder.

Vs. 16–23. *And if he smite him, etc.* The main distinctions here made by the law between *manslaughter* and *murder*, and which the judges were especially to regard in deciding upon the cases that came before them, were the following: If the slayer appeared

put to death; *for* he *is* a murderer:
the revenger of blood
shall slay the murderer when he
meeteth him.
22 But if he thrust him suddenly without enmity, or have
cast upon him any thing without laying of wait,
23 Or with any stone, wherewith a man may die, seeing *him*
not, and cast *it* upon him that
he die, and *was* not his enemy,
neither sought his harm;
24 Then the congregation[r]
shall judge between the slayer
and the revenger of blood according to these judgments;
25 And the congregation shall
deliver the slayer out of the hand
of the revenger of blood, and the
congregation shall restore him
to the city of his refuge, whither
he was fled: and he shall abide
in it unto the death of the high
priest which was anointed[s] with
the holy oil.
26 But if the slayer shall at
any time come without the border of the city of his refuge,
whither he was fled;
27 And the revenger of blood
find him without the borders of
the city of his refuge, and the
revenger of blood kill the slay-

r ver. 12. Josh. 20. 6.

s Ex. 29. 7. Lev. 21. 10.

---

to have struck the person slain with an unlawful and unsizable weapon, obviously sufficient to cause death by a single blow, as a sword, crowbar, huge club, or a great stone, etc., it was to be looked upon as a design upon life, and to be adjudged wilful murder. In all such cases the nearest relation of the person slain might kill the murderer wherever he met him, nor should his flying to a city of refuge be of any avail to him. So again, in like manner, any other mode of taking life by violent means, as by a forcible thrust, push or stroke, evidently prompted by a spirit of enmity and with malice prepense, was to be adjudged murder, and to remain unrelieved by the provisions of the present law. But if, on the contrary, the outrage were apparently committed in a sudden fit of passion, without premeditation or antecedent threat, grudge or malice, then it was to be pronounced mere manslaughter, and the righteous judgment of the congregation was to absolve the slayer from the guilt of blood.

V. 25. *The congregation shall deliver, etc.* After trial and acquittal the involuntary man-slayer was sent back to the city of refuge to which he had betaken himself, and was there to live retired without stirring out of the place till the death of the then living high-priest. There was doubtless a degree of severity in this enactment, considering that the man had been pronounced guiltless, but it would naturally have the effect of a warning to all men, lest by heedlessness or negligence they should endanger the life of a fellow-being. Moreover, the retirement and absence of the slayer would tend to soften the resentments of near relations and friends, and prevent the execution of revenge.

Vs. 26–28. *If the slayer shall at any time, etc.* If through impatience of confinement, or other cause, he should venture beyond the prescribed limits, and the relations of the deceased should then find him, they might put him to death without being answerable for murder, though still in the sight of God he might not be accounted guiltless as having

er; he shall not be guilty of
blood;
28 Because he should have remained in the city of his refuge
until the death of the high priest:
but after the death of the high
priest the slayer shall return into
the land of his possession.
29 So these *things* shall be
for a statute of [t] judgment unto
you, throughout your generations, in all your dwellings.
30 Whoso killeth any person,
the murderer shall be put to
death by the mouth of witnesses [u]: but one witness shall not
testify against any person *to
cause him to* die.
31 Moreover, ye shall take
no satisfaction for the life of a
murderer, which *is* guilty of
death; but he shall be surely
put to death.
32 And ye shall take no satisfaction for him that is fled to
the city of his refuge, that he
should come again to dwell in
the land, until the death of the
priest.
33 So ye shall not pollute the
land wherein ye *are;* for blood
it [v] defileth the land: and the
land cannot be cleansed of the
blood that is shed therein, but
[w] by the blood of him that shed it.
34 Defile not [x] therefore the
land which ye shall inhabit,
wherein I dwell: for I [y] the LORD
dwell among the children of Israel.

t c. 27. 11. *u* Deut. 17. 6. 19. 15. Mat. 18. 16. 2 Cor. 13. 1. Heb. 10. 28.

v 2 K. 24. 4. Ps. 106. 38. Mic. 4. 11. Mat. 23. 31–35. *w* Gen. 9. 6. *x* Lev. 18. 25. Deut. 21. 23. *y* Ex. 29. 45, 46. 1 K. 6. 13. 2 Cor. 6. 16.

---

slain an innocent man. This enactment goes on the supposition that the man was accessory to his own death, which he might have avoided by keeping within the bounds set for him. "He should have remained in the city of his refuge."—*Jarchi.*

V. 30. *By the mouth of witnesses.* No evidence should be sufficient to convict a man of wilful murder but that of living, competent, and sufficient witnesses, of which there should always be at least two; it being unreasonable to put a man's life to hazard solely on what might be the prejudice, passion, ignorance, or caprice of a single person. See Deut. 17:6. 19:15.

V. 31. *Ye shall take no satisfaction for the life of a murderer.* A murderer once legally convicted shall be incapable of pardon. Neither interest nor influence of any kind was to be available to the purchase of his life.

V. 32. *Ye shall take no satisfaction for him that is fled, etc.* In like manner, the person guilty of manslaughter shall not be able by the proffer of any sum, even of his whole estate, to buy off his confinement to the city of refuge till the death of the high priest.

Vs. 33, 34. *So ye shall not pollute the land wherein ye are.* Murder being the highest of all injuries against human society and against God, in whose image man is created, it is but just in itself that life should pay for life, and so therefore it is the will of God to have it. Accordingly, were any Israelite, but especially judges and magistrates, through a mistaken leniency or a culpable remissness, to fail in the execution of so important a law, the failure would be sure to bring a polluting stain upon the whole land, for the defilement of blood can only be cleansed by the blood of him who has shed it. If,

CHAPTER XXXVI.

AND the chief fathers of the families of the children of Gilead [a], the son of Machir, the son of Manasseh, of the families of the sons of Joseph, came near, and spake before Moses, and before the princes, the chief fathers of the children of Israel:

2 And they said, The LORD [b] commanded my lord to give the land for an inheritance by lot to the children of Israel: and [c] my lord was commanded by the LORD to give the inheritance of Zelophehad our brother unto his daughters.

3 And if they be married to any of the sons of the *other* tribes of the children of Israel, then shall their inheritance be taken from the inheritance of our fathers, and shall be put

a c. 26. 29. b c. 26. 55. 33. 54. Josh. 17. 3.

c c. 27. 1, 7.

---

therefore, they would preserve the sanctity of that holy land which the Lord had consecrated by the symbols of his special presence, let them guard with the most sacred solicitude against contracting the guilt of disobedience in addition to the guilt of the shedding of blood.

CHAPTER XXXVI.

Law regulating the Inheritance of Daughters.

V. 1. *And the chief fathers, etc.* Heb. "The heads of the fathers." Gr. "The princes." The regulation here recorded was consequent upon the case mentioned ch. 27, where we read of a special provision made for the female branch of the family of Zelophehad, who belonged to the tribe of Manasseh, the son of Joseph, but to that half of it which was to settle on the western instead of the eastern side of the Jordan. Moses had indeed secured them an ample inheritance among their brethren, but some of the heads of that family, foreseeing a great inconvenience likely to result in the case of the marriage of these women, came before Moses with a new petition bearing upon the point of the apprehended grievance. While gratefully acknowledging the provision kindly made for them by the commandment of the Lord, they represent that in case these female heirs should marry into other tribes, the inheritances accruing to them would of course be alienated from their own tribe, and be transferred to that into which they married. This would appear to be contrary to the divine arrangement, by which a certain portion of territory was assigned by lot to each tribe, and this would of course be diminished to the extent of whatever was taken out of it. This is now to be guarded against. Should it be objected that this is a case which the divine omniscience would have been expected to have foreseen and provided for without being previously applied to for the purpose, we deem it a sufficient reply to say, that he evidently preferred that his people should learn his will on many points only as the emergencies arose which prompted them to consult him. On this head we subscribe to the very appropriate remarks of Calvin:—"God designedly withheld his decisions until they naturally arose out of the circumstances of the case. He allowed himself to be interrogated familiarly in regard to doubtful points of no primary

to the inheritance of the tribe
whereunto they are received:
so shall it be taken from the lot
of our inheritance.
4 And when the jubilee [d] of
the children of Israel shall be,
then shall their inheritance be
put unto the inheritance of the
tribe whereunto they are received: so shall their inheritance
be taken away from the inheritance of the tribe of our fathers.
5 And Moses commanded the
children of Israel, according to
the word of the LORD, saying,
The tribe of the sons of Joseph
hath said [e] well.

d Lev. 25. 10, etc. e c. 27. 7.

6 This *is* the thing which the
LORD doth command concerning
the daughters of Zelophehad,
saying, Let them marry to whom
they think best; only [f] to the
family of the tribe of their
father shall they marry.
7 So shall not the inheritance
of the children of Israel remove
from tribe to tribe; for every
one of the children of Israel shall
keep [g] himself to the inheritance
of the tribe of his fathers.
8 And [h] every daughter that
possesseth an inheritance in any
tribe of the children of Israel,
shall be wife unto one of the

f ver. 12. Gen. 24. 3. 2 Cor. 6. 14. g 1 K. 21. 3. h 1 Chr. 23. 22.

importance, in order that posterity might recognize his reply as a proof of his fatherly indulgence. Meanwhile let us bear in mind that if heavenly things are the subject of as much anxiety to us as earthly things were to the children of Manasseh, the rule that we should observe will always be made clear to us."

V. 4. *And when the jubilee of the children of Israel shall be, etc.* The jubilee was an institution returning every fifty years, when all manner of alienated inheritances returned to the original possessors. But it is here intimated that this will not remedy the difficulty, since the inheritances would go by the rights of marriage into another tribe, and just so much would be withdrawn from the portion of the tribe of Manasseh as the daughters of Manasseh should take away with them. This they regarded as a prospective injury for which they feel that they ought to have some redress

V. 5. *The tribe of the sons of Joseph have said well.* Moses admits the validity of their plea, having referred it to the Most High himself, and thereupon is moved to utter the divine sentence regarding the case, to wit, that these daughters and heiresses of Zelophehad should not only be restricted from marrying out of their own tribe, but that even within the limits of that tribe they should connect themselves with some branch of their own family. This is the import of the words, "Only to the family of the tribe of their father shall they marry," and also of the similar clause, v. 8. The reason of the law, moreover, was that the family as well as the tribe might be preserved; and the daughters of Zelophehad, when they besought an inheritance, said, ch. 27 : 4, "Why should the name of our father be done away from among his family?" This was, doubtless, one of the grounds of the law requiring the marriage of a brother's wife. Deut. 26 : 6.

V. 8. *Every daughter that possesseth an inheritance, etc.* Heb. "That is heir of a possession;" the father having no son to inherit his estate. The passage

family of the tribe of her father,
that the children of Israel may
enjoy every man the inheritance
of his fathers.
9 Neither shall the inheritance remove from *one* tribe to
another tribe; but every one of
the tribes of the children of Israel shall keep himself to his
own inheritance.
10 Even [i] as the LORD commanded Moses, so did the daughters of Zelophehad:
11 For [k] Mahlah, Tirzah, and
Hoglah, and Milcah, and Noah,
the daughters of Zelophehad,
were married unto their father's
brothers' sons.
12 *And* they were married
into the families of the sons of
Manasseh, the son of Joseph;
and their inheritance remained

i 2 Chr. 30. 12.

k c. 27. 1.

---

designates those to whom the law applies. It was not intended to restrict other women who had no inheritance; and even of those who had, it is supposed that if they were willing to abandon their inheritance they might marry whom they pleased. Priests and Levites, having no inheritance, were at liberty to marry into any of the tribes. 2 Chron. 22 : 11.

V. 9. *Neither shall the inheritance remove from (one) tribe to another.* Heb. *lo tissob, shall not go round, revolve, devolve.* Gr. "Shall not be transferred."——¶ *Shall keep himself to his own inheritance.* Heb. *yidbeku, shall cleave, shall stick close to.* The term is emphatic, implying the tenacity with which they were to adhere to the divine ordinance in this matter. The design was to preclude, as far as possible, all danger of the confusion of tribes. Vulg. "That the tribes be not mingled one with another, but remain so as they were separated by the Lord;" which, however, is rather a paraphrase than a translation. According to the construction opposite to this, if a woman were married into another tribe, and her father and all her brethren should afterwards die without children, the inheritance would fall to her, and consequently the possession devolve from one tribe to another, viz., to that into which she had married. According, however, to the letter of the present text, the inheritance was rather to descend to the next of kin to the woman, than be carried by her out of the tribe to which it belonged.

V. 11. *Were married unto their father's brothers' sons.* This would imply, according to the strictness of the letter, that they were married to their first-cousins; but as the phrase "father's brothers' sons" may, according to frequent Scriptural usage, denote "father's brothers' descendants," we cannot affirm the literal construction as the true one.

V. 12. *They were married into the families of the sons of Manasseh.* Heb. "They were married to some that were *of the families, etc.,*" i. e., to one of the families of Manasseh, from whom several other families descended.——¶ *Their inheritance remained in the tribe of the family of their father.* Heb. "Was unto the tribe, etc." So Dan. 1 : 21, "And Daniel *continued* even unto the first year of king Cyrus." Heb. "*Was* even unto the first year." Ruth 1 : 2, "And they came into the country of Moab, and *continued* there." Heb. "*Were* there." The clause might be more literally rendered, "And their inheritance was (remained) in the tribe (even) the family of their fathers.

in the tribe of the family of their father.

13 These *are* the commandments and the judgments, which the LORD commanded by the hand of Moses, unto the children of Israel, in [l] the plains of Moab, by Jordan, *near* Jericho.

[l] c. 26. 3. 33. 50.

V. 13. *These are the commandments and the judgments, etc.* The distinction between these two terms is probably that between precepts relating to worship, and precepts relating to civil ordinances, both which classes we find in the preceding chapters, from ch. 26 to ch. 36.

THE END.

1981-82 TITLES

0102	Blaikie, W. G.	Heroes of Israel	19.50
0103	Bush, George	Genesis (2 vol.)	29.95
0202	Bush, George	Exodus	22.50
0302	Bush, George	Leviticus	10.50
0401	Bush, George	Numbers	17.75
0501	Cumming, John	The Book of Deuteronomy	16.00
0602	Bush, George	Joshua & Judges (2 vol. in 1)	17.95
2101	MacDonald, James M.	The Book of Ecclesiastes	15.50
2201	Durham, James	An Exposition on the Song of Solomon	17.25
2302	Alexander, Joseph	Isaiah (2 vol.)	29.95
3001	Cripps, Richard S.	A Commentary on the Book of Amos	13.50
3201	Burns, Samuel C.	The Prophet Jonah	11.25
4001	Morison, James	The Gospel According to Matthew	24.95
4102	Morison, James	The Gospel According to Mark	21.00
4403	Stier, Rudolf E.	Words of the Apostles	18.75
4502	Moule, H. C. G.	The Epistle to the Romans	16.25
4802	Brown, John	An Exposition of the Epistle of Paul to the Galatians	16.00
5102	Westcott, F. B.	The Epistle to the Colossians	7.50
5103	Eadie, John	Colossians	10.50
6201	Lias, John J.	The First Epistle of John	15.75
8602	Shedd, W. G. T.	Theological Essays (2 vol. in 1)	26.00
8603	McIntosh, Hugh	Is Christ Infallible and the Bible True?	27.00
9507	Denney, James	The Death of Christ	12.50
9508	Farrar, F. W.	The Life of Christ	24.95
9509	Dalman, Gustav H.	The Words of Christ	13.50
9510	Andrews & Gifford	Man and the Incarnation & The Incarnation (2 vol. in 1)	15.00
9511	Baron, David	Types, Psalms and Prophecies	14.00
9512	Stier, Rudolf E.	Words of the Risen Christ	8.25
9803	Gilpin, Richard	Biblical Demonology: A Treatise on Satan's Temptations	20.00
9804	Andrews, S. J.	Christianity and Anti-Christianity in Their Final Conflict	15.00

TITLES CURRENTLY AVAILABLE

No.	Author	Title	Price
0101	Delitzsch, Franz	A New Commentary on Genesis (2 vol.)	27.75
0201	Murphy, James G.	Commentary on the Book of Exodus	12.75
0301	Kellogg, Samuel H.	The Book of Leviticus	19.00
0901	Blaikie, William G.	The First Book of Samuel	13.50
1001	Blaikie, William G.	The Second Book of Samuel	13.50
1101	Farrar, F. W.	The First Book of Kings	16.75
1201	Farrar, F. W.	The Second Book of Kings	16.75
1701	Raleigh, Alexander	The Book of Esther	9.00
1801	Gibson, Edgar	The Book of Job	9.75
1802	Green, William H.	The Argument of the Book of Job Unfolded	10.75
1901	Dickson, David	A Commentary on the Psalms (2 vol.)	29.25
1902	MacLaren, Alexander	The Psalms (3 vol.)	43.50
2001	Wardlaw, Ralph	Book of Proverbs (2 vol.)	29.95
2301	Kelly, William	An Exposition of the Book of Isaiah	13.25
2401	Orelli, Hans C. von	The Prophecies of Jeremiah	13.50
2601	Fairbairn, Patrick	An Exposition of Ezekiel	16.50
2701	Pusey, Edward B.	Daniel the Prophet	19.50
2702	Tatford, Frederick	Daniel and His Prophecy	8.25
3801	Wright, Charles H. H.	Zechariah and His Prophecies	21.95
4101	Alexander, Joseph	Commentary on the Gospel of Mark	15.25
4201	Kelly, William	The Gospel of Luke	16.95
4301	Brown, John	The Intercessory Prayer of Our Lord Jesus Christ	10.50
4302	Hengstenberg, E. W.	Commentary on the Gospel of John (2 vol.)	34.95
4401	Alexander, Joseph	Commentary on the Acts of the Apostles (2 vol. in 1)	27.50
4402	Gloag, Paton J.	A Critical and Exegetical Commentary on Acts (2 vol.)	27.50
4501	Shedd, W. G. T.	Critical and Doctrinal Commentary on Romans	15.75
4601	Brown, John	The Resurrection of Life	13.25
4602	Edwards, Thomas C.	A Commentary on the First Epistle to the Corinthians	16.25
4801	Ramsay, William	Historical Commentary on the Epistle to the Galatians	15.75
4901	Westcott, Brooke, F.	St. Paul's Epistle to the Ephesians	9.75
5001	Johnstone, Robert	Lectures on the Book of Philippians	16.50
5401	Liddon, H. P.	The First Epistle to Timothy	6.00
5601	Taylor, Thomas	An Exposition of Titus	17.50
5801	Delitzsch, Franz	Commentary on the Epistle to the Hebrews (2 vol.)	29.95
5802	Bruce, A. B.	The Epistle to the Hebrews	15.00
5901	Johnstone, Robert	Lectures on the Epistle of James	14.00
5902	Mayor, Joseph B.	The Epistle of St. James	19.25
6501	Manton, Thomas	An Exposition of the Epistle of Jude	12.00
6601	Trench, Richard C.	Commentary on the Epistles to the Seven Churches	8.50
7001	Orelli, Hans C. von	The Twelve Minor Prophets	13.50
7002	Alford, Dean Henry	The Book of Genesis and Part of the Book of Exodus	11.50
7003	Marbury, Edward	Obadiah and Habakkuk	21.50
7004	Adeney, Walter	The Books of Ezra and Nehemiah	11.50
7101	Mayor, Joseph B.	The Epistle of St. Jude & The Second Epistle of Peter	15.25
7102	Lillie, John	Lectures on the First and Second Epistle of Peter	18.25
7103	Hort, F. J. A. & A. F.	Expository and Exegetical Studies	29.50
7104	Milligan, George	St. Paul's Epistles to the Thessalonians	10.50
7105	Stanley, Arthur P.	Epistles of Paul to the Corinthians	20.95
7106	Moule, H. C. G.	Colossian and Philemon Studies	10.50
7107	Fairbairn, Patrick	The Pastoral Epistles	14.95
8001	Fairweather, William	Background of the Gospels	15.00
8002	Fairweather, William	Background of the Epistles	14.50
8003	Zahn, Theodor	Introduction to the New Testament (3 vol.)	48.00
8004	Bernard, Thomas	The Progress of Doctrine in the New Testament	9.00
8401	Blaikie, William G.	David, King of Israel	14.50
8402	Farrar, F. W.	The Life and Work of St. Paul (2 vol.)	43.95
8601	Shedd, W. G. T.	Dogmatic Theology (4 vol.)	49.50
8701	Shedd, W. G. T.	History of Christian Doctrine (2 vol.)	30.25
8702	Oehler, Gustav	Theology of the Old Testament	20.00
8703	Kurtz, John Henry	Sacrificial Worship of the Old Testament	15.00
8901	Fawcett, John	Christ Precious to those that Believe	9.25
9401	Neal, Daniel	History of the Puritans (3 vol.)	54.95
9402	Warns, Johannes	Baptism	11.50
9501	Schilder, Klass	The Trilogy (3 vol.)	48.00
9502	Liddon, H. P. & Orr, J.	The Birth of Christ	13.95
9503	Bruce, A. B.	The Parables of Christ	12.50
9504	Bruce, A. B.	The Miracles of Christ	17.25
9505	Milligan, William	The Ascension of Christ	12.50
9506	Moule, H. C. & Orr, J.	The Resurrection of Christ	16.95
9801	Liddon, H. P.	The Divinity of our Lord	20.25
9802	Pink, Arthur W.	The Antichrist	10.50
9803	Shedd, W. G. T.	The Doctrine of Endless Punishment	8.25